A Coach's Reference Guide

The Last 9 Seconds

The Secrets to Scoring Goals on the Last Touch

A Psychological Perspective

PLUS New Insights into Player Development

By John DeBenedictis

The Last 9 Seconds

ISBN # 978-0-9868399-0-0

Printed in Canada by:
DirectImage Media
4325 Steeles Ave. W. Suite 524
Toronto, ON M3N 1V7

www.directimageinc.com • 416.488.8845

Distributed in USA by Cardinal Publishers Group

Printed in USA by Versa Press

First Edition - January 2012

Second Edition - January 2013

Credits:

Editor: Bernard Lecerf
Diagrams and Illustrations: Jo-Anne Godawa
Photographs: Les Jones
Photographs: Action Images
Cover design: Anton Tielemans
Layout Design: Paul Di Murro

To my Dad, (Danilo) for getting me into soccer and always offering a different point of view on many things in soccer and life.

To my Mom (Angelina) for always offering positive support, love, and good food too.

My Dad and Mom: Danilo (Danny) and Angelina DeBenedictis

To my wife (Angela) for her patience while I'm away coaching soccer or writing this book.

To my sons, Joseph and Marco for their understanding while I've been focused on writing this book and for all their support.

To all the family members who have offered their advice throughout the writing of this book.

To all the players I have coached who have shaped my opinions and provided me experiences in soccer who without, the game would not have been enjoyable to coach.

To all the coaches who have been to my goal scoring sessions and provided me great feedback.

PREFACE

First of all let me start by thanking you for picking up this book and reading about what I have to offer you on the topic of scoring goals. After over 35 years of coaching and thousands of hours studying, learning, and analyzing the game of soccer and how to teach it, I have finally decided to put all the information I have gathered which pertains specifically to scoring goals down on paper. I hope the information provided in this book offers you new ideas on teaching your players how to score more goals. I hope that this book offers you some unique ideas on a topic very dear to me but also allows you to discuss, critique, and comment on what I have written. It may help shape your own ideas into how to teach your players how to score goals.

Gender

Please note that throughout the book, players and coaches have been referred to as 'he'. This is simply for convenience and in no way reflects an opinion that soccer is a male-only game.

For Coaches

This book is written for coaches. It includes much of the background information coaches will need in order to teach young players the psychological aspects of scoring goals. All the information is presented in a way that prepares coaches on how to communicate with their strikers. Different personalities will need a different approach and coaches are encouraged to read through the first two parts of the book before applying the third, fourth, and fifth parts of the book in the most effective ways so that success is immediate and long lasting.

The Golden Goal Scoring Course

I have developed a course for players aged 14 and up that is designed specifically for strikers. It's based on psychology and is run over 3 days intensely for 20 hours. I work with very small groups and administer 60% of the course in the classroom and 40% on the field. I call it 'The Golden Goal Scoring' course.

I first ran my course in 2004 to a small group and then again in 2005 to another small group. The results have been so dramatic that I wanted to hold off running any more courses until I finished this book. I started again with two courses in 2009 and one in 2011 prior to the completion of this book. Once again, the results were incredible and beyond my expectations. The key to my training techniques is the psychology. I run the course intensely and over a short period of time. This book mirrors what I teach in the classroom component of the course.

Reference Guide

The book is also a great reference guide for coaches who have taken the Golden Goal Scoring Course. The book is designed so that coaches will be quickly able to find the information they need to solve certain psychological problems that their strikers may be having. Simple chapter titles and subtitles should help the coach find and recall key information presented in my Golden Goal Scoring Course.

Editions for players

There is a simplified edition of this book for players. It leaves out much of the background information that explains to coaches the thinking behind how to teach players the psychological factors about how to score.

Coaches can visit my website to get more information on my courses, books, and DVD's
www.goldengoalscoring.com or www.thelast9seconds.com or www.thesecretstoscoringgoals.com

FOREWORD

"John DeBenedictis is to be congratulated on this remarkable book, one of the most comprehensive ever written on the subject of goalscoring. The research on this important aspect of the game coupled with the attention to detail make it a must read for students of the game. The chapter on beating the goalkeeper is especially relevant and the practices listed should be part of every training session."

Dick Howard

- Former professional goalkeeper in the NASL
- TV soccer analyst
- Author
- Member of FIFA Technical and Development Committee

"Within a few pages of reading this book you will come to the conclusion that John DeBenedictis is an incredible student of the game of soccer. His writings give a new perspective on the game – particularly in relation to the art and science of scoring goals.

Years ago I learned much of my goalkeeping from an old friend, Verdi Godwin, who in his playing days was an old-fashioned English centre forward. He looked at goalkeepers from the other side of the bargaining table. He knew what goalkeepers didn't like and hence, he would attempt to take advantage of that. He also knew what he didn't like to see in an opposing goalkeeper. For instance, one that came out, narrowed the angle, stayed big and didn't anticipate.

In the book John talks about the Jekyll and Hyde personality duels between attackers and their opponents – and in particular, the striker and opposing goalkeeper.

So this book is for every coach and every player. It may concentrate on the last 9 seconds before a goal is scored, but that is the focus of each player no matter what their position – as it is with every team and every coach."

Tony Waiters

- Former goalkeeper with the England National team
- Former Coach of England's National youth team
- Former coach of the Vancouver Whitecaps in the NASL
- Former coach of Canada's National Men's team
- Author
- Respected clinician and coaching instructor around the world

CONTENTS

Coaching the Psychological Aspects of Scoring Goals

PART ONE

PART ONE

Les Jones/Covershots

PSYCHOLOGY

CHAPTER 1

Introduction

I first decided to start specializing on scoring goals as a special topic after watching endless games where my favorite teams, Italy or Canada lost games because they failed to score when they had great scoring opportunities. Of course, Italy made up for that with their victory at the 2006 World Cup. But as a more important inspiration for this book, I'm tired of listening to critics of soccer here in North America constantly complain about the lack of scoring in the game. Although most of those critics do not understand the beauty of a good game of soccer regardless of the amount of goals scored they continue to criticize soccer. But what really frustrated me was to watch more and more games where good finishing could turn a 0-0 game into an exciting 3-3 game and thereby silencing the critics of soccer.

Finally, having played goalkeeper as a semi-professional in a pro league and been a student of the striker, I thought that I could use my knowledge in my attempt at stopping strikers from scoring on me to help others score more goals. In a selfish way, I avoided telling my secrets to other goalkeepers or strikers outside of the players I coached. Endless criticism from anti-soccer reporters and the importance of sharing information with others compelled me to put my methods in writing.

But first I had the challenge of putting my knowledge and experience to the test through in-depth analysis to make sure my assumptions and theories about scoring goals were accurate. What I had set out to do was to lay out a very specific set of teaching guidelines for all players who get chances at scoring to follow. This should result in more success in the amount of goals scored in a game.

In the process of writing this book I studied many different aspects of the great goal scorers in soccer from both a physical/skill perspective and a mental/psychological perspective. My background apart from playing and coaching is in the Science of Health and Physical Education having obtained an Honours Bachelor of Science degree in that area of study. I continued studying and gathering in-depth information over the past decade on many aspects of the human body and brain, specifically how it pertains to perception, psychology, and human kinetics.

I delved myself in the subject and found many interesting facts, behaviors, and so-called secrets and tricks that existed in this aspect of the game. Journalist Simon Kuper, in a March 2003 article for the *Financial Times*, on the English Premier League strikers wrote that "most goalscorers know how they do it. Fearful of revealing their secrets, they seldom talk about it".

I lectured on the topic of scoring goals for the first time in 2003 and shared some of my findings. I received tremendous positive and unique feedback from coaches and players over the past number of years and have refined the information and I am excited about helping players improve and inspire change on how to teach one of the most exciting parts of the game of soccer. Goals create more excitement in the game for players, spectators, and future stars. Goals are not exciting for the goalkeepers who give up goals but without a doubt the potential for goals is the reason so many spectators follow the game. Over the years coaches have organized their defenses so well that goal scoring has been on a decline. The 2010 World Cup had the lowest goal total since allowing 32 teams in the finals.

In preparing to write this book I got to know the habits of strikers both in a general sense and in very specific ways. This was not as difficult for me because I played as a goalkeeper and was fortunate to play with and against some top caliber players. While still in my prime as a player I also started coaching youth players. I had to stop shots but then coach my kids on how to score. I had to try and read the game not just from a goalkeeper's and player's perspective but also from a coaching perspective so I could make my players play better. As a keeper, I knew I was limited in speed, flexibility, agility, height, and power and therefore had to really try to get inside the head of the striker in order to give myself the best chance to succeed and prevent goals.

Because they say, goalkeepers are different, expect a number of different perspectives on the subject.

Be prepared for a host of unique and original ideas on how to teach goal scoring. I hope you enjoy this book.

The 2010 World Cup had the lowest goal total since allowing 32 teams in the finals. "145 Goals"

Picture 1A: 2010 World Cup had the lowest goal total since allowing 32 teams in the finals. Spain were the 2010 World Cup Champions. Photo by Action Images

CHAPTER 2

Scoring Goals
The Last 9 Seconds

In this book, I will explain what the player needs to know to be able to score. In particular, what he needs to do and think about in the last 9 seconds or less prior to a goal being scored. That is all!

The book does not give you methods of creating chances as a team or building the play up from the back. It does not offer you systems of play or special tactics or strategies to use to create scoring opportunities. It does not offer you combination plays for strikers or any other team concept information. It simply stresses how you should coach the players on an in-depth individual basis about how to prepare to score, which usually takes 9 seconds, or less. It will help you communicate with your players so that they will get more chances to score and convert more of the chances that they get into goals.

It's Psychology 101, Soccer Style!

I will help you coach your team for those few but precious seconds. Those few seconds where there is an opportunity to score can be the most influential in a 90-minute match. They can determine whether your team wins or loses. They can change careers of players and coaches. Unbelievably, most coaches simply touch the surface when coaching the psychological aspects of scoring to the players on their team who get the most scoring chances in a game.

I hope to convey in this chapter that "The Last 9 Seconds" before each goal and what is happening in the mind of your players in those last few seconds before a potential goal scoring chance presents itself, can be the most important part of your coaching career.

In coaching the athlete in this aspect of the game, one needs to prepare for what a friend of mine, Norm Tsolakis, calls "The Complexities of the Mind". Tsolakis uses this concept in the context of business dealings and I have since adopted it in my teachings. Every athlete thinks differently and reacts to different stimuli. Key factors that may affect one athlete can be completely different for another athlete. The way the mind works is very complex. The state of mind of the player in a scoring situation can vary considerably according to the circumstances. It can make players brilliant, or prevent them from reaching their potential. Those who can overcome some of the stresses of trying to score can become great goal scorers without the refined skill and physical attributes of others.

All the practice and skill in the world can often not suffice as we see great players miss chances to score because they have not been coached enough in how to score on an individual psychological basis. Of course, basic skill is necessary in kicking, passing, and heading a ball, but once that is acquired the rest is psychological.

Each athlete is different. Some chapters will help some players while others will help others. No one really knows which will work with each athlete and, in the courses that I have taught, all players have improved their goal scoring conversion rate and, yet, different factors and information have influenced them.

In a press release from June 13, 2004 from the W-League after the Toronto Inferno lost to Long Island 2-1, Inferno General Manager Tony Marmo said, "It's frustrating because our players are getting a lot of chances. However I think there's just a lack of confidence when it comes to finishing". The press release went on to say, "Coach McManus feels that his players need to be better prepared when scoring chances occur." How often have coaches shared these sentiments?

The Importance of Psychological Training for your Strikers

Let me explain the importance of working on the psychological aspect of scoring goals with your key players. Your key players are the ones that get the most chances to score.

Let's assume that your team does not give up more goals than the scoring opportunities your team generates. In other words, assuming your team gets chances to score, if they converted those chances to goals then a loss or draw could be converted to a victory. If on the other hand your team concedes 4 goals but only generates 2 scoring chances a game, then converting those chances to goals would still result in a loss and therefore, you need to work on a number of other things to win games. In that case, this book will not solve your team's problems.

But if your team is creating chances but not converting them to goals, then I suggest you spend more time on the players who get the most scoring opportunities and work on the psychological aspects of scoring. Doing anything else with the players on your team who get most of your scoring chances will be less effective in bringing your team better results. You can work on things such as fitness, defending, set plays, passing, shooting, tactics, and strategies, but your strikers' problems are probably psychological. How many coaches put this problem into the correct perspective?

In all the years I have played, coached, or watched soccer, I have yet to see a game where the number of chances where players should have scored or at least taken shots at goal or hit the net, are fewer than the goals actually scored!

After that thought, I leave you with these questions:

How much time do you spend on the players on your team who get most of your goal scoring opportunities outside of practicing team scoring or shooting on goal?

Is it not worth spending more time on the mental and psychological preparation of your key players so that they can focus on *The Last 9 Seconds?*

CHAPTER 3

Coaching the Striker to Score More Goals

How many times have you scratched your head and rattled your brain about teaching scoring? For the most part coaches are creative and try different things to get the point across. But nothing is more frustrating than when for that instant, your athletes forget everything you have told them or taught them. The excitement, stress, pressure of the moment, overtakes all the things you have tried to teach them.

What I present for you in this book is probably not too different than what you have told your players over and over. But, through years of experimentation, I have found that, when working on the mental aspects of scoring, better results will be realized using the information in this book. I use abstract visual and mental cues that will hopefully make the athletes block out the pressure and stress of the moment so that they can concentrate on the facts. This will enable them to focus on performing the skills properly because they have made the right decisions on what to do in that instant more so than ever before.

The topic of coaching players to score in "The Last 9 Seconds" can be broken down into different elements. What you need to do is make a mental connection with the athletes so that they remember what it takes to perform at the spur of the moment. You need to provide players with different options, using key words, phrases, or visuals that allow them to make the correct decisions in scoring situations.

Are Your Players Ready?

First we need to consider the age of the players you are coaching. This book is NOT for players under the age of 13 nor is it for players who play recreational soccer who have not mastered the basics of kicking and passing a soccer ball. Do not proceed to work on the mental aspects of coaching your strikers if they are not at this point because it will only confuse and frustrate them. The players MUST be able to pass, kick, and head properly.

At the younger age levels, more goals are scored due to the sheer speed of the players.
Fast players tend to score more goals because their speed gets them many more chances.

With age, defenders and goalkeepers get better. Few players want to be defenders at 8 years of age. The leading goal scorers at this age tend to have speed to outrun opponents. This trait will often prevail until players turn 14 or 15. Often young players also have a big or powerful kick and score goals on short goalkeepers by shooting high on them on large goals. As defenders become specialized and goalkeepers start to read the game better and grow taller, speed and power will no longer provide as many goals as before. Those players with the mental skills and fortitude to finish consistently will be the ones who will continue to score. The others will not.

In coaching "The Last 9 Seconds", you need to know all the different aspects that affect the decision making process of the athlete. They include psychology, soccer facts, human motion, biomechanics, opponents, probabilities and possibilities of different situations and different training techniques.

To be most effective in coaching your players you will need to focus on the key elements that make a complete player who can score goals. These are the areas I will focus on:

1. **The Mind**
   As a coach, you need to understand the players and how they think and then use strategies to improve their mental aspect. I will present strategies that many athletes use to prepare for games such as visualization and relaxation and also new strategies to help players score.

2. **The Body (Human Movement)**
   If players can read human motion using the principles of physics and biomechanics, then they should become better players if they can apply them to reading defenders and goalkeepers. I will present some key areas where players can improve their ability to read their opponents.

3. **The Mind with the Body**
   Being able to apply both of the above points to performance takes a special ability. In order to speed up the learning process, learning will need to be accelerated so that instinctive decisions are made quickly and accurately. I will outline methods using the mind with the body to make the players make more correct decisions in a game under pressure. Teaching players how to concentrate and apply these principles in a game will be covered.

4. **The Soccer Facts**
   I will present relevant facts that will help your players make correct decisions based on them. In my studies I have discovered many scoring facts that are unique. By analyzing goals and presenting the findings in a unique and creative way I will provide you more details on what to coach your strikers in a variety of specific situations they will encounter on the field: for example, when to shoot and where to aim.

5. **The Soccer Application**
   It will take time and mental energy for players to apply many of my techniques. Often it will require stepping away from the game and using examples from other areas of life to help recall the proper information when needed.

6. **Training the Goalscorer to Apply all of the Above on the Field.**
   Once the athletes "get it", then you need to teach them the mental skills to take it to the field on a consistent level and provide them with exercises that they can practice on the field so that they can score consistently.

7. **Mind/Body Perception Training Techniques**
   These are special training techniques I have developed to help players become more natural at certain skills.

What to Tell the Players

You will need to give power to your strikers. In order to understand how to do this, you will need to see what I would tell players. When I work with players on my teams or in my goal-scoring course my main goal is to shift the balance of power from the defenders and goalkeepers to the strikers. I want them to believe that scoring is easy and fun. I want to give them the mental, visual, and factual information and trigger cues that gives them the confidence to feel that scoring is simple. Yet I want them to have the power to use failure as a method of exciting themselves to try to do better again because they have the knowledge. In turn, they WILL get better without a shadow of a doubt!

In some cases I will present some of the material as though I was talking directly to your players. This way, you will see what I'm trying to get across to players. ***The text will be bold and in italics***. I believe you will have a better understanding of how I deal with teaching the players the psychology of scoring goals by knowing exactly what I would tell young players. Your goal as a coach will be to persuade your players that they can score.

CHAPTER 4

Goals in Soccer are Precious

It's no secret that goals in soccer are rare and precious, and they make each game captivating and unique. Right from the opening whistle, fans know that one goal can decide a match and the anticipation of that goal can bring the crowd to a frenzy. Just the goal scoring opportunity often creates excitement. Even with a near miss, we find that fans of the attacking team start to chant and sing louder.

The higher one advances in playing or coaching the game, the harder it gets to score. As a result, when players do not score, they take on unnecessary stress with them to the next phase of their game. Players often feel that they have played poorly and all the spectators, coaches, and even teammates are talking about them if they do not score.

Coaches also often are down when their key players do not score. Even without being disappointed with their strikers, often their body language can show it. But even if that is not the case, there is no doubt that strikers who do not score will put undue pressure on themselves and start doubting themselves and their abilities. This will even take place if the players have done nothing wrong: in some games, they do not get scoring opportunities because of poor service, their opponents' skills or bad bounces.

This is when you as the coach need to make sure that your players do not feel as though they are letting you or the team down. In fact this becomes vital.

You need to understand that goals are precious and hard to come by. I challenge you to take a cross with no opponents including no goalkeeper and score from 8 yards out with one touch on a consistent basis. You will be amazed how often you will not score.

And it is with this fact in mind that you must start to train your key attacking players. Goals are precious and hard to come by. Make them understand that scoring is not easy. But at the same time, delicately, you must give the players confidence. You will do this in many ways. But to start with, you must make them feel that YOU are not upset at them if they do not score.

You will need to stress this over and over. Players can be moody and top goal scorers tend to be the most difficult to deal with. (Outside of goalkeepers but that's only because they are different). They can be cocky when they score and blame everyone else when they don't, yet they can also be quick to blame themselves when the scoring stops. This book is not about how to deal with these players' personalities but it remains that it is better to have confident strikers than ones who doubt their abilities. Also, I want to answer some questions about scoring.

Practicing is important and we have all scored that great goal in practice and possibly even in a game. But it doesn't happen enough. Why?

Some players will practice just as many hours as others but for some reason, some players will consistently score more goals. Why?

Do some players have better eyes? Are they blessed with natural ability? Is it heredity? Is scoring teachable?

Many think it's an innate gift. The Dutch speak of "a nose for goals." The answer to all these questions has to be that they do not need amazing magical skills. It's not in their genes and they do not need superhuman x-ray vision. You must convey to your players that ANYONE can be a brilliant striker provided he applies his mind to it.

Glenn Hoddle, once said Michael Owen, his country's best striker, was not a "natural goal scorer".

Consistency is the key and that is what coaches want. Keith Eddy, former coach of the Toronto Blizzard of the old North American Soccer League once said to me, "Every player that is good enough to try out for our team has the skill to play the game but the difference between those that make it and those that do not is that the ones that make it can do the skill correctly 8 out of 10 times. The ones that don't make the team are good enough to use the correct skill or make the correct decisions just like the best players on the team. The problem is that they only do the right thing 4 or 5 times out of 10. That's the difference at the pro level."

This point was well made and one that we should not forget because it applies even more to strikers. I state this to the players I teach all the time. I tell players that coaches want consistency. Success in scoring will come from practice but with the energies in the right place. We want players to think of what they need to do each and every time they need to score and this becomes just as important in practices as in games – even when they practice on their own without coaches in the park.

But to practice and want to get better, players must have a passion for the game. They must enjoy the game. They will seek new information because they enjoy the game so much. Quite often I see players lose this enthusiasm. There are various reasons for this as young players pass through adolescence. If you want your players to work hard and get better, then they need to become passionate about the game and if they are not enjoying and looking forward to practices and games or to go play on their own, then you may need to re-evaluate your coaching methods. Quite often, it's the coach who stops making the game fun and leading good potential players to quit.

Your top strikers must enjoy playing and scoring and if they lose the passion for the game, they will not and cannot become great goal scorers. This was evident in my research on the Great Goal Scorers. Remember: Goals are precious but so are the players who can score more often. They make the game better for everyone. Do not lose them!

CHAPTER 5

How to Motivate Your Players to Focus on the Details You Will Give Them About Scoring Goals

Many young players are looking for that opportunity to move up to the next level. For some it can be playing for a high school team while for others it's about getting a soccer scholarship. For some players it's about making a State or Provincial Team. At some point players may get an opportunity to play for a youth National Team or get a tryout at a pro camp but the opportunities do not come often unless players are of the highest skill.

For every superstar there are many other professional players who start out as fringe players until they make their way up to a higher level. Sometimes all they need is that one chance. But one way to get more opportunities is to score goals. In soccer, since goal scorers are highly sought after, anyone who can score on a more regular basis than the next player, will always get that second look or opportunity.

Everyone knows that the goal scorer gets all the publicity and that crosses into all other sports from Pele, to Maradona, to Rooney, who captured stardom by scoring a few goals in Euro 2004, to Gretzky and Crosby in hockey, to Jordan, Carter, and James in basketball. Those who score more points get the most attention. That's a fact!

Picture 5A: The photo of Pele was taken by Anton Tielemans of Tielemans Design. Anton Tielemans commissioned artist Michael Dudash to paint this action photo of Pele taken at the 1970 World Cup Final in Mexico City. Pele, known as "The King" scored a total of 1,282 goals in his career. In this picture he is standing in front of artist Michael Dudash's art of him in action. Pele signed 1,282 limited edition prints of this piece of art. Dudash is an American artist know for creating some of the most memorable posters for Hollywood films. Tielemans' web site is www.tielemansdesign.com.

Pele, known as "The King" is the only player to score over 1,000 goals in his professional career. (see Picture 5A) Thirty years after his retirement he still draws big crowds wherever he goes. The goal scorer will get the attention of the scouts in spite of the perception that the athlete may give off about not being good enough. They said that Maradona was too small or, in hockey that Phil Esposito (former great with the Boston Bruins) was too slow and that Wayne Gretzky (often called "The Great One") was too weak. No matter what sport, the player that can rack up points will get noticed. And in soccer, where goals are hard to come by, players can improve their goal scoring output by a large percentage by just scoring a few more goals in a season.

I Almost Dropped a Future Superstar.

I tell players that they never know when someone is watching. They may only score one goal a season but if the right person is there scouting, they never know what can happen.

In 1981, I was appointed head coach of the National Soccer League's U19 Select team. This was Canada's top U19 league and we were to select a team to play in a tour against some of the top US Division I Colleges. We had to scout all 20 teams in the league and quickly put together a team because the League had committed to a series of games in the fall. After the tour our team was to train over the winter to represent the National Soccer League in The Dallas Cup the following April. I was appointed coach in late August when the league was nearing its last month of play so my assistant and I would only get to watch each team play once.

When choosing a select team and scouting players I can usually spot the players who I want on the team quickly and accurately when it comes to most positions on the field. But, and I would assume that most coaches would concur, the two toughest positions to select are goalkeepers and strikers. Both require strong mental strength because so much of what they do stems from psychology. For example, a keeper may be great at practice. He can be athletic, powerful, agile, fit, and look natural at shot stopping but make some errors in a game that has nothing to do with his technical abilities. Mental errors by your keeper can cost you games. That's why I tend to take a long and hard look at goalkeepers. Sometimes, the keeper who is less skilled technically but who is composed, in command of his box and teammates and makes fewer or no errors is the best choice. I recall watching a young Toronto FC goalkeeper named Stefan Frei in his first pro game (picture on page 2). Even though he was very young for a pro keeper I saw something in him that made me say that he would eventually become the starting goalkeeper. Shortly afterwards, the former starting keeper was released as he won over the starting job.

Strikers are even harder to figure out. In my study of strikers, I have not been able to come up with a consistent formula that predicts a future great striker. I have not been able to say that a particular physique is better than another. Pele was average in height; Ronaldo seems a bit heavy and built like a tank; Owen and Maradona are small; Luca Toni is tall, and Roberto Baggio was relatively small. Gary Lineker was awkward and slight while Landon Donovan is small as well (picture 5B). Christine Sinclair is fairly tall and stocky and seems slow while Mia Hamm is of average height. It is just impossible to determine what a perfect striker should look like from the outside. That leaves the inside, the brain, which is where things differ and that's why selecting a striker for my select team was so difficult.

The one thing I can say about strikers is that no matter how clumsy, awkward, unfit, or slow strikers are, if they score goals consistently in big and little games, I CANNOT CUT them. For players reading this, you read correctly:

I CANNOT CUT PLAYERS WHO SCORE
on a consistent basis.

Coaches will toss and turn as they try to sleep at night over a decision that they may have to make regarding a striker that seems to score but does not fit the part. To the casual observer it would seem that the player may not look like a naturally gifted athlete. He may even seem outclassed in certain parts of the field but when he gets a chance close to goal, if he scores, it takes all that is bad about his game away. Coaches succeed or fail by their decisions and, as a coach, I do not want to fail, so I will think carefully about my striker and if an awkward player scores lots of goals, I want him on my team rather than scoring against my team.

I always remember watching Giorgio Chinaglia of the New York Cosmos when he played against my beloved Toronto Blizzard in the old North American Soccer League. He looked slow, clumsy, tired, and ready to have a seat and a cigar for most of the game. Then, in an instant, he would get the ball for a split second, score a goal and go back to sleep for the rest of the game all while our team lost by that one goal.

While scouting for my National Soccer League's U19 Select team, I went to watch one particular team and there was a player who constantly missed glorious goal scoring opportunities. In fact it was amazing how often this player missed chances. In that game he missed breakaways, and close chances, including an open net opportunity inside the 6-yard box. His team won the match by 3 or 4 goals but he missed too many great chances to be invited to the tryouts. The player looked clumsy and awkward and miskicked the ball too often.

After not choosing this player, I received a call from his manager Guy Fracassa, who asked that I give this player another chance. He told me he had a bad game and rarely missed so many chances. I decided to heed his advice and to invite him to try out for the team. As it turned out, he made the team. In fact he was only one of a few players who went on to play pro soccer. Most players who made the team had scholarship offers from US Colleges. He started with the Cleveland Force of the Major Indoor Soccer League. When the league folded he moved to the new National Professional Soccer League, an indoor league and became one of the top scorers. His name was Gino DiFlorio. He possessed a dangerous left foot, and he sits as the fifth highest goal scorer in league history. He had a successful career playing indoor soccer making very good money while the league was at its peak. His first pro coach, Timo Liekoski said, "he had a powerful left foot and was very quick at releasing a shot".

I tell young players this story all the time because it helps them get motivated to pay attention to the details of what I have to say. Much of the information in this book is very detailed and very specific and young players tend to drift away when you speak to them. As a coach you need to keep them wanting to learn more, especially about the psychological points because they will just want to get on with playing and kicking a ball. I recommend that you work one on one with your key strikers instead of in a group situation. Teach them that small increases in consistency in applying the skills they already have can have huge positive consequences. Here is what I tell players when speaking to them directly.

> ***"You never know who is watching. An opportunity can come and go with each game but scoring goals will improve your chances of being moved up to a higher level tenfold over not scoring. Any advice you can attain to gain an edge over an opponent is worth listening to."***

To further this point I bring up some simple math.

> ***"If you go from scoring on 2 out of 10 chances to 3 out of every 10 chances, that's huge! You will score 10% more goals on the chances you get. In some cases, it may take 5 games to get 10 scoring chances in soccer. But if I can teach you to get 3 scoring chances in a game instead of 2, that's huge too! That's a 50% increase in scoring chances, which will increase the number of goals you score in a season by quite a bit."***

Some players may have problems with math but for the mathematicians I go on by saying the following:

> ***"If you get 50 scoring chances a season and score 10 goals a season but we can increase your conversion rate by just 10% then you will score 15 goals a season on the same 50 chances. That's a 50% increase in goals that you will score over the course of a season. That is significant and may get you and your team to the next level."***

Of course, as a coach, your stature in the soccer community will also grow if your team is scoring more goals, but please do not let the players know this! Tell them how it will benefit them personally. But soccer is a team game and you're afraid that your strikers will not want to pass the ball. To handle the selfish players, you will need to help them decide when to shoot and when to pass (but keep in mind that players often simply do not take enough risks in trying to score). Let players know that if they pass when they should pass then they will still get goals because they will get passes back from teammates when their teammates should pass to them. Do this with each of your strikers privately. The real question is, can they score when they get that pass back and a scoring chance presents itself?

Continuing with high school math I go a step further with players by saying something like the following:

> ***"Now that you are scoring 50% more goals by converting just 10% more chances, what will happen if you get more chances to score per game? What if I can show you how to get 3 chances in a game instead of 2. What will happen to the number of goals you score over the course of a season?***
>
> ***Getting 3 chances to score instead of 2 per game means you will get 75 scoring chances a season instead of 50. As before, assuming you increase your conversion rate to 3 out of 10 from 2 out of 10, then you will score between 22-23 goals a season instead of your original 10 goals. That's a 130% increase in goal production. Imagine the possibilities and opportunities that you will have with that kind of an increase."***

I finish off this segment by telling players:

> ***"Concentrate on what I am about to teach you and pay attention to the littlest bit of information because the accumulation of those little things will make you a better player, guaranteed!"***

You must keep in mind that you are coaching the players one on one and working to motivate them to listen carefully to what you have to say. Once again, do not let them know how your own coaching career will improve and how you may have to book your tuxedo because you'll be up for the "coach of the year" award!

Motivate your players to want to learn the littlest of pointers and be on your way to developing better goal scorers. You need an eager audience who will be prepared to absorb your information regardless of how odd it may seem at first.

In terms of learning, I have a rule that helps me stay focused on teaching players different skills, tactics, and strategies of the game I call my 20/60/20 rule.

The 20/60/20 Rule

This formula has passed the test of time as a result of my experiences when teaching very specific skills and when the players were required to think.

- 20% of your players will never really get what you are teaching them.
- 60% will get it right at practice. But they will not get it totally right and thus will get it right half the time in games. Sometimes it will be a fluke and sometimes it won't be. Usually under extreme pressure the skill fails them.
- 20% of the players will be absorbed by your information on new skills. They will be intrigued by them. They will know why, when, and how to do the advanced skills. They will consider them their own little secrets and they will enjoy the challenge of knowing what you taught them and work to perfect the skills. They will look forward to their next game just to be able to try what you have taught them. They will make mistakes but know quickly what it is they have done wrong and look forward to trying it again to perfect the skills. As they get better, they will want to do it over and over again. It will become a bit of a high for them. You will notice that they will be able to perform the skills under pressure in game situations and be more successful than any other group. These players will become your superstars.

Look for these trends and be aware of the limitations of the first group. Some of your 60% group will move into the third group (the top 20% group) once the light bulb goes off in their heads about what you are teaching them, so don't give up on them.

Thinking and Skills

I first came up with the 20/60/20 rule while I taught my players the Wiel Coerver ball possession and dribbling techniques after first meeting him in 1984 in Philadelphia. I was the first to bring his techniques to Canada, and they gave our team a unique advantage over many other teams. They are magnificent, because they really deal with human movement. The true magnificence about his techniques is that Coerver studied human movement when putting them together. Although he offered the details on beating and taking on opponents, the player had to be able to pick out which move to use in which instance.

At the time I was coaching a team in the U19 division so I had to teach new skills to players in their late teens. It's not easy for players to become instinctive in a new skill when it is introduced late in their developmental process. At the time, playing soccer in the street everyday as soon as you can walk was not normal in North America. But the Coerver techniques made it possible for players to think through these new skills and use them effectively as though they were a natural instinct. Never before had the art of dribbling and ball possession been so wonderfully broken down in so specific details.

The Ideas

In the same manner that the Coerver dribbling and ball possession skills marry complex techniques with instinct and soccer intelligence, I hope that this book can accomplish the same goals in coaching and teaching the specifics of goal scoring. Developing the unique ideas I present in this book is the result of a long process of research, analysis, and working with players. I have refined them over the years, and they work. Some of your players may not get them at first, but be patient with them and challenge yourself to add your own spin and creativity to the information presented.

Picture 5B: Strikers come in all shapes and sizes. Landon Donovan of the USA is relatively small at 5' 7". Action Images/Guy Jeffroy

CHAPTER 6

Thinking Outside The Box

I believe that the exceptional strikers play the game from a different frame of mind in comparison to other players on the team. In my research on strikers, I found there is something definitively different about the best of the best and it's definitively not in raw skill.

Each athlete is unique in his or her own way. For a coach, the challenge is "how do I teach this mental thing, and what is it exactly?" Unfortunately, I cannot tell you what triggers any particular athlete. What I can tell you is that there is something there and all you can do as a coach is work on a number of things and hope that something will set off a light bulb in their head and sink in. What we do know from the scientific world is that when the brain thinks it perceives something, i.e. receives a stimulus, it triggers signals for the appropriate behavioural response immediately and stereotypically (Rubinstein et al., 2001). The stimulus needs to exceed a preset threshold before action is taken. In other words, before your body reacts to something it needs a stimulus, but that stimulus has to be strong enough to elicit a response. The point where a stimulus causes a reaction is called the threshold.

Perception

I believe teaching goal scoring is all about perceptions. According to studies by Schinke, da Costa and Andrews (2001), perceptions are learned and unlearned in social contexts. There are many types of perceptions that we need to consider. Perception of what is reality is one main area of coaching. Coaches even have different perceptions of player development. At what point do the athletes go beyond just being good players with skill to becoming exceptional players? Where in player development do players vastly improve? What are the facts about scoring goals and how do the strikers absorb them? How do the players perceive their environment, that is, does what the players see and hear or think they see and hear, translate into providing the best physical response to a particular situation?

What I can say is that the exceptional players who can score goals perceive things differently and, as coaches we need to help them develop this mindset. To train this, I have to get the athlete to "think outside the box".

Tell Your Players to Think Outside the Box

Thinking outside the box is a term used in advertising but young players have to be receptive to this concept and be excited and prepared to hear things in a different way. We need to make the players believe that they have the ability to become better and to believe that all the best athletes of any sport go through this process regardless of how odd or different it may seem. Players with an open mind will be able to improve their goal scoring. In my work with athletes on this topic, I have found that some players pick it up quickly while others find it very challenging. Be patient with the information I'm presenting when sharing it with your players. Sometimes it may take a while before something will suddenly click and what you have told them will start to register. The age of your players may play a part in how quickly they take in the information. Some players will be cocky and not be able to think outside the box until others start to surpass them. I tell them to think outside the box to prepare them for the information. That may mean making it funny or even entertaining so that they relax about taking in the information.

In this first part of the book I concentrate on the psychological part of teaching goal scoring. Seeing the big picture and the little picture is another business term I like to use with athletes as I prepare them in my classroom sessions. Here is how I relate the points to soccer when speaking to my players.

"The Little Picture"

> ***"There is a hairdresser who can do amazing things with hair. The hairdresser is an expert at picking out what style fits each person and how to cut, trim, and style each strand of hair. This is equivalent to the player who can juggle the ball a thousand times,***

has all the moves to beat defenders, and can read the opponents so that he can go past them. These skills are all very important to have. BUT . . . ."

"The Big Picture"

"This highly talented hairdresser decides to go into business on his own. He opens up a shop but business is very slow. He can't figure out why business is so slow considering the talents he possesses. One day the landlord wants to know why the rent is behind. After another month business does not improve and the hairdresser goes out of business.

When the hairdresser was asked about the business he did not know why his business failed because he did not see the big picture. Then a friend figured out why he failed. He had set up his shop in an area of town where most residents were of a religious group who could not cut their hair. He had the talent but not the smarts to see the big picture."

In soccer, you can have very talented strikers but they may not be able to read the game or make correct decisions as to what to do in order to score. All the skills can be useless if your players cannot read the game and make correct decisions. The little picture is important but the big picture can be just as important if not more important when it comes to goal scoring.

In fact, for strikers quite often it's better to have fewer skills but be masters of some very specific skills relating to scoring goals rather than be an expert in all of the skills of the game. This point is important for your players to understand so that they can relate to key points in this book. How often do you see a player who is highly skilled not make a team in place of another who consistently makes correct decisions? This applies to all positions on the field of play but it is especially relevant to the striker.

For many soccer players in North America where soccer is not played on the streets every day, seeing the big picture can overcome some of the short falls in their skills that they have in comparison to players coming from countries where they play soccer every day.

I will clear up the picture for you, the coach, in a way that will make it easier for you to convey the key points of scoring goals to your players. Your players have to know why goals are scored beyond knowing the skill of kicking a ball! That's the big picture!

CHAPTER 7

The Natural Athlete

I have closely researched the so-called "Natural Athlete", a term that commonly refers to players who become superstars in their sport. Basically, there can be two ways we define such a player. We can define the superstar at the pro level and the superstar at the youth level. I have found that many players who make it to the pro level were given the "Natural Athlete" title when they were playing in their youth. When these players end up in the pro ranks they are no longer considered "Natural Athletes" unless they are superstars in their sport. When you think about it, any player good enough to make it their profession at the highest leagues must be very, very good.

The Recipe for the Making of Superstars

When I looked at the superstars of pro sports I did find many similarities between them. In this case, by superstars, I mean the Peles, Maradonas, Beckhams, Zidanes, and Messis of this world but also superstars from other sports. So the big question is: are these superstar athletes born or made? Is it heredity, instinct, or practice? Do they come out of the belly differently?

I believe that, although some people will never be top athletes just as some others will never be rocket scientists or brain surgeons, most superstars are made and not born. And they do display common traits in a variety of areas.

Traits of Superstars

- **Passion:** They love playing their sport whenever they can.
- **Dedicated Time:** They spend hours upon hours practicing their sport because they are passionate about it.
- **They Want to Learn:** As they grow older they are sponges for information about their sport.
- **They Love to Practice and Play:** These future superstars love practices as much as games. They may not enjoy the fitness component of practicing but they enjoy the parts of practicing that involves a ball or a puck just as much as an actual game.
- **Perception of Surroundings:** They have an amazing ability to know where everyone is in relation to themselves. In soccer we call it vision.
- **They Have Secrets:** These are little things that make a difference.

Passion

If your athletes do not have passion, you are fighting an uphill battle. In an article in the NSCAA *Soccer Journal* called *Soccer's Age of Innocence Lost?* (2001) by Tim Schum, a club in central USA studied the effects of having state coaches spend countless hours with athletes only to have them drop out before they could reach their potential. The study involved players that were identified as being elite in the state and also had the potential to make it to the national level. The question of course was two-fold. Firstly, why do we lose potential National Team players in whom we invest time and money into? Secondly, can we identify players who will give up or decide not to continue playing at the highest level and as a result give other players the opportunity to receive the highest qualified coaching possible? They also explained that there is a cost factor involved when top-level state coaches spend time to develop players who will eventually quit at the expense of other players who did not get that opportunity. The underlying problem was that the players who decided to quit lost their passion for the game.

At the recent UEFA EURO 2012 Final, TV commentator Jason DeVos, was explaining to viewers about the success of the Spanish team in their victory over Italy in the final. Talking specifically to coaches and parents of young aspiring players he stated that today's game requires great technical skills from players, but in order to develop these techniques the players have to have a passion for the game. In picture 7B, the Spanish players celebrate their second consecutive Euro Championship to go along with their 2010 World Cup victory.

Many reasons why players quit sport exist, but we need to make sure they are enjoying the game and are passionate about it. It cannot become 'a job'. Players have to look forward to playing. If you are sensing that some of your players are not enjoying the experience, you will need to re-evaluate your coaching methods. Coach passion and you will have successful athletes and a successful team. On the other hand, you will find players that do not really have that passion. My 20/60/20 rule will apply when assessing players.

Dedicated Time

Players will only dedicate time to something they enjoy. Beyond that, they will need to strive for something. In the process of investing their time, they cannot lose their passion. Keep an eye on players for this – you'll be able to tell. Everyone will go through life facing different issues at home, with friends and teammates, in school or at work, but if they love doing something, that passion should not disappear. In this day and age when young players have so many choices such as computers, the Internet, iPods and video games, a lack of passion will distract them from putting in the time to get better.

On the other hand, we do need to give players a break from the structured game. I believe all players should take some time off from the game. The Great Gretzky used to tell hockey parents to allow their kids to play other sports in the summer season. He discouraged parents from having their kids play year round and go to too many hockey camps. That's coming from a hockey icon.

Pele said in a panel discussion in the 1994 NSCAA Coaches Convention in California that he didn't start playing organized sports on a full 11 a-side team until he was 12 years old. Before that it was just fun in the park and in non-structured school programs and small-sided games. Often players at a young age are driven too much by parents and coaches and become disenchanted. Everyone needs a break. Fortune 500 companies know the value of providing vacation time to their employees. It's no different in sports.

They Want to Learn

With passion, players want to learn more about the game, tactics, strategies, and about their heroes. Players will actually enjoy the knowledge. They are inspired to work harder and learn more. All the superstars I researched had heroes or other players that they wanted to emulate. In North America, where soccer may not receive the media attention that other sports receive, coaches need to educate their players on who the key players in the sport are. I urge coaches to spend time in practice to talk about some key players and what they do and whom they play for. It's just another ingredient in the mix needed to develop players who are passionate about a sport. It still comes down to passion. I will come back to this subject in the next chapter, which is called "CAM".

They Love to Practice and Play

The future superstar likes practices as much as games. They love playing in the park with their friends and kick a ball whenever they can. They know that games cannot take place every day and therefore are happy to attend practice to learn. Of course, there will be some parts of practices that they will not enjoy but whenever there is a ball involved, they are eager.

Perception of Surroundings

If there was one of these traits that may have a connection to heredity or instinct, it would be this one. There is no doubt some players will have huge advantages over others but when it comes to scoring goals, great goal scorers have all sorts of different physiques. Some are small and quick, others are tall and slow and there are a host of types in between. There is not one type of physical quality for a goal scorer. This is good because it means anyone can become a great goal scorer. Your athletes can stay positive knowing this.

Learning to read human motion is vital to optimal performance and I will elaborate on this in Part Two of this book. I believe we can speed up the ability of a player to become better at reading the game and react instinctively using the principles of human motion and physics. And through "Perception Training", a term I have come up with, players can speed up their cognitive and body perception of their immediate surroundings.

Secrets

Secret is a key word that I like to use when training players to score goals. It's a powerful word and everyone likes to know a secret. Just the word itself creates curiosity. Magicians have secrets. Chefs have secret recipes. Businessmen and businesswomen have trade secrets. I will dedicate chapter 15 to secrets because it's a major motivator to training the goal scorer to want to get better.

Superstars: Why are There so Few?

Picture 7A: True superstars Zidane, Ronaldo, and Ronaldinho greet each other before a match at the 2006 World Cup. The best of the best have some similarities that we want to duplicate as coaches in terms of giving young players the right inspiration to learn, develop, and reach their abilities. Picture Supplied by Action Images/Charles Platiau.

What makes superstars different? To become better goal scorers players need to want to study the best players at their position and try to understand what makes them different and believe that one day, they CAN become superstars too. You need to make your players understand that pro strikers can be made and are not born. Players will tune out if they feel they have no chance to become good goal scorers. I also believe that you can turn good strikers into goal scoring superstars at their own level. This in turn will give them a better chance to make it to the next level.

Gary Lineker, the highest goal scorer of the 1986 World Cup who played as a reserve at Leicester City realized that he did not have some of the physical attributes of some of the players he had to try and beat out for a regular spot on the team. He figured that he had to learn how to score goals so he began working out how to score them. He studied this aspect of the game and came up with his own method. Soon he started scoring goals when he got the chance to play. At some point, his coach could not leave him on the bench. Lineker scored goals. He didn't do drugs or go on a special fitness program. He simply studied the game and got smarter.

He was one of the most intelligent players of the time and explained how he scored, as related in the article by Simon Kuper from *Financial Times*; "Everyone says it's about being in the right place at the right time, but it's more than that. It's about always being in the right place." In fact, he was at the right place almost every time. It was not about instinct or heredity.

In hockey, Brett Hull, who played most of his career with the St. Louis Blues in the NHL was not chosen to play for Team Canada because he was not fast or tough enough. Many thought he would never make the NHL, but he scored over 700 goals in his career. In an interview at the 2007 All-Star game in Dallas, he was asked about his scoring abilities. He said, "It's a matter of knowing where to go. I'm there, then it's a matter of having the player with the puck find you. That's why players like Sidney Crosby are so successful and great to play with. They find you but at the same time you got to be there so you have to know where to go."

Hockey and soccer are similar in many ways and the point here is that scoring goals is a lot more than just skill. Scoring prowess comes with the ability to think in the heat of the moment.

Picture 7B: Spanish players celebrate their second consecutive UEFA Euro Championship to go along with their 2010 World Cup victory. Action Images/John Sibley

CHAPTER 8

"CAM"

"CAM" stands for what I call "Captivating and Absorbing Moment". In order to have passion for something, people usually have a moment in their lives where they are captivated by something. This is a prerequisite to developing a passion for any subject. We usually have any number of these moments in our lives, some that fizzle, some that stay longer and others that develop into passions and stay with us for many many years and, for some, even a lifetime.

Have you had a "Captivating and Absorbing Moment?" My guess is that you have and when it comes to soccer, your reading of this book may even be the result of such a moment. In other words, you have been captivated by the game and want to learn more. That's why you're reading this book. For your players, any one of the specific bits of information from this book can be an absorbing and captivating moment, or it may be a defining moment, which I will discuss in chapter 18.

The difficult part of "CAM" is that you, the coach, cannot coach it or decide for the athletes when they will be captivated by the sport to really put in the effort and get better at it. It will happen on its own and all you can do is present as many situations as possible when it may occur. That's it.

What Exactly is a Captivating Moment?

I refer to a captivating moment as a specific moment in one's life where a person has to take action to find out more about something or get interested in something more than just knowing a bit about it. For example, you watch a movie about a subject that you knew nothing about but suddenly you want to learn more about it. You focus on that item and do everything possible to find out more about it. Once you have dug out as much information as possible on the subject you will decide whether to continue or, having been satisfied, you may no longer seek more information on that subject.

I'll use three examples to clarify what I mean by a "Captivating and Absorbing Moment." I recall watching the movie *Amadeus* which won numerous Oscars at the Academy Awards. The movie portrayed the life of Mozart and was made in a unique way that made me leave the theatre with a lot of questions about the life of Mozart. How accurate was the movie? How much was real and how much was fiction? For the next month or two I was captivated by this film and wanted to know more. I went to libraries and bookstores to read up on Mozart. I was captivated by him and spent the time to seek out more knowledge. Once I was satisfied with the information I had gathered, I was content and no longer sought any more information nor did I want to learn how to become better at playing the piano. Although I took piano lessons as a kid, I knew my limitations and was not musically inclined to try harder at learning the piano. I was only interested in Mozart's life.

I had a moment when I was captivated and absorbed by something. This happens to everyone and does not on its own make one a future star athlete or musician but it does leave a lifelong impression which is good for the subject. I purchased a tape of some of Mozart's music at the time. If you captivate a player on the game of soccer, at worst you will have gained a lifelong fan for the game.

Here is another example of what I mean by a "Captivating and Absorbing Moment". One summer, while on vacation, I visited my friend Patrick Abate in Montreal. After dinner, my son Joseph, who was 13 at the time and Patrick's 15-year-old son Dominic disappeared to his bedroom. Dominic had an electric guitar and proceeded to show Joseph how to play it and how he could learn through the Internet. Once we came home from vacation Joseph relentlessly requested that we buy him an electric guitar, and we eventually obliged. Within two weeks he was playing the guitar quite well so we had him take private lessons to make sure he developed good habits just in case he would want to pursue this new passion. He has not stopped playing since and now writes music and plays in his own band, and has recently recorded some songs. He is passionate about his music and is very good at it. In fact, his song "Feel The Game", which is about soccer, is included in the documentary film "Make Goals Not War." He also made a music video for the song which is on "You Tube". Joseph needed that captivating and absorbing moment in order to develop the passion.

As a final example, when it comes to playing soccer, I always liked the sport ever since my father took me to games at our local stadium but my captivating moment came when my father took me to watch World Club Champions Santos of Brazil. They played against our local Toronto team, the Toronto Metros of the old NASL. The stadium was packed and the game was one of the most memorable I had ever seen. The Toronto Metros took an early 2-0 lead over the powerful team from Brazil. That brought out the best in the Pele and his teammates who went on to take charge of the game and brilliantly attack Toronto in waves. But Toronto's goalkeeper, Dick Howard, made save after save turning in an outstanding performance. Although the Brazilians went on to win 4-2 after Toronto went down to 10 men for over half the game, both Pele and Howard were brilliant. That made me appreciate the skill level of the Brazilians but, at the same time, inspired me to play goalkeeper. That was my "CAM" experience. Passion developed later as I realized I could play the game provided I worked hard to move up to a higher level.

Every kid wants to be a singer, a movie star, or a professional athlete when he or she grows up, but at some point that 'want-to-be' turns into 'I have to find out more on how to become that'. That's the captivating moment. It does not necessarily turn you into a star, but that step has to happen. Some kids want to read all about a team or a player, or watch games all day long. Some want to practice a lot. At some point, the athletes will make a decision. Do they enjoy what they were captivated by or not? If the answer is yes, then they will play and practice more often, and get better and like the game even more. When the sport becomes a passion, then we are on the way to potentially having the correct formula for developing a future professional player. If this does not occur, the player will not develop. As you cannot build a car without steel, you cannot build a future professional or National team player without passion.

Heredity or Opportunity for "CAM"

Quite often people think that the reason certain things are passed on into the next generation within a family is because of genes or heredity. When a child grows up with his or her parents and is surrounded by many things that are involved in their occupations, the child is exposed to more things related to their professions. Because of this entire stimulus and information, there is a better chance that a child finds something in his or her parents' profession that is captivating and absorbing. Although this is not always the case, there is something to be said for the percentage of players or actors that follow their parents' footsteps and become some of the best in the world at it that has nothing to do with heredity.

If you coach young athletes you may have some players on your team who have yet to reach a "Captivating and Absorbing Moment". Others may have discovered soccer and have been captivated by the game but have yet to develop a passion while others have developed that passion and are looking to you to keep it. Understand your role in each player's life because each player will be at a different state of mind when it comes to playing sports.

What Types of Things can you do to Create CAM?

Obviously, the media will play a lot into this as people get interested by things they see on television, in movies, in papers and magazines or in books. Do not forget the live experience of being a fan of soccer. World Cup 94 in the USA introduced the game to many new people in North America. For many Americans who attended a World Cup game for the first time it also clarified why millions of people around the world follow the sport. The media gave it lukewarm coverage but the spectators who went to the games in person were suddenly captivated by the game. Many journalists who had otherwise ignored soccer had now found out why the game is so popular worldwide. For some of them it was a CAM experience. The US Olympic Women's gold medal in Atlanta drew huge crowds both at the stadium and on television. Prior to that event, the US Women's National Team was virtually unknown. All of a sudden they captured the imagination of millions of people. Young children as well as their parents became interested in the game. For some it was a CAM experience. In the US, it was the start of something big that led to record breaking attendance and audiences for the women's game (Picture 8B).

Coaches need to take their players to games, and give them information on what is going on around the world in the game. They need to advertise the game so that their players are captivated in some way. Take them to the movies whenever soccer shows up in a film. The film *Bend it Like Beckham* (2002), where a young girl practices to bend a ball past a wall like Beckham (picture 8A), has inspired many young girls in Europe and in India to take up the game. Some of the best commercials for soccer footwear come with the feeling that soccer is "cool" to play and be a part of. Help provide exposure to local professional teams or national team players to your team members as soccer competes with many other sports for media time in North America. "Captivating and Absorbing Moments" are impossible to manufacture but, as a coach, do your part to give it a better chance.

Picture 8A: David Beckham crosses the ball by bending it around defenders to create a scoring chance. The movie Bend It Like Beckham has inspired many young girls all over the world to take up the game. Photo by Les Jones/Covershots

Inspiration Not Perspiration

Inspiring and motivating players to do more to improve their game usually comes from making the game interesting and fun – not with endless fitness sessions where players start to get turned off, especially at the younger ages. I have seen coaches turn players off the game who were not technically competent by overworking them to make them fitter. If the limiting or determining factor in performance is skill on the ball, then do not spend too much time on non-skill parts of the game. Fitness can be acquired in a short span of time. Becoming a great footballer with vision and skill needs repetitive practice with the ball. Playing with the ball is also more fun and the basis for having passion in the game.

Future goal scorers will need to be captivated by the game in order to become better and then look to seek the more specific information found in this book to get even better.

Picture 8B: The 1999 World Cup Final between the USA and China in the Rose Bowl in California, USA, broke an attendance record for a women's sporting event. Photo by Les Jones/Covershots

CHAPTER 9

General Strikers Skills

Statistics are available that offer information about strikers and some of their attributes. It is important that the strikers you coach know some of them. English FA Coach Dick Bate made these observations about strikers at a video conference presentation in Ottawa in 2001 and updated them in St. Louis at the 2009 NSCAA Coaches Convention:

- Central Strikers cover distances of about 10.5 km per game – all types of movement.
- Cruising speed and top speed make up 10% of running.
- The number of high intensity movements in a game at high speed – 83.4.
- The strikers operate in front of and behind defenders.
- They read the game well.
- They drag defenders away to allow goal scoring opportunities.
- Strikers think of attacking when defenders win the ball by providing outlet passes.
- They have good ball holding skills.
- They delay the opposition when possession is lost and force the opposition in a certain direction.

On the mental skills that strikers possess, Dick Bate made these observations:

- They display courage. They are brave.
- They are persistent in their decision making.
- They are always involved and available.
- They are creative.
- They have concentration, intelligence, composure, perception.
- They focus on their personal performance.
- They check their own game.
- They read defenders well.
- They think ahead.
- They think under stress.
- They have determination and awareness.

Strikers need to take responsibilities by being in a scoring position where there is a chance to score. They need to set up defenders with dummy runs. They must often be first to the ball. Strikers are good at attacking space behind defenders and are very good at keeping the ball under pressure especially to link play when they get the ball and bring teammates into the game with vision, accuracy, variety, and imagination.

The best goal scorer's in the world
only score ONE goal in every two games.

In 2001, Dick Bate of the English FA noted that the best goal scorers would score one goal in every two games and a decade later it is slightly less. Dick Bate has also identified some key skills required by strikers. They are:

- Able to get away from tight marking. This can be practiced using man to man games.
- Good at changing direction and changing pace at the right time.
- Able to support teammates around the penalty box and in deep positions.

They have:

- Good turning skills.
- Effective 1 vs. 1 skills.
- Imaginative distribution skills.
- One touch on-demand skills to score.
- High intensity finishes.

Other skills such as accuracy in shooting and kicking, and being good in the air are also good to have. Speed is a nice luxury but strikers without blazing speed have been able to find success.

In an analysis of goals scored in the 1998 World Cup the following observations were made and published by Professor Lee Harvey of the *Centre for Research into Quality*.

- To score goals it is essential that once the ball gets into the opponents' half, it is moved forward only. The fewer the 'moves' thereafter the more likely a goal will result.
- 59% of goals came from open play and the rest from penalties (11%), free kicks (16%), corners (10%), and throw-ins (4%).
- Most of the open play goals (50%) were from direct attacks and few were from indirect attacks (9 %). Indirect attacks involve one or more passes backwards during the course of an attack in the opponent's half.
- 65% of direct attack goals involved three or fewer moves.
- Despite the rhetoric about intricate and clever play only 9% of the goals in the tournament resulted from indirect attacks. Of the 16 indirect attacks that resulted in goals, 13 involved a single backward pass.

This general information on goals is good for coaches to know when planning their strategies and practice sessions. I urge coaches to continue finding more information as it becomes available. A good source for match analysis type information comes from FIFA's technical studies. They send technical experts to each major FIFA competition to compile interesting and very valuable information. Of course, coaches need to use their own philosophies and know what their players are capable of when deciding how to play. Nonetheless, this information is available and is invaluable.

The success of coaching your players to score more goals does require some team strategies and the above information can help you build your strategies to get your team more scoring opportunities. But as we are not looking at that part of the game in this book, let's get back to working on the mental state of your striker on a one-on-one basis.

CHAPTER 10

Perception is Reality

I write about perception quite a bit throughout the book and talk about it whenever I lecture on the subject of goal-scoring, but as I stated earlier I use the term perception in many different ways. In this chapter I will be focusing on the advertising type of perception and how it affects players and specifically, potential strikers. The athletes must separate what they perceive to be true or real and what is real. If you cannot get past this stage with your strikers, you will struggle to achieve success.

The strikers must understand clearly what we are talking about in this section and I would advise to bring examples outside of soccer to make things absolutely clear. You need to break down preconceived notions in regards to how goals are scored and about how they perceive themselves when they score goals. You will need to remind players constantly about these points. They will forget (picture 10B). It's human nature.

We are talking about brain re-programming and you need to tell players quite clearly that they will need, first and foremost to re-program their brain before they can be the best that they can be. They must erase what their brains think about scoring and overcome emotions and self-doubt as they reprogram their inner computers (picture 10A).

Picture 10A: Like computers, we need our strikers to erase their memory and reprogram their brains about how to score goals.

Younger players may need more of an explanation than older players, but generally things do not appear to be as they seem. Use examples from advertisements such as the following ones and make sure they are age-appropriate for your players.

For example, when watching certain beer commercials on television, the advertiser wants you to get the impression that for those who drink their brand of beer, life is great, fun, and the beer will make your life better and will help you make more friends. That's the perception the advertiser wants you to believe. Reality is that only you can make friends, not the beer.

Other ads suggest that certain shoes will make you a better player. Reality is that practice will make you a better player, not the shoes. Convey this message to your players about this type of perception.

In regards to scoring goals, there are many perceptions that players have that are not accurate. For example, players think that there is a certain area of the net that goals are scored in. As I will point out throughout this book, the realities of how goals are scored are usually different from what many players think.

In the next four chapters, I will explain how I change the focus of scoring in the brain of the players I work with.

Picture 10B: Gygax of Switzerland reacts to a missed goal scoring opportunity at the 2006 World Cup. The situation Gygax had to score was a classic case of where perception of the situation was not reality. In other words, most players in that situation would have done what Gygax decided to do because of the visual stimulus provided by his eyes. But the correct decision requires mental strength to do what is illogical based on what the eyes see but logical in terms of how to score. A better decision could have turned a 0-0 game into a 1-0 victory for his team against France. Action Images/Pascal Lauener

CHAPTER 11

Goal Scoring is an Individual Sport

I believe that you must convey to the players that, to be great goal scorers, they must understand goal scoring is an individual sport like tennis, badminton, and golf. Athletes of individual sports have to have a different mental makeup because they cannot blame anyone else for their loss or win. They have to study the game more because they have no one else to lean on but themselves. In tennis, the player who makes the fewest mistakes usually wins. The world's best strikers usually make the fewest mistakes when getting chances.

This understanding is vital and I have taught players who have totally understood this and transformed their game almost immediately. This point made them pay attention to my information and material more than any other point. Getting this fact into their psyche is key to progressing quicker and getting your athletes into the correct frame of mind to want to learn more. This understanding will make them want to take more responsibilities for their own performance as it relates to scoring goals and is essential in self-analysis, which I will discuss later.

Eliminate Errors and you Will be More Successful

The key to victory or success in any individual sport comes down to eliminating errors. The golfer who gets a hole-in-one and then a triple bogey on the next three holes will not win the competition too often, if at all. The tennis player who misses an easy shot has to be mentally strong enough to overcome a mistake and focus on the next shot. Tennis player Roger Federer (Picture 11A) has an amazing ability to stay focused, eliminate errors, and stay consistent without being too flashy to get the job done.

Bronze Medal at Olympics

I remember watching my sister-in-law, Julie Cirone-Foley play beach volleyball in the Canadian pro circuit as she tried to qualify for a berth on the Canadian Olympic team. While she played in the tournament on her court, another match had started at Centre court that had attracted a lot of attention. The tournament was held just outside Montreal, Canada. The match on Centre court featured Heese and Child, the Men's Olympic bronze medallists at the 1996 Olympic Games. Every few minutes one could hear some loud cheering from the crowd, so, after my sister-in-law's game, I rushed to catch the men's game. Heese and Child were playing against the Quebec home town fan favourites. Each time the Quebec pair scored a point they did it in dramatic fashion diving all over the place to grab a point. They showed great athleticism in getting those points and the local crowd cheered enthusiastically. After about five minutes, I was looking for the scoreboard wanting to see what the score was. I expected that the Quebec pair had a comfortable lead judging by all the diving around they were doing, scooping balls out of nowhere to score points, and from the cheers from the crowd. To my astonishment the score did not reflect what I had perceived. It was totally the opposite with Heese and Child winning the game by a wide margin.

Heese and Child won their first match and I continued to watch them closely for the next match. The game took on the same attributes as the first. The local team played some exciting points and had the partisan crowd behind them but the experienced Olympians remained composed and focused and they eventually ran away with the game. In the end Heese and Child won two straight games to eliminate the local and flamboyant team to move on to the next round. Heese and Child lost points whenever their opponents made unbelievable plays but scored points whenever they could not. They made very few errors and it always took a perfect shot to score a point against them. Without unforced errors they won handily and showed why they were Canada's best. They were mentally focused, playing as a team but each player was focused as though they were playing an individual sport making sure they made the simple plays all the time without making errors.

Picture 11A: Roger Federer has an uncanny ability to stay focused even after he makes a mistake that costs him a point. Successful athletes in individual sports, have a certain mental make-up that strikers must also have if they are to be successful goal scorers. Picture supplied by Action Images /Henry Browne

I recall a goalkeeper I used to coach who was my second string keeper on my U13 boys rep team long ago. He could not come to grips with the fact that he was not even close to being as good as the first string goalie. One day, our team played against the Canadian champions from the previous year in a league game. Our team had just moved up a division so we were down by the bottom of the standings and had lost to this team previously by a score of 9-0. In this particular game we were short of players due to injuries and holidays and had to play against the defending champions with 9 players. Our first string keeper was away on holidays for that game. We won the game by a score of 1-0, and our second string keeper played well and made some great saves, including stopping a penalty shot. Many of the saves were more luck than anything but he did play well.

After that game he went on to play his usual game worthy of a second string position at the time. Unfortunately, he consistently went on to remind me how great he played that one game against the defending champions and why he should start more often even though he played poorly after that game. He did not improve over the next season and a half and was no longer good enough to play rep soccer. Our team had improved to become one of the top teams in the league over a two-year period but he did not improve with others. That probably came from the fact that he perceived himself to be better than he actually was therefore he could not possibly be concentrating on getting better if he already thought he was better than he was.

The point I'm making is that in order to get better, players must be able to analyze their game and pick out areas where they can improve. This player should have used his positive experience to try and get better and duplicate his efforts instead of trying to convince his coach he was better than he was. This ability to self-analyze is relevant to players in all positions but nowhere more meaningful than for strikers. If Gary Lineker had thought that he could not score because the ball was not played to him when he was open and shunned the responsibility, then he would have never been one of the world's best goal scorers. When thinking like an athlete in an individual sport, the players can look for ways to improve based on their performance and not based on their teammates' performance.

Strikers need to believe that scoring goals is like playing an individual sport.

Most strikers do not think this way enough. This type of thinking will get the players in the correct frame of mind to study their position as though they are on their own and help them be consistent. The great players in tennis are consistent. The great players in golf are consistent. They make fewer mental errors. Every hit or stroke must be good. They need to stay focused on their task with each shot. Only they hold the cards to their own destiny. Consistency is vital. Eliminating errors is even more vital. Stress this to your players. No doubt that in soccer the opponents will have a great deal to do with the outcome of a scoring chance. But the defenders will have nothing to do with the outcome if the players who get the chances are not focused and botch it all up when they should have scored.

When they fail to make a shot, players in individual sports are quick to analyse their performance and try to immediately find what the cause of the error was. They identify it and move on. They have a mental ability to learn from their error and move past it. The successful athletes do this well. Sometimes, even the best players in the world have mental lapses and sometimes it takes more than just a few seconds or minutes to get their game back in control. In some cases they completely lose it for some reason or another and cannot get back in that particular game or tournament but are strong enough to come back in the near future and compete at the highest levels. Those that cannot do this will get down and never succeed. The key to athletes' success in individual sports is consistency. Being consistent at the highest level also means being very skilled which takes long hours of practice and repetition. When strikers see themselves as athletes in an individual sport, they have the power to be even better than their skill level suggests.

Using Math to Change Perception to Reality

Small changes can lead to big improvements and simple mathematics can illustrate this point very powerfully as pointed out in Chapter 5. Remember, your goal as a coach is to capture the attention of your players to focus on their own performance when having an opportunity to score and to take the result into their own hands and not anyone else's.

Expected Response

"I want to know more. I'm willing to accept responsibility for my success and I can't wait to play again." That's what you want your players to be thinking after you have taught them how scoring is like an individual sport. You want them to take ownership of their own ability to score. You want them to start to think differently about practices so that they develop the consistency in performing even the simplest of skills.

Although much of this seems like common sense, you will be amazed at how some players do not see their game in this way, especially your key strikers. They often are the quickest to blame others for their lack of scoring or scoring chances. They can also be the first to take the credit when a goal is scored. That's the nature of the beast. When discussing the individual sport comparisons with your strikers, be careful not to overstate the point because it will sound like you are lecturing them rather than advising them. Some young players turn off when an exciting point becomes a repetitive lecture.

I would advise that when focusing on many of the psychological points I make in this book, that you do not make many of the points part of your team lectures but rather in a one-on-one format with certain players. Each player will be able to take in certain information and the timing of it will be different with each player. Often, it's better to bring in an outside person to get into some of the psychological aspects of soccer. Many sports teams have sport psychologists on staff to deal with each athlete on an individual basis because each position can be looked at as an individual sport in some way. But by far, the strikers and goalkeepers are your two most individual sport-like positions on the field.

In 1999, the USA Women's National Team won the Women's World Cup. They had sport psychologist, Dr. Colleen Hacker on staff. Coach Tony DiCicco stated in a lecture at a NSCAC video conference that, while the Chinese players were probably more skilled on a one-on-one basis, the difference that resulted in the USA winning the World Cup was probably that Dr. Hacker was on staff and working with each athlete individually. The Chinese team did not have a sport psychologist on staff.

CHAPTER 12

Scoring is Not Easy

Now that you have convinced the players to look to themselves for their performance as though they are playing an individual sport, you must prepare them for their biggest challenge: overcoming failure.

You may be thinking that in Chapter 3, I was telling you to make the strikers feel that goal scoring is easy and fun, and now I'm telling you the opposite. Not only do I do this when lecturing to coaches but also I'm quick to make the exact same point to players. The point is to make sure that the player does not get down on himself when unsuccessful. Hopefully, I will have trained them to analyze their own performance and realize that scoring should have been easier, and then quickly identify what went wrong. This becomes motivation for their next opportunity and should help them focus on doing the simple things required to convert chances into goals.

There is no doubt that scoring is not easy. It's not easy to score. Even the best players will not score on every shot even with no opposition or goaltenders. The ball is moving; the body is in motion, the conditions are different in each instance. Things are changing constantly. The player must understand that missing is going to occur and must be accepted.

We Are Only Human

Rafi Srebro in his excellent book on mental training for soccer, *Winning With Your Head* wrote, "real mental strength comes from the acceptance that you are only a human being! You are neither superman nor a star, even if it is written in the papers. Real strength comes with your awareness of your weaknesses!"

This is an important factor because each player is only human and each is unique. Even the best players in the world make mistakes. Our brains cannot possibly be in deep cognitive thought all the time. We have weak moments not just in sport but in life as well.

No Player Can Bat 1000

I like to compare scoring to baseball especially when trying to make sure the athlete understands the point of this chapter. In baseball the batter gets a minimum of 3 chances to hit a ball. He can attempt to hit the ball when the ball is in the strike zone and get to pass when it's not. He can mis-hit the ball provided it's not caught and still get another chance to swing at it. There are no moving defenders to worry about and he doesn't have to move to get to the ball because the pitcher actually has to pitch it to him exactly where he is. To top it all off, he has a coach or manager on the sidelines telling him what type of pitch to expect based on statistics. He gives the player this information by way of signals. In picture 12A, first baseman Justin Morneau of the Minnesota Twins swings at a baseball. Wouldn't it be nice if your strikers had this luxury when attempting to kick or head a ball into goal off a cross?

Imagine: no opposition, the ball has to be placed in a perfect area so you can kick or head the ball and a coach telling you what to do every time you get a chance to score. In soccer even if you hit the ball towards goal you only have one goalie to worry about preventing you from scoring. In baseball, you have nine goalies, perhaps a minor disadvantage. It still must be simple. But it's not. In baseball, if you fail to hit the ball safely 8 out of 10 times you can say goodbye to making it to the next level. But if you fail just a bit less, say 7 out of 10 times, you not only make the next level but you are considered a superstar. And if that were in the majors, you would be worth at least 5 million dollars a year!

Fail Just a bit Less and you Make the Next Level

If you fail just a bit less, you can make it to the next level. In order to be able to do that you have to accept failure 7 out of 10 times in baseball and adjust your game just enough to fail a bit less. The baseball players need the same mental makeup as players playing an individual sport. They accept that hitting is not easy and focus on getting better rather than getting down. No player can bat 1000. In soccer, the problem is that a player will not get as many

Picture 12A: Minnesota Twins first baseman Justin Morneau (33) receives signals from his coaches to help him try and hit a baseball. He still fails 7 out of 10 times to get a hit. Overcoming failure is essential to baseball players because failing just a little bit less could be the difference between not making a team or being a superstar. Picture supplied by Action Images/Jan Cole

chances to score as a baseball player does so they will have to make the best of it. A swing and a miss in soccer can be a slightly mistimed run or a failure to focus on performing the skill correctly.

Sport Psychology Only Helps Players who are Coachable

When using sport psychology in coaching, we need to make sure the player is coachable. Most players are, but some don't like to show that they need help in front of their peers. Work on psychology away from the team. The players will be more receptive to your advice in overcoming failure. Those who get down on themselves may need an extra pat on the back but at the end of the day, they will need to address this on their own and in their own minds during a competition. Knowing that <u>you</u> know they are only human and know that scoring is difficult will give them the confidence to seek to do better and get excited about the next opportunity rather than get down about their mistakes or near misses. I refer to the baseball statistics when I see strikers get down on themselves for missing. Since scoring chances do not come often in games, when a player misses, all the spectators, teammates, and coaches see the opportunity and feel let down by the miss. This can play on players' mind, especially the young ones. The great goal scorers make it their challenge to do better on the next opportunity by analyzing what went wrong.

At this point in training the mind, I do not want to complicate things by talking about defenders and evading them. That will come later. I want to concentrate on the player being able to score on the chances that he is already getting because he <u>has</u> evaded the defenders. Often enough, this can be the difference between winning and losing for your team. Before moving to the next step, the player has to understand that scoring is not easy that they will fail and that's OK.

Tony DiCicco, in his book *Catch Them Being Good*, had to learn how to deal with female athletes after having coached male athletes with previous teams. Without going into too much detail, DiCicco noted that his approach to coaching women athletes had to be completely different from coaching male athletes. It wasn't until he realized that there were major differences between males and females from a psychological standpoint that he started achieving success. He was successful in learning how to work with them and changing his approach. This change of style helped his team win the Women's World Cup. For soccer coaches who are accustomed to coaching males and switch to coaching female teams, I recommend they read his book.

The Higher up you go the Harder it is to Score

When coaching youth players you will need to pay attention to their development because things will change. Quite often players who scored lots of goals when they were younger can no longer score as many as they used to. As they grow, players can get down on themselves as they no longer dominate because of speed or height, and they possibly lose confidence when they can no longer score at a rate they were accustomed to. Players may have great skills and you may have invested time to develop them. You would not want to lose these players because they have the potential to be great. Make them understand that the higher up you go, the harder it is to score. Tell them they need to understand this, accept it and move on. Challenge them to be better at their new age level and encourage them to enjoy the game.

When I coached an U16 boy's team I had a player that came to me from U14 the previous year and was one of the leading goal scorers in the league. But when he moved to my team he was U15 playing up in U16 and he also moved up a level from his local league to a district league. He was no longer a big goal scorer and his speed was not an advantage anymore as the players in U16 were bigger, faster, and more talented. He found it difficult to get away with things he was able to at the lower age and skill level. I knew this player had the potential to improve and become a much better player but he had problems adjusting to the new level of play. He was not good enough to play striker at this level but was a good wing midfield player. He lamented not playing as a striker and did not improve. He could not understand why I did not play him at striker so I gave him an opportunity to play a game at the striker position later that season knowing that he would not find his form and score as he had done in the past. After half a game at the striker position without success he asked to go back to his wing-midfield position and played his best game of the season. He came to grips with reality and that goal scoring is not easy, and started vastly improving almost immediately.

The funny part of this was that at the start of the season the player came with a bit of an attitude until he realized things were not so easy. By year's end, and especially after he realized how hard it was to score, he became a pleasure to coach.

Often we lose players when they face reality. I have a problem with losing players when they stop enjoying the game because quite often some of them get into bad pastimes. Our youth is precious and regardless of how far they go in the game, I make it a personal goal to do my best to keep kids in sports.

Coach of the Year

I will never forget a panel discussion I attended with Pele, Tony Waiters, (renowned author, former Canadian National team coach, and former English National team Goalkeeper) and Dr. Tom Fleck, (Director of Coaching for the Florida Youth Soccer Association) as guest speakers. The topic was player development. One of the most important points that I came away with from that discussion was Dr. Fleck's statement about who should win the "coach of the year" award at the youth level. He said, "The coach of the year award should be given to a coach who retains the most players in the game the following year as opposed to the coach who has the most wins."

Earlier I discussed coaching passion. This is the key to developing players because once the players you coach have a passion for the game and take that passion away with them off the practice fields and into the parks and streets, then you will have better players, and eventually teams.

It's not Easy to Score Goals

I tell players:

> ***"You will miss your share of chances. You will go through slumps, which may simply be because the team is not providing you with chances or the opposition has defended well. Great players who score goals also go through slumps. You will go through hot streaks as well. Keep challenging yourself to do what it takes mentally to do better and keep getting excited about when the next opportunity to score may present itself. Do everything in your power to study the game to get more chances to score and then convert them.***
>
> ***I will not be upset at you for missing. Just promise me that you will analyze and ask yourself, what possibly could have gone wrong? Do not be afraid to ask for my opinion."***

In this chapter I have prepared the players for failure because they will fail to score more often than actually score. Being mentally prepared for this actually relieves stress and prepares players for success. Dale Carnegie, in his best selling book, *How to Stop Worrying and Start Living,* gives some simple advice:

1. What is the worst that can happen?
2. Prepare for the worst.
3. Proceed to improve on it.

By making sure players know scoring is not easy, you are preparing them for the worst and then asking them to think over what they could do better next time and improve on their performance.

CHAPTER 13

The Brain and Stress

Many strikers fail to get to the next level because of stress that they put on themselves. Players are always thinking and worrying about things before the game, during the game, and after the game. But the brain is complex and affects performance more than any other factor as I have stated before.

Rafi Srebro, in his book, *Winning With Your Head*, writes about stress being a result of our own thoughts, "In sport, most threatening situations are a result of thoughts and they exist only in our imagination or mind."

How can coaches help relieve stress for the athlete? Obviously, making the player as skilful as possibly is essential and teaching players how to perform the skills of shooting or passing under different situations is vital. I will not discuss this aspect of goal scoring. There are many books and videos that do an excellent job of going through the step by step methods of performing a skill. Books will cover everything from where to keep the eyes and plant the support foot, to what part of the foot to use in each situation, to where the body and the knee should be in relation to the ball. This information is very important but not the main context of this book. DO NOT forget the importance of teaching the proper technique and skills.

But apart from skill, the coach can relieve the stress players put on themselves by trying to figure out what their strikers are thinking during games as it relates to skill. For example, if your players are thinking that in a particular situation he should trap the ball and take on a defender and beat them before they can shoot to score, but the correct decision is to do a quick give-and-go with a team-mate and then shoot to score, then we need to work on the player's mind so that he makes the correct decisions in each situation.

Trying too Hard

Getting through to the player is not easy but if players continuously make bad decisions, they will fail more often than they should. Using the example from above, this can lead the player to try harder to attempt to beat an opponent to get a chance to score. But if it's still the wrong decision to make, then they will still fail which will make them put more pressure on themselves. How often do we hear that when players are not scoring that they may be trying too hard to score? Often the remedy is simple and it's about making better decisions and not a lack of skill.

So in essence, I'm presenting as many possibilities as possible so that you will make the correct connection with your players. How often have you been in a situation at school when you are having problems understanding the concept of a topic be it math, science, physics, or another subject? But then, all of a sudden, someone explains it to you in a different way and you completely understand it. I'm suggesting that you may need to explain things differently to your strikers when they are having problems converting scoring chances. Try to find alternate methods of communicating with them.

The Cognitive Development of Athletes

Understanding stress is important in trying to improve performance. In his book, Srebro looks at stress using the following flow chart:

Causes of stress > your thoughts > your feelings
> the things you say to yourself
> the explanation and definitions you give to situations.

This shows that stress is under each individual's control. The athlete must believe in this concept.

But improvement in performance can also come from making correct decisions in a game. The more correct decisions players make, the more confident they become. In scoring goals, helping players make correct decisions is THE most important factor in scoring. Most of the times, when players have failed to score, they have made poor decisions. They may have made poor decisions in what to do, or in which skill to use, or in assessing where they are on the field, or where their opponents are. Some of the decision-making process can be trained instinctively even later in life through deep cognitive thought. Others aspects of the decision making process will come with making a player "smarter" and a student of the game. Knowing how to read the game quickly by having knowledge of the game will help players make more correct decisions. I'll help you educate the strikers on this component of the game in Part 3 of this book.

Here then are some factors that will help coaches decide what to work on with their strikers.

Cognitive perception in mind/body skill training.
This means that you will need to find methods to make the players more skilful by helping them in making certain skill decisions instinctively. Repetitive training is the only method to achieve this and I will cover how to speed this type of training up in more detail in the Human Body section in Part 2. Not all players will have this ability.

Deep thought is needed by the athletes so that they can analyse themselves.
The players will need the information necessary to evaluate their performance. In other words, they will need to think like a coach. Coaches usually know what went wrong when a goal is not scored. The players will need to acquire this skill.

Players must know when they were consciously in the state that produced cognitive thought during performance. If an athlete does not have this ability, then only repetition training can produce automatic responses.
Can the athletes feel a difference in their performance when they are in the mental state that produces better results and better self-analysis? Often we call this state "being in the zone". This comes from being able to deal with stress.

The successful players will keep practising their mental portion of their game and really think of their finishing touch needed to score.
As a coach, you want to narrow their choice of which skill to use in each goal-scoring situation they get. You want to be the baseball manager in their head giving signals to them as the ball is played to them so that they can pick the right thing to do to score. The soccer facts I will provide in Part 3 of this book will be the information you will need to give your players in order to help them make better decisions on which skill to use to score more goals. This information will help them deal with stress. They will have less self-doubt about what to do.

It's important to note that some players will absorb the information you provide while others will not. You cannot pester players or get on their backs when they are not ready. It will only hinder their development. I suggest that you try different approaches and stress different points when communicating with them. Remember to keep this part of training one-on-one and do not single players out in front of their peers.

Sport psychology itself can be a questionable subject for some athletes, but without question, it can be a very powerful tool for others.

In the training of strikers it is important to focus on two psychological issues that must be dealt with. Both are important to working with strikers to make them perform better.

- The first is to give the player as much information about not letting bad plays affect future performance. (Chapter 14)
- The second is to tell the player that some of the key information to scoring goals is 'top secret'. (Chapter 15)

CHAPTER 14

"Che Sera, Sera"

Players that get chances to score will invariably miss their share of glorious opportunities. Or so that's what they may appear to be. I have often watched these glorious goal scoring opportunities in slow motion and often saw that the shooter was not always at fault for missing. Sometimes, a great last minute effort is made by the defender to prevent the goal or the goalkeeper pulls off a heroic save. In other instances, a bad and unlucky bounce occurs just prior to the player playing the ball. But of course, there are instances where the player should have scored and deserves to be benched.

Did you really think I was serious about the benching? If you did not agree with that statement, then you know how players who miss can start to doubt their own abilities. Often, missed glorious opportunities, even if the goalkeeper makes a great save, cause some psychological damage to the players because they feel that everyone is watching and knows that they missed a great chance to score. They start to feel more pressure especially as the game progresses and when that chance could have been crucial to the outcome of the game. You will not want your players to be in this state of mind because they will be more likely to miss again.

I found that the best goalscorers and players I feared most when I played goal were the ones who did not let a miss or save bother them. In fact, they went about playing with the confidence that it was just a matter of time before they would score on me. This confidence factor is very unsettling for the goalkeeper. On the other hand, I could tell if a player was rattled and affected by a missed chance. I found that they missed even more often. Of course the opposite would occur occasionally. But the player that was confident and knew what he did wrong couldn't wait for another chance to ruin my day. He did not seem to let a failed attempt deter him from scoring later in the game even under extreme pressure. On the other hand, the player who had low self-confidence needed just a bit of stress to lose focus and miss or shoot the ball right at me.

The Panic Attack

Players who get great chances often get a panic attack. Many thoughts come across their minds as they get close to scoring. Srebro explains: "When the brain recognizes a real or imagined stressful situation the body prepares for immediate reaction." It's not often the correct reaction. Often it happens at the moment of skill execution. Just as they try to volley, head, or kick, something forces them to lose focus at the last second just enough to miss. At other times, their mind is not thinking correctly and they choose the wrong skill or make the wrong decision on what to do. This happens regularly with players. Those we see at the pro level have already improved on their ability to make better decisions. That's why they are there.

Picture 14A: Often players, including pro players, get excited about scoring chances that look very appetizing and easy. They are salivating over the chance they are presented with and often make the wrong decision and miss the opportunity. It's like kids getting excited over something. They just lose their composure with excitement and anticipation.

You Get So Excited!

The opposite of the panic attack is the excited feeling of anticipation one gets when a chance presents itself. Sometimes players get so excited that they forget the secrets (the basics) to scoring a goal. It's a bit like how kids look when something excites them. (Picture 14A) They lose their composure with excitement and anticipation.

These two extremes can be illustrated by my own experience in another sport. In one instance I get a panic attack whenever I get a chance to score when I play hockey. Scoring chances are very rare because I'm a defender and when I get one I often get a panic attack and rush my shot or over-anticipate instead of being calm about it. I think that someone is all over me ready to stop me from scoring. In the other instance, I sometimes get excited rather than panicky and I mess up as well, especially when a situation seems to be a certain goal for me.

The brain works in mysterious ways and in both instances, players lose their focus on what they need to do to score.

Here is how I explain it to players who attend my goal scoring course,

> ***"You will miss. You will make mistakes. You are only human. Rather than get upset about it or get down on yourself, what you must do is quickly analyze your play and find out what you did wrong. Based on the secrets from my course, ask yourself what went wrong and then imagine yourself in the same position doing the right thing. Then get excited about doing the right thing next time. Keep focusing on your next opportunity. Stay tuned-in with the game to get another chance and then get excited about doing what you know you can do to score.***
>
> ***DO NOT let the past affect the future in a negative way. If anything, make it a positive thing. Ask yourself, can I control the emotions and options that I have racing through my mind when I get a chance simply by focusing on what I know needs to be done because that's what I learned in this course? The key is that you know what you will do next time regardless of the situation.***
>
> ***What you need to do is be thrilled with the fact you are playing a sport you love to play and be excited for your next chance. You will be happy being where you are. Do not worry about the people watching. You can do nothing about what happened. Just get excited about what can happen when you score later because you will be more focused and you will use your secrets. Often you missed the scoring chance because you forgot for an instant the secrets I have told you."***

I end my speech by singing a song, an old team song our team sang. I'm talking about the York University team I played on which went all the way to win a National Championship. We used to sing this song on the bus. The song was an old Doris Day Song called "Che Sera, Sera[1]." Now you wouldn't think a bunch of tough looking guys would sing a song such as "Che Sera, Sera" but we did, starting with a long Cheeeeeeee before we continued the song. "Che Sera, Sera," in Italian means, "whatever will be, will be," because, as the song goes, "the future's not ours to see, what will be, will be, che sera, sera."

I explain the meaning of the song and I want the players to use that in their minds to get over their misses and get on with the game. It's a happy song, so it works well. Sometimes, the coach can be the one using these words to remind the player about not getting down. It can help refocus the players to analyze what they did wrong and focus on scoring on a similar chance at a later time or the next game.

Coaches Gerry Gentile and Michael Ruscigno who took my golden goal scoring course with their players told me that they used this technique to remind their players about the basics (the secrets) of scoring. In the first half of a league game, Analisa Romano, (their top scorer, who had taken the course) had just missed a great scoring chance by forgetting the basic secrets to scoring. She had reverted back to some old habits. Gentile, knowing this could affect her, said the phrase "che sera, sera" when she got close to the bench. She smiled, knew what he meant, and relaxed about the miss and started focusing on her game again. She had a brilliant second half and scored an absolutely magnificent goal to seal a victory for her team. I received a copy of the DVD of her game and watched her score that goal and one could see exactly what she was thinking as she set up to score. She knew what to do and this time there was not going to be any mistakes.

Confidence Must Be High

Without question players need to feel confident that they can do what they want with the ball. You do not want their mind to be saying, "oh my gosh, here comes the ball, I hope I can trap it or keep it." Or, "I hope I don't mess things up." If your players are having these thoughts, then this is a problem and they are more likely to miss.

Michael Owen, (Picture 14B) of England said this about scoring in an article by Simon Kuper from *Financial Times* in 2003, "When confidence is high they flow, and when it's not they dry up". The point of this chapter is that your players will all go through this lack of self-confidence at some point in their careers. What you need to do is give them the comfort level so that you are not upset at them and that they are good enough to score. Let them feel the confidence.

Players that feel more comfortable with the ball also tend to be more confident players. One way to train on-the-ball confidence is something all players can do in their spare time: ball juggling.

Athletes of individual sports have to be very good at not allowing the past affect the future or they will not advance in their sport. Former number one ranked men's tennis player in the world, Roger Federer, said that after years of playing tennis he has found peace on the court. He used to be "wild' on the court before becoming "number one" because he'd get frustrated: "Now I can handle it. If I miss shots, I say, 'Okay, I hope the next one goes better'. So I can just always see something positive in my game".

The examples above illustrate why you need to consider the delicate state of mind of strikers when they miss. As coach, your actions, your reactions, your body language and what you say or do to the player who missed can be the difference between winning and losing. This is where your skills as a manager of people will be tested.

A final note on missed opportunities: tell your players never to take blame for a missed chance where they did everything correctly but a great defensive play or save by the goalkeeper saved a goal for the opponent. Tell your players to admire their opponents' efforts and skills. It's what makes sport so exciting. Hopefully, the goalkeeper will also admire and respect your strikers' efforts when they score. Often this respect does not present itself until after players retire or age. Old-timers always come back to say that they really respected their former competitors for both their mental and physical skills once they have analyzed their careers.

1. The term "Che Sera Sera" was first used in a movie called *The Barefoot Contessa* where actor Rossano Brazzi's family motto was "Che Sera Sera." The motto in the film was in Italian, but Evans and Livingston, the composers of the song, switched the "Che" to "Que" because more people spoke Spanish in the US. The song won the 1956 Oscar for Best Song. It was used in the Alfred Hitchcock movie *The Man Who Knew Too Much* and later in the 1960 film *Please Don't Eat The Daisies*. Later the song became the theme song for the sitcom *The Doris Day Show*, which ran from 1968-1973.

Picture 14B: Michael Owen scores against Brazil in the 2002 World Cup. He says, "when confidence is high they flow, and when it's not they dry up." Action Images/Ian Waldie.

CHAPTER 15

Secrets

As I stated earlier the word 'secret' is a very powerful word and one you should use to help develop great goal scorers. Because of the powerful implications of the word you will not want to address goal-scoring secrets presented in this book to the whole team. Use the information in this book to coach your strikers one-on-one.

The first point I make about how to teach your strikers to score more goals is that I have to make them believe in the principles outlined in this book. The only way to approach this topic is that the striker must know that some of the specific information they are receiving from the coach truly are secrets. They must "make it their own" to be most effective and the coach must work one-on-one to coach this aspect of scoring. You cannot give out secrets to a whole group. And the coach must tell his players to keep the information secret.

General shooting information and drills can be taught to the whole team but some of the specific details in this book must be taught to individual players. Do not underestimate this recommendation. It will pay great dividends. In teaching secrets to individual players, use examples from other sports. Often athletes of other sports offer great information that would seem like secrets to soccer players – especially, the psychological information.

Since there is so much psychological information out there, what you hope to do is find something that will connect with each of your players on an individual basis. Secrets give confidence. I will not get into the specifics of some of the secrets at this point, as they will be noted throughout the book. Some of the information I provide may not seem like secrets but I present them as secrets to players.

What I want to emphasize in this chapter is the fact that players tend to lend an ear to the word 'secret'. And as magicians do, tell your players to keep secrets a secret. At 15, my son Joseph was an avid fan of magicians David Blaine and Criss Angel. He studied them so closely that he could perform many of the magic tricks they do. Often he got hired for house parties to entertain. As I watched him perform, occasionally there were other magicians in the room. To watch them is as much a treat as watching the show itself. They are right there pretending to be fooled and keeping quiet. It's an unwritten rule. Magicians can never reveal their secrets. They never reveal how a trick is done. In picture 15A my sons Joseph and Marco met magician and illusionist Criss Angel in Las Vegas.

Picture 15A: Criss Angel is the creator, executive producer and director of his #1 rated television series on A&E (Criss Angel MINDFREAK). Criss has received numerous awards throughout his career. He was named 2001, 2004, 2005, 2007 and 2008 Magician of the Year. The CRISS ANGEL Believe Cirque du Soleil show is ongoing in Las Vegas' Luxor Hotel and Casino.

Here is what I tell strikers who attend my goal-scoring course.

> ***"It's a competitive world out there. Do not go revealing the secrets I teach you to anyone. It's the little secrets that will allow you to beat another player for the starting position. The little secrets you will learn, plus the tricks and facts you will learn, must be stored in your memory as such. Take possession of them as your own. Use them over and over again. As simple as some of them seem, pretend that you own them all by yourself and go out and enjoy trying them. Most magicians' tricks are so simple yet most people do not know them. Goals scoring secrets are the same.***
>
> ***Practice them and get better at using each trick or fact. This information is a secret of the great goal scorers. Like magicians, other good goal scorers won't tell you their secrets so make sure to keep yours to yourself. There are not many of you who will know them, so keep it quiet. When you move up to the next level and someone else does not, do not make fun of them, but remember, your secrets are precious."***

If you were a player and listened to that speech on a one-on-one basis, would you not get excited about these secrets, trying them, practising them and trying to excel? We are all human beings, and all humans seem to love a secret. It puts them in an elite and special group. Have you ever been left out of a secret when you knew that there was one going around? Does that not drive you crazy when someone does not want to tell you his secret?

The word secret is used in marketing all the time. Kentucky Fried Chicken restaurants use a 'secret' recipe. There are advertisements about the 'secrets of weight loss' or the 'secrets to becoming rich' everyday in the media. You feel privileged when you're let in on a secret.

But when you know there is a secret out there and no one is telling you, your hair stands on end and you become frustrated. The brain can emit an emotional/chemical response in our bodies just because of this word and how we interpret it. Is it working for you or against you?

Coaching your strikers and goalkeepers, especially as they get into the higher leagues and into their teens and onward, becomes just as much as a psychological challenge as it is and technical challenge. Most coaches do not deal with this aspect of coaching enough and many who do, work on it with the whole team. But consider the state of mind of both the goalkeeper and the striker. Both positions have negative undertones associated with them. The best way to truly understand these undertones is to be a parent of a striker or goalkeeper watching a son or daughter play. My nephew, Daniel plays competitive hockey and whenever I go watch him play I find it more stressful than usual. When I ask my brother Mark how he handles the stress of being the father of a goalkeeper he tells me that it's not easy because it's the only position on the team where you start with zero and go minus one, or two, or three, or four or more. Even when the team wins, the keeper ends on the minus side of things unless he gets a shutout.

As I state in my lecture session, many strikers find it harder to score as they get older and into more competitive soccer. The number of goals goes down. Often players who scored at a young age because of speed or a big kick can no longer score with the same regularity. Goalkeepers get taller and defenders start to become more specialised. At the highest levels there are not as many goals scored in a soccer game. This statistic from *FIFA Magazine* reveals the most common results of soccer matches.

FIFA MAGAZINE SEPTEMBER 2004

The most common result in Soccer is 1-0
(19% of matches end with this score)
10% of matches end 0-0
23% of matches have 2 goals
20% of matches have 3 goals

Playing Striker is a Psychologically Negative Position

To truly understand the negative vibes inherent in playing the striker position, think of it in this manner. If there are three strikers per team who share 90 minutes in a game, that means that only one player of six will leave the game with a goal in 29% of the games. Five strikers will have had an unsuccessful game when judged by goals scored. This is the scenario once every third game. And if two goals are scored in a game then only two out of six players will have something to be positive about after the game. Now what if a midfielder scores a goal once in a while or a defender moves forward to score? That makes the probability of a striker scoring even less. What happens if the team loses and the striker does not score? Who gets the blame?

Even if the strikers had no good balls to score from, the pressure will still be on them especially from the media. Going into a game, the average fan is expecting a goal from each of the strikers. How unfair! Most strikers come away from a game on a negative note when judging their personal performance based on goals. So if strikers can't deal with this pressure, then, regardless of their skill level, they may fail to reach their true potential. Coaches need to understand this and work on the psychology of their strikers more than any other players on their team. Using secrets as a coaching tool is one way of helping out the strikers to help them gain confidence.

Coach Geoff Fleck of Pickering, Ontario, who was at one of my lectures, sent me this e-mail. "Loved your presentation and came away both informed and inspired. Your discussion on the secrets that the coach shares with the strikers alone reminded me of something I'd seen in a movie. The scene was an adventure camp. The time was twenty years later and these thirty-something friends were reliving their summer adventures from twenty years previously. One of them asked if he could remember what super secret Indian name the camp co-ordinator had given him twenty years previously. The camp co-ordinator told him 'Whispering Eagle'. Another asked the same question and the camp co-ordinator also gave him the name 'Whispering Eagle'. The point is that the secret was between the camp co-ordinator and the kid – nobody else knew the secret or so they thought."

The Secret Recipe

What I consider secrets as they relate to scoring goals often seems obvious but unfortunately the information is not used enough to make players better because coaches do not stress them enough. I want to stress the simplicity of scoring and take away the mystery to scoring goals to my players while at the same time, to others, it will seem mystical or magic. If you saw how some of the most amazing card tricks are done, you would be amazed at how simple they are. You would want to slap yourself for not thinking about them yourself. Scoring is the same. But remembering the simple stuff during a game seems too simple to worry about. All of a sudden, it's too late. After the missed scoring chance coaches get caught up in trying to explain the misses using fancy technical explanations: "She didn't have her knee over the ball when she shot and her centre of gravity was off balance." That may be true, but it will not connect with a player for the next chance. If your players can do the skills correctly under no pressure, that is kick and pass a ball, then the secret to scoring is simple. On the other hand if players are still kicking with their toes all the time, you will need to work on their basic skills.

So Then, What is a Secret?

I found that you could categorize secrets differently for the players who are the natural superstars and for the players who become good by thinking their way to succeed without having superior natural physical abilities.

Natural athlete superstars don't even know some of their own secrets when it comes to the instinct portion of their skills. Players like Zidane, Beckham, C. Ronaldo, Hamm, Jordan, Bryant, Carter, Ovechkin, or Gretzky are so good that they do not study the game in the same way that other players such as Lineker, Owen, Rossi, Vieri, and Chinaglia do. The super skilled superstars who were brilliant all their lives did not have to deal with certain issues when beating players or scoring because their skills were superior.

The players who had to think through their limitations in ability had to study the game from a different perspective.

Ironically, once retired, the players who had physical skill limitations and had to be more analytical in their game are more likely to become coaches, colour commentators, or sports analysts. Rarely do we see the superstars with the physical skills superior to their peers become good coaches or analysts. That's because they didn't have to think through their skill development as much as others. They were so good that everyone else was trying to out-think them and figure out how to stop them from doing what they did so well.

For the natural superstars such as Christiano Ronaldo, and Messi, some secrets are subconscious while others are not. In many cases the superstar natural athletes think others share their way of thinking. But less naturally talented players are not thinking like them because their minds work differently. While these athletes have to think of doing their skills correctly, the superstars are already past that point and thinking of other things. Later in life they realize the gift they had. Their brains interpret visual cues differently without thinking.

Most players try to figure out how they can bring the smallest part of their game up to a higher level by watching every move of their competitors. Both types of players have secrets, usually of a different nature. As has been documented earlier, the best goal scorers are weary of revealing their secrets because they do not want to lose their jobs. Top strikers know that the mental skills they possess can be easily learned by any intelligent player so they don't want to let anyone in on their personal secrets. They do not want to lose their position on the team. It's a competitive world out there and they do not want to jeopardise their advantage.

Can Secrets in Sports be Learned?

I believe many secrets can be learned provided the athlete makes a conscious effort to learn some of the little things about performance and mental skills. Players will not be able to learn all the secrets but just perfecting a few may will make them good enough to enjoy playing the game more.

The secrets must be taught to the athletes and then they must be able to retain the information and apply it at the right time during a game. This is key. In essence, mental skills must become habit so that correct decisions are made on which skill to use and what to do in each circumstance.

Here is a revealing quote from Darren Tilley, former player with the Rochester Raging Rhinos regarding a good goal scorer. "The top goal scorer scores against top teams as much as against weak teams." Tilley led the A-league in scoring a number of years in North America. In other words, when the opportunity is similar, a top goal scorer can score on the best and not just the poorest players and teams. Obviously, a stronger opponent may limit the scoring opportunities players have in a game, but, nonetheless, when they present themselves, the conversion rate is the same. Good goal scorers know the secrets, which really means they know the basics, the simple stuff needed to score.

CHAPTER 16

Relaxation

Sometimes, no matter how much we try to eliminate the players' stress and give them positive feedback, or give them confidence through secrets, they are not able to eliminate their fears or perceptions. At this point I like to give players some self-help techniques to help them not get all stressed out.

Before big games, some players get so emotional and therefore stressed that, instead of getting ready to play well, they are getting ready to perform badly. These athletes will go from bad to worse if they make an error early in the game. Coaches will need to find out which players thrive on pressure and which players crumble. For those who crumble, relaxation techniques are good to know.

The soccer player and particularly the striker has to be in a fairly relaxed state of mind when it comes to having the skill available when it's needed. Pele called soccer 'the beautiful game' partly because of the grace and elegance shown by players and their ability to maneuver with a rolling ball. Players cannot be too stressed or uptight and expect to delicately control, pass, or kick a ball. American football players or rugby players may need to be in a tough and rumble state of mind before a game, but this will not work for soccer. The strikers should go over the simple basics and secrets to scoring reminding themselves to stay composed and focused while playing the game.

Prior to games, players can do some relaxation exercises. When I first tried them in a lab for a sport psychology class at university, I was very impressed. Along with twenty other students, I was asked to lie down on the floor on a mat on our backs. Then the professor gave us instructions on how to relax. The lights were turned off and there was a soft noise of a fan in the background. The professor had a calm soothing voice as he went over what we should do to help us relax. The eyes had to be closed and we started with deep breathing slowly listening to our breath. Then he told us that the body was full of energy: the energy is built up inside us waiting to be used but in order to relax we had to release this energy from the body.

As we lay there, he told us to relax with each breath and start to see the energy lift away from our bodies. He asked us to feel the body start to relax and pretend to see the energy leaving our body into the air. After about 5 or 10 minutes he said that now we had to squeeze the rest of the energy out like squeezing water out of a wet blanket. To do this we had to go through each and every body part starting one by one from the feet. He asked us to tighten all the muscles in one foot and hold that for 15 seconds. Then the professor said to relax that body part, breath out and feel the last bit of energy leave that part of the body. He instructed us to do the other foot and then the other leg up at the calf and so forth. We did this all the way through the body up the thighs, the buttocks, the stomach, the back, each arm, and the neck, up to the head. Then he went through the tiniest of parts on the face including eyelids, nose, cheeks and temple. He may have gone on to say at lot more but at this point I was sawing logs and snoring.

In a matter of 15 minutes in the middle of the day, I was having the best sleep I could ever remember even to this day. When it was time to end the class and wake up, I thought it was morning and it was time to get up except that I wasn't in my own bed. I was a bit out of it for the next hour while I tried to wake up while going to the next class.

There are many different types of relaxation techniques. In our next class we learned another method, this time using visualization: being on a beach and hearing the ocean waves. I don't usually sleep that easily but yes, I crashed out again. The key is deep breathing. Rafi Srebro's book *Winning With Your Head*, offers similar techniques including one with simple breathing. Provided you empty thoughts from your head and focus on the techniques, they will work. I would recommend to all athletes and coaches to get more information about this aspect of sport.

Picture 16A: Marco Fabian from Mexico, is on his knees doing his own relaxation routine right on the field prior to the kick-off of the London 2012 Olympic Gold medal game. Or he could be simply praying knowing that their opponent is the mighty Brazil!
Photo by Les Jones (Covershots)

CHAPTER 17

Top 2 Reasons Why Goals are NOT Scored

In this chapter I bring the whole point of this book down to two simple facts about goal scoring. In coaching presentations I make this point early but when dealing with the players I hold this back until half way through my course. The reason I do this is so that the coach has this point in the back of his mind and therefore reminding himself as to why players do not score enough. I do not want to stress this to the players too early because I don't want them to think about these points and stop concentrating on the rest of the material.

Here then, are the top two reasons why goals are not scored (apart from not being proficient at the skills of kicking, heading, or passing a ball.)

Reason # 1

The player with the ball...

...does not shoot

(which really means the player is not prepared to score).

... Reason #2

The player with the ball...

...misses the net

(or does not hit the net).

These Two Reasons Define This Book.

I can say that, from a goalkeeper's perspective, without a doubt, these are the two main reasons why players did not score on me as often as they should have. If more players would have figured out these two points, I may have been scored on a lot more often probably to the point where I may not have made some of the teams I played on.

As a goalkeeper, I cannot tell you how many times I was at the mercy of players in a perfect shooting position. So perfect and close to goal that they even had the ball and the correct body position for taking the shot at goal but did not shoot. And then for the other half of the time, when they did shoot, I was so relieved that they missed the net. In a few seconds I experienced the feelings of hopelessness and relief when an opponent was in a good goal scoring position and then either didn't shoot or shot and missed the net. And in most of those cases, I knew that had the shot have been taken or the player hit the net, my chances of making the save were slim. I feel that unless you have played goal, you will never really understand how major these two factors really are.

For a long time I had to figure out how to teach players about overcoming the reasons why they fail to shoot or how they miss the net when there is no solid reason to miss. For such a simple concept, you would wonder why I needed a whole book to explain how to shoot and how not to miss. The fact that the blockage to scoring usually starts in the brain means that there is a lot more to scoring than just striking a ball. After years of research I believe that the concepts in this book cover in the utmost detail some of the problems you will face when teaching players to score more goals. Keep in mind that some information will work with some players while other information will work with other players.

It is not easy to know which points are more relevant to players than others. Mysteriously, I found that some points that totally connect with some athletes did nothing for others. On the other hand, other points that I felt maybe were not so important in fact managed to change how players scored. In older players, (16 years and older), I look to make some special connection so that they "see the light" or are faced with some "startling revelation" that catapults their game to a new level. I like to call these moments, "defining moments".

CHAPTER 18

Defining Moments

I call defining moments in a player's performance instances where a player improves dramatically over a short period of time. This is different from CAM (captivating and absorbing moments) because CAM has already occurred at this point in their careers. With CAM, the player has been inspired to want to learn more and get better. But every player that loves a sport wants to learn and get better. Coaches work hard at reiterating certain points while they teach skills or certain aspects of the game and players generally improve over time. That is normal.

Defining moments are when, for some unknown reason, a player improves dramatically to the point where someone who has not seen him play in a month or so and then sees him play again says "wow, what happened to him? He seems to have really improved!"

I have seen it happen to players many times and I know it's happened to me even if it was just in my own mind. There is a sense of confidence that seems to be emitted by the athlete once this occurs. And this is different for everyone. Often defining moments happen more than once. A player may have catapulted to a new level one year but remains at that level for a while and then another part of his game dramatically improves again. When you see players who have made it to the professional ranks, you will often see that they have had defining moments.

How often do you see fringe players who start their careers by barely making the team suddenly improve so much that they cannot be left off the starting roster? I have already discussed how this happened to Gary Lineker (Picture 18A) from England. In my research, I have found that defining moments usually come from a sudden burst of confidence that comes from the tiniest bit of information. At other times it comes from being successful at something for the first time which gives players the confidence that they can do it again.

Observers of the player can see when he has had a defining moment by the sudden improvement in that player's performance. Players who have defining moments can often feel them but there is no formula to coach them that is guaranteed to work for players. We as coaches feel that every point we make should bring a player to the next level but it doesn't work that way.

The interesting thing about defining moments is that they can happen to older players as well. Quite often players who seem to have reached their peak even in their thirties suddenly seem to have been rejuvenated and continue their career at the top of their game for many more years. Their body may have lost a step, but they draw on their experience and knowledge of the game to have more defining moments. Some older players often gain a step mentally and stay in the game longer. Some players play into their 40s while others drop off earlier. Healthy players who drop off early probably stopped having defining moments to keep up with the game.

Often a defining moment comes from someone saying something to an athlete that he has probably heard over and over again from his coach. The difference is that another person may have said the same thing differently and in a way that made a special connection with that individual player. Once again, I stress that defining moments are noticeable and often originate from simple bits of advice. Any of the points already made in this book or any of the little bits of advice or facts in the upcoming chapters may be enough to create a defining moment for your strikers. I have seen it occur to some of the players I have worked with in my course. I'm confident it can affect some of your players too!

My Secret on Stopping Breakaways was my Defining Moment

I started playing goal at 15 after my captivating and absorbing moment with Dick Howard's performance against Santos and Pele of Brazil. I worked hard to improve by reading books, practising how to dive on my bed and then land properly without hurting myself. I made the all-star team after my first season in goal even though I posted a goals against average of 8. (My recommendation to goalkeepers: look for the worst team to play on so you get lots of shots and the scouts will actually see you make some saves rather see you do nothing in getting a shutout.) At

Picture 18A: Gary Lineker, the highest goal scorer of the 1986 World Cup in Mexico. Lineker played as a reserve at Leicester City when he realized that he did not have some of the physical attributes of some of the players he had to try and beat out for a regular spot on the team. He figured that he had to learn how to score goals so he began working out how to score them. He studied this aspect of the game and came up with his own method. Soon he started scoring goals when he got the chance to play. Lineker kept scoring goals and his coach could not leave him on the bench. Photo supplied by Action Images

any rate, when I played, there were very few coaches at the time that specialized in teaching goalkeepers as there are today. Although playing on the varsity team in my first year at York University was great, I knew I made some mistakes that may have cost the team a chance to qualify for the play-offs.

In my second season at York, a new coach took over the team who had some experience in playing goal. One of my problems was that when a player broke through the defence, I was mediocre at stopping the ensuing breakaway, often giving up a bad goal by being beaten. Nothing can bring a player or team down more than looking bad on a goal by having a player waltz around you. Coach Eric Willis of York University gave me a little pointer that seemed so minor yet so major that I like to call it my defining moment.

He told me that players move in steps and to look for the moment a player dribbling towards me touches the ball with his foot. At that precise second, the player has virtually lost possession of the ball until he plants that foot and brings the next foot up to touch the ball again in his dribble. He told me that what I had to look for was to try and time my attack to get the ball for that split second when the attacker gave up the ball before he regained it. He stressed that, once the player touches the ball with his foot, he has actually given it up and there is nothing he can possibly do to alter the path of the ball until he plants that foot and brings the next foot up to regain possession. "Wow! That's magic stuff", I remember saying to myself. So I spent the rest of the practice diving at feet.

It wasn't easy because one cannot simple think they can just do it. The players are moving very quickly and so is the ball. The timing of the dive was not easy at all. It wasn't until I really stopped and focused on the task, getting into a trance-like state of mind, before I was able to use the information successfully to get the ball. I had to be in a certain frame of mind where I was thinking a step ahead in order to get the timing right.

Although I had a few bumps and bruises, my confidence rose dramatically once I achieved success. By the end of the practice I couldn't wait to try this approach in a game. From that point on, I never ever gave up another goal off a breakaway where a player waltzed around me to score for the rest of my career. I had so much confidence in that situation and was so focused on concentrating on the steps of the players that I made it very difficult for players to score on me off a breakaway from any angle even if they tried shooting instead of going around me. In fact I preferred breakaways over long high shots from 40 yards out. They were easier to stop!

My own Little Secret

I called this my own little secret and never told anyone until I finished playing. In the finals of the National Championships, we were down by a goal at half time. Thanks to our potent attack we went ahead 2-1 in the second half but the other team started attacking in droves once we took the lead. On two different occasions the opposition had breakaway-type opportunities but I was so focused on the task at hand that the play seemed to develop in slow motion. In both instances I came off my line to gather the ball up from an opponent's feet and this ended up in a minor collision. With the adrenaline flowing and with the ensuing victory celebration of a National Championship, I hadn't noticed or felt the pain in one arm. Halfway home on the bus trip a couple of hours later, I started to feel pain in the arm and it had swelled up. I couldn't remember when I had hurt it and I couldn't move it. The team trainer recommended going to the hospital to get it x-rayed before going home.

Team manager Norman Crandles took me to the hospital for x-rays and stayed with me in the waiting room with a room full of patients. There was a TV set in the waiting room and manager Crandles convinced all the patients in the emergency waiting room to switch the TV channel to catch the National sports report on CBC. Our National title was covered and everyone was forced to watch the report on our victory. Crandles made sure everyone in the waiting room knew we had won the National Championship. He even sang our team song for those waiting for the doctor to see them. He brought a smile to everyone there and a big cheer. I don't know how to call that kind of moment! The other good thing is that I did not break my arm when I made that crucial save.

I bring out this story in my course because I could have missed the point Coach Willis was trying to make because it was very specific and needed deep concentration and thought during a game to perform correctly. I want to keep the players in the course focused on the littlest of pointers in order to find something that can change their game.

I tell players who attend my course:

> ***"Remember that the difference between being good and being really good can be so minor. You are here looking to improve your game that little bit that can be enough to make a big difference. Listen carefully to all the points I make because that seemingly little pointer can be so dramatic in elevating your game just as it did mine."***

After this defining moment I was challenged to keep trying to focus on the little things to improve my game even further. After all, if something so minor could make such a difference, then there must be a host of other little things that I had missed out there for me to learn or figure out. As I said earlier, I was already coaching while still playing at the University level and this little pointer made me more aware of little things as it related to all positions on the field. I wanted to provide information to the players I coached that would also be a defining moment for them and their careers. I was intrigued with sport psychology as well as human body motion and visual perception. I have continued to study that to this day. New information is coming out rapidly on this aspect of sport.

In chapter 5, I touched on Dutch coach Wiel Coerver, who presented his ball possession and dribbling techniques in 1984 in Philadelphia at the National Soccer Coaches Association of America (NSCAA) convention. He provided specific information with a "lot of little things" about maintaining possession of the ball and taking on and beating an opponent one-on-one. His material was revolutionary and I was captivated by it. I used it with my players at the time (U19 boys) and made a presentation of the Coerver techniques to Canadians coaches for the first time. For some players on my team, the Coerver techniques became their defining moment. Some progressed rapidly once they understood them and mastered some of the moves and skills. But not all of them did as per my 20/60/20 formula, which I covered in Chapter 5.

Céline Dion Country

"Captivating and absorbing moments" and "defining moments" are very important when teaching strikers because I truly believe that a coach needs to inspire players in finding their personal moments that can change their interest in the game and also hopefully help them rapidly improve their game. Here are more examples of defining moments and captivating and absorbing moments.

When my son Joseph just turned 8 in October 1996, he played soccer at the recreational level and was just an average player. That month I was in charge of the year-end banquet for the club I volunteered with. So I wanted to do something differently to try and inspire more kids to learn more about the game and hopefully become fans of the game and not just participants. Unfortunately, in North America, there was a major lack of media coverage for soccer, which hindered the opportunity for kids playing the game to find heroes and have dreams of playing pro. The period was just after the 1994 World Cup and before the MLS started. Although the World Cup garnered media attention in 1994, this was not the case in following years.

In North America this is somewhat of a problem. Professional teams and National teams are still trying to figure out how to turn the hundreds of thousands of participants into avid supporters of the game in order to make professional soccer viable. For my part, I wanted to bring different components of the game to the youngest players, from 8 and up. Many do not follow the game outside of the team they play on because their parents don't follow it either. In North America, football, baseball, basketball, and hockey are the dominant sports. I am glad to see that things are changing with David Beckham and Thierry Henry now playing in North America. And clubs like the Toronto FC and Seattle Sounders FC have brought the excitement of a World Cup atmosphere to every home game. The media is taking note, as all games have been virtual sell-outs in those two cities. But at the time this was not taking place.

So I brought hundreds of youth soccer players together in an auditorium in October and put on various exciting videotapes that covered many angles of this great game on a giant screen. I also brought in a great sound system to enhance the experience. I wanted young players to know who the superstars were. I wanted them to see great goals, hear excited and singing fans up close, watch some funny moments and observe some exceptional skills.

My show lasted 45 minutes and was followed by the year-end awards presentation and then by a live show with two very talented players who called themselves the "FreeStylers" (Steve Elias and Richard Lissone) photographed with me in picture 18B and 18C. They performed some unbelievable tricks with a soccer ball on stage. My son was with me because he played soccer but also to tag along while dad was doing his thing. It gave my wife Angela, a break to look after our younger child, Marco. Joseph liked the show but especially the hot dogs that came at the end, (or so I thought).

Picture 18B: I'm with Steve Ellias of Freestyle Soccer. Player development often comes from being inspired to practice soccer skills as Steve and his team does across North America.

Picture 18C: I'm with Richard Lissone who also inspires kids by perfoming soccer skills with his crew around the world.

In April of the following year, in Toronto, when the weather was finally getting warm enough to go outside and kick a ball in the park, Joseph wanted me to come in the backyard and watch him try to juggle a soccer ball. As a good parent I obliged with the anticipation that he would keep the ball up two or three times as was the case the previous fall. To my total surprise, the first time he juggled the ball, he kept it up over 20 times. On his second attempt he was close to 30 and he was particularly good at keeping the ball up with his head. This was from someone who didn't like heading the ball.

In 5th grade, he was on stage all by himself at the school talent show juggling a soccer ball and doing all sorts of tricks with the music of "La Bamba" in the background. It happened to be the same song PUMA used for a Diego Maradona promotional piece they produced while Maradona juggled a ball while warming up when he played for Napoli in Seria "A" in Italy.

I asked him how he got so good. He said he practiced in the basement all winter after school and wanted to be like "The Freestylers and Maradona". In that instance at the banquet he had a "captivating and absorbing moment". He was driven to get better. Believe me, I did not put the show together to inspire him. I thought he would be too young to be affected. I was wrong. I have no idea if my presentation inspired any other kids. Needless to say, his ball control improved dramatically. He was a much better player the following year.

A few years later, Joseph was still playing soccer at 14 and playing in the inter-district league. By this age group many players have already quit. I don't like to push my kids into anything but I was glad that he still wanted to play the game at a reasonable level. I was glad that his CAM lasted this long.

I mentioned earlier in Chapter 8 that on our trip to Montreal, we also visited Charlemagne for the National Beach Volleyball Tournament to watch my sister-in-law Julie Cirone-Foley. It became evident very early that this small French town outside of Montreal was the home of "Céline Dion". You could see how proud this little town was of their star singer. While the ladies went out one evening I took my kids for a drive along the St. Lawrence River eastward and about half an hour later found another small town overlooking the St. Lawrence. One of the first things we found was this lovely looking soccer field, beautifully groomed with a grass pitch that you just wanted to run on. It was a wonderful evening and I emptied my trunk with the 3 or 4 soccer balls I took with me on the trip. I thought that this was the time to really test some of my newest concepts found in this book with my son Joseph for the first time.

Joseph played as striker most of the time because he was too slow to catch up with anyone at defense or midfield. But he had a good touch and could shoot well. Unfortunately his lack of speed hindered him from getting many goals. Most of the players on the team ran faster backwards than Joseph ran forwards!

I knew that Joseph was never going to get many chances to score playing at the U15 age group where his lack of speed was a big disadvantage so I worked with him to make sure he scored as often as possible in the few chances he did get. We spent the next 2 hours one-on-one on the psychological aspects of scoring I mention in this book. Right away, I could tell he was "getting it". On the ride home back to the hotel we discussed the concepts.

I pretty much left the topic for the rest of our stay in Montreal until we got to New York, where we went to visit our friends, Sal and Sue, in Long Island. He impressed our friends with his amazing ball juggling skills. Joseph and my other son Marco played small 2 v 2 games with Nicholas, Thomas, and Irene Formica on their front lawn using tiny goals all day long. I also stressed the importance of chopping the ball correctly as per the Wiel Coerver techniques to Joseph in Montreal. My friends' kids did not play soccer and were all younger than Joseph yet all the kids had fun playing. Joseph got to try some of his chopping on the little guys.

A week later, we were back in Toronto and Joseph's first game back after holidays was coming up. I took Joseph out to the field one more time for a couple of hours prior to that game. I also went over some of the off-field psychological points in the next few days. In the next game, Joseph scored two goals on the only two chances he received. In the game after that he scored another two goals. He ended up scoring 9 goals in the last 5 games of the season. Prior to my trip, he had only scored 2 goals in the first 12 games of the season. In the following year he was second in the team in scoring but scored in most of the chances he received. He consistently led his team in scoring on the chances he received. Joseph had a defining moment with something I said, which made him improve dramatically.

He is always the slowest player on the team. Even when he plays recreational hockey, he's a slow skater but has the mental fortitude to concentrate on the task of scoring whenever an opportunity presents itself and is always towards the top of the league in goals scored. He also creates more opportunities for himself by following some of the advice presented in Part Three of this book.

Superstar Players Have the Power to Give Others Defining Moments

Pat Quinn, former NHL coach and coach of the 2002 Canadian Olympic Gold medal hockey team and 2004 World Cup champions stated in an interview on TSN (The Sports Network) that there are a number of things that can change how a player plays and then improves dramatically. He stated, "Sometimes it's just playing at a higher level". But Quinn saw vast improvements in some of the younger players in a short amount of time when they played with veteran players. He said, "Often it was watching a superstar veteran go out and do some of the non-glorious things like back-check and block shots. Moments like that can really improve a younger player."

Defining moments can even happen in the dressing room when someone makes a positive comment about another player.

I had defining moments in hockey too. I play recreational non-contact old-timers hockey. I don't consider myself a very good player but I felt a major improvement in my own skating ability and puck handling ability halfway through one season after I started applying my own bio-mechanical perception techniques from Part Two of this book to my hockey game. My defense partner at the time, Ken Evans noticed almost right away and said after one game, "John, you had a good game tonight, you seemed to be flying out there." Later that year, when shaking hands after a game, a player I used to play with, now on another team, said "John, good game, I didn't recognize you out there, you really improved." Compliments from peers, especially the ones players perceive to be better, can lift them up just as much as good advice from a coach.

To help elevate your team's game, I suggest you look for players on your team who have the ability to offer sincere compliments. And if you have one who is talented, you have found a diamond. This player can often do more for your team than anything you can coach.

Can Teams Have Defining Moments?

I remember the year my university team won the National Soccer Championship (picture Appendix F). We started the year with two ties. Our captain, Nick Plessas was a very skilled midfielder and a veteran of the team. However, he had one problem: every time I made a mistake I heard it from him. If I miskicked the ball or threw it out poorly, I would hear it from him. It took me off my game so you can imagine how bad I felt after letting in a bad goal. Apparently, other defenders from the team got the same vibes. After a practice the defenders and I stayed back and discussed this with Eric Willis, our coach.

To this day I do not know what happened after that meeting but all I could say was that at the next game, when I made a mistake our captain was the first to say it was okay and told me not to worry about it. It caught me totally by surprise and it made me feel good and more confident. The great thing about this was that Nick said it and meant it in a genuine manner. This continued and never once did Nick make negative comments to our defense. It made the year very enjoyable and, to this day, I believe Nick was the best captain I ever played for and was probably a main reason we won the Championship. Do teams have defining moments? It starts with little things within each individual that works to build a championship team. Players on our championship team from 1977 still get together when they can and are always glad to see each other. I think Nick, coach Willis, and manager Crandles had a lot to do with the success of that team.

CHAPTER 19

Confidence Helps Skills

Michael Owen was quoted by Simon Kuper from *Financial Times* as saying "when confidence is high, they flow, and when it's not,they dry up."

Skills improve when players are more confident. Confidence comes from being positive about oneself. Players need to stay positive but to achieve success at creating a great striker you need to provide them powerful facts that will help them make more correct decisions on the field. As I present powerful soccer facts to scoring throughout the book, your delivery of them to your strikers could be the determining factor of whether or not they will have the impact needed to give your players more confidence to make better decisions. To help their confidence, remind them to keep them as secrets.

When asked whether he was nervous about his performance in an upcoming game, Paulo Rossi of Italy's 1982 World Cup winning team said, "It's not a matter of if I'm going to score, it's a matter of when I'm going to score." That's confidence.

Ronaldo of Brazil said, "I am always aware that I will define the game." (Picture 19A) That's pressure and confidence.

George Klas, a teammate when I played in the U18 age bracket was our top goal scorer in the two seasons we played together and was always difficult to stop even at practice. He possessed a booming shot but, more importantly, exuded a confidence about his abilities to score. George was offered a US soccer scholarship at Princeton University plus a try-out with a First Division team in England. His immigrant parents from Macedonia were not about to allow their son chase a dream of playing pro soccer when getting an education was foremost in their minds. Consequently, he studied dentistry and eventually became my dentist.

We recently met up for lunch and we discussed my goal-scoring course. Intrigued, he offered some thoughts about his game. Consistent with most of the world's top strikers he said, "I'd think about the game right from when I'd wake up in the morning. What I thought to myself about was, 'Am I going to score 1, 2, or 3 goals today?' It was never a question of, 'Am I going to score?' That never entered my mind. It was always, how many? I know some players who would wonder if they would score or get stressed out about how to score. For me it wasn't about that at all and I could never understand why a striker would not expect to score every time."

When asked about his best quality as a player, German World Cup Star Jürgen Klinsmann said, "I always felt we could win, even if we were down two goals in the 90th minute" (Connolly, 2003). That's confidence too.

Picture 19A: Ronaldo currently holds the record for most goals scored at the World Cup. He knows that there is pressure on him to score but accepts the pressure as a psychological role the striker has to assume. He says, "I'm always aware that I will define the game." He scores against Costa Rica in the 2002 World Cup. Action Images/Tony O'Brien.

CHAPTER 20

What you Think is Real May Not be Real

Former NHL hockey coach of the Toronto Maple Leafs, Pat Quinn said, "what you think is real may not be real."

Quinn was talking about the mental aspects of playing and discussed what players need to decipher in their minds as to what is happening on the ice and what they think is happening. This can apply to many different sports and positions.

Here is how I approach this subject with players. I want to break down for them what is real and what is not real about scoring goals. My first step is to define a goal.

What is a Goal?

1. A goal is scored when the ball completely crosses the goal line.
2. Goals are not always a thing of beauty.

That seems pretty simple except point number 2 may come as a surprise to players. Why would I even mention this point? We need to clear up some misconceptions about scoring, especially for young players. While many players play, they also watch soccer. They watch the game on TV, in videos and DVDs or on the internet and they talk about it off the field with friends and teammates as well. When it comes to goal scoring, what do people always talk about? They talk about that great goal that a superstar scored. Everyone wants to score that great goal. And what is a great goal? To find out, watch any highlight video or DVD package of the greatest goals.

The Brain is Watching the Highlight Reel Goals

Goals that constantly get shown on television are usually the nicest goals, which are commonly called "highlight reel goals". Unfortunately, most kids who watch sports highlights think that most goals are scored that way. Therefore, when they are playing in a game and get a chance to score, they try to score these types of goals. That's what their brain is telling them to do.

For example, when you analyze the top 10 goals in the Women's 1999 World Cup, you will find that about 7 of the 10 goals appear to go in at the top corners. There are a couple of long-range shots off the low posts and one other goal comprised of some unbelievable dribbling skills that finish with a goal. This is consistent with most highlight goals shown on TV. So then, what is the first thing your players will shoot for when they are equipped with some soccer balls and an empty goal? The answer is obvious: they are all aiming for the top corners. That's natural. They see themselves scoring that beautiful goal that bulges the top corner of the goal and makes them look brilliant. They see the fans cheering, going wild, and their teammates mob them. They see themselves on the highlight reels that evening on the sports report. They want to be on TV looking good.

Making the Net Bulge

In my analysis of goals, most highlight reel goals make the net bulge towards the top and bottom corners of the goal, which gives an illusion, that the ball actually went in at the corners. In picture 20A, we see the net bulge as the ball goes in the net. This causes young players to make wrong assumptions as to how goals are scored.

The problem with highlight reel goals is that highlight reel goals are not real goals as a percentage of the total goals scored. Those beautiful goals are an exception rather than the rule. Thus players lose focus of what it actually takes to score goals. When we analyze where most goals are actually scored, we see that the story is much different than what your players would expect.

In diagram 20B, I have plotted, where the brains of most players ***THINK*** the ball is entering the goal when a goal is scored. Note that I have divided the goal into 9 sections: the top third, the bottom third, and the middle third, and the left third, the centre of goal, and the right third. The dots represent where players often think they need to shoot in order to score goals.

Picture 20A: When the ball bulges the netting after it goes into the goal, it causes young players to make wrong assumptions as to how goals are scored. Spain's Xavi (2ndL) scores past Russia's goalkeeper Igor Akinfeyev (L) during their Euro 2008 semi-final soccer match in Vienna. Picture Supplied by Action Images/Kai Pfaffenbach

Diagram 20B

HIGHLIGHT REEL GOALS – WHAT YOUR BRAIN THINKS

Diagram 20B: Each dot represents where most people think the ball goes into the goal when it crosses the goal line.

Most players have this type of picture in their mind as to where goals are scored when the ball crosses the goal line. You may believe so as well. In diagram 20C, 20D, 20E, 20F, and 20G, I have plotted where the ball was as it crossed the goal line and entered the goal for the 1999 Women's World Cup, the 2002 Men's World Cup, the 2006 Men's World Cup, the 2010 Men's World Cup, and the 2012 UEFA Euro Cup.

Diagram 20C

Point of Entry of Ball – Women's 1999 World Cup

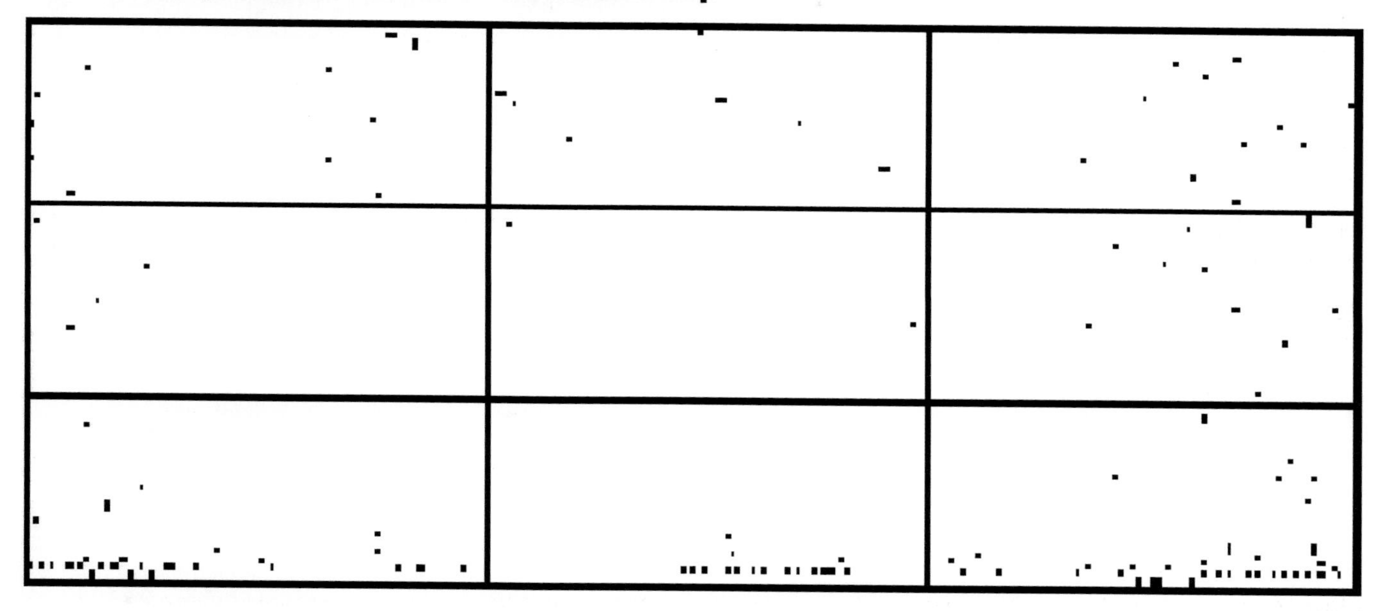

Diagram 20C: Each dot represents the point in the goal where the ball crossed the goal line. I have divided the goal into 9 sections. Vertically I have divided the goal into the top third, middle third, and bottom third. Horizontally, I have divided the goal into the right third, centre third, and left third.

Diagram 20D

Point of Entry of Ball –Men's 2002 World Cup

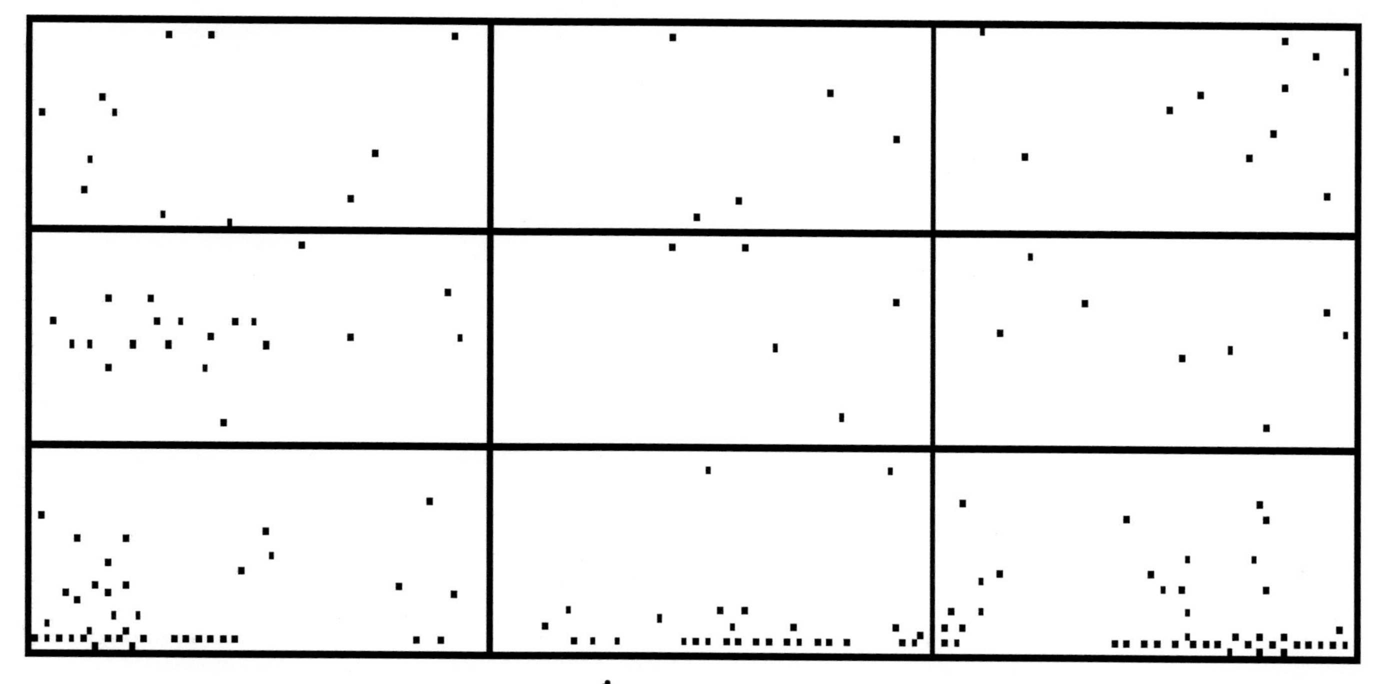

Diagram 20E: Point of Entry of Ball –Men's 2006 World Cup

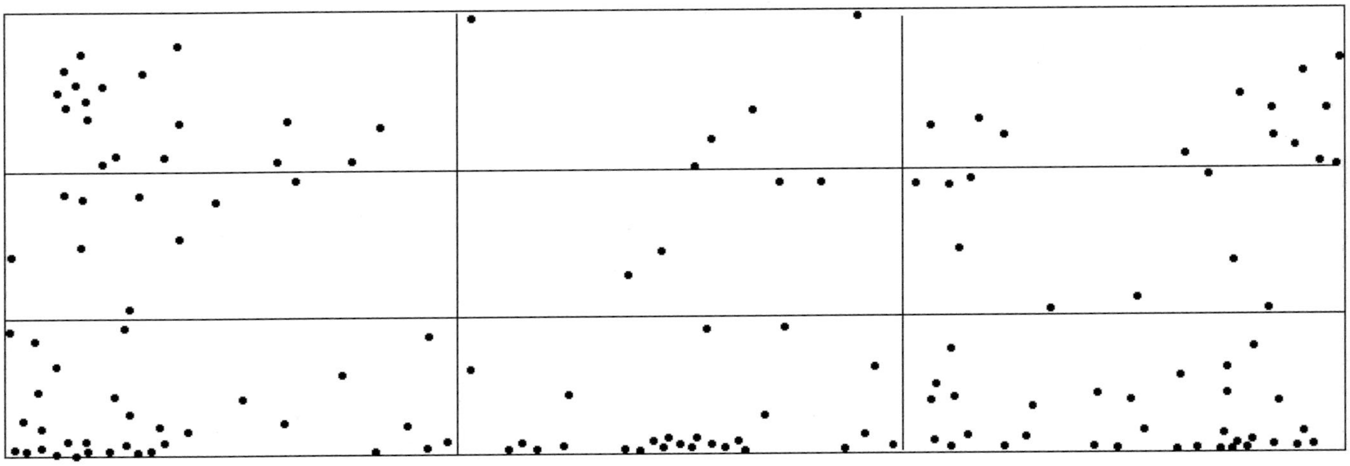

Diagram 20F: Point of Entry of Ball –Men's 2010 World Cup

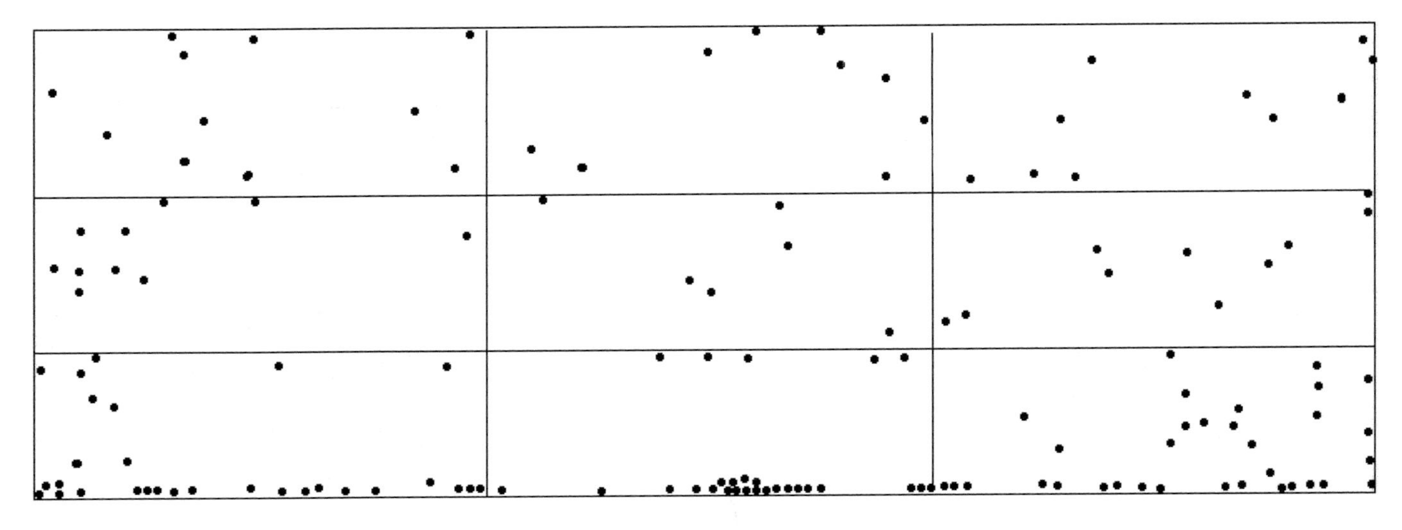

Diagram 20G: Point of Entry of Ball –UEFA 2012 Euro Cup

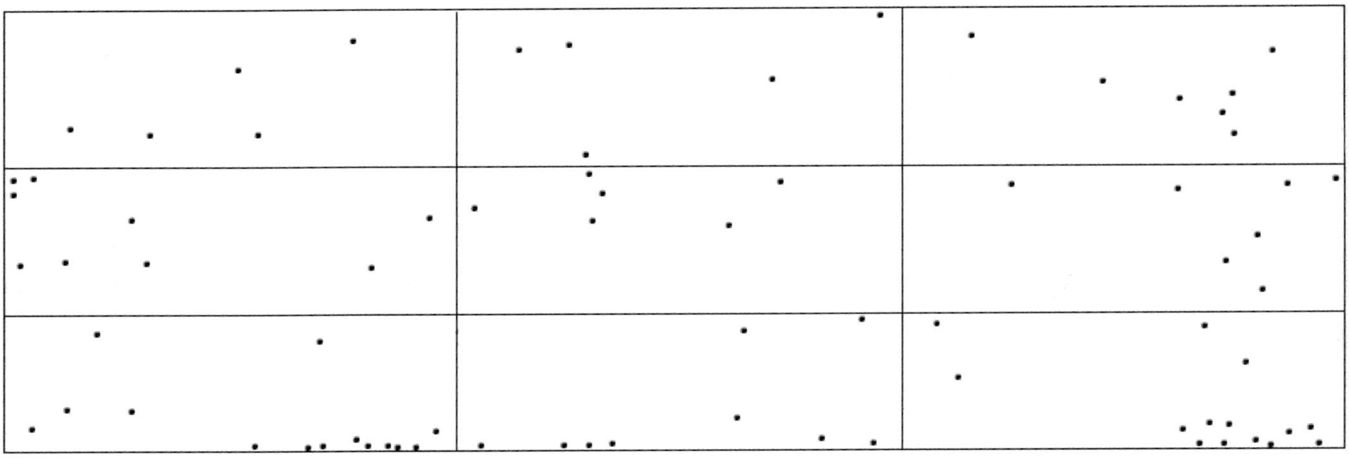

What is Real?

As you can see from the actual plots of where the ball entered the goal, what your brain thinks and what is real are very different things. The dots are not all hugging the posts and crossbars at all! This fact can be enough to get your players re-thinking about what is reality. It's a very powerful fact.

Here is how I explain it to young athletes.

> ***"When you get a chance to score, your brain may already be watching the highlight reel instead of concentrating on scoring first and foremost. Most goals are actually scored all over the place."***

This explanation is very powerful, has a psychological effect on the young athlete, and strikes home with a lot of punch.

> ***"The statistics at the end of the day do not tell you how the goals are scored. Your name is there on the score sheet or in the newspapers with the goal you scored. That's it. The statistics do not explain how you scored. Pretty top corner goals DO NOT count as two goals. They still only count as one goal. In a game like soccer where goals are very precious, no coach at a higher level can ignore the player who scores goals. Being consistently there with your name attached to goals will turn eyes. The players who score will make it to the next level over the players who do not regardless of what the player looks like on the field. It doesn't matter if you're clumsy, pretty, ugly, tall, short, or athletic looking: if you score you're going places."***

Reality may start to set in when young players study these diagrams. I continue by saying:

> ***"The reality is that most goals are not top corner goals or a long range blast or a magnificent dribble around half the team, so get it out of your mind. Attempting those types of goals will only make you score less goals because you will miss more chances than you should."***

"Not a Pretty Goal but Still a Goal!"

Picture 20H: Senegal's Papa Bouba Diop (right) scores against French goalkeeper Fabien Barthez (left) as France's Emmanuel Petit (2nd Right) and Youri Djorkaeff defend at the 2002 World Cup in Seoul. This goal was your typical ugly goal as the ball bounced around before Diop kicked the ball in the goal while sitting down. But the celebration was outstanding as Senegal went on to defeat France 1-0. Picture supplied by Action Images/Jason Reed

I like to show my players lots of goals that are not the type of goals that will show up on the highlight reels. As you can see from the diagrams, there are a lot of goals scored in the bottom third of the goal and in the centre third of the goal. Goals scored in the bottom third of the goal far outnumber goals scored in the top third. These types of goals are not usually your pretty goals. Picture 20H shows a very basic goal that dribbles past the French goalkeeper after a scramble in front of goal at the 2002 World Cup. Picture 20I shows the type of goals I want my strikers to get out of their minds.

I say to players:

"Get This Type of Goal Out of Your Mind"

After showing the players pictures such as these I'll say this to them to conclude this point.

> ***"Most goals are not pretty but they still count and put your name on the score sheet. There is no secret about that. It's a fact. And you know what? The celebration is the same because it's Fun to Score."***

Picture 20I: Goals that seem to enter the goal in the top corner are not goals that occur often. Players must get these types of goals out of their mind when shooting to score. In this goal, the ball actually crosses the goal line a yard inside the post but the ball will bulge the net to the outside and the spectator will think that the ball went in right at the corner of the post and crossbar. Photo by Les Jones/Covershots.

CHAPTER 21

It's Fun to Score

Sam Kucey, former editor of *NewSoccer Coaching Newsletter* wrote in an article in 2003 that joy might be your 12th player. He was writing about a discussion he overheard by some of the girls on the team he was coaching. One of the previous coaches of some girls from his team devoted a full practice to celebrating. They practiced celebrating goals in a positive way. The girls were 8 or 9 at the time. Around the world people genuinely celebrate after EVERY goal. That includes games played on the street with friends.

After all, it's fun to score. Scoring goals signifies success and celebrating a goal is celebrating success. But when trying to turn average players into great goal scorers, what I'm looking to do is shift the focus in the brain away from scoring a highlight reel goal to scoring any kind of goal, ugly or otherwise. I focus on the fact that scoring is just as fun regardless of the beauty of the goal. At this point I like to show players game footage of all sorts of celebrations of ugly goals. As a coach, you know there is no such thing as an ugly goal. Every goal is beautiful, but your players are in a different state of mind most of the time. They actually think that aiming for the top corners is the only way to score. They think that if they do not aim for the corners, they cannot score. This results in reason #2 in Chapter 17 on why goals are not scored: it's because they miss the net.

The diagrams from last chapter should clarify to players that goals are not scored from picking corners. They are scored in all the areas of the goal. An amazing number of goals are scored in the middle parts of the net. In cases where goals are scored while a player attacks from an angle and beats the keeper to the far post, quite often the ball will cross the goal line 2 to 3 yards away from the post. But even though the ball crosses the line away from the far post the ball will hit the mesh on the inside of the goal at an angle. This creates a visual illusion as it looks like the ball went into the corner right by the post. In reality, the ball may have crossed the line 2-3 yards away from the post. This is not always the case but it occurs quite frequently. To some players this is an amazing revelation. They were under the assumption that most goals were scored in off the far post. When a shot from an angle bulges the net, fans, spectators, and even players on the field are tricked by this visual illusion.

In picture 21A, the camera is behind the shooter, David Villa, who scores the goal. The ball crosses the goal line almost 3 yards away from the far post, but the ball will make the net bulge. If you are watching from the stands or other parts of the field, the goal will appear to go into the corner and looking very pretty as the net bulges. It is vital to correct this misconception due to wrong assumptions. It's why I write about perception being reality for some players. They think goals are scored in corners so they believe it to be reality. With these thoughts, players would have no other option than to shoot for the corners of the goal because in their mind, they feel that if they don't aim for the corners, then the goalkeepers will save the shot. When they keep aiming for corners, they are more likely to miss the net. State, and re-state this important fact to your players. Players would not normally aim for a spot three yards away from the post in practice because it's not exciting enough for them. This is especially true if there is no mesh behind the goal.

The key coaching factor is: Does the player who is given this important information make more accurate decisions at the spur of the moment on the field? I have seen players who continue to forget this important fact at key moments. That is why you may need to use some of the psychological ideas presented so far in this book in order to make the player recall the facts about where goals are scored from when the ball crosses the goal line. Diagram 21B shows what often happens when the ball goes in from an angle. The ball hits the meshing and bulges the goal to the side. The fact is that in many cases, the ball crossed the goal line 2-3 yards away from the post. Based on its trajectory, the ball may actually travel 2-6 yards past the goal line before it stops after a goal is scored. Over time, I have found different ways to make players recall and act on the facts that I present. I have found that by showing players the diagrams from chapter 20 along with highlights of goals showing how far the ball is from the post in many goals, that it can have a powerful affect on some players to improve their shooting habits. What works for one player does not necessarily work for the next.

Many goals are scored when shots or headers are taken from angles. In fact very few goals are scored from directly

Picture 21A: This goal will bulge the net but the entry point is far from the corner. Spain's David Villa (L) scores past Sweden's goalkeeper Andreas Isaksson at Euro 2008. Picture supplied by Action Images/Miro Kuzmanovic

in front of the goal with the ball traveling parallel to the length of the field. Most balls do not enter the goal at a right angle to the goal line. So the chance of a ball ending up hitting the mesh from an angle is high. Balls kicked into the goal from an angle tend to make the net bulge more. This looks good to the eye and causes players to forget where the ball actually crosses the line before hitting the mesh.

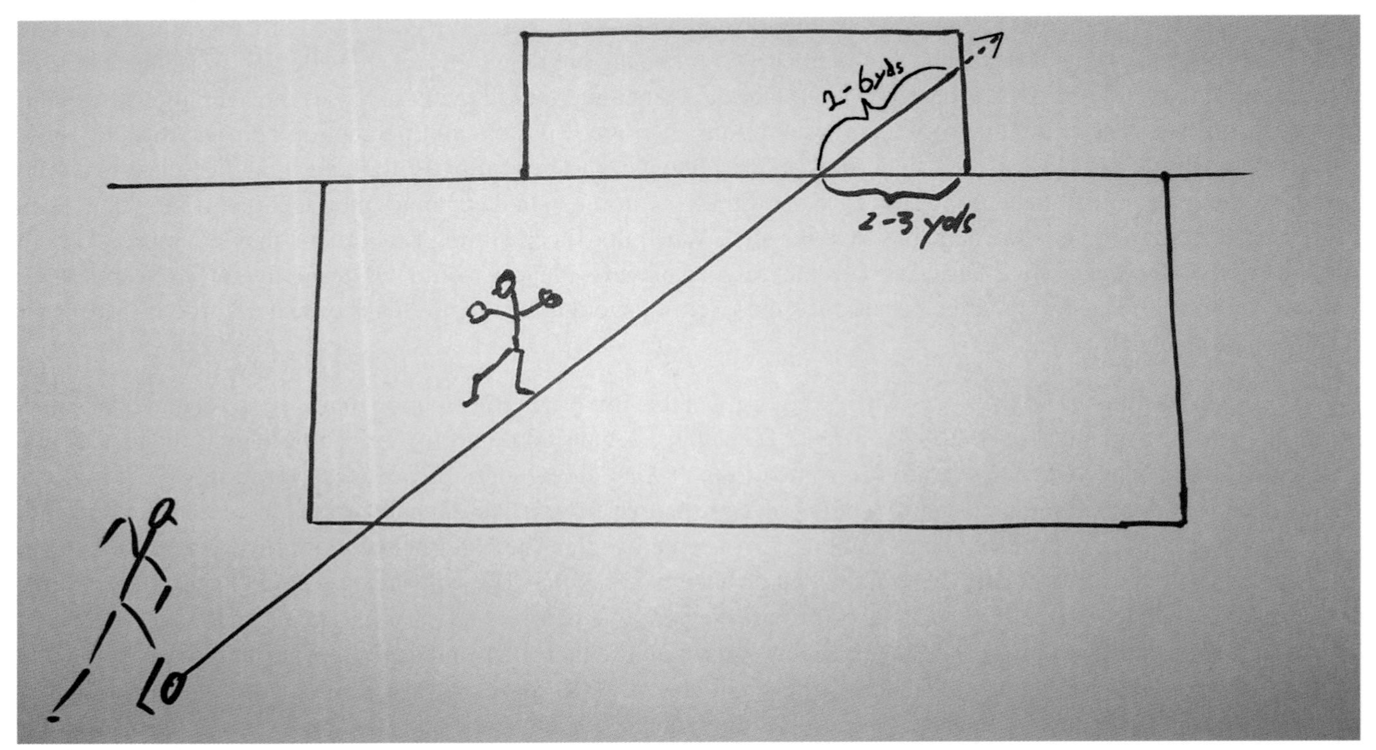

Diagram 21B: This diagram shows the path of the ball from the shooter's foot to the goal. Often the ball enters the goal 2 to 3 yards away from the post but still bulges the mesh, giving the illusion that the ball enters the goal near the post. After crossing the goal line, the ball may travel as far as 6 yards before it actually bulges the netting and stops.

Picture 21 C: Arjen Robben of Holland scored against Serbia & Montenegro in the 2006 FIFA World Cup in Germany by hitting the ball right by the goalkeeper. The ball is not scored anywhere near the corners of the goal. It's not a highlight reel goal, but nonetheless, an important goal! Picture supplied by Action Images/Yves Herman

Players who want to score more goals need to keep this in their minds when presented with a scoring chance. The temptation to aim for a corner to score is very high especially if the keeper saved a goal in an earlier attempt. If this temptation prevails, the next goal scoring opportunity can result in a shot missing the goal altogether, eliminating any possibility for a goal.

Stress the importance of hitting the net by making sure your players understand that goals that are not perfect are just as fun to score because the celebration is the same. Many goals will enter the goal from more than 1 yard away from the post. The key is to not miss the net. I like to show strikers in my goal scoring course players celebrating after scoring ugly, non-highlight reel type goals as in picture 21C and 21D because it's fun to score!

Picture 21D: Everyone is happy when a goal is scored regardless of how ugly a goal may be. Robbie Keane celebrates scoring a goal. Regardless of how ugly a goal may be, **it's Fun to Score ... and the celebration is the same!** *Photo supplied by Action Images /Brandon Malone*

CHAPTER 22

More Reality

Once I have convinced the players of the fact that goals are scored all over the goal I start bringing in more facts. Based on diagrams 20C, 20D, 20E, 20F, and 20G in chapter 20 showing where goals are scored, more facts can be derived. The next revealing statistic is this:

Most goals are scored in the bottom third of the goal.

In the 2010 Men's World Cup

60.7% of goals were scored in the bottom third of the goal.

In the 2006 Men's World Cup

62% of goals were scored in the bottom third of the goal.

In the 2002 Men's World Cup

63% of goals were scored in the bottom third of the goal.

In the 1999 Women's World Cup

60% of goals were scored in the bottom third of the goal.

Players who think they need to pick top corners to score must erase this misconception from their memories. The facts say it clearly: Most goals are not scored in the top corners; most goals are scored in the bottom third of the goal.

Here is how I explain it to players.

"As you can clearly see, most goals are not highlight reel goals and almost 2 out of every 3 goals scored are scored low and on the ground. They are the boring and ugly looking goals but they still count. The player who scores the goal goes ecstatic and is energized because it's fun to score. When you score, the statistics don't tell you that you picked the top corner. All they say is that you scored a certain number of goals and if your name is up there, you will be noticed as a goal scorer.

It's also important to keep in mind that the statistics I present are based on games where the best goalkeepers in the world were playing at the World Cup level. They are the best-trained goalkeepers and fittest keepers that have the best chance of stopping low shots. They still let in most goals down low and not precisely in the corners. Surely, the goalkeepers you are playing against are not that good. And not only are the keepers you are playing against not as good, the size of the goal is the same. Therefore you should be scoring more goals on the goalkeepers you play against by shooting at the bottom third of the goal and not picking corners.

Remember the facts. Most goals are not scored because players do not hit the net, which often is a result of players trying to pick corners or bulge the net. Now you know a couple of secrets. Goals are scored all over the goal when looking at the point of entry of the ball into the goal and most goals are scored in the lower third of the goal. Therefore, just concentrate on hitting the net and remember that the celebration is the same because it's fun to score."

In Picture 22A, the goal that won Spain the World Cup was scored in the bottom third of the goal and close to the centre of the goal.

Picture 22A: The goal that won Spain the 2010 World Cup was scored by Andres Iniesta. The ball went into the goal close to the centre of the net in the bottom third. Action Images/John Sibley

CHAPTER 23

Training the Brain to Focus

The facts presented in the preceding chapters must be used in such a way that a player can recall them under the stress of a game. Players often forget key facts when there is a chance to score. I have found that even though players may know the facts about scoring, some need better mental skills to perform them.

Players in goal scoring situations often lose focus and then need to retrain themselves to focus again. The first step is to go back to the basics. The highlight reel goal is embedded in most people's minds. When players step onto a field before a game or a practice they tend do two things wrong right off the bat. First, they strike a dead ball and secondly they aim for the corners. When aiming for the corners, their first choice is to aim to the top corners. This is another error. We need to start right at the practice field and get our goal scorers to think differently. First of all, they should hit moving balls and secondly they should stop aiming at the corners. They need to concentrate on scoring where most goals are scored. That is in the lower third of the goal.

As stated earlier, I play non-contact hockey and after the game, we usually head upstairs to the bar for a few drinks. My teammates, Gary, Jeff, Al and Mike, know about my book and as we were watching the highlights of the Champions league game between Lyon and the Glasgow Rangers we discussed the missed opportunity by Rangers player, Jean-Claude Darcheville. He missed what appeared to be a simple tap-in, but hit the cross bar instead. A goal at that time would have tied the game and changed the complexion of the game. As it turned out Lyon scored a bad second goal and went on to win 3-0. A goal by the Rangers at that point in the game would have probably changed the whole outcome of the game. I stated that Jean-Claude Darcheville obviously knew what to do to score but was not focused on what had to be done at that moment.

Which was similar to a situation in the game we had just finished playing. One of our players, Rick May, noticed that the opposing goalie liked to go down early and shouted to everyone on the bench to shoot high if we were to get a scoring chance. As it turned out, in the very next shift, Rick had a great opportunity to score himself and he shot low. On the ensuing rebound, he also failed to get the puck up high enough to score. I remember saying to him at the next face-off, "Rick, shoot high, shoot high!" He replied, "I know, I know".

The excellent goal scorers are often mentally much more into the game than many other players that play different positions on the field. I would say that the goalkeeper is the only other player that would rival the top goal scorer in terms of mental energy in relation to physical energy needed to be most successful. A player may have all the physical attributes to be a great striker but if he loses focus at the wrong time in games then he will not achieve top level success. As a former goalkeeper, I know from experience that the best goal scorers were different than the average players in their mental makeup. There was something about them. I'll explain some of those ideas later in Part 4 when I cover the psychology of beating a goalkeeper.

Our job as coaches is to help keep our key strikers focused right up to the last second. In numerous studies in sport psychology the terms being in "the zone" or having a "flow experience" come up all the time. Athletes talk about it often and there certainly is something to being "in the zone" that we want to go over with young athletes. Being "tuned in" is a key characteristic of great athletes and goal scorers. In Chapter 16 we went over relaxation techniques. Now we need to help athletes focus and one skill all athletes should acquire as they move up to higher levels is visualization techniques.

Simon Kuper in his article *On The Game,* made numerous observations in discussing goal scoring with some of the best scorers. Marco Simone from Italy said, "The goal is a moment, the goal is centimeters. The trick is to finding those centimeters."

French star Thierry Henry calls it "a fox in the box". Hakan Sukur knew that for those crucial moments when an opportunity presented itself, he had to be sharper than the defenders.

Michael Owen stated in the article, "Goal scoring requires a mental quality; on entering the penalty area, goalscorers grow hyper-alert. All contours become sharper. They clock everyone else's position."

Deep cognitive thought is necessary for players to be fully successful. They need to get better at focusing and trying to be in "the zone". I like to discuss what being "in the zone" is, and try and do some exercises with players so that their curiosity to find out more information will be tweaked. Each athlete is different and there is a great deal of information on mental preparation in books and on the internet. Coaches can encourage their players to do their own individual research as well. For some of the more detailed and specific points I make throughout the book, players will need to get better at focusing and trying to be in "the zone".

CHAPTER 24

"The Zone"

I remember when I was 17 playing in the U18 division, called the Junior Division of the National Soccer League in Canada. Junior teams played some of their games prior to the pro games later in the evening. Our team, called Wexford, was playing against the top team in the league and I got the start in goal. The buildup to the game was no different than any other game I had played except that very early in the game I made a save on a high ball whereby it seemed as though the ball was coming at me in slow motion. It was a weird feeling and it set the tone for the rest of the game. I was in deep concentration in the game but for some unknown reason it was different. Everything seemed to be taking place in slow motion and all sounds, spectators, and opponents seemed muffled and not clear. On the other hand, the ball was very clear and so were the opponents who were shooting and trying to score on me.

It was probably the best game I had ever played up to that point because it seemed as though the opponents had an endless barrage of shots directed at me but none that went in. All saves seemed easy. Even crosses, which were a problem for me, seemed to go in slow motion, and picking them up seemed effortless. I even recall the other team's players talking to each other about their frustration. The pro game that followed our game was between the top two teams in the league and by the end of our game over 10,000 people were in their seats. What timing for a good game!

It was an unbelievable feeling and I consider that in that game I was "in the zone". It was my first true experience of "the zone" and all I can say was that I wish all games were like that. It was not easy to duplicate "the zone" experience thereafter and in fact it was over a year before I figured out how to prepare myself to be in that state of mind more often. Preparing to try and get in the zone did not guarantee you were in it. It just gave you a better chance of doing so. I would imagine that players that make it to the top level actually play in "the zone" more often than those who do not.

I am not the only person to have felt "the zone" experience. Some people call it "the flow experience." If you have never experienced it yourself, you may have a harder time understanding it but similar experiences can take place outside of sport. "The Flow Experience" can be described as the matching of demand to skill where there is an absorption in the task at hand. The flow response requires rapid consideration and choice between many cognitive precepts or rules, which guides the body's actions to complete a particular task. When in "the zone" the brain makes rapid correct decisions that will result in the desired response for that situation. Thus, a mountain climber, surgeon, or athlete would have to rapidly choose between many variants of each successive behaviour or cognitive precept, each of which if chosen wrong could result in a bad fall, a dead patient, or an unsuccessful move or action. Even great musicians and chess players have experienced the feeling.

Here are some other descriptions that have been used to describe the "flow experience" of being in "the zone".

- Players have described their feeling similar to being in a trance.
- "An optimum state of experience is one in which there is order in consciousness." (Csikszentmihalyi, 1990)
- Increased cognitive efficiency that occurs when one is performing an absorbing task.
- The flow occurs because psychic energy is invested, consciousness is ordered, undreamed states of consciousness are reached and when we are immersed into activity.
- The flow is distinctive among motivating processes because it is not only signalled by a perception of a matching skill to demand, but it also incorporates, self-actualization, and psychic energy. (Marr, 2001)

In trying to explain this state, scientists and psychologists have identified some neuropsychological evidence. Goleman found a reduction in brain metabolism, as represented by brain activity, such as EEG. (Goleman, 1995). The cerebral cortex is enervated, and no manner of direct stimulation, electrical or physical or otherwise results in sensations that would otherwise be reported as pleasurable or painful. Mesolimbic dopamine (DA) activity has been conceptualized as a reward signal that marks the importance of perceptual events (Horvitz et al., 1997) and promotes the effective processing of afferent signals simultaneously arriving at midbrain. A cascade of perceptual events would presumably accentuate DA activity and facilitate the switching among alternative cognitive perspectives, and thus enhance decision making and creative thinking (Ashby, Isen, Turken, 1999). This neurochemical activity would not only facilitate the rapid efficient focusing of the mind on a wide range of images, but would also be frequently interpreted as highly pleasurable (Koepp, 1998; Marr, 2001).

Do not to Take your Strikers out of "the Zone" when they are in it!

Sometimes, you will notice when some of your players are in this state of mind. Encourage them to talk about it and see if you can help them achieve this state again. But during a game, you need to be weary of taking a player out of this state. If one of your players appears to be in "the zone" be careful not to take him out of "the zone". Players can lose focus with criticism, bad tackles against them, bad referee decisions, or key errors. Often the temperament of the players plays a part in how quickly they can be taken out of "their zone". The defenders who are able to distract strikers and take them out of their element often are your best defenders. In soccer and most sports, there are forces working against each other on more levels than one. You want your defenders to distract your opponents' top strikers while at the same time you need to train your attackers to stay focused and in control. The now famous head butt by Zinedine Zidane on Italy's Marco Matterazzi in the 2006 World Cup Final may have cost France the World Cup. The defender succeeded in taking a key striker out of "the zone" (and out of the game).

Strikers are often heavily marked and therefore must be mentally focused to outsmart, outwit, and outscore their opponents. They have to deal with two or more players and then beat a goalkeeper in order to score. The best players do. In picture 24A, Italy's Christian Vieri manages to get a head on this cross to score despite many defenders and the goalkeeper challenging for the ball. To get to the end of this ball, Vieri was probably in "the zone." Being in "the zone" also helps one focus on the task at hand which includes being brave and risk injury to achieve the result.

Picture 24A: Italy's Christian Vieri heads the ball for a goal against South Korea goalkeeper Lee Woon-jae. Vieri fought off defenders to get to the ball by staying focused on his task, which takes great mental strength for most strikers. His Italian teammate Alessandro Del Piero is also up for the challenge in this World Cup match. Picture supplied by Action Images/Jason Reed

Being in "the Zone" – Vince Carter

In a *Toronto Life* Magazine article, picture 24B, (Callaghan, 2002) former 8-time NBA all-star Toronto Raptor and New Jersey Nets basketball superstar Vince Carter, now with the Orlando Magic, explained his mental state:

> "I always play with the beat. It all depends on the move, the possible situation in the game.
>
> I sit back, I analyze, I am looking at players, their reactions to different situations, things normal players wouldn't do.
>
> When I get the ball, I always look at the court to see where everybody is standing at that point in time, and I try to pick their brain within two or three seconds. I say time, two or three seconds, because a man is guarding me, and I am always thinking when I go by him, there's the guy on the baseline and the guy who is standing on top of the key, and is that guy going to run, or is this guy going to run? I look at where I am, if I am close to the sideline; I can only go one or two dribbles to the right, or it's out of bounds. If I go left, who is going to be there? What is going to happen?

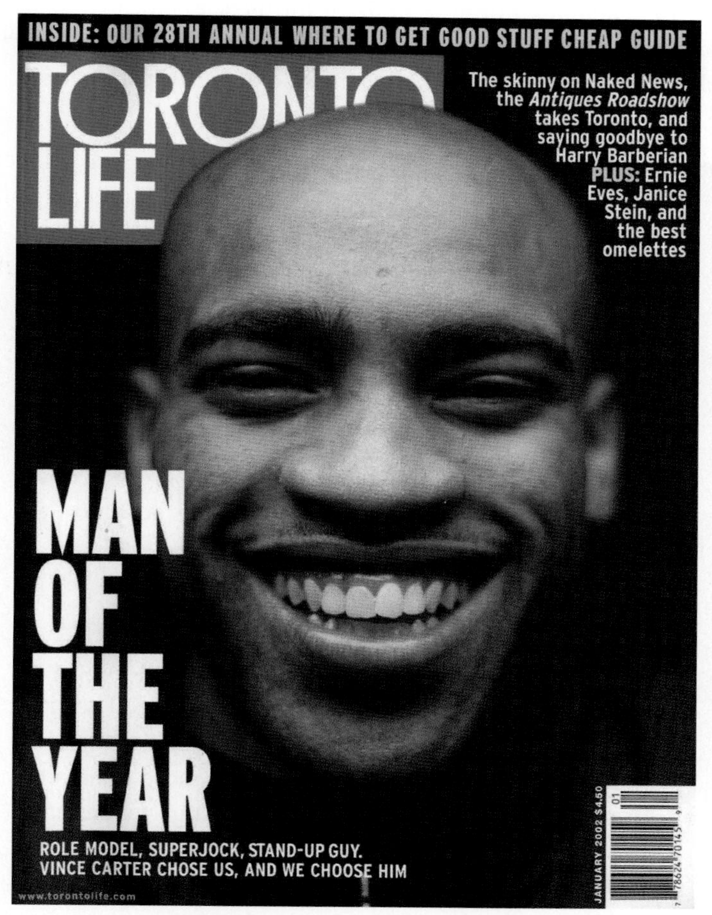

Picture 24B: Basketball 8-time all-star, Vince Carter was featured in a Toronto Life magazine article and described his mental state when he was in "the zone". His description of this mental state is similar to many other athletes when they are also in "the zone."

Athletes often feel good when in this state. Some describe it as a rush where they don't want the feeling to end because things are going so well. Things flow for them without the need to think about it. It's like being on automatic pilot when performing. Everything just blends in together nicely. (Csikszentmihalyi, 2004)

This cover is used by permission of Toronto Life. Picture of Vince Carter is used with permission of photographer Bryce Duffy. Website: www.bryceduffy.com

> Like a chess game, I see the pieces moving, people moving, and I try to figure out their path before they take it so I can make mine.
>
> When I'm in the zone, I shoot and I see the ball going in before it actually goes in. Sometimes, I don't even look back to see, because I know where it is. I've seen it already."

Some players may question the value of sport psychology and having a sport psychologist as part of the coaching staff but in today's modern game this person is not only a valuable part of the staff, but sometimes credited with saving players' careers. As coaches, we have all seen players who appear to have all the attributes and skills to be a future professional player but fail to make it. Often it's because of their poor training habits or some "unexplainable" reason as to why they don't seem to perform up to their capabilities. It is likely that these highly skilled players who fail to make it to the next level are lacking the mental skills to do so. In teams that may not have the budget to have a sport psychologist on board, many coaches are reading up on the basics of the discipline in order to pass on important information to their players.

Getting in "the zone" was a problem for me. It was unpredictable. Sometimes, I would prepare mentally and figure I'd have a good game and get that "zone" feeling but it wouldn't develop that way. At other times, I would not think much about the game or the opponents and then have a great game. Actually, over time I found more success by spending as little time as possible worrying about the game and rather looking forward to playing the sport. After all, it's just a game and there are lot worse things in life to do than play. This mentality kept me as loose as possible and

I played each game as though it was just another game regardless of how important it was. I found that the more importance and stress I put on myself, the tenser and less effective I would be. That's not to say I wouldn't try and find out about the other teams best players and their tendencies but I wouldn't dwell on it too much.

Game Face

Players have their own methods of getting into a game and getting in "their zone". In baseball, people have said that one of the most pleasant players in the game is Darin Erstad formerly of the Chicago White Sox and shown in picture 24C with the Houston Astros. Hours before a game he's loose and fun with everyone. He likes to play crosswords on game days and often ask for help from the batboys and ball boys. But then he goes to batting practice two hours before the first pitch. He comes back into the dressing room with his game face on. His personality changes completely. He's 100% focused on the game. He doesn't talk to anyone and his teammates don't talk to him.

For some players getting in "the zone" may mean doing things a certain way and going through an exact routine. Sometimes getting in "the zone" includes having superstitions. For some, superstitions just help them get ready for the game mentally and getting into "their zone" rather than actually doing something for them that brings them luck. For example, I always got dressed in a certain manner. Our team sat in the same order in the dressing room. Although these little things can be considered a good luck ritual, they are more likely a method of getting in a certain comfort zone as each player gets mentally ready for the game.

Picture 24C: MLB baseball player, Darin Erstad of the Houston Astros has his game face on as he concentrates on the game. Erstad changes personalities once the pre-game warm up begins as he tries to get in "the zone" to be able to perform at his best. Picture supplied by Action Images/Romeo Guzman

Ivan "Pudge" Rodriguez formally of the Detroit Tigers Baseball Club always wants the batboy to set up his catcher's equipment so that it's staring at him in the dugout whenever he takes it off before going up to bat. It helps him stay focused. Derek Jeter of the NY Yankees would always give the bat to manager Joe Torre after every at bat. He also has to chew Bazooka sugarless bubble gum every game.

Provided superstitions don't go overboard, for many athletes, it's their way of helping them get into "the zone."

We all Dream of Greatness

Everyone daydreams of doing something they want to do and being good at it. This is normal. The time used in daydreaming as though we are in "La La Land," can be put to better use with more controlled dreaming. We can use daydreaming to actually improve performance. But we do not like calling it daydreaming in sport. So the sports world invented the terminology, visualization and imagery. Providing visualization skills to goal scorers can help improve their game. This is because the goal scorers need to be aware of situations that come up in a game and know what to do in those specific cases. Visualizing different situations that they may be in during the course of a game with an ensuing successful result can actually improve performance. We shall look into this in more detail in chapter 25.

CHAPTER 25

Visualization

Can we dream ourselves into being great? I can visualize myself getting ready to discuss visualization to a group of snarky 16 and 17 year old kids. I'm going to try and convince them that dreaming in a controlled fashion is going to make them better players. What I also see is the smirking and feeling of disbelief amongst some of the players at the back. I know it will happen but for the sake of those who really want to improve their game I say to myself, "the show must go on". If I can capture most of them to have faith in visualization, then I know my team will be better, and to do so I start out with a scientific study that shows the power of visualization. It should convince most to take me seriously. I know visualization (also called mental rehearsal or imagery) works because I have used it to improve my skills both physically and mentally. I want the players to know the facts on visualization and imagery so I point out the following studies.

Dreaming of Greatness

This study done with college basketball players taking and learning free throws has been repeated and documented many times (Wiese, 2002). We take 3 players and after a warm up we do the following:

- Each player takes 20 free throws and records the number of baskets.
- For the next week, player 1 does not practice taking free throws at all.
- Player 2 takes 10 free throws per day.
- Player 3 does not practice with a ball at all but instead practices taking 10 free throws a day mentally. The player closes his eyes and pictures himself standing at the free throw line looking at the basket. He thinks about having the ball in his hand, doing the usual dribbles he might do before taking the shot, and finally making the shot itself. He also pictures the ball going in.
- After a week is over, the three players return to the court to each take 20 free throws. Both the player who actually took the free throws (player 2) and the one who mentally took free throws (player 3) do about the same. The player (player 1) who did neither scores lower.

Visualization and imagery is believed to work in much the same way as physically repeating an activity does. Both mental and physical practices reinforce the messages that are sent from the brain to the muscles to coordinate the movement, so both can lead to improved performance. It's important to note that the eyes do not always need to be closed when visualizing.

Knowing this information on visualization usually helps players focus on learning the techniques.

Visualizing Goals

Even though visualization can improve performance, players still need to practice the skill in the first place to build up the muscle perception/feeling. Players will need to have the basic skills to kick and pass a ball for visualization to work.

Visualization Mistakes Teenage Players Make

What I tell strikers in my classroom sessions is to visualize themselves scoring goals. But when I ask them how they scored their goals in their minds, most say they saw themselves scoring a highlight reel goal. In one session a player actually went into a very specific description of scoring a goal where he beat 5 players and the goalkeeper and then picked the corner of the goal. Another player saw herself volley a ball from 18 yards out. And yet another player saw himself scoring on a bicycle kick. And there was also the student who visualized herself scoring off a diving header. I was not surprised at this but I was surprised how all of my students had visualized themselves scoring brilliant goals. This type of visualization to create better goal scorers will do more harm than good because these situations are not real. They rarely occur. The video sports editor of the highlight reel tape in the news department has cut out all the ugly goals. This type of visualization will actually cause the players to miss more goals because they are not real.

Proper Visualization Techniques for the Striker

At this point I ask the players to close their eyes and visualize themselves celebrating the goal rather than see themselves scoring the goal. I ask them to see themselves in different types of celebrations. Here is what I would say to them in my course.

> ***"Really see yourself celebrating. Do not worry about how the goal went in; just concentrate on the celebration after the goal has gone in. See the excitement in yourself having scored an important goal for your team. See your teammates mob you. Hear the fans cheering your efforts. Feel your players hug you. Doesn't that feel good? Wouldn't you like to score more goals so that you can get the feeling of celebration a few more times? Now I can make that happen for you more often.***
>
> ***Remember when I said that most goals were scored in the bottom third of the goal? Some were at the centre of the goal. Now see yourself shooting the ball in the net on a low shot 2-3 yards inside the post and visualize the ball going in. Did that not start to get you excited? Why? Because you have already started to see yourself getting excited about the celebration. Go ahead, see yourself scoring an ugly goal and start seeing yourself in an amazing celebration because the goal won you the game. Feel the jubilation."***

In the book *Winning with your Head*, Rafi Srebro asks players to see themselves going for the ball and to feel the movements. He wants players to hear the contact with the ball and listen to the roar of the crowd.

I tell players to return to the final touch of the ball before a goal a couple of times from different places on the field. Srebro says to players, "try to imagine yourself succeeding in every action." He states that players cannot allow negative thoughts to enter their mind when visualizing and they should concentrate on the present and pretend it's happening now. Not in the past and not in the future.

Using visualization before games can help prepare players for a better chance at success. Srebro states in his book that he wants players to take responsibility to prepare themselves mentally to get in the game. The coach can assist in this but only the players can prepare themselves.

Visualization and Relaxation Bring Confidence

I tell players to use visualization techniques in many different circumstances. For instance:

- Between games when I want them to focus on certain skills.
- When I want them to read opponents movements, which we will discuss in the upcoming chapters, I need the players to get good at using visualization.

Often players can make the best use of visualization together with relaxation. When I want players to reprogram their instincts to do something different than what they would normally do, I need them to be able to see themselves correct their errors. For example, shooting low instead of shooting high, or when reading an opponents last moves step by step, I will want them to see themselves doing the correct things. I want them relaxed and also in tune while visualizing themselves scoring.

I then ask players to see themselves score calmly, just doing the easy thing over and over with confidence. Most players do not score when they should even though they have the technical skills to score. Often, when players don't score, it's not because they don't have the skills. They don't score because they panic, get tense, and then make bad decisions. Scoring is like fine art and goal scorers are like artists. Scoring requires finesse and one cannot do precision like work if the body is all tensed up, agitated, stressed, or disturbed. The great goal scorers have all their emotions under control. Relaxation and visualization can assist in this. Of course the players need to be fiery and aggressive to win balls but the confidence needed to finish the goal requires composure. It takes mental strength to be aggressive, alert, and then calm when you need to put the ball in the goal.

Goal scoring is like surgery. The surgeon's job gets a bit messy when cutting someone open and then stitching that person up again. But when the surgeon is fixing a heart valve or taking out a gall bladder he or she'd better not be all tensed up when performing the operation. Goal scorers and surgeons need to be calm, confident, focused, and precise with their fine motor skills to do the job. This is the state of mind you want your goal scorers to be in when the chance to score is there and they have only one more touch on the ball before they score.

Using Visualization After a Missed Opportunity

Visualization can also really help a player after he has missed a chance to score. I want players to quickly ask themselves what they did wrong or could have done better. Then I ask them to see themselves doing better and then knowing the secrets mentioned in chapter 26 and throughout the book; I want them to get excited about their next opportunity. I want them eager and sharp for the next chance but also calm and confident that they can score on the next chance because they will make the correct decisions and do the right things. If players step back for 15 seconds and visualize on the field, this is quite appropriate. The key is to not let the missed chance get them down. I stress in the course that they need to get excited about the rest of the game. Why? Because they know what they should have done because they know the statistics, rules, and secrets to scoring and they can't wait to do it again.

This excitement is important. I play non-contact hockey and often make mistakes. But I think about the errors, get them off my chest with my defence partner between shifts and can't wait for the next shift to try some of the little things that I have learned about skating or defending. I visualize the correct response. Fortunately, my defence partner, Gary Nasu, offers a sympathetic ear to my self-analysis. Gary played professional hockey in Japan and now we play on the same old-timers hockey team. Gary has an excellent skating style and vision on the ice and I even visualize myself skating like him. It gets me more excited about doing some of the little things he does well in my own mind on my next shift. I usually don't let myself worry about my mistakes and it usually works. My other defence partners who I play with on occasion (Mike Brady, Jeff Bowers, and Al Moffatt), also tend to lend an ear between shifts.

Visualization techniques are great for pre-game preparation, during game self-evaluation, and between-game reflection. Sometimes it's the tiniest bit of advice or information on a very specific part of a skill and the ensuing ability to help the decision-making process that can make a vast difference in performance. Just one of the many bits of information provided in this book can really have a profound effect on a striker. The striker may want to concentrate on these small points when visualizing himself score right down to the smallest detail.

Dr. Paul Schienberg, (2003) has written about mental training and visualization and offers a step by step guide for athletes to help them visualize. It can be found on his website www.psychedonline.com. Also Shane Murphy, in his book, *The Sport Psych Handbook* (2005) offers some good insight on imagery.

As I go over very specific skills later on that require deep thought, you will see that visualization is a necessary technique for strikers. They must see themselves score the simple goals using the correct techniques over and over and over.

Here is what I would say to players about visualizing specific things:

> ***"I don't want you to visualize the general things in a game. I want you to visualize yourself doing very specific things all in the last nine seconds before scoring -- from the simple things I have stated about scoring to getting down to some very specific details. Everything you visualize must be very specific. See yourself scoring from your eye level. Do not visualize watching yourself from a high camera angle. Oh, and don't forget the celebration."***

Picture 25A: Alan Shearer, preparing for a game. Relaxation and visualization techniques may have been part of his pre-game mental preparation. Photo by Les Jones/Covershots.

CHAPTER 26

The Secret to Scoring Goals

I have developed four fundamental rules to scoring goals, which I call **The Key Secret** to scoring goals. I use these four rules over and over. They are quite basic but so obvious that you will wonder why you did not think of them yourself. And if you have, it's fantastic.

Before you reveal the secret of scoring goals to your players make sure you build the suspense so that the impact will be more dramatic. The four fundamental rules will guide your players for years to come. But I urge you to wait for the right moment to reveal the four rules of scoring to your key strikers, just like a good comedian knows when and how to deliver the punch line.

When I make the presentation in my Golden Goal Scoring classes I use the moving slide method using PowerPoint so that players cannot see rule 2 until they have seen rule 1. I present a slide with rule # 1 and then move to a new slide with rule 2 and so on to rule 4.

How to Make Sure Your Players Will Never Ever Forget These Rules

Although you need to be brief when explaining each rule, take your time and create suspense as you move from rule 1 to rule 4. Hesitate a while so that the rule you just mentioned sinks in with your players. In fact, repeat the rule a few times keeping that rule on the screen. Please remember that you are working on the players' mind so you must present these rules in such a way that the anticipation for each rule is very strong and that they will never, ever, forget these rules mainly because of your delivery. Your presentation of the rules in their order from rule #1 to rule #4 will be very important if you want your strikers to remember them in key situations on the field.

The 4 Fundamental Rules to Scoring Goals:

Rule # 1) Direct The Ball at the Net

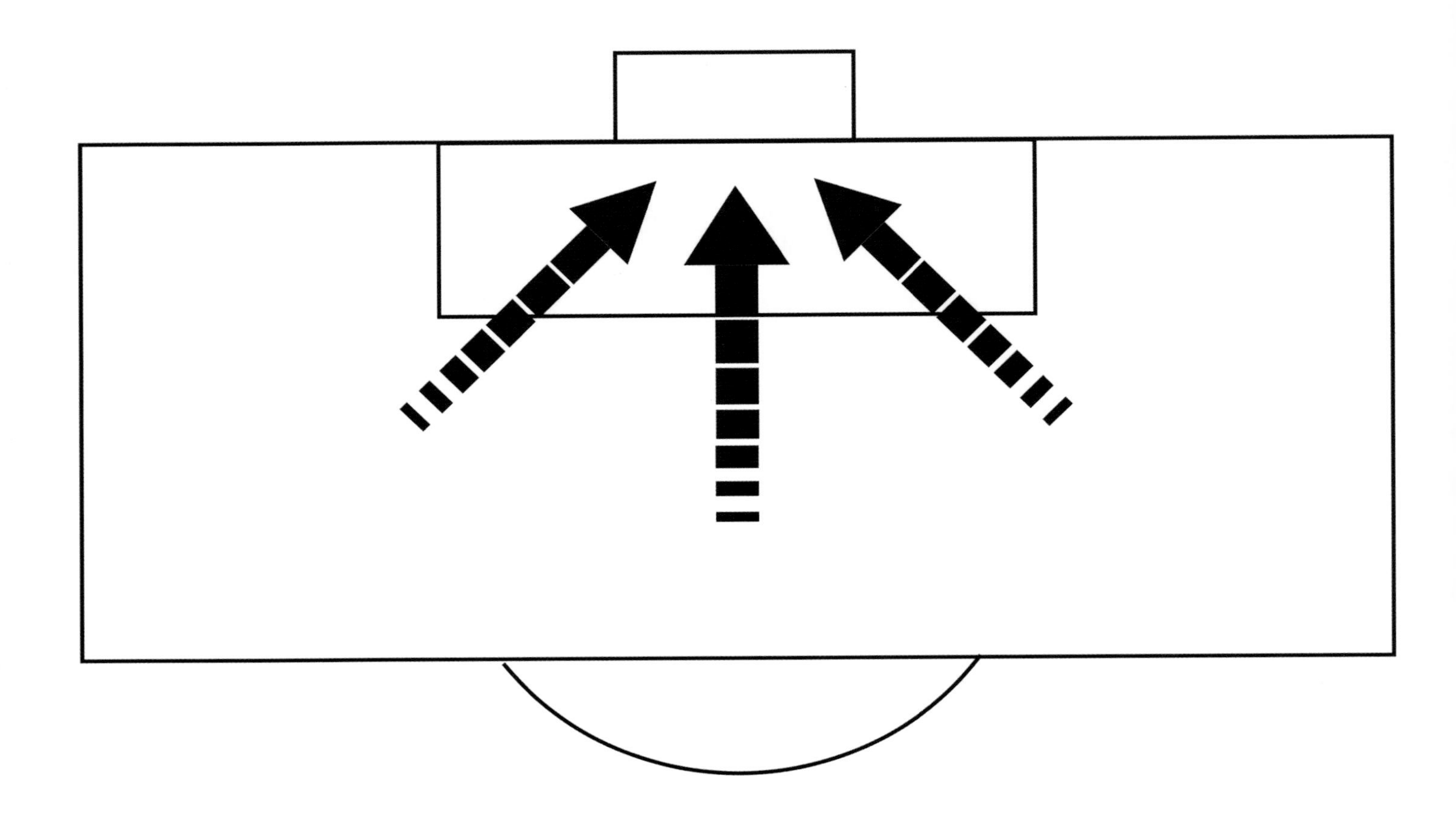

Rule # 2) Hit The Net

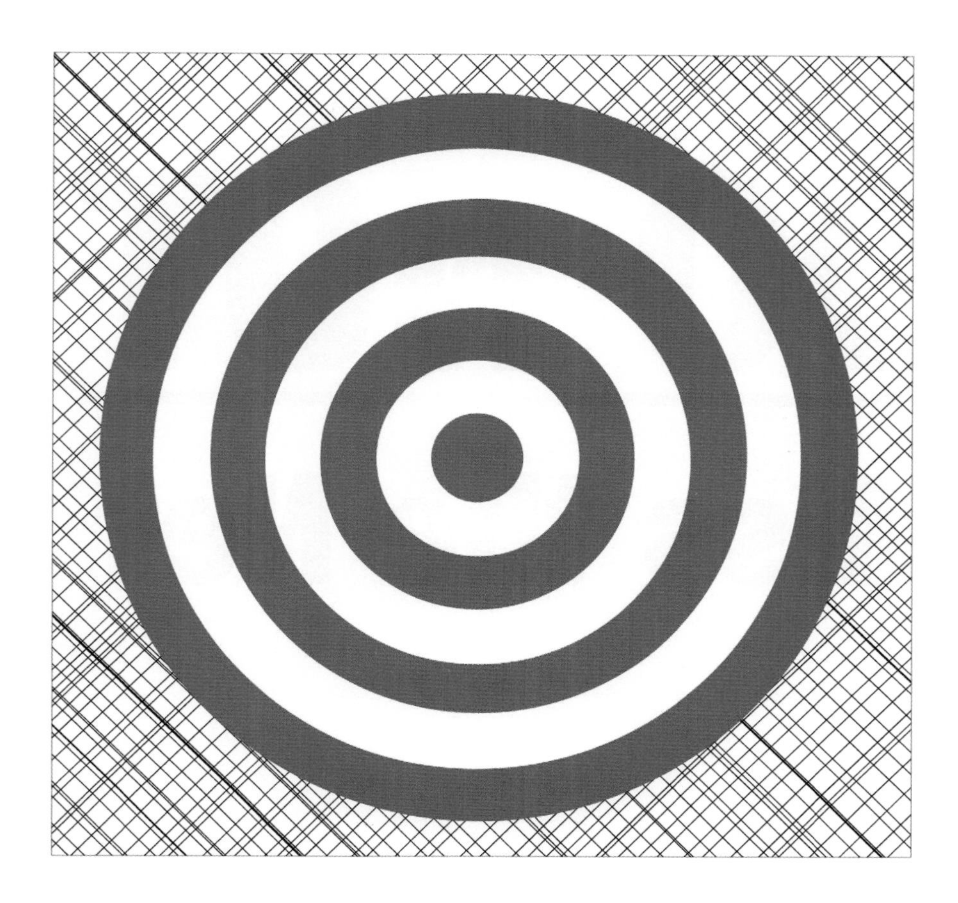

Rule # 3)

DO NOT

Miss the Net

Rule # 4) If you are having problems with rules #2 and #3, revert back to Rule #1.

Rule # 1) Direct the Ball <u>at</u> the Net

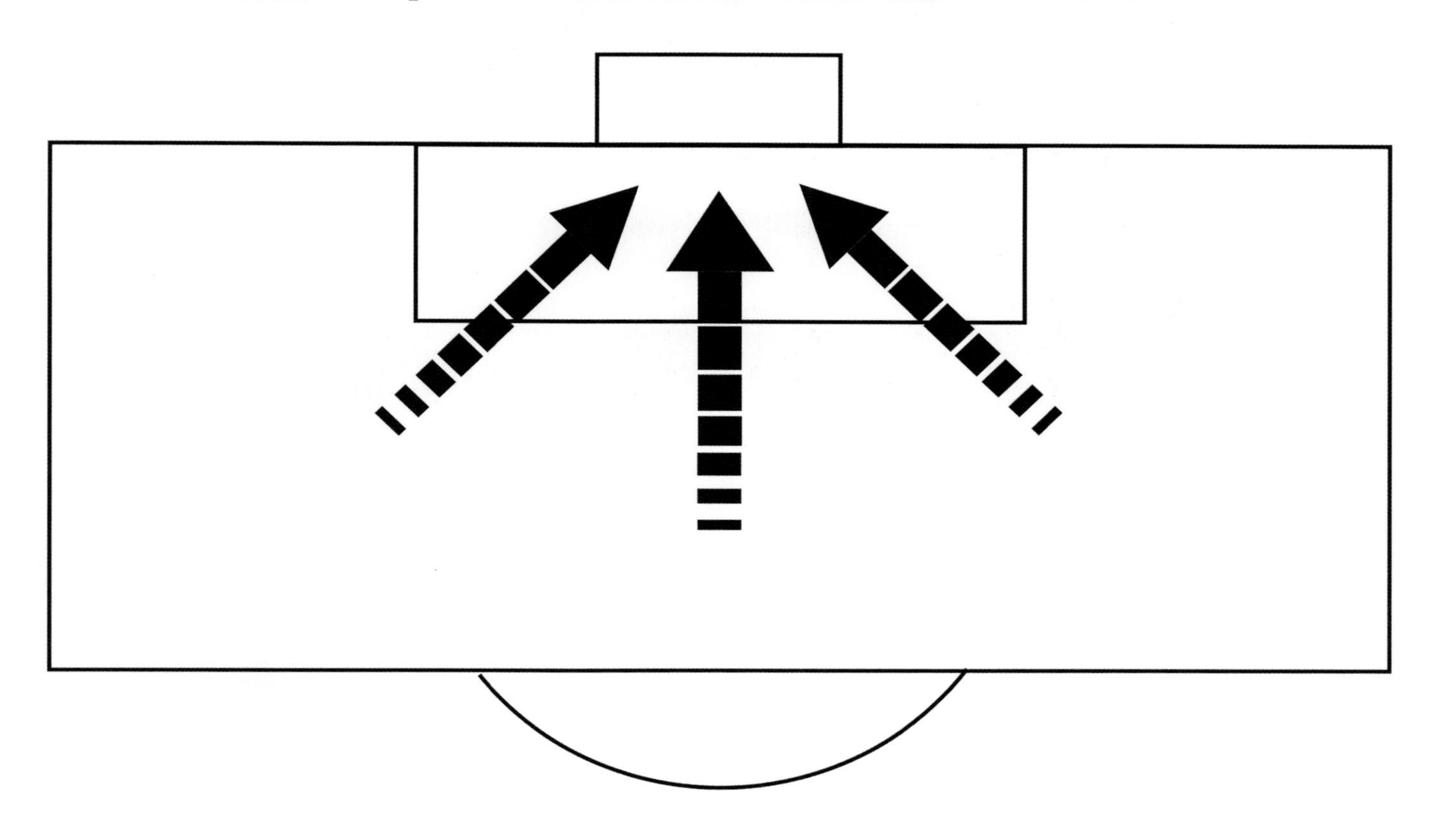

These are "The 4 Fundamental Rules to Scoring Goals". You'll have a chuckle but you'll remember. Especially since you were expecting some major scientific revelation. Imagine what your players will think. If you deliver the message correctly, they will have a laugh and they will think you're joking. The reality of course is that it's true. If you would like to summarize and re-word the rules and wrap them up into one here it is:

HIT THE NET

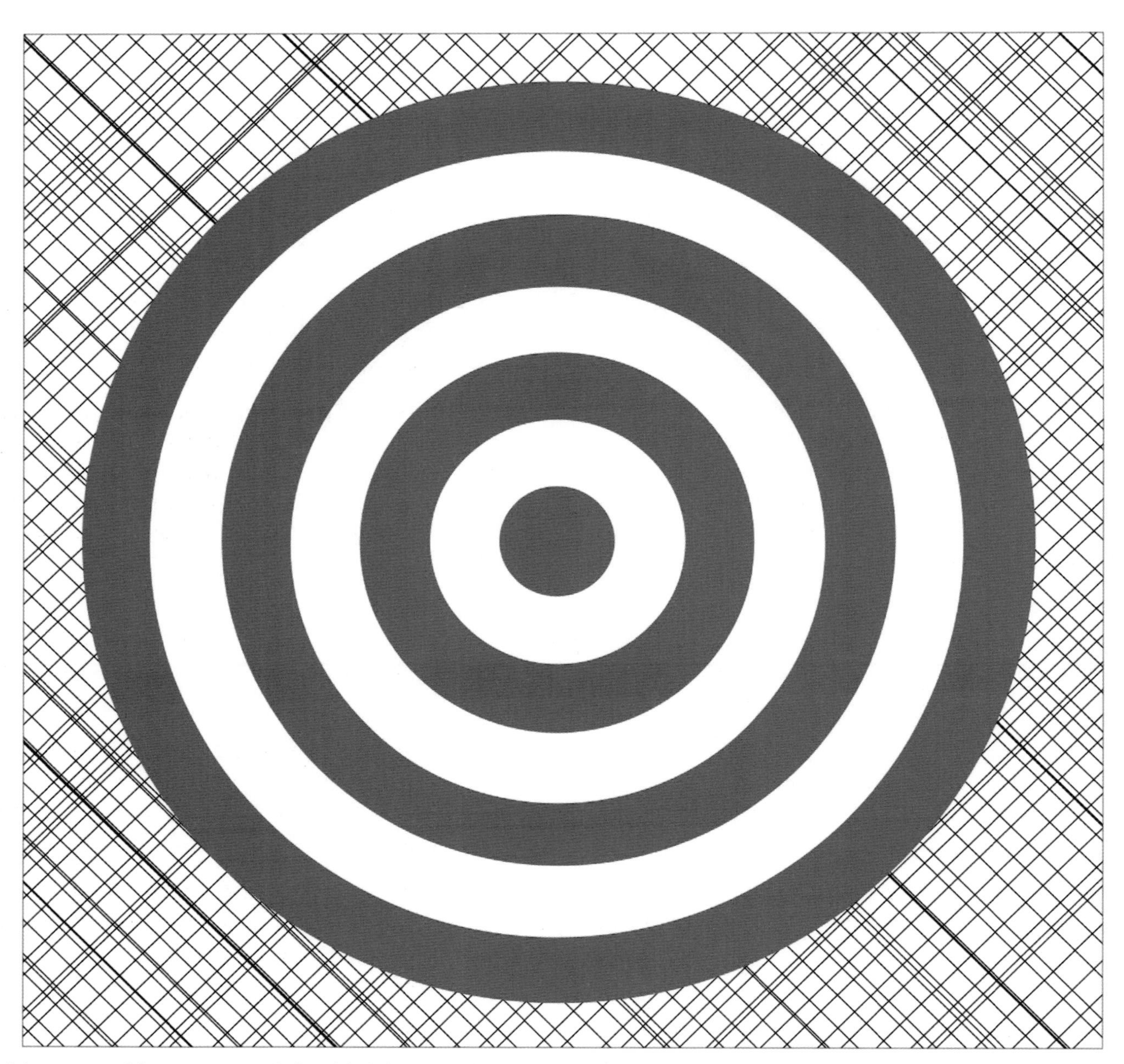

It's a pretty big target. It's 8 feet high by 8 yards wide. That's pretty big!

Or if you prefer:

DO NOT MISS THE NET!!

These are very simple concepts but without a doubt they are the second most important reason as to why goals are not scored apart from not having the technical skill to pass and shoot. When you see players miss a scoring chance by missing the net when they should have scored simply by directing the ball at the net, remind them of these four rules.

When you see a player miss the net remind him that if he had directed the ball at the net (Rule 1), then he would not have missed (rule 3). Keep reinforcing these four rules over and over at practice. Do so in a nice way of course, until the player gets tired of hearing you tell him of the importance of the four rules.

Here is an interesting point I make to young players about focusing on the ball and hitting the net:

> ***"I do not understand how you can miss the net. You must concentrate on directing the ball at the net. Not away from the net. This should not be that complicated unless the defender has done an excellent job, but you will find that quite often, even though you have beaten the defender, you will miss the net. Why? Does the net move? The net stays in the same spot all game. That's a guarantee. Your attention should be on getting the ball on target. Obviously you need to know where it is at all times. Once you are aware of its whereabouts, why would you not be able to find it? It's 8 yards wide by 8 feet high. That's pretty big. What's the big deal about the defender coming? If you can get the ball away, you should always hit the net because the net is not going anywhere!"***

As coach, you need to make it seem simple to score. Take away their fears of on-coming defenders, the goalkeeper, and anything else. Make them feel that, if they hit the net, even if the goalkeeper makes the save, you are happy with their effort. I will guarantee you that if your team gets 10 chances at goal and scores 1 goal, the goalie stops 3 and your players miss the net on the remaining 6, that your team will have more success if all 10 shots hit the net. Maybe the one that went in would have been saved but at least 2 out of the 6 that were missed would have gone in and your team would have scored on 2 or 3 out of 10 instead of 1 out of 10. That's a 100-200% improvement for every 10 chances your team gets on the number of goals scored.

At the National Soccer Coaches Association of America's (NSCAA) annual convention in Charlotte NC, I presented a lecture session on the psychology of scoring goals and about 6 months later I received an e-mail from a coach.

Coach, Jack Baer from Howland High School Girls Soccer in Ohio had this to say about the four fundamental rules of scoring. "The first time I introduced the four rules of scoring, they thought I was a goofball. Over time, they have begun to realize that scoring is really that simple. Of course, some kids pick it up faster than others, but most of them have had success." The team saw a vast improvement in goals scored after they adopted the rules.

That's exactly what you can expect from players, especially those between 14 and 18 years of age. Some will even roll their eyes. Then you must keep catching them miss the net and you must keep reminding them that they missed. Do this in a positive way, not a critical way. At some point, you will get your message across loud and clear and you will be well on your way to training players to score more consistently. Here is what I tell players in my course:

> ***"Let's start with making sure you force the goalkeeper to make a save by hitting the net because if the goalkeeper does not save it, then it's a goal. If you miss the net because the ball is not directed at goal, then the goalkeeper does not have to make the save at all. You will not score. Final!"***

Jasmine Merith one of my students e-mailed me this message about a month after she took my course, "I use the four fundamental rules every time I'm on the field. Since taking this course, my "last touch" has improved significantly. High flying balls over the cross bar are a thing of the past."

Remember:

HIT THE NET!

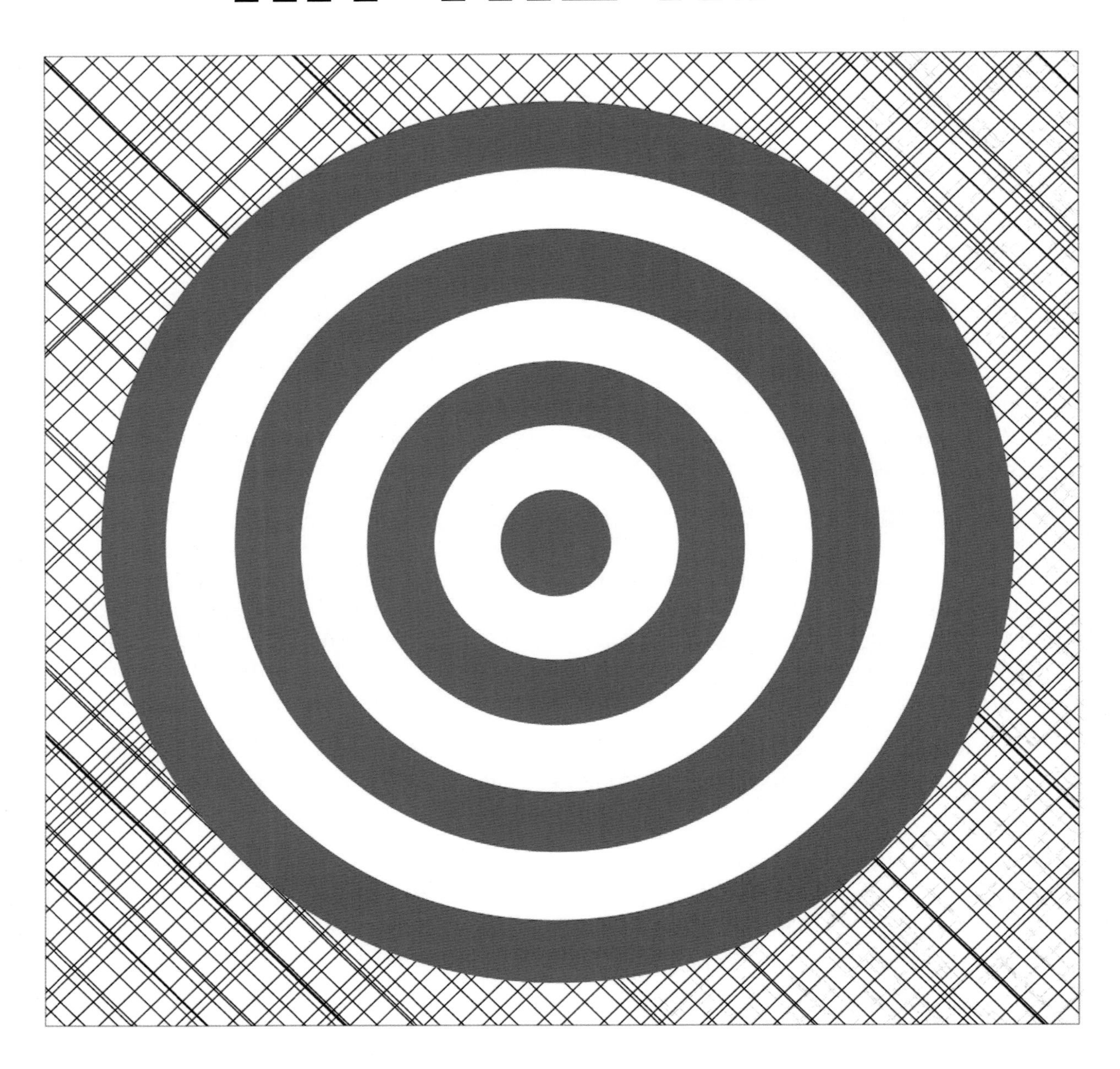

PART TWO

Understanding Human Movement and Muscular and Visual Perception and how it Affects Player Development

PART TWO

Action Images/Max Rossi

PLAYER DEVELOPMENT

CHAPTER 27

Switching Focus

Up until this point, we have looked at the psychological aspect of coaching players to become better goal scorers. As you know, this is only one aspect of developing great strikers. There are many other factors including perfecting some of the skills. And at this point I'm still going to assume that players have the basics down pat on passing, heading, and kicking a ball. We will assume that our players are now mentally strong, having taught them to accept failure and deal with stress. We have given them information to help them get in "the zone" and introduced them to visualization and relaxation techniques. We have also given players some simplified rules to scoring goals. But some players will still have problems matching their knowledge to the skills that they have. In other words, they know what to do in terms of making correct decisions based on the rules and they have the skills but they are having problems making the correct decision before applying the rules. What we still need to do is to help them make more correct decisions based on what's going on around them. Once we have improved this decision-making process then they will be able to match the correct skill to each specific situation. After we have helped them in this area, we can go back and give them more facts and information.

If a player follows all the rules (shoot low since most goals are scored in the bottom third of the goal, and hit the net) then that's great, but what if the player used the wrong skill? What if the player should have done something else but wasn't able to see what that other, possibly better option was? Does the player have the ability to see what is going on in relation to himself? The naturally gifted superstar seems to have this ability as described by basketball player Vince Carter, earlier in the chapter on "the zone" (chapter 24). What if you have taught your player to visualize, but when push comes to shove, the player doesn't actually read the game quickly enough on the field. It's great to visualize things with no pressure, but can the player really do it? And even if the player is able to, can we improve his ability to be even better?

Earlier, I talked about my goalkeeping secret on stopping breakaways, but I also had to seriously learn to read the motion of players in action. Can we teach this to our players? Coaches need to understand some details of human motion and how the muscles, eyes, and brain have to work together to make the player more instinctive in some of the things they do. I will go through some aspects of human motion and visual perception so that you know the theory behind some of my teaching methods. When I teach players in my goal-scoring course, I usually do not go into too much detail, but I feel that it is important for coaches to understand why and how I teach the young athletes certain things. It applies to strikers, as well as other positions.

Making the Average Player Play More Like a Natural Superstar

In Part Two of this book, I reveal some of my greatest coaching ideas and principles, which I have developed over years of research and experimentation. Although I use these ideas and principles with players in all positions on the field, I find that the quickest and most noticeable results come with strikers. This is because I can see improvement immediately. For midfielders and defenders who want to improve and "get it", their improvement takes longer to actually notice and see. With strikers, it's easier to see results because the measuring gauge is the number of goals scored. Other parts of the strikers' game may also improve but they are less noticeable to the average person. I focus on the strikers because of their impact on the game. As stated in the introduction, the game needs more goals.

I believe that, using my unique "Feel Good Perception Training Techniques" described in Chapters 37 to 44, that players who truly understand them and work hard to perfect their game will see remarkable results.

Please note that the naturally gifted athlete, who has many natural instincts but just cannot put the ball in the net, need not be taught what I will present in this section (Part 2 of this book). If your strikers are very talented then Parts 1, 3, 4, and 5 of this book will suffice to make them unbelievable goal scorers. What type of player is this? Any player who can control a ball effortlessly and dribble past players, who can pass and shoot, who is one of your best players on the team except that he fails to score when he should. Many things will come naturally to this player because he is very co-ordinated.

Part 2 of this book will help the player who is good but not naturally gifted. Maybe this player does not have the speed or natural coordination but has the ambition and drive to succeed. Part two of this book will work wonders with that type of athlete, assuming he has the mental ability to comprehend the information. Trying to coach naturally gifted athletes on how to get instinctively better when they already have the skills can actually confuse them and get them thinking about things that they don't have to think through to perform. This part of the book will help average players improve their natural abilities dramatically. I find the material in this part of the book exciting to coach to athletes ready to be coached because of the intrinsic feelings that they will get when they succeed. Also their subsequent improvement will be dramatic. These players will also thank you for your help and guidance.

Basics to Human Visual and Muscular Perception

To coach my techniques you will need to have a basic understanding of how the human body, eyes, and brain work together. Having some knowledge as to how the body works can only improve your ability to coach some of the most complicated and finer details of certain skills. Also you will see where I am coming from in relation to why I do certain things when teaching a goal scorer to become great.

I have outlined a number of factors that determine how human motion takes place, is perceived, and then performed. I will go into more depth in the upcoming chapters for each of these factors.

1. First, the eyes see things.
2. Next, the eyes send what they see to the brain.
3. Next, the brain interprets the images it sees.
4. Then, the brain looks inside its stored memory to see if there are past experiences similar to those the eyes have just seen and it has interpreted that can help it make a decision as to what to do next. The stored information helps the brain decide what to do but no two situations are 100% identical.
5. When recalling the information, the brain looks for similar experiences where the response provided a positive result. These answers pop up to the forefront and will help the brain decide what it should instruct the muscles to do next. Based on this positive history, the brain would give a response to what it sees and makes assumptions as to what will happen in the future. If there is not much memory in the background of positive results for similar situations, the brain will be more likely to choose a response that is not correct.

The brain is making assumptions all the time to predict the future so it can tell the muscles what to do. Positive responses provide a "feel good" feeling which both the brain and muscles enjoy and want to duplicate.

Imprinted in Memory

It is quite obvious that repetition is important in skill training. Athletes spend hours performing their specific tasks so that the brain and muscles coordinate movements in the skills required for their sport. Each time the athlete performs a task, the proper nerve path that carries the messages to the muscles as well as the proper sequence of muscle contractions that produce the skill are reinforced. With repeated practice, the information for the skill becomes imprinted in the memory of the brain and can be recalled the next time that it's needed for the same skill. The problem is that it is not easy to duplicate all the other factors that take place in a game (such as things the eye catches through peripheral vision) in a practice situation.

That's why players have to practice, practice, and practice so they experience as many of those situations as possible. When practicing, the players must be put in situations that are likely to occur often in a game. If this is not accomplished, the players may choose the incorrect response more often than you would wish in a game. We have to strive to find these situations as often as possible for skills to become instinctive.

Let's go though each of the stages one chapter at a time.

CHAPTER 28

(1) The Eye

It all starts with the eyes. What the eyes see is the start of everything. The eyes usually are not an issue unless players actually have vision problems. If this is the case then you will need to ask your players to go see an eye doctor.

The eye sees through the pupil. The image goes through the lens, which flips the image as it hits the retina at the back of the eyeball (diagram 28A). Then the image is passed on to the brain so that the brain can figure out what it sees and what to do. It gets there by way of the optic nerve. The optic nerve sends its signals to the area of the brain that looks after vision. That part of the brain is called the visual cortex.

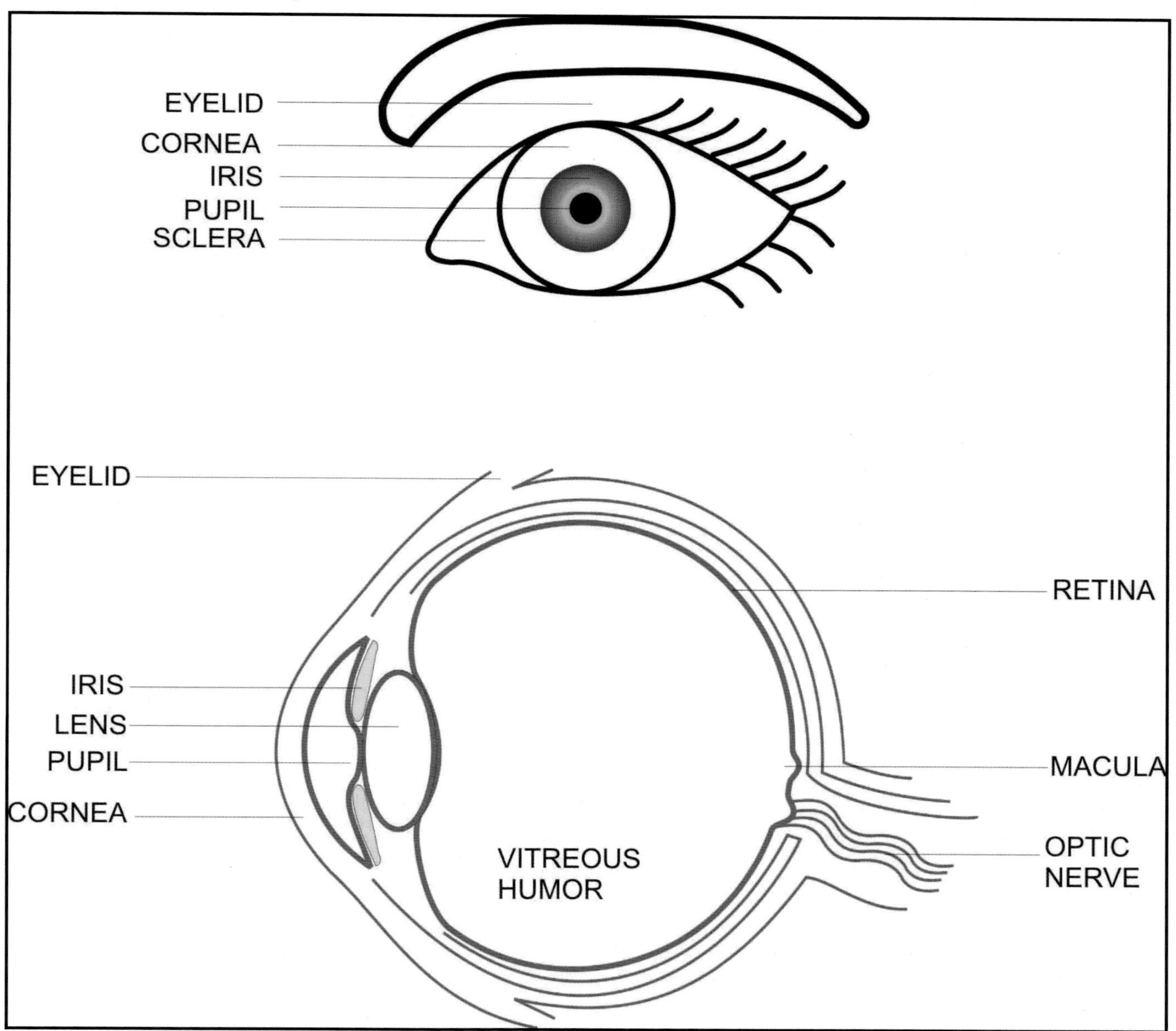

Diagram 28A: The diagram of the eye from the front view and from the side view is shown. We see through the pupil. The image goes through the lens to the retina at the back of the eyeball. The lens inverts the image. The optic nerve sends the image to the brain for interpretation. Diagram by Jo-Anne Godawa.

What the eyes see is not in the form of a TV screen, which is rectangular. What we can see is more cone-shaped. The closer the object is to the eyeball, the less we can see immediately around us. The farther away we look at an object, the more area we can see. Also, we are able to see things in three dimensions.

As we shall see later, good vision and good depth perception is certainly important for athletes to have in order for them to successfully predict where they actually are in relation to their opponents, teammates, and themselves. But good vision alone is not the only important aspect in a player's development. The brain, which detects vision, must be in good working order as well. Also, the portion of the brain that deals with motion and perception must function properly. And of course, the connections between all those components must be in good working order too. Even though the brain has ways of dealing with all of this, it still makes mistakes, as I shall point out in the upcoming chapters.

CHAPTER 29

(2) The Eyes Send What They See to the Brain

The optic nerve is the highway that the image takes to get to the visual cortex. It's the part of the brain that takes in what the eyes see. In studying the athlete and how things affect performance, I like to bring in motion. How does motion affect vision? Things move all over us but we can see motion in three different ways. For example we can keep our head still and be able to pick out a ball moving from right to left without moving our head or eyes. In fact, we don't even have to look at the moving ball to know that it is moving (diagram 29A). We can also see motion by keeping our head still by following the ball with our eyes (diagram 29B). Finally, we can keep our eyes still and focused on the ball but move our heads and follow the ball (diagram 29C). In each instance we know in our brain that there is movement going on.

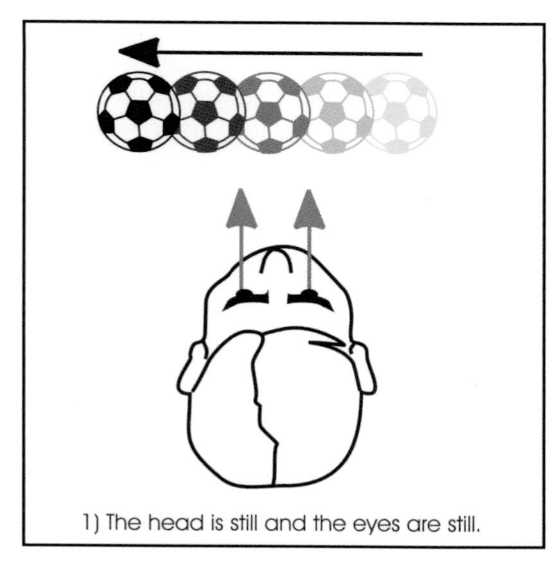

Diagram 29A: The head and the eyes stay still and are focused on an object straight ahead and we can detect motion without looking at what is moving.

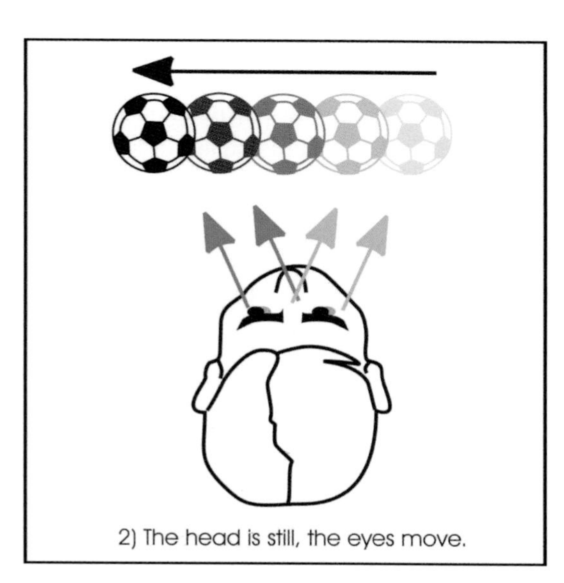

Diagram 29B: We can detect motion by keeping the head still; the eyes move and follow the object.

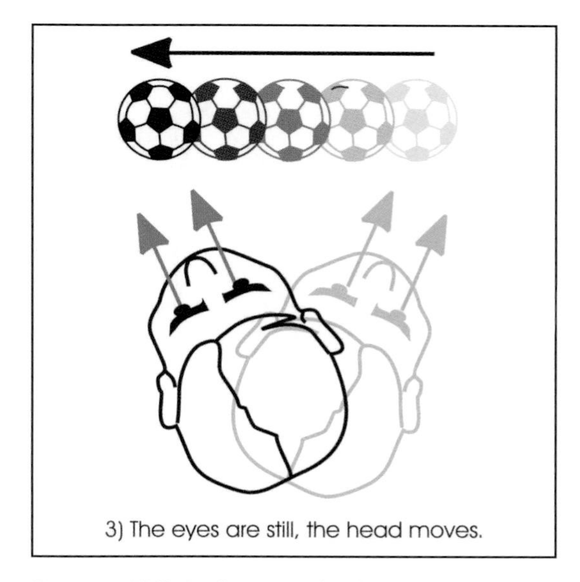

Diagram 29C: In this example, the eyes are still but the head moves to follow the moving object. We know that the object is moving in this situation as well. Illustrations by Jo-Anne Godawa

As a coach you may wonder how it is that, in all three situations, different things are happening, and yet the brain can interpret all three correctly and know exactly what is going on. The image on the retina is different in all cases but the end result is that we can detect that there is motion and in all cases detect that the ball is moving from right to left. The last one is particularly interesting because the head moves and motion is detected. This means that there has to be a connection between how our body moves and what our eyes see in order for us to actually see what is happening. How is it that, when being upside down, we know what is really up and what is really down?

How do we Know What is up and What is Down?

Regardless of where we are, we always know what is up and what is down. When we are lying in bed and looking up we know what's up and what's down. When we are standing up, we know what's up and what's down. When we are lying face down, we still know what's up and what's down. And when we are running or walking we know what's up and what's down. When we are half up and half down falling or diving, we still know what's up and what's down. We can still tell even when things are moving all around us. Pretty amazing isn't it?

How does our brain know all this? Believe it or not, the ears give us this information.

Inside the inner ear are the cochlea and three semi-circular canals. The semi-circular canals, utricle, and saccule make up the vestibular system and are involved in balance (diagram 29D). There are tiny hairs attached to the insides of the three semi-circular canals, the utricle, and the saccule. The canals are filled with a fluid called endolymph, and when the head moves, the fluid moves the hairs and bends them as water in a stream bends the plant life growing at its bottom.

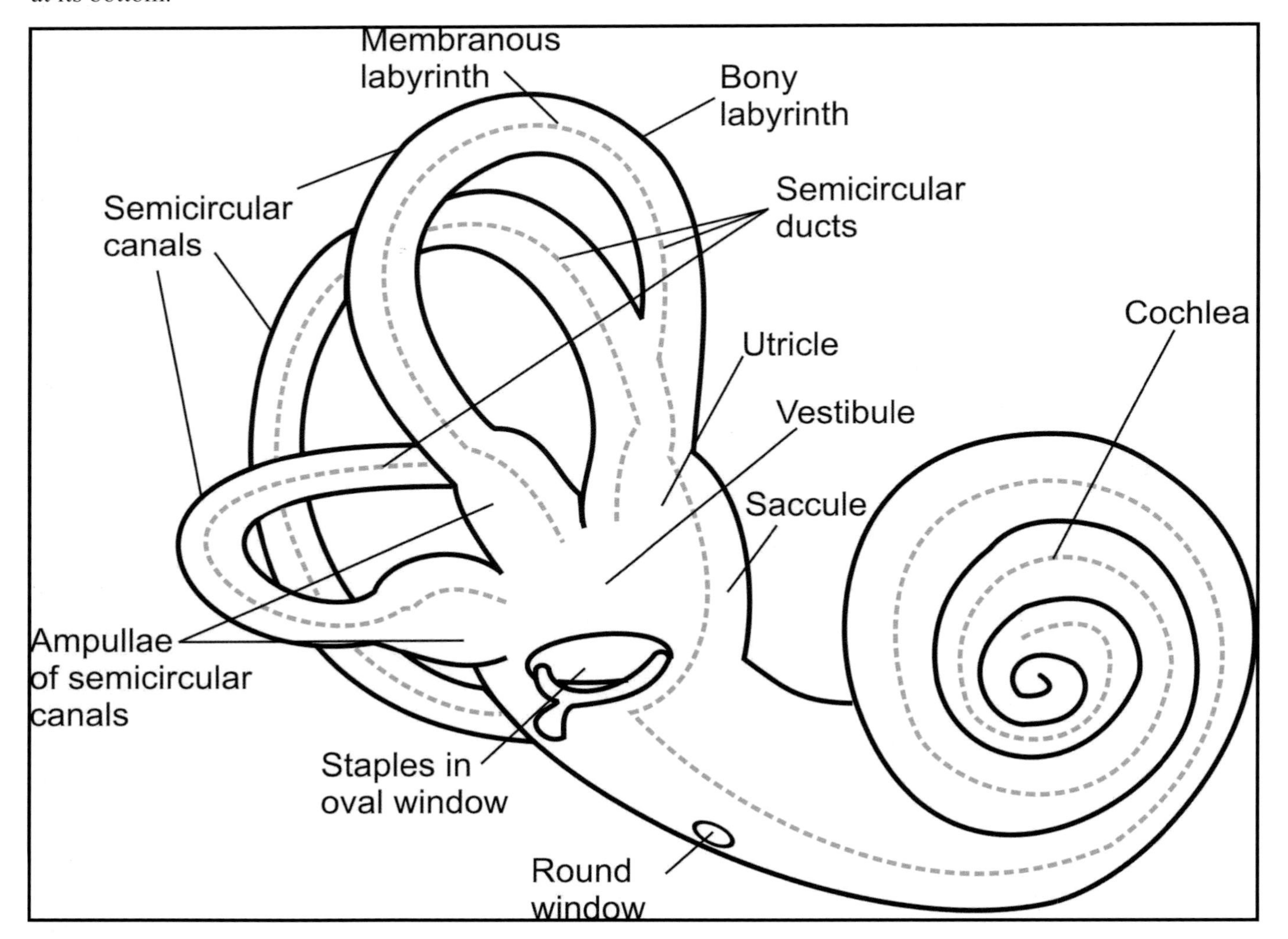

Diagram 29D: Balance is detected by the vestibular system made up of the cochlea , three semi-circular canals, utricle, and saccule. Illustration by Jo-Anne Godawa

Sensory nerve cells can detect small movements of the hairs in the fluid in all three semi- circular canals. The three canals are at right angles to each other in three planes so that together, they can send signals to the brain as to what position the body is in relation to the ground. The brain accounts for the force of gravity on the hairs and as the head is tilted the fluid inside the canals moves the hairs (diagram 29E). This movement is picked up by the sensory nerve cells and sent to the brain via the vestibular nerve. The nerve impulses then reach the temporal lobe of the cerebrum (areas of the brain that control coordination, balance, movement, blood pressure, and consciousness).

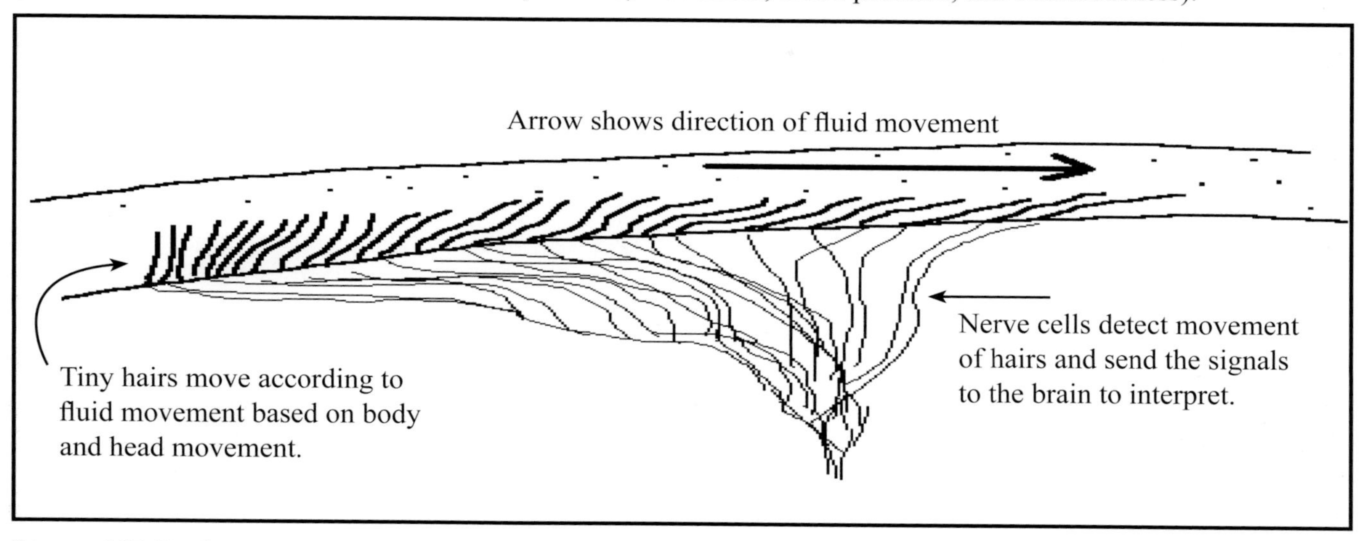

Diagram 29E: Tiny hairs inside the vestibular system help detect motion based on the head movement. Head movement makes the fluid inside the system move, which in turn moves the tiny hairs. This movement is detected by the sensory nerve cells, which send the messages to the brain via the vestibular nerve. Diagram by John DeBenedictis

When we lose balance, the hairs are tilted within the cristae in each canal and the information goes to the brain. By combining the input from each of the three canals, the brain can create a representation of the vector, which describes the instantaneous speed of head rotation relative to 3-dimensional space. The brain then makes the correction and tells the muscles how to behave in order to keep us in balance.

This is one reason why doctors are concerned when young children get ear infections. They are not only concerned with potential hearing problems but also potential balance problems in the future. Things are more complicated than what I have just described because there is a system in place that accounts for what the eyes see while everything is going on. The good news is that we will leave all this scientific stuff to the scientists. We will take what we can from it and apply it to the game and specifically, the goal scorer.

Things That Can Cause the System not to Work

As an aside, there are methods of confusing the brain even though the inner ear system and the eyes are all working well and is telling us what is up and what is down and what is moving and what is not. A few things can go wrong. For example, all the information goes to a certain section of the brain to get processed. But sometimes that area of the brain is slightly damaged. It can occur from a blow to the head, which can cause one to feel disoriented and lose balance. A severe blow to the head could cause a concussion, even for a few seconds, and once again we would lose our balance. A stroke to the area of the brain that affects balance can cause permanent damage and affect our ability to maintain balance or walk on our own.

The brain can also be affected by alcohol or drugs, which can leave us with a loss of balance or perception of where we are in relation to others and the ground.

Also, there can be a problem in the inner ear. Vertigo is usually associated with a problem in the inner ear balance mechanisms (vestibular system), in the brain, or with the nerve connections between these two organs. Sometimes this occurs when we are spinning for a while with our eyes closed. If you were to be spun around in a chair, at some point you would have no clue as to which way your were facing, or whether your chair was still spinning or not. In fact you will actually think you are turning in the opposite direction. This weird sensation is a result of the fluids in your ear catching up to themselves as you spin around. Your brain is getting all sorts of mixed messages and gets totally confused and as a result you become disoriented. If you were to try and stand up after being spun around for a while, you would probably feel dizzy and fall. This condition is called vertigo.

A Great Strategy to Disorient Defenders

A good scoring strategy would be to spin a defender around a few times so that the player gets disoriented and then one could walk around him and score. Or you could offer the defender a drink or two of Sambuca before a game. That would throw him off and he would be happy at the same time. This would not be an easy thing to do but if you could, it would work. Enjoy my true "Sambuca Story".

THE SAMBUCA STORY

As I have stated before, I play in a non-contact old-timers hockey league, and that year, our team reached the finals. This was my first time with the team in a while after missing almost two seasons while recovering from an injury. As we were getting dressed and preparing for the grand finale, the captain pulled out a bottle of Sambuca. (Sambuca is a sweet, strong liqueur.) I thought this was strange because usually you have champagne, but after the game, if you win it. To my total shock, the captain took a drink from the bottle and passed it on to the next guy. This was before the game even started! Next in line was our goalie and then the bottle went around the room. I was trying to figure out what was going on as the bottle got closer to me. My teammates told me that this is tradition and each time they get to the finals, they have a swig of Sambuca for good luck. Apparently, it's worked in the past so I took my turn, not to be a party pooper. Don't forget this is recreational hockey. Nothing serious for sure.

How a Bottle of Sambuca Can Affect Your Game

The bottle went around and back to the captain. Since there was some Sambuca still left, the goalie, who was beside the captain, took the bottle from him and had another sip. There was still a bit left so he took another gulp to finish the bottle. Early in the game, the other team had possession of the puck. Their player playing on the left wing came inside our blue line with the puck. I was defending him from that side. Suddenly the player took a long weak shot from just inside the blue line and at a bad angle to our goal, practically touching the boards. This was a routine shot, which should have resulted in a routine save. As I turned my head to follow the path of the puck I noticed, to my astonishment, that our goalkeeper was standing to the side of the goal protecting the boards instead of the goal. The goal was left completely open. The puck went in easily and I knew that our goalie was seeing double. We lost the game 5-2 and except for one goal against us, the goalie let everything in from all distances and angles. His perception was definitively affected.

Superstitions Can Start in the Weirdest Ways

The Sambuca good luck superstition came to an end but the tradition had started a few years earlier. Our hockey team, called 'The Pickups,' started the season as a bunch of guys who had no team to play on and came together at the last minute put together by the league. We finished the season in last place but in recreational hockey, every team makes the play-offs. I blew out my knee in the first round of the playoffs and missed the rest of the season. Somehow, the team managed to win a couple of games and the team found itself in the Championship Final.

For the final game another player had injured himself and our best player and leading goal-scorer, John Mason, had to miss the final game due to work commitments. The team we had to play in the final game was a team we had never beaten so the Cinderella story was sure to come to an end. The remaining players figured that we didn't have a chance of winning so they thought, 'why not have a drink before the game instead of after it?' The co-captain brought with him a bottle of Sambuca. Miraculously, even without our key players and to everyone's surprise, the team won the championship and the Sambuca tradition began.

The team won again the following year, which I missed so that took us up to that game where it all came to an abrupt end.

CHAPTER 30

(3) The Brain Interprets What the Eyes See

Nerve cells communicate electrochemical impulses. They use chemicals to send an electric signal. The brain alone contains 100 billion nerve cells. Sensory nerves collect information about the environment and change this information into sensations (cold, hot, touch, pressure, and pain). The information goes to the brain, which then decides how to react. The brain sends messages to other nerves called motor nerves, which direct muscles to move.

In sports, we need very quick reaction times. Can we improve our reaction time? Reaction time is the amount of time it takes for a message to travel from the brain to the muscles and cause a movement. Some of this is done in the primary motor cortex, which is the area of the brain that causes movement but does not initiate movement. For example we have all tried the reflex test where we drop a ruler between our fingers and see how quick we react when the ruler is dropped. In this experiment shown in diagrams 30A and 30B, the eyes see the drop of the ruler and this information is sent to the brain to give a response to squeeze the fingers to catch the ruler. We measure our quickness by how many inches or centimetres the ruler has dropped by the time we squeeze our fingers and catch the ruler.

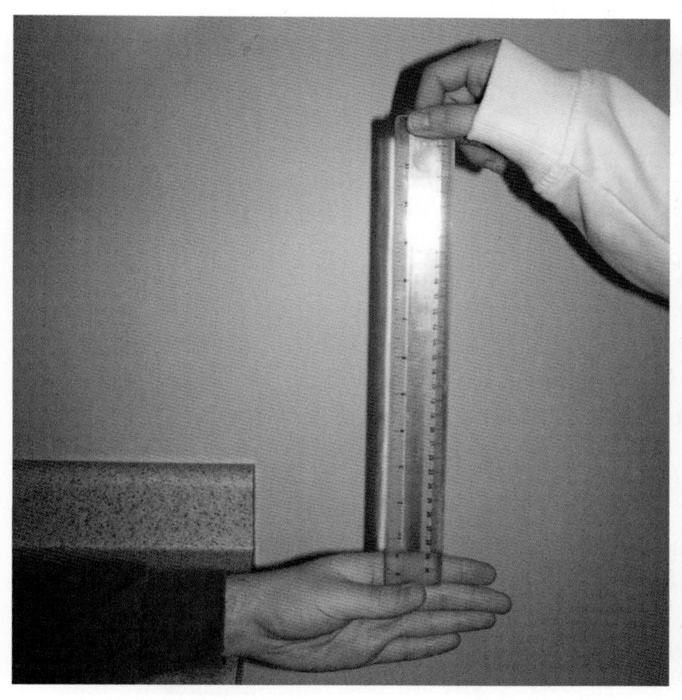

Diagram 30A: In this reflex test someone holds a ruler between the subject's finger and thumb. The ruler is held so that it ends where the subject's finger and thumb are. The hand must rest on a desk and stay on the desk. Once the ruler is dropped, the subject must squeeze the ruler to catch it.

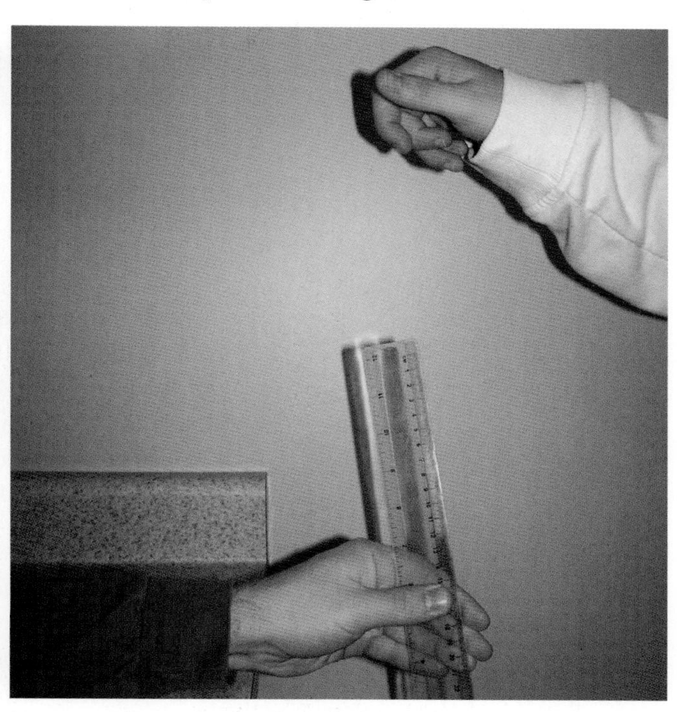

Diagram 30B: At the conclusion of the reflex test, the subject will squeeze his finger and thumb to catch the ruler while keeping the arm on the table. We can measure the quickness of the subject based on how many inches or centimeters the ruler dropped when it was caught. To get a correct measurement of reaction time, the subject should not squeeze the ruler until he sees it being dropped. There will be a tendency to guess before the ruler is dropped.

But How does the Brain Know, it Needs to Squeeze the Fingers and not the Toes?

A lot is happening in our brain for such a simple exercise. But how does the brain know it needs to squeeze the fingers and not the toes? Without going into a lengthy explanation it's safe to say that many of the reactions we do are based on us having done them before with positive results, thus the brain builds a memory bank for recalling the correct response. If you are interested in more details on how this works, see recommended reading in the footnotes at the end of chapter 31.

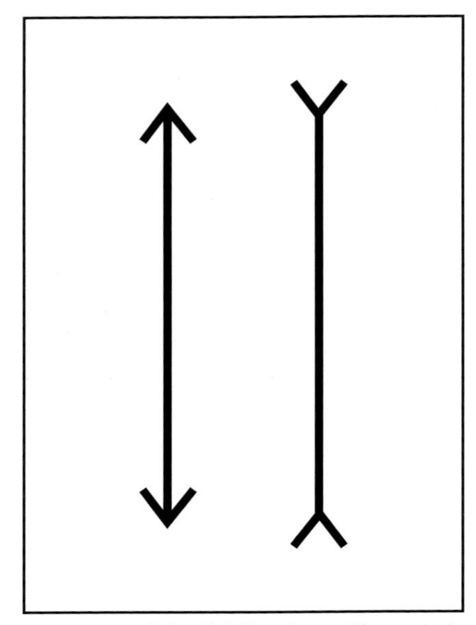

Diagram 30C: (Müller-Lyer illusion) In this popular illusion, the distance between the top and bottom tips of the arrows is identical between the left figure and right one, but appears to be longer in the latter than in the former.

The Brain Can be Fooled

Even though we are blessed with a pretty good system for taking in information and deciphering what is going on around us, it's not perfect. Once in a while things get mixed up and the brain gets totally fooled. Occasionally, the eyes and the brain are on a different page. But the problem is usually a result of the psychological (cognitive or thinking) part of us and not the physiological (eyes, inner ear, sensory nerves, brain) part.

For example, the brain can interpret things incorrectly because we are in the wrong frame of mind. Our brain predetermines what we think we should see and makes assumptions based on prior similar experiences in our memory bank. It does this instead of interpreting what is actually there. Here are some well-known visual patterns that provide good examples. In the well known Müller-Lyer illusion shown in diagram 30C, the lengths of the two vertical lines are perceived as different, while their actual lengths are in fact identical.

In this case we are fooled. There is nothing wrong with our eyes and nothing wrong with our sensory nerves. We have had no drinks or no blows to the head yet we make wrong judgements. Why?

What we think we see and what we actually see is heavily dependent on memories and past experiences (learning). In other words, we use past experiences to make assumptions about things even in highly specific areas such as vision.

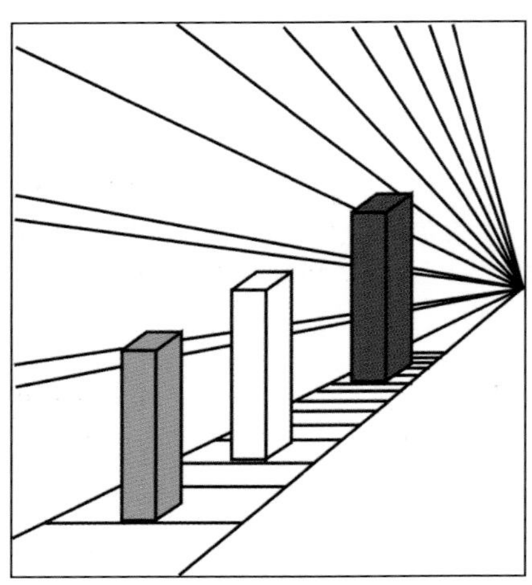

Diagram 30D: When perceiving three-dimensional images on a two-dimensional plane, depth can be distorted. The brain has been conditioned to perceive objects that are far away as smaller but yet all 3 bars are equal in size in this drawing, but we assume the bar to the right is bigger. Illustration by Jo-Anne Godawa

We also make errors in depth perception as well as 2-dimensional perception as shown in diagram 30D. In the following example, our brain is trained to see things in the 3D world and when asked to compare the size of these three blocks in real size instead of perceived size we make errors. All three bars in diagram 30D appear to have different sizes but in reality they are all the same size. Once again our brain is fooled.

The brain has a mountain of stored information in it about everything, which it calls upon to make decisions. We make decisions on how to coach based on your experiences from previous games, books, coaching sessions etc. Our instincts or our automatic response system makes similar decisions based on its previous experiences. That's why we make the mistakes we make in diagrams 30C and 30D. We have based our thoughts on stored information.

Earlier I quoted a common phrase used in advertising, "Perception is Reality". This occurs when we take things as being real because that's what people want us to believe. Or we believe them but they may or may not be real. Now I will introduce a new play on that phrase, "Reality is Perception" (DeBenedictis, 2004). As we saw from the above illustrations, in these cases reality is perception. That is, what is real is perceived to be different than what is real.

This happens because the brain interprets what the eyes see and makes errors for what is actually there because its stored memory of similar situations is different than what they are seeing.

I will go into more detail about this in the next two chapters. The information will help you understand my "Feel Good Perception Training Techniques". My techniques will not only help your players make less errors on skill choice but, as a consequence, also improve players reaction times once the correct skill is chosen because they will become more instinctive.

CHAPTER 31

(4) The Brain Looks Inside its Stored Memory

Our brain is capable of remembering everything it sees, hears, smells, or feels. Our brain's stored capacity is almost endless. It's a most powerful piece of equipment. And things that are stored eventually can be retrieved provided they are found. As we age and experience more and more things in life, the brain stores more and more information so finding the information becomes harder and harder. Our brain then uses methods to retrieve information based on what it uses most often. For example, when we see or talk about certain people everyday we can easily recall their names but we often forget names of people we don't see or talk about as often. The brain is using a technique that helps it recall information that's stored in our memory bank called "association".

We like to organize things and associate things together by way of experiences. We are not born with them. For example, when we hear certain types of music we can become scared by them. On the other hand when we hear a song like rock-a-bye-baby, we become relaxed and happy and mushy. These reactions are not due to heredity. We do not have genes that like certain types of music and have them affect our feelings. All this is learned and it affects our emotions and our muscle movements. We don't get tensed up with baby music. Amazing, isn't it?

What happens in our muscles is not all heredity. A lot less than what we think. A lot of decisions made are based on our experiences including how we perceive motion. In the game of soccer there is a lot of movement. The opponents, teammates, and even the background fans and coaches move along with the ball. Things are moving everywhere at the same time. Can the brain make mistakes about motion and movement?

Motion perception is detected in the ascending limb of the inferior temporal sulcus. Without this region the perception of motion would be impossible but it does make errors in detecting motion.

Amazingly the brain can be fooled when it comes to detecting motion just as it does with stationary perception. How often have you been in a car and just come to a complete stop but then all of a sudden you get the feeling that you are moving backwards but then quickly realize that you are not as it is the car beside you which is moving forward. The brain gets fooled. You think you are in motion but you are not.

Check out the circle in diagram 31A and stare at the inner circle of the diagram. Really focus on the inner circle in this illusion called the Ouchi apparent motion illusion. A Japanese artist named Ouchi first came up with this illusion.

Does it not appear that the inner circle is moving side to side just a little bit? Our brain does not perceive the motion correctly. In reality, nothing is moving. "Reality is Perception".

Once again the brain is fooled or deceived. The fact that we get fooled when trying to identify motion is interesting because with some motion type errors, often comes some major physical consequence. Vertigo is one consequence and dizziness and even epileptic seizures can be another, although rare. Errors in motion detection when driving a vehicle can result in serious accidents.

Motion perception is amazing and fascinating and one can find a host of information about it on the internet or in books. When the brain gets fooled, it can actually affect us physically.

For example, one website actually has this warning:

"Caution: This page contains some works of 'anomalous motion illusions', which might make sensitive observers dizzy or sick. Some of the pictures on this website can cause dizziness or even epileptic seizures. The latter happens when the brain can't handle the conflicting information from your two eyes. Should you feel dizzy, you had better leave this page immediately."

It comes from the Department of Psychology from Ritsumeikan University in Kyoto Japan. Professor Kitaoka Akiyoshi's web-site is: www.ritsumei.ac.jp/~akitaoka/index-e.html

You wouldn't think that a computer could be so dangerous. It may be safer playing soccer on the street! All those superstars and natural athletes actually did play soccer in the street or in the park for hours on end. That's how they trained their motion perception abilities so that they make fewer errors in perceiving motion.

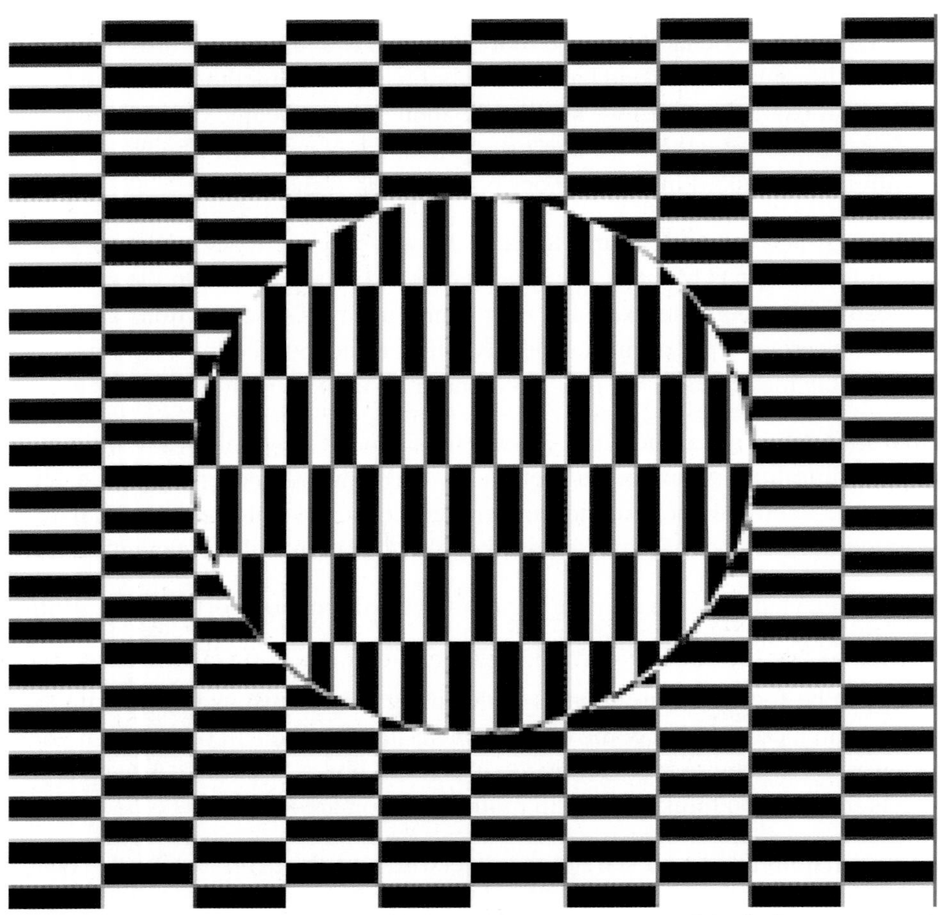

Diagram 31A: Ouchi apparent motion illusion. A Japanese artist named Ouchi first came up with this illusion. When you stare at the inner circle at the centre of this diagram for a while, it will appear to move.

What I have illustrated is that what we see is often not what's real and the mistake happens in two areas of the brain. One directly related to the job of seeing or staying in balance and the other, based on stored information from past experiences. Both are important and in both cases our brain can make mistakes.

When relating it to the psychology of scoring goals, you can see that scoring is not easy. The player with the scoring opportunity has enough problems dealing with defenders, goalkeepers, crowd noise and a moving ball, he also has to deal with the fact that what he thinks he sees can be completely wrong! No wonder soccer is such a low scoring game!

With all this happening, the coach needs to understand that players will miss scoring chances. Simplifying the information that the athlete is absorbing, deciphering, and trying to compute to give out the proper response is not simple at all. Can we make some of those responses more automatic or instinctive? Can we tell our muscles to do the right things more often?

For more reading:
Kaufman, Lloyd, *PERCEPTION*, *The World Transformed*, New York 1979 by Oxford University Press Inc.
Howard, IP & Rogers, BJ, (2001) *Seeing in Depth*, I Porteous Publishing
Howard Ian P, Rogers, Brian J, *Binocular Vision and Stereopsis*, Oxford Psychology Series No 29, 1995 by Oxford University Press, Inc.

CHAPTER 32

(5) When Recalling the Information, the Brain Looks to Similar Experiences

Every movement that we make in response to something is stored in our memory bank. In soccer, each situation is different from another. When the brain gives a command to its muscles on what to do for each situation, it gives it based on past experiences. But before giving the command, the brain uses past experiences to help it predict future events so that the command it gives its muscles is more likely to result in a positive experience. For example, if a defender makes a move to try to prevent the striker from scoring, the next move that the striker will choose will come from what the eyes have seen and the brain interpreted. Once this is accomplished the brain has to figure out what to do and, when this is done, tell its muscles to make the desired movements. Maybe it's to shoot, cut back, pass, take another stride, whatever. The brain is trying to make an educated guess on what to do because it does not know what the next move the defender will make. These guesses will be based on its history of similar situations from the past.

The more often the brain gets the responses correct, the more likely it is to give the correct response again next time in a similar situation. The idea in training is to make the responses automatic so that the brain does not take up too much time figuring out what to do. Split seconds for the striker can cause missed scoring opportunities. In the case of a race car driver, a split second delay may cause an accident or even cost a life. A wrong decision can also cost a life. In fact, one doesn't have to look to the car-racing world to see how important making quick and correct decisions can be. Our highways and roads call for reactions to what is perceived every second. In fact the study of vision and motion perception is very important in the automobile industry as car manufacturers constantly try to build safety mechanisms so that the driver will make fewer motion perception errors when driving (picture 32A).

Picture 32A: Errors in motion perception can result in wrong decisions made by drivers, which can cause accidents. In this picture, a major highway was blocked for hours due to an error made by one or more motorists. Photo by John DeBenedictis

The automatic response system can be trained so that our muscles instinctively react to each situation correctly or with a smaller margin of error. The best and most naturally gifted players tend to be excellent at this. They tend to make quick, accurate decisions more often than other players do. To train this system so that the correct response is more likely to occur as often as possible, the memory bank must be full of positive responses to that exact situation. To improve the performance of your players, you want them to react to situations quicker by helping them make correct decisions on what skill to use and then follow through with the correct technique for that skill.

Picture 32B: Finding the mouth involves visual, mental, and muscular perception requiring repetitive practice with success. Conor Foley (child in picture) would not be able to improve his fine motor skills if he did not receive positive reinforcement by having success.

Quick decision making alone is not going to improve performance because if the decision made was the wrong decision, then it won't matter how quick it was made and the performance will not and cannot improve. You want to improve the speed of decision making and the accuracy of choosing the correct response to each situation whether it be, run, accelerate, stop, cut, turn, control the ball, dribble, pass, or shoot. This can be trained by combining the two factors that affect a reaction becoming instinctive.

1) Build the Memory Bank

The player is to build the memory bank with as much stored information as possible for each situation he may come up against. This is not easy and requires lots of playing time.

2) Deliver Correct Responses

Secondly, in order to deliver the correct responses to situations consistently, the correct responses must have occurred enough times to create positive feelings in the brain and muscle nerve pathways so that they become instinctive.

The key words here are positive experiences. The two factors above are so important that they cannot be mixed up when understanding how to coach your players at becoming more instinctive. Your players need similar positive experiences to occur again and again for the instinctive correct reaction to occur consistently. This is built with increasing the frequency of doing the correct skill or manoeuvre at the right times.

In order for a skill to become instinctive it needs to be repeated successfully many times just like when we were babies learning to put food into our mouth. We try over and over and over and at first we make a mess. Then each time we get a positive experience (good tasting food), we are more likely to repeat the action. At some point we get really good at this and can actually do it with our eyes closed. Our brain has learned through positive experiences. The baby will make a mess at first trying to put food in his mouth as shown in the picture 32B and the picture 36A but we learn to get good at it. (Apparently, too good. A lot has been written lately about how more children than ever before are overweight in North America. That's another issue for another book!)

No Bloody Nose

We become so good at some things that even when we close our eyes and try and touch our noses, the brain sends the signal to the muscles and we get it right all the time. But even though we know where our nose is, why don't we give ourselves a bloody nose? We are so good at training ourselves that we not only know where our nose is but we also know how hard or gently we can make our muscles move while touching the nose. We can do all of this with our eyes closed and without hurting ourselves. Amazing isn't it?

But our nose does not move and there are no defenders trying to stop us from touching our nose so it doesn't take that long to train our brain and muscles to work together to accomplish this task. In soccer, things are much different and there are many possible scenarios.

Defenders Everywhere

If you were a striker trying to score a goal, you may be faced with situations such as this one: One minute you have a defender to your left, the ball is coming from an angle from your right at 15km/hr and the goalkeeper is 7 meters away. Another defender is 4 meters away to your right running at 10km/hr at a 45-degree angle towards you. The next time you get a chance to score the ball is in the air coming at you at 20km/hr from your left and the defender is 1 meter to your left at a 35-degree angle from you. Your body is at right angles to the goal. Another defender is to your left at a 45-degree angle to you but already in the air. The keeper is in your sight but 5 meters away moving to his left at 6km/hr. The sound you hear is from 3 meters behind you and you suspect it's a defender. There is a lot going on!

How can we possibly experience the exact same situation over and over again and provide a positive response so that the brain and muscles do it more instinctively? It is very hard (picture 32C, 32D, 32E & 32F). Without question, playing the game as often as possible will do wonders for the goal scorers and that's why I stress throughout the book about teaching passion or a love of the game. Passionate players who become superstars and natural athletes actually did play soccer in the street or park for hours on end without coaches offering advice every two minutes. It's unpressurized play that was fun. Those players will get more situations where they will experience things more often and they will get more positive responses and therefore automatically become better than the players who do not. That's how they trained their motion perception abilities.

Picture 32C: Every time the player has the ball or the ball is coming to him, a different set of circumstances will exist. It's hard to recreate identical situations unless players play often. This photo cannot be duplicated very often. Les Jones/Covershots

Picture 32D: How do you re-create a situation like this very often so that the brain can get a positive response regularly and then proceed to make the muscles perform the right action to "get it right" more often? Les Jones, Covershots

Picture 32E: Louis Jourdan Brasil from my team with the Pickering Soccer Club, has defenders all around him in this picture. Photo by Philip Yates

Picture 32F: Brazil's Neymar surrounded. Photo by Les Jones, Covershots

CHAPTER 33

It's All About Repetition and Having Fun

Many experts are concerned with the lack of free play that our youth are experiencing today. There are numerous problems that we are facing today in developing more creative players and blame is being fired in many different directions. Two factors seem to contribute to the lack of free play.

1. The coach is either over-coaching and driving players away, or the coach is under-coaching by not teaching or coaching passion. This is a key component that coaches often overlook. As coach Karl Dewazien, coaching director of the California Youth Soccer Association puts it, "there is one thing that you have to teach kids, and that's to learn to love to play soccer".

2. In today's western world, society offers our youth too many options for things to do outside of going out to play sports and having fun.

The German Soccer Federation made a presentation at the National Soccer Coaches Association of America's (NSCAA) coaching conference in 1998 and stated that they were concerned with their own lack of a superstar player that would make a major difference in their National Team program. They cited that too many kids were at home playing Nintendo or Sony PlayStation or other computer related games or just had too many choices of programs to watch on TV and therefore were not going out to play enough.

German World Cup Star and former German Men's National Team coach, Jürgen Klinsmann, who now resides in Southern California said in an article by Marc Connolly in *Soccer Journal* (2003), "soccer in my opinion, is self-teaching. The more you play, the better you get. You don't see American kids playing in the park these days. It's only in an organized environment. Similar problems are taking place in Europe. I kicked the ball around three to four hours a day."

Playing in the park everyday helps provide more opportunities for the eyes, brain, and body to get more specific experiences and therefore help in making certain decisions become instinctive. It's about repetition. A great goal scorer needs to make decisions very quickly because time is most precious around the goal. As Frank Cirone, hockey coach of the boy's varsity team at Holderness School in New Hampshire and former leading goal scorer in the Professional Roller Hockey League, says, "If you have to <u>think</u> about where you have to be or what you have to do, it's already too late."

You may be coaching players at the high school and college age brackets and have to work with a group of players of varying skill levels. You hope that some of them are very good. If you do not have the cream of the crop because your recruiting tools are not good enough to give your team enough players with great instinctive skills, do not lose enthusiasm. Some coaches believe that it's too late to develop the players' motor skills if they haven't already got them by this age bracket. You may have some players who are very good but others who are still having problems juggling a ball 5 times. This does create some problems for many coaches and I always admire coaches who can make their teams competitive creating a fun environment when dealing with those types of situations.

Bob Bigelow, former NBA player was interviewed by Michael Jones in an article titled, "We're losing our late bloomers" in the July-August 2009 issue of *Soccer Journal*. He discussed how potential superstars are overlooked at too young an age before they hit puberty. Because of this, many players who may develop their motor muscular skills later may quit because they get rejected at a young age.

Scoring Goals at the Right Time can do Wonders for a Player's Career

I don't believe it's too late to start playing and become very good even as late as 14, 15, and 16 years of age. Many players I have coached who started at that age range went on to play professionally, semi-professionally, or at the varsity level. I recall an episode with one of my players who started playing soccer at age 14. My rep team was short of players and I asked my players to ask friends if they knew anyone who may want to play. One of our players brought a friend for a training session and I liked his enthusiasm. We signed him so he could play in our next game. Halfway through the game, I was ready to give him his first-ever chance to play organized soccer. I called the referee for a substitution and then went to the player, Kenny Dodd, and said, "OK Kenny, you go play on the left wing striker position."

Kenny started happily trotting on the field and after about 5 or 6 paces stopped and turned back and said, "Coach, where is left wing?" I quickly realized that this kid had no idea about positions on the field so I told him to come back so I could give him an idea of what he had to do. He went on 5 minutes later. At 19 he was the leading goal scorer in the National Soccer League's U21 division and training everyday with the Toronto Blizzard of the North American Soccer League (NASL) with the likes of Roberto Bettega (Juventus and Italian National Team) and Ace Ntsoelengoe (South African National Team). He joined the team halfway through their season after scoring a big goal in the final of The Robbie International Soccer Tournament for our team. The coach of the Toronto Blizzard, Bob Houghton, was the colour commentator for the game, which was televised locally. Kenny was invited to the reserve team (Picture 33A) a week later and scored 5 goals in their next 3 games and was quickly called up to train daily with the first team. He was about to be drafted in the next draft but the league folded that winter. I believe that when it comes to strikers you can train average players to be very good fairly quickly using my "feel good perception training techniques".

Before I go into the specifics of those techniques, I want to address player development at the younger age groups so that when they come into your age bracket, there are a lot more players with great instinctive talents to choose from. I believe that every professional, college, high school, and higher level club and even provincial or state level coaches can improve things in their community. In communities where there may be a lack of experienced coaches, I urge you to get involved in passing on your coaching skills to younger players through educating coaches and overseeing their activities. Many higher level coaches like working with highly skilled, older players. This is normal because it challenges them as coaches and can be more rewarding financially and from a career point of view. But do not forget to give some of your time and some of your wisdom and foresight with the coaches of our younger age groups. Meet with club executives or new coaches and share your knowledge. Preach to coaches of younger players in your area to make playing the game fun. Work with the local clubs and associations to implement changes so that visual, mental, and muscular perception is more likely to improve at the younger age groups.

Picture 33A: Players from my team that played on NASL Toronto Blizzard Reserve team. Kenny Dodd is #19. Bill Pagonis, #11 started playing rep soccer at 15. #10 Cam Walker also played on Canada's U19 team, #4 Peter Norde, Bill Mackrel (arms crossed), Clem Leca, #25. Guess which player moved up to the first team out of this group? The one who scored the most goals and the player who kicked a ball for the first time at age 14!

In chapters 34-36, I will share with you some stories and articles that I have used in influencing player development at the younger age levels. I want to make sure the children are having fun so that we keep kids in the game. I'm delighted to report that many of the clubs I have spoken to have accepted this information and instituted change to help the game. When you can institute wholesale changes that help keep kids in the game and make them enjoy it more, it becomes very satisfying. Positively affecting hundreds and thousands of kids is as rewarding as winning a championship because you have made a difference in people's lives. Try it.

In chapters 37-43, I will offer shortcuts to help players improve their instinctive abilities using my "feel good perception training techniques" and also my "tiny perception learning techniques".

CHAPTER 34

Pass the Passion

Learning takes place much more quickly when we get positive feedback and results, like the baby learning to put food in its mouth. Tony Waiters, former English National Team Goalkeeper, NASL Coach, Canadian National Team Coach and respected author and clinician was a pioneer in identifying some of the problems first encountered in North America in regards to not seeing enough kids playing in the streets and getting the experiences they need. He also noted problems with how the game was organized at the youngest levels because it did not provide enough incentive for the kids to go out and organize themselves in their backyards or parks to play soccer. The once a week 7-aside games they were playing was not turning young players into passionate players.

In the USA and Canada, the media's coverage of soccer is generally poor. Also, with games such as Nintendo, Sony PlayStation, or X-Box and computers and iPods, kids have so many other activities to choose from that seem more fun. Kids play street hockey in Canada and the NBA has been making great efforts to organize 3 v 3 basketball tournaments across North America. Soccer is fun. Why are kids not playing soccer as freely in the parks?

Picture 34A: David Beckham's arrival in North America helped spur media attention that the game desperately needs to help kids find heroes to give them dreams of becoming professional soccer players. Photo of David Beckham at MLS all-star game by Les Jones/Covershots.

The Media is Very Powerful

Tony Waiters needed to make some changes in how the game was being taught in the youngest age groups so that eventually more players would emerge with better skills especially after the North American Soccer League (NASL) collapsed and less soccer was evident in the media. Waiters, who resides in Vancouver, Canada, has often said to me that he still gets more people stopping him in the streets reminiscing of his days as coach of the 1979 Soccer Bowl Champion Vancouver Whitecaps, than as a former National Coach for Canada. That's even though his tenure as coach of the Canadian National team came after his time with the Whitecaps. He noted that the Whitecaps were in the news almost every day. The media is very powerful. The MLS grabbed media attention thanks to the signing of David Beckham (picture 34A). This attention to the game of soccer in North America can only help create dreams for kids and is good for the game.

Waiters developed a concept called Micro Soccer ™ in his book Coaching 6, 7, and 8 year olds with Bobby Howe, another former NASL coach. He understood that in North America many moms and dads did not grow up playing the game and were often begged to help coach. Waiters' revolutionary book was geared to guarantee success, achieved through the enjoyment of the game made specific to kids and not adults. "Kids want to kick a ball", Waiters states in the book. Even in 7-aside soccer the "swarm" effect continues. Micro Soccer is based on the concept that kids need to touch the ball as often as possible to learn and enjoy the game thus he developed Micro Soccer™ (3 vs 3 Soccer).

Since its inception in 1988, more and more soccer clubs have introduced Micro Soccer™ to their youngest age groups and therefore more kids are enjoying the game and learning. The success of the US National Men's Team and Women's team can be attributed to young players becoming passionate about the game without all the media assistance that other sports have enjoyed. Waiters' philosophies and ability to convince many troopers like myself to institute change has helped this process. With success comes more media attention, which soccer needs to help build heroes who inspire our youth to go out and play.

Waiters has always said, "the game is the teacher". Here is an excerpt from the book, *Coaching 6, 7, and 8 year olds*:

> "Areas in the world where kids have little to do, often depressed areas are soccer's breeding grounds. Kids and young men play soccer morning, noon, and night. Those conditions continue today in some parts of South America and Africa, as well as in parts of Europe. Where do kids learn their soccer skills? Not through coaching! They play small-sided soccer, 2-a-side, 3-a-side, and 4-a-side almost always on an improvised soccer field. It's from this kind of environment that most great players have emerged and this environment does not exist in North America and is disappearing in Europe. But the requirement to have fun, kick the ball, and develop skills most certainly does. Coaches need to re-create the conditions under which kids had great fun and learned the game. This is the purpose of Micro Soccer™"

I recommend this book to all coaches of players of all ages because some of the activities in them are just as effective for adults as they are for children. When I took part in some of those fun activities at his coaching clinics, the coaches there enjoyed them just as much as the kids did! To help coaches organize their practices for different age and skill levels, Waiters has developed an on-line tool for coaching called Byte Size Coaching.

Another coach who has spent many years promoting fun in soccer in North America is Karl Dewazien, Director of Coaching for the California Youth Soccer Association. He has written a number of books and lectured throughout North America on Soccer FUNdamentals. His speciality is in working with children from a number of perspectives including child psychology. Here are just a few of his quotes from his book *Practice of Champions:* "Create an atmosphere where players are teaching themselves. Duplicate the excitement of the game in your practices. The genius of good coaching is to make hard work seem like fun. They will continue to participate if they are having fun."

So what does this have to do with goal scoring? Everything. You want players coming up through the system that have developed a broad range of instinctive responses that will bring out the correct skill responses to different situations especially as it applies to scoring. Coaches cannot complain about players coming up through the system if they don't pay attention to the skill levels of the younger players within their clubs and communities. This is one of your responsibilities. It's not just for soccer, but for sport and health in general. Let's help make soccer so fun that kids will leave those computer games behind and go for a run and play and socialize a bit more. It seems harder and harder for parents to get the kids to play on their own. Often Marco, my younger son, says, "Dad, even when I want to play, none of my friends do. They're all busy playing video games!" Maybe organized sports are our only hope. Let's at least make that environment more conducive to providing positive experiences for players to improve! Go ahead, pass the passion around.

CHAPTER 35

The Centre Field Wall

You will need to find ways to create successful experiences for skills to develop in younger players in your communities. Find out what is happening at the lower recreational levels in your community and see if you can help institute programs using 3 vs 3 or 4 vs 4 as described in chapter 34. If you are coaching at the rep or competitive level or high school or college level, many youth clubs would be honoured to have your input and help in doing what is best for the kids.

One of the larger soccer clubs in Toronto (over 4,000 kids) were still playing 7 v 7 on big fields for players under 8, and after a few years of trying to convince them to change, I finally got them to make changes after making a presentation to them. I wrote an article called "The Centre Field Wall" which appeared in various soccer publications and web sites prior to my presentation. I presented the executive with this article and within a week, the club had decided to institute 4-a-side soccer for children under the age of 8. In fact I received e-mails and comments from across the continent on this particular article stating that I had helped convince clubs and associations to make changes. Once again, I was just trying to spread Waiters' and Dewazien's message in my own way. I wrote it in a different style keeping the reader guessing as to what I was talking about. That article follows.

THE CENTRE FIELD WALL

It's game day and the players are restless all day long. In most cases it's because the day seems so long especially when it ends with a soccer game. The game is not foremost on their minds so there is no need to get all worked up so early about it. In fact, when the game actually approaches it will seem like the next day. So much will have taken place from morning until the pre-game meal.

The pre-game meal makes the players realize that the game is about to begin. Right there as the pasta comes out, a player's favorite food, the concentration is intense. One cannot possibly sit still knowing the game can only be minutes away when in reality it's hours away. But not to these players because the game is not just another game like the last game. That game is as if it was played decades ago. The score becomes obscure and of no interest. All that one can think of is today's game. So much so that the players don't even want to finish their pre-game meal. Utmost on their minds is putting on that uniform and getting on the field.

The drive to the field seems like an eternity and the game takes on significance of astronomical proportions. It is of no importance as to who is the leading scorer or what the standings are because this game is as important as a World Cup Final. And so it should be because these players have worked so hard at trying to get there faster that they can already see themselves on the pitch playing the game. This pre-game ritual becomes paramount for optimal performance according to the World's top sport psychologists.

As the players warm up, the teams' spectators size up their opponents, and as usual, both sides, feel their opponents look huge. That doesn't deter the huge crowd at the game from cheering on their teams as they get set for the kick-off. The players look around as the coach gives last minute instructions. As they look at the crowd they are mesmerized by the noise and feel the electricity of the spectators, which they estimate to be in the tens of thousands. The players on both teams are looking rather dapper and the faces of the combatants are quite varied. As they wait for the whistle to start the game some are looking rather intrigued at the whole proceedings and others are looking rather uninterested as if to try and take away some of the pressure that the huge crowd is expecting of them.

..."holy cow" I say to myself, "I can't believe what I'm seeing."

I, of course, am quite calm in comparison to the others at the game. I'm looking to make observations that can improve the game at this elite level, the highest level in this bracket. I'm as excited about what I'm about to observe as the players because I know before the game is even started that I will have plenty of comments about the game. I casually finish my conversation with the person in the seat beside me and then I hear the whistle to start the game. I turn my head to watch the kick-off and "holy cow" I say to myself, "I can't believe what I'm seeing." I didn't expect to find something to write about so early in the game. The coach of the team defending the kick-off had just developed a completely new strategy, which I had never seen before. He had his seven players form a wall just outside the center circle to defend the kick-off. What a gutsy move. I've heard of a wall on a free kick just outside the box and even a mini-wall at a corner kick but never had I seen this. A wall to defend the kick-off. And guess what? It worked. The players defended well, won the ball quickly, went into attack and stayed in the opponents' end of the field for nearly five minutes and almost scored a goal. A brilliant strategy that I just had to investigate.

After the game I approached the coach identifying myself and telling him that this was something I had never imagined. When asked about his strategy he had a brilliant answer.

A new soccer strategy for all you coaches

"I thought that if I positioned my team outside the center circle (which is only five yards away), in a wall, we could block their kick-off. Also, a 4 and 5 year old cannot kick the ball hard enough or high enough to clear the wall and they would not have the skill or understanding to pass it around our wall. Therefore we would win the ball quickly and have numerical superiority immediately to push the ball via the scrum up the field into their end and hopefully score a goal."

So there you have it, a new soccer strategy for all you coaches of 4 and 5 year olds (sorry, I'd better be administratively correct, under 6).

As the game progressed the superior players of each team were quick to spot. They ran the fastest and were not claustrophobic. These two or three players out of 16 on the field controlled the game and the ball. In the game I watched, the final score was Stephanie 6, Michael 4. (Who says females can't compete with males?) The remaining 14 players barely touched the ball but I don't think they actually came to play soccer. Follow the leader is a more appropriate name of this game as some were not quite so impressed with this game called soccer. One player did not want to go on the field for his last shift citing that he never got a chance to kick the ball as his excuse. Tears followed as the parents tried to convince the player that soccer is a great game to try and play. Saving the day for this little chap was the Popsicle promised at the conclusion of the game.

Four and five year olds mostly tend to run with their weight forward because they are head-heavy. The growth of their body and their co-ordination skills have not caught up with the growth of their head. Therefore as they chase the ball, it is quite often that a player will fall. As one can imagine when 14 people are all chasing the ball in close quarters, when one falls, quite a few behind them will also fall. Sometimes with not so pleasant consequences. The game was stopped five or six times for injuries usually of minor proportions but, when accompanied by a pool full of tears; it seemed much more serious. That Popsicle seems to cure all wounds although in one of the injuries the player tripped over the heel of another and fell with enough force to whip his head on the ground causing a scratch on the chin. The player had to be carried off on the outstretched hands of the coach, who surely needed earplugs to soften the high pitch overtone of the accompanying sonata.

"Why are the parents going nuts?"

The crowd of 50 or 60, which seemed like thousands to these 4-year-olds, cheered at every opportunity and shouted words of encouragement. When I focused on them it was hard to imagine grown adults looking so foolish. Watching them was certainly just as enjoyable as watching the game. As one player finally caught up with the ball, he ran with it whichever direction the ball wanted to go, turned his head towards his parents, and smiled. It drew a big laugh from the crowd, as big a laugh as when the players tried to score in their own goal. Whenever a goal was scored the crowd let out a huge cheer with applause but all the players on the field froze while trying to figure out what they should be doing next.

"Did our team score?"
"Are we supposed to cheer?"
"Why are the parents going nuts?"
"Why are they laughing at us?"
"Why are some people looking rather let down?"
"Did I do something wrong?"

The game ended and most of players came out with the proverbial question "Did we win?" They were not sure. The kids were told to line up to shake hands. They rushed through that ritual because they knew what was next. The Popsicle! Did they care whether they won or lost? No. Did they know the final score? No. Were they looking forward to their next game? I'm not so sure. Well I guess so. Because of the Popsicle of course!

My assessment of the situation is not one of positive conclusions for the game of soccer. In reality, it shocks me that adults who administer the game cannot see all that is wrong with the above scenario. Over 50% of these four and five year olds will play a whole season of soccer and not score a goal. Some will barely touch a ball over the course of the year. Many players will only want to play again because of the uniform they get as opposed to the game itself. The spontaneous play that occurs off the field, at home with friends in the form of small-sided games will not occur naturally. Many clubs still try and jump right to 7 or 8 aside with big goals and a field 60 by 40 yards. The Dutch and Brazilians develop players using small-sided games at the younger age levels.

Soccer is not fun when players barely touch the ball, don't shoot and don't score. The novelty of being in a uniform or getting the Popsicle will eventually wear off and the kids will eventually want to quit. Dr. Tom Fleck said in a panel discussion a few years ago that the "coach of the year" should be the coach who brings back the most players the following year. Nothing is more fun than kicking a ball and trying to score. If you can't touch it, you will never score and there goes the fun.

There are plenty of ready-made programs available to help clubs organize themselves for small-sided games. Two key coaches who have written and presented methods of scaling the game down to young players are coaches Karl Dewazien and Tony Waiters. Karl Dewazien is State coaching director of the California Youth Soccer Association and offers his FUNdamental soccer program. Both coaches have an assortment of books and DVDs on the topic. They are both pioneers in making soccer fun to play so that the game becomes the motivating factor in future development. You can find more information on their programs on-line.

Please do your part in influencing clubs who haven't already converted to 3 or 4 a-side soccer to do so as soon as possible before we lose those kids to other sports.

Feel free to reprint this article for your needs but please include the reference.

At the Pro Soccer Camps in West Virginia in July 2011, I had the pleasure of meeting Larry Paul who was an avid messenger for scaling down the game for younger age groups. He has produced excellent DVDs on 4 vs. 4 soccer training methodology based on the KNVB Dutch system but tailored to North American youth players. Many clubs in North America have made the switch to smaller sided games but many clubs still need to scale the game down.

Picture 35A: Coaching staff at Pro Soccer Camp in West Virginia

Before I leave this topic, I recommend coaches bring the documentary film, *Pelada* to their communities. It's an inspiring film about how soccer touches people around the world. The film follows two American players, Luke Boughen and Gwendolyn Oxenham in their quest to find soccer outside of the professional stadiums, bright lights, and manicured fields.

Now that you have understood the importance of contributing to your community, I want to discuss a few things you can do to improve the opportunities for "right feelings" in your players' brain and muscle patterns. Once again I see problems in our youth systems that hinder perception learning. In the next chapter, I include another article that can help institute change of a different variety.

CHAPTER 36

Player Development Starts at the Socks

Perception learning is learning how to be more instinctive. In chapter 24, I mentioned how Vince Carter, basketball star, is able to predict where his opponents are going to move before they actually move. By guessing correctly where everyone is going, he is more successful with what he is going to do. His decisions on what to do are impacted by past positive experiences. Each time he predicts correctly, the brain records the experience and then when that situation presents itself again, the brain is more likely to instinctively provide the same response correctly again.

What else can the coach do in his community to encourage perception learning? One method is to go watch what is happening at the youngest levels and see if things are in place for perception leaning to take place. Most youth clubs start on the wrong foot, or shall I say sock, right off the bat. The following article has appeared in many publications and web sites around North America. Once again it has initiated change with some youth clubs to create a better environment for perception learning to take place. This is especially important in communities where not enough street play exists. My article follows in its entirety and contains segments that are included from previous chapters. Feel free to reprint it and please provide proper credits.

PLAYER DEVELOPMENT STARTS AT THE SOCKS

Have you ever watched the best players in the world and wondered: how did they do that? They perform a brilliant pass, finding a player in the open while being under extreme pressure. Or they score a brilliant goal and it seemed as if the player knew where everything and everyone was and then made the right decision under pressure. It may be a quick dribble into a space that didn't even seem to be there but suddenly appeared.

The best players seem to have that sixth sense. Although to some it may come naturally, I do believe that to a large extent, it can be improved in all players. It takes mental perception. What do I mean by that? It has to do with the ability of players to quickly assess who is around them and which way they are moving in relation to themselves. Coaching this is not easy and occurs with repetition and success over a long period of time. For the player to become good, the brain has to make certain decisions automatically and correctly. It's a bit like a baby learning how to put food in its mouth.

At first, it takes time to properly grasp the food and then there is a challenge in coordinating the hand movement to actually find the mouth. With repetition the child gets really good at this. So good that the child can do it with its eyes closed. The brain is well adapted to learning. But the training is done every day.

The ability to teach players to make certain things instinctive comes with knowing what is around them. Unfortunately, in game situations there are opponents who want to make life difficult for them. They want the ball. In order to beat them or find a teammate to pass to, players must make decisions quickly. They must quickly process information that their eyes see, and then make a quick decision as to what to do next. The brain has to make these decisions in a matter of milliseconds because it has to send signals back to its muscles on what to do with every step or muscle movement. To complicate matters, things change every second as teammates, opponents, and the ball are all in motion.

In soccer, in most cases the ball is on the ground. The player has to make some decisions and in making these decisions, he/she has to look at the ball to see where it is. In that split second that the player is looking at the ball, the brain has to take mental pictures, process them, and spit out a decision on what to do next. Visual perception of what's going on here is key. Split seconds are critical. Quite often, the player is under so much pressure from opponents while also trying to read the motion of the ball (is it spinning? etc). In order to make a decision the brain will have to make a certain amount of assumptions based on what the eyes see. Based on these guesses, the brain gives back a response to its muscles and tells them what to do. If the guesses are wrong then there is less chance

Picture 36A: Finding the mouth involves visual, mental, and muscular perception requiring repetitive practice with success.

of success. If the guesses are correct the chance of success is better. Achieving success is vital in successful training. For example, if you have to guess a number between one and three or a number between one and ten, then you will obviously make more correct decisions when guessing a number with less chances of error (in this example picking a number between one and three).

In analyzing player development over a number of years, I have found that the player who consistently makes more correct decisions will get to know what it "feels like" to be correct and then use the correct skill more often. This will result in the brain making more correct decisions on which skill to use in each situation. The skill will become more instinctive if successful over the years. The player who uses a certain skill under certain conditions and does it successfully more often will eventually start to become natural at that skill in the right situation. Repetition and getting the "feeling" of getting it right is key to training the brain. That player will not even be able to explain what he/she may be doing because the brain just does it.

But if players are put into a condition where the chances of getting those assumptions correct are so rare that they will not get the "feeling" of doing it right enough times then the brain cannot learn to instinctively make the right decisions consistently.

For the first 5 years of their soccer playing careers, many soccer players in North America are making too many poor decisions because, for the most part, they do not play the game enough every day. Most play once a week and train once a week. Although that's not enough, the clubs cannot provide more games during a season mainly due to the lack of fields and the short season. For the first 5 years, the bulk of the players are playing at the recreational or house league level. Hopefully, the coaches of these kids will make their players enjoy the game so much that their players will look to play with their friends in the park between games.

"Which black socks and black shorts belong to my team and which belong to my opponents?"

But in some clubs across Canada and the US, player development is being stifled by a simple lack of understanding of human perception and cognitive learning. In those clubs, while children are playing the game in huge numbers, they are not making enough correct decisions to train the brain to become better. When children are 5, 6, or even 9 and 10, they are just learning and they are having enough challenges, under no pressure at all, to pass a ball, dribble it, or shoot it. Take them in a game situation and what do you find? When a player gets the ball, there are lots of players around him. He will have very little time and room to make a decision. Also, their heads and eyes are focused on the ball.

When a player has the ball in a game, he/she is looking at the ball and his/her brain must make a decision based on what the eyes see in a split second. So what does a house league or recreational league player's eyes see and how does the brain process the information so that the correct response is elicited?

Information is processed in the brain and based on what it sees. The brain sends back signals to the rest of the body to react to each situation. In many cases, the response is instinctive, based on past experience, similar to the situation where the baby is learning how to find its mouth. With enough correct guesses, the baby will eventually train its muscles to know where its mouth is. The key to getting really good at something is to be successful and in soccer and many other sports where motion is involved, the player has many more variables in finding the correct response to each circumstance. It goes through an extensive process, which involves an executive control process to process this information. The brain does not always give its muscles back the correct response because it has to make a certain amount of guesses or assumptions on what's going on in each split second of the game. It also has to predict what's going to happen in the future.

Bringing it back down to the simple level, when a player has the ball he sees lots of feet, primarily socks, and shorts. It catches some shirts. Now the brain has to make a decision and the question the brain has to decipher and ask is which socks and shorts belong to my team and which belong to my opponents? And also, which belong to the referees? How can the brain of a young child, and even of an adult for that matter, make the right decisions on a more consistent basis if it doesn't know who's socks and shorts belong to his/her team? It can't because in many house leagues or recreational leagues across North America everyone is wearing the same colored socks and shorts. It will take an extra split second for the brain to figure out whose black socks and black shorts go with the blue shirts and whose black socks and black shorts belong to the white team?

Picture 36B: In many clubs, all players wear the same color socks and shorts even if they are opposing teams. This can slow down the decision making process for young players. Special Note: The baby from picture 36A is the player in blue. Photo by Mike Pochwat/ News Advertiser

Since the brain needs more time, and it does not have it in soccer, it will make more errors and the player on the ball will quite often make the wrong decision because there is more chance of errors in what the brain is processing. It is a bit like picking a number between 1 and 10 instead of between 1 and 3. Therefore, many young Canadian and American players make more wrong decisions in their earlier years simply due to the color of the socks.

Saving Money at Expense of Player Development

If the clubs were to purchase different color socks for each team, then the young brain would be able to process information more accurately and make more correct assumptions. It does so by reading the motion of all the players around better. This would help give the player the "feeling" of making the right decisions more often in a game. This is vital in training the brain to be able to read the game better and perform the correct skills more instinctively. And a player who is successful more often also enjoys the game more and is more apt to take his or her positive experiences to the park with friends outside of team practices.

Manufacturers try and save production costs by convincing clubs to give all teams the same colored socks and shorts. Uniform suppliers save money because they will need to carry less inventory of colored socks and shorts and take less time to package teams together. Clubs do save some administration headaches in case they have to exchange players to balance teams. The clubs are sold on this convenience factor at the expense of helping the cognitive development of their players at an early age. If clubs are committed to player development, then making sure each team wears different colored socks should be their first order of business.

This seemingly small point is much more important than one would think especially for our youth players and it is so simple to correct. Any player development model must make it mandatory for clubs to issue different colored socks to our youngest players.

In the club I coach, all 3,300 house league or recreational league players used to wear the same colored socks and shorts. I coached my son's U12 boy's house league team a few years back. My team started the year with 4 straight losses. I tried to teach them to pass the ball, look for space, and then find each other to pass to. After working on this in practice I noticed that in a game situation, where there is more pressure, the kids were making too many poor decisions. So I went out and purchased a set of bright yellow socks for all my kids and we did not lose another game for the rest of the regular season, going 10 games without another loss. Maybe it was the socks, or maybe it was psychological.

My recommendation to clubs is to act immediately!

For Canadian and American youth players, let's get started on the right foot. My recommendation to clubs that run house league (recreational) programs is to look at purchasing different colored socks for each team **immediately** if they are not already doing so. I'm happy to report that my local club has instituted my recommendations. The earlier our youth start training the brain, the better it will be for the future. Socks would be more important than shorts since socks are closer to the ball. It will help player development in Canada and the US and besides, make my home videos and DVDs of my kids' games much more colorful too.

Please use the article above if you wish to help convince your local association to institute changes but please include source and author.

This article appeared in the July/August 2012 issue of Soccer Journal.

CHAPTER 37

Get the "Feeling Good" Feeling

Getting the feeling of doing something right really speeds up the learning process because you get an inner feeling of accomplishment when successful and it's a feeling you want back. Your brain will go search its memory bank to retrieve that information faster than all the other information it contains. It wants and likes that "feel good" feeling.

You can see many examples of this in every aspect of your life. Why not bring it to the development of your players? Skills improve with practice and cumulative successful experiences (Schinke et al., 2001). Great goal scorers get this feeling more often because it's fun to score.

Now that you have understood the importance of contributing to your community, I want to discuss a few things you can do to improve the opportunities for "right feelings" in your players' brain/muscle patterns. I always look for ways to give the players as many touches on the ball and, without a doubt, juggling a soccer ball is an important skill. It's a skill that can be self-taught when kids have no one to play with. They can make up little competitions with themselves on how to keep the ball up. Give them ways they can challenge themselves.

Tricks to Train Ball Control and Perception

Another thing I like to do with players is use a smaller ball once in a while in mini games – one size lower or sometimes even a size 2 mini ball, just to change things around, will help. When working with heading I like to use a lighter ball, especially with younger kids who are still trying to learn the proper technique on heading. I had a Micro Soccer™ ball around the house and as I mentioned earlier, my son Joseph wanted to juggle a ball like Maradona and the freestyle ball jugglers. Having a light ball gave him the confidence to head a ball and learn it properly. Today he can juggle a ball 100 times in a row without any problems. He could walk down a mall with a ball on his head if he wanted to. And he scores most of his goals with his head. The Micro Soccer™ ball was first invented by Tony Waiters to help kids gain confidence with their game. It helps kids kick a ball and lift it at a younger age. They get a sense of accomplishment and it gives them a good feeling. You can see it in their faces. Once again, good feelings are necessary for training the motor muscular system.

You might be thinking I am giving Tony Waiters lots of credit. He is indeed a pioneer in his thinking and teaching and realized that there were obstacles in promoting the game in North America. He wanted to speed up the learning process of kids who did not grow up watching soccer like in Europe and South America. I want to give credit when it's due.

Getting the right feelings is most important in developing great players in any sport. When I studied some of the superstars of various sports, perception of their own bodies and their surroundings were a common thread. Players like Maradona juggled a ball at half time of a pro game when he was just a young boy. David Beckham won various ball-juggling contests while just a kid even getting on national TV in a talk show. That's before anyone knew who he was.

The Great One

In hockey, the Great Wayne Gretzky (picture 37A) was doing similar things. His father was another genius as he trained his son. He built an ice rink in his backyard each winter so that Wayne could practice. Gretzky would spend hours outside not because he was forced to but because he loved it. In hockey, skating is a key component of the game and it's one sport where you need to start earlier than most only because of the skating. Gretzky's father had him stick handle a tennis ball. Many people would laugh at this exercise and asked why would he want to stick handle a tennis ball on the ice instead of a puck? Gretzky answered, "Well, a tennis ball would bounce and be more difficult to handle on the ice so if you can handle a tennis ball well, then a puck would be simple."

If you have seen Gretzky play hockey, you understand why it's not a fluke that he owns practically all the goal scoring records available. It's because he started his perception training at a very young age.

Perception training is finding ways to train your instinctive system to choose correct responses instantly without really thinking about them. To train this system, you must get "good, positive feelings" and achieve success. Look to give these intrinsic opportunities to develop in your athletes.

It's all on Auto-pilot

Don Crowther of Racine Wisconsin, said it nicely and so precisely in his October 2004 '*Great PR Newsletter*', published by 101PublicRelations.com, that I called him to request permission to include this excerpt in this book. He wrote,

> "Virtually every one of us has spent time on a team or in a gym class learning how to shoot a basket, swing a bat, spike a volleyball, or throw a pass. We practice these physical skills, where we teach our nerves and our muscles the exact pattern necessary to execute the skill, thus freeing up the conscious mind to be able to make adjustments for that specific situation. I played basketball in high school and to this day, when a shot is going to go up, I automatically move to the most likely spot to grab the rebound. I box out who ever is within range, time my jump, grab the ball and sprint down to the other end of the court. It's all on auto-pilot. That's how my body's been trained. I honestly have to consciously think to disturb and adjust those patterns."

Picture 37A: Wayne Gretzky had phenomenal muscular perception skills due to the type of training exercises he did when he was a child. Photo supplied by Action Images/Rocky Widner

Crowther uses this example and relates it to business systems. He makes interesting points about disturbing certain patterns. He is correct; players do need to intentionally think of some changes, especially if some of the patterns have become instinctive but provide unsuccessful results. Changing an instinctive response that is wrong can be accomplished but it will need more time and deeper mental thought from the player in order to correct.

It's possible that what used to work for players when they were playing at a younger age level no longer works. Sometimes this means making corrections to do something better than usual. Your players may do some things well and feel good about them but they are not getting the results you think they should. Their instinctive reactions are good but not the best. How do we, as coaches, help them make some changes to improve some of their results when it comes to scoring goals? I will tackle this issue in the next few chapters.

CHAPTER 38

WARNING: You may have to Re-train

In previous chapters, we reviewed how human muscles learn. For whatever reason, some players are better skilled than others are, even when the less skilled players spend the same amount of time playing, training, and enjoying the game as the better players are. Often, less skilled players spend more time training than players with a higher skill level do and yet they can never catch up. In the parks and the streets there are players of different abilities. As coaches, we want to help players with certain things. We all offer advice and demonstrate skills and put them in drills, which will hopefully take the players to a higher level. It's good practice to go one-on-one with certain players giving them individualized advice to improve the tiniest of things that can have huge results. In the same way my coach Eric Willis gave me some individual advice on reading human motion when stopping breakaways, I want to proceed with details and facts about human movement to take the goal scorer to the next level.

WARNING!

Giving the superstar natural athletes very detailed information may have no effect on them. If you see a player that has the instincts and usually correctly predicts where the defenders or goalkeepers will move and acts accordingly, then skip this section for them. You may be hindering them by giving these types of players too much information. Unless they are having a specific problem with one of their skills or decision making process, less is better. But in instances such as the ones experienced by basketball superstar Shaquille O'Neal, you need to intervene. In picture 38A, superstar basketball player Shaquille O'Neal practices free throws.

Picture 38A: Phoenix Suns Shaquille O'Neal shoots a free throw during practice at the team's practice court in Phoenix, Arizona, in February 2008. Picture Supplied by Action Images/Jeff Topping

Even great athletes do not do certain things correctly all the time. The great basketball player Shaquille O'Neal barely threw 50% from the foul throw line. So in order to improve his team's chances in the playoffs he practiced his foul throws three hours a day thinking that, if he could only improve his success rate from 50% to 60%, it may be enough for his team to win some key games. But the problem here is that if his technique is wrong then all he will be doing is continue to train what is wrong and get better at being wrong. The sports psychologist that worked with him told him that it did not matter whether he was training three hours or one minute a day if what he was doing was wrong. So what needed to be done was to think through the skill and retrain the mind, body, and automatic response system to do things differently. This can only be done with deep cognitive thought at this stage in a player's career. As the saying goes, "it's hard to break old habits". It actually takes more mental effort to do so. Scientifically, this makes sense.

Taking the Striker to the Next Level

When young children play in organized leagues but small sided games are not included as part of their training, the players who score most of the goals in league play at the youngest age levels may be learning the wrong scoring techniques. This is especially true if they are using regular size soccer goals. In these cases, kids who can kick far and high score more goals as they can kick a ball over the goalkeeper's head. They receive positive feedback after the goal. The parents on the sideline cheer, teammates pat them on the back and hug them and the coach probably sends positive messages. This success continues until the goalkeeper gets tall enough to stop most of those shots. Eventually, what used to succeed no longer does. The players who want to succeed again in scoring goals will need to retrain their automatic, instinctive tendencies in order to convert their technique to score again. To take the players to the next level, retraining is needed. In fact, most coaching can be called retraining. Coaches constantly help players do things correctly or better. The younger the players, the easier it will be to teach them skills correctly because they will not have experienced as many incorrect responses as players who are older.

Trying to ReLearn Muscular Responses to Stimulus to Get Better

An automatic response comes from a stimulus. We can help players change wrong responses to stimuli by making sure they think through the information provided. Also here is where all the points made in Part 1 about 'Secrets' and 'It's fun to score' can help your players choose different options that, as stated by Don Crowther, disturb the normal pattern of response to a certain stimulus. In a way, we are going to focus on getting the player untrained and retrained like the dog or pigeons in Pavlov's famous stimulus-response experiments.

The first part of perception training is to teach players how to read the body movements of their nearest opponents. I actually get very excited in my goal scoring course talking about teaching players how to read their opponents because of the effect it had on me. However, I don't always feel I'm connecting with each player. This is why I will present you with different options to use with your players. Also, as a coach, you may come up with your own methods which I hope are in tune with what I'm trying to accomplish. You may also look for someone who has studied human bio-mechanics to help you work with a player who has the potential to turn your season around by scoring just a few more goals a year. Like I mentioned before, we should try anything (that is legal) to get inside the head of our key players who get opportunities to score goals assuming our team is getting the chances.

In essence players need:

1. information that will help them read the motion of their opponents.
2. powerful mental cues to help them identify certain situations and start their retraining process.

In chapters 39 to 44, I'll delve into some of the methods I have used when working with young high school and college aged athletes that seem to have had the best results. Communicating to them on how to read human movement of their opponents is not simple. I remind you of my 20/60/20 rule mentioned in chapter 5 when teaching this aspect of the game. If we can make a mental connection with the athlete, the results can be dramatic and it can change the striker's game completely.

CHAPTER 39

Mind/Body Perception Training

The key to my mind/body perception training is to train the players to be able to accurately predict the motion of players around them. To do this they will need some tools to help them read human motion.

All players have forces acting on their bodies throughout the game. The ball also has forces acting on it. For example, if a ball were to be put in motion by a kick, without forces acting on the ball, the ball would travel forever. If you were to kick a ball into space, where the force of gravity and air does not exist, it would travel a long way, maybe millions of kilometers. This is Newton's first law of physics. **Every object in a state of uniform motion tends to remain in that state of motion unless an external force is applied to it.** Without the force of gravity and air the ball would travel forever.

Even as we walk, we put a force on the ground to push us to move. How do we define this force? Newton's second law of physics explains this: **The relationship between an object's mass m, its acceleration a, and the applied force *F* is *F = ma (force = mass times acceleration).*** Acceleration refers to a change in motion or direction of an object. In physics, this change can be a decrease in speed or an increase in speed.

Newton's third law called the *Law of Action and Reaction* states that when an object exerts a force on a second object, the second object exerts an equal and opposite force on the first. **(For every action there is an equal and opposite reaction.)** Thus a force can cause a change in the velocity of an object. Velocity is defined as the change in position of a body per unit of time.

These basic laws of physics can help explain how to start using my mind/body perception training techniques. For example, let's say two players were pushed with an exact same force. This would cause the players to accelerate. The rate of acceleration would be dependent on the mass or weight of the players. Therefore a smaller player would accelerate more than a bigger player would. According to Newton's law *(F = ma)* the acceleration would equal the force divided by the mass *(a=F/m)*. So if we measure a force, let's assume it measures 100 units and the mass of one player (#1) is 100 units while the other player (#2) is 50 units. Then the acceleration of player #1 would be 1 (100/100=1) while the acceleration of the other player would be 2 or twice as much (100/50=2).

But it's not that simple because players of different sizes can generate forces of different strength based on a variety of things. A person with large muscles may be able to generate more forces than someone with smaller muscles. Cardiovascular conditioning may affect the ability to generate forces at different times in the game. The shape of the body would also affect how much force can be generated. For example one individual's legs may be proportioned differently than another. The hips, arms, and neck could be of different sizes even for players of the same height. There are a variety of factors that affect what forces a player can exert to perform an action in a game.

The body has to work to produce the force in order to move. In order to perform work, the body needs energy. The body gets its energy in the form of food energy, which is measured in calories. How many calories and what forces act on the body can be measured in scientific terms. For example, it may take 8 calories to do a task such as running around the field according to a scientific calculation, but the body is not 100% efficient and therefore may actually use up to 10 or 11 calories to perform the task. Nutrition may even become a factor in a player's ability to exert energy to create a force. Some players are more efficient than others are in converting calories (energy) to accomplish work.

To coach players to use my mind/body perception training techniques it will be important that you understand how the body moves and then be able to simplify what is happening when communicating to your players. To explain this I find that Newton's third law is the most applicable in explaining forces and motion. Diagram 39A shows a body moving in a direction from left to right with an arrow showing the force being exerted by the foot into the ground by the player. As the player pushes into the ground, the ground pushes back and propels the player forward and upward. A heavier player will need a larger force than a smaller player to move in the intended direction will.

Friction, gravity, and drag prevent a player from running forever without exerting any more energy.

Friction with the ground slows the player down unless he exerts more force in the opposite direction to keep him going. As the athlete pushes backward with the foot, he is also pushing vertically downward but gravity keeps him from floating up in the air. Gravity causes the player to come back down to the ground where friction will slow him down again. On earth, unlike in space, humans will get resistance from air, called drag, which again will slow the body down. So in order to keep moving forward, the player would need to keep exerting a force into the ground. Since the ground pushes back in an equal and opposite direction, then the player will move in that direction.

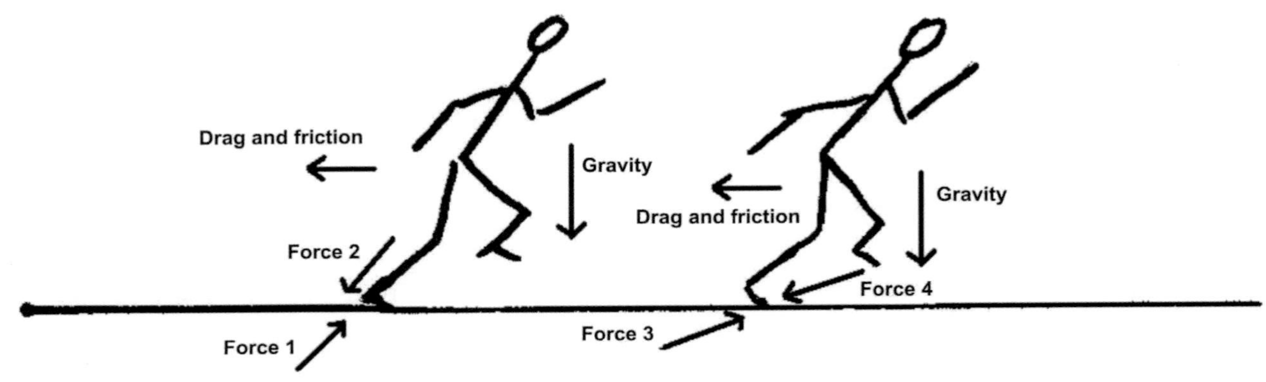

Diagram 39A: Arrows represent forces in action to cause motion.

So to recap diagram 39A, the player's leg applies a force down into the ground at an angle (Force #2). The ground pushes back applying an equal and opposite force, (Force #1) propelling the body forward and upward in the intended direction. As the player moves forward from his heel to his forefoot and toes, the player continues to push into the ground at a more horizontal angle (Force # 4). This moves the player less upward and more horizontally and helps acceleration. The ground pushes back (Force #3) making sure the player goes in the opposite direction. As the player moves forward, drag from air and wind resistance will cause the player to slow down between steps. Also, gravity is working to bring the player back down to earth. Once the next foot touches the ground, there will be friction, which will slow the player down even more. But unless the player wants to stop, he will apply more forces to keep him going forward, and so on.

Picture 39B: MLS and Team Canada player Adrian Serioux is pushing against the ground down, backwards, and to the right. The equal and opposite forces acting on his body will move him upwards, forward, and to his left. Photo by Les Jones/ Covershots

As players change direction and turn, then they will apply forces in different directions to produce the desired movement. In picture 39B, the player is in action applying forces against the ground so that the ground pushes back and propels him to where he wants to go. Note that he is not only applying a force backward but also sideways to his right so that he can cut to his left and go forward.

Each time a player's foot touches the ground and exerts a force, the player moves.

In between those steps, nothing really is happening that will continue to make the player accelerate or change direction. It all happens when the force is exerted when the foot touches the ground.

When the players are in the air, nothing is going to change where they touch down. Humans cannot generate more force that will increase their acceleration while in the air. Other bodies making contact with them may affect how they turn, rotate, and therefore land, but there is no place where they will be able to apply a force, which will propel them and make them accelerate any more. We cannot flap our arms and go forward like birds, which use their body shape and wings to apply a force against air and wind to make them accelerate in the air. It would be nice if our strikers could do this and tower above defenders but, unfortunately, it does not happen. In picture 39C we can see that once the body is in the air, it becomes easy to predict where it will land.

Picture 39C: Costa Rica's Ronaldo Fonseca battles with China's Li Weifeng for a high ball. It's quite simple to predict where the bodies will land since neither of the two players will accelerate while in the air. Action Images /John Sibley

Being able to analyse human movement will help you train your strikers to predict in advance where their opponents will most likely take their next steps and how much force can be generated by their bodies. Another factor that will help you teach players how to read their opponents is the old saying: "The foot bone is connected to the leg bone, and the leg bone is connected to the hip bone and the hip bone is … etc." With each bone, there are muscles that work to move it to create motion.

Another principle of human motion is that the transfer of energy for maximum use of that energy is to start the large muscles first and then work down to the smaller muscles right to the smallest muscle. An efficient athlete will do this properly and look very co-ordinated. An athlete that does not transfer this energy smoothly may look awkward and therefore not be able to apply as much force as possible to create motion. He may take more energy to do the same thing assuming everything else is equal.

Players will need to think logically through some of the movements of their opponents, keeping in mind their own abilities for motion in order for them to speed up their instinctive abilities for the many tasks required for scoring goals. With deep concentration on body movement of their opponents and a proper response, I feel that those "feel good feelings" can be manufactured. Often the players will need to be "in the zone" to accomplish this because their natural instincts have not experienced these feelings. Perception learning will start to take place as positive experiences are built up in the memory bank. Great strikers need to learn the tricks to reading human motion. Naturally gifted strikers like Messi (Picture 39D) are doing this already, as they don't have to think through it.

Picture 39D: Lionel Messi has incredible instinctive mind/body perception skills. Action Images/Enrique Marcarian

CHAPTER 40

Training the Mind to Read Human Body Movements

Humans move in steps. The left foot always follows the right foot. We can start to read human motion by watching where players must plant their next foot. Once one foot has pushed off, the other foot must make contact with the ground before that foot touches the ground again. And a split second after one foot pushes off, the other foot must be planted unless the player is jumping in the air. I want my players to see if they can predict where the next step of the opposing player or players closest to them will land. I want them to think deeply about each step that their opponents take. Once they start to look for these moments, they will gain confidence in their ability to read opponents. Learning to watch where the opponents' next step will be is a major hint as to what they are going to do next. The players need to really concentrate on identifying this hint. It's like predicting the motion of a swing (Picture 40A). You know where the swing is going. Once it reaches its maximum height, you can predict exactly where it's going next. That's easy.

Picture 40A: When watching a child on a swing, it doesn't take much thought to predict what happens after maximum height is reached.

I want my players to use the same formula for predicting where a player may step next. With deep concentration the striker can predict what may happen next. The quicker strikers can ascertain what's happening, the more time they have to predict future movement. If strikers can make an educated guess as to what the defender is going to do next, then there is a better chance of making a better decision on what to do to try and score.

The muscles can offer more clues. There is a transfer of energy from the large muscle groups to the small muscle groups with movement. What that means is that the body's biggest muscles initiate the motion followed by smaller muscles and finishing with the smallest group. If the order is upset, the athlete may look awkward and will probably not be a star athlete at all. For example, in order to get a powerful throw, a baseball player will move his shoulders and upper arm first, followed by the lower arm, wrist, and finally, the fingers. Knowing this can help players read motion. It's like the engine of a train that leads the way. It takes a bit longer to get the bigger muscles moving but when they do, the others usually follow and it becomes harder to stop the train once motion has begun. Looking closely for major muscles moving can assist in helping players predict motion.

Players Have Springs Under Their Feet

The final part of predicting motion is to understand the forces that act on the body.

The main forces involved here are the forces between the ground and the feet. I find that by interpreting Newton's Law that, "a force is countered by an equal and opposite force," in an unconventional and unique fashion, that a young player can understand the effect that forces have on the body without getting into physics. I try and plant a mental image of what's happening to the body. I have tried many ways to get young players (aged 14-21) to grasp reading human motion. I have found that the following techniques and explanations seem to work the best for the 60% of players in the group that I state in the 20/60/20 rule from chapter 5. The top 20 will just "get it" without needing this explanation. The key method I use to explaining forces is to assume that players have springs under their feet (picture 40B).

Picture 40B: Assuming players have springs under their feet may help some players predict the motion of the nearest defenders that they are trying to elude in order to score a goal. Do they have big springs or little springs under their feet at any given time?

Here is how I put it to players to help them read motion:

> ***"To read which way the opponent is going to move, you need to predict how far or fast the player can push off with the foot that's touching the ground. In deciding your next move it would help if you knew how much time you had to do something by knowing how much time it would take your opponent to move in his intended direction. To take a big step sideways, the foot on the ground is going to have to stay on the ground longer in order for the player to spring sideways. Another factor that will decide how the player is going to move would be their weight, speed, and momentum.***
>
> ***Imagine then that your nearest opponent has springs under his shoes. In order to move in any direction, when he plants his foot on the ground, the spring first has to crunch together before it expands again and springs the player forward. Can you see (imagine) if your opponent has big springs or small springs under his feet? This changes all the time and it depends on how hard or fast the player plants the foot on the ground. If your opponent is moving fast and has to stop suddenly to change directions, then you can imagine that the player's foot that lands on the ground to stop and start again has a huge spring under it. So you know that:***
>
> ***a) you will have more time. Why? Because this big spring first has to contract before it can push out. Therefore, since it's a big spring, it will take more time for the spring to contract.***
>
> ***b) when it expands again and pushes out, it will propel the player further in the direction he wants to go because it's a big spring.***
>
> ***If the player is taking small steps and starts with little or no motion then the player will have small springs under his feet. This tells you that the player will move in the direction he wants to go quickly, and he will not be able to go as far on his next step. Just by reading and imagining that the player has springs under his shoes can help you try and make more accurate predictions on the player's next move."***

Then I give them some diagrams to read. The questions I ask in class are these:

1. How big are their springs and how much have they constricted?
2. Where is their next step going to be?

In picture 40C, I have drawn imaginary springs under the defending player's feet. The feet planted on the ground have their springs constricted and are ready to push the player in the intended direction. Can a player imagine how big that spring is so they can predict how far the defender can go on his next step? The size of the spring will be based on the weight of the player and how fast the player is moving. Once that foot touches the ground, the spring under that foot will need to crunch up first before it can push the player in his intended direction. If it's a big spring, it will push further but also take longer to crunch up before pushing off. I find that players who use this visualization technique to analyze their opponents' movements, tend to learn and understand what I'm trying to teach them. It forces them to think and get into a deep concentration mode easier. After a while, they will not need to think of springs under feet anymore as they will know what to expect quicker.

Besides using the spring method to predict how much time a player has and how much force he is going to push off with, you can also teach them to predict in which direction they are more apt to go. If the spring is angled sharply one way, then they can only go sharply in the opposite direction. If the angle of the imagined spring is not as sharp, then they will have more flexibility as to where they can physically move in their next step. The forces are at work according to Newton's Law of physics as the ground presses against the foot to allow the athlete to move in an opposite direction.

Picture 40C: Imagine springs under the feet of the nearest opponents. How big are the springs under the foot that's planted on the ground? How much can the player move when it springs him? How big is the spring under the foot that he's going to plant next? Ronald De Boer from Holland can attack the defender along the wing. Photo by Les Jones/Covershots

In picture 40C, Dutch player Ronald De Boer with the ball can try and quickly assess what the defenders can and cannot do. The defender to his left has both feet on the ground and his legs are quite far apart meaning he cannot push forward too far on his next step. The springs under his feet are small. When a player has his feet spread wide apart, it means they are not in the best defensive position. The player closest to him has his weight on his left foot and therefore that foot is frozen. The right foot will touch down next and has a small spring. In this case, the defender is vulnerable on the outside but the inside track is not looking too good because the defenders next step will be to his right foot and there is no space to move between the two defenders. A quick dart up the wing seems to be De Boer's best option. For the defender to chase him down the wing, he would have to place his right foot down, and create a big force to push himself left while turning to chase him. He will need a big spring, which he will have to create by shifting his weight. This will take time. Time will be the defender's enemy if the attacker has read this situation properly and takes advantage of it by accelerating past him now.

Here is what I add when speaking to players:

> ***"When first learning how to use this technique to predict player motion it may be a good idea to take mental pictures at first. To help you analyze your nearest opponents try and take mental pictures as though you are stopping time and then try and concentrate on what's going on with the forces that will dictate in which direction they can physically move. Remember that humans move one step at a time. We cannot fly and get somewhere when it's impossible to get there in just one step. It's amazing what the body can't do. We are not birds nor do we have four feet.***
>
> ***So, to repeat, try and take pictures of the springs under the foot that's about to touch the ground and predict what players can and cannot do with their bodies. As you get better at***

this, tempt yourself to be a step ahead and try to beat a player where you think he actually <u>cannot</u> go. If it works, then you are doing great. If it doesn't, you must ask yourself, where did I go wrong? Was I too slow in figuring out what the player was doing? Did I know what he was going to do but I messed up my reaction?"

We need to train the mind to take pictures. As I show the players pictures of situations on a big screen I also have the sound effects of a camera clicking with each picture. Sound effects help make the point. Look at pictures 40D and 40E and ask yourself, where will the defender's next step be? How far to the right or left, forward or backward can the defender move on his next step?

In picture 40D the defending player #21, Lassana Diarra of France has a tiny spring under his left foot and therefore will not be able to move laterally to the right too far. The force he will be able to exert is small because of his balance. His knee is fairly straight. Imagine that the spring under his left leg is slightly crunched up so his spring will be little, unless he tightens the spring up more by bending his leg and exerting a force into the ground. Once this is done, he will be able to spring much further to the right. Crunching up the spring more will take more time. On the other hand, he has a small spring so he can quickly move to his right foot where his right foot can touch down and spring him in the opposite direction to his left should Alessandro Del Piero go to his left.

Picture 40D: Pay attention to the defender and try to predict his next step or two. Alessandro Del Piero of Italy is trying to read his opponent's body movements. He's not looking at the ball but the defenders feet and body position. Photo supplied by Action Images/Lee Smith

Italian striker Del Piero will need to try and predict what the defender can and cannot do. Since Diarra has small springs under his feet at the moment, it means that whatever he does, the defender can quickly change feet to spring in whichever direction he may want to go to stop Del Piero. Ideally, Del Piero will want to force the defender to commit himself by forcing him to create a big spring under one foot and then go where that big spring cannot push the defender to because he has taken him in the wrong direction. Del Piero's eyes are focused on the defender's feet to try and read his opponent's movements. His eyes are not on the ball. Notice the concentration of the striker.

Little springs means that a player can quickly shift feet to get to a ball in either direction but will not be able to exert large forces and move the body great distances to block shots. Large springs usually means that a defender can exert a larger force and move laterally a larger distance, but is vulnerable in the opposite direction.

In picture 40E, French player Patrick Vieira (#4) had a big spring under his right foot before pushing off. Notice how much distance he has covered with his big step. But also notice that once his left foot touches the ground, the defender will not be able to generate much force in any other direction. He is in a vulnerable position and is hoping to block the shot. Vieira will also be in a poor position to challenge for a rebound should there be one. If Mauro Camoranesi of Italy can pass or shoot the ball past his extended foot by accurately predicting where Vieira's left foot will land, then he will have a good chance to score on the shot and also be in a better position than Vieira to chase any potential rebound. Did Camoranesi read this early enough to make the correct decision? To score or not to score can be a matter of predicting player movements by only inches and centimeters.

Picture 40E: Mauro Camoranesi of Italy sees the large step that the defending player, Patrick Vieira from France, has taken. Has he predicted this early enough to know exactly where the defender's left foot will land? Picture supplied by Action Images/Lee Smith

The key to the spring analogy is to get a feel for how much the spring is constricted with each step. A slightly coiled spring will generate a weak force while a tightly coiled spring will generate a larger force. A tightly coiled spring will give the player less control of his body. What often determines how much a spring will tighten and coil up is the speed at which a player is moving. The faster a player approaches a striker in his attempt to stop him, the easier it is to beat him because he has less control of his body. The problem is that a defender coming at speed gives the striker less time to react to make a decision and to get his body in a position to beat the defender.

A defender coming at an attacker faster is easier to throw off in the wrong direction with a fake. In this case, the tiniest move or feint can beat an opponent by sending him in the wrong direction. The forces (springs) under the defender's feet are so huge that to stop and spring back in another direction cannot be done fast enough assuming the striker has already made correct predictions as to what the defender can and cannot do. When a defender commits to an attacker with speed, he is also more likely to commit a foul because he cannot control his body, should the attacker predict the motion of the defender correctly. Sometimes, the defenders know this and know they have been beaten so they don't try to avert the foul because it may have drastic consequences depending on where they are on the field. A defender that is practically stopped and in control of his body, will be harder to beat. In such an instance the striker will need to put on a bigger fake to cause the defender to take a bigger step in the direction he wants the defender to go so that he can go in the opposite direction.

The Ground has Springs

Another example I use to connect with certain players to explain forces is the thought that the ground has springs underneath it like a mattress and acts like a trampoline (picture 40F). Just as most kids bounced on their beds when they were young we can use the same ideas in explaining forces. For example, vision a body or a ball bouncing on a spring mattress. If the ball is coming fast and is big like a soccer ball, as shown, the spring under the mattress will take longer to contract and then expand again but the ball will bounce fairly high. If the ball is dropped from a distance very close to the mattress, then the spring underneath will contract only a little bit and therefore the ball will not bounce back up too high.

Picture 40F: Some players will understand how to predict human motion by using the spring analogy as though the ground is a mattress. You are looking to help players learn how to predict human motions and whichever works best for your striker is the correct formula for that particular player. I'm offering suggestions that have worked quicker for some of the players I have worked with.

Also if you bounce a tennis ball instead of a soccer ball, the tennis ball will take less time to bounce back than a soccer ball because the springs under the mattress will coil up a lot less than a heavier ball or body.

Making Educated Guesses

Players need to be in deep thought as they learn to read the body movements of opponents near them. There is an element of guesswork going on because, as things move, the players will need to make educated guesses on what's happening all around them. Not just the player's move, the ball is moving too. As we demonstrated earlier, we can't even rely on our eyes to see what's really happening because our brain misinterprets the information quite often. The goal is to guess correctly as to what is going on most of the time, and then react correctly. This will give the player a 'feel good feeling' which will immediately expedite the future response to a similar situation provided it happens again without too much time elapsing.

For this new learning to take place, the player has to actually be in deep thought and consciously make lots of correct decisions. Correct decisions occur because the educated guess has to be correct quite often. It can't be a fluke. I believe that, using the principles of human motion and Newtonian physics and deep cognitive thought, that players can actually train the body to be more instinctive and thereby make up for lost time due to the lack of free play in the streets when they were younger. It can also be a useful method of correcting instinctive tendencies that do not work.

CHAPTER 41

Practice Makes Perfect

I don't know of too many coaches who don't say to their players that practice makes perfect. In this case, I don't mean practicing skills such as shooting, passing, dribbling, or heading. I'm talking about practicing to read human body movement.

Ask your players to try and read human motion and predict future motion by looking at pictures. Whether they use the spring analogy as expressed in the previous chapter or not is not the issue. The issue is can we get players to concentrate deeply on what's happening around them in relation to the specific movements of their opponents? Doing so at practices is important because it cannot happen automatically in games.

Picture 41A: This is not a good picture to analyze because it's too late to predict what the defender may do. Photo by Les Jones/Covershots

I present strikers pictures of defenders in situations where they can fairly easily predict what the correct response could be. Do not expect your players to get anything from a picture where the outcome is not controllable as in picture 41A.

Why do I want to spend so much time on getting my strikers to read human movement? Let's go back to chapter 17 and check up on the number 1 reason why goals are NOT scored: The player with the ball does not shoot, which means he is not prepared to score. As a goalkeeper, I can tell you that the main reason the player in a shooting position does not shoot is because he has not read the body position and future movement of the defenders that are trying to stop him.

Here are a few pictures to look at and guess what's going to happen next with the defender. Ask your strikers to look at pictures like these and see if they can see what is happening to the defender. Can they get a shot off? Can they take the ball in a certain direction to avoid a tackle? Get them to look for these types of moments as they focus on their task.

Once the player has learned how to better predict the opponent's next step you will want him to try and read more than one opponent at the same time. Another skill you will want your player to acquire is to predict his opponent's next two steps and not just his next step. This will take time and will require lots of trial and error in small-sided games.

Another factor to consider when reading a player's motion is that even with the biggest or largest forces, the human body can only move so far with each step and with each movement side to side or forward and backward. If the body is going one way, it cannot possibly go in the other direction until it stops and pushes off in the opposite direction.

In picture 41C, the Manchester United player Paul Scholes has read the body movement of the player to his right by pushing the ball past where his maximum reach will end up. Once the defender lands his right leg, the player will be practically hopeless. In his next touch of the ball Scholes will need to react to the player coming at him from his left. Will he get to the ball quickly enough to beat that player too?

Some players can get so good at predicting motion of opponents because they have had many positive experiences in similar situations that they no longer have to study these movements in detail. They instinctively react correctly most of the time. That's the overall goal in coaching this aspect of the game.

Picture 41B: Where is the defender's next step going to be? Where can the defender go with the step after that? Has Ryan Giggs of Manchester United got the defender where he wants him? Photo by Les Jones/Covershots

Real Estate is About Location, Location, Location

Real estate is always at a premium around the box, which makes it harder for the striker to find those inches and centimeters to maneuver in and get a shot off. Real estate is so precious that defenders will often resort to illegal or questionable methods to deny the striker time and space as shown in picture 41D. Kaka of AC Milan has to deal with defender John Arne Riise of Liverpool trying to stop him by inadvertently pushing on his private parts.

Picture 41C: Manchester United player Paul Scholes has a player on both sides to contend with and try to predict what they can and cannot do. Photo by Les Jones/Covershots

Picture 41D: Kaka of AC Milan has to contend with arms, as well as opponents pushing and grabbing him when entering an area of the field where a goal is possible. Picture supplied by Action Images /Michael Regan

Finding space to get a shot off in the box means having great motion perception abilities from strikers. In picture 41E Mia Hamm of the US finds it frustrating to get away from cover from the Chinese defender in the 1999 World Cup Final.

Picture 41E: One of the world's best female strikers, Mia Hamm of the USA, finds real estate difficult to find in the 1999 World Cup Final against China. Photo by Les Jones/Covershots

Picture 41F: Alan Shearer, one of England's most prolific goal scorers prepares mentally in the pre-game warm up. Photo by Les Jones/Covershots

When asking your players to read pictures, ask them to look at them, then have them close their eyes and then see themselves on the field in the position of the player reading the opponent. Make sure your players see themselves from the perspective of the player with the ball or about to receive the ball. Getting them to visualize themselves in a game situation before the game scoring a goal or getting a shot off with defenders in frozen positions like in these pictures is helpful. You want to stress to your players that they are not just looking to visualize themselves scoring but that they need to visualize the last few seconds before the goal and the specific movements of the defenders.

The players must remember that, although they look at pictures such as these as spectators, they must pretend the camera is in their eyes and that they see things through the eyes of the strikers. Practicing by going back and forth between a picture which is taken from one angle and then to pretending to be on the field with the ball at a real angle is good. Can they do this accurately?

This is definitively not easy especially when they may also have the ball. Often strikers do not have the ball but are about to receive the ball so they have to watch out for the ball as it approaches them and also try and figure out where their opponents are going to move next. No wonder scoring is not easy. In picture 41F Alan Shearer of Newcastle United and one of England's best strikers is in deep thought as he prepares for the game in the pre-game warm up.

It is important to note that these techniques to read human motion are not just useful for strikers. They work just as well for the midfielders, defenders, and goalkeepers. In fact, great defenders are brilliant at reading the motion of forwards and throwing them off and thus are able to predict what they can and cannot do and defend well.

In the 2006 World Cup, Fabio Cannavaro of Italy showed how, despite his height disadvantage, reading the game and the body movements of his opponents seemed simple for him. In picture 41G, defender Cannavaro predicts what the Roma attacker, Perrotta will do next so that he can get in a position to stop a scoring attempt.

The defenders will always have the advantage because they know that the strikers not only have to worry about the defenders, but they also have to take the ball with them or connect with a moving ball to score. That's not simple and it is one reason why goals in soccer are hard to come by.

Picture 41G: AS Roma's Simone Perrotta (R) tries to score as Real Madrid's Fabio Cannavaro predicts correctly and gets in the correct position to block a shot and stop a scoring attempt during their Champions League match at the Olympic stadium in Rome, 2008. Picture Supplied by Action Images/Alessandro Bianchi

Attempting to Block Shots Can Be an Illusion

A player who throws his body in one direction, such as when he makes a last second attempt at blocking a shot from a striker, will be very vulnerable for a few seconds until he lands and regains his balance and composure. This last ditched attempt at stopping a striker from scoring as shown in picture 41H of Alan Shearer, is often a result of some good attacking skills in reading defenders by the striker. At this point the defender has been beaten and throwing himself at an attacker may be enough to provide a visual distraction and cause the striker to miss the net. If the defender can get any part of his body in the striker's field of vision, he may be able to create an illusion in the striker's mind that he has less time to shoot than he really has. This can cause the shooter to hurry his shot, which may result in missing the target. Missing the net is the second reason why goals are NOT scored. A striker who is in "the zone" and concentrating on the task of shooting, will not miss the goal. Unfortunately, many young players get distracted in these situations and fail to hit the net.

Picture 41H: Alan Shearer eludes the defender to get a shot on goal. By lunging, the defender hopes to force the striker to shoot wide by creating a visual distraction. Photo by Les Jones/Covershots

Defending Secrets

In many situations where the defender lunges to stop a striker from shooting, the defender's attempt may not be enough to block a shot, but the visual distraction that a lunging player has on many strikers may cause the striker to delay his shot. When speaking to my defenders, this is what I tell them when they are in a position where their opponent has beaten them.

> ***"Although you may not be able to do anything else to stop the striker physically, you can still affect his final decision or technique by trying to throw him off visually. If you can get any part of your body in his visual field, then there is a chance that he will interpret what he sees as something that will make him fail to complete the task of scoring. He may think you are closer than you really are and therefore decide not to shoot when in fact he should have. Or it may take his focus off the ball and make him rush his shot and therefore miss the net. It may take him out of "the zone" if he is in one and make him make an error. It's your last chance and therefore DO NOT give up your attempt to save a goal even though you may not be able to get there physically. Do anything to try and get in his visual field."***

Any kind of delay in taking a shot where a shot should be taken can actually take away the opportunity to shoot. A striker's peripheral vision may catch a defender's motion in the lunge and create the illusion that he cannot get the ball to goal (even though he is able to) thereby causing him to refrain from shooting. I always say to strikers, "early shots pay, late shots may never happen". A defender may recover when a shot is not taken and should have been taken. Often when a player does not shoot, the chance to shoot does not come back in that segment of play as the defender has recovered enough to end the scoring opportunity. Although there are times when the shot would have been blocked, quite often an intended shot at that time would have actually found its way to goal. That's why learning to get "in the zone", to block out visual distractions and read human body movements is so important for the striker. In picture 41H, Shearer decides to shoot.

Picture 41I: The German defender lunges to block a shot while the striker concentrates on shooting. Photo by Les Jones/Covershots

In picture 41I, the German player lunges to block the shot from a different position than the previous picture. Notice how the striker's eyes are on the ball and he is concentrating on getting a shot away.

In picture 41J, Dwight Yorke of Manchester United makes a decision not to shoot. Did the defender distract him? Should he have taken a shot since he was in the box? Did he get it wrong and not get off a shot at all while in the box?

Strikers who get to the pro level make less judgmental errors. They manage to figure out the situation and decide what to do early due to the lack of time and space in the box. But even the best in the world make errors in visual perception. They reach the professional level because they make less of those errors. See if your players can study pictures and learn to take mental pictures in a game at key moments to help them decide what they should do.

To get better at visualization techniques players have to see themselves in different situations on the field. In order to learn quickly through visualization, players need the ability to place themselves in different areas on the field with opponents. Staring at a picture without the ability to place themselves in it from field level will be a fruitless exercise. Once on the field, they need to concentrate and look for opportunities to read human motion. Self-analysis should constantly take place. Players must be able to rate their own performances in how they read human motion. They need to keep studying how opponents move. They can even get personal as they get better at reading opponents. For example do certain defenders have certain tendencies? Can they place specific defenders that they may be playing against in their images as they visualize themselves scoring?

At this point, the question coaches may still be asking is, how can I use this information to help players improve and provide positive experiences so that they will become more automatic? Once players become more instinctive it will require less thought so that it frees up the mind for other considerations. If a player is so focused on reading the opponent step by step, is it possible that he will forget some of the other aspects of his game such as team strategy or play? It's very important to move on to the next stage which is to get lots of positive experiences by being successful at reading player movements so that it becomes instinctive.

Picture 41J: Dwight Yorke decides to halt his attempt at goal because the defender has made him believe that the shot will not get through to goal. Did he make a good decision? Photo by Les Jones/Covershots

The biggest question of all is how can we guarantee that our players will take what they have learned in theory and make it work on the field? What if the player tries to read the motion of his nearest defenders but doesn't always get it right? The game may be too fast for him and things happen too quickly. There may not be enough positive experiences for instinctive perception training to occur. This question plagued me until I came up with my tiny perception training techniques.

CHAPTER 42

DeBenedictis' Tiny Perception Training Techniques

What you are about to read in this chapter is something that I revealed in my first lecture on scoring goals in 2003. In all the courses I have taken at university, in all the readings I have done on player development, in all the soccer lectures and courses I have attended, I have never heard of the player development suggestions I will address in this chapter as it pertains to soccer. They cover motor muscular and visual perception and the ability to make something instinctive later in a player's development to make up for lost time. They also address problem areas that even the best and most naturally gifted athletes may be having. They are so powerful that I was surprised that they have never been mentioned and/or thought of in the fashion that I will reveal. Yet the concept is so simple.

Discoveries Often Happen by Accident

I play non-contact hockey, and I started using my techniques on reading human motion to improve my game while researching this topic prior to 2003. I'm not a very gifted skater having started skating later in life than most in Canada, but I do feel as though I can stickhandle decently. That's because I played lots of ball hockey on the streets. But my lack of confidence in my skating makes me want to pass the puck quickly and get rid of it a bit like a "hot potato". But while preparing my goal-scoring course I thought to myself, "why am I not using some of the basic body movement skills my old soccer coach offered me?" I used them to stop breakaways. I use them when I coach soccer and in particular when teaching any of the Wiel Coerver dribbling and ball possession techniques, so why not use them in hockey? I started trying to predict which way the nearest opponent was going to go. If I could do this, then I wouldn't have to always get rid of the puck as though I was in a state of panic.

Skating should actually be easier to predict than running because the skate is straight and the glide should be more predictable. So I tried it a few times in games with disastrous consequences. Skating was still a problem and I did not achieve success enough times to make me feel confident to hold onto the puck a bit more. I'm a defender so I shouldn't be holding it too long anyway but whenever I tried, I would give it up in my own end and now I gave away scoring chances. At about the same time, I was watching my son Marco play hockey for the first time. He seemed to drag his feet rather than lift them up to plant and push in order to go faster. It occurred to me that maybe he should do a little hop or mini jump to get started. When you watch closely, hockey players take this little hop all the time to gain momentum. But while trying to correct my son, I realized I didn't hop either when I skated and maybe that would help me speed up and get to the puck ahead of on-rushing forwards, and give me a chance to try to carry the puck a bit more.

After that, everything happened very fast, and, like in any discovery, things happen by accident more often than expected. As I kept telling Marco to hop more, I realized he did improve his speed. I also noticed that it seemed to improve my speed too whenever I tried the hop or jump-start. It felt great at public free skating but when I went back to a game situation I would completely forget to do the hop while under pressure. Even between shifts I would talk to myself, but in the heat of the moment, I would always forget. It was no problem in the pre-game skate but it became a problem during the game. My brain was unable to make the hop or jump-start instinctive because I could not think of it fast enough to do it in a game.

Then one Foggy Christmas Day, Santa Came to Say...

"John, with your nose so bright why not guide yourself tonight?" And that I did. We rented the ice for our annual Christmas hockey game. My kids, 9 and 13 at the time, along with my nephews (Michael, Peter, Stephen, and Daniel) and some of their friends got together for a parent-kids hockey game. We had the ice for a couple of hours and this time I convinced myself that I would seriously think of my own skating and hopping in a game situation. I would try and read my opponents' body motions before they would occur and try to predict which way they could go and which way was safe for me to go. Well, guess what happened? I now had time to think of what to do because the players were tiny and slower in comparison to me. And it was quite "a rush" to be able to do the jump, and read the players' movements and then waltz around them. It felt great. The difference was that I tried to get in some sort of "a zone" to be able to try and read the movements, step-by-step of these little kids and make decisions based on their movements as opposed to basing it on my ability to overpower them. I was able to use deep cognitive thinking to try and apply my own techniques to my game. It was another defining moment.

For the whole pick-up game, whenever I had the puck, instead of using size, strength, and the fact that these little kids were slower than I was, I really studied their steps and strides and used that to make my moves. Humans, big or small, still move in the same fashion. But since the kids were slower, it gave me more time to get used to reading them. With each attempt at reading their movements, I made correct predictions more often and I realized that I beat the players using cognitive thinking rather than sheer size, speed, or strength. In terms of skating, I also had time to hop to pick up speed. Also, because the little guys outnumbered us, these chances to test my ability to read human motion in hockey came often. It felt great and the feeling was addictive.

That's the right word, "addictive". I really felt something different and couldn't wait to try it with the big guys at our next game. It felt that the instinctive system had kicked in really quick. Needless to say, when I played with my regular team again, I still needed to think about what I wanted to accomplish and do but, almost immediately, it was easier to do so. When I actually jump-started as I went back to get the puck after the opponent dumped it into our end in my next game, I actually got there way ahead of my opponent for the first time. It was an amazing feeling. The nerve pathways were quickly gaining more experiences and positive ones at that. Then, once I got there first, I actually tried reading the adult players who were coming at me and, almost miraculously, their movements were not much different than the little kids'. I was able to hold on to the puck with more confidence immediately and do more with it. "Wowed", was how I felt after my first game with my team after the experiment with the little kids. Again, I couldn't wait for the next game to try it some more and be even more confident.

This didn't happen when I stopped thinking about what I had to do, but it was easier to get the thinking part going because I had felt that "feeling good feeling" and my muscles and brain wanted it to happen again. After each shift I made sure to ask myself if I did the jump with each forward stride and if I tried to consciously read my nearest opponents. At times I did, while at other times I didn't, but each time, I couldn't wait to go try it again. In the same way as when I learned a little secret about stopping breakaways, I felt young again!

In my first game after the experiment with the smaller, less talented kids, my defense partner told me after the game that I had played a good game and said, "John you were flying tonight." While I was a fairly slow skater, but in comparison to my previous performances, he noticed that I had made an instant improvement.

I like to believe that this does make sense scientifically because we do learn through positive experiences when it comes to motor learning. Without enough opportunities for positive experiences, your players cannot learn perception skills. That's a fact! And this certainly supports all the studies I have done with superstars and so-called natural athletes. One other factor about being in deep cognitive thought while reading those around me is that I had to be in "The Zone" in some form even when I played with the little kids. This was certainly true while learning to read human motion while applying my techniques.

Player Development and Playing Up

Often coaches talk about player development and making sure players play up a level or two to get experience playing with better players. There is no doubt about the importance of this. I have seen players improve dramatically when given the chance to play at a higher level. But, if the timing is not right, it can also hinder a player and retard the player's development. Every player development program I have read stresses that at some point, players must play at a higher level to improve. Experts' opinions differ regarding the age at which this should occur. But playing up will not address all of the needs of a player's skill development.

Player Development and Playing Down. Way Down.

When it comes to improving a player's perception abilities when he is not reading things properly, the best way to improve this aspect of his game is to play down a few levels. Like in my own scenario, when correcting or improving an aspect of a players game that requires reading opponents and deep thought, the key is to play way

Picture 42A: Mia Hamm was a superstar with the US World Cup Champion National Team. She was always the best player on her school team, playing against inferior female opponents and developing her motion perception skills. This allowed her to play up and become the youngest player in history, male or female, to play on a national team. Photo by Les Jones/Covershots

down. The best superstars of all time, players that excel above others, have always played way down as part of their training even though they didn't know they were doing so. Having studied the history of most superstars in a variety of sports and followed their lives, I can confirm that many of them were the best at their particular age groups as they were growing up. Maradona, Beckham, Ronaldinho, Messi, Hamm, Gretzky, Jordan, were all the best at their age categories and benefited from playing with and against inferior players as they were developing their superior perception abilities. It's true that they were also improving by playing with and against older players but the fact that they were always the best in their age group while they were younger also meant that they were the best and played down most of the time if not all the time. With their superior perception skills, as they moved to older age groups, they quickly became the best in their new age groups. When they moved to pro, they were the best very quickly.

The Best Cannot Play up!

These superstars played against inferior opponents more often than with players better than them as they grew up. If then, the assumption is that players must play up as often as possible to develop, then why is it that all the players that played with these young superstars did not surpass them? If players only improve by playing against and with better players, then everyone else, at some point, should have surpassed them because they were no longer capable of playing with players better than them because there weren't any. They were the best. In fact, as they were growing up, hardly anyone was close to them in terms of skill when they played in the streets, parks, or backyard rinks. These future superstars dominated their park or street games all the time. Why were all their friends' not becoming great as well? According to most player development programs that stress playing up, all the friends and teammates of these superstar players they played with should have improved more than any other kids because they played with the best. Reality is that many of their friends did not even come close to pro but their presence was paramount to the success of the superstar in training their visual and mental perception skills.

When players like Mia Hamm, David Beckham, Alessandro Del Piero (picture 42C), George Best, or Pele are already one of the best by age 18, 19, or 20, how is it that they are still the best at 26 or 27 if they can no longer play up with and against players better than them? The reason is that they are playing down all the time and playing down is an important element of player development when it comes to training the instinctive perception system. Positive feelings are reinforced over and over and consequently they get even better as they reach their prime between 23 and 29.

As I am very interested in the development of superstars, I always ask about their past whenever I've been fortunate enough to talk to one. I had the pleasure of meeting the late George Best and was able to spend some quality time with him in 1977 over a couple of days (picture 42B). What stood out in my mind from our conversations was what he said about his youth. He told me that he used to play for hours everyday on the pavement in front of his house with his friends until his dad came home from work. If his friends were not around, he would play with his younger siblings. Even when his ball or his friends' ball got flat or lost, they would make a ball out of rags and played for hours. Best was one of the youngest players to ever play in an international match when he played for Northern Ireland.

In playing street games, which all superstars played, they often played against players of different ages. You don't go to the park, rink, or court and say, "sorry this game is for U12 or U15 only." Whoever shows up plays. Kids vary greatly. Sometimes the 12-years old is playing with older kids who are 13-15 years old and at other times they are playing with younger kids who are 9, 10, or 11. They see what the older kids do and try to copy them but without those younger kids in the playing fields to try out their stuff, they may not get successful experiences to build their instinctive repertoire. That's where they often get those positive "feel good feelings". All superstars have received plenty of positive experiences playing on the street and in parks in their neighborhood.

"Perception of Their Surroundings"

Today, sports are often too structured. There is not enough free play and experimentation with players of higher or lower skill levels. That's why we are starting to see more and more star players from countries in Africa and South America filter into the top European leagues. Those kids have fewer toys to keep them from playing street games. North American and European players have umpteen TV channels to watch, computer games to play, and Internet options. A key to player development is for players to have a good "perception of their surroundings" and be provided with this type of learning environment through small-sided games with inferior opponents. One way to make up lost time is to consider "tiny training by use of deep cognitive thought and human motion principles."

Coaches must understand this concept in order to understand how they can train their players in their perception abilities even if they themselves have never experienced these "great feelings". In training the striker, perception skills are vital and although playing with older kids and better players is an important part of player development, learning to read human motion should be done by playing with younger or inferior players. It's as simple as that. This training should help players make more correct decisions provided they are practicing while in deep thought and focusing on reading human body motion of their inferior opponents. I call this simple concept my "Tiny Perception Training Techniques". When working on reading human motion with strikers I purposely try and arrange for inferior opponents. The results are usually very impressive and in accordance with my 20/60/20 rule from chapter 5.

In all the player developments programs that I have researched, it's never stated directly that players should play down. While it's true that all player development models state that it is important to get players to play in the parks and on the streets, none state why or how it relates to building players perception abilities. None state that, at some point, a player, even later in life, can be retrained by playing way down. In the United States Soccer Federation's Player Development Model, a 70-page document, playing down is not brought up even once. This simple but powerful point is not found in the KNVB, English FA, or any other major player development model that I have read.

The most noticeable part of the game where my "tiny perception training" can improve a players ability significantly is in the striker position because results are obvious and immediate. I call it "tiny perception training" because tiny means to play with smaller players and also to focus on a few tiny little things to improve greatly. Reading the player's movement by a foot placement as tiny as a few centimeters can be the difference between finding the space to shoot and score and not shooting at all. In most cases, an average player who 'gets it' can become a great goal scorer. I love it when I teach kids and see the progress of those who "get it" develop so quickly. Not only does it work, but their new goal scoring attitudes and mental skills are long lasting.

When I brought the Wiel Coerver techniques in 1984 to my 18 and 19 year-old players, I was totally amazed at how quickly some of them made them instinctive moves. It started with the players being excited about Coerver's techniques, which made them train long and hard. Then, shortly afterwards I started a soccer camp program with the Coerver dribbling and ball possession techniques as a main focus of the camp. I used players from the team I coached at the time as instructors. Besides teaching them using my methods of analyzing the movements of opponents, they also played with the kids in fun games each day. We often played small games with the kids and instructors. This was their "tiny training" for the moves. In retrospect, it was playing down with the little campers that made them improve significantly over the summer. Within those 5 or 6 months, my most serious players made some of the techniques instinctive enough where they could use them successfully in games at the highest level in North America. This gave them great opportunities to play professionally or at a higher level.

What coaches must do is provide players with more opportunities where the skills that deal with reading human motion can be experimented and success will be the result. Players who did not play endless hours of park or street soccer will greatly benefit from my "tiny perception training". Also players who are late developers or players who cannot get to the next level can use the "tiny perception techniques" to improve. The key to my "tiny perception training" is to combine some deep cognitive thinking to correct or improve a skill and then make sure it's successful in a game situation with inferior opponents. This type of training does not really train skill such as how to pass, kick, or dribble. It trains the players' ability to perceive the environment around them. Please note that there is a difference. If your players do not make certain decisions on which skill to use and when, you can still make corrections to their decision making process.

The DeBenedictis tiny perception training techniques are all about playing way down and reading human motion while in deep thought. That means you get better by playing way down and using mental thought to read human motion and not brute physical speed or force. The body needs to get accustomed to making decisions very quickly based on what's constantly changing in a motion sport. This perception must come from being in that decision-making environment as often as possible, getting positive results, and enjoying it. Training with inferior players can be a huge factor in player development from a motor/muscular/perception perspective.

Picture 42B: I'm with the late George Best. I was able to spend some time with him and his wife during his stay and was curious about his development as a soccer player during his youth, and asked many questions in that regard.

Picture 42C: Alessandro Del Piero, still one of the better players at age 37, is the all-time leading goal scorer for Juventus. Starting at Juventus at 19 years of age, he practically always played down against inferior oppenents. This actually helps improve his motor-muscular perception abilities. Photo supplied by Action Images/Lee Smith

CHAPTER 43

Good Coaches Manage Their Players

Up to this point in the book, I have looked at the psychological factors that will affect a striker when it comes to scoring goals. I have outlined a number of problems you may encounter coaching your strikers and different things you can work on from a psychological standpoint. Then I have gone through some basics of the human body and how it works both from a visual perspective and physiological perspective as it relates to perception. I have covered the importance of trying to help future players become more instinctive in how they do certain things on the field by providing you with some ideas, from a perception standpoint, on how to improve youth player development in your local community.

I have also covered how to speed up the learning process in regards to perception and making better mental decisions by learning how to read opponents as it affects the striker from a striker's point of view. I'm sure you can relate to how both the psychological and physiological components of coaching the striker intertwine. For example, reading a defenders next step will require some deep concentration. The use of visualization techniques may help the player master that skill.

The next phase of this book, covered in Part 3, will be about bringing more soccer facts and skill factors into the equation as they apply to scoring goals. You will use what you learned about the psychological factors of coaching the striker in Part 1 along with the human motion and muscular perception factors you learned in Part 2 to build your complete striker with the information I will present in Part 3. In Part 4, I will get into specific methods on how to beat a goalkeeper. In Part 5, I will cover other areas of coaching the striker that have not been covered in the first four parts.

Your intuition as a coach will help you decide when you will need to bring certain points up with your strikers and at what stage in their careers. Each individual is different and will react differently to some of the things you try with him. A good coach understands the individual needs of his players. In many parts of the world a coach at the professional level is called a manager because he manages people and their personalities to form a cohesive unit. Each player needs special considerations. The striker is usually one of your most challenging players.

The Message is Simple: Put the Ball into the Goal

In sport psychology, one of the goals is to try to group different player characteristics so that the coach can deal with them. But at the same time, each coach will have his own personality and set of characteristics that may affect what will work and what will not. You know your own coaching style and now you have the background information to pick and choose how to deal with your strikers for each situation. In fact, you may need to talk to each of your strikers in a different way to get the same message across. At the end of the day, that message is simple: put the ball into the goal. It's amazing how such a simple objective is so difficult to achieve.

It's important to understand the power of what you have already read in making your players grasp the information better. As I have already stated, although this book is geared for coaching the striker, most of the information provided so far pertains to all players on the field. My main point is that if you spend more time with your strikers, your team will improve quicker assuming your team is getting chances to score. The information in Part 3, 4, and 5 is much more specific to the striker.

Remember that the information from the previous chapters about playing against inferior and younger players will be a total waste of time in terms of learning to read human motion to help with goal scoring if players do not actually stop and think about what they are doing. They need to be reading, reacting, and trying things according to the principles of human body motion and movement.

Before I move on to Part 3, I will introduce you to some physiological factors that take place in the human body as they relate to perception, making decisions, and reacting to those decisions. I want to give you a little bit more about motion perception and muscular perception from a physiological perspective so that you know a bit more of what is going on inside the body. Although you will not need to know specific details, knowing a little bit will help you appreciate the learning curve of the human body as it applies to motion and muscular perception. I have covered how the eyes and the brain work together to decide things. Now, I want to get deeper in the muscles after the brain has done its thing with the hope to inspire you to learn more about this element of the human body as it relates to sport.

CHAPTER 44

Task Switching

I would like to introduce you to a term used in human perception and performance analysis called "task switching". Generally, this term refers to a situation where muscles are prepared to do one thing, then in the middle of that task, are asked to stop that action, and quickly do something else.

This change in action occurs very quickly before the previous task is completed. In most cases it's partway through completing a task before it's asked to change action. Often more than just one muscle is required to make the change. Whole groups of muscles are often affected and even more than one muscle group as well.

This seems simple because you do it everyday. For example you may be starting to write something with a pen and then suddenly lose control of the pen. Your muscles have to adjust quickly to try and prevent you from dropping the pen. Muscles in the fingers, hand, arm, and shoulders could all be involved in this task that has suddenly and unexpectedly occurred.

Muscles operate by expansion and contraction. While one side of the muscle is contracting (flexing), the other is expanding (extending). To quickly change from doing one thing to another must take some doing. What is going on in the brain? What is going on inside the muscle that allows it to change what it was doing and quickly do something else? Many studies have been done in this area especially as it pertains to motion, vision, and driving a vehicle.

From a coaching standpoint, I like to break it down further into two different types of "task switching". The first is partially under our control because there is just barely enough time to think consciously about what body movements we can change. The second is so fast that we have no time to think about what our brain tells our muscles to do. This type of "task switching" is more instinctive and comes from perceptual experiences.

There are various theories as to how the brain switches between tasks. The common belief is that the brain operates as though there is an "Executive Control System" in place. Often, the brain and the body are multi-tasking – they are performing more than one skill at once. For example, the player needs to dribble while also seeing opponents and teammates and then consider options as to what to do next. All this occurs before touching the ball again on the next step. Executive Control is a process where the brain supervises selection, and initiates execution and termination of tasks.

In the Executive Control Process, There are two Stages:

Stage 1) Goal shifting: the brain changes what it wants to do.

Stage 2) Rule activation: the brain uses stored rules to make decisions on how to tell the body what to do in an orderly manner. (Rubinstein, Meyer, Evans, 2001)

When the brain thinks it perceives something (a stimulus) it shoots out signals for the appropriate muscular motor behaviour immediately and stereotypically to accomplish a goal for the muscles based on the information it received. But in order for the action to take place, the stimulus needs to exceed a preset threshold. No action will take place until the threshold is met. (ATA Model Norman and Shallice, 1986) I'll come back to that threshold shortly.

In deciding on the action the brain wants the body to perform, it bases everything on the perceived stimuli (which could be wrong) it receives. There must be a stimulus in order to get a response. (Rubinstein et al., 2001) The key to a behaviour is that there is a perceptual stimulus. The need for a response to something is based on the perception that an action is needed. Keep in mind that the brain can make errors in what it perceives, as we saw in chapter 30.

If the goal is to perform a task (A) and the stimulus is (S), then a response (R) is produced.

To produce a response there are movement production rules that need to be followed. Something must happen within the muscle group before something else can happen: before you can kick a ball a number of things must happen before the foot makes contact with the ball. Throughout the task, the body must maintain balance. Various muscles are all working together to accomplish the task. Task 1 takes place, then task 2, and task 3 and so on. The concept is that there are rules for each task in perceptual motion for the different motor components.

The Executive Control Process defers movement production for task 2 until task 1 is completed. A Response Stimulus Interval (RSI) allows time for responses to take place in orderly fashion. This ensures responses do not interfere with each other. Muscles groups must work in unison. If they don't, the task cannot be completed properly and a disaster can occur. The correct responses come from working memory, and these are built up over time.

While the various muscle groups are performing a task to get to the overall goal, there can be some interference messages being picked up by our eyes and other senses and sent to the brain. There are lots of messages coming into the brain all at the same time. Why do some elicit responses and others not? According to some experts, the "Executive Control Process" uses inhibitory mechanisms to keep order. In other words, some messages that we receive are brushed aside and ignored so that the original task can be accomplished. However, there must be some messages that do require a "change of plans". When a new stimulus is received that exceeds the threshold for a "change of plans", a new goal is set. If this is the case, the individual task that each muscle is performing must be changed. In the middle of an action (e.g. flexion or extension of a muscle and/or group of muscles) the task is switched and the new goal is introduced. New messages are sent to the muscle group to perform different functions to reach the new goal.

Goal Shifting

In order for the task to be switched, there must be a change in the final goal. The brain has made a decision to change the goal it must achieve. For example, in a game a player may be ready to shoot but now decides to stop the action and do something else as seen in picture 44A of Dwight Yorke. This is called "Goal Shifting". The goal has been changed and therefore the individual tasks of each muscle and muscle group must also be changed. A stimulus has come into the brain that is strong enough not to be discarded or ignored and therefore the goal must be altered to accomplish the new goal. "Task Switching" entails two functionally distinct stages of executive control: goal shifting and rule activation as stated before.

Stimulus Identification Stage

A key component of "Task Switching" is receiving a perceptual stimulus and identifying that stimulus. This is called the "Stimulus Identification Stage" of processing information. In order for a stimulus to cause a reaction, it must exceed a pre-set threshold before action is taken. Once a threshold is met, things are set in motion or "triggered". When certain conditions are met based on a perceived stimulus, the specific response is selected at the "Response Selection Stage". This selection is made from what is available in working memory. For soccer, this is based on past experiences from playing soccer. Experiences are placed in memory for response selection to take place using rules from memory.

The ability to perform instinctive movements can be broken down to what's happening in the brain and the muscles and "Task Switching" is the component that affects the athlete more than anything else. As coaches, we want to change the pre-set threshold of certain stimuli as they apply to muscle movements so that it caters to the skills required to play the game. Starting right from the beginning when teaching players to play soccer, we show players how to kick a ball properly. Hence we are setting new thresholds every time to get the player to do what it takes to kick a ball properly. Once successful, the player eventually knows what to do without thinking as the responses needed for kicking a ball are placed in memory to be used when required.

Then we want the player to repeat a variety of kicking actions for kicking in different situations so that a series of responses are ready for the body to choose from to make them play the game better. Many of the skills of the game are not normal reactions used in everyday life. Chesting, heading, or turning with a ball are not natural body movements in real life. Our muscles do not automatically want to perform a function to bring the head and neck back and then forward again to head something that is flying at us in the air. More information and research on "Goal Switching" and "Task Switching" can be found in studies in experimental psychology and human perception and performance such as some provided in the references.

As we coach these skills we are resetting thresholds for different types of stimuli and changing how we react to them. Other factors affect these thresholds. For example, it's important to note that a stimulus that reaches a pre-set threshold to cause a reaction in one situation may not cause a reaction in another situation even though the stimulus is exactly the same.

Thresholds can be different depending on the circumstances. For example, while having dinner, a fly enters your field of vision and you automatically move your arm and hand to try and swat it away because it's bothering you. Now take an instance in an intense soccer game while you are in the process of tackling a player or dribbling and a fly enters your field of vision in exactly the same spot as when you were having dinner. In this instance you will most likely not even notice the fly and you will not stop what you are doing to try and swat it away. In this case, the stimulus (the fly in your field of vision) did not result in stimulus identification because the stimulus did not reach the pre-set threshold to cause an action and therefore any "goal shifting" and thus "task switching" does not take place. The goal does not change. The goal is still tied to the game and not the fly therefore since the goal does not change or shift, then the tasks required to achieve the goal also do not change.

Picture 44A: Dwight Yorke makes a decision to change the goals of what he wants to do in this situation based on the feedback he receives from his eyes. The eyes send the signals to the brain, which is where the decision is made. Now the brain has to send signals to each of the muscle groups to stop what they were about to do and give them new tasks to realize a new goal. Photo by Les Jones/Covershots

Pre-set Threshold Levels can Change due to Injuries

Thresholds in stimulus identification can be reset when an injury occurs. Injuries can play a big part in helping decide what the body wants to do and not do. If an athlete has received a painful injury by making a certain movement, either accidentally or not, the body will memorize the unpleasant experience and avoid it by setting the threshold level higher for a similar stimulus that caused that reaction. For example, take a case where a player tries to cut to his left by planting his right foot but accidentally makes contact with a defender. If this contact causes the foot to stay planted on the ground and stresses the knee ligaments causing major knee damage, then future similar actions will be inhibited, even though that may have been the correct response to beating that opponent to take a shot on goal. Chances are that after recovery, that player will have issues with trying the same thing because the brain's executive control process will not allow it to happen since the threshold level for that reaction to that stimulus has been changed. This can be a problem for strikers because the action that the player should take to score more goals can be discouraged by the brain's "Executive Control System" due to past painful experiences. Players may need psychological help to return to form.

In picture 44B, player #16 lands awkwardly and injures her back. If the injury is very severe, her threshold for a stimulus making her do the same thing in a similar situation may change so that the body will not want to attempt the same move or challenge in the future. Fortunately, this did not result in a severe injury and the player's willingness to go for challenges from this angle will probably not be affected in the future. In picture 44C, she ices her back to ease the pain.

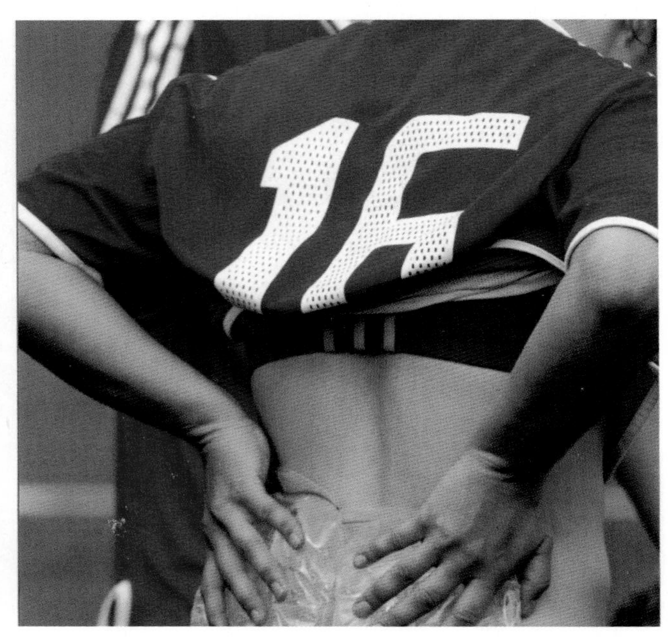

Picture 44B and 44C: Player #16 lands awkwardly, injures her back, and then applies ice to ease the pain. In most severe injuries, the brain remembers the circumstances that resulted in the injury and resets thresholds so that the body does not put itself in similar situations in the future. Photos by Les Jones/Covershots.

For coaching education purposes for strikers, I like to break down "task switching" into two types, which I will call:

1) <u>Instinctive "Task Switching"</u>

Instinctive "task switching" is when the muscles and brain automatically change what they were doing to do something else that may turn a half-scoring chance to a full scoring chance.

2) <u>Cognitive "Task Switching"</u>

Cognitive "task switching" occurs when a player is in deep thought and picks out something that makes him change what he wants to do that may interrupt normal tendencies. This means he will change his goal, which in turn will change the individual tasks to accomplish the new goal. Cognitive "task switching" may come from deciding to change an action based on some of the psychological information already provided in this book. Or it may be based on some of the facts that will be provided in Part 3 or 4 of this book. In essence, "task-switching" occurs due to remembering some of the points made about scoring goals that may be different than what the eyes see or the body would normally do that do not result in many goals. If we can coach this aspect of "task switching" so that decisions based on some of the concepts in this book supercede what would be normal for a player but do not result in goals, then we are on our way to coaching the player to score more goals. But even more importantly, we hope that our player will make a habit of making better decisions that will result in more goals scored, thus making the process of scoring instinctive.

Invariably, the striker's ability to "task switch" either instinctively or cognitively will decide the fate of how successful the striker will be in today's game. In diagram 44D, at the end of this chapter, I have attempted to simplify "task switching" and the "Executive Control Process" using a practical example from Dwight Yorke's attempt at scoring from picture 44A.

Strikers Change What they do Constantly in Order to Try and Beat an Opponent to Score

In all cases, strikers must be changing what they do all the time – reacting to the movement of the ball, their opponents, and their teammates. They need to be able to read the game very well to be successful. With new training methods available to players and coaches that make players fitter than ever before, you would assume that goal scoring would not be as frequent. One would assume that the defenders and midfielders could pack the defense more often as their fitness capacity increases. Defenses are also better organized than ever before. The increase in video technology also helps coaches analyze opponents and find better ways to defend.

Fortunately goals have been keeping pace due to a variety of reasons. One is the development of the ball. Newer soccer balls are harder for the goalkeeper to stop as more power and accuracy can be attained with today's soccer balls. Better shoes; also help the striker shoot with more accuracy. But goal scoring is still very difficult and the players who can switch what they are doing to react to the defenders' actions will score the most goals provided they follow some of the simple rules I have already mentioned.

In Part 3 of this book, I will outline more statistics, rules, and psychological points to help your strikers score more goals on a more consistent level.

Explaining Task Switching and Executive Control Process

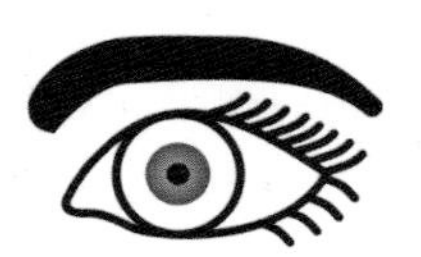

The eyes see the ball, opponent, and goal. The stimulus of what the eyes see is strong enough to elicit a response.

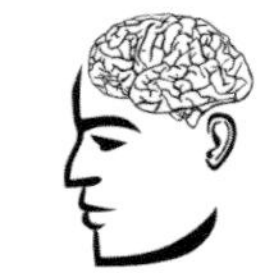

Brain interprets what the eyes see and sets a goal. The goal is to kick the ball at the net.

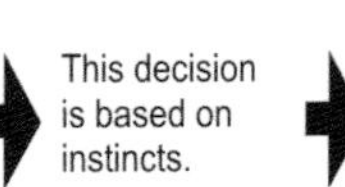

This decision is based on instincts.

The brain has to select a response to accomplish the goal. In The Response Selection Stage, the brain chooses a response based on past experiences from working memory.

The brain sends messages to the muscles based on movement production rules.

Each muscle has to perform a task to start the shooting motion. Collectively the muscles work in synch to accomplish the goal.

As Yorke starts the shooting motion, his ears hear the sound of the crowd get louder.

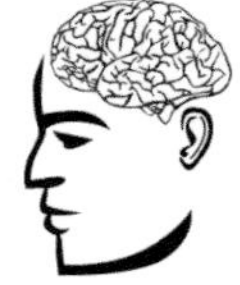

The stimulus from the ears is not recognized as being important by the "Executive Control System" as it relates to the goal and is therefore inhibited from having an effect on the tasks being performed.

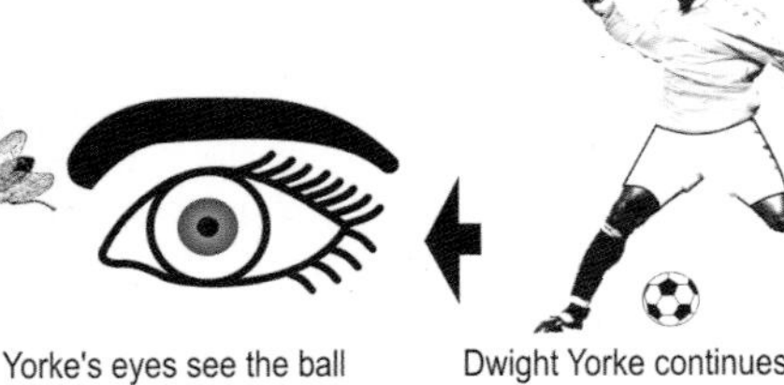

Dwight Yorke continues with each task to reach the original goal, which is to shoot.

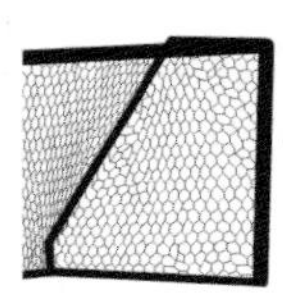

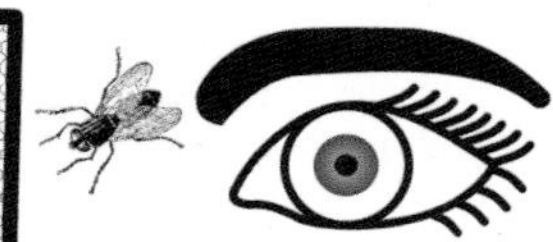

Yorke's eyes see the ball and the target but let's assume an insect (fly) enters his field of vision

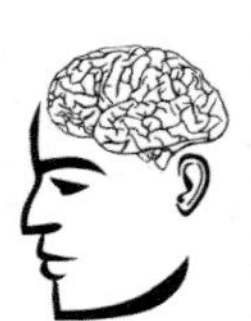

The stimulus in this case is a fly in Yorke's field of vision. This stimulus does not cause a reaction because in this situation, the stimulus does not reach the threshold that would cause a shift in goals. The goal to shoot is stronger than the goal to swipe at a fly therefore the stimulus of the fly is inhibited and not allowed to cause a change in action.

The eye now spots an opponent in its field of vision and sends this information to the brain.

This time the stimulus of the opponent is much stronger than the fly or crowd noise. What will the brain decide?

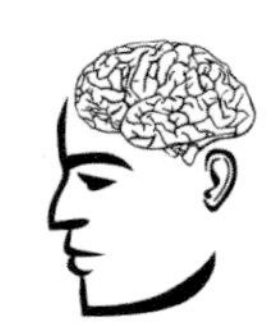

At the Stimulus Identification Stage, the stimulus is identified as being important and it reaches the threshold to cause a response. Based on instincts, the brain decides to change its goal. It thinks that it's better not to shoot.

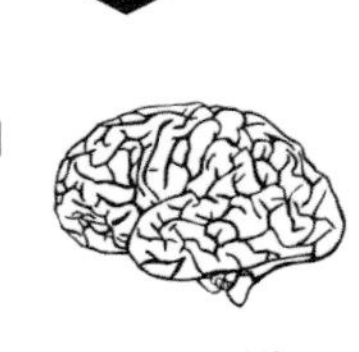

The goal has shifted. Now each of the tasks that each muscle had started to do or got ready to do according to the movement production rules must also be switched.

Each muscle must now do something different. Once again, the brain looks at past experiences for a response.

The front leg must now put on the brakes; the kicking leg must stop its swing and switch to a new task to accomplish a new goal, which is to stop kicking. The brain will then shift its goal again once it decides what to do. The player may decide to dribble further and each muscle will receive its new task again. Thanks to the stimulus response interval, Yorke is not tripping over his feet as muscles work in unison with one another to accomplish the different goals. As you can imagine, goal switching and task switching is going on every second of the game.

THE END RESULT:
Manchester United did not score on this attempt. Dwight Yorke did not shoot but rather, chose to take a few more steps and then crossed the ball to a teammate. It was not a bad option since another defender did well to prevent Yorke's teammate from scoring. But, since Yorke did not shoot, could he have missed a scoring opportunity since the cross did not result in a shot on goal either?

Instincts can be changed to better instincts through cognitive thought

Using some of the powerful psychological information provided so far in this book, a player can overrule the instinctive tendencies and decisions made by the brain in these types of situations that do not result in goals. Through cognitive thought they can make better decisions that provide a better statistically based chance to score. Over time, the better decisions that are made according to the ideas and facts in this book should make these new and better decisions more instinctive.

Diagram 44D: From picture 44A, Dwight Yorke of Manchester United enters the box with the ball. His instincts tell him to take a shot on goal based on the stimulus provided by his eyes. Illustration by Jo-Anne Godawa

SOCCER FACTS and Simplifying the Mystique of Scoring Goals Psychologically Using "The Power of Statistics" and "Visual Cues"

PART THREE

PART THREE

SOCCER FACTS

Action Images/Paul Hanna

CHAPTER 45

The Coaches Role in Using Soccer Facts

In this part of the book, I will provide powerful facts and visual cues that you can use when coaching your strikers to reinforce the fact that they must score goals in the chances that they get if they want to further their career in the striker position. Actually, players who get scoring chances whether they are strikers or not, should work to improve their conversion rate. The problem is that, although in practice players may do all the right things to score a goal, in the heat of an intense game, they often make simple psychological errors based on poor decision making. For example, in Euro 2008, Luca Toni of Italy failed to score a goal in normal play despite having numerous scoring chances. In most of the cases where he should have done better, he made poor decisions. Consequently, the 2006 World Champions bowed out of Euro 2008 because they failed to score when great scoring chances were not converted to goals which goes to prove that even some of the best players in the world make poor decisions in the heat of the moment. In picture 45A, Luca Toni looks to the heavens for answers to why he missed.

Picture 45A: Luca Toni of Italy missed several great chances to score at Euro 2008 because he made some poor decisions on what to do in the situation he was presented with. Here, Luca Toni (#9) reacts after missing an opportunity to score as France's Eric Abidal applauds during their Euro 2008 soccer match in Zurich. Action Images/Ruben Sprich

In baseball, managers are armed with pages and pages of statistics on every aspect of the game. Due to the slowness of the game, they are often able to use these statistics to instruct their players on what to do with each and every play or pitch. They do so with the use of signals. There is time for the manager to communicate to his catcher what type of pitch his pitcher should throw and make that information available to the pitcher. He can tell his players how to align themselves for each batter and even for each pitch based on the count. The team on offense or up to bat also passes on signals so that they have a better chance of scoring. The players need to make fewer decisions on their own because all of the probabilities and possibilities have already been worked out for them.

Wouldn't it be nice to be able to do the same thing for your strikers? In this section you will give your players powerful facts and statistics that should help them make better decisions when it comes to scoring goals. Unfortunately, you will not have time to signal them what to do. Therefore, you will need to make sure the players remember the facts and hopefully pick the best response for each situation. We want to bring in more facts and visual reminder cues to help the players decide what to do. This will require the players to think quickly and stay focused.

We have already discussed methods of getting players ready for success by overcoming failure by telling them that scoring is not easy (Chapter 12). Coaches will need to constantly remind players of the facts to scoring goals, which will help them make the best decision in order to score each time. Powerful reminders that include specific cue words and facts need to be repeated in a way that the player feels they are his private secrets. Interpreting the facts and communicating their meanings is where your skill as a coach in managing people will come to the forefront. Each athlete is different and will be triggered by different methods so have patience with your players as they learn the secrets to scoring goals.

Bill Beswick, sport psychologist for Middlesborough FC in England stated in a presentation at the 2005 National Soccer Coaches Association of America's (NSCAA) convention in Baltimore that in a game he analyzed, his team attacked 78 times and failed 77 times to score. But there was success once. A striker will need to be able to deal with a great deal of failures before success comes. This takes a special mental ability. The striker has to be different. At the same convention in my presentation on goal scoring, I had a slide that I directed at the coaches. Here is what it said:

Coaches: Do Not Show Disappointment

- **Not only by what you say!**
- **But by how you behave and react.**
- **Coaches may need to practice this.**
- **Glow in your skills as people manager.**
- **It's OK to fail.**

Coaches often give off signals that show major disappointment when players miss chances. The players know when they have missed. The team knows, the fans know, everyone knows. As a coach, now is the time for you to calm the players down, give them the feeling of reassurance that it's not easy to score and give them some cue words to get them excited and ready for their next chance to score. Chances are that they will get another chance and it could still be the difference in the game. If the error was due to their forgetting some of the facts about scoring, then find a way to remind them of this. Bring them to the touchline and in a calming voice tell them, "don't forget the secret" (whatever it is for that situation). Don't forget the smile!

CHAPTER 46

Powerful Facts

I extensively researched and watched game films to find out how many touches the goal scorer took to score. The statistics were similar in almost every game and tournament I analyzed. Here are the facts from the 2002 Men's World Cup.

Number of Touches by the Player who Scores the Goal

Facts from the 2002 Men's World Cup (Not counting penalty shots)

- **106 Goals** were scored **on ONE TOUCH**
- **22 Goals** were scored **on TWO TOUCHES**
- **11 Goals** were scored **on THREE TOUCHES**
- **7 Goals** were scored when the player who scored took **MORE THAN THREE TOUCHES**

When I first looked at these numbers, I was so surprised by the overwhelming majority of goals scored on two touches or less that I went back and watched every single goal again to make sure that I hadn't made a mistake while counting.

These facts are so powerful that your strikers must look at scoring in a different light. The vision of them dribbling around half a team and finishing with a goal is more of a dream than reality. Of course the "goal of the 20th century" which gets shown over and over is just one of those goals. The goal where Diego Maradona takes the ball at centre field and proceeds to dribble past the whole English team in the 1986 World Cup was considered "the goal of the century" (Picture 46A). His first move, where he spins to beat and get away from three English players is now commonly referred to as "The Maradona Move" in many circles. Yes it was an amazing goal, but if your players are trying to score on some brilliant dribble, they are actually less likely to score. The statistics show that the more often your players touch the ball, the less likely they are to score.

Picture 46A: Maradona's "Goal of the Century" in the 1986 World Cup in Mexico. Maradona dribbled past most of the English side to score. Most goals are not scored in this manner but young players emulate these types of goals and give themselves less chance of scoring. Photo provided by Action Images

Interestingly, in the same game Maradona scored the famous "hand of god" goal. For those who don't recall that goal, Maradona went up for a cross but realized he could not jump high enough to get his head on the ball. So, he cleverly brought up his fist and placed it beside his head and moved his head in such a way that one thought he got to the ball with his head. Even the sharpest eye had problems catching the fact that he had punched it in with his fist, which he conveniently hid behind his head. He celebrated as though he actually scored with his head and the referee awarded the goal. The English keeper knew what had occurred as did some of the defenders, but no one else could be certain. Until of course, you went back and saw it on replay later. The goal stood. Argentina went on to beat England and eliminate them from the tournament.

If you're thinking that this is another secret to scoring goals, think again. Today, you would be red carded and suspended. Maradona, being a great goal scorer at only 5' 4" tall was the deciding factor in many games and although he didn't get his head to that ball by only a matter of inches, his perception of where he had to go was spot on.

In his actual "goal of the century", Maradona made some instinctive moves to beat players which clearly shows his ability to switch tasks quickly and accurately. I have watched that goal many times and his instinctive "task-switching" and "goal-shifting" perception abilities were in full display in his run.

The statistics on goals scored by the number of touches it takes for the striker to score a goal will be one of your most powerful tools when coaching the striker one on one. Here is a similar statistic based on the 2006 Men's World Cup.

Facts from the 2006 Men's World Cup

Number of Touches by the Player who Scores the Goal

(Not counting penalty shots, and own goals)

- **83 Goals** were scored **on ONE TOUCH**
- **25 Goals** were scored **on TWO TOUCHES**
- **11 Goals** were scored **on THREE TOUCHES**
- **4 Goals** were scored **on FOUR TOUCHES**
- **8 Goals** were scored when the player who scored took **MORE THAN FOUR TOUCHES**

The number of goals scored on two touches or less is a powerful statistic to use as a secret when coaching your strikers. 87.7% of goals scored in the 2002 Men's World Cup were scored on two touches or less. 82.4% of goals scored in the 2006 World Cup were scored on two touches or less.

Things didn't change much in the 2010 World Cup. 96 goals were scored on one touch, 26 goals were scored on two touches, 9 goals were scored on three touches, 5 goals were scored on four touches, and 9 goals were scored when the player who scored took more than four touches. The trend continued at Euro 2012 with 48 goals being scored on one touch, 17 on two touches, 7 on three touches, and only 4 on four touches or more. That translates to 84.1% and 85.5% on goals scored on 2 touches or less, respectively, for World Cup 2010 and Euro Cup 2012. These are very powerful numbers for you to use when coaching your strikers.

Call them secrets if you wish and keep in mind that secrets are a powerful tool to give your players more confidence to complete the task. Do not under estimate this.

CHAPTER 47

Be Prepared To Score

The facts from chapter 46 can help us coach our players in making the correct decisions when a scoring chance presents itself. Keep in mind that one of the top reasons why goals are not scored are that players do not shoot. Having played goalkeeper, I can't count the number of times when players have a chance to shoot and do not shoot. That's because they want to make that extra move and take that extra touch, because they think they will get a better chance to score by doing so. This is simply not the case most of the time.

Judging by the facts presented in chapter 46 that show that the largest percentage of goals are scored on only one touch of the ball, one could conclude that it's possible that a player with the opportunity to shoot who does not shoot was not mentally prepared to score on his first touch. You could also conclude that he did not prepare his body to shoot on one touch. In the next best case scenario, players should think of shooting on their second touch using their first touch to prepare their shot.

Quite often, from the bench, the coach will not be able to see a scoring opportunity due to the angle that he is in. The goalkeeper can see how often players don't shoot when they have a clear path to get the ball at goal. Chances to score present themselves more often than one would think.

When I put on a field session with highly competitive high school and college players (mostly strikers) aged 15 to 20, I always get the same result. I stand with soccer balls at the 18-yard line and place players at about 12 to 15 yards out from goal with their back to the goal. I serve the ball in the air and simply ask the players to score a goal. There are no defenders or goalkeepers in this exercise. In almost every session, after going through all the players, not one player will instinctively put the ball in the goal on one touch. Most players take 3 to 4 touches to turn and shoot the ball at the goal. This tells me that they are not strikers prepared to score. They are not thinking about scoring.

In these sessions, I say this to the players:

> ***"Why are you all taking 3 or 4 touches to put the ball in the net? We just went over the facts about scoring goals and overwhelmingly, most goals are scored on one touch. That touch is your last touch before the goal is scored. Do not take more than one touch."***

In one particular session a player (Teresa Hintz) looked at me in astonishment. She asked, "how do you expect me to score on one touch when my back is to goal and you are serving the ball in the air?"

Now I could have gone into many different technical aspects of turning a ball towards goal on one touch. But my course is on the psychology of scoring. I know that the players have the skill to turn and strike a ball properly so my response was this:

> ***"You figure it out. You know the statistics, you know you only have one touch because that's what it takes to score, you know what you have to do, try doing it!"***

I do not think the players were ready for that kind of response but they got the message. Basically, a great goal scorer has to get his body in a position while the ball is in flight so that he can (rule # 1) direct the ball at the net. This means he has to be prepared to score both mentally and physically by getting his body ready to score on one or two touches. This takes mental strength and practice.

As I served the ball again, the players all started to change their body position so that they could get the ball at goal on one touch. By the end of the session, all players were re-directing the ball at the goal on one touch. This occurred without any technical information. I just worked on their brain. The players had to be more aware and focused on the task at hand as soon as possible. I made the decision for them on what to do as the ball was served, that's all. Not all shots at goal were power shots but they were able to get the ball to goal, which quite often is all that's needed. And on many occasions they also took some brilliant strikes at goal.

As for Teresa, she immediately started to direct the ball at the goal on one touch and then went on to score a key goal in her first game after taking my goal scoring course. Her goal gave her Seneca College team a 1-0 victory in a game that decided which team would get an all-expense paid trip to China to play some friendly games and tour the country. She stated that the psychological information from the course helped her score that goal. You could say that it was a $40,000 goal. And, her younger brother Adam, who was at the same course, also scored a goal in his first game back which helped him make Bryst International's Academy touring team run by former National Team coach, Gary Miller.

In picture 47A, I did the same exercise at a coaching conference in California. The girl who I used to demonstrate in picture 47A had the exact same problem. In the next few serves after my advice she changed her body position and scored on a goal that was behind her back and is not shown in the picture. At the end of this exercise after scoring 5 times in a row, she received a standing ovation from the crowd.

When the ball is directed at goal on one touch, the goalkeeper is less likely to be prepared to stop the shot. And that's because the player is "PREPARED TO SCORE".

Coaching Goes Hollywood

I like to show the players a scene from the classic Hollywood movie, *The Princess Bride*. There is a scene in the movie where the character Inigo Montoya, is trying to revenge his fathers death by tracking down his killer. When he finally meets him and prepares for a sword fight he continues to express his feelings and psyche himself up. He says to his father's killer, "Hello, My name is Inigo Montoya, you killed my father, prepare to die!"

Picture 47A: At this coaching session in Santa Clara California, I was working with Hervi Rualo's excellent U18 players as demonstrators. I was showing coaches how to work on the psychology of the striker. In this exercise, I served high difficult balls to the player with her back to goal and expected her to turn the ball towards the goal on one touch. She received an ovation from the coaches at the session after she successfully completed the task numerous times in a row with some incredible strikes at goal after having problems at first.

As the killer runs away, Inigo catches up to him and meets him again repeating those words. Even though he gets stabbed in the arm, he finds the inner strength to fight on to accomplish his lifelong mission. He repeats the words again as he prepares to fight, "Hello, my name is Inigo Montoya, you killed my father, prepare to die!"

I won't ruin the movie for you but this powerful scene is a classic and actor Mandy Patinkin is forever remembered by these lines. When I show this scene to my goal scoring students (and coaches) it brings a laugh but it also drives the point home. Prepare to score!

I tell strikers to go into each game saying, "Hello, my name is (insert player name), prepare to score!" It's just another visual and mental cue that I want to be able to use with my key strikers to give them the confidence they need in order to score more often in the chances that they get in a game.

All great strikers have to have this confidence. Alan Shearer, English National Team striker and one of England's top strikers for over a decade said, "When I miss, I say it's OK, I will get the next one!" Ronaldo, the golden boot winner in the 2002 World Cup for Brazil was quoted as saying, "I am always aware that I will define the game."

Sometimes the ball does not land in the perfect spot for a player to take a textbook type of shot or pass at goal, but if the striker is always prepared to score from a mental stand-point, then he can adjust his plans to direct the ball, as soon as possible, at goal. In picture 47B, Ronaldo is surrounded by four players all coming at him with speed and closing down his time and space so he quickly directs the ball at goal with his toe. Consequently, he caught the goalkeeper by surprise and scored a key goal for Brazil against Turkey in the 2002 World Cup Semi-Final. Had he waited for the ball to be at the perfect spot to hit the ball with his in-step, it would have been too late as the opportunity would have evaporated. Strikers must always be prepared to score any way they can. You could say, "Brazil won the game by a toe."

Picture 47B: Ronaldo takes Brazil to the World Cup Final, which they eventually won by being prepared to score any way he could. In this Semi-Final game at the 2002 World Cup, with four Turkish players closing in on him, his only hope of getting a shot on goal was to use his toe. The ball went in the goal as the goalkeeper was surprised with his shot. Photo supplied by Action Images/Ruben Sprich

Your goal as a coach is to pay particular attention to your strikers on a one-on-one basis. They are different and they will need to be handled differently. Bill Beswick, sport psychologist for Middlesbrough Football club in the English Premier League likes to call strikers "artists". Defenders are soldiers but attackers are artists. They are creative and like all great artists, they are different. Coaches need to be creative in dealing with attackers and use their imagination in communicating with them.

One Touch Instead of Shoot!

My under 16 team was in a tournament a few years ago and our top scorer during the season was having a bad start to the tournament. We had beaten some teams that were favoured to beat us in the first round with good defense and just enough goals to scrape through to the semi finals. But my top striker, Renad Mansour, had yet to score. He was my son's best friend and I drove him to the game. I knew that to go further, the team would need him to contribute with a goal especially if he got one of the few chances our team was likely to receive in the semi finals against a better team.

On the way home I reminded him of the facts to scoring and especially the fact that most goals are scored on only one touch. Renad had a habit of wanting to take the ball in close to the keeper and try and dribble it around him or take a few extra touches to try and get away a power shot off. I said to him, "Renad, when you get the chance I want you to prepare yourself to score on only ONE TOUCH. Do not take any more than one touch when you are close to goal." The next morning I picked him up and again reminded him of the importance of shooting on one touch.

So, shortly after the start of the game, he received a ball that pierced the defense and sent him clear on goal as he chased the through pass. Everyone including fans, parents, players, and myself were shouting from the sidelines. Shoot! Shoot! Renad proceeded to touch the ball two, three, four times as he tried to dribble past the goalkeeper. He failed to get a shot away and did not score. It was difficult to not show disappointment but I worked hard to say 'it's OK, nice try'. Reality was that it was a terrible try because he made the wrong decision again, even though I had talked to him about it in the car. As the ball came to the sidelines for a throw-in, I called Renad over and said to him. "Renad, that was a nice try but you forgot about shooting on one touch."

His reply, "Oh yea".

I said, "Trust me Renad, if you just try shooting on one touch you will score!" I smiled. He smiled and the game went on. With about 5 minutes to go in the first half our team got another opportunity with a long drooping through ball. Renad ran to the ball in a similar fashion as before. The fans were all shouting "shoot" as before and it looked as though Renad would once again forget what to do and try and dribble around the goalkeeper who was coming out. This time though, due to the type of lob pass, I had time to shout "ONE TOUCH" instead of "shoot". Immediately, you could see from Renad's body reaction that he heard me shout "one touch". He adjusted his response to try a one-touch shot instead of trying to dribble around the keeper. He did manage to shoot the ball on one touch. It was a gentle shot that was simply directed at goal and it went in. The team went nuts as we just tied the game at 1 and it seemed as though Renad had discovered something. This was a 'defining moment'. There was a big smile on his face and you could tell that he felt good about the goal and that he must have felt, 'wow, it's that easy to score?'

At the half the team was quite happy with the score and Renad came to me and said, "Hey coach, one touch."

"Yup", I said, "I told you it would work. It's about time. Let's do it again."

Midway through the second half Renad once again received a ball close to the goal and I shouted "one touch". I don't think he heard me this time, but he knew what to do. He prepared his body for a try at goal on one touch. He scored again. We won the game 2-1 and went to the finals. Later that day, we played the final, and again Renad scored on a one-touch goal as we won the game 1-0 to capture the championship. Later that year, I drove my son to school on a rainy day and picked up Renad to drop them off at school. As Renad entered my van he said, "Good morning coach, ONE TOUCH!"

CHAPTER 48

Changing the Frame of Mind

Over 80% of goals are scored in two touches or less. I want my strikers to always keep these statistics in their minds while in a game situation. To do this, I like to change their frame of mind so that they can think of what to do more often. Players often get back to old habits in a game, such as waiting for the perfect opportunity to shoot when in fact the chance may have already existed. Coaches often teach players to concentrate on their "first touch". The term "first touch" is used the world over and is common language in soccer. This helps coaches teach players the importance of getting a good first contact with the ball whenever it comes to them. Thinking, "first touch" as the ball approaches, helps the player bring the ball under control without using any more touches to control it. Once the ball is under control the player can work on his next moves. Players don't often have time to take three touches to control the ball in higher levels of play so we tend to brainwash them to work on their "first touch".

This method of coaching is very very good because it gets the young players thinking while the ball is approaching them. We want players to think ahead. We want them to know what to do with the ball once they get it. Without a good "first touch", the players will not be able to do what they are thinking of doing. I do not suggest coaches change this aspect of their coaching...... except...... when dealing with their strikers when they are close to the opponents' box.

The "First Touch" is Not Really the "First Touch"

I want the strikers to think differently when they are close to the opponents' box. Once again, I tell them that this is a secret. If most goals are scored on one-touch, then the "first touch" is also going to be the "last touch" before the ball goes into the net. But when using the term "first touch", you are implying that there is going to be a "second touch", or "third touch". At least this is how the brain feels. Therefore I want my strikers to think "LAST TOUCH", not "first touch" as the ball approaches them in the box. I want their brain to automatically know that if they want to score they must prepare their brain and their body for a one-touch chance to score. In practice I talk about the "last touch" to my strikers, not the "first touch".

It's amazing, when you try this, how differently the players' body movements are as the ball approaches them. Instinctively almost, this allows them to get in a better position to make their last and only touch a shot at goal or a pass to goal. All we want to do is direct the ball at goal (Rule # 1). In cases where goals are scored on two touches, I want them to think of the touch before the "last touch" as the "second last touch" instead of the "first touch" to set up the goal. I believe the term "first touch" takes up too much room or memory in the brain. It takes up too much energy. It's a bit like thinking of flying from one city to another but stopping over and changing planes to catch a connector flight as opposed to flying non-stop directly. Just the thought of the stopover tenses up the body and mind. You feel more relaxed knowing you are flying direct. Although you're still going to get to your destination, the brain gives signals to the rest of the body when even the smallest bit of stress occurs.

Stress, imagined or real, often causes us to lose focus and make mistakes. Imagined stress can cause players to miss goals just as much as real stress. If you're the striker, having a defender standing beside you trying to stop you from scoring can cause you to miss. But thinking there is someone there although there is no one standing there can cause you to miss just the same. Scoring is mostly in the brain. I want my strikers' brain to be as stress-free as possible so I like using the terms: "Last Touch," "Second Last Touch," and "Last Step," in order to "Be Prepared to Score!"

LAST TOUCH,
SECOND LAST TOUCH,

And

LAST STEP,

In order to

BE PREPARED TO SCORE!

The "last step" is useful when players are having problems getting their body in the correct position to score. The last step is often a key to their accuracy. When shooting or passing, the "last step" before contact with the ball by the support foot tends to be a bit bigger than your ordinary step. When shooting with power, a small last step will mean the player is not bringing his full momentum into the shot. Also, the placement of the support foot and where it is pointing can help the coach correct accuracy. Generally, the support foot should point at the target. If the support foot is pointed away from goal, then the player will most likely miss the goal. So planting the support foot and concentrating on the "last step" can also help you correct technical skills.

For players who have the technical skill to pass and shoot, these cue words are all that is necessary to change their mental frame of mind so that they will think differently and think according to the soccer facts related to scoring more goals. Do not get wrapped up into the technical details if you feel the problem is in their mind. Too much technical information can actually confuse the picture. If you know that your players have the ability to be technically sound in the skill of passing or shooting and if they have performed the skill correctly at some point, then you know that there is some memory in their motor-muscular nerve pathways for this skill. Bring it out in your strikers more often by using cue words such as "Last Touch", "Second Last Touch", "Last Step", and "Prepare to Score" instead of technical jargon. As in my sessions with players who could not turn the ball towards goal on a serve with their back to the goal, your players too will start to hit the net more often and score. Keep their minds focused on scoring on one or two touches. Eventually, as they see and feel success, they will instinctively perform the skill correctly.

CHAPTER 49

The Second Last Touch

We want the players to prepare mentally and physically to score every time the ball is played to them close to goal. At least if they are prepared, there is a better chance that they will not miss a scoring chance. At times, even with the best preparation, there may not be a chance to score or there may be a better option for the team, but let's not allow an opportunity to go by without being prepared. Keeping players in the game and alert and focusing on the task of scoring is not always easy. There are many distractions.

Thierry Henry, the great goal scorer from France and winner of the most goals scored in the English Premier League while with Arsenal in their undefeated season described himself as "a fox in the box". That is what a great striker is.

Michael Owen said, "On entering the box, goalscorers grow hyper-alert. All contours become sharper." And Marco Simone said, "The goal is a moment. Centimeters. The trick is to find those centimeters." All those quotes came from Simon Kuper in an article from *The Financial Times* (2003).

The key is to teach young players to be mentally ready. Cues such as "the second last touch" and "the last touch" are just that. If players see a ball coming at them while in the box that is physically impossible to turn into a shot or pass at goal on one-touch, they must be thinking to score on two touches. They should say to themselves that their "first touch" is actually their "second last touch" before their "last touch", which will be a goal, which will be followed by a celebration.

When a player has made the assessment that a one-touch goal is not possible, I want their brain to start concentrating on the "second last touch" immediately. This way they can prepare to play the ball to a spot where they can direct the ball at goal on their next touch, which will be their "last touch". The "second last touch" sounds a bit awkward, but keep in mind that this book is about training the psychological aspect of goal scoring. This must be engrained in their brain. The term, "second last touch" gets the players ready and immediately makes them make a decision as to what to do next. If the players have to think too long to decide what to do, it will be too late to score. The "second last touch" gets the players in the right frame of mind earlier for situations where they will need a minimum of two touches.

For years I have coached the "first touch" to prepare for the shot. Although it works fine, I still saw times when players took too long to decide what to do. Since using the term "second last touch" I find that, from a coaching standpoint, the reaction time and decisions making process is generally quicker with players. Their mental state is better when it comes to scoring and also their body position to prepare themselves to get the ball at goal is also much better.

Knowing what they must do in order to score can free up their mind to concentrate on performing the skill. If players are still thinking of what to do when a ball is played to them then their brain will be too clogged up in deciding what to do instead of doing what it should do. For example, many young players wait to receive the ball before deciding what to do with it. For the striker, this wait to decide is not going to produce many goals. As players try to focus on the ball, their peripheral vision will spot many things that will be a distraction.

Assuming the players must take two touches to score, then they should be thinking in the following manner:

1. They must focus on the ball, deciding where to put the ball on their "second last touch" in relation to the nearest defender and their position on the field.
2. They must decide where exactly they can play the ball so that their next touch will result in a goal. The object of the "second last touch" is to play the ball into a spot where there is a pathway to goal, and where the player can take a good "last step" to get the body in the best position to make contact with the ball.

By reading the motion of the nearby players, hopefully your players can think about where their "second last touch" should be and make the correct decision. Usually you want your players to play the "second last touch" to a position so that the ball is not trapped under their own body as this would make it difficult to take a proper "last step" to finish the job on the "last touch".

In picture 49A, Alan Shearer of Newcastle United must be thinking where he can play the ball so that on his next touch, he can get a shot away. Although players like Shearer will be already programmed to instinctively look for these spots, younger strikers can start the thinking process by thinking "second last touch" in their minds to help them realize that their "last touch" must be a ball directed at the goal.

In summary, you need to be clear about the verbal cues you give your key strikers. You want them to think they are hearing your cues while the ball is being played to them during a game. Simple but effective cues, "Second Last Touch", "Last Step", "Last Touch", "Prepare to Score". That's it!

Picture 49A: Alan Shearer should be thinking, "Where is my 'Second Last Touch' going to be so my 'Last Step' will be a good one so I can get a good 'Last Touch' and score with it". Photo by Les Jones/Covershots

You don't want your players thinking, "Oh, I'd better get my left foot back and my hip turned to the right and my shoulders leaning back to the left and my knee over the ball." You don't want them to continue thinking, "I'd better get my left foot planted beside the ball and I'd better keep my eyes on the ball and I better make sure to keep my head steady and hit the ball with my instep, or side of the foot." All this requires too much thought in a game situation. Keep it simple and free up the mind so that the focus stays on the ball and the mind doesn't wander while deciding what to do.

The decision has to be made early in the player's mind. The cues are just there as a reminder. You could casually walk by your strikers before certain games and remind them of the secret you share with them. The secret of using terms like, "The Second Last Touch, The Last Step, The Last Touch, Prepare to Score."

CHAPTER 50

"The Last Step"

"The Last Step" is another mental cue I like to use to help make the strikers aware that they need to place their body in a position where they can get the ball to goal. It reminds the players that they have only one more step in order to prepare the body to score. Again, it helps reduce the clutter that's going on in the brain as the players set up to take a scoring opportunity. "The Last Step" clearly states that it's the last. What I'm telling players with this verbal cue is that there will be no more chances to adjust their body before contact with the ball. Therefore, make it a good one.

As we know, the players can only process so much information in the time that it takes for an opportunity to come and go. I don't want them to be thinking of keeping the shoulders square or neck tight or whatever it is they need to do. In a game, this should already be automatic. The mind must concentrate on the job of finishing. "The last step" reinforces this. Also, a good last step will help them correct many technical problems they may be having.

"The Last Step": A Great Coaching Tool

Besides using "the last step" as cue words for players, coaches can analyze their shot on goal by focusing of the placement of the support foot as they set to shoot. When teaching young players how to kick and shoot, keep an eye on their last step. It will help you correct technical and skill related problems. You can derive lots of information to base your feedback to your players as a result of their last step. The placement of the non-kicking foot or support foot is very important. The last step before a shot always tends to be bigger than the previous steps. This occurs because, when shooting, you want the most power going through the body and the momentum from the previous steps to go into the shot. In passing long balls, it's the same. You want a good pass that will get to its destination.

Coaching the "Instep Drive" by Observing "The Last Step"

Picture 50A: Notice that Wayne Rooney's support foot is even with the ball at the moment of contact and pointing at the target. The player's eyes are down and on the ball. Action Images/Henry Browne

Watch for the last step as they go into the final kick and last touch. It can be a good coaching tool especially if you notice that your players are not getting enough momentum behind their kicks or passes. When shooting at goal, the support foot should be beside the ball, not too close or far from the ball. Ideally, the toe should be level or slightly behind the front of the ball. In picture 50A of England's Wayne Rooney, note where the support foot should be when the kicking foot makes contact with the ball. If a player wants to kick a ball high and far such as when taking a goal kick or making a long lofted pass, then the support foot should be behind the ball. This will force the body to reach for the ball and hit the bottom part of the ball. When shooting to score, the kicking foot should hit the ball at the centre of the ball or slightly below the mid-point of the ball. Use the placement of the support foot to base your feedback when teaching players to shoot on goal. If the support foot is too close to the ball, then a good smooth swing with the kicking leg will not be possible and the player is likely to miskick the ball. If the support foot is placed too far ahead of the ball, then the power generated by the kicking leg will go into the ground instead of forward. This will result in a weak shot on goal since the main force will go into the ground.

Even more information can be derived from the last step. Players who plant their support foot too far behind the ball will need to reach for the ball and they will probably send the ball high, over the crossbar. The last step should be a nice smooth step and bigger then the step before it. As the support foot is planted on the last step, the player will stop most of his forward motion as that foot acts as a break, but the momentum will transfer to the kicking leg which should carry forward that energy. If done smoothly and fluidly, the kicking foot should contact the ball at the instep while reaching maximum angular velocity causing a good powerful shot. In Picture 50B, the US player gets a nice "Last Step". From another angle such as in Picture 50C, you see that Francesco Totti of A.S. Roma gets a big last step which will give him maximum power.

Picture 50B: The player shooting is taking his "Last Step" before his "Last Touch" of the ball. Coaches can focus on the "Last Step" to help decide if the player is using the proper technique to shoot. The "Last Step" before a shot is usually bigger than the steps before "The Last Step." The support foot is pointing at the goal. Eyes are on the ball. Photo by Les Jones/ Covershot

In picture 50D, you can see the angular velocity created in the leg swing. This will add power to the shot. Also, watch for where the toe is pointing in the non-kicking foot. It should be pointed at the target. If it is not, then the body will adjust itself as it comes to meet the ball. This will result in a shot that will probably miss the net.

Coaches of young players should be aware that when explaining to take a big last step, some of them will take a jump upwards in order to take their big last step. The resulting big step may be big but the ball will go nowhere. Be careful to pick this out. The jump will send the body up which will mean that their momentum will be heading down into the ground instead of forward towards the goal. This will result in a poor and weak shot. The last big step should be on the same plane as the player approaches the ball with. In other words, you should not see the player change the height of their body throughout the movement before the support foot touches the ground. The body's momentum should always be going forward and never vertically.

Picture 50C: AS Roma's Francesco Totti gets a great "Last Step" as he prepares for his "Last Touch" which is a shot on goal. He points his support foot at goal and keeps his head down and his eyes on the ball. Knowing this is his last touch, the last step will slow his run as it breaks but the energy generated from the bigger last step and run up to the ball will get transferred to his kicking leg and create a more powerful shot. His arms are out for balance, which will be necessary to make everything flow smoothly. Picture Supplied by Action Images/Max Rossi

Picture 50D: This photo is taken with a slower shutter speed, which shows the movement of the kicking foot. At the moment of contact, Totti gets the maximum velocity in his leg swing. Notice that his head is down and eyes are on the ball and his support foot is right beside the ball. Action Images/Kieran Doherty

Coaching the "Banana Kick" by Observing "The Last Step"

In most cases the non-kicking foot should be pointing at the target. An exception to this is when using the outside of the foot to kick the ball with. In that case, the shooter is attempting to curve the ball by hitting it to the side of the centre of the ball. Commonly know as the 'banana kick', an outside of the foot shot requires the support foot to be behind the ball and pointing in the opposite direction to where the ball should curve towards. The 'banana shot' can be deceptive because the defender and goalkeeper do not expect the shot to go in the direction it will go because of the position of the body. The toe and ankle of the kicking foot are pointed down and in to give the ball spin so it can curve. It appears that the player taking a 'banana kick' is miskicking the ball because it makes contact with the ball off to its side. Many goals are scored with outside of the foot shots and passes. In picture 50E, David Beckham of the L.A Galaxy, just made contact with the ball with the outside of his foot. Note the position of the support foot.

The Last Step to Correct Shooting Errors

Finally, here is another cue to use when teaching players to hit a ball properly using the information from the last step. Note that, if the ball is running away from them when they are preparing to kick, the support foot must be planted ahead of the ball. This is necessary so that at the moment of contact of the kicking foot with the ball, the support foot is beside the ball. If the player plants his support foot beside the ball while the ball rolls forward, then by the time the kicking foot makes contact with the ball, it will be in the position where the player will hit the bottom of the ball and send it high. This is a common problem for young players. In Picture 50F, Canadian player #16 plants her foot ahead of the ball and points the toe at goal. In this case, the ball is rolling forward and by the time the kicking foot meets the ball, her support foot will be where it should be, which is beside the ball.

If the ball is coming at the striker, then the last step will be behind the ball so that when the ball makes contact with the kicking foot, the support foot will be beside the ball. Using information about the last step will be very effective when correcting technique.

The Goal Scorer's Last Step

Getting back to the psychology of teaching players how to score goals using "The Last Step" as cue words, note that the last step before a shot or a header always tends to be a bit bigger than the previous steps. Even when heading a ball to goal, the last step may need to be the step that catapults the player ahead of onrushing defenders, or above other players in the area. If by chance it's a diving header or a fling to throw a body part at goal in order to redirect the ball to goal, you will notice that the last step as in picture 50G, is almost always the largest.

Picture 50E: David Beckham swiped through the ball with the outside of his foot. Note the support foot is behind the ball and not pointing in the direction the ball is heading. The ball is heading to his right. Action Images/Brandon Malone

Picture 50F: In this photo, Canadian player #16 plants her foot ahead of the ball as the ball is rolling away from her so that when contact is made with the kicking foot, the ball will be beside the non-kicking foot. The toe of the non-kicking foot is pointed at goal. Photo by Les Jones/ Covershots

The cue words, "Last Step" are to remind players to get their body in the best position to score on what will be their "last touch". This also prepares them for the psychological aspect of scoring. For example, in the drill where I served balls to the players with their back to the goal as shown in picture 47A from Chapter 47, originally players were not thinking to position their body for a one or two touch shot at goal. In diagram 50H, I show how the player who is facing back to goal must prepare to score in his mind. The ball is served at different angles and heights at about 8 to 15 yards out from goal. The server must vary the serve. The player must concentrate on directing the ball to goal consistently with no defenders. Make sure the player is focusing on the ball and making the right decisions all the time.

Players need to be thinking that they only have one touch, (two at the most) in order to redirect the ball to goal. When the ball is served to them, they need to be mentally focused to perform this action.

The Defenders "Last Step"

Picture 50G: Fernando Torres of Spain stretches with his last step to try and redirect the ball towards the goal in the Final of Euro 2008. The last step to reach the ball to redirect it at goal is usually the largest. Action Images/Eric Breatgnon

In the section on biomechanics and body movement (chapter 40), I discussed how players could try and read the motions of their nearest opponents. I like to use the term "Last Step" also as a reminder for my strikers to perceptually try and read the defenders' "Last Step". Although I have used the cue words, "Last Step" to refer to the striker's last step, in this example, I want to use the cue words, "Last Step" to start off the thought process when reading defenders.

Most goals come on one single touch of the ball. Let's assume we freeze the action at that time. While the goal scorer is taking his last touch, the defender will also be taking his last step to try and prevent the ball from going in. This last step is actually a last ditch effort by the defender in doing his job. The pressure on this defender is enormous because he can do the job perfectly for 89 minutes and 59 seconds in a game. But for one second, he may fail to prevent the attacker from getting to the ball to redirect it at the goal. That one-second can cost his team the game if the attacker is successful. Since humans are not perfect, there will be times when this defender will not be able to prevent a shot directed at goal. So, although the defender will have the advantage for most of the game, the reality will be that he will not always be there to stop the attempt at goal. It's impossible.

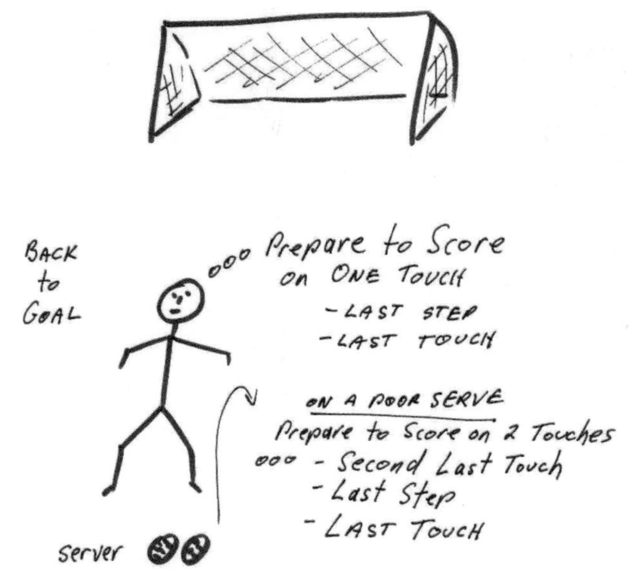

Diagram 50H: Thought process on 1 or 2 touch shot on goal. In this case the player has his back to the goal.

Here is what I say to my strikers in my course:

> ***"Defenders have a lot of space to cover and more than one attacker to be concerned with. They will also make some bad decisions. When they make an error, are you ready to pounce and score? In every game there will be chances. Defenders cannot possibly be 'on' every second of the game. Stay focused and in 'the zone' because your chance to score will come. Try and read the defender's 'last step' as you plan your 'last step' and 'last touch'. Remember the rules, and facts about scoring. Be prepared to score all the time!"***

Give your players the confidence that, if they are mentally alert and "in the zone", the chance to score will come. And to find this moment, maybe we can study the defender's "Last Step" and see what they can humanly do and not do to stop your players from scoring.

Picture 50I: The defender's last step is still not enough to block the attempt at goal by Wayne Rooney of Manchester United. Many players will think the path to goal is not there when in fact the ball can get to the goal unobstructed even if it goes right by the foot. Action Images/ Darren Walsh

You want your players to be so focused that they know where their "last touch" will be, and thus guess if their defenders will actually be able to get there to block the attempt. The defender is only so big, tall, fast. If the attempt to stop a shot is coming from the foot for example, the foot is only so long and the defender's last step can only be so long. Is it always long enough to block a shot at goal? The answer is no, but players often think it is and therefore they do not shoot. In picture 50I, Wayne Rooney has read the defender's attempt to stop him from shooting correctly and is getting a shot past him.

Analyzing Why Players Don't Shoot From a Perception Point of View

The body can cover only so much area. And the key is that it doesn't matter how far the defender's foot is away from the ball, if there is no blockage to prevent the ball getting through to goal when a shot is taken, the ball will get past the defender. That includes a case where the toe is only millimeters away from the potential path of the ball. The problem is, can your striker visualize and accurately identify when a clear path to goal actually exists? Players often don't shoot because they think their shot will be blocked but they are often incorrect in this assessment. One reason why this perception exists is that the player's eyes see things differently from what is actually happening where the ball is. While the striker's head is up and often sees obstacles, the path from the ball to the goal may actually be clear. You have to train your strikers to see the goal from where the ball is and not from where their eyes are.

Carefully following the defenders last step will help your players read where the defenders will plant their foot and what they can possibly cover. This perception training can be accomplished by having the coach move in slow motion to exaggerate the nearest defender's last step and also by having your strikers play down against inferior opposition and looking for these critical moments when shooting or passing.

Once strikers are able to read the defenders' movements accurately, they will get those "good feelings" that come with learning. Eventually, they will be making more correct decisions in their ability to read their opponents. They can help their decision-making process using the cue words presented. The cue words will help bring out the correct skills needed to score more often.

The next obstacle of course is the goalkeeper. But how often do players not even get to the shot because they fail to see the opportunity or they fail to prepare their mind and body to score? I can tell you, having played goalkeeper, that it remains the biggest reason why goals were not scored against me. Many players in the situation as the one Rooney is in, as depicted in picture 50I where the shooter can get a ball to the goal, will not shoot. The shooter is very close to goal and the chances of scoring are quite good. But, he must shoot in order to score!

I recall watching an FA Cup match in 2005 when Wayne Rooney of Manchester United scored two brilliant goals against Middlesbrough. He had mastered the decision-making process to scoring in that game. In the two one-touch goals Rooney scored, you could see that he prepared his body in mid-stride to score. He made correct decisions under extreme pressure to score. In his second goal, a volley, he had to quickly slow his step so he could adjust his body to get it in position to score. His last step changed to allow him to get his kicking foot on the ball. It was as if he had his mind clearly made up. It seemed as though he was saying to himself something like this:

> "I know I score more goals on just 'one touch', so I'm going to score on my 'last touch'. But I'd better concentrate on my 'last step' so I can make my 'last touch' a good one because the ball is coming at me in the air. Let me focus on the ball and nothing else because I can tell that if I get the ball off in 'one touch', the nearest defender doesn't have a chance to stop my shot. Here comes the ball, I'd better adjust my run to take into account the flight of the ball and where it's going to land. OK, Wayne, don't take your eyes off the ball. My 'last step' will be here. OK, here comes my 'last touch'. Keep the eyes on the ball. Just hit the net and then it's up to the goalie to stop it. Focus. 'Last Touch'. Oh Yea, a goal. I love this game!" (Picture 50J)

Maybe he didn't think it through exactly this way and maybe it just happened automatically. If so, that came through lots of hours of training and studying the game. The decision-making process does not start out automatically. It comes with deep thought and can be the fastest thing to train. I can train a striker to make decisions faster with regards to scoring than many other decisions that have to be made by other players on the field. Of course, the striker has to have the skills to be able to kick, pass, and head a ball properly. If you can get your players to think in this manner using cue words as coaching tools, and if they are focused to see the skill through to its conclusion, then the goalkeeper will only become a minor obstacle. We shall look at how to beat the keeper in Part 4 of this book.

Picture 50J: "My last step will be here. OK, here comes my last touch. Keep the eyes on the ball. Just hit the net and then it's up to the goalie to stop it. Focus. 'Last Touch'. Oh Yea, a goal. I love this game!" Action Images/Darren Walsh

CHAPTER 51

"The Last Touch"

"The Last Touch" is my personal favourite new coaching term I use to help coaches coach their strikers. "The Last Touch" refers to the last touch by the player who shoots and hopefully scores the goal. I first presented it to coaches in 2003 in coaching sessions to replace the standard term, "First Touch" that coaches use. Specific to the striker it should get the mind thinking about finishing the job to score. Similar to "finishing", coaches now have another term to communicate to players. The last touch on the ball before a goal is scored can be the most important touch in the whole game. If there are three goals scored in a 2-1 game, then there are really only three touches in the whole game that will decide the outcome of the game from a scoring point of view. Similarly in a 1-0 game, there is only one touch (one second of time) in a 90-minute game that will have any meaning on the score-sheet and in the papers the next day. That touch is the all-important "Last Touch" that puts the ball into the goal.

To put the last touch in perspective, think of it this way. You as a coach spend hours upon hours training your team and at the end of the day your whole season and all your efforts can come down to just a few seconds of each game. If your players do not make "The Last Touch" a good one, everything else seems wasted. Are you spending enough time, one-on-one with the players on your team who you are counting on to make that "Last Touch" count? When players fail to score it's often because of a simple mental breakdown.

Picture 51A: Mia Hamm receives a through ball and takes more than one touch on the ball and tries to go around German goalkeeper Silke Rottenberg instead of taking a shot directly on her first touch which should have been her "last touch". Action Images/Anthony Bolante

I want my key players to think about their last touch in a number of ways. Firstly, as suggested, I want them to think that they only have one touch to score in most cases. I want them to use the term "Last Touch" to remind them that most goals are scored on only one touch. Knowing this fact and remembering it in a game can make a world of difference to a striker as I stated in my story in Chapter 47. The term "One Touch" or "Final Touch" can work well too. The overwhelming evidence on goals scored on one touch should be enough for players to remember, but even the best in the world get caught up in the moment and revert back to old habits. In picture 51A, Mia Hamm, of the USA fails to prepare to score on one touch after receiving a through ball in a semi-final game at the 2003 Women's World Cup. She probably would have scored if she had taken a one-touch shot on goal, but instead, she decided to try to go around the German goalkeeper. The German keeper made a great save by coming out quickly and preventing a shot. Germany won that game and went on to win the 2003 Women's World Cup, and eliminated the USA from defending their title.

A Perfect Touch

I also want my strikers to think "Last Touch" to remind them of a key technical issue when shooting, heading, or passing a ball. I want them to use the term from a point of view of making that "Last Touch" a perfect touch. A "perfect touch" will most likely result in a goal. I want my striker to know that I will only accept four reasons and only four reasons to prevent the goal from being scored when there is a good chance:

1. a great save by the goalkeeper.
2. a brilliant defensive play by the last defender.
3. being fouled.
4. field and weather conditions.

Nothing else is acceptable. I definitively don't want my striker to fail to score because they messed up their last touch. They must focus on making it perfect and consistent all the time, starting from practices. Actually, staying focused in practice is crucial to performing the skill under pressure in games. Young players often take it too easy at practices when it comes to the final touch.

For the last touch to be good, the players should stay focused on accomplishing the task at hand. Often this means being "in the zone". The key to the "Last Touch" is to keep the eyes on the ball and actually watch and see their last touch as their body touches the ball. That can be the foot, the head, or even the thigh. They must keep their eyes on the ball. When a defender or keeper truly makes a great play to stop my player from scoring, I encourage my strikers to acknowledge their skills. I want them to congratulate the defender or goalkeeper for their efforts and then look forward to the next challenge. I want them to stay positive and confident while they wait for their next opportunity to apply all the psychological advice I have provided them. If your strikers are in a negative state of mind, they are more likely to fail in a future attempt. Here is a slide I show players to explain the above point.

It all Goes Back to the Eyes

The biggest mistake players make in completing the skill of scoring is to take their eyes off the ball a split second before contact. Many players maintain eye contact with the ball right up until the last moment. Then, just at the last split second, for some reason, they take their eyes off the ball. This often takes the body out of a good position into a less advantageous position to complete the skill. It may come from habit from playing other sports like basketball, lacrosse, or bowling where the player's eyes are on the target. Sometimes, the player is anxious to see the result before completing the task.

This is a problem I have experienced when playing golf -- I should say, trying to play golf. It's hard keeping the eyes on the ball and the head down. Funnily enough, it's probably less necessary in golf than in soccer because the golf ball is not going to move when the player starts his swing. The soccer ball will. A friend of mine and avid golfer, Dino Cirone, tells me that this is a common problem amongst golfers. He says that, "players are in a hurry to see the result of their shot before they finish taking their shot!"

Actually, lifting the head at the last split second before contacting the ball in a golf swing will bring the body out of synch and that can mean topping the ball or slicing the ball. The same thing happens when trying to make that final touch in soccer. The movement of the eyes off the ball to see where the ball is going to go will automatically cause the head to lift up. When the head moves, even the slightest bit, it will cause the whole body to move as well. In golf, a slight movement will cause the player to mis-hit the ball.

In soccer, one would think that a small movement of the head and eyes would not affect the outcome of the shot because the ball is so big in comparison to a golf ball. In a game, the soccer ball is usually in motion and there are defenders trying to distract the player from scoring. The fact is that the head movement will affect the rest of the body and also cause the player to mis-hit the ball. Striking the ball too high, low, or off to the side will affect its flight just as in golf. You have to admire the mental strength of some superstar athletes as they ply their craft consistently in their sport. Golf's Tiger Woods is very strong mentally to be as technically perfect each time as possible (picture 51B). Notice how his eyes are still on the ball. This helps keep his head down so that he makes a perfect shot.

Picture 51B: Tiger Woods keeps his eyes on the ball as he hits the golf ball. Photo supplied by Action Images/Shaun Best

Go back and look closely at some of the pictures from chapter 50 and you will notice that the great players keep their head down and eyes on the ball right up until they make contact with the ball. In picture 51C, you can see that Canadian player number 9 starts to lift her head and eyes off the ball. Her eyes should be clearly on the ball. Her chances of scoring will be diminished greatly in this situation.

The use of the term "Last Touch" reminds strikers to keep their eyes on the ball right to the end. I want the players to concentrate on their "Last Touch". These cue words help deliver a specific message.

Players also take their eyes off the ball because they think they need to see where the goalie is or the defenders are. Or, they may take their eyes off the ball because a nearby player is distracting them. It can also occur as a result of a shout from a teammate who may be calling for the ball. It takes deep concentration to maintain good eye contact with the ball and still see what's going on around them. Through their peripheral vision, players should be able to see and read the position of their nearest defender and possibly also the goalkeeper's. Nonetheless, the goalkeeper's position won't matter if your strikers take their eyes off the ball and then miskick the ball and miss the net.

Two Parts of the Brain Are Fighting With Each Other

One thing is certain: the net does not move. As long as the player always knows where he is in relation to the goal, he does not have to stare at the goal when shooting. Since the ball is moving, it is harder to track and focus on it than on the net. Thus, the eyes should be focused on the ball. But the eyes are eager to see the result of the upcoming shot. Here is where we need to coach the player to think through this dilemma. The striker's brain should be telling the eyes to focus on the ball. Why does the brain wander and forget to tell the eyes and head to stay focused on the ball? One part of the brain is fighting with another part. In picture 51D, we see a typical example of where a striker gets a good scoring chance. He has pressure on him and is aware of that pressure but he's also excited about a possible goal coming up.

This is where the emotional part of the brain is getting excited and wants to see the ball go in the goal from the front row seats (picture 51E). As shown exaggerated in picture 51F, often the eyes and head come up off the ball at the

Picture 51C: The player's head comes up and eyes come off the ball, which will reduce her chances to score. Photo by Les Jones/Covershots

Picture 51D: In this picture we see an example of where a striker (#10) gets a good scoring chance. He has pressure on him and is aware of that pressure but he's also excited about a possible goal coming up. Players in Photo: Left to right. Lucas Caridi (white #9), Nicholas Rodrigues (navy #2), Marco DeBenedictis (white #10), Shayne Branigan (goalkeeper), Jan Lang (navy #4), Alex Von Gemmingen (navy #3)

last split second before making contact with the ball. This can cause a player to miskick the ball and miss the goal. Or often, the player makes poor contact with the ball and takes a weak shot at the goalkeeper.

There are also many situations where the player will think his shot will get blocked so he will not even attempt the shot and try getting closer, which will reduce the chance of a goal being scored. Common sense often leaves the player even though we tell him over and over again. I tell myself the same thing (keep my eyes on the ball) before I swing at golf balls and then I suddenly do the opposite. What kind of battle is going on in my brain?

As a coach, I try to use powerful cue words to keep the common sense part of the brain away from the emotional side. That's why I find that repeating the words "Last Touch" at practice helps players I have worked

Picture 51E: Players often miss scoring chances because they are in a hurry to see the result of their shot. It's as if the emotional part of the brain is excited and wants front row seats to see themselves score and bulge the net.

Picture 51F: Players are in a hurry to see the result of their shot before they finish taking their shot and often take their eyes off the ball and lift their head before making contact with the ball, as shown.

with more than any other term. The results with the players I have worked with have been spectacular. When players lose focus I often say to them,

"Try to read the writing on the ball as you touch it. What brand is it? That's how focused you should be."

Here is a slide I like to use in my presentation to players that makes the point.

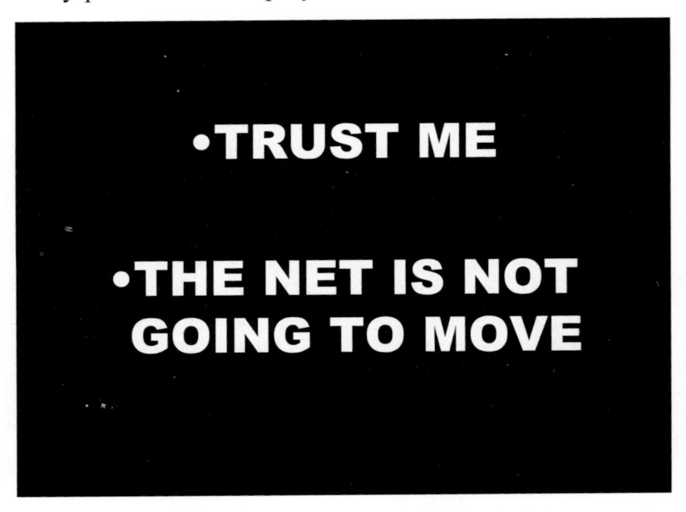

Here is how I explain it to players:

> ***"Trust me, the net is not going to move. The flight of the ball is not often going to change in mid-flight so keep your eyes on it as you shoot. If it does change direction due to a deflection then you will probably not score anyway but if it doesn't and you are unprepared because you got distracted from focusing on the ball by players around you, then you will miss an easy goal scoring opportunity. Your 'last touch' usually does not have to be a great powerful shot; it just has to be on goal. You have to make good contact with the ball and be accurate to make it the 'perfect touch'. Hitting the net is good enough in most cases. Focus, keep your eyes on the ball, you will score more goals!"***

In picture 51G, A.S. Roma's Francesco Totti is not looking at the defender or the goalkeeper. He is focused on the ball and scores against Inter Milan, beating the defender's attempt to stop him by only centimeters.

Picture 51G: Totti's "Last Touch" is perfect in this goal against Inter Milan. He displays why he's one of the league's leading scorers with deep concentration and by keeping his eyes on the ball. Photo provided by Action Images/Giampiero Sposito

CHAPTER 52

Focus – "Click-Click-Click"

Regardless of what part of the body players use for their last touch, they must focus on the ball and stay mentally alert and "on". Focusing on a moving ball with defenders, teammates, and the goalkeeper all in close proximity is not easy. It's even harder with shouting coaches, players, and fans adding to the strikers' stress level. Staying mentally alert takes practice. I like to tell players to block everything out except the ball. They can experiment with what works best for them. Often using cue words to remind the players can be part of a pre-game ritual where your strikers visualize themselves scoring by keeping the eye on the ball until the end. I show strikers powerful images such as the pictures from Chapter 51 that clearly show how the players who score maintain composure and stay focused with their eyes on the ball.

Picture 52A: Hasan Sas from Turkey scores a goal with a beautiful volley by maintaining composure and not getting distracted from striking the ball perfectly on his "last touch". Action Images/ Desmond Boylan

In picture 52A and 55C, Hasan Sas of Turkey maintains composure and is focused as he keeps his eyes on the ball and his head down as he concentrates on making contact with the moving ball. In the picture, the ball has been played from a fair distance away over defenders. Sas prepares his body and maintains focus. For players who miss the goal in this type of situation, quite often the head is already up by the time the ball is moving towards the goal. That would suggest that the eyes came off the ball even before that. This goal was one of the most skillful goals of the 2002 World Cup and it was scored on none other than the eventual 2002 World Cup Champions, Brazil.

If you watch some of the great players score goals, you can see how focused they are on keeping the eye on the ball even through traffic. I also like to show players some great pictures where the ball has come through traffic to get to the player who scores as in picture 52B. The player who scores is probably "in the zone".

In picture 52B, taken in the World Cup Final in 1998, Zinedine Zidane concentrates on hitting a moving ball in flight by keeping his eyes on the ball. This is not easy. The most common error is to take the eyes off ball just before making contact, or in a case such as this, to allow others to distract the player from concentrating on getting his head to the ball and direct it towards goal.

As a coach, I have learned to pull out as many tricks out of my hat as possible to get players to focus on being consistent in these situations. The cue words, images, and ideas presented in this book are the ones that have worked best. Others didn't seem to trigger the mind with many of the young players I worked with over the years. Another mental technique I use is to tell strikers to imagine taking pictures as the ball comes at them. I suggest that they pretend to take three pictures with the last one being when the ball touches the foot, head, or body part.

Picture 52B: Zinedine Zidane (#10) scores against Brazil in the 1998 World Cup Final in traffic by picking out the ball in a crowd. Action Images/Michael Craig

I'll say this to players:

> ***"As the ball comes towards you, take three pictures to score. In the first two pictures make sure you follow the ball with deep thought as it comes to you. Ignore defenders' arms, legs, or anything else that may get in the way. Each time you take a picture, hear the camera clicking. Assume the ball is not going to change its flight pattern, make sure you are there when it comes down, and focus on your 'last touch' to score. Take a picture just as you touch the ball and make sure the camera (your eyes) is in focus."***

Boom-Boom-Boom

I tell players to hear the camera click three times (click- click- click). It's just something that will hopefully remind them to concentrate. The camera has to be in focus in order for the picture (in this case, the last touch) to be good. In classroom sessions, I'll show pictures and have the sound of the camera clicking three times with each picture. Another term I like to use instead of click-click-click- is boom-boom-boom. I tell players to hear a drum beat 3 times as they say the words in their head. Also with each boom, the ball needs to get closer to them. Teenage players seem to resonate with hearing these words when I asked them what things they remembered most from my course. Do not ask me why. There must be a song that connects with young players with these words.

Visualizing cue words and sounds while scoring goals before the game can help the player get "in the zone" and stay mentally focused. Each player will be different and each will have his own ritual. Sometimes a player's ritual will stem from superstition but the coach has to reinforce that the "last touch" is all that counts and that the player must stay sharp at the moment the ball comes to him. Players must stay focused to make sure that the quality of the final touch is perfect because in most cases, there will only be one touch needed to score a goal. That touch is "The Last Touch"!

CHAPTER 53

3 Ways to Score Goals

In my research on goal scoring and thorough analysis of goals, I have come to the conclusion that goals are scored in just three ways (except for goals scored by the defending team on their own goals!).

1. Power shots into the goal
2. Balls re-directed at goal
3. Passes into the goal

Let's review these three methods of scoring

1) Power Shots into the Goal

One method of scoring is what everyone thinks is the most common way to score and that is the power shot, or, if the ball is in the air, the power volley. This skill usually involves using the instep and when you actually analyze goals, you will find that most goals are NOT scored on a power kick with the instep. No doubt though, it will be useful to be able to kick with power because there are situations where goals can only be scored with some power. I will go over some teaching methods for the instep power drive in chapter 55.

2) Re-directs

The second method of scoring goals comes from re-directing the ball at goal. Often these are goals that can be classified as passes as well as goals re-directed at goal. In my analysis I classify re-direct goals as goals where the ball simply needs to be re-directed to goal in order for the goal to be scored. There is no real passing skill needed. In all cases the body acts as a wall similar to the wall pass for the ball to go in. No kicking motion is necessary in these types of goals.

Goals that are scored by the head are considered re-direct goals because the ball came towards the player and simply had to be re-directed.

Some goals are scored off deflections. When the player tried shooting the ball at goal by a power shot or a pass and it was deflected off a defender, I classify the goal as a goal from re-direct because if the ball had not have been deflected, the goalkeeper would probably have made the save or the ball would have missed the net.

3) Passes into the Goal

Finally, the third method of scoring comes when the ball is "shot" into the goal in a variety of ways that would otherwise be considered a pass. It could be an inside of the foot pass, an outside of the foot pass, a chip pass, a long lofted pass and any other methods players use to pass a ball to a teammate. Scoring goals by passing the ball into the goal is basically exactly the same skill as used in passing a ball to a teammate. So I always say to players that, when they are near the goal, they need to pretend they are simply performing the skill of passing the ball into the net. Surprisingly to many players, scoring by passing the ball into the goal results in the most goals.

I say this to players who miss goals by not thinking that a shot on goal is actually a pass:

> ***"Scoring with a pass should be easier than passing to a teammate because your target is so much larger. In regular play when passing to a teammate, in order to make an accurate pass; you need to play the ball past defenders, being careful not to make the pass too short or too long. Also, your target area for a successful pass is only a yard to either side of the intended receiver, even less if you are close to him. Passing accurately is not easy. When passing to score, your intended target is actually 8 yards wide and if you kick it too hard, the intended receiver will still catch the ball and control it: that's***

what the mesh is for. Also, your teammate is 8 feet tall (the height of the goal!). How can you miss?"

Most players are quite good passers. Why do they have problems passing the ball into such a big target? It is true that the defender (the goalkeeper) can use his hands. But the game would be quite different if there was no goalkeeper. Such a game is hard to imagine and the defenders would have to use new methods for stopping the strikers, otherwise we would have basketball-like games with scores like 48-45. Even with the goalkeeper having the use of the hands, the strikers still have a target 8 yards wide by 8 feet high.

You want to stress to your players that, just like for passing to a teammate, they need to use passing skills to score. In fact most goals are just that: passes. Yet when players think of scoring, they think of striking a ball with power and then bulging the net, which looks cool. Yes it does, but with this method, they won't score too many goals. But, like in passing to a teammate, the pass must be strong enough so that it gets to the goal. It must be accurate enough so that it goes into the net in an area where the goalkeeper or the defenders cannot stop the ball. Passes make up most goals.

Players Want Proof

The reason I classify goals this way is to clearly show strikers that goals come from ways they would not have assumed. Most people assume most goals are scored from great power shots, amazing diving headers, and by picking corners and that shooting accurately at those corners is the way to fame. You need to dispel this theory in your players' mind. By classifying goals into power shots, re-directs, and then passes, you can accomplish this task better.

Players will challenge you with proof of what you are trying to coach them, so here are the facts from the 2006 World Cup and UEFA Euro 2012. Please note that there are times some goals can be classified into either category so I have split those types of goals equally. For example, if 4 goals could be classified as either power shots or passes, then I have classified 2 as power shot goals and 2 as passing goals.

In the 2006 World Cup	Euro 2012
40 Goals came from power shots (27.2%)	**Power Shots - 22 Goals (29%)**
49 Goals came from re-directs (33.3%)	**Redirects - 28 Goals (37%)**
58 Goals came from passes (39.5%)	**Passes - 26 Goals (34%)**

These are powerful numbers that should get the message across to your strikers who think most goals are scored from power shots. When you watch the "Top 10 Goals" of the official FIFA 2006 World Cup highlight package, 6 of them were power shots of which 5 out of those six went in the top corners of the goal. The other one, by Zambrotta of Italy, went in the bottom corner of the goal. Not one of the re-directed type goals made it to the top 10 goals highlight package. It's no wonder young soccer strikers miss as often as they do. They are trying to score unrealistic goals.

If goal-scoring practice just involves power shooting, then you are neglecting to practice how to score nearly 75% of all goals. Even if you do practice for all types of goals in your practice sessions, how will your strikers practice their goal scoring skills when they are out on their own? The temptation will be to find someone who will play goal and then fire the ball at him from around the edge of the box. Also, you can be certain that they will practice scoring typical highlight reel goals. In my Golden Goal Scoring Academy coaching sessions, I outline some scoring practices you can present to your players to try when they are out on their own or with a couple of friends that will cover all aspects of goal scoring.

I believe that presenting strikers these goal-scoring facts in the manner that I have will mean that practicing goal scoring should now take on a completely different meaning. We will look at each method of scoring in more details in the next three chapters.

CHAPTER 54

Passing the Ball into the Goal

Passing the ball into the goal is not a new method of teaching players how to score. Yet amazingly, it baffles me to see how often players in close proximity to goal lose their composure and forget the concept of scoring via the pass. It's as if a mental block exists somewhere in the brain and players just have to try and blast the ball as hard as possible when all they need to do is get the ball at goal by way of a simple pass. I would say that if you see fellow coaches pulling their hair or losing their hair or prematurely turning gray, it's probably because of this simple failure from their strikers.

So what I intend to do in my goal scoring course is to make as strong and powerful a case as possible to overcome this mental block whenever the temptation is there to blast the ball. It doesn't always work but I find that the success rate is quite good.

There are other factors that can contribute to a player's performance in a game that causes these types of mistakes. My son Joseph became quite good at scoring goals since working with me. He was one of the slowest players on the team but he converted most of his chances and was the team's leading scorer outscoring players who were faster and had more chances. After one particular game I questioned his decisions in regards to situations where he usually does not err. I asked, "Why did you just try to blast the ball all the time?"

He answered:

**"Because I was mad at the other team.
The other team were jerks!"**

The opposition had distracted him early in the game and told him that he was no good and got him off his game. It evidently worked because he made poor decisions and forgot to pass the ball in the net when he had great chances to score close to the goal. The best can overcome these pressures. This is gamesmanship. But we are human and these things happen. That's why we need to give our players the skills to overcome these weaknesses. Those who can are more successful. Those who cannot are not. It's quite a simple thing and it's mostly mental.

Serena Williams vs. Lindsay Davenport: Tennis Breakdown

I was watching the 2005 Women's Australian Open tennis championships and Lindsay Davenport was ahead 1 set to 0 against Serena Williams and staying close halfway through the second set. Then Davenport had the opportunity to break Serena Williams and take a commanding lead in the second set. She had 7 break points and numerous opportunities to win one of the games in the second set. She failed. Shortly afterwards, in the next game, Davenport had Serena Williams at 40-love but missed a simple shot that should have put the game away and tied the set at four games apiece. After that miss, the game, set, and match were practically over. You could see it in her body language and reaction. I remember saying to myself after that miss, "It's over, she's given up unless she composes herself". She proceeded to lose total composure after that miss and lost that game ending it with a double fault. She then lost again to lose the second set. In the third set Williams won 6-0 and won 2 sets to 1 to claim the Australian Open Women's title. She was unable to mentally overcome her errors and she broke down so quickly it was sad to see such an even match turn so one-sided in such a short time.

Your goal scorer is a key piece of the puzzle that makes up your team. Goal scorers are also often some of the most difficult players to deal with but yet, you need to come to grips with their abilities and faults and do your best to make their decision making process as simple as possible while also giving them the tools to succeed. I can't stress enough this aspect of coaching a player to become a great goal scorer.

Picture 54A: David Beckham passes the ball towards an onrushing attacker in front of goal using a long lofted pass at the MLS all-star game in Toronto. The cross is a pass but the skill of this type of pass is also used to score goals. Beckham has made precision passing an enjoyable skill to watch. Les Jones/Covershots

Passing the ball into goal is a key area that I find works wonders to help the player relax in making the right decisions and then finish the task. In a game or practice session, passing is often much less stressful than shooting and there is a better success rate. Players like David Beckham have made passing an enjoyable art form. The pressure from this skill is much less than that of shooting (Picture 54A). The body and mind are in a much more relaxed state.

We need to bring this relaxed and confident approach of passing to scoring. Tell your strikers that this is a secret. Bombard them with the statistic that shows that nearly 40% of goals come from passing the ball into the goal. Convince your strikers to think that a pass is a good way to think GOOOOOOAAAL!

There are different types of passes players make to score goals. The push pass or inside of the foot pass is the most common. The outside of the foot pass is another method of passing the ball into the goal. When a ball is in the air and the ball is played through the defense and the goalkeeper is coming off his line, the chip is often a good pass. A simple gentle chip over the keeper's reach is a common way to score. The long lofted pass can be used to catch the goalkeeper off his line from a distance and often goals from free kicks are passes bent around defenders. Many players who take penalty shots actually pass the ball at goal making sure to give it enough pace. Watch carefully which part of the foot the player uses to score. Often it's an inside of the foot push pass.

Players need to keep in mind that, like in passing, the ball needs enough pace or velocity to get to its intended target. The famous "hospital ball", which usually refers to a ball that is passed to a teammate but not strongly enough leaving the teammate in a situation where the pass barely gets to him, can be a dangerous pass. This is because a weak pass often enables a defender to come in and challenge for the ball putting the receiving player in a situation where an injury can occur. Coaches need to get players out of bad habits with weak passes.

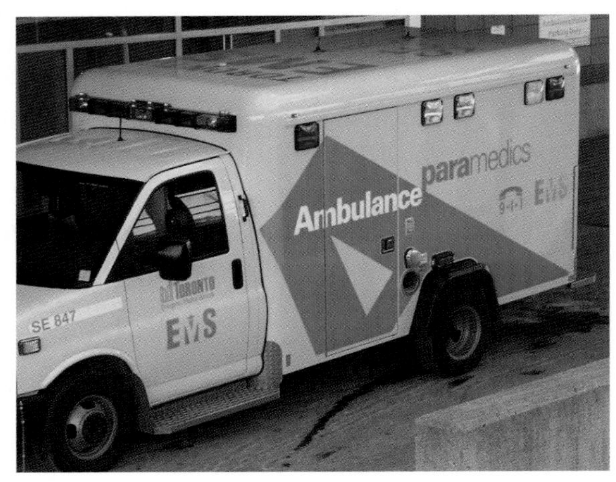

Picture 54B: "The Hospital Ball" is a weak pass that can put a teammate in the hospital. To score, passes need to have some pace to them so that they get to the teammate, which in this case will be the back of the net. Photo/John DeBenedictis

Finally, a goal that looks like a brilliant volley and power drive at first is often a well taken and timed pass to goal and not an instep drive. Without the use of slow motion replay, one would often assume that a volley, especially off a cross, is a powerful kick when in fact it's a pass with the side of the foot. Once again our eyes are fooled and the player dreams of a similar goal without realizing that the volley shot was actually a pass.

Picture 54C: Ronaldo scores Brazil's 2nd goal against Costa Rica in the 2002 World Cup by passing the ball into the goal with an inside of the foot pass. He found an opening to the side of the goalkeeper on the ground as if he was passing the ball to a teammate through defenders. Action Images/Tony O'Brien

It's imperative to keep the eyes focused on the ball while completing this task. Often in passing, the super keen eye and attention needed for scoring are not quite as important because the pressure is not as intense. Also, passing errors are not as obvious as errors made when missing a good scoring opportunity. When passing to score, the concentration must be much more intense because the opportunity to pass the ball into goal in a game is much less frequent than the pass to a teammate situation. Players cannot lose their focus when the chance to score does occur.

Practice Passing to Score

Most coaches believe that shooting practice is when the team practices to score. But since most goals are passes, your strikers should see every passing drill as their own personal scoring drill. Make it their little secret. In picture 54E this standard passing drill can actually be considered a goal scoring drill for a striker. In picture 54F Christine Sinclair concentrates on making an accurate pass to a teammate. Reality is that a great goal scorer sees every completed pass as a GOAL! That means extra concentration on the "last touch" and "second last touch" on every pass in games and practices.

Can your key strikers afford not to take passing practices seriously? You cannot spend all practice shooting and there are many more things you will do that involve passing than shooting so why not tell strikers that, unlike other players on the team, they should consider their successful passes as goals? This is their challenge in each and every passing practice session.

Here is what I tell players:

> ***"Never again, should you NOT want to concentrate fully on making a perfect pass because to you, it's a goal! You ARE a striker. You want to score more goals. You want to celebrate the goal. You need to make passing part of your practices more important for you than any other player on the team. Focus as you would in scoring the goal when you make passes in practice so that your brain learns to concentrate and block out distractions. Read the movement of the ball and players around you. More goals are scored by passing the ball into the net than shooting it into the goal. To a goal scorer any passing drill is really a goal scoring drill."***

At the very least, using this approach will keep your strikers more focused at practice. As discussed before they can become a bit cocky so you want them at their best all practice long. Not only for themselves, but also for your goalkeepers and defenders who need to practice defending against strikers that try hard at practice. I emphasize this to my strikers this way:

> ***"Look how easy it is to practice goal scoring. You do not need a goal. Your defenders are your goalies. Your teammates are the back of the net. The opportunity to train your brain to score is there almost every minute of your practices and games. Don't forget to keep your concentration in the game and complete your passes."***

You want all your players focused on the game at all times but especially your strikers because they can go for long spells in a game without receiving a ball. When the ball comes to them, you want your strikers focused so that they can receive a pass as a target man without giving up possession of the ball with poor control. Staying in the game is important for strikers because they may receive a ball after minutes of not seeing it and be the start of an attack. If they are not focusing, they can just as easily give it up and have to wait a while before the team wins possession again.

Often, when coaches arrive at a practice session, they leave a number of soccer balls on the field while preparing to start the training session. I like to observe young players while they wait for all their teammates to arrive. Most of the time players practice their shooting in unrealistic situations. Quite often, players are shooting at goal while the ball is not moving. Except for set pieces, this does not happen in a game. Then, I like to see where players aim. They are all trying to bulge the net by hitting the ball into the top corners or off the posts. While this is exciting for them, these types of goals are not real. Let your players have fun but make your passing sessions more valuable to your strikers by reminding them of the facts to scoring. Concentrating to make an accurate pass is a more realistic goal scoring exercise than kicking a dead ball from outside the area. The facts clearly support that.

Game Warm-up to Prepare Strikers

As your players warm up prior to a game, occasionally remind your strikers about passing the ball into goal. Ask them to stay focused. Many teams get in a circle with a player in the middle and the rest of the players try to keep the ball away from the player or players in the middle. Better teams are restricted to one touch or two touches. Ask your strikers when doing this exercise to try and focus on passing the ball right by the defender's supporting leg as they would against a goalkeeper (as I shall cover later). Ask them to get focused in the warm up with reading body motion. Have your strikers use the warm-up to get in the game mentally. You don't want your strikers shooting at your starting keeper and scoring on him all the time. This will ruin your keeper's confidence. To the strikers, each successful pass should be considered as a goal in your warm-up. It's a good idea to do some shooting on goal during the warm-up but don't use your starting keeper for this exercise unless he is of the mental makeup that giving up goals in the warm-up will not affect his performance.

You also want your strikers to try and feel the game ball before the game. They need to get a feel for its flight. Some balls fly faster than others or tend to float more while others are heavier. In wet conditions, you want them to do the same. A good pre-game practice for your strikers is to take a variety of short and long passes and turn the ball to a teammate on one or two touches to see how the ball spins or plays especially in wet conditions (See Diagram 54D). Remind your strikers that goals are scored low as they do this drill. That means that the pass from O (the striker) to X2 has to end up on X2's feet. The ball played to O from X1 should be a variety of types of balls. It can be a short ball, long ball, high ball, or chip type of pass and also come from different angles. Playing the ball preferably on one touch to X2 will help the striker get in the game mentally to prepare to score.

Midfielders may have other needs from a similar warm up. X2 could be a defender who needs to play a long ball to X1 to warm up his touch for long passes. Use your warm ups to get your players in the game both mentally and physically but pay particular attention to your strikers. Younger players will need to be reminded more often. As players play at higher levels and gain experience they tend to know what they need to do.

X1---------------------→ O ---------------------------→X2

Diagram 54D: Warm up drill: X1 passes to O (the striker) who has to get the ball to X2 in one touch or two touches to score. O has to think, "Prepare to Score", "Last Touch".

The First 5 Minutes

You want your strikers in the game as soon as possible. Since scoring chances do not occur often, they need to be alert from the starting whistle. Also, the opponent often tends to be over-relaxed or over-stressed depending on the situation before a game and can be vulnerable in the first 5 minutes. You do not want your strikers to miss a golden goal scoring opportunity that can change the whole complexion of the game and turn it in your favour right away. In the 2002 World Cup, Hakan Sukar of Turkey scored a goal in the first eleven seconds of the bronze medal game when he and a teammate pressured the Korean defender right off the kick-off. After having analyzed this goal repeatedly, I could tell that the Korean defender was too relaxed at the start of the game. His body language suggested that he was still enjoying the crowd reaction as the hometown fans gave a rousing ovation to their team's progress in the tournament. Hakan Sukar and his teammate caught the Korean defender off-guard and forced an error that resulted in a goal. That mistake changed the game. It helped silence the pro Korean crowd until they tied the game shortly afterwards only to go down 2-1 again in the thirteenth minute. Early defensive breakdowns helped Turkey win that game.

There is a fine line between reminding players and nagging players. As players get older they do not like being talked to as though they are kids. Strikers can be sensitive. Use your people management skills here.

Picture 54E: In this standard passing drill, the striker can consider this their personal goal scoring drill.

Picture 54F: Canada's Christine Sinclair is a prolific goal scorer who knows that concentrating and being focused in performing passing skills is important for the striker. Les Jones/Covershots

The Power Pass-Shot

With today's new soccer balls that travel faster and longer due to their composition and construction, a shot taken with the front inside of the foot with little follow through can provide more accuracy and enough power to beat many goalkeepers. Many free kicks, penalty shots, and shots from around the box can be taken with a pass-like shot that has enough power in it. The area of the foot to use is the black area of the inside part of the shoe shown in picture 54G. It's important to keep the eyes on the ball and keep the toe up and pointing slightly to the side with this type of shot. Notice the use of the inside of the foot with the toe up in pictures 54H, 54I, and 54J as the player uses the power pass-shot to shoot on goal from outside the box. This type of shot is not to be confused with the full-out power shot I shall cover in chapter 55.

Picture 54G: Using the black area of this shoe, a player can make a hard pass-like shot that has enough power to beat many goalkeepers from around the box. In this type of shot, the player will keep the toe up and pointed to the side and there is little follow through like the one used in a regular power shot as described in Chapter 55.

Picture 54H: Samir Nasri of France scores a goal at UEFA EURO 2012 with a power pass-shot from the edge of the box. Today's soccer balls travel faster and longer due to their composition and construction. A shot taken with the front inside of the foot with little follow through and with the toe up can provide more accuracy and enough power to beat many goalkeepers, as shown. Action Images/Lee Smith

Picture 54I: Atiba Hutchinson tries a power pass-shot from just outside the box. Beating a goalkeeper with this type of shot is more possible than ever due to the composition of soccer balls today. Photo by Les Jones/Covershots

Picture 54J: Ryan Johnson tries a power pass-shot from just outside the box. Notice how he keeps the toe up in this type of power pass/shot. The toe stays up in the follow-through as well. Beating a goalkeeper with this type of shot is more possible than ever due to the composition of soccer balls today. Photo by Les Jones/Covershots

CHAPTER 55

The Power Kick

The ability to kick a ball with power in order to score is sometimes overemphasized but, nonetheless, it is a very important skill that all the best strikers must have. Over 25% of goals still come from power shots and volleys. Most often, the power comes from good contact with the ball and from paying particular attention to keeping the eyes focused on it right up until making contact with it. There are many great books that go into detail about all the proper mechanics of the individual skills needed to play soccer. In this book, I concentrate on the types of feedback you can provide your players when teaching how to shoot with power. The feedback I provide will produce the correct results without too much technical information. That is, technical information that teenagers can relate to and that works. For more information related to technical details of the power kick or volley, I would recommend the book by Hubert Vogelsinger titled *The Challenge of Soccer*.

Vogelsinger's step by step instructions on all the skills are the best I have seen and his accompanying videos are also excellent. He breaks things down for coaches in many different ways and coaches can use his analysis to help coach players on the most advanced skills. Vogelsinger runs successful camps throughout the USA and was one of the most successful pro coaches in the former North American Soccer League (NASL). His methods and details in teaching to kick with power are excellent. His detailed analysis of volleying a ball is also outstanding.

I like his method of teaching young kids how to use the instep to kick a ball properly by making them learn barefooted. Using the toe to kick a ball will hurt when playing barefoot. It's one of the quickest methods of teaching a young player what part of the foot to use. To learn volleying, playing beach soccer is a great way to improve volleying skills as the game is more successful when the ball is played in the air.

Sometimes in North America the opportunity to teach a player correctly at a young age is not there because free play is not a natural occurrence. Often coaches of recreational teams at the youngest ages do not have the technical knowledge to teach correctly. Also, many recreational players don't play often enough on their own to practice the skills that some of the coaches have taught them. With these limitations in mind, I like to speed up the learning process by replacing technical information with giving the players mental and visual cues that produce the desired results quickly and help inspire players to go try things on their own.

When coaching to shoot with power, there are a few things I like to concentrate on. In no particular order, here are the things you should focus on and base your feedback to your players on.

1) Use of the Instep

Players must use the instep or shoelace area of the foot when making contact with the ball keeping the toe down. When kicking for power, many kids in North America aged 10-17 take a typical kick where the support foot drags a bit and the follow through is with the toe up. But if kids had learned to kick with their bare feet at a young age, they would have quickly learned that keeping the toe down was paramount and striking the ball with the instep is the best place to kick a ball because it hurts the least. This would then lead to following through with the toes pointed down. The ankle is pronated. Vogelsinger asks players to pretend they are holding grass in their toes when kicking with power. This forces the players to keep their toes down. When introducing shooting to new players I actually find that girls who have taken ballet seem to find the sweet spot for making contact on the foot quicker than boys do.

2) Eyes on the Ball

The shooters must keep their eyes on the ball. This is a key area to focus on because players will often take their eyes off the ball a split second before making contact. The reaction to lifting the eyes and head to see where the net is or where the ball will go is very strong and very natural. It's so tempting to see what's going on that it's hard to resist the urge. Look for this error, which is more of a mental error than a technical error because the brain knows what to do, but for some reason, it does something else. The key here is that the athlete can physically do it correctly. That's when it gets frustrating as a coach and one reason why scoring is not easy. Our brain quickly forgets and wants to take shortcuts. Sometimes success will still come but room for error increases immensely. I like to tell players to read the logo on the ball.

3) The Location of the Non-Kicking Foot

The location of the support foot should be beside the ball at the moment the kicking foot makes contact with the ball. Focusing on the placement of the non-kicking foot can help you decide what may have gone wrong. If the player's foot is ahead of the ball when contact with the ball is made, then the power created by the leg swing will go into the ground. If the support foot is planted behind the ball, then the body will tend to lean backwards and send the ball sailing high. The key for coaches when analyzing the technique is to focus on where the support foot is when the kicking foot touches the ball rather than where the support foot is when it touches the ground. If the player kicking is chasing the ball, he will need to plant the support foot in front of the ball so that by the time the kicking foot touches the ball; the support foot will be even with and beside the ball. If the ball is coming towards the shooter, then the placement of the support foot should be behind the ball so that by the time the kicking leg touches the ball; the ball is beside the support foot.

4) Volleying the Ball

In the case where the ball is in the air and a volley is necessary, the player should wait for the ball to be at its lowest point possible. When you analyze the volley in slow motion, players are often surprised by how low the ball actually is to the ground at the moment of contact. In real time, it appears the volley contact point is much higher than reality. Planning for a low contact point must occur in the "Prepare to Score" stage of the body movement before the last step.

Now the Real Secrets to Coaching the Power Shot

- The Last Step
- The Support Foot coming OFF the Ground
- The Landing of the Kicking Foot and
- Where to aim

Let's look at each secret separately because it may be the difference between getting good power in a shot and getting no power at all. As I mentioned earlier, the failure of the Canadian National Men's team to qualify for the 1998 World Cup was one of the reasons I started my in-depth research into the psychological factors that affect the coaching of goal scoring. I noticed that too many glorious scoring opportunities went to waste. I also noticed that there wasn't any player that threatened the opposition with a long powerful shot from outside the box. Even though not many goals are scored with the power drive, the threat that someone can potentially score from a distance can put added stress on the defense or goalkeeper in how they defend. Other team scoring opportunities can emerge as a result of having a player who can score with a power shot from a distance.

Having coached the power kick to young players, I found that many players in their teens in North America did not get enough power on the ball due to poor acceleration and momentum going into the kick. I found that those who did kick with the proper area of the foot but were unable to generate power needed some key mental cues to quickly and effectively help them develop power in their shot. As you know by now, I like to call them secrets.

5) The Last Step

In order to generate velocity in the ball, the power or energy that goes into the ball must come from our body. It must flow from our body to the ball through the foot. That means that the foot must be travelling at the fastest possible speed in order to transfer that energy into the ball. The transfer of energy must also be in the direction of the goal. A punter in American football will need to get power into a kick but his goal is to send the ball as far as possible and as high as possible, therefore the point at which the energy is transferred will be different.

In order to develop power the body usually needs a running start. This helps it build up its energy. To pass as much energy from the body to the ball, the body needs to stop abruptly and then transfer that energy to the foot kicking the ball and then to the ball itself. We can actually measure the force that is transferred to the ball during a kick using physics and high speed cameras to measure angles, torque, acceleration, momentum and body velocity. A personal story on this is in the upcoming text box titled, "One day in my life I will never forget..."

Sometimes there is not enough room or time to take a running start to create velocity. Throwing the body forward with a large step can make up for some of the energy not created by a running start. When stopping a forward moving body with a large step, it's important to keep the momentum and transfer of energy moving smoothly to the kicking leg. The player cannot stop completely and lose the momentum gained by the big step. All the built-up power is carried forward to the kicking leg and then to the ball which must be struck at the center or slightly below the center in order to lift it a bit above ground.

In coaching, you will see that the last step may be the easiest way to teach the player to get as much behind the ball as possible to give it power. The size of the last step can drastically help increase the velocity of the ball. When players approach the ball, their last step should be huge: much bigger than the previous steps and with all the momentum that the body has built up going into this last step which literally puts the brakes on while the body transfers its energy to the foot swinging and then kicking the ball. Ask your players to visualize themselves taking a giant last step and throwing everything into their kick. Planning for this bigger step does take some effort. If the player misjudges the location of the ball in relation to his body, he may cram his last step, lose all momentum, and thus get very little power into the ball.

I like to use visuals of players taking that last step just as they plant the foot. Still images of good players kicking with power shows the importance of this last step in power shooting. See Picture 50C from Chapter 50 of Francesco Totti taking a power drive. Focusing on the last step should help improve the rest of the kick, which will include the windup of the kicking leg from a position sharply bent with the heel practically touching the buttock to its unwinding and swing to make contact with the ball.

Picture 55A: Joe Cole of Chelsea is about to take a shot. Notice that the heel of the kicking leg is practically touching his buttock, as it is about to swing downward with speed. This will transfer energy to the ball and give the ball power. Action Images/Toby Melville

In picture 55A of Joe Cole, notice the position of the kicking leg as it begins its swing towards the ball. Also notice that the arms are out for balance. This also looks very athletic. Concentrate on coaching the importance of getting a big last step and many other technical aspects of the power kick will simply fall into place on their own.

ONE DAY OF MY LIFE I WILL NEVER FORGET AND IT INVOLVES A WORLD SUPERSTAR CHAMPION AND THE POWER KICK

It was a cold winter day in February and I was about to leave for a "university reading week break" with my father (Danilo) and brothers (Mark and Danny) to visit Los Angeles, California. Hollywood, here we come!

We were supposed to be at the airport around 3:00 pm to catch a late afternoon flight. But I had an important project I had to start for my biomechanics class. We had to analyze an aspect of human performance using super high-speed cameras and study the results in the lab. Being a varsity soccer player, I chose "The Power Kick". No other student chose a soccer skill, which was not surprising at all.

I wanted to compare a recreational player who played intramural soccer with a professional player. Luckily enough for me, the old Toronto Blizzard was training at our university in February before they went down to Florida for their annual training camp. I talked to numerous players after their training sessions and in particular, the goalkeepers who all identified the late Brian Budd as the player with the hardest shot on the team.

Brian Budd was very supportive and agreed to show up early on the following Monday morning before his training session started to be filmed for my assignment. I was lucky enough to get the player I wanted to analyze. I was also fortunate to have him arrive early so that I could get through the filming and then scoot off to LA. I used 16mm film shot at 100 frames per second to analyze his shot.

At the time, Brian Budd was one of the best known athletes in North America because he won the 'made for TV' World Superstars competition featuring athletes from different sports competing with each other on fitness events. The World Superstars competition was held annually from 1977 through 1982. After the initial competition, it was followed by three straight wins for Canadian soccer player Brian Budd. Budd was not allowed to enter again because of a new rule barring anyone from competing in a World Superstars competition after his or her third victory. His victories were music to my ears as it clearly showed how fit soccer players needed to be in comparison to athletes of most other sports.

After the filming, I turned in the film for processing which would be completed by the time I would arrive back from my holidays for analysis. At around 11:00 AM, I was rushing home to finish packing and getting set for the flight. When I arrived home, the house was empty and no one was anywhere to be found. Shortly afterward, I received a call from my mother (Angela) from the hospital. My father had suffered a major heart attack and was in intensive care. Thankfully he survived and is still with us today.

Unfortunately, Budd passed away in 2008 from a heart attack. He hosted a soccer show on a sports channel called "The Score". His kick was very powerful and showed he possessed all the correct mechanics to get off his booming shot. It was one hectic day that I will never forget. As for the assignment, it went very well and delivered some interesting results and is one reason why one of my favourite skills to teach players is how to kick with power.

Needless to say, our trip to Los Angeles was cancelled and Hollywood is still waiting.

Picture 55B: Wayne Rooney of England just releases a power shot. Notice that his back foot or supporting foot has come off the ground. This is a result of attaining maximum velocity of the kicking foot which carries the body forward as it exerts all its energy into the ball when shooting with power. Action Images/John Sibley

6) The Support Foot Coming off the Ground

The next thing to coach which may help you communicate the importance of the last step is to tell the players that if they have lots of power going into the kick, then their back foot will automatically lift off the ground. In fact, this will be unavoidable because the player will have so much momentum coming off the last step and swing that it will force the body to lift off the ground. In picture 55B, England's Wayne Rooney's back foot is off the ground after taking a power drive.

Keep a close eye on the support foot after the kick has been taken. Coaches like to focus on the ball after the kick. In my power kick analysis with Brian Budd and the non-professional player, it clearly showed that the non-pro player actually stepped backwards after his kick instead of forwards. The support foot stayed on the ground throughout the kick. With a proper power kick, the support foot should lift off the ground and land ahead of where the ball was contacted.

7) Land on the Kicking Foot

When taking a power shot the player should always land on his kicking foot after the shot has been taken. This piece of advice is my most powerful bit of information when coaching the power shot. Players of today are so into looks that I teach power shooting based on how a player should look. Because so much power has gone into the kick, the player's back foot will lift off the ground, which will subsequently have the player in full flight with both feet off the ground. This power will result in the kicker needing to land on the same foot he kicked the ball with. To simplify the explanation, I tell the player taking a power shot to "land on their kicking foot". I remind players who are shooting for power to land on their kicking foot again and again. The funny thing is that it's hard to demonstrate this aspect of kicking in slow motion. I keep reminding them to land on the kicking foot but what some players may end up doing is taking a hop after the kick. It looks funny and I'm sure you have all seen this happen.

The key to teaching this is to get a big last step along with good timing on the approach to the kick. I like to show young players who are having problems with this that landing on the kicking foot looks "cool". The psychology often works better than the expert technical advice. I like to show pictures of what I mean and describe it to them this way:

> ***"When you take a big step, you can see that you will look like you have power built up inside you. The kicking foot is tucked back under your butt ready to explode out with velocity. Then when you make contact with the ball, notice how the eyes are on the ball and the head is down. This makes you look very focused and ready to unleash a blast. Then, see how the back foot lifts off the ground. That shows you had power. Finally, see yourself landing on the kicking foot. Check out the picture. It looks cool. It looks very athletic. It looks powerful and you want to look like this."***

The images of players in full stride can look very athletic. These images make it obvious what players need to do to get power. See pictures 55C and 55D of Hasan Sas scoring at the 2002 World Cup for Turkey. From every angle the power shot looks spectacular when you focus on the power generated by the kick and when you see Sas in mid-flight after striking the ball as he prepares to land on his kicking foot.

Picture 55C: Hasan Sas scores a goal on a powerful volley against Brazil in the 2002 World Cup. He beats the goalkeeper (Marcos) on the near post. His back foot is off the ground as is his kicking foot. He will land on his kicking foot. A well-taken power drive will look gracious and spectacular. Action Images/Jason Reed

8) Where to Aim

When it comes to power shooting, this point gets the most reaction, both from known goal scorers and from young players wanting to learn. The reason is that the great goal scorers feel I'm giving away too many secrets and the young players I'm teaching are surprised by what I say about where to aim.

When you are going to shoot for power with your instep, there really is only one place to aim for. And that's right down the middle of the net. Close to the ground about a foot off the ground is fine. Aiming just a bit off the ground allows for errors and keeps the shot that ends up hugging the ground still powerful.

If I were to film the reactions of young players when I say this, I could produce enough footage for a whole episode of America's Funniest Videos. To most young players what I say about where to aim comes somewhat as a shock. But some of the best reactions have come from players who are or were very very good at scoring. One retired player in particular who played college soccer at Alderson-Broaddus in West Virginia in the US and at the highest possible leagues in Canada during the eighties and early nineties was Johnny Williams. He won numerous scoring titles in the various leagues he played in. Unfortunately he was part of "the lost generation" in North America. He was in between the demise of the NASL, (North American Soccer League) which included players like Pele, Beckenbauer, Cryuff, Eusebio, and Best, and starting a career in life outside of soccer while waiting for a pro league that could pay the bills to start up again. That's a good topic for another book.

His reaction when I first told him about my course and this specific secret of power shooting was at first amazement, then shock that I said it, laughter as he couldn't believe what I said, and finally one of those "how did you know?" responses.

Picture 55D: Hasan Sas pictured taking a power shot in the 2002 World Cup. It doesn't matter which angle you see him take a power shot from. When done correctly, it looks like a piece of brilliance. Picture supplied by Action Images

"Hey," I said, "I used to play goalie, you know!"

It was a moment of enlightenment because we laughed about this simple concept and how he used this secret all the time. We talked about it for a while. Others have reacted similarly but not quite as dramatically. I'm pictured with Johnny Williams in my office in picture 55J.

The reason for aiming at the centre of the goal makes perfect sense. When you look at the area of the foot that the player strikes the ball with in a power shot, it's very narrow. See pictures 55E, 55F, and 55G. The instep of the foot is fairly narrow. As a ball is moving and even spinning, and often in the air, with players around, and with a limited amount of time, what are the chances of a player striking a ball so perfectly that it goes exactly where he aims it at all the time? Chances are not good. You have to go with the odds. Go with the odds!

If players actually aim for a corner, they're going to have to hit the ball perfectly centered on their foot. The point of contact can't be off even a bit. With a moving ball that may be spinning or bouncing, and with defenders nudging them trying to throw them off, what will happen if they mis-hit the ball just the tiniest of inches or centimeters? There is no way the players will actually hit the target right on. In fact, in other sports where a player has to hit a target such as in archery or darts, not all shots hit the bulls-eye. In those sports, there are no defenders trying to distract them, so what would make your players think that they will hit the bulls-eye in a game when the ball is also moving?

New shoe technology is coming out to try and make the perfect part of the shooting area of a foot larger by a shoe company called Concave. I'll elaborate on this later.

Picture 55E: The kicking area of the foot is very small.

Picture 55F: The ball is much bigger than the width of the foot. Hitting the perfect part of the ball with a small foot area is not easy.

Picture 55G: The foot is relatively small in comparison to the ball. Will players be able to hit the ball with the perfect part of the foot all the time to make the ball go exactly where they want it?

In diagram 55H, I have set up two targets for the shooter to aim his power shot at. A red circle in the top corner of the goal depicts one target and the other target is depicted by a blue circle at the centre of the goal and about a foot above the ground. Let's assume a player was to hit a ball perfectly and it would go just inside the post in the red circle where he was aiming for. If the player mis-hit the ball by only a fraction of an inch or centimeter, then the perfectly aimed shot would now be slightly off. Chances are the player will now miss the net on most of his shots taken as shown by blue dots in the diagram.

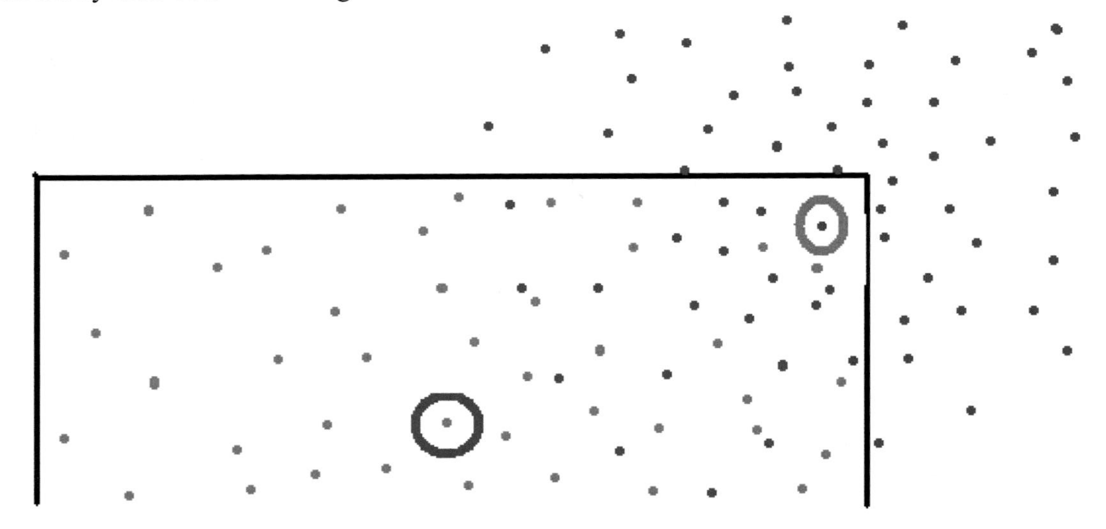

Diagram 55H: If a player aims for the red circle in the top corner, then most balls would probably miss the net if the player missed the target for any reason (as depicted by the blue dots). If a player aims for the blue circle at the centre of the net and a foot off the ground, then most balls will probably still hit the net even if the aim is off (as depicted by the red dots).

If, on the other hand, the player aims for the center of the goal, and hits it right at the goalkeeper, surprisingly enough, his chances to score would be very good because a power shot will be hard for the goalkeeper to stop. In picture 55I, Michael Owen takes a power shot right at the goalkeeper while taking a penalty shot. Notice how both his feet are off the ground. Because the ball has power, it can go into the goal very near to the goalkeeper, therefore why not aim it at the centre of the goal? A player's chances to score on a power shot will be better than aiming for a corner and missing.

Picture 55I: Owen of Newcastle, scores on a power shot while taking a penalty shot. The ball goes in the net right under the goalkeeper. Notice that both feet are off the ground after he has taken the power shot. Action Images/Lee Smith

If the player mis-hits the ball when he aims at the centre of the net and a foot off the ground, he will probably still hit the net as depicted by the red dots in the diagram. Even if it's practically shot right at the goalkeeper, he will not have much time to move.

Think of it this way, what if a striker mis-hits the ball by a fraction of an inch or centimeter either way? In that case that shot that should have hit the centre of the goal would now miss the centre of goal and go somewhere else. Players can't possibly miss the target by 4 yards can they? If the player shoots for the centre of the goal and mis-hits the ball, he would have to have mis-hit the ball enough to send it 4 yards away from centre of goal and 7 feet from the ground not to score. If a player is going to miss the net by that much, then his aim is horrid and chances are he would have never hit the target even if he aimed for the corners.

Based on diagram 55H, I'll guarantee you that the player who hits the net more often in a power shot by aiming at the centre of goal will score more goals than the player aiming for that highlight reel goal in the corners, especially when shooting or volleying with power.

So as a consequence of a slightly mis-hit ball, a player's shot will potentially go in just inside the post or under the bar. Here is what I told Johnny Williams and what I tell players in my course.

> ***"Here is the biggest secret of the day because it's two secrets in one. You can't tell anyone.***
>
> ***Secret # 1.***
>
> ***Aim for the centre of the goal about a foot above the ground. Because the chances of you hitting the ball slightly off from the centre of the instep or someone nudging you and throwing your support foot off are very high – higher than the chances of you hitting the ball perfectly off the centre of the instep. Your power shot will now miss the centre of the goal. There is a good chance your error will result in a beautiful highlight reel goal that enters the goal just inside the post or in the top corner.***

<u>Now here is secret #2.</u>

Without mocking the opponent, celebrate the goal like you would any other goal. But under <u>no</u> circumstances will you tell anyone that you were <u>not</u> aiming for the top corner. If anyone asks, tell them that's exactly where you were aiming."

Well at this point Johnny Williams turned away laughing so hard and he really couldn't believe what I was saying. He said, "No, John, do not go around telling everyone that. For years I told all my friends and fans that I was always aiming for the corners. They believed me. You're going to make me look bad!"

To top it off, I give players a great reason why they should keep this a secret. I tell players this:

"Now remember not to reveal your secrets about where to aim when taking a power drive. Here is another reason why: if you make your competitors believe that you had to aim for the top corners in order to score, then they will believe you and just keep aiming for those highlight reel goals. That's OK because what will happen is that they will keep missing the net more often than scoring. Meanwhile your name creeps up there on the score sheet. And when the scouts look at the statistics, they'll see your name there and not anyone else's. Hey, it's a competitive world out there. Take any advantage you have. Give up your secrets and you could be giving up your place on a team now or down the road."

With this last story, Williams couldn't believe how I was the first to nail this point to him right on the head. We laughed it up and reminisced about soccer over lunch. Williams is doing well in his business life working for Adidas, the company that makes those shoes that players like to score in. He is also coaching in his community and still scoring goals and winning scoring titles in the old-timers team he plays with.

I have watched countless goals while researching my subject and learnt how important where to aim is in scoring. When you see the placement of the support foot, it tells you where the player is intending to aim. When you see the results, they are quite baffling in two ways. A slight spin or bad bounce or contact from another player can throw the balance off enough to direct the ball in another part of goal. The second amazing fact is that so many power shots actually go past the goalkeepers very close to their body. Why risk missing the net when power can overcome accuracy. Remember rules 2 and 3 in scoring goals. Hit the net and don't miss the net!

Picture 55J: Johnny Williams is with me in my office as we discuss the secret of where to aim when taking a power shot. Photo by: Mike Salvatore

CHAPTER 56

Re-Directs

The final category of goals comes from re-directs. Often these goals can be also described as passes and headers. In my analysis, re-direct type goals are goals scored when the ball simply needs to be re-directed to the goal. There is no real passing or heading skill needed beyond getting a foot or head to the ball. In most cases the body acts as a wall which has to be hit for the ball to go in.

I consider all goals scored from headers as goals from re-directs because the ball comes towards the goal and simply has to be re-directed. Some goals off re-directs are scored off deflections. In cases where the player tries shooting the ball at goal by a power shot or pass and it deflects off a defender and goes in the goal, I classify those goals as goals from passes or power shots and not-re-directs. The reason I want to break down goals this way is for communication purposes to clearly show my strikers that goals come from ways they would have not assumed. Most people assume goals are scored from great power shots, amazing dribbling runs and by picking corners and that shooting accurately at those corners is the way to fame. I need to dispel this theory in my players' mind. By classifying goals into passes, power shots, and then re-directs, I can accomplish this task.

The key to scoring goals from re-directs is to get to the end of the ball's trajectory when it gets close to the goal. Re-direct goals are always scored on only "one touch" of the ball. This is because the ball is coming from a different place than from where the player is coming from. That means there has to be a point of intersection for this type of goal to occur. This point is not often easy to predict because the ball is coming at speed and the player is also working to get there at speed. A player could be waiting there for the ball but if a player simply stands there and waits, then it's not likely he will score because a defender will mark him. Therefore the player will need to position himself so that the space he runs into is where the ball will end up. The good goal scorer will need to plan his approach to the ball and be 'bang on' with when to get there while avoiding defenders. That's not easy.

One Second to Score, Nine Seconds to Think!

That's why I like to call scoring goals, "The Last Nine Seconds". Although the contact with the ball occurs in one second or less, the actual ability to be mentally alert needs to be at least 9 seconds prior to contact with the ball. The striker must be super focused both mentally and visually on the path of the ball. He must estimate the ball's velocity and time of arrival at where he plans to intersect it in order to re-direct it at goal.

It's important to get there when the ball gets there. The player needs to place his body where the ball will be as a wall and make sure that the body part he uses to make contact with the ball can re-direct the ball at the goal. As you recall, this is rule #1 to scoring goals: direct the ball at the net. This also means that the player must always know where the net is because re-directs are all "one-touch" goals. The player must ALWAYS know exactly where the goal is or he cannot score these types of goals. Remind your players that the net does not move. It is their job to always know where the net is in relation to their body and the ball. Stress this fact to your players and then remind them that all they need to do in order to score is to keep the eyes focused on the ball right up until the moment of contact. There is no need to occupy the brain with technical detail at this point. Even players who never kicked a ball in their lives can score this type of goal in the game of soccer. A player simply making himself available as a wall to re-direct the ball at the goal can score these types of goals.

How many goals have you seen where players threw themselves at the path of the ball just to re-direct the ball with their body? I've seen players slide as though they are stealing second base in baseball and get a toe on the ball to score. No finesse technique is required there, rather, just a sense of timing and the ability to focus. See picture 56A where Ronaldo scores a goal by diving for the ball to re-direct it into goal in the 2002 World Cup.

Just Get a Head on it!

Picture 56A: Ronaldo throws himself in the air to get any part of his body to the ball off a cross and redirects the ball into the goal for Brazil's first goal against Turkey in the 2002 World Cup. Action Images/John Sibley Digital

Many goals scored with the head are simply re-directed at goal with any part of the head. If the ball is played with some velocity close to goal, a player just needs to get a head on it to score. Quite often the player who scores a re-direct goal off the head does all the wrong things in terms of heading technique that coaches teach their players. For example, they don't use their forehead, they close their eyes, they don't arch their back and they still score. That's because the head simply acts as a wall instead of what we would usually consider a goal from a header. See Picture 56B where Christian Vieri of Italy beats out a number of players to the ball to re-direct it at goal resulting in a goal in the 2002 World Cup. In the picture, his Italian teammate Alessandro del Piero, also tries to get to the ball in the event that Vieri misses it. There is lots of traffic in front of the goal and since the cross has pace and is inside the 6-yard box, all it takes is a glance off someone's head in the direction of the goal for a goal to result. Both Italian players are trying to gain position and get a re-direct. Neither of them is using the proper technique used for heading such as keeping the eye on the ball and using the forehead. In many re-direct type goals, the object is to get any part of the body to the ball as long as it re-directs the ball at goal. Many re-direct goals come off crosses, which I shall look at separately.

Picture 56B: Italy's Christian Vieri gets a head on the ball for a goal against South Korea in the 2002 World Cup. In this picture the ball glances off the side of the head of Vieri to score. Action Images/ Jason Reed

Often the key to scoring is knowing how to get to the ball while eluding the defenders and the goalkeeper. I'll go into more detail on that later in chapter 58 called "3 ways to fame". Whenever your player is approaching the goal to re-direct a ball, keep in mind that it is always easier to get to the ball getting there going forward than going backward away from goal. I want my player to stay focused and think "last touch" and present any part of the body to the ball so that the ball will just go in off the player and into the net. That often means selecting the largest possible area that will be able to get to the ball and handle a deflection or odd bounce. The inside part of the foot for example is better than the instep to re-direct the ball from a low cross because it presents a larger surface area for the ball to bounce off of.

In picture 56C, Wayne Rooney of Manchester United re-directs the ball into the goal with the inside of the foot. He uses the largest part of the foot to form the barrier for the ball to glance off to re-direct it at goal. The important thing is for the striker to get to the ball and focus on re-directing it at goal. Nothing fancy is needed. So many young players (and professional players for that matter) try to swing at the ball and blast it into the net only to miss the ball completely. Or they take their eyes off the ball because they either get distracted or too confident that the job is easy. Strikers cannot miss these types of glorious opportunities because one goal in soccer can decide the game. Soccer is a low scoring game.

Picture 56C: Wayne Rooney of Manchester United scores a goal by re-directing the ball into the goal with the inside of the foot. He uses the largest part of the foot to form the barrier for the ball to hit off. Nothing fancy or technical is needed in this situation but strikers cannot miss these types of glorious opportunities because one goal in soccer can decide the game. Action Images/Lee Smith

Soccer Ball Technology Geared to try and Create More Goals

Judging the speed of the ball as it travels is not easy. In fact it's one of the hardest things to do. Fortunately today, soccer balls are designed so the eye can judge the spin on the ball easier and this allows the player to be able to focus on the ball easier as it approaches. The designs used for the Euro 2004 ball, the 2002, 2006, and 2010 World Cups soccer balls make it easier for players to keep their concentration on the ball because as the ball comes to them they are able to follow it as it approaches. In many previous soccer ball designs where the patterns are very repetitive and blend in together, it's easy to blur the brain, and can cause a slight loss of focus for even the shortest time. Players who lose concentration as the ball is played to them will not be able to make up for lost time if they have not anticipated properly and therefore are too late or too early to get to a ball to score.

Ball manufacturers are studying these minor points all the time in order to improve scoring. All fans want to see more goals to make the game more exciting. The development in soccer ball technology has come a long way in recent times. But occasionally, what may seem to work in the lab does not work in real game situations. In the 2002 World Cup, players often complained that when they struck a ball in the normal way, the new balls tended to rise thereby going over the goal instead of resulting in a shot at goal. This problem was rectified at Euro 2004. In 2006, the seamless ball was supposed to cause less air resistance when the ball was in flight. Despite advances in ball technology, fewer goals were scored in World Cup 2006 than in 2002. For Euro 2008, Adidas manufactured a ball with dimples similar to a golf ball with the intention of adding more power to a player's shot. This was changed again for the 2010 World Cup ball to provide a perfectly round ball with other new features. After the players complained about the flight of the 2010 World Cup ball, it was changed again for UEFA Euro 2012.

Brain Technology is More Important Than Ball Technology to Score Goals!

The object of each new technological advance is to increase the striker's chance of scoring goals. Poor goalkeepers! Unfortunately, the advances have not made a significant impact. Working on the player's state of mind when scoring chances present themselves will ultimately produce more goals. In this chapter, I want to make sure the players know that scoring from re-directs is a big part of the game and needs to be practiced.

Many times re-direct type goals come unexpectedly. For example, a ball may have deflected into a position where a re-direct is necessary to score a goal. How can the coach give players more advice to prepare them to score off re-directs? Many re-directs come off crosses when players are in the right position at the right time. In chapters 57 and 58 I'll provide more hints that will help players score more goals off re-directs from crosses.

From a psychological point of view, coaches need to stress to their players the importance of expecting a re-direct type of goal. Spell out the statistics because they reveal that a third of all goals are scored this way as stated in Chapter 53. To practice this aspect of the game, a player should stay focused in practice. I like to say this to players at my course:

> ***"The number of goals that come from re-directs is much higher than you would expect. Approximately a third of all goals scored can be classified as re-direct type goals. This means you have to be at the right place at the right time in order to score. In other words, you can have no technical skill in how to shoot or kick a ball at all but have the mental skill to know where to be when the ball arrives while eluding defenders and you can score a third of all goals scored in a game. Think about that for a second. Some kid who has never played soccer in his life, can study the game, hear what I have to say about positioning and reading the game to score and voilà, he can become a leading scorer in a short time. Don't let others propel ahead of you because they are practicing hard and smart. If you have the technical skills AND the mental skills to score, YOU can be this leading goal scorer.***
>
> ***You practice for long periods of time on how to shoot to score but usually when in a practice situation you often do not consider the importance of scoring every time on a chance by way of the re-direct. Many players take this nonchalantly and too casually in practice. They play for fun and try hard but they do not bring their brain into the practice with deep concentration and focus on the little things. But it's these little things that make the difference between a great goal scorer who moves up to higher levels and a player who is left at a certain level. Often in close games a winning or tying goal can come from a re-direct because the attacking team may press forward in numbers to create more chances to score. This causes more goals off deflections and re-directs. A non-focused player can miss a great scoring opportunity.***
>
> ***The thing is that most re-direct goals can be scored by anyone. The actual skill involved in scoring them takes no special technical skill: just concentration, determination, and anticipation. Get these habits into your game or someone else will. And at the end of the day, the creative ball dribbler or fantastic power shooter who is cocky but never scores will be replaced by the hard working kid who always happens to be there to score. If you are trying to win a spot on the team, this part of the game can take you there. If you have a spot and won it by talent and skill alone, watch out because the student of the game who is thinking and working hard will catch you. It's a part of the game you can also attain."***

Once again I tell my strikers that this is a secret bit of information. Some coaches whose players have attended my course have seen their players become better practice players– especially those overconfident, cocky, and somewhat hard to coach, strikers!

CHAPTER 57

Scoring From Crosses

Most goals that come from re-directs actually come from crosses. In fact, a surprising number of goals come from crosses. In my analysis, I consider any goal that originates from a ball being played from the side of the goal, and ends up in the net, to be a goal as a result of a cross as shown in diagram 57A. Many players assume that goals that are a result of a cross come from heading the ball into the net. Based on my analysis, most goals from crosses are not from headers. Many goals do come from headers but not the majority. In fact in the 2002 Men's World Cup, not including penalty kicks, 24% of goals came off headers: 36 out of 149 goals. But 8 of those 36 goals (22%) came from one team (Germany).

In the 2006 World Cup, 41% of goals that were scored directly off crosses came from headers. That's less than 50%. More goals did not come from headers off crosses than from headers. Again there is a perception problem for many players, as one would assume that most goals from crosses are headers. What is also somewhat revealing is that the total number of goals coming from crosses overall is higher than one would assume. In the Men's 2002 World Cup, not including goals from penalty shots, 50% of goals came from crosses.

Statistics on Crosses

(These include goals from the head, the foot, or any other part of the body)

In the 2002 Men's World Cup, excluding penalty shot goals

- **50% of goals came from crosses**

In the 2006 Men's World Cup, excluding penalty shot goals

- **42.5% of goals came directly from crosses and 48% of goals started from crosses**

Coach George Pallecaros from "Soccer Tutor", (a UK based software program designed for coaches) produces regular video coaching sessions on their web site. In one of his sessions he had this to say, "I was watching the English Premier League highlights for games played on Sept 13th and 14th, 2008 and I wrote down these statistics for goals scored. Here is what I found:

- Goals that originated from wide areas, i.e. crosses : 14
- Goals that originated from central areas, i.e. through balls centrally: 14
- Goals originating from corner kicks: 4
- Goals originating from free kicks: 3
- Goals from penalty kicks: 3

What does this mean? I thought it was quite interesting because it ended up 14-14."

Thinking psychology and perception, I e-mailed coach George to find out what he meant by 'interesting'.

He answered, "I thought the statistics were interesting because of the high number (of goals) from wide positions and the fact that it was 14, 14. Also I truly believe a good attacking team should mix up play from wide and through the middle so I was pleased with the results."

In fact, when you add in corner kicks and take away penalty shot goals, you can see that over 50% of goals scored during that time span came from crosses of some sort. Even coaches are often unsure of the number of goals coming from crosses because based on what type of goals get most of the attention and get shown over and over again on television, goals from crosses tend not to be as spectacular. In fact, in FIFA's official World Cup 2002 DVD, not one of the "Top Ten Goals" came from a cross. Six out of the top 10 came from shots outside the box. These types of goals are the ones most often shown on game-day highlights on TV. This is not at all representative of the real facts on how goals are scored.

You are probably wondering exactly how goals are scored off crosses. Here are the facts from the men's 2006 World Cup.

The Last Touch of goals scored from crosses from the 2006 World Cup

- Head: 25 - 42%
- Inside of the foot: 18 - 29%
- Outside of the foot: 4 - 6.5%
- Instep shot: 4 - 6.5%
- Toe poke: 1
- Sole of foot: 1
- Shoulder: 1
- Knee: 1
- Thigh: 1
- Own goals: 5 - 8%

TOTAL GOALS SCORED DIRECTLY FROM CROSSES: 61

An additional 8 goals came from rebounds after a cross

If your strikers don't practice scoring goals in the manner that goals will occur in games, then you are reducing your team's chances of scoring. Since you don't have time to work with your strikers individually all the time, you need to make your strikers use many of your other drills and small-sided games as their personal striker drills. For example, they can take one of your practice drills and turn it into a goal scoring drill by thinking differently about how to perform in the drill. In order to convince your strikers of the usefulness of this type of thinking they may need some more convincing as to what you are trying to describe to them. One fact that I like to use to change their way of thinking about scoring drills is to bring in more information about scoring from crosses.

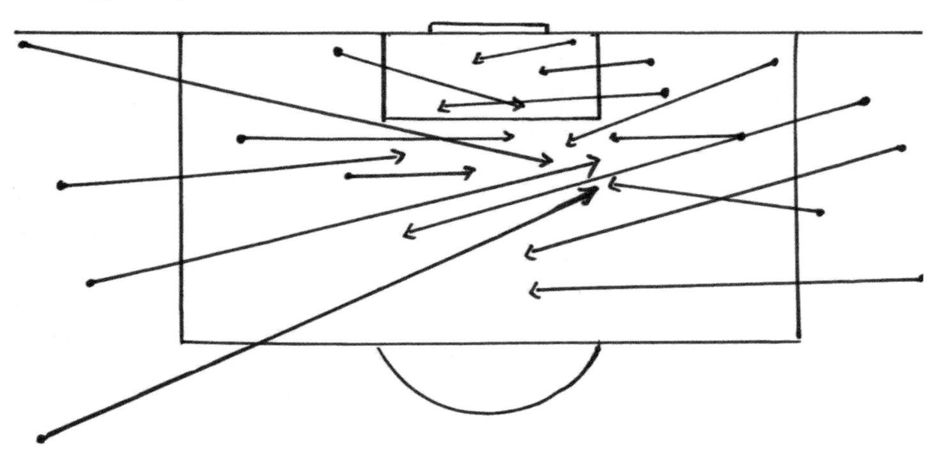

Diagram 57A: In my analysis, I counted all balls played across the goal starting from many different areas of the field as shown, as crosses. This diagram gives you a general idea of where a ball can originate from and be played to in order for me to have classified it as being a cross, for the purposes of coaching strikers and getting my points across to them.

If about fifty percent of goals come from crosses then a striker should spend about 50% of his scoring practice time scoring from a cross. Goals off crosses are usually 'one-touch' goals. Armed with these statistics, a player can immediately understand that becoming a great goal scorer is not all about dribbling and shooting. Since most goals from crosses are actually balls that just need to be re-directed at the goal, then the secret to increasing your team's goal output is to find out how to teach your striker to get to the ball that's played in from some sort of a cross. That really takes more mental skill than physical skill.

Do not under estimate the importance of technique but all the skill in the world will not help players score from a cross if they are unable to anticipate and predict where the ball will end up or when to get there. In many cases, goals come from knowing how to elude a defender to get to the end of a cross unmarked. Lastly, when players get to the ball at the end of the cross, once again all the skill in the world cannot help them if they lose focus and concentration when the ball arrives. Players that can shoot, dribble, pass, and dance with a soccer ball with superior skills will not be able to score if they get distracted just before the ball gets to them off a cross. Without the mental ability to read the game, study the defenders, and keep the eye on the ball as it arrives, players will not be able to score goals in a consistent fashion.

A Coaching Dilemma: Whom do you Play?

I have seen some brilliant players with all the talent in the world who do not have the ability to read the game, focus, and thus just cannot score goals in relation to their skill level. Then I have seen players who looked clumsy, slow, uncoordinated and less skilled on the ball, and yet had the magical ability to be at the right spot at the right time and then be able to concentrate and finish their last touch and become great goal scorers.

For a coach, seeing talented players continuously miss chances can be very frustrating especially when deciding on whom to play. You are compelled to play the player with more talent but when you have a less talented player who seems to have a knack for scoring sitting on the sidelines, it makes you start questioning yourself. This scenario can drive you crazy. Do you play the talented player or the one who is less talented? The choice is usually obvious to the player who is skilled, the rest of the team and all the fans. Yet as a coach, you are trying to win and you often have to go with the player who has the ability to score. If he doesn't, you get blamed for playing the wrong player.

In 2009, I ran my goal scoring course in Edmonton, Alberta, for the Edmonton Juventus U14 boys soccer team. One of the starters could not attend the course but the rest of the attackers did. Rob Mosele, the club president who brought me in to run the course told me that when the substitutes that took my course went in to replace the more talented striker who could not attend, they would continuously score. Mosele said, "Scoring consistently makes a case for a player to be considered as a starter."

Based on skill, the choice is often obvious but the scorer can never be overlooked. As a coach, this is your dilemma. You may give up more scoring opportunities by taking off the more talented player in place of the goal scorer who is less talented. For example, when your less talented player receives a ball at midfield as a target player but loses it, then your team will be defending more often than with the more skillful player on the pitch to start an attack. It's almost a no-win situation. This is always a tough choice for coaches but I keep telling the strikers in my courses that as long as they keep scoring, the decision not to play a goal scorer will become harder and harder for a coach. At some point, the less skillful player who consistently puts the ball in the net will win a permanent spot on the team.

The Edmonton U14 boys team went on to win the National Championship later that year while setting a record for most goals scored in the U14 boys finals competition (41 goals in 5 games).

Statistics can really shed light on why an average player can suddenly start scoring more goals. Practicing and learning to read crosses is a very important factor. If players can learn the secrets and tricks to score from crosses, they will score many more goals. And to think that many of these goals come from re-directs is more amazing. That's because we can teach someone who may not be as talented as another player but is willing to learn to become an instant great goal scorer on the team. If we can take a player with great technical skill and teaching him how to read the game, then we'll have a dynamite striker.

Facts can Clear the Striker's Mind to Practice Better

So what I'm doing then by revealing the facts about crosses to my strikers is giving them a more realistic perception as to how goals are scored. Almost 50% of goals are scored off crosses and less than 50% of them are scored via the head. When you tell players that you are working on scoring off crosses, most players will assume balls will be played from outside the box and from the sides of the field and that they will be practicing heading the ball to goal. Maybe you thought the same. Knowing these statistics can make you concentrate on redesigning your scoring practices to relate them to scoring goals as they actually occur in a game.

Sometimes as a coach I do a crossing drill and get caught up on spending most of my time commenting on the heading portion of getting to the end of a cross rather than all aspects of coaching scoring from a cross. When a young player misses a header off a cross, often the focus is on the quality of the serve or the failed header. Everyone tends to stop when a poor serve arrives. All balls need to be played to conclusion with all players trying hard because less than 50% of goals off crosses come from the head. Why do most coaches and players settle down when there is a poor cross at practice? Defenders need to stay sharp as well because if they are going through the motions after a poor cross, then the attackers can't practice these situations correctly. Focus on maintaining a high tempo in your crossing practices.

A Passing Drill is a Scoring Drill to the Striker

Since you need to work on more than just crossing, you can make your strikers practice their scoring off crosses in many other drills you do. You can take a typical passing drill and tell your strikers to look at the drill differently. Then, you can modify it a bit so that you can bring out some situations which strikers are more apt to encounter in a game. The rest of the players can use the drill to work on their passing while the strikers can use it to work on their scoring. For example in diagram 57B, we have a common passing drill. While the players work on their passing, you will tell your strikers separately that for them this drill is actually a goal scoring drill. Tell them to really focus on the ball to make an accurate pass, which is a goal to them in their own minds. Many crosses along the ground are re-directed at goal like a simple pass. In diagram 57B, the player has to pass the ball to a player across from him and then run to the back of the line he is passing to. Since two lines are going to criss-cross each other at the same time, players have to concentrate on making good crisp passes. The strikers should also try to make their pass a 'one-touch' pass while the rest of the players may not be restricted to one touch.

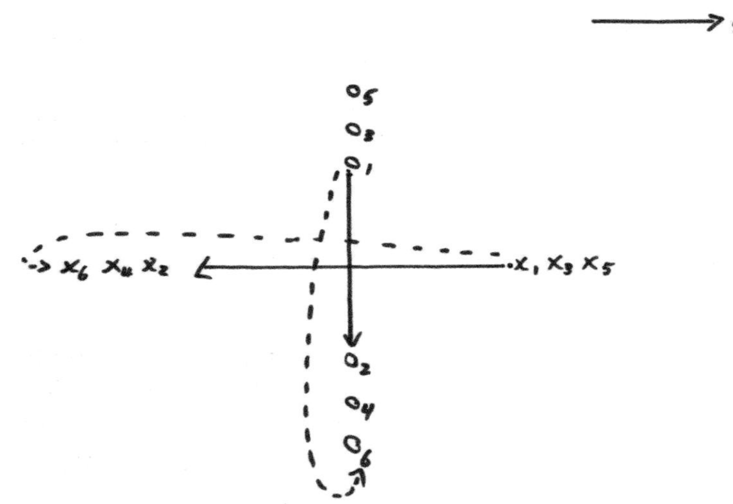

Diagram 57B: In this common passing drill, X1 passes the ball to X2 and runs to the back of the line he passed the ball to. X2 will then pass the ball to X3 and so on. At the same time O1 will pass the ball to O2 and then run to the back of the line he passed the ball to. O2 then passes the ball to O3 and runs to the back of that line. In this simple passing drill, the striker can concentrate on the ball and keep his eyes on the ball to pretend that a successful pass is actually a goal. The striker must be on his toes before the ball gets to him and expect the unexpected such as a bad pass from his teammate. Since most goals are scored on only 'one touch' he must adjust his body to make a successful pass in one touch. Other players may be allowed more. Also, since most goals are scored low, passing drills actually help train the striker to keep the ball low. Your strikers need to look at every passing drill as a goal scoring drill with the same intense concentration needed to score. Another component of this drill is that the passer runs to the back to the line he is passing to. Get on your strikers in particular, to sprint to the back of the line assuming they are following up a ball in case of a rebound.

Now you can take this drill and change it a bit to suit a situation that a striker may face while receiving a low ball along the ground from the side (diagram 57C). In this slight variation of the drill, you will change the order of the passing so that the pass goes to the middle. The player from the line to the side as shown in the diagram, will come forward to intersect with the ball to pass it to the line straight in front of him, which will be where the goal would be. While the rest of the team thinks it's another passing drill, you will be looking for something different from your strikers because you have designed this for them. Ask your strikers to make a small loop to get their body in a better position to re-direct the ball to the next line, which will be like the goal to them. Make sure the support foot points to the target. The pass should usually be made with the inside of the foot. The small loop the player makes or "looping run" is done so that the striker opens his body position to meet the ball at a better angle in which to re-direct the ball at goal.

The point I want to make is that a typical passing drill can also be a goal scoring drill for your striker provided he sees it as such while the rest of the team sees it as a passing drill. As a coach, look for ways to modify passing drills to include goal-scoring situations more often. Since the statistics clearly show that many goals from crosses do not come from headers, then your strikers must concentrate more on getting the job done on all drills because they will replicate a goal scoring chance.

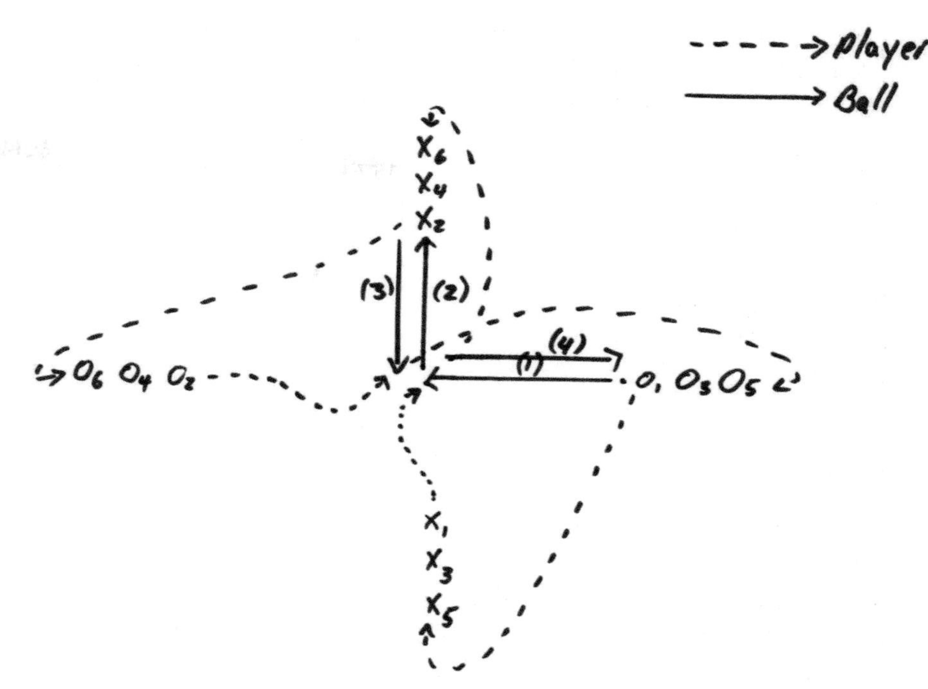

Diagram 57C: Using the same format as the common passing drill from diagram 57B, you can change a couple of things to suit your strikers. Use one ball instead of two. The first pass (pass #1) will be from O1 to the centre of the four lines. X1 will run to the centre to get to the pass and re-direct it to X2 (pass #2). To the striker, (X1 in this case) X2 represents the net. The pass to the centre from O1 will act as a cross along the ground. X1 will run as if to get to the low cross in a way that will put his body in the best position to score. The striker will do this by creating a little loop to change the angle he approaches the ball. He will point the support foot at X2 and get the ball there in 'one touch'. He will run to meet the ball as if a defender were marking him. After the pass, X1 will follow forward as if preparing for a rebound but move to the back of the line he passed the ball to.

Continue the drill with X2 passing to the middle (pass #3) and O2 going to meet the ball to pass it to O3 to score (pass #4). After the players understand where they go you can introduce two balls going at the same time.

Your striker will start to do what is necessary to get the ball to the next player in the drill. But often, when you take the situation from the drill in diagram 57C and add a goal net as in diagram 57D, your strikers will think that they have to blast the ball. Because of this urge, they will play it differently and may miss the scoring chance by missing the net or even missing the ball. Although the drill is essentially the same, players will be tempted to bulge the net and hence miss more often. If they think of it as a simple passing drill, they will score more goals. I want them to really pay attention to making simple decisions based on facts. Statistics will prove over and over again that more goals are scored in the bottom third of the net by way of a pass rather than a hard shot.

I like telling strikers to use passing drills as their personal scoring drills because in most cases, the pass has to end up on the teammate's foot forcing the ball to be played low. In many cases, such as a wall pass, the pass is really just like a re-direct type goal. In diagram 57E, I have plotted the point of entry of the ball when a goal is scored from a cross. Amazingly, 66% of goals scored off crosses are in the bottom third of the goal. The percentage of goals scored in the bottom third of the goal off a cross is higher than when goals do not come from crosses.

Review of my Psychological Approach to Teaching Goal Scoring:

1. I tell players that many goals come from re-directs, which anyone can score.
2. I tell players that 50% of goals scored come from crosses, which need to be re-directed to goal.
3. I remind players that most goals from re-directs are 'one-touch' goals.
4. I remind players that most goals off crosses are scored in the bottom third of the goal.
5. I remind players to 'be prepared to score'.
6. I tell players that to 'prepare to score' the player needs to get his body in the best possible position in order to increase the chances of success.
7. I tell players that they need to focus on the ball and its trajectory by keeping the eyes on the ball.
8. I want players to be at the right place at the right time.

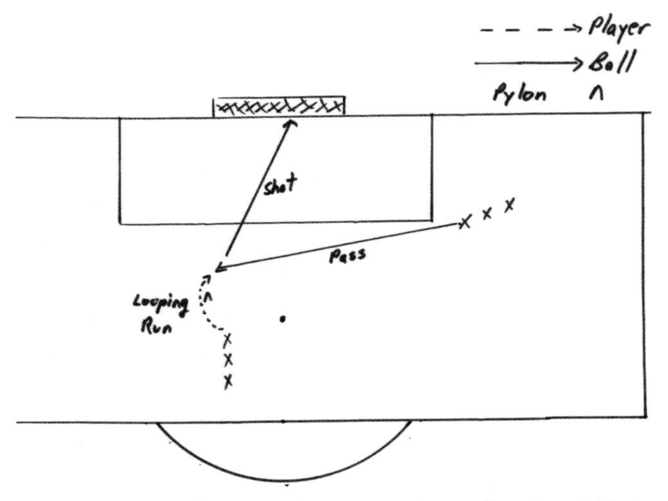

Diagram 57D: In this more obvious crossing and scoring drill, the player receiving the ball can make a 'looping run' around a pylon in order to get his body in the best possible scoring position off a cross. Players want to get their shoulders turned so they are facing the ball as much as possible. What coaches will find from this drill is that many players will try to blast the ball towards the goal to bulge the net. If they think back to the passing drill in diagram 57C, players will remember to pass the ball into the net, keeping it low. Statistics prove over and over again that more goals are scored in the bottom third of the net by way of a pass rather than a hard shot provided the pass is not a hospital ball.

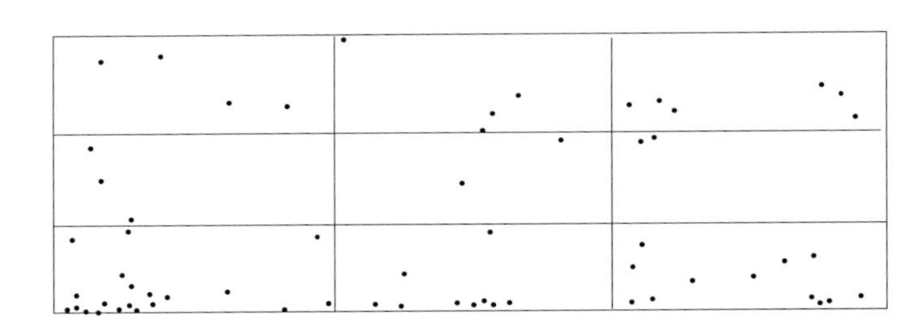

Diagram 57E – Point of entry of ball on goals scored directly off crosses from the 2006 World Cup. 66% of goals were scored in the bottom third of the goal. With almost 50% of goals coming from head height, a huge percentage of goals are still scored in the lower part of the goal.

Gary Lineker, golden boot winner in the 1986 World Cup for England, was one of those players who was very average. He was a reserve at Leicester City when he figured that he had to find an edge in order to make his way up to the First Division (now the Premier League). He started studying the game and found out where he'd have to be in order to get scoring opportunities. People always said that he scored, "those types of goals" where he seemed to always be at the right place at the right time. Lineker's answer to that was that even when the ball didn't get to him, had it made it through, he would have been there. He said that he was at the right place all the time, not only when he scored. The thing is, no one notices when you don't score. That's what teaching players about scoring off crosses is all about. The next step is to give them some help finding the right place and helping them with their timing.

"It's about being in the right place all the time"

"People just don't notice when the ball doesn't come"

Gary Lineker (Reserve at Leicester City) From *Financial Times* article by Simon Kuper (2003)

CHAPTER 58

3 Ways to Fame

In my psychological approach to teaching players to score off crosses I now move on to providing more specific information, in a simple way, as to where I want my strikers to go. What part of the field should strikers get to when they know a cross is going to be played? I want to take some of the guesswork out of the thinking process for my players. No formula is 100% correct but we need to bring a bit of baseball mentality here. That is, using powerful statistics to help players make decisions. Since we cannot signal a play, we need to come up with methods so that the players can quickly recall the statistics and make choices that will increase their probabilities of scoring. It's simple math. You're more likely to score if you go with the best odds.

I want my strikers to know where goals from crosses are scored. In Diagram 58A, I show the location where the last touch occurred in goals that came from crosses from the 2002 Men's World Cup.

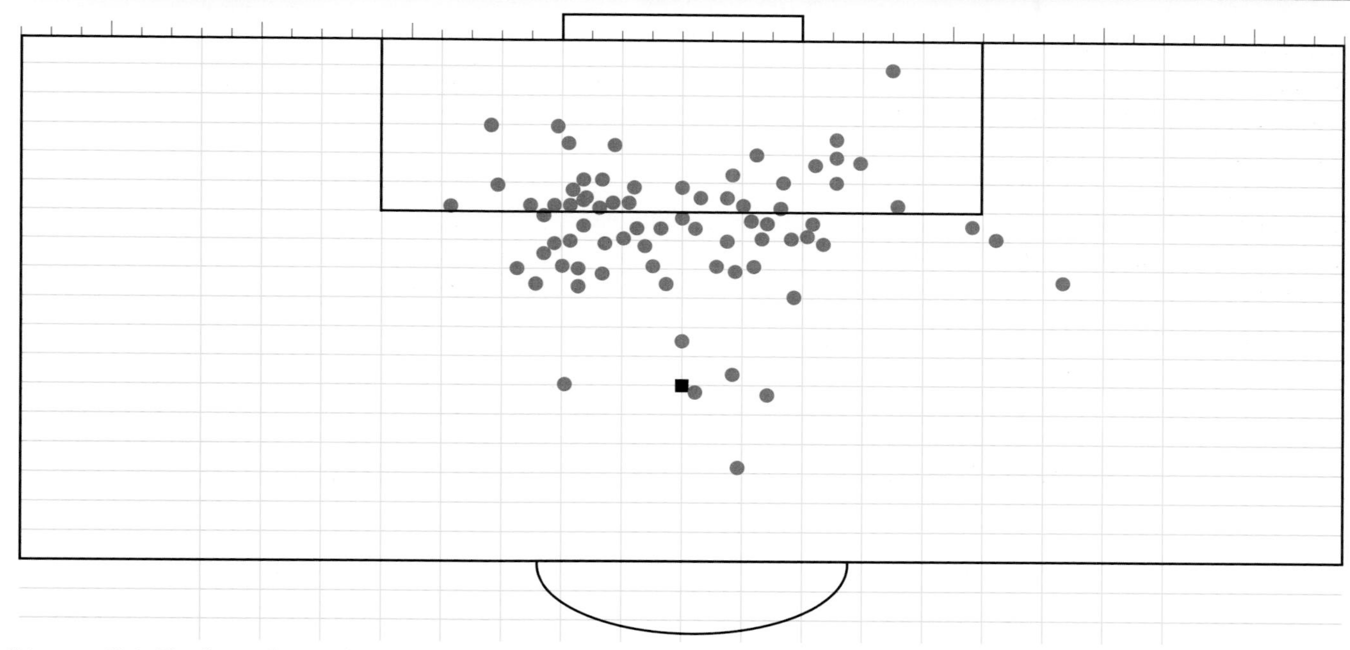

Diagram 58A: The dots indicate where the last touch was played on goals that came from crosses. The reality is that they may be different than one would assume.

As you can see from diagram 58A, there is a very small area where the last touch occurs on most goals scored off crosses. Coaches often talk to their players about going to the near post or far post. But this does not tell the whole story. In fact, based on diagram 58A, there is little difference between goals scored at the near or far post from goals scored anywhere else including the centre of the goal. If all goals were to actually be scored at the near or far post then diagram 58A would look more like diagram 58B.

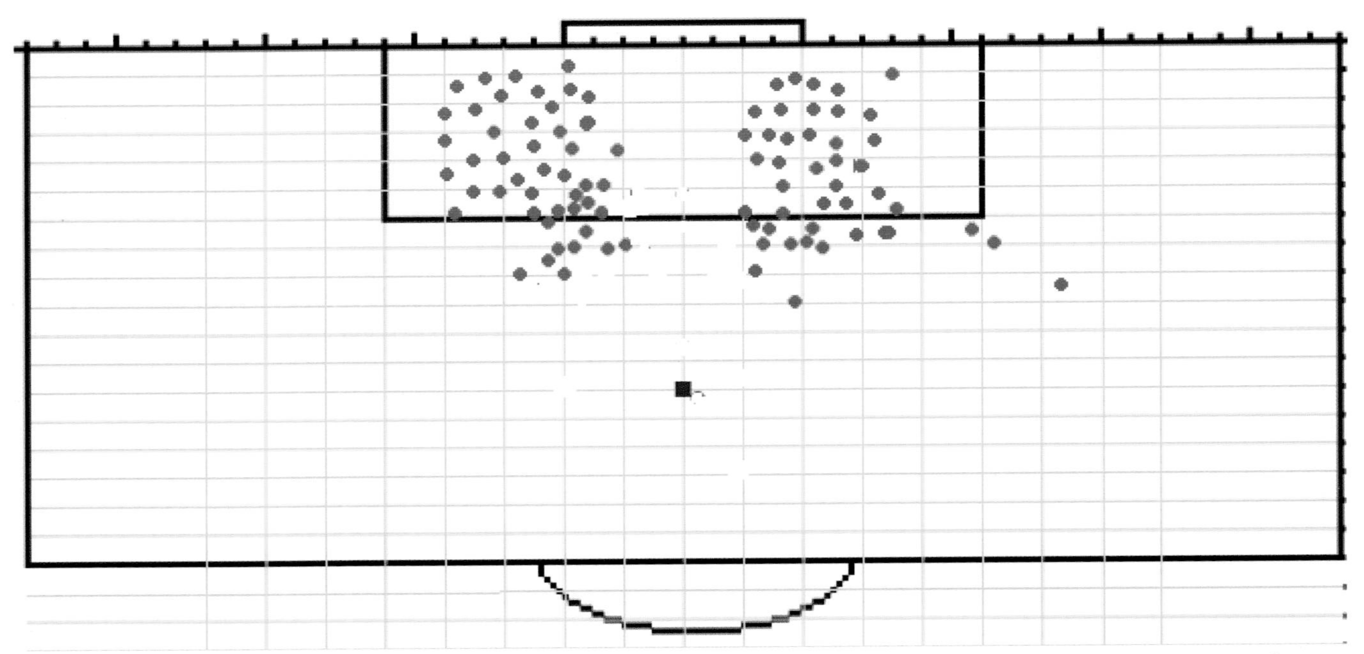

Diagram 58B: Based on coaches and sports announcers talking about near and far post runs and crosses, players may assume that most goals from crosses come from these parts of the goal area.

Once again there is a perception problem here on where players need to go. Coaches ask players to make near post or far post runs knowing that those verbal cues will help determine the path to take to goal and not necessarily define exactly where the goal will come from. But what we say as coaches and what young players interpret in their brain is not always the same. Young minds take things more literally. That's probably why parents and teenagers have a communication problem in their everyday lives. So, in my course, I redefine some concepts and clarify what I want my strikers to do so that there is a greater probability for a goal.

To start with, I want my players to know where goals from crosses come from. The statistics clearly show that most goals from crosses come from a very small area. There is not much difference in where the goals are scored from in terms of goals scored by the head or by the foot. In the 2002 World Cup, 66% of goals scored from crosses came between 5 and 8 yards out from the goal line. When you add a yard either way you find out that 85% of goals came from between 4 and 9 yards out from the goal line.

When I looked at goals that came from outside of the posts, assuming you draw a line out from the post towards the centre of the field, I found that most goals were scored no more than 1 yard away from either side of the post. A whopping 86% of goals were scored in this area. So where to go to increase a player's chances of scoring is quite clear. No closer than 4 yards away from goal and no farther than 9 yards away and in a 10-yard area no further than 1 yard away from either post. The visuals are quite clear on this and the statistics were similar for other World Cups and league games.

The diagram (58B) showing where players are led to think goals off crosses are scored does not represent reality: most goals are not scored in the near post and far post areas.

In my course, I actually plot out an area using cones to indicate where the last touch usually comes from on goals from crosses as shown in Picture 58C. I want to make this perfectly clear in my strikers' minds. This is what I tell my strikers:

> ***"Take a look at where your last touch should be in over 85% of goals you will score off a cross. Do not get any closer to the goal and note that it's not really just the near post and the far post. It's the middle of the goal area as well."***

Picture 58C: In this view, I have outlined the edges of the area where most goals are scored from. The last touch on most goals scored off of crosses comes from inside this area. I want my players to clearly visualize this and know where this area is. Photo by DeBenedictis 2009- (Special thanks to the Pickering Soccer Club in Ontario, Canada, for use of the turf field for the photo shoot.)

Knowing where goals come from is only part of the teaching progression for scoring off crosses. Players with this information can still miss scoring chances if their timing is off. Rather than using near post and far post too often, I like to be more specific in where they need to go. In my analysis of goals off crosses I found three ways to score and I like to call this approach "Three ways to Fame". This terminology is easy to remember, catchy, and should tell players to concentrate on a few things as they plan their run into the scoring area. Here are what I consider the "three ways to fame".

"Three Ways To Fame"

1. In front of defenders: Be first.
2. Behind defenders: Be last but be there.
3. Delayed and dropped back: The "magic spot" or blind spot or sneaky position.

I will look at each one in a bit more detail. Remember that the coach needs to connect with the strikers in any way possible to help them time their run and get to the right place. The coach also has to offer suggestions as to how to elude defenders. Once again, use a lot of one-on-one coaching with your key strikers. What you will tell one player may not work with another, and vice versa.

1) In Front of Defenders

An analysis of goals from crosses clearly shows that many goals are scored when the attacker gets to the ball before the defender. These types of goals are almost always re-direct type goals. The striker must time his run so that he manages to get a part of his body to the ball just before the defender does. Often, the player who scores the goal comes from slightly behind the defender and suddenly appears to beat the defender to the ball. Often, this catches the defender by surprise. That is why I like to teach players to make "looping runs" as they get set to attack the ball as it is crossed.

"Looping runs," means that the attacker actually runs away from the intended location of where the goal is going to be scored. This is done in order to prepare the body so that it approaches the ball in a position so that it is facing the ball and the goal. It helps the player get his shoulders square to the ball. Running away from the ball (even the tiniest of loops or steps) before it is crossed also helps the player attain a position where he can see the play better and predict when the ball will be crossed by a teammate. Finally, a looping run helps the attacker elude the defender because the defender must keep his eyes on the ball while trying to figure out where the attacker is.

As shown in picture 58D, if the attacker is slightly behind the defender then the defender will have a hard time keeping his eyes on both the striker and the ball. This can allow the attacker to suddenly sprint ahead of the defender to get to the ball first. It also puts the striker in a position to change his path to goal if he thinks there is a better chance of scoring by scoring from behind the defender (the 2nd way to fame). Decisions will have to be made quickly based on the position of the defenders and the player crossing the ball. Packing a defense may be one way to prevent a goal as shown in picture 58D although goals do result from these situations.

The striker should decide which defender he will need to get in front of in order to score. Coming from behind that defender or his blind side can have a psychological effect on him. If a defender cannot see the striker, he may get a false sense of security. The defender may feel that he has more time and space than he actually has to clear the ball. Often in goals that are scored from 'in front' of defenders, the defender will stand in one location to clear an oncoming ball rather than go meet the ball. Suddenly, when it is too late to react, the striker will jump in front of that defender to be first to the ball and score. In these types of goals, the body reaction from the defender is clear. He knows he should have beaten the striker to the ball because he started with good body position to clear the ball. But he failed to do so because he didn't think the striker was that close behind him. Once beaten to a ball in front of him that results in a goal, he feels down, as he knows the keeper will look at him with a hopeless look, putting blame on him without saying a word. He also knows his coach will look to him for answers. It's a psychological letdown that can be taken advantage of again later in the game.

Picture 58D: Go behind to get in front. Before working to get in front of a defender to beat him to a ball it's best for the striker to get behind him in his blind side. Two Celtic players are positioned behind Roma defenders as they await a cross while another is trying to run behind his defender as he prepares for a potential cross. Defenders will have a hard time keeping their eyes on the ball and the striker at the same time. Amazingly, even with a packed defense, often goals will result by running in front of someone. DeBenedictis/2004

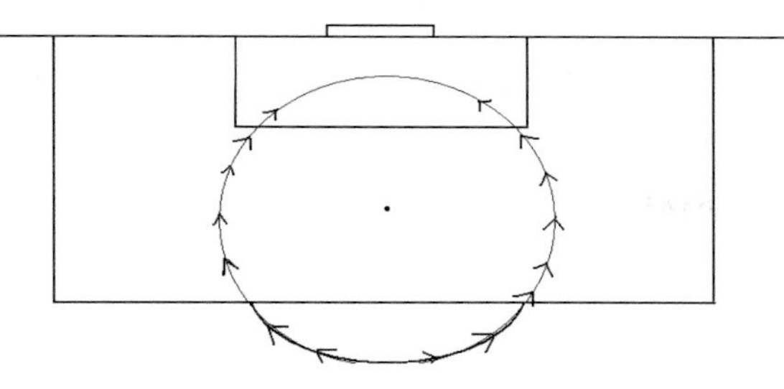

Diagram 58E: "Going round the bend" is one way to get your strikers to make runs into the box that help them get their body into a better scoring position. It also helps players learn to come from behind defenders or on their blind side. Ask your strikers to imagine that the D is part of a full circle. Ask them to follow the D and its continuing imaginary circle as they approach the goal. If the ball is coming from the right side of the field, then the player takes the path created by the left side of the D and vice versa.

Picture 58F: Cones laid out on the field give a good visual image of "going round the bend" or to make a "looping run" to get blind side of defenders and to help get the body turned towards the ball so that converting a cross can be made easier. The actual location of each run will vary based on the circumstances, but the idea of how to approach the goal is what we're looking to coach.

Picture 58G: Shown from another angle, the player, Lucas Caridi from the Pickering Soccer Club, shows how to follow the bend and the importance of not getting too far ahead of oneself. Players approaching the goal to receive a cross must be patient and wait for the right opportunity to run quickly to get to the key goal scoring area as shown in figure 58C. Waiting back in the box is more effective than waiting too close to the goal.

The "looping run" or start of the approach towards the goal area is an integral part of coaching strikers to get to the key areas to score off crosses at the right time and in the best body position to make it easier to re-direct the ball to goal. Darren Tilley, former top goal scorer and professional player in Toronto and with the Rochester Raging Rhinos said that he went "round the bend" in his approach to goal. Tilley said, "A coach in Britain once told me to go around the bend, which meant to follow the natural curve of the D at the top of the penalty box. Extend the circle of the D as if it was actually a full circle and follow its path towards goal. It prepares you to get into a better position to score and gets you coming at goal from behind defenders." (see diagram 58E)

Whether you call it a "looping run" or "going around the bend" or any other way, the objective is the same. Many players, especially young players, just take the shortest route to goal and drive straight for the goal. Unfortunately, this type of run makes it harder for players to see where the ball is coming from. It also makes it difficult for the player to convert a cross and re-direct it at goal when the intersection point between the ball and the player is at a 90-degree angle. This does not mean going as wide as this imaginary circle all the time or even most of the time. Sometimes there is little time to do a major loop but the players must always attempt to get their body around in such a way that, if they time their runs correctly, they can convert the chance more easily. Making a looping run is effective for scoring goals when the striker needs to get in front of defenders and also when scoring from behind defenders. The cue "looping run" or "going round the bend" is about thinking about how to get into the correct body position and preparing to score.

To make sure players understand this concept, lay out cones on the field as shown in picture 58F and 58G. Young players will also have a tendency to get ahead of their teammate who is about to cross the ball. They must have patience when heading towards the goal. To help them make the right decisions in a game I tell them that they should never be ahead of the ball while awaiting a cross. They can always speed up to go forward to make up the distance needed to meet the ball while a ball is in motion. Being ahead of the ball practically eliminates the opportunity to score if the ball is played behind the striker.

Pick out a Defender

Once I make sure players understand how I want them to approach the goal with the body in the best position to score, then I specify what I mean by scoring in front of defenders. Scoring by getting in front of defenders or being first to the ball is often called a near post run by coaches. I like to give my strikers more specific details, which more accurately explain that goals are not always scored on the near post by beating a defender to a ball. They also occur at the centre of goal and at the far post. One of the ways to fame is to score goals by getting in front of a defender. Players have to do their best to get a half a step ahead of a defender so that they can get a foot or head to the ball before the defender does at the moment the ball comes. The last touch is not necessarily at the near post but rather just in front of a defender. Sometimes, the ball is played behind one defender but still in front of another defender. Your strikers must identify which defenders they must beat to the ball and then be able to read how fast these defenders can move. Then the strikers must figure out what they need to do to beat the defenders to the ball by coming in front of them just at the last second.

This is not easy and will require some deep concentration in predicting the path of the ball as it approaches. If the striker gets there too early, the defender can take up a position that will allow him to block the re-directed ball. If the striker gets there too late, the defender will beat the striker to the ball or be close enough to block the re-direct as well. Timing is everything. Practicing crosses is essential, but at practice the strikers must be in deep thought to always try and score. They need to analyze when they failed and try to correct how they read the cross and the defenders. An unfocused player at practice will not be able to learn how to make quick decisions necessary in a game.

Pay Attention to the Support Foot on a Low Cross

Technically, the players must present an area of their foot or body so that the ball gets re-directed at the goal. When scoring from in front of defenders the last touch will be relatively close to the goal as shown in diagram 58A. This also means that the ball will often just need to be directed at goal to score and no additional power should be needed to beat the goalkeeper. Missing the net because players are trying to kick the ball with power must be unacceptable to you. Let the players know this. They are often too close to goal for the goalkeeper to be able to stop the shot. And finally, in cases where players miss with the inside of the foot, pay particular attention to the placement of the support foot. Make sure they turn it at the goal. This will make it easier for them to re-direct the ball at goal. It will also help them use their body and shoulder to shield off the oncoming defender (See picture 58H).

Picture 58H: Note that the player who scores (White #10) is now in front of the defender and is about to point his support foot at the goal. Pay attention to this little point when coaching players to convert low crosses with their feet into goals. The goal, not shown, is to the right of the photo. The ball was played to the player from the left side of the goal and is considered a cross. The attacker, # 10, came up on #4's blind side to surprise him and has good position on him. The support foot also acts as a block. Attackers don't always have time to plant this support foot but the mind must be thinking about turning this foot to re-direct the ball at the goal. Also note the second white attacker. He is looking to get in front of his marking defender, #2 and behind #4, should the ball get past both his teammate and the defender. Photo/DeBenedictis/2009

Often, there is no time and space to get a support foot in front of the defender. It may be necessary to lunge at the ball with the outside of the foot closest to the goal with one leg to beat the defender. The important thing to tell your players about scoring in front of defenders is to identify which defender they need to get in front of in order to score and concentrate more about that aspect of scoring instead of about the near post. Also, with a clutter of players usually around the goal area, a player may find it easier to focus if he is picking out which defender he should look to get in front of in the event that a ball is played there.

2) Behind Defenders

The second type of goal scored from a cross comes when the attacker is behind the defender scoring from a ball that has usually crossed the front of the goal. In this type of goal the defender has not been able to get to the ball and the ball travels across the goal area unobstructed. A missed opportunity in this type of cross upsets coaches more than anything. How often do you see a ball crossing the whole goal and the attacker was not at the end of the ball behind the defenders to tap in the easy goal? It's most frustrating when an attacker was in proximity but did not plan to be behind the defender to tap in a goal. Often, the striker lost concentration of what to do and gets lost in "nowhere land" waiting for the cross in an area that will not likely result in a goal being scored. The alert player will decide which players to run in "front of" or which players to be prepared to run "behind", should a ball arrive. This type of thinking will keep the player mentally alert.

The goal scored by running behind defenders is often called the far post run. For a goal to be scored at the far post, the ball probably had to travel past some defenders, behind them, and out of the reach of the goalkeeper. Knowing the scoring areas from diagram 58A, the striker should start to prepare to decide where to go as the possibility of a cross presents itself. The furthest players from the ball will need to make their decision based on the position of their teammates who are closer to the player crossing the ball. Teach your players to see what their teammates are doing. For example, if one player is running to get in front of a defender, then the furthest player from the cross should prepare to get to a ball that may be played past that defender. In picture 58H, the second attacker is looking to get behind defender #4 and in front of defender #2. It's often quite amazing how many balls go past defenders and there is no one there to score an easy goal. In some cases, two players run to the same space. This is not good and a failed goal scoring opportunity is due to bad decision-making and not lack of technical skill.

Defenders are only human. Their legs are not 10 feet long. They cannot cover all possible crosses. Tell your players to stay alert to get behind defenders to score. While this may occur at the far post, it can also be at the near post behind the defender at the near post. The secret is to elude the defender.

Part of the secret for an attacker to elude a defender is making the defender believe that the attacker is in a different spot than he really is. This deception can result in the defenders losing focus of where they are in relation to the striker and ball. If the defender cannot see the ball and the striker at the same time, it makes it difficult for him to be correct in his decision making process all the time because part of his decisions will be made based on assumptions. When defenders lose focus on a cross because their attention was on the perceived location of a striker that they are supposed to cover, then they may react slowly to a cross. A good attacker will have a feel to where the ball will end up. The striker will need to clear the path to that location by taking his defender away in another direction. Sometimes the defender is taken away mentally and not physically. As stated earlier, the looping run helps the attackers distract the defenders because the attackers will get on the blind side of the defenders. Alert strikers can prepare to sprint to get "in front of" defenders or prepare to get "behind" defenders if they think the defenders will not be able to get to the ball.

Do not Wake up a Defender

Another part of eluding defenders is to deceive the nearest defenders so that they do not think that the players behind them are actually there or that they will be there when the ball arrives. This deception can cause the defenders to get too comfortable with their position in relation to the ball and the attackers. Clever attackers will not make their run too early which can 'wake up' the defender to mark them.

The goal scored from behind defenders can also be a goal scored in front of another defender. Have your players think 'in front of' or 'behind' in order to help them predict where to be in order to score from a cross. Practice and more practice will help players judge correctly. Often, the player who is crossing the ball and the striker must be in sync as to where the cross is going to go. Perfectly timed runs can be difficult to defend especially in goals scored in front of defenders.

Many young players often rush into the goal area only to get there too early and too close to the goal. A ball played into the goal area that no one gets to is a tragedy especially if a striker made a bad decision in his run and got too close to goal. I often tell players who are responsible for scoring from behind defenders to hold their runs towards goal because they can always move forward and speed up to get there. They should be able to see if a ball will potentially clear everyone and thus give them the opportunity to score from behind defenders. They will have more time to react when running behind defenders to score than when running in front of defenders. Goals scored in front of defenders will need a quicker start than goals scored from coming behind defenders.

A Brilliant Goal that Doesn't seem that Special at First but is "6 Seconds of Magic!"

In the 2006 World Cup, Argentina beat Serbia and Montenegro by a score of 6-0. They totally dominated the game with some brilliant attacking decisions combined with wonderful skill. Everyone talks about the goal that involved 25 consecutive passes as one of the best World Cup goals ever, which by the way would have meant nothing had the last touch not gone into the net. But Crespo scored the goal that really defines this chapter and the next. It was "6 seconds of magic". I have summarized the goal in diagrams 58I and 58J. Argentina is pictured in navy blue and Serbia & Montenegro is in white.

The play starts on the left side of the field with Crespo offering himself as a target at the top of the D. His central attacking teammate is behind him. The ball is played up the left wing to Messi. Immediately, Crespo turns to run away from the ball as if "going round the bend". He runs behind the defender at the top of the box noticing that his teammate is making a run to the goal area. Crespo quickly decides to go behind all defenders as he sees two defenders follow the run of his teammate.

At the start of his run away from the ball, he moves at half speed. He quickly turns his head to face the ball. Because he runs behind defenders he notices that potential marking defenders are watching the ball. While his nearest defender is watching the ball he makes his move to sprint around the bend to get behind him. At this point, the defender notices him but he has lost a step on Crespo because Crespo deceived his intention. As the ball goes up the wing and is ready to be crossed, the defender tries desperately to catch up to Crespo. The ball is crossed and no other player gets to the ball as it comes across the goal due to Messi's precision cross. The defender who tries to catch Crespo lunges desperately to intercept the pass but it's too late. Crespo is there to direct it into the goal. In the end 4 players beat 7 defenders and a keeper to score with intelligent play.

From a technical aspect, the most important part of scoring from behind defenders after a cross is to focus on the ball because there will be lots of visual distractions as the ball comes across the goal. The view may even become partially obstructed at times but if your players can block these distractions out then they will not miss the opportunity. The actual final touch on the ball will probably be easier than for other types of goals. The challenge is to not let other players' movements take your players' focus off the ball.

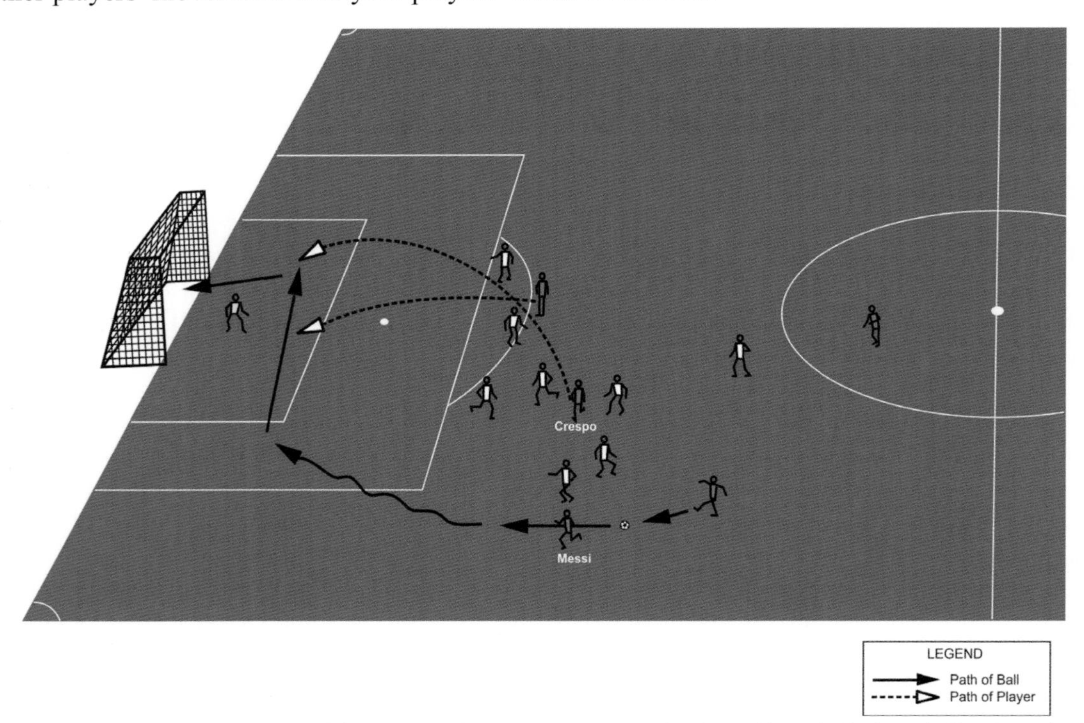

Diagram 58I: Argentina's Crespo scores a goal from a cross by Messi. Crespo makes himself available for a ball to feet when his teammate has the ball in the midfield. Once the pass goes up the wing instead of to his feet, he takes off away from the ball to run around and get behind defenders as he sees a teammate go to the near post. It takes between 5 and 6 seconds from the moment the ball was played up the wing until his last touch to score. Illustration by Jo-Anne Godawa

If we look at the same goal by Crespo from another angle (diagram 58J), we can see how easy it is to miss the ball as the last touch approaches. The ball actually went under the leg of the nearest defender to the crosser (Messi). The ball went by the goalkeeper's left, then past two other defenders who were in the line of sight between Crespo and the ball as the ball made its way across the front of the goal. Crespo also had a visual distraction from the last defender who slid to try to intercept the ball and may have actually touched it a bit. Crespo maintained his focus to redirect the ball into the goal despite having 5 players close to the ball trying to distract his attention. In fact, his own teammate blocked part of his view of the ball as he fell in front of the goal. A world class goal by a world class player.

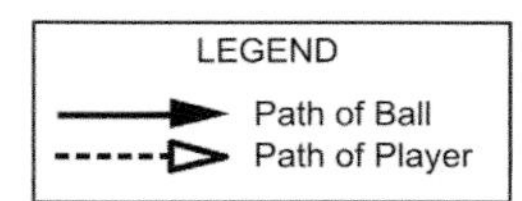

Diagram 58J: Crespo's goal from the opposite angle. Note the position of Crespo, the eventual goal scorer in this diagram at the moment the ball is crossed. The ball actually went under the leg of the nearest defender. It went past two other defenders who were in the line of sight between Crespo and the ball. The ball made its way across the goal and went behind the last defender who slid to try to intercept the ball and may have actually touched it a bit. Crespo maintained his focus to redirect the ball into the goal despite having 5 players close to the ball trying to distract his attention. In fact, his own teammate blocked part of his view of the ball as he fell in front of the goal. A world class goal by a world class player. Illustration by Jo-Anne Godawa

This goal was an incredible goal from a psychological and mental perspective. Crespo had to make numerous decisions in the 6 seconds that it took from the ball not being played to him to his run and then his last touch. He made lots of quick decisions, some instinctive. This is why he's on one of the world's best teams.

This is what I tell players:

> ***"I'm always baffled by the amount of players who let distractions affect their performance in getting to the end of a cross behind defenders. Once the ball is in flight it is not going to change. Focus your full attention on the ball and then simply re-direct it at the goal. If a ball does get deflected and causes you to miss, that's OK. You probably would not have scored anyway. Just don't miss the ball when it gets to you unobstructed."***

The Wrath of the Coach will be Coming

Scoring behind defenders with timely looping runs also cause defenders to lose confidence for the rest of the game. When defenders get beat because they did not pick up an opponent that they should have, they will probably get the wrath of their coach, keeper, and fellow defenders. After Crespo's goal, one of the defenders who did his job by marking his man was clearly upset at his fellow defender for allowing Crespo to get behind him to score. What psychological effect did this have on the defender for the rest of the game?

3) Delayed and Dropped Back ("The Magic Spot")

The final way to fame from crosses is to find the special spot where a ball is likely to be played or end up after a cross that is different from the previous two places to go to. I'll call this spot away from defenders, "the magic spot". In hockey this spot is called, "the slot". It's not near post or far post. This magic spot is often in front of the last row of defenders and behind or beside the location from where the ball is coming from. This magic spot obviously changes as the ball moves but it's a key goal scoring area. Often players move to this spot late knowing that it's the spot to get to. On other occasions the attacker gets ahead of this spot and moves backwards into it. The striker who is looking for this area of the field must adjust himself as the ball moves and must always see a clear path to this spot from where the ball is going to be at the time of the cross. In some cases, a defender occupies this "magic spot" but by the time the ball is played to it, the defender will have vacated this spot.

As a guide I'll say that this "magic spot" is at least three yards away from the striker at all times until the ball is actually crossed or played there. Usually it is ahead of or to the side of the striker. Based on picture 58C, the magic spot is towards the back part of the main area where goals are scored from crosses. In some cases it is even outside this area. This means the spot is usually 7-11 yards away from the goal. The strikers may not be able to see the ball clearly from where they are as they move into the goal scoring area since the view to the ball may be blocked by opponents but the ball will eventually have a clear path to the "magic spot". This spot is usually most noticeable when the ball is deep into the attacking zone and played backwards or sideways to it. Diagram 58K gives you a better idea of where the "magic spot" may be. Please note that it moves based on the position of the ball and the defenders and teammates. The striker must find this area when this cross is "on". The diagram explanation will give the coach some guidelines of what is happening when goals are scored from this area.

Diagram 58K: The "magic spot" or area that's dropped back from the defenders is shaded. From the defender's point of view, it's in front of the last line of defenders. The eventual goal scorer will be at least 3-yards away from this spot before the ball is played into it. Both A3 and A2 can score from it but only one of them should go to the spot. It's a dangerous area to leave vacant therefore almost every goal scored from this spot is a one-touch goal. As the ball is played there, defenders at the last line will pressure and defenders coming back to defend will also pressure. If more than one touch is necessary it will be because of a weak pass that has allowed defenders to close this space down too fast. In such an instance, the striker may need a touch to change the shooting point.

Another important factor when finding this space is to note that most defenders (D1- D2- D5) will be facing the ball and not see the striker because they will have their eyes on the ball. The defenders who will see the eventual goal scorer (D3 and D6) will think that other, closer defenders, will pick them up and therefore let their guard down and not assume responsibility for them. Defensive mental errors can be created when the striker approaches the magic spot from the blind side of defenders. Illustration by Jo-Anne Godawa

How do you coach a player to find this spot? That's not always easy because it moves and the striker creates it in the course of play. The striker must read the game to be able to find this spot at the right time. The teammate with the ball has to have the vision to see it as well and find the striker. If the striker goes to this spot at the right time, the teammate with the ball will be compelled to pass it to the striker heading there most of the time because it truly is a place to score from. Goals from this spot will be further from the goal than goals scored from 'in front of' defenders or 'behind' defenders. You want your players to look for this space and plan to get there at the best possible time. Getting there too early will make it easy for defenders to cover the player. Getting there too late will mean that the striker has not read the teammate with the ball properly. Generally your striker should look to get to the blind spot of the defender covering the near post. The striker will have to be patient when moving into this area so that the back defender feels that he is not a threat or that someone else will cover the striker.

When moving backwards or sideways to this space, the striker may have to "check", or pretend to go in the opposite direction before quickly moving to the 'magic spot'. Checking means to fake to go in another direction in order to elude or flatfoot a defender before heading for the space to try to score from. A check can be a few steps or as little as half a step.

This special area is always moving and not easy to find. Great goal scorers can find the 'magic spot' and when the ball gets to them, they are going to be under extreme pressure to score because the near post and far post defenders will both quickly attack them to block their attempt at goal. Also, other opponents from the side or behind them will also try and deny them the shooting opportunity. And finally, this magic spot will disappear in a flash. Good goal scorers have to convert quickly and "be prepared to score", because if they are not, the defenders will close this area down quickly as it's too dangerous an area to allow a player to stay unmarked.

Picture 58L: Trezeguet finds the magic spot in the Euro 2000 overtime final to score the golden goal to win the Euro 2000 Championship for France over Italy. The cross comes from Trezeguet's left in this picture. He moves to this spot after faking to go somewhere else. Action Images/Peter S. Bennett

Italy lost in the Euro 2000 Final by way of the Golden Goal when David Trezeguet scored from this spot. Trezeguet delayed his run, prepared his body but almost got too close to the goal before deciding to find the magic spot based on Rober Pirès's run. He cleverly and skillfully realized where this spot was and deceived the marking defender by faking to go in one direction but going in the opposite direction to "the magic spot'. He converted the cross to score the winning goal and give France the 2000 European Championship to go along with their World Cup from two years earlier. Goals from this area are usually scored by the feet and on one touch. Picture 58L and 58M show the last touch by Trezeguet.

Diagram 58N shows this "magic spot" in the goal from Trezeguet. He faked to go forward by taking a step towards the goal and then came back to the "magic spot (shaded area). This area changes depending on where the ball and defenders are. Players who score from this area sometimes are referred to as being "cheeky" or "clever" for finding this area. The striker usually is alert, quick-thinking, and "on" when scoring from this area. The passer is also alert to see this pass while being under pressure.

Picture 58M: This is the same goal as in picture 58L but from a different angle. Notice how Trezeguet is left totally unmarked right in the most dangerous part of the field and at the most crucial time in the game. Trezeguet found the magic spot at the right time moving into it unnoticed until it was too late. The ball was played from a wide left position close to the end line as shown in diagram 58N. Trezeguet sneaks into the magic spot, which was on the blind side of both Italian defenders #15 and #16. He was also away enough from #3 (Maldini) shown in picture 58L so that Maldini assumed that someone else would cover him. Trezeguet flat-footed Maldini by 'checking' before moving into this space. Action Images/Andrew Budd

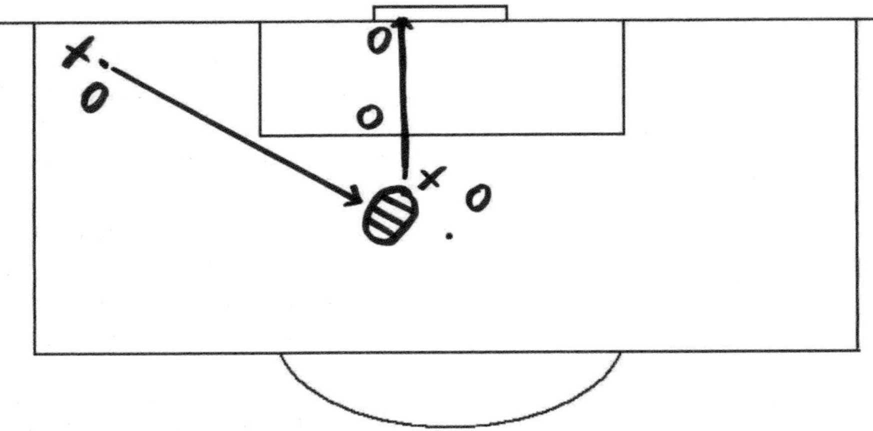

Diagram 58N: The shaded area shows the "magic spot" in this situation from the Euro 2000 Final. The ball was played there before Trezeguet moved to the "magic spot."

The Decision Making Process: Where to Go?

In the next example I will explain the thinking process and decisions that need to be made by a striker moving forward and deciding where to go if it is indeed the 'magic spot'. The striker we are focusing on in diagram 58O is labeled X9.

In diagram 58O the play is developing as a player (X7) enters the penalty area having beaten O3. The striker (X9) who is moving forward to assist X7 must make a decision based on a number of factors to get in the best position to score off an ensuing cross. O1 is the keeper and will play a part in the decision making process. Defender O2 will be the player to elude in order to have the best chance of scoring. The first order of business is to prepare to score by getting the body in a position turned toward where the ball will most likely be played. Running behind O2 is an advantage because O2 will need to make some assumptions as to where the striker, X9 is. The longer X9 can stay out of the view of O2 the better his chance of scoring will be. Defender O4 is also approaching. The final decision will be based on the position of his teammate, X7, and where his last step will be before the cross and how the keeper will play the attack. At this point I want my striker to be thinking 3 options and only 3 options.

1. Do I run in front of O2?
2. Do I get ready to run behind O2 or
3. Do I have to go to the magic spot?

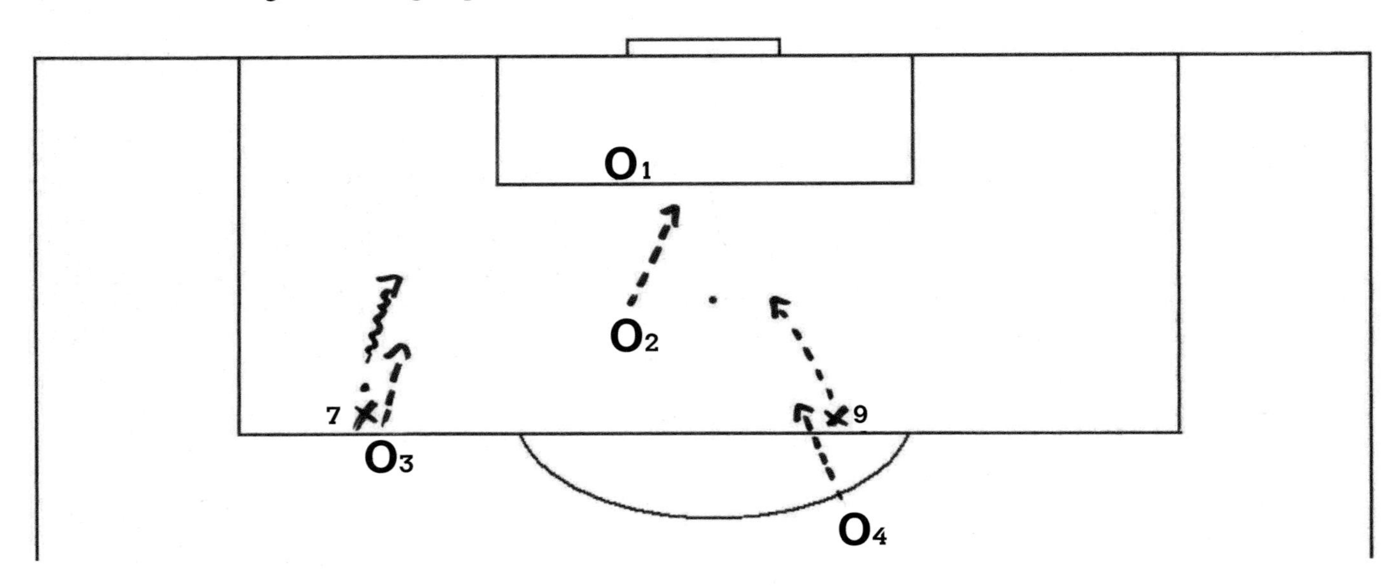

Diagram 58O: X7 has the ball and has beaten O3 who is chasing X7. O1 is the keeper. X9 needs to find the magic spot in order to score. Can you point it out?

Each situation may require a different correct answer but in this case I'll give an example of when the magic spot is the best option. In diagram 58P we see what has developed as X7 is ready to kick the ball. Will he shoot or cross the ball to X9? If the goalkeeper comes off his line to cut down the angle for a shot, then shooting may not be the best option. If O2 is still running back to protect a cross in front or behind him then X9 may have to look for the magic spot. Based on the fact that there is little room for the ball to pass between the goalkeeper (O1) and defender (O2) then a magic spot develops. It is in front of the last defender but delayed and dropped back away from the defender. Because X9 is coming from behind O2, then the space that's dropped back from O2 becomes open as highlighted

Diagram 58P: X7 is moving at pace down the side from a poor shooting angle. The goalkeeper, O1 is coming out to cut down the shooting angle. O2 is facing the ball and his goal and is having problems knowing where X9, the nearest striker is going to go. X9 pretends to go to the far post but suddenly cuts to the magic spot as highlighted. In this situation, this is where the magic spot is. Interestingly, O2 runs right through this spot as he goes back to defend. Illustration by Jo-Anne Godawa

in the square in diagram 58P. I call this area the "magic spot" and X9 must know where that spot is but disguise his run into that area as long as possible so that O2 and O4 will assume that he will not go there. If X7 spots this as well and passes the ball there, then X9 will have a great chance to score in one of the most dangerous parts of the field.

In this case X9 'checks' and suddenly cuts back to the magic spot. If X7 spots this and passes the ball there then X9 should score provided he hits the net. But X9 will have little time because O2 and O4 will both attack the striker because this is a key scoring area. X7 will need to score on his "last touch" which will be the only touch that he will have time for. In picture 58Q, we see the conclusion of this play.

Picture 58Q: Pauleta, #9 (X9 from diagram 58P) scores for Portugal against Angola in the 2006 World Cup. Figo (X7 from diagram 58O) provides the cross. Portugal beats Angola 1-0. Action Images/Alex Morton

From a skill related technique perspective, note that the support foot (right foot) is pointed at the centre of the goal. Young players in this situation receiving a ball across the goal from their left will often fail to turn this foot around and point it at the target.

Another tendency that attacking players have in these types of situations and crosses is to try to hit the ball hard. It's tempting to try to bulge the net. Anytime a ball is played backwards towards an oncoming striker, for some reason, young players want to hit the ball too hard. Consequently players often hit the ball over the bar. Also young players who have the urge to want to hit the ball hard may have to take a back swing to get power. The extra time needed to generate power can also allow the defender that split second of extra time to get in the way of the shot. Re-directing the ball to goal from a cross usually does not require power especially since the ball is close to the goal. Also when a ball is played backwards, less energy is needed from the body to get pace on the ball.

Another technical error that young players make in a situation similar to the one shown in diagram 58P and picture 58Q is that a right footed player may want to use his stronger foot rather than the nearest foot to score with. As you can tell from picture 58Q, if Pauleta had used his right foot instead of his left foot to score, then his shot may have been blocked.

The important concept that will help you coach players to find these places to go to is that, in all cases, the strikers must get to the magic spot and not stand and wait for the ball to come to them. Although this is not rocket science, sometimes, when dealing with high school and college aged players, we need to make them understand that they cannot get in front of the goal and wait for the goal scoring opportunity to just come. It will not. That's why I like to tell players that there are "three steps to fame." This is another special cue that will help them remember how to time things correctly more often.

CHAPTER 59

3 Steps to Fame

A key error young players make is to rush to the front of the goal and then wait there for the ball. The problem with getting there too early is that the defenders and the goalkeeper can communicate with each other to make sure the attacker gets marked. To solve this problem I give players a rule. When I looked at goals from crosses, in almost every single case, (there are a few exceptions) the player who scored the goal, took a minimum of 3 steps forward (occasionally backwards) to score the goal. Sometimes the steps were small and short, other times long and fast but the fewest always seemed to be 3. In most cases the goal scorer took more than three steps. The average number of steps taken before scoring from a cross is much more than 3.

So, because of this fact, I give players in my course a rule. I say:

> ***"There are three steps to fame. If you want to score off a cross, you better have taken at least 3 steps forward to score. If you do not, you will go against statistics which means you will score less often. Knowing this rule, and knowing in which area of the field you need to get to for your last touch, plan your runs accordingly. If you get to the front of the goal expecting the cross and the cross does not come, remember the rules of scoring off crosses. 3 steps to fame. If you take 3 steps forward from where you are standing, ask yourself, where does that take me? If it takes you outside the key scoring area, then you better make back those 3 steps because your chances of scoring are going down should the cross ever come."***

It's like sending signals similar to the ones the baseball manager sends to his batter. The three-step rule makes decision-making simple, easy, and logical. It can cure those bad habits young players have when they get to the front of the goal too quickly. They need patience when attacking the goal if the cross is delayed. Sometimes, when a cross does not come when they get to the scoring area, they need to go backward to get back in a position to go forward. Young players rarely use this approach.

It's Hard to Dispute Facts. Have them Working for Your Strikers

If most goals from crosses are scored from 4-9 yards from goal and the scorer needs to take a minimum of 3 steps forward to score, based on statistics, then a player waiting for a cross at the 7 yard mark is making a bad decision on his positioning. If the facts state that a player will need to take a minimum of three steps forward to score, then 3 steps forward will take the player to the 4 yard line thus eliminating all the chances to score that come between the 5 and 9-yard line. This fact is hard to dispute. Hopefully it will be something that is simple to convey to players. It's quite normal for players to make forward runs to get to a position to score from a cross but how often does the cross come as first expected? Often it does not because a great defensive play or an extra dribble by the attacker can change the timing of the cross. This should change the impending run and positioning of the potential goal scorer. The secret is to adjust the path, speed, and run to goal. A good goal scorer will take mental notes and make more correct decisions.

Go back to chapter 58 and look at picture 58D. The Celtic players waiting for a cross are patient around 9 and 12-yards from the goal line, not in the scoring area. This is the case even though they can move to as close as 4 yards away from the goal without going into an offside position. Young players make this mistake and get too close to goal. Professionals show how to be patient. Roma players are well organized by staying in central defending positions in numbers.

In the run to the "magic spot" in diagram 58P, Pauleta of Portugal took over 12 steps to get to the scoring area. In the goal by Argentina from diagram 58G, Crespo took over 16 steps to score. There was no standing around waiting.

Crespo started slowly but changed speed as he felt the cross coming. If he had made his sprint too early, the defender would have had time to cover him and he may have been too far ahead to convert the cross. Teach your players to remind themselves of the rules and facts based on the statistics I have provided. "Three steps to fame" is just another psychological form of stating the obvious for memory purposes. Hopefully your players will use these cues to get to the right spot to score and then concentrate and focus on finishing the job on their "last touch."

Many coaches like to plan who goes where and who does what. For example, you may want certain players to go to the near post and others to look after the far post. You may have scouted the opposition and may prefer all crosses to go to the far post because the goalkeeper or defenders are weak on those types of crosses. These are strategies, which make up an important part of the game. You may have set limits on your players on where you want each one to be on a cross. But the final conversion to score will still be defined by players making correct decisions based on speed, angles, trajectory, and just plain physics of a ball and bodies in motion. Specific mental decisions for the athlete are what I'm trying to focus on. Even the player whose job is to go for the near post will need to get there at the right time and get in front of a defender to score. This is the mental aspect of the game that you want your strikers to be able to read. Those last nine seconds of their performance within your system and strategies is what will define their success rate in scoring.

A friend of mine, Barry Johnson, who coaches highly competitive volleyball in Whitby Ontario, likes to call the mental aspect of sports "beyond the skills and strategies". This is where champions excel.

CHAPTER 60

Heading to Score

Although I have downplayed the number of goals scored by the head in the past few chapters, they still make up a large percentage of goals. In fact, considering that the game is played mainly with the feet and is called "football" in most parts of the world, there are actually a large percentage of goals scored by the head. In the 2002 men's World Cup, 24% of goals came off headers. In the 2006 World Cup, 42% of goals scored from crosses came from headers.

In fact, the ratio of goals scored to attempts at goal with the head is much higher than the ratio of goals scored to attempts at goal with the foot. If we turned all the missed scoring chances to goals in a typical game, then we would find that we would have scored many more goals from the foot and not the head. The actual percentage of goals scored by the head would go way down if the chances missed by the foot would have gone in. I would estimate that the ratio of goals missed by the foot as opposed to goals missed by the head would be close to 10:1 in favour of goals missed by the foot.

Picture 60A: Wayne Rooney of Manchester United gets a step up on Paul Stalteri of Fulham in this mid-air challenge while trying to score. Jumping up a split second before the defender will give a player an advantage in beating the opponent to a ball in the air. Action Images/Eddie Keogh

Why is that? The main reason is that there are fewer decisions to be made when the ball is in the air, which reduces bad decisions when it comes to finishing. For example, the major decision that does not have to be made when trying to score from a header is how many touches the striker should take. Goals scored by the head are always only one-touch attempts at goal.

Jump First

Goals scored by the head are more about timing than any other factor– another reason why all the details regarding timing from chapters 58 and 59 are so important. The "Three Steps to Fame" chapter is important because, besides taking steps to go meet the ball, there is often some jumping involved in scoring by the head. Strikers will need to climb above defenders in some situations. The key to getting above defenders is to jump slightly before the opponent. The first to jump usually gets the upper hand. It's difficult for a striker to outjump his defender if the defender has taken off first because he will be under the defender when he starts his jump. Unless the defenders completely mess up the timing and are on the way down when the ball is coming, the strikers will be less likely to get to a high ball when starting the jump after the defenders.

In picture 60A, Wayne Rooney of Manchester United gets the upper hand on Paul Stalteri of Fulham by leaving the ground a fraction of a second before him. That's your first secret when teaching players to score by the head. You want your striker to take off a fraction of a second before the defender when jumping for a ball in the air.

When I got deep into analyzing goals I kept finding that many goals scored by the head were not textbook heading goals. In fact, at first I was so surprised by this fact that I didn't want to show my players some of the pictures I had that demonstrated goals scored by the head because they break many of the rules that we teach our players. For example, from picture 60A, you see that Rooney has his eyes closed as does Stalteri, the defender. Rooney heads the ball from the top of the head instead of the forehead. Picture 56B from chapter 56 also shows Christian Vieri using the wrong part of his head to score. But, if your striker scores with the back of his head, how can it be the wrong part of the head? What we need to understand is that there are two types of goals scored by heading a ball.

Two Types of Goals From Headers

I have classified goals from headers into two categories for the purpose of my analysis to help me coach the striker to score more goals. The coaches need to be clear in their minds as to how goals are actually scored. The two methods are fairly evenly split at 50% each.

The Head as a Wall

In one type of goal, the head acts as a wall to re-direct the ball. Any part of the head will do the trick provided it is ahead of the defenders to re-direct the ball at goal. The object is to place the head in an area where the ball can glance off it towards the goal and preferably down. Many of these types of goals happen when the striker runs 'in front of' the defender to score. Your strikers will want to protect the head from injury and may take their eyes off the ball. Do not be too concerned with proper heading technique if the scoring opportunity is based on getting to the ball first to re-direct it. Concentrate on getting your strikers to gain the mental courage to go challenge for the ball. A striker with the courage to go for balls in the air will provide bigger dividends than a technically perfect striker who is afraid to go in for a challenge on a cross. A striker who cannot score by use of the head will not be able to score 25% of those goals that come off of headers. That can be a significant number and one that may decide if a player makes the team at a higher level or not.

One piece of advice I give to help players who are hesitant to challenge for balls in the air is to suggest they use a headband at practice. There are protective headbands available on the market for players to use. This can help them gain confidence to challenge for balls in the air. Once the confidence grows, you will find that the thrill of scoring will help overcome fears of injury. Eventually, your strikers should be able to provide a challenge to a ball in the air without protective headgear. As you can see from both pictures 56B and 60A that the players are concerned for their safety but in this situation, goals were scored. By the way, defenders are just as interested in protecting their head.

Heading the Ball to Score Like we Teach it

In the other type of goal scored from a headed ball, coaches will feel good because it follows more of what we teach players. It requires using the forehead and keeping the eyes on the ball. It includes arching the back and swinging it forward to get some power to the header. Some goals will require the player to jump and turn the ball towards the goal all in one motion as shown in picture 60B. In this case it's Cristiano Ronaldo of Manchester United who scores a goal from a ball crossed into the danger area. He scores this goal by scoring from 'behind' defenders. His body position is such that it is facing the ball and his shoulders are square to the ball. Because he ran on the blind side of defenders he has caught all the defenders by surprise as no one picked him up. They were all caught ball watching. You can see how surprised the Chelsea defenders are when they turn to face the ball that has gone behind them. Ronaldo takes his minimum of 3 steps towards the ball to help give him lift and he keeps his eyes on the ball. He also gets an early jump

Picture 60B: Cristiano Ronaldo scores the first goal for Manchester United in the 2008 Champions League Final against Chelsea by perfectly timing his jump. His heading technique in the air is superb. He keeps his concentration and his eyes are on the ball while performing the skill. Action Images/Scott Heavey

which helps him tower above everyone to score. A well-timed jump where the striker gets a slightly fast start can prevent the defender from getting any height at all. In picture 60B, we see Cristiano Ronaldo tower above his closest defender to score a goal.

Turning a Ball and Changing its Direction Towards Goal with the Head

The next technical thing to look at when scoring by the head and turning the ball to the goal is to make sure the player turns his body at the hips to whip his head towards the ball to direct it at the goal. The striker must turn the ball by using his forehead and not the side of the head or temple area of the head. Not only is heading with the side of the head at the temple not the correct method of directing the ball at goal, it is also dangerous. Young players will think that they have to use the side of their head to re-direct it at the goal. It's still the forehead that is used and the turning takes place at the hips and torso. Usually the player takes off with the foot closest to goal using his arms to help him gain height and to turn in the air. In picture 60C, taken a split-second after picture 60B, Ronaldo has used his arms to twist his hips to turn his forehead to re-direct the ball towards the goal. He has kept his eyes on the ball.

Picture 60C: Cristiano Ronaldo of Manchester United times his jump perfectly to re-direct the ball at goal by twisting at the hips. He makes contact with the ball with the forehead but turns the body to get his power to re-direct the ball towards the goal. He does not use the side of the head to re-direct the ball at goal, which many young players attempt to do. Action Images/Scott Heavey

Turning the ball at goal takes place at the trunk of the body even when the striker is not jumping. As shown in picture 60D, Russia's Roman Pavlyuchenko scores by using his forehead to re-direct a low ball to goal. It is easier to redirect the ball if the body position is facing where the ball is coming from. This is where a looping run helps get the body in the correct position. The player will consequently come to meet the ball squarely with the shoulders turned towards the on-coming ball. Many young players will fail to make this simple adjustment in their run towards the goal. Performing the skill of twisting the hips to make sure the forehead makes contact with the ball and not the side of the head will be something to focus on. Meeting the ball to head it in will be easier with the body facing the ball.

Picture 60D: Russia's Roman Pavlyuchenko scores his teams only goal of the game by re-directing the ball using his forehead and not the side of the head. He maintains concentration on the ball with his eyes throughout the skill. Action Images/Juan Flor

Can you Score from Underground?

Once you have helped your strikers with the heading techniques and helped them overcome some of the fears of heading, you will need to give them some specific information as to where to aim in order to score. The answer here is no different than most other types of goals but the assumption that players have towards where to aim is often wrong.

Players need to aim the ball down at the ground. Most goals from headers are scored in the bottom third of the goal. In the 2006 World Cup, about 66% of goals from headers were scored in the bottom third. What helps create a false perception of where goals are scored from headers is that the head and the ball are already above the ground so one would assume that a header to a top corner would be easier than trying to place the ball down low. But here is the most astounding fact on goals scored from headers: in about 50% of goals score from headers, the ball actually contacts the ground before it enters the net.

That suggests that the ball would have gone under the ground if the ground were not there to stop it. This point alone should help you convey the message that to score from a header, your strikers will have to erase any preconceived notions they may have about where to aim, and aim to head the ball to the ground and not at the same level as their head. If your players are still trying to head the ball to the top corners then please bring out the following statistic.

From the 2006 World Cup, 74% of goals scored in the bottom third of the goal by heading the ball to score, actually touched the ground before entering the goal. That percentage would go way up if you were to include goals that crossed the line and hit the ground within a yard behind the goal line. The pros know where to aim. Getting above the ball and making contact with the head on the top half of the ball is important to get it to go down. This fact also clearly shows that the goalkeeper will have a harder time stopping a ball down at the ground than one at mid-height. When players don't aim the ball down at the ground, the problem is not that they can't do it. It's that their immediate instinctive system has other ideas. This is normal and this is where you as a coach will need to make sure your players are changing these instincts by re-training their natural tendencies as outlined throughout this book. Please read on for more insight and ideas.

How many goals from headers actually touch the ground before entering the goal?

50%

Key to Scoring: Head to Ground

In picture 60E, Robbie Keane of the Republic of Ireland heads the ball down to score. Since most goals from crosses are scored between 4 and 9 yards out from the goal line, heading a ball down and making sure to hit the net will give your striker the best chance to score. Goalkeepers will have little time to react to a ball that is placed low at the ground level. One reason the keeper will have a hard time making a save on a ball played at the ground from a header is that the ball will be coming from a higher point than from someone's foot. The keeper's body position will typically be higher when the striker's last touch is by the head than by a foot.

Picture 60E: Robbie Keane of The Republic of Ireland scores against San Marino in a UEFA Euro 2008 Qualifying Group D match by heading the ball down. Note the position of the keeper's body. He is positioned too high to stop a ball directed at the ground. Keepers tend to stand higher than normal when defending a cross and expecting a header. Action Images/Scott Heavey

That's because the keeper's eyes are looking at the ball at eye level or higher, which will lift up the rest of his body. When looking at something at eye level or higher, the head will automatically come up. The lifting of the head will cause the rest of the body to lift up as well. This will mean that it will take the goalkeeper a split second longer to get to a ball played low than had his head and eyes been facing down at the ground.

Note how high the goalkeeper's body is in picture 60E even though the ball was low before Keane heads it. So the secret to score off of a header is to tell your striker to aim down to the goal line and not to the middle third or top third of the net.

Can we give players any more information to help them decide how to score from heading a cross? Each situation may require a different action but generally, the rules for scoring from headers are the same as for most other types of goals. The main difference is that because the ball is in mid-air most of the time, the strikers will have a different view of the goal than when using the foot. The background view that the strikers may have will be that of the goal itself. It

Picture 60F: When heading a ball to goal the background in the field of vision will be different than when having the head down to kick a ball from the ground level. Although the eyes will be focused on the ball, the brain may detect motion from the keeper, which should help the striker score. This field of vision can also fool the striker by tricking the brain into thinking that the middle of the goal is vacant thus forgetting the key rule to scoring from a header: to aim the ball at the ground. The other error that can occur is to take the eyes off the ball and look at the goal instead of the ball at the last second thus making poor contact with the ball. Photo/John DeBenedictis

should be unfocused but still evident. Also, the movement of the goalkeeper should be noticeable. Provided that strikers do not lose focus of the ball, the fact that they may be able to spot the movement of the goalkeeper should be an advantage in making decisions as to where to place the ball.

The Illusion of Seeing an Empty Net

The danger with this view is that the goal will often look big and the middle of the goal will look appealing. Because of this, players may tend to forget to aim low at the ground. How often have you seen a striker in a great scoring position head the ball right into the keeper's hands at the centre of the goal? Since the ball is usually displaced laterally on a cross across the front of the goal, the moment the striker gets a head to the ball, the centre of the net will look empty. This is because the keeper is still making his way across the goal. The temptation to head the ball in the middle of the goal at mid-height

Picture 60G: The top third of the goal and the middle of the goal looks very appealing as a spot to aim to score.

is very strong. In this case, shortly after the ball leaves the player's head, the keeper should be arriving as he comes across laterally. The keeper will therefore make an easy glove save. The accompanying reaction will be that the striker will hold his head as if to indicate he has a headache. This reaction is normal, because the striker knows he should have done better. In fact, the coach will get the headache because he will pound his head against the wall trying to figure out how to get the striker to score!

The coach will not be able to correct the situation in the future if he cannot grasp what is happening in his striker's field of vision during such an instance. Picture 60F and 60G shows the soccer ball just before the striker heads it towards the goal. The camera is where the eyes are. The moving ball should be clear in the player's eyes because he is focusing on the ball. The background will be fuzzy but the brain may detect the goal and the fact that the keeper is nowhere near the centre of his goal. The moving keeper may or may not be in the immediate field of vision behind the ball but the keeper should be heading towards the middle of the net. In some cases, the eyes spot this movement. Coaches should let players know that if their striker can spot the motion of the goalkeeper in the background, then they should score fairly easily because the first decision has already been made. That decision is to head the ball down towards the ground in front of the goal line. Strikers need to avoid one of the most common errors is attempting to score from a header, which is to take the eyes off the ball at the last second and thus make poor contact with the ball.

I stress to my strikers that it's very important to have already decided that they must head the ball down to the ground. Having made this conscious decision, then they can use the fact that they have the advantage of seeing the goal and possibly the movement of the goalkeeper in the background to decide where to place the ball. For

Picture 60H: Michael Owen scores for England by heading the ball in the opposite direction that the keeper is moving and into the near corner of the net by aiming low. The ball will touch the ground prior to going into the goal. On some goals from headers, the striker will be able to see the keeper's motion to help him decide where to place the ball. Action Images/Alex Morton

example, if the keeper is moving from where the ball originated from across the goal, then heading the ball back in the direction it came from may be the best place to aim. The keeper will have a hard time changing direction to stop the header.

In picture 60H and 60I, Michael Owen of England heads the ball in the same direction the ball came from because he was able to spot the keeper's motion before deciding on where to place the ball. Sometimes, the opposite corner is the best choice. It all depends on the cross and the position of the keeper. Except for the decision to aim low and the physical ability to get to the ball, the placement of the ball can be decided at the last moment. This is an advantage the striker has on headers.

Scoring from heading a ball from a cross is one of the toughest skills for coaches to teach because there is an element of fear that enters the picture. This makes it quite difficult. Similar to many other types of goals from crosses, timing, where to run, getting proper body position and then focusing by keeping the eyes on the ball as long as possible are most important. Scoring from a header is not an easy feat by any stretch of the imagination. Good luck!

Picture 60I: The conclusion of Michael Owen's goal shows the keeper going in the opposite direction than the ball is heading. The keeper was put in this position because of the cross coming from the keeper's right across the front of the goal. Since goals from the head originate higher than goals scored by the foot, notice how high the keeper's hands are in comparison to where they should be. Players who forget to aim down will miss a great scoring opportunity. Action Images/Alex Morton

CHAPTER 61

Through Balls

There are a lot of goals scored as a result of a ball being played through the defense with the striker running past the last defender to collect the ball and then beat the goalkeeper. These are called through balls or penetrating passes that pierce the defense. This type of pass is usually the last pass before the striker has a chance to score. On many occasions the combination play that creates this final through ball is practiced in detail by the coach and is part of the team strategy to create a great scoring opportunity. Each coach may have a different strategy in creating this situation. Often the coach looks at the strikers he has to work with when deciding how to create these scoring situations. A striker with speed will likely get more of these types of chances than a slow one. Coaches with fast strikers may try and play more through balls than coaches without. Whatever strategy you take with your team is not what I'm covering in this book therefore I'm not going to spend any time offering suggestions as to how you want to create chances for through balls. But, in the event that you have a player breaking through the defense with a chance to score, I do want to make sure I provide you with some things you can use to make sure that your striker scores.

Many of the previous chapters have already indirectly covered this issue. The most relevant information is covered in chapter 46 called "Powerful Facts", which provides information regarding how many touches a player needs to score a goal. Players that have received through balls and are free of the last defender often take too many touches on the ball thus negating the great scoring chance a through has created. There are a lot of potential decisions to be made. How can you help your striker make more correct decisions that will result in goals?

You must remind your strikers that after receiving a through ball there will be a lot of things going against them that will cause them to miss. The most obvious will be that all the defending players close to your strikers will be chasing them at maximum speed. Also, the goalkeeper will in all likelihood be coming off his line to close down the shooting options. The ball may be moving in a different direction opposite to the striker, making the first touch difficult. The ball may come in the air, needing good control. The striker may be on a collision course with the keeper. The ball may be spinning. The turf may be wet causing a different type of bounce. The ball played through could hit a bump in the pitch that could send it in an unfavourable direction. The spectators will be cheering or getting nervous depending on which team is the home side. Everyone will be expecting the striker to score. The stress of the moment is on the strikers. Or is it on the goalkeepers? I want my strikers to think that the stress is on the goalkeeper.

All these factors can play into the striker's situation. The striker can get over-anxious and totally botch up the opportunity. Each situation will be different depending on where on the field the ball is played and where the defenders are. The striker will have many decisions to make. He may be thinking 'Do I dribble, shoot, take a few more touches, is there someone on my back, do I pass it off?' Probably the biggest question will be where to aim. In Part Four, I will provide some mental cues that will help you make your striker make more correct decisions on how to beat the goalkeeper and score.

Dealing with Offside Issues

But for now, I want to bring up some issues that you will need to deal with. Making runs past defenders to chase through balls always involves great timing between the striker and the player playing the through ball. Making sure not to go offside is one of the biggest obstacles to overcome. Sometimes, even though the play may not be offside, the referee assistant can call the play offside. In many cases, the play is so close that it's hard to call accurately. In youth leagues where there may only be one referee, the referee will have more problems calling the play accurately than with assistants. As a general rule for the referee, it's better to call a bad offside than give away a bad goal. If the referee doesn't call offside when he should have and the non-call turns out to be a goal, it will have more effect on a game than calling an offside that wasn't. Some players and coaches totally lose their cool when there have been some calls against them which they think were wrong. It can affect your striker for the rest of the game if his personality can't handle the perceived injustice.

Strikers should try and keep their emotions in check when they have been called offside. Different players react differently to bad calls but I have seen good players lose their finesse after being called offside wrongfully because they have lost their composure. In the event that a scoring opportunity presents itself later, you want your strikers to coolly and calmly put the ball in the net. Good strikers will coolly and calmly turn through balls into goals on a fairly consistent basis. As a coach, you want to make sure your strikers will have this composure when needed most. You may need to have a chat with your strikers if they need to be calmed down.

Some strikers live for the ball that sends them clear. Filippo Inzaghi of AC Milan has made a career of beating the offside trap. Although he also probably also holds some sort of record for being called offside the most, he has been able to play in one of the world's top leagues and national squad for over a decade. He's not the fastest player to have worn a national team jersey or the tallest, toughest, or most skillful but he has endured.

Timing is a big part of getting in the open for a through ball. Through balls are usually created with diagonal runs and/or diagonal balls. Similar to crosses, runs through the last line of defenders occur in front of some defenders and behind others. Generally, the successful striker runs behind more defenders than in front of them. Often a couple of passes at feet to other players help create the final pass to space behind the defenders. If defenders get hypnotized by watching the ball then the chance for a through ball may be created. Combination plays involving more than just one pass usually creates successful through balls. Sometimes a through ball comes as a result of a turn over and the striker is quick to react to find space to run to accept a through ball. One of the biggest challenges for strikers is to deal with a ball that is going one way while they are going in another direction. In diagrams 61A and 61B, I provide two typical examples of the type of through balls that a striker may receive.

In diagram 61A, the striker who is running on to the ball (X2) is coming from a similar direction that the pass is coming from. The angle of intersection between him and the ball is low. In diagram 61B, the striker receiving the ball (X2) is running from right to left while the ball was played from left to right. The angle of intersection in this case is 90 degrees. This type of through ball will be harder for the striker to deal with. Often, the striker will need an extra touch to control the ball. If both the ball and the striker are going at a fair speed, then the first touch will be difficult. A poor first touch may negate the opportunity especially if the striker plays it too far in advance or back in the direction of a defender. Also, the teammate who is passing the ball will find it harder to make the pass accurately and weighted perfectly because if the ball gets there too early, the striker may miss it and then have to go retrieve it before heading for goal. If it gets there too late, the striker may be in an offside position or may have to go back to get it and thus allow defenders to recover.

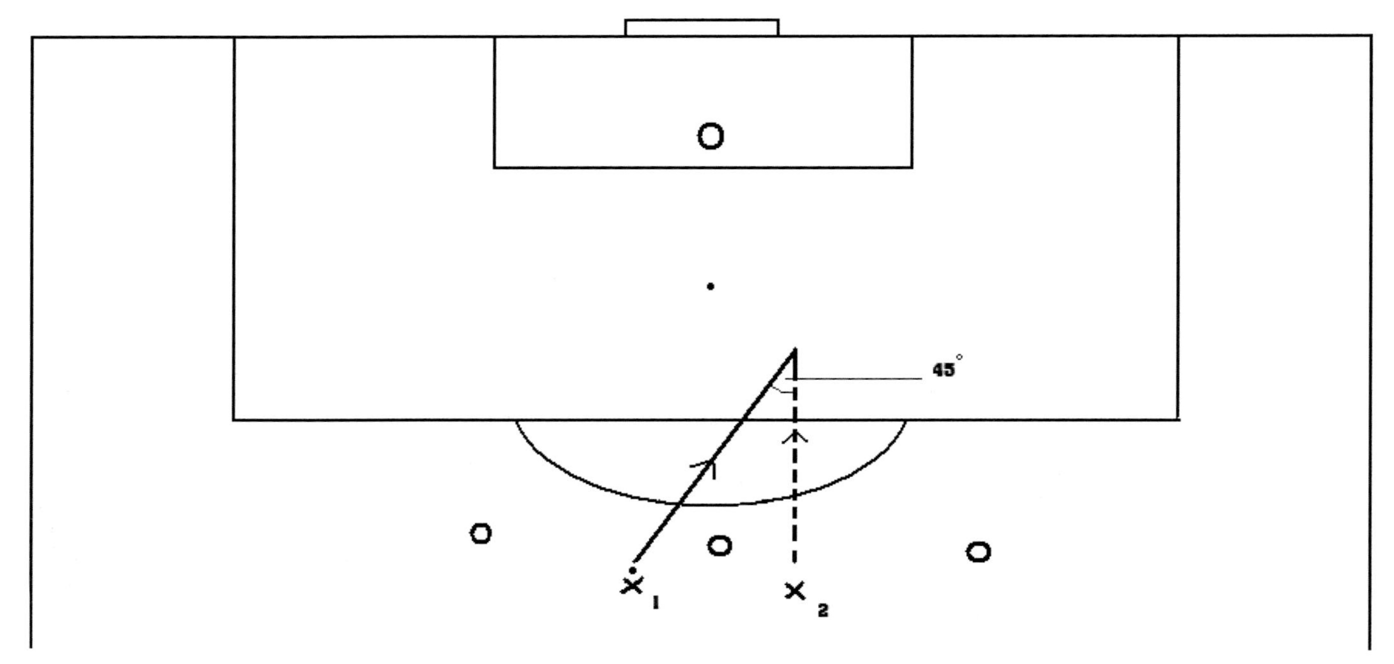

61A: X1 plays through ball past the Os with the angle of intersection between the ball and the player receiving the ball (X2) being at about 45 degrees. (The path of the ball is a straight line and the path of the player is the dotted line.)

On the other hand, a smaller angle between the ball's path and the striker will make it easier for the striker to play but other problems may arise. For example, if the ball is played directly at the goal the goalkeeper may be forced to come off his line and hence be on a collision course with the striker. If the through ball is played closer to centre field than the edge of the box, then a different set of circumstances will develop. Each situation will present its own set of problems.

I often see young players make poor decisions in their runs for through balls. They almost make it impossible for the through ball to succeed. These players get weeded out before they make it too far if they cannot think their way through certain obvious problems. In diagram 61C, the Xs are attacking the Os and are presented with two different through balls and two different runs that players can make. Let's look at these scenarios.

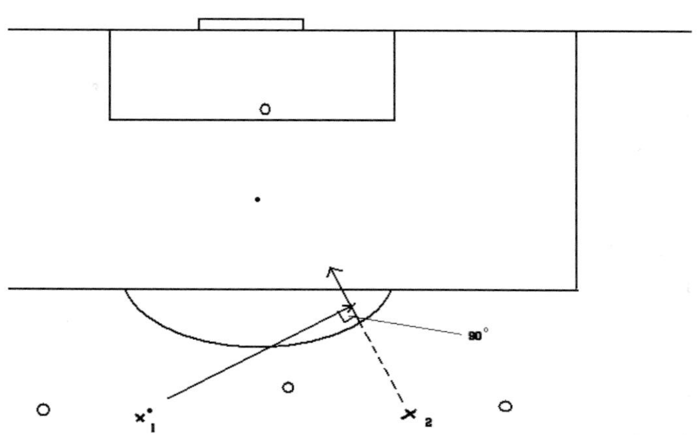

Diagram 61B: X1 plays a through ball past the Os with the angle of intersection between the ball and the player receiving the ball (X2) being at about 90 degrees. The larger the angle, the harder it is to control the ball. For teenage players who are still developing their touch, more goals are scored when this angle is smaller. Keep in mind, that for every example, there will be cases when this principle will not apply. In training strikers, I want to give them advice that will increase their probability to score based on facts.

Scenario 1

X1 plays the ball through with a ball straightforward (P1). In this case X2 can run behind O4, O2 and O5 and in front of O3 to collect the ball (Run R1). Because the angle is 45 degrees, he should have no problem collecting this ball.

He may even want to pretend to run to the outside of O3 before cutting in front of him to collect the through ball.

Scenario 2

X1 plays the ball through on a diagonal (P2).

X2 has two options to collect this ball.

make run R1 or

make run R2.

By making run R1, the striker will intersect with the path of the ball at 90 degrees. Many young players will make this run and consequently miss-time their run or have problems controlling the ball when they get to it.

The better run is R2 because it's on the blind side of O3 but also because it will be easier for the striker to control the ball when he or she meets the ball. The striker will also have a better view of the goal and has more options on his first (or last) touch.

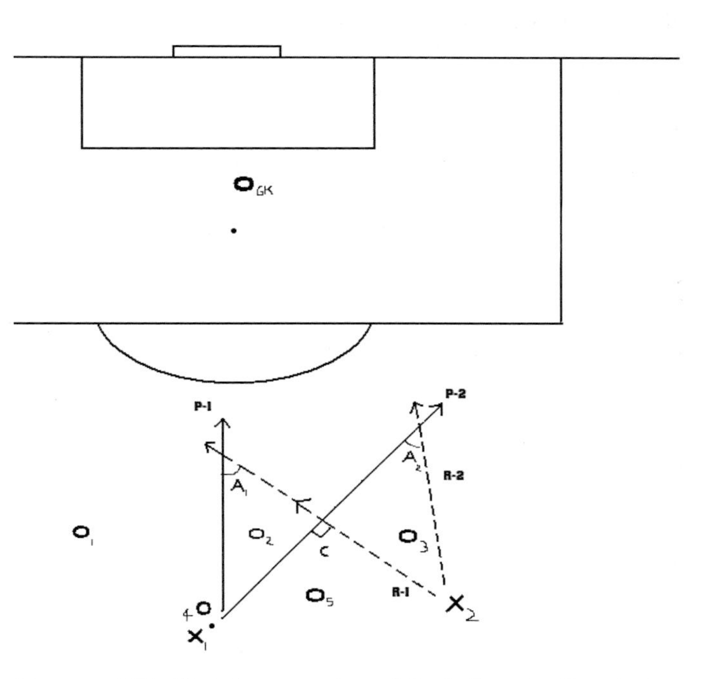

Diagram 61C: X1 is in possession of the ball and will make two different through ball passes for X2. P1 (pass 1) is straight through and P2 (pass 2) is a diagonal ball. X2 will make two runs: diagonally, signified by R1, and straight signified by R2. A1, A2 and C are three potential intersection points between the ball and the player. A1 and A2 have approximately the same low angle while C is a right angle.

Correcting Poor Through Runs: Use Geometry

Look for problems based on poor decisions when your players make runs through the defense. In scenario #2 from diagram 61C, many young players in North America make run R1 to expect a ball at intersection C. I see this so often with young players that I start to wonder if this is a North American problem or just a worldwide problem with young players. In North American sports such as basketball, American football (and even hockey and lacrosse), this type of run is an effective attacking play. But in those types of sports, the player making a run at full speed to collect a pass uses his hands (or stick controlled by the hands) to collect the ball (puck) while the feet do the sprinting (skating). In soccer, the feet will do the sprinting and also need to control the ball and thus the first touch is going to be very difficult.

As a rule, when the through ball is played close to the edge of the box, an ensuing shot or pass into the goal should occur on one touch. That's one reason a smaller angle at the intersection point between the ball and the striker on through balls is more likely to result in a goal. Larger angled through balls may need an extra touch and thus reduce the chances of scoring.

Of course, I make the point of angles (geometry) to remind players what types of runs are better to help them make better decisions. In reality, runs should have some element of loops to them that will have the striker running in the final direction towards the goal as shown in diagram 61D.

If your strikers can make runs that reduce this angle then they will give themselves a better chance to score. Often patience is required before the strikers make the sprint past the last line of defenders. A slight hesitation or a run parallel to the offside line for a few steps is all that may be needed to prevent an offside and turn this opportunity into a real chance instead of one that's called back. Through balls or penetrating passes can be very exciting for the spectators, as there is a feeling of anticipation of a goal. Keep your strikers focused on hitting the net on their attempt at goal. The striker may be approaching the goal directly from the centre of the field or from an angle. By and large, in most cases the striker will be approaching the goal from a slight angle.

Consider Passing the Ball into the Goal to Score all the Time

Some through balls are played just outside the box while others may come around centre field. When a ball is sent through at centre field, the strikers may have to take more than one touch because they are too far from the goal for a shot at goal. In such an instance, they may have more time to take a look at the goal and see where and what the keeper is doing. The problem with through balls from a fair distance from the goal that sends coaches and fans into a state of disbelief is that too many such opportunities are missed. In some cases the strikers have too much time to think and may change their mind a few times before deciding… on the wrong option. They often end up missing the net or not getting a shot off at all and completely botch up the chance. If this happens to your strikers, make sure to deal with their psychological state because all the fans, teammates, and coaching staff will think they should have scored. The players who missed will feel the same way and you want them to forget about it and move on.

The end result of a through ball is that the final touch should be a pass into the goal and not a power shot at goal. If your strikers are thinking about taking a power shot to score from a through ball then they will have made the wrong decision most of the time. Through balls usually require either inside of the foot or outside of the foot type passes in order to score. On occasion, a chip pass over the goalkeeper's head is the best option. Make sure your strikers don't get too close to the keeper when trying a chip pass or they will chip it right into the keeper's hands. Usually the ball should be played low but on occasion when the ball is bouncing, a chip pass into the goal over the keeper's head is easy to perform. Most chipping type efforts should take place at the edge of the box or further.

Another option may develop from a through ball and that is one where the striker dribbles past the keeper to either side and then passes the ball into the empty goal. This method of scoring did produce 5 goals in the 2006 World Cup. Using the term "dribbling around a goalkeeper" may give the wrong impression. Touching the ball to either side of the goalkeeper and then quickly passing the ball into the goal on the next touch is a better description of this type of goal. Strikers who must do this to score must do so with as few touches as possible in order to succeed. In picture 61E and 61F, Filippo Inzaghi of Italy beats Czech Republic's goalkeeper Petr Cech by going around him after receiving a through ball at the centre field line.

This goal by Inzaghi in the 2006 World Cup was 9 seconds of brilliance. Diagram 61D shows the goal and each of Inzaghi's touches. Even though he was over 50 yards from the goal when the ball was passed forward, he still only took 3 touches to score. A key component of beating the goalkeeper by going around him is to touch the ball to the side of the on-rushing keeper on the second last touch. This touch must be far enough to the side that it will avoid a diving goalkeeper's reach, which is quite far because he can use his hands. Notice the distance of his second last touch as he beats the keeper by going around him. It's 8 to 10 yards long before his last touch. Errors occur when the striker does not play the ball far enough to the side to avoid the goalkeeper's lunge and reach.

In chapter 51 and picture 51A, a similar touch to beat the keeper by Mia Hamm was not long enough or far enough away to beat the German keeper. Since this touch has to be fairly big, a striker must make sure that there are no defenders close enough to where the ball is being played to prevent the potential scoring chance. In most cases, I will still prefer that my striker attempt to score by passing the ball past the keeper instead of going around them. When a goalkeeper convinces the striker to try and go around him, it buys time for a defender to sprint back and intercept a shot at goal and it usually gives the striker a poorer angle to shoot from. In this example, Filippo Inzaghi makes no mistake.

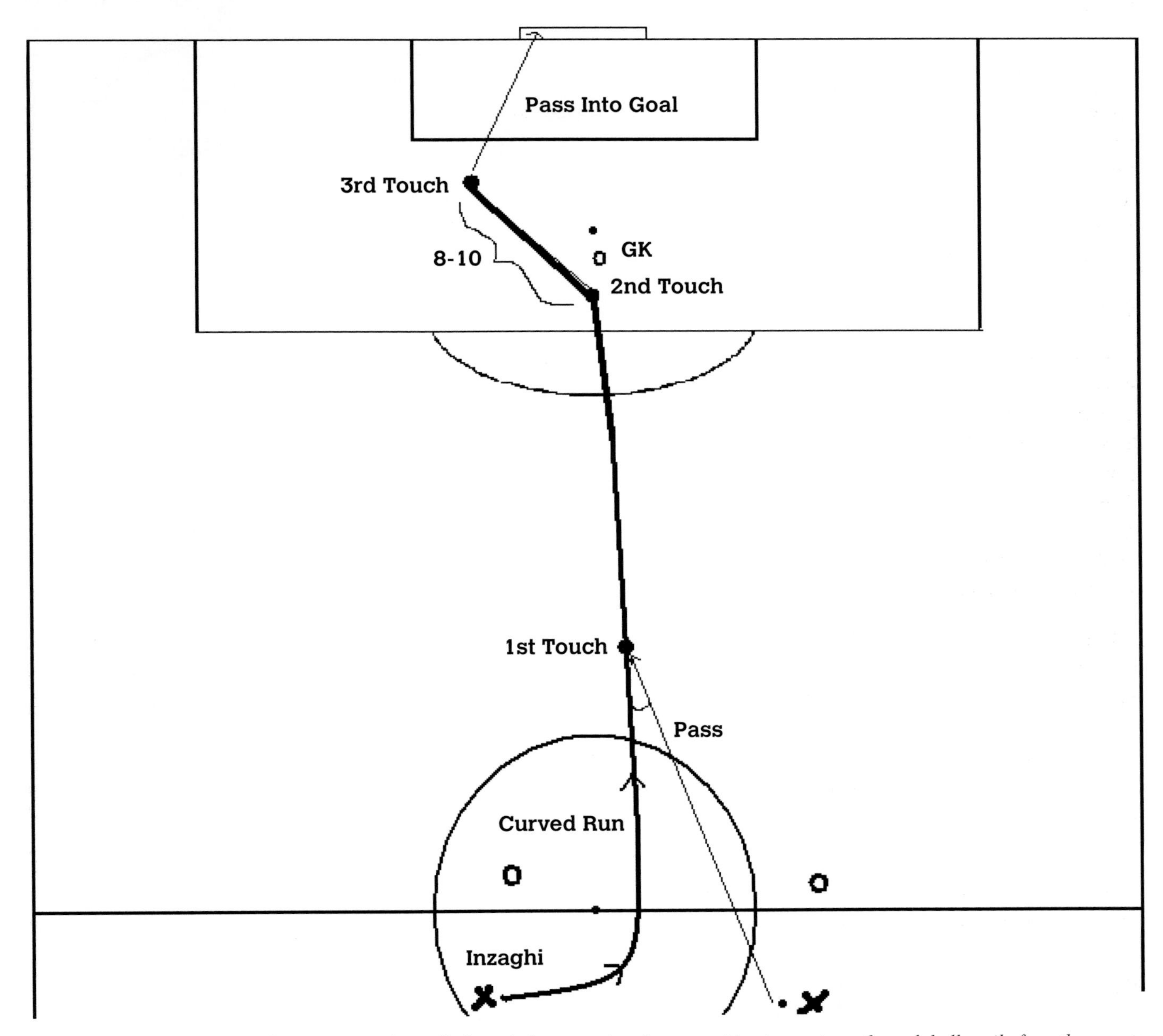

Diagram 61D: Inzaghi loops his run to avoid an offside and also to get in a better position to receive a through ball easily from the pass to make his first touch easier. His second touch is 8-10 yards in length and clears the keepers reach. His third touch is a pass into goal.

Picture 61E: Czech Republic's goalkeeper Petr Cech cannot stop Filippo Inzaghi of Italy as he takes the ball to one side and then passes it into the goal. Inzaghi beats the offside trap at centre field to take a through pass that sends him one-on-one against the keeper. When going around a goalkeeper, the striker must push the ball enough away from the goalkeeper to avoid his ability to dive to get the ball. This is often further to the side than one would first assume. Action Images/Lee Mills

Picture 61F: Filippo Inzaghi goes around Petr Cech far enough from him to prevent him from getting to the ball. Inzaghi's second touch is perfect. It's further to the side than one would first assume. Action Images/Jason Cairnduff

I would think that most readers would be surprised by the low number of goals scored by the through ball in the World Cup or the Euro as a percentage of goals scored in comparison to goals scoring in this manner at the youth and college level.

At Euro 2008, only 10 of 73 goals came as a result of a through ball compared to 50% of goals that came off crosses. Less than 20 goals of the 147 goals scored in the 2006 World Cup came from a direct through ball and 5 of those came from the striker going around the keeper. That's fewer goals then goals scored from the head. The 2002 World Cup revealed similar statistics. There were also more misses, saves, and more shots not taken, that should have been turned to goals from through balls than misses from heading chances. Why? I believe that there are many more decision-related problems when a through ball is involved. We need to reduce the options players have in deciding what to do.

I also believe that many poor habits are developed over time that carry on into older age brackets. At the youngest levels of soccer, from 7 year olds to 9 year olds, I would say that most goals come from a through ball. Coaches and parents are shouting, "pass it", or "kick it", or "through" all the time as the attacking team approaches centre field. Then the fastest kid runs like a horse and eventually scores a goal. Defenses and goalkeepers are not skilled or organized enough to stop this type of attack. As players get older, the through ball still produces many goals – certainly far outnumbering goals from crosses. When watching a scrimmage or game of players 10 to 17 years of age, we keep hearing players and coaches shouting, "send it, send it", meaning to "send the ball through." Even at the lower levels of recreational soccer, players over 18 years of age into adulthood, we hear players calling for through balls and as a result getting opportunities to score.

The odds are that while there are many one-on-one opportunities to score at these levels of play, many will miss the chance to score but since so many opportunities present themselves, players will generally score their share of goals. As players move to the highest levels of play and defenders are better at defending through balls and keepers are better at coming off their line, scoring opportunities by way of the through ball start to diminish. Only the best players – those who convert their chances to goals – remain at the highest levels, the others don't get past a certain level.

Strikers need to learn to minimize errors, misses, and make the right decisions when receiving through balls. In Part 4, I will present ideas that will help your strikers avoid making the wrong decisions, even at the highest level of play. In particular, I will show how they can learn to read the goalkeeper's moves and thus make better decisions.

BEATING THE GOALKEEPER

"Insight into shifting the advantage to the striker"

PART FOUR

PART FOUR

THE GOALKEEPER

Les Jones/Covershots

CHAPTER 62

From a Goalkeeper's Perspective

So far, in this book, I have almost totally ignored the goalkeeper in coaching the striker. That was not done by accident because, as a former goalkeeper, I always felt that I was the least important reason why players did not score on me. That's not because I was useless. I did play on a National Championship team with York University, had an invitation to attend an open tryout with the Fort Lauderdale Strikers of the NASL, and eventually played as a semi-professional in the National Soccer League, a professional league based out of Ontario, Quebec, Michigan, and Upper New York State. I didn't fancy my chances with Fort Lauderdale Strikers after they signed Gordon Banks but I was lucky enough to try and stop some top class strikers in games and practices. Some of these players played in the NASL, National teams and in Europe, and in trying to stop them from scoring on me, I found that most of my saves were non-saves.

I felt that my presence in a shooter's field of vision was as much a deterrent to the striker as anything. Coming out to narrow shooting angles, being in the right spot, would often be enough to cause players to try too hard to hit a perfect shot and, as a result, miss the target or better still, not even shoot. I also thought that my voice would distract a shooter from shooting or chasing a through ball. I would shout "keeper" as loud as possible when coming off the line, to hopefully slow down the striker so I wouldn't get hurt. I'd shout to my defenders to challenge players who were ready to shoot and I would notice that they wouldn't shoot even though they would have gotten the ball past the challenge and probably past me to score. I actually believe that some of my best saves occurred when the player either did not shoot or missed the net, because I won that psychological battle.

Although I think a good part of coaching the striker involves all the details as outlined so far that do not include the goalkeeper, in the end, the goalkeeper is someone who is a factor in the outcome of a scoring attempt. However, I feel that the goalkeeper is too much on the mind of the striker. Of course the goalkeeper's ability to stop a shot or header cannot be totally neglected, but I think that most strikers fear the goalkeepers too much or give them too much respect for what they can actually do. Goalkeepers don't have as much say in the matter as strikers think they do. In reality, the goalkeepers can't do anything until a ball has been directed at them. Yes, they can make themselves look big or have a say in the matter, but when you think about it, the keepers can't decide for the strikers. The keepers can't tell the strikers where to shoot, how hard to shoot, where to aim or when to shoot, or even how to beat them or their defenders. Goalkeepers are playing a 'wait and see' game with a lot of 'hope' thrown in.

So the final part of teaching strikers to score comes with dealing with the goalkeeper. While goalkeepers may be upset that I bring out some of the secrets to stopping goals they should not worry, as strikers will still forget what to do in the heat of the moment if they do their part right.

When there are not many goals scored in a typical game, everyone assumes that the goalkeeper had the advantage. Statistics will tell you that. Have you ever watched a game where goals seemed to just flow in for both teams? Not only are they exciting to watch, but it seems as though players have such an unbelievable confidence in their abilities to score that it seems like every shot goes in. Why do these types of situations not occur often enough? I think that strikers in general lack composure and forget some of the basics to scoring. To offset this, I want to give my strikers the goalkeeper's perspective to scoring goals.

Just a word of advice before I go on: If you have one of those rare strikers who has the confidence, composure, and instincts to score regularly, you probably don't need to go over what follows because it may get them thinking too much and reverse their success rate.

To start with, I want my strikers to think that they have the advantage over the goalkeeper when trying to score.

Look at Your Net. It's Pretty Big!

Here is what I tell my strikers in my goal scoring course:

"So let's be the goalkeeper. Look at your net. It's pretty big."

In picture 62A, you can see how small the goalkeeper (Kasey Keller of the USA) is in relation to the big goal that he is defending. It's 8 yards wide (24 feet wide) and 8 feet high. Tell your strikers to stand on the goal line and see how much of a chance they think they have to prevent a goal with a player shooting at them from 7-10 yards away. Ask your strikers to feel the pressure on them to make a save if they were a goalkeeper.

I tell them this:

> ***"If you're the keeper, 21 other players plus the coaches and all the fans will be there waiting to judge you in the next instant after a shot. Your performance will be judged by the goals you allow not by the wins or losses. In an instant, you can become a goat or a hero. Fans don't understand that the goal is so big. They expect you to make the save. And you thought you had pressure on you as a striker! Think again!"***

Take a few shots at them from 7 to 10 yards out while they stand on the line. You should score every time without kicking the ball too hard. Now tell them this:

> ***"See how easy it is to score and how little chance you have? As a striker, you can shoot harder and more accurately than me. If you miss the net, you won't score. Seeing that the keeper has little time to react, you should always hit the net. Look at your body as a goalkeeper; you have no pads, helmet, or hardly any other protection."***

Picture 62A: USA goalkeeper Kasey Keller looks small in front of the big soccer goal. This view gives the impression that he will not be able to cover much of the goal to stop a shot. In fact, in this picture the ball has already left the striker's foot. Unless the ball will be struck right at him or very close to him, you would think that a goal is imminent because the goal is so big in relation to the keeper. Photo by Les Jones, Covershots.

Also in many cases at the youth levels, the front of the goal is the worst part of the field. Often the grass is worn out so the keeper has to dive around in the worst part of the pitch. There can be dirt, rocks, and mud on the field that make life unpleasant for keepers. I want my strikers to know and feel how hard the ground is for the keeper to dive on in a hot dry day where the field is like concrete. Goalkeepers don't want to dive or go down on that terrain. I make sure that my strikers really see how bad things are for the goalkeeper. Strikers put too much pressure on themselves to pick corners in order to score and beat the goalkeeper but the keeper should be the least of their concern because the pressure is on them more than the striker's. I want to clear the mind of my striker to stop thinking of what the goalkeeper can do and shift the balance of power in the mind of my striker to thinking of what the goalkeeper can't do.

I want my strikers to think that the goalkeeper can't stop them because the goal they are defending is so big, the terrain is bad, the sun may be in their eyes, the shot gets there faster than they can react and so on and so forth. In my course, I show videos and DVDs of misses where players should have scored. I show them misses where players missed the net and misses where players didn't shoot. Once strikers see how hard it is to stop a shot, they can start to see things from a different perspective. Sometimes, if your strikers are failing to see shooting opportunities or missing the goal too often, have them play in goal in your scrimmages. They will be amazed at how many scoring chances exist but are not taken. This exercise will be fruitless unless they know why you want them to play goal. Have them look for situations where teammates don't shoot when a chance to shoot is there. Use this exercise to remind them of how simple it is to score when they follow the basic rules already presented in this book.

Players in scoring positions often feel that scoring is harder than it should be because goalkeepers use a variety of techniques to make the goal appear smaller than it really is. They come out to block the angles, and they use giant keeper gloves that make their hands look bigger. The facts are simple. Regardless of what the keepers do, the goal is still going to be 8 yards wide by 8 feet high and even big keepers can appear small in comparison to the goal when put into perspective. I want my strikers to keep this in mind. I want them to believe that they have the advantage because they have the ball and control the situation, not the goalkeepers. In picture 62B, a big keeper like Italy's Buffon can look relatively small in the goal. In picture 62C, Laura Twidle scores for Central Michigan University. The net looks huge in comparison to the goalkeeper. This mind set is important for the strikers. Good strikers have this aura or confidence about them that practically shouts this mind set out loud. I'm not saying that the strikers have to be cocky but rather that they need to have the inner confidence to score.

Getting strikers to re-focus is a big part of coaching them. Sometimes, they are on a roll and do things right and then for some reason; their confidence may wane. The coach has to keep coming up with new ideas to get the strikers

Picture 62B: Italy's Gianluigi Buffon looks like he can only cover a small portion of the goal as he watches the ball go in the net in the 2006 World Cup Final. Buffon is a relatively big keeper and is known as one of the best in the world yet he looks small in the penalty shot shootout. Action Images/Tony O'Brien

to score when they should. In the process of studying the striker to come up with numerous different coaching ideas to help them make correct decisions on the field, I came up with an interesting fact. I tell my strikers it's one of the biggest mind-boggling facts. I find it really helps them with their confidence. It also helps them keep focused on the facts and rules to scoring. It's what I call, "The Big 7". It's so revolutionary, that I'd like to patent it, but it's not really patentable because the facts are there for everyone to see.

Picture 62C: Laura Twidle, a Golden Goal Scoring Academy student, scores a goal for Central Michigan University. The goalkeeper looks relatively small in the goal. Photo by Bob Twidle

CHAPTER 63

"The Big 7"

When most people look at goals, they don't pay attention to how far or close the shooter is to the goalkeeper. Many shots, headers, or re-directs are taken from a lot closer than what people realize. When you realize how close the shooter really is to the keeper, you'll see that goalkeepers don't have that great a chance of making a save.

Here are some amazing facts:

Distance from the Goalkeeper

From the 2002 Men's World Cup ------ of 163 goals scored
127 Goals were scored by the feet
36 goals were scored by the head

In the 127 goals scored from the feet:

- 72 goals were scored when the shooter was 7 yards or less away from the goalkeeper.
- 36 goals were scored when the shooter was between 7 and 12 yards away from the goalkeeper. (15 of those were from the penalty spot)
- 6 goals were scored when the shooter was between 12 and 18 yards away from the goalkeeper.
- 13 goals were scored when the shooter was over 18 yards away from the goalkeeper.

In the 36 goals scored from the head:

- 32 goals were scored when the goal scorer was less than 7 yards away from the goalkeeper.
- 4 goals were scored when the goal scorer was between 7 and 12 yards away from the goalkeeper.

"The Big 7" means that 7 yards is a magic number. Unbelievably, 104 out of 163 goals scored in the 2002 World Cup came from when the goal scorer was less than 7 yards away from the goalkeeper! A further 40 goals were scored when the goal scorer was 12 yards or less away from the goalkeeper when the shot or header was taken. 144 or 88% of goals were scored when the goal scorer was 12 yards or less from the goalkeeper when the last touch was taken. The key point here is that these facts show the distance the goal scorer is from the goalkeeper and NOT the goal. Only 12% of goals come from shots taken when the shooter was more than 12 yards away from the goalkeeper. But, in both the official FIFA 2002 and FIFA 2006 World Cup DVD's, 50% of the "top ten" goals of the competition came from goals where the shooter was more than 12 yards away from the goalkeeper. Another example of how the media distorts reality for young aspiring strikers that dream of becoming world class strikers.

So what do these statistics really reveal? Why have I broken them down in this manner? I do so because I want to make powerful points that convince the players' mind of what does actually happen. 12 yards is the distance that the ball is away from the goalkeeper when a penalty shot is taken. What chance does the goalkeeper have in

Picture 63A: Korea's Ji Sung Park scores his goal against Portugal in the 2002 World Cup by shooting and hitting the net while being less than 7 yards away from the goalkeeper on his last touch. Action Images/Tony O'Brien

stopping a penalty shot? Approximately 80% of penalty shots are converted to goals. More importantly, what do most goalkeepers do when they try to stop a penalty shot? They try and guess where the shooter is going to shoot and start moving in that direction before the shot is taken. Why do they do this? It's obviously not because they want the shooter to score on them. Quite simply, it's because the goalkeeper does not have enough time to see where the shot is going and then react to the shot to make the save.

Go to picture 63G to see Michael Owen's penalty shot goal. Is it not amazing that Michael Owen shoots from 12 yards out and puts the ball barely a yard away from the goalkeeper and still scores? How is it possible that the goalkeeper does not have enough time to make a save on a ball that's played only 1 yard away from him? The reality is that on a well taken shot, the goalkeepers, even professional goalkeepers, will not be able to get many balls unless the ball hits them (see a more detailed analysis in chapter 66). Check out the pictures in this book where you see the goal scorer and the goalkeeper in the same picture and you will find that the goal scorer is usually quite close to the keeper. In picture 63A, Korea's Ji Sung Park is less than 7 yards away from the goalkeeper when he shoots to

Picture 63B: The touch that won the 2010 World Cup was Andres Iniesta's shot taken from less than 7 yards away from Holland keeper Maarten Stekelenburg. Missing the net could have cost Spain the World Cup. Iniesta made no mistake keeping the ball low and hitting the target. Action Images/John Sibley

score against Portugal in the 2002 World Cup. The keeper looks to be in a great position to make a save but from this close a distance, keepers will not be able to react quickly enough to stop the ball unless the ball happens to hit them where they are standing.

In picture 63B, Andres Iniesta's goal in the 2010 World Cup final wins Spain the World Cup and he is less than 7 yards away from Holland's goalkeeper when the shot is taken.

The point of "The Big 7" is that whenever attacking players are in the box and ready to shoot, there is a good chance that the goalkeeper will be standing 7 yards or less away from them. Almost certainly the goalkeeper will be standing no more than 12 yards away from them. So if the goalie is not quick enough to react and make a save on a shot from 12 yards out, what makes it possible for a goalkeeper to be quick enough to move and make a save on a shot less than 12 yards away?

Goalie Saves are Often Good Guesses

To further research this, I analyzed the movements of the goalkeeper when shots were taken at the goal. The results were surprising although they showed things I probably did as a goalkeeper. After watching thousands of goals, paying particular attention to the goalkeeper, I found that in many cases where a goal resulted, the goalkeeper actually moved to try to make a save before the shot or header had actually been made. In many cases, even the best goalkeepers in the world made the mistake of guessing and moving before the shot was taken. In many instances, the goalkeepers are guessing to make a save! But when goalkeepers guess, they often guess incorrectly and they allow a shot to go in where a save would have been in order if they had stayed big and maintained their position. In many situations, when the keepers guess incorrectly they actually help the striker score. Since many goalkeepers guess when they shouldn't, especially in the non-professional ranks, the scoring opportunities are greater than they should be.

The goalkeepers should avoid guessing and moving before shots are taken. Assuming they have narrowed down the shooting angle properly and they are in a favourable ready-position just prior to a shot being taken, their chances of making a save will be better if they maintain their position as opposed to trying to anticipate where the ball is going to go. In cases where the goalkeepers have to move while getting in position and have no time to get set to block a shot or header, then they are truly scrambling to try to block a shot. For example in pictures 65F and 60I, you see the goalkeeper come across the face of the goal in a desperate attempt at getting in a better position to stop a shot or header from going in. In such cases, they often have a better chance of making a save by praying than by counting on their skills! See picture 63C about a goalkeeper who did his best to call on the soccer gods. The striker who misses the net will have answered the keeper's prayers. But in so many instances we see strikers miss the goal when a simple shot, pass, or header directed at goal would have resulted in a goal.

Picture 63C: Oh God, help me! Goalkeeper Craig Forrest of West Ham United faces a red-hot Manchester United team at Old Trafford that put 9 goals behind him. He had no chance on any of the goals and even stopped a penalty shot in that game. Action Images/John Sibley

In his book on goalkeeping *Keeper II*, Tony Waiters points out the 10 key principles of goalkeeping. His principle number 7 states "react – do not anticipate" which is the opposite of what I want my striker to be thinking when thinking about "The Big 7". I want my strikers to think of the number 7 because I want them to know that in most scoring situations; the goalkeeper will be 7 or fewer yards away from them and will be guessing and anticipating instead of waiting for the shot. The whole point is that because of these two probabilities, the strikers should always direct the ball at the goal and never miss the net.

"Oh God, Don't Shoot"

It sounds like a line out of a western movie but what most goalkeepers are saying to themselves when they see a striker in a shooting position is, "Oh God, Don't Shoot." Goalkeepers know that their chances of making a save are not that great if the shot doesn't hit them. Goalkeepers know that the shooter is usually a lot closer than they think they are. Keepers are hoping that by being close to the attacker, they can distract the shooter from shooting on goal or force them to refrain from shooting altogether. As you know, when not counting penalty shots, 70% of goals are scored with the scorer being less than 7 yards away from the goalkeeper. That's a pretty big number and one that a striker cannot and should not ignore.

Here is what I tell players in my course:

> ***"The Big 7" is what I want you to think of so that you don't fail to score by missing the net when you are in the box. Without looking, whenever you are in the box, you have to assume that the goalkeeper will be off his line and be barely 7 yards away from you. You know for a FACT that goalkeepers have to guess in order to stop a shot from 12 yards away on a penalty shot because their reactions are not quick enough to make a save. If you prepare to score all the time when you are in the box and focus on the ball and get***

Picture 63D: Michael Owen scores on Brazilian goalkeeper Marcos in the 2002 World Cup. Notice that the keeper is less than 7 yards away from the ball at the moment of contact of Owens's foot with the ball. Also notice that the moment of contact has not yet taken place in this photograph. The keeper is guessing as to what Owen is going to do. It actually looks as though he is moving out of the way so that Owen can shoot straight ahead and score. In fact Owen does not panic nor does he miss the net as he proceeds to score. Action Images/Ian Waldie

> ***a shot or header away, then you should score a lot of goals because the goalie will not have time to react to make a save. Unless of course you take a weak shot or make a weak "hospital ball" type pass to the goalkeeper. Do not let the goalkeeper affect your ability to get a shot on goal. Don't lose focus by worrying about him. Make good contact with the ball. A shot, header, or pass with good pace, even if it's really close to the keeper has a good chance of going in. Certainly a 100% better chance of scoring than if you don't shoot or miss the net!"***

The next step in this portion of the psychological coaching of my strikers is to make them believe that, when they are stopped from scoring by the goalkeeper, in many cases it's because the goalkeeper has guessed correctly. The fact is that when the goalkeeper moves before a shot is taken, you can tell your strikers that the goalkeeper is doing his best to move out of the way of the shot so that the striker can score.

Check out examples of this in pictures 63D and 63E. In picture 63D, Michael Owen of England scores easily when the keeper decides to guess and guesses wrong before Owen's last touch.

I tell my strikers this:

> ***"It's a huge goal that the goalkeepers have to protect. Even though they come out to cut down angles, your job is to hit the net in your shot. Think of it this way. When a goalie makes a save from 7 yards away and sometimes even 12, he has guessed correctly. The goalkeepers will be guessing most of the time. They will move before you direct the ball at the net. Often they will move out of the way for you to score. DO NOT miss the net and let someone who is guessing, stop you from scoring. And you thought that goalkeepers made great saves with their lightning fast reflexes. Chances are you were wrong. They outguessed you. Or put in another way, they outsmarted you. That's a fact. No secret there. Do not let the goalkeepers outsmart you. Hit the net!***
>
> ***... and even if the ball happens to hit the goalkeeper, he will not be able to react quick enough to hold on to the ball most of the time and the rebound can cause you or a teammate to score. Make sure you are ready for a rebound from your shot or a shot by a teammate because in many cases there will be one."***

In picture 63E, Van Nistelrooy comes in from an angle, puts his head down and fires straight ahead. Being a world class goal scorer, he knows where the goal is and knows it's not going to move. He takes only two touches to score and also knows that he's less than 7 yards away from the keeper. He also knows that his main task is to hit the net.

Ruud Van Nistelrooy sees the keeper moving in his peripheral field of vision from right to left. The brain can detect motion easily without the eyes focusing on the moving object. Therefore, the logical thing to do is to put the ball on goal. Because the keeper has moved out of the way in order to help Van Nistelrooy score, the ball beats the keeper to the keeper's left. In picture 63F, you see where the ball beats the keeper.

The key to scoring in these situations is for the striker to remain composed and use the facts I have noted to decide what to do. If a visual cue is detected that can help make the goal even more certain, then the striker can use this to his advantage. But more often than not, the visual cues that keepers give do more to distract the shooters than help them.

Young strikers often detect visual cues that goalkeepers provide. In their lack of experience they allow the visual cue provided by the keeper to affect their decision making process. Even experienced strikers can be affected by these visual cues, which cause them to make poor decisions when it comes to scoring. The logical part of the brain is affected by visual cues that appear to make things seem different than they really are. Check out pictures 68K and 68L of Manchester United's Wayne Rooney. He makes a poor decision based on the visual cue he received as he was preparing to play the ball. The illogical and maybe creative side of the brain overrode the logical side of the brain.

Picture 63E: Ruud Van Nistelrooy of Holland scores against Ivory Coast in the 2006 World Cup. Although the ball just left the foot of Van Nistelrooy in this picture, the goalkeeper had actually started his movement to his right before the ball was struck. He was guessing. Van Nistelrooy placed the ball close to the centre of the goal and scored without a problem. Action Images/Michael Regan

Picture 63F: In this picture, taken right after Picture 63E you see that Ruud Van Nistelrooy of Holland scores against Ivory Coast by putting the ball right where the goalkeeper should have stayed. Instead, the keeper tried to be smart and guess where Van Nistelroy was aiming for but the world class striker notices motion from the keeper in his field of vision and consequently places the ball toward the centre of the goal to score. "The Big 7" as a mental cue should be a way to make sure strikers don't miss these scoring opportunities. Action Images/Tony O'Brien

How can we make sure strikers do things that will provide the best chance of success? As coaches we need to come up with mental cues that work in making and keeping the logical decision making process intact while receiving varied visual cues from goalkeepers and defenders. The keeper's job is to distract the strikers and provide visual cues that actually hinder them from attaining success. The coach must make sure that the facts to goal scoring override visual cues that keepers emit, which, in most cases, are designed to put the attacker off.

Unless it's a certainty that the strikers will score, they should stick to the facts instead of the visual cues that they may detect. Sometimes, the visual cues are so strong that the strikers have to take them and score because of the obvious. For example a goalkeeper may play his angles poorly and make the visual cues provided too strong to ignore. Young strikers may be faced with inexperienced goalkeepers or goalkeepers that do not play very well positionally. Young strikers may score a lot of goals because of this but as they move up in age groups and levels of play; they will be unable to cope with goalkeepers and defenders who play better if their abilities to understand the secrets to scoring goals do not improve. Their goal scoring numbers will go down and their chance to play at a higher level will diminish.

"Outsmart and Outwit the Goalkeeper and you will Outlast your Competition"

As goalkeepers get better and more experienced, they will get better at doing the right things more often which include providing visual distractions that can put off strikers. In fact, I believe that goalkeepers are illusionists. They have to make things seem different than they really are if they are to force errors from attackers. In pictures 63E and 63F, we see that Van Nistelrooy is unfazed by the keeper's attempt to distract him. He places the ball right past the keeper barely a yard away from his body. The key to the psychological cue "The Big 7" is to reinforce the fact that the keeper is very close to him and therefore has little chance to react to a ball played past him, even a yard away. I want the striker to know instinctively that the goalkeeper probably doesn't have time to react to a shot (and that includes a ball played inches away from the keeper's body as in picture 63G), rather than to think that in order to beat a goalkeeper he has to place the ball just inside the post or under the crossbar. The main objective becomes avoiding hitting the keeper, which I'll go into in chapter 66.

Here is what I tell players when concluding my section on "The Big 7":

> ***"You know the facts to scoring goals; you know that the goalkeeper is close to you and just guessing to try to stop you; and you know that all you have to do is make sure to hit the net. Make sure you take the shooting opportunity when in the box and do not miss the net! You know that there will be cases where the goalkeeper will make the save either by guessing correctly or by staying big and blocking your shot. But in the end, I guarantee you that you will score more goals when you take an early shot and hit the net then by waiting too long to shoot or trying too hard to place the ball just inside of the post. In order to outlast your competition and make it to the next level, remember the rules and facts to scoring. Now you have the tools to outsmart and outwit the goalkeeper to help you score more goals. It's a competitive world out there so it's all about 'survival' if you want to play at the highest levels"***

In the sequence of pictures 63H, 63I, 63J and 63K, note that the goalkeeper appears to move after the shot has been taken. If that's correct, why did he decide to go in the opposite direction to where the ball went? The answer is that, in reality, the goalkeeper had already made up his mind which way he was going to go. His muscles had already been told what to do and they had "gone over the cliff". It was too late to switch tasks. He was guessing because he knew that, if he didn't, his reaction time would be too slow to stop the shot. The goal scorer, Hulk, is less than seven yards away from the goalkeeper when he takes the shot.

Picture 63G: Michael Owen takes a penalty shot with power. Knowing that a shot is coming, the goalkeeper still does not have quick enough reaction time to stop a shot less than 1 yard away from his body. Action Images/Lee Smith

Picture 63H

Picture 63I

Picture 63J

Picture 63K

Picture 63H, 63I, 63J, 63K: In picture 63H, at this moment, Hulk of Brazil makes contact with the ball to shoot at the goalkeeper. Note that the ball is less than 7 yards from the goalkeeper. Although it appears that the goalkeeper can now decide to drop down to his right to make the save, he dives to his left instead. Why would he do this? The answer is that the goalkeeper made the decision which way to go before the shot was taken. It was an educated guess. You could even say that it appears that the goalkeeper moved out of the way so that the ball would go into the net. Note that the ball entered the goal close to the centre of the goal. All photos by Les Jones/Covershots

CHAPTER 64

2 Too Close

Before I move on to more information about the goalkeeper, I want to point out one more fact about scoring goals and distances from the keeper.

Based on the 2002 FIFA Men's World Cup

- On shots, only 1 goal was scored where the shooter was less than 2 yards from the goalkeeper, (i.e. in front of the goalie) at the moment of the last touch
- Most goals were scored from 2-7 yards from the goalie

The fact that only 1 goal was scored when the last touch was less than 2 yards away from the goalkeeper is something you should know but I'm not too sure if and when I would tell my strikers about this statistic. In order to come up with this fact, I had to stop the action many times to calculate exactly at what distance the last touch occurred when the striker seemed close to the goalkeeper. Interestingly, when watching goals at regular motion, in almost all those type of goals, it seemed as though the striker was closer to the keeper than 2 yards away. However, when I played them in slow motion and paused, I found that in fact they were 2 yards or more away from the keeper at the moment of the last touch.

In some cases, after the last touch, the striker would end up colliding with the goalkeeper because one or both of them were moving towards the other. This made it seem as though a fair amount of goals were scored when the striker was less than 2 yards away from the keeper at the moment of the last touch. It was not the case at all. Only through stop action replay, was I able to ascertain that rarely did a goal result when the last touch was closer than 2 yards away from the goalkeeper.

Picture 64A: Manchester United's Roy Keane is less than 2 yards away from West Ham goalkeeper Craig Forrest as he stretches to touch the ball on his last touch to try and score. Forrest has come out to narrow down the shooting angles and does not guess which way the ball will be re-directed. Forrest maintains good body position in this instance. Action Images/John Sibley

When goalkeepers get very close to the shooters, their chances of stopping goals increase dramatically. The chances to score at the 2-3 yard distance is still very favourable for the striker but many strikers fail to take the shooting (or passing) opportunity from this close because they think they will not score. Since things are often happening quickly, players in this position may actually think they are only 1 or 2 yards away from a goalkeeper when they may in fact be 3 to 4 yards away. This will happen when the keeper is still moving forward towards them. They think a chance to score is no longer there. In picture 51A from chapter 51, Mia Hamm does not score because of this assumption. Although the picture does not show this, she had a chance to direct the ball at the goal when she was 3 yards away from the keeper. But she decided not to, probably because she thought the keeper was closer to her than she actually was and felt that she could not score.

Picture 64B: Canadian Craig Forrest, goalkeeper for West Ham United, maintains his position rather than trying to guess where Roy Keane would direct the ball, and makes the save. Forrest increased his chances to make the save dramatically by getting within 2 yards of the attacker when the ball was last touched. Picture supplied by Action Images

In picture 64A we see Roy Keane of Manchester United trying to score from closer than 2 yards away. Goalkeeper Craig Forrest of West Ham United has narrowed the angle perfectly and does not try to guess where the ensuing re-direct is going to go. In picture 64B, Forrest makes the save. In these pictures Roy Keane probably had no other options but to slide to get a foot on the ball to try and score. If in fact Forrest had tried to guess where the ball was going to go and moved in that direction, it's possible that Keane would have scored. This is precisely one reason why I may not even bring this point up to my strikers. It's just a good point for the coaches to know so that they are aware of the facts.

Coaches can use the "2 too close" mental cue if their striker is always trying to get too close to the keeper before shooting. In that case, you may want to point out this fact to your strikers but I suspect that strikers who think they are too close to the keeper and don't shoot, decide to try to go around the keeper as an alternative. Their problem is more likely to be that they think they are closer than they really are and therefore don't shoot and thus try something fancy. You may have to alert them to the fact that they can be very close to the keeper and still score.

Picture 64C: Fernando Torres of Spain scores the only goal of the Euro UEFA 2008 Final to win the championship for Spain by scoring his goal when his last touch was less than 2 yards away from the goalkeeper. Lehmann came out to close down the angle but Torres decided to direct the ball at the goal instead of trying to go around the goalkeeper. This is never a bad idea regardless of what the statistics have to say about shooting from closer than 2 yards away from the goalkeeper. Action Images/Tony O'Brien

Encourage your strikers to shoot even when they think they are too close because, when they don't shoot, it usually is because they will have misjudged their perception of distance. What may appear to be less than 2 yards to them will in fact be more than 2 yards most of the time and therefore a shot at goal is the best decision to make.

Make sure your players are alert and anticipating a rebound even when they shoot from within 2 yards, because there will be a good chance that there will be one.

In picture 64C, Fernando Torres of Spain is only 1.5 yards away from the keeper when he touches the ball past the keeper to score in the Final of Euro 2008 to win the trophy for Spain. I believe that a ball directed at the goal from within 7 yards of the keeper is never a bad idea and that includes when the striker is closer than 2 yards away because most likely there won't be any other better options. Spanish fans were glad Torres did not pay attention to the statistics. Sometimes when the goalkeeper is within 2 yards of the striker and guessing to make a save, a chip pass over the keeper is the best option. Definitively better than attempting to go around the keeper.

A Small Psychological Point that can pay big Dividends

In pictures 64A and 64B, Forrest not only cuts down the shooting angle and holds his position but also provides no rebound. And in cases such as these when good goalkeeping saves a goal, I like to encourage my strikers to applaud the goalkeeper and give them a pat on the back for making a great save. I want my striker to realize that he didn't do anything wrong and that the keeper did very well. In this way, my striker can stay positive instead of getting down on himself for not scoring. It's a small psychological point that can keep your striker in the game and excited about the next opportunity.

CHAPTER 65

Goalkeepers are Illusionists

In chapter 63, I briefly touched on the idea that goalkeepers are illusionists in some way. Keepers have to try and make the attackers do something that they want them to do. In order to do this, they have to make things appear in a certain way to the strikers so that they believe what the keepers want them to believe. The goal is to block a shot by making the strikers shoot where they want the ball to go, or by forcing them to miss the target or to not shoot at all. Illusionists, also called magicians, make you think that something is happening when in fact it's not. By tricking you into believing something that you think is real but is not, they actually do what seems to be undoable or magical. It doesn't really happen as you think you see it. It's quite amazing how we can be fooled. This is also a job of the goalkeepers. It will allow them to make saves and prevent goals.

Illusionists and magicians are lifelong students of their craft and are always thinking of how they can pull their next trick. I believe goalkeepers are very similar. In fact I believe that keepers that are not students of the game can only go so far in their careers. The poorest magicians will be left off the team at the higher levels of play. I recall being at a goalkeeping session with Dick Howard, chairman of FIFA's technical study group. He was lecturing about what some keepers did to try and stop shots. He was talking about some of the theories different goalkeepers from around the world had about their uniforms. Some keepers would go out before a game and check out the colours that strikers would see behind the goal and felt that if they could blend in with the background, then the strikers would not be able to clearly see them. They would look for a uniform colour that would blend in with the background. They believed that this would force the shooter to shoot the ball at the centre of goal having assumed that the keeper is not really there. Then they would suddenly appear out of nowhere to save a shot that was directed right at them.

Other goalkeepers would think in the opposite manner. They would wear something bright so that when the shooter would glance up to take a shot, the bright colour of their shirt would attract them to shoot the ball right into their chest. Other keepers found fabrics with dazzling design patterns to custom manufacture their jerseys. The artistic and blurred jerseys were meant to partially hypnotize the shooter and throw them off. These types of jerseys were prevalent in the 80's. The point is that keepers are always thinking of ways to distract shooters.

I also think that good goalkeepers have their own secrets about how to create illusions and play their positions. Their secrets would include general things but also very specific things as well, such as knowing the tendencies of certain players that they may play with and against. Keepers will keep their own secrets on players on their own teams because they never know when that player may be playing against them down the road. And I'll also bet you that most goalkeepers, although team players in many aspects of their game, will not divulge their personal secrets to their teammates or other keepers on the team. They'll even keep secrets that can help the team.

Call us a bit selfish but there is only one goalkeeper on the field at once and competing for a position is very intense. We will avoid giving away secrets about a striker on any aspect of goalkeeping that will give other keepers an edge over us. In fact, we honestly believe that other goalkeepers will be withholding some information from us. That's not to say we don't share some of the more obvious traits that other players or coaches tell us about certain players, but it's the ones we find out about on our own that may remain secrets for a long time.

Being a good illusionist has to be one reason why goalkeepers improve with age. Have you ever wondered why goalkeepers tend to be at their best when they are in their 30s and even into their early 40s, while the rest of the players on the field tend to go down drastically once they hit their 30s? At Euro2008, over 47.9% of the goalkeepers in the competition were over 29 years of age. Of all the positions on the field, goalkeepers had the oldest average age. In fact, the next position closest to goalkeepers in players over the age of 29 were defenders who had only 29.75% of players in this category. That's almost 20% more goalkeepers over the age of 29 than the next closest group. The spread gets even greater with midfielders and strikers. The reason for this cannot be because their reflexes and agility get better once they hit their 30s. In fact, you would think that for a position that requires quite a bit of acrobatics where the body gets punished for it, the younger, the better. Quite contrary to what seems to make sense isn't it?

<u>% of Players at Euro 2008 over the age of 29 by position</u>

Goalkeepers 47.9%
Defenders 29.75%
Midfielders 28.8%
Strikers 17.3%

Source: euro2008.uefa.com

With age, obviously comes experience and with this experience keepers will become better at guessing what can and may happen. They instinctively make more accurate guesses based on previous experiences. Their skills at being illusionists are obviously better. I certainly wish I could have taken this ability to predict the future to the casino!

A NICE STORY:

The trick is for the young striker to learn the secrets to scoring as presented in this book <u>before</u> the goalkeeper becomes experienced!

The point I want young players to understand about goalkeepers and their age is that scoring <u>will</u> become harder. If young strikers want to move up the ranks to college, state or provincial teams, and eventually youth National, Olympic, and pro academy teams, they need to impress scouts and coaches with their ability to score goals when goalkeepers are less experienced. It's one of the quickest ways to advance above others and "get noticed".

Analisa Romano, a U16 girl playing with Vaughan Azzurri in Toronto, took my course in June after her season had started and she struggled with scoring. Although she played at the highest youth level for her age at the time, she got passed up for a spot on the Provincial team. The day after she started taking my "Golden Goal Scoring" course, she scored 4 goals in 1 game. By the end of the season, she won the league scoring title. In September of the same year, she went to Italy to do some training with a youth program. She kept scoring and because she had Italian parents, she was eligible to play for Italy. She got called to train with the Italian National U19 team. This all happened in a 3 month span.

No one can improve his or her technical skills that rapidly in just 3 months. To play at a club level in one month but not being good enough to move up to the next level locally but then being able to move up to a National team level in such a short time on skill alone is virtually not possible. This shows that in the case of strikers, the ability to score goals is what sets them apart and not just their technical skills. A coach may see lots of talented players who can perform magic with a soccer ball, but in the case of strikers, they are looking for that scoring touch.

It was the mental side of training that she acquired in the course that got her there and got her noticed. And because she grasped the concepts so well in the course, her advancement was quick. Her coach, Gerry Gentile, also attended the course and was instrumental in constantly reminding her of the mental things covered in the course. The time to change things for the striker and make fast progress is when goalkeepers are young, less experienced, and not so good at being illusionists and predicting the future.

The human visual system, which occasionally falls for illusions, is probably based on survival in some way. It's designed to protect us. Motion is interpreted in the brain very quickly so that we can predict what may harm us and thus make us move in ways to avoid injury or death. I stated in Chapter 30 how the brain can be fooled when the eyes see one thing and the brain interprets it as something different causing a reaction to what it interprets instead of what it actually sees. It's probably a good thing that this condition exists within the human visual system for the goalkeeper. In other words, if the visual system was not able to quickly notice motion and make predictions then keepers would virtually be able to stop nothing. The human body is often just not quick enough to react to some situations as stated in the example about stopping a hard shot from the penalty spot. The human body and brain are designed to react by making predictions when it involves motion so that we can instinctively protect ourselves to survive. For example, have you ever noticed that whenever something appears in our field of vision and is close to our head, that we react with lightning fast reflexes to get our hands up to prevent something from hitting our head?

Whether it is a fly, or someone pretending to hit us in the head, our visual system and motion perception system in our brain pick this movement up quickly enough to allow us to make predictions and then quickly move our hands up to protect our head just in case something might harm it. In order to help us protect ourselves, our visual and motor muscular systems allow for errors in interpretation of motion perception. This is a good thing for keepers because it gives them the opportunity to try to do something to fool the strikers, which may work and often does. Thus the expression, "the hands are quicker than the eyes". For the purposes of survival, our system allows us to make errors and be fooled. Because this is possible, the keepers have the opportunity to fool strikers by being good illusionists.

Here are some of the things that keepers can do as illusionists

Goalkeepers as Illusionists

What keepers have to accomplish to improve their game

1) Distract attackers while they try to perform their skills.
2) Make strikers assume there is more pressure on them than there really is.
3) Appear closer to the shooter than they really are.
4) Make the strikers believe that there are no shooting options available.
5) Make attackers think that the only way to beat them is by beating them just inside the posts to score.
6) Make the attacker feel as though they can get hurt if they challenge for the ball.
7) Try and force the attacker to shoot on their good side.

I want to look at each of these points individually.

1) Distract Attackers

Once an attacker has cleared all other obstacles to shooting or heading such as those pesky defenders, it comes down to a battle between the shooter and the goalkeeper. At this moment in time the goalkeeper has exhausted all other options to stop an impending attempt at goal. His only and last recourse is to try and distract the shooter from hitting the net and beating him. Goalkeepers know that this is a tall order but they will not give up. They have a number of tricks up their sleeve that may work.

How can goalkeepers make the strikers mess up? As I've mentioned before, the best two options they have are to make the strikers not take the attempt to score, or have them take it but miss the net altogether. The final option is to have them shoot it right at them or where they will move to in order to get in the way of the ball.

Goalkeepers know that if there is some way that they can make the shooters take their eyes off the ball, then their chances for distracting them and make them mis-hit the ball will be greatly increased. So here are some of the tricks goalkeepers use to distract strikers. Fooling the strikers' senses of vision and sound are two things that may help accomplish the desired results. If the keepers move closer towards the strikers or get in their field of vision on crosses or while shooting, then the strikers may take their eyes off the ball and consequently miss it or partially miss it. If they shout loudly and cause the strikers to look to see where they are while a ball is in motion, they may cause them to take their eyes off the ball and miss it.

Goalkeepers like to make the net look smaller by cutting down angles and also having their hands up rather than down. The hands being up will block more of the view of the net for the attacker than having the hands down. The only time keepers keep their hands down is when the shooter is very very close to them and they need to cover the bottom part of the goal to make a save. In such a case, creating an illusion when the striker is very close to them is no longer an option. It is a key component of their repertoire when the shooter is over 3-4 yards away.

Part of the reason keepers keep their hands up while preparing for a shot is to try and distract the shooter. It's not always the best position. For example, when the keeper has his hands down as in picture 65A, it will appear that there is more room for the striker to shoot at than when the keeper comes out with his hands up as in picture 65B. Big hands up in the face of a striker will make the net look smaller and the keeper look bigger. In reality, the keeper is covering the exact same amount of space. Both pictures are taken with the ball at the same distance away from the goalkeeper. Also, goalkeepers wear gloves that are much bigger than their hands. Large gloves block more of the goal and the contact area with the ball is larger.

Picture 65A: The goalkeeper's hands are down as he challenges the shooter. From the strikers' point of view, it will appear as though they have more room to shoot at than when a keeper's hands are up as shown in picture 65B. Goalkeeper is Matthew Caldaroni. Picture by John DeBenedictis

Picture 65B: The keeper's hands are up as he challenges the shooter. By keeping the hands up, it will appear that the striker has less space to score as the goalkeeper's body and hands cover up more of the goal than when the hands are down. In reality, they will cover the same amount of space but if the goalkeeper in this picture forces the striker NOT to shoot or to take an extra touch to try and displace the keeper, then the keeper's chances at preventing a goal will improve significantly.

In picture 65C, we see Gianluigi Buffon of Italy who is a tall goalkeeper, cover a bigger portion of the goal than a shorter goalkeeper. Although he may not cover a much bigger portion of the goal in his ability to stop a shot at goal, when coming out to cut down the distance between himself and the shooter and getting into the strikers field of vision, he will take up a much bigger percentage of the striker's field of vision than a shorter keeper would. The illusion that a taller goalkeeper will leave on the shooter's mind will be more powerful than what a shorter goalkeeper can elicit. When a striker with very little time peeks at the goalkeeper before shooting, he will feel as though he has less chance of scoring on a taller goalkeeper as opposed to a shorter goalkeeper because of this illusion. This will often result in the striker trying to score by placing the ball in off the goalpost. This is just one of the reasons why taller goalkeepers are desired.

2) Make Strikers Assume There is More Pressure

As a goalkeeper this was one of my best secrets. I know that if the strikers feel that they have little or no time to shoot when in fact they may have lots, then they will rush their shot and are more likely to make a mistake. How do keepers pull this magical trick? They are very vocal usually directing their defenders. Voice carries quickly. Also, early in a game, coming out to challenge strikers aggressively even if it is not needed can make the strikers feel that on every ball

Picture 65C: A taller goalkeeper like Gianluigi Buffon covers a much larger area in the shooter's field of vision than a shorter goalkeeper does. Without making a save, his size may deter players from shooting. A taller goalkeeper who covers a larger part of a shooters field of vision may result in the shooter trying harder to pick corners and consequently missing the net altogether whereas a shot on goal may have resulted in a goal. Coaches like tall goalkeepers for other reasons such as coming out for crosses but their shot stopping abilities are often not any better than smaller keepers. But their ability to cover more of the shooters field of vision creating an illusion that makes them look even bigger than they are can be an asset. Strikers must realize that the net is still relatively large in comparison to the goalkeeper and the chance to score is still very good provided they do the simple things well. In this picture, Buffon follows a ball that misses the goal just in case he got his positioning wrong. Action Images/Christian Charisius

played towards the keeper, they will come out quickly for the ball.

Also, I always wanted my defenders to get a leg in the way. I wanted my defenders to lunge to try and distract a shooter from shooting. Many strikers will think their defender is closer to them than they really are and consequently will not shoot.

There are always discussions as to what the keepers should do on a through ball. Should they stop at some point and get set for a shot or should they keep coming and get as close as possible to the shooters and hope that an ensuing shot will hit them? Inexperienced strikers may be fooled by an oncoming keeper who may force them to rush their shot. This can cause strikers to take their eyes off the ball and miskick the ball or miss the goal altogether. Composed strikers should be able to distinguish between real pressure and manufactured pressure. In chapter 66 on reading human motion, I provide my strikers with some ideas on how to score every time when a goalkeeper keeps coming at them. At the same time, a keeper coming out too quickly with no self control may be susceptible to being beat by having the striker push the ball to either side of him and then passing the ball into the open goal.

3) Appear Closer

This point is very similar to the previous one because when goalkeepers make themselves appear closer to the shooters than they really are, the strikers will assume there is more pressure on them than there really is and thus hopefully force them into an error. Standing tall with hands up may make them appear bigger. When coaching strikers, I want them to know the tricks that keepers use to stop them from scoring so that they can remember these tricks in the heat of the moment. I like to use many different visual cues to make them think straight. The picture of the side view mirror in the passenger side of a car such as the one in picture 65D makes quite an impression on players. Because of the curve in the mirror, which allows the driver to see more of the road, the objects in the mirror are closer than they appear. This is written right on the mirror. This is what I say to strikers in my golden goal scoring course:

> ***"Similar to the illusion in the side view mirror in a car where the inscription says that 'objects in mirror are closer than they appear', you need to say to yourself that this is exactly what the goalkeeper wants you to believe. They want you to think they are closer than they really are. As a striker you have to change the wording a bit in your mirror (mind). Say to yourself, "Goalkeepers are farther than they appear". Take your time, be cool and composed and place your shot where the keeper must make the save in order***

to stop you. Do not miss the net by rushing your shot. Do not mis-kick the ball by taking your eyes off the ball or by rushing your shot thus making it an easy save for the keeper to make."

Picture 65D: A play on words with this graphic may help your strikers make smarter decisions to execute the skill to score properly. They should change the wording to read "Goalkeepers are farther than they appear". Goalkeepers want your strikers to think that they are closer to them than they really are.

4) Believe There are no Options. Keepers have to be Good Mathematicians

Without question good goalkeepers have to be some sort of mathematicians. Not only do they have to know the probabilities and possibilities of doing certain things that may result in them stopping more shots but they also have to have a good grasp of geometry. Angles will be an important part of their repertoire. The best possible method of narrowing the shooting options for the striker will be to come off their goal line to cut down the distance between them and the shooter. This will make the net appear smaller and themselves bigger. The challenge for the keepers will be to be at a correct angle. Poor positioning and understanding of angles will reduce their chances of stopping the shot.

The easiest way to get the correct angle is to come towards the striker from the centre of the goal directly towards the ball. For example in diagram 65E, the goalkeeper (O) is preparing to stop a shot from player X2. If the keeper comes out from the centre of his goal and heads directly towards the ball, then he will be in position O1 and would properly cut down the angles. The dotted line represents the keeper's path from the centre of the goal to the ball, which he must intersect to get the best position. The attacker's view of the goal will be intersected by the goalkeeper right down the middle, which should make him aim for just inside the posts. This is what the keeper wants to do. It's easy to come out and cut down the shooting angles when the ball is stationary or moving towards the goal. But if the keeper is coming off the line and the ball is not rolling directly at the goal prior to a strikers' last touch, then the keeper will be challenged to narrow the shooting options properly. If the ball is moving across the face of the goal from right to left or vice versa, the distance the keeper has to move right or left to cover the goal and reduce shooting angles will be difficult to judge.

Here is another area where experience will come in handy. In diagram 65E, let's assume X2 passes the ball to X1. The keeper will have to change positions to narrow the angle properly. If the ball travels 10 yards to the right of the keeper, in order to cover his goal properly, the keeper will also have to shift to his right. How many yards will he have to shift laterally? The keeper will not have time to go back to the centre of the goal to come out again. If the goalkeeper does not move far enough as in position O2, then the shooter will have a clear path to goal at the near post. If the keeper moves to position O4 and goes too far, then the shooter has a clear and easy shot to the far post. Even experienced goalkeepers may not find position O3 all the time.

When balls are moved laterally, the striker can gain an advantage because the keeper's attempt to create an illusion may be challenged. Make sure your strikers are aware of their advantage in a situation where the keeper has come out to narrow shooting angles and then the ball is played across the face of the goal. The striker must be cognitively aware that although he may be shooting from more of an angle and his chances to score seem to have been reduced, in fact they haven't because the keeper has to shift positions to cover the angles correctly and is more prone to making errors. Also, the keeper may be in motion and not have time to get set for a shot. These two factors will leave the striker who is composed and knows what to do with a great chance to score. Andres Iniesta of Spain, as I will explain shortly, caught the keeper moving laterally and converted his chance perfectly in the winning goal at the 2010 World Cup Final in South Africa.

So, as in the example from diagram 65E, when the goalkeeper is faced with a situation where a ball is played from X2 to X1 and where X1 would run forward and be clear to take a shot, what would you expect the goalkeeper to do? I would say that many goalkeepers would try and create an illusion to make the striker miss the goal. If they are getting ready to stop a shot from X2 by standing in position O1 and then are forced to move to try and stop a shot from X1 from a different angle, they know their angles may be off. They will not have time to go back to the centre of goal and then come out again to face a shot from a new angle and prepare properly. They will have to think quickly and part of their plan will be to get as close as possible to the new shooter. They'll try and take up position O5 instead of O2, O3, or O4. This will allow room for errors in their judgment of their angles because by being close to the shooter, it will make the striker think that his shooting angles are narrow and thus the striker must place the ball inside one of the posts.

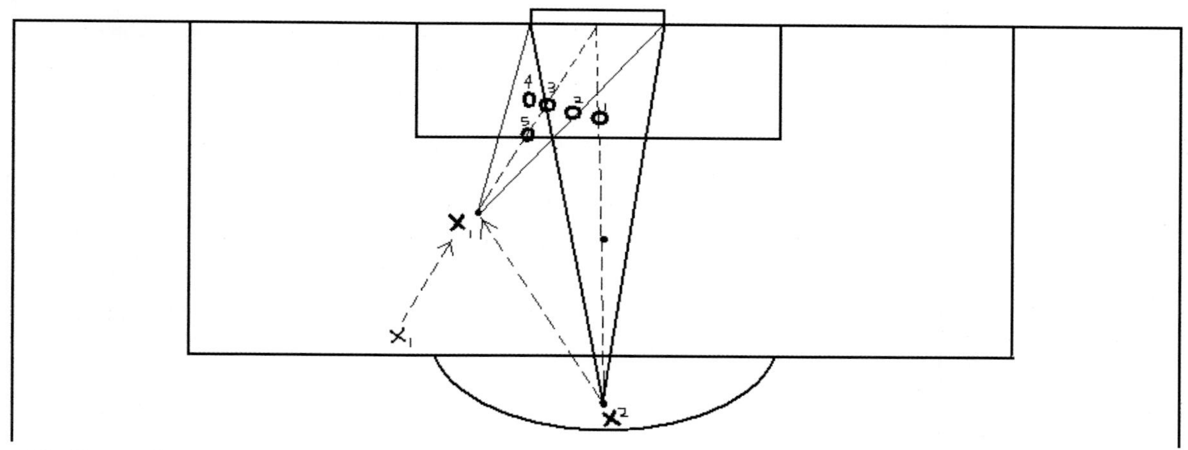

Diagram 65E: The goalkeeper must try to narrow the shooting angles to have a better chance of stopping the ball. The main purpose of narrowing angles is to create an illusion. The illusion being that in order for the strikers to score, they feel that they must attempt to place the ball right inside the posts. Often keepers are successful in creating this illusion in the strikers' mind as they proceed to aim there and then miss the goal altogether. Experienced strikers like Del Piero in the next picture are not always fooled by such an illusion.

In picture 65F and 65G, Italy's Alessandro Del Piero maintains his composure and does not let German goalkeeper Jens Lehmann distract him by making him try to put the ball in off the far post. Del Piero made sure he hit the target in this semi-final game at the 2006 World Cup in Germany. The ball actually crossed the line more than a yard from inside the far post.

In picture 65G, Del Piero shows his composure but notice how he does the simple things right. When you watch this goal on TV you can assume that his eyes are on the net while he is shooting but this picture shows that when it comes down to business, the striker must focus on the ball and let nothing else distract him. Notice how he uses the inside of the foot to pass the ball into the goal. Young strikers may let the goalkeeper distract them from keeping their eyes on the ball and from making sure to hit the net. Del Piero knows that Lehmann was displaced laterally and now he has a great advantage since the keeper may not have his angles covered properly.

In the 2010 World Cup Final match between Spain and Holland, Andres Iniesta executes his final touch absolutely perfectly. A thing of beauty from a coaching perspective although I'm sure the Dutch were not so impressed. The pass from Cesc Fabregas that pierced the Dutch defense and sent Iniesta on course to shoot to score, forced the Dutch goalkeeper (Stekelenburg) to move laterally to try and stop the shot. This is where Iniesta was brilliant because he "Prepared to Score". Young players may have taken an extra touch to prepare to shoot. Iniesta, who often tries to get too close to the goal to shoot, prepared to score perfectly on "one touch" this time. Knowing that he had a charging goalkeeper coming out to cut down the angle and a defender throwing himself down to block the shot, he maintained his composure by not panicking in any way. He was careful not to over-hit the ball causing a miss or to shoot too softly to allow the keeper to react to stop the shot.

As you can see from picture 65H, Iniesta kept his eyes on the ball right up until he made contact with the ball. He knew where the net was and did not need to look to see where it was. His full concentration was on striking the ball properly and keeping his eyes on the ball and hitting the net. He knew that the keeper was displaced laterally and thus shooting where he came from was the best option. He also knew that keeping the ball low would give him the best chance to score. In picture 65I, which was taken right after his contact with the ball, you will notice that his head is still down, showing that he was fully concentrating on the ball at the time of contact and not being distracted

Picture 65F: Germany's Jens Lehmann is forced to come out in desperation after he got set to stop a shot from the center of the goal area by Italy's Gilardino. Instead Gilardino sent a lateral pass to Alessandro Del Piero. Lehmann closed down the shooting angles as much as possible to try and force Italy's Del Piero to shoot wide but Alessandro Del Piero scores his team's second goal of the game by putting the ball more than one yard inside the far post. Action Images/Kieran Doherty

Picture 65G: Del Piero, pictured at the moment of his last touch prior to picture 65F where he is watching the ball go into the net. Notice that his head is down with his eyes focused on the ball. He uses the inside of the foot to pass the ball into the goal. He knows where the net is and makes sure that the keeper does not distract him. Lehmann plays the ball in textbook fashion, moving quickly across his goal to cut down the angles and set himself up for the shot. With the shooter less than 5 yards away from him, he knows his reflexes will not be fast enough to stop a shot past him. But by being big and close he is hoping that Del Piero will hit part of his body to stop the shot or miss the goal altogether. Del Piero knows that the keeper was displaced laterally and therefore an error on his part can cost his team an important goal. He cannot miss the goal. Action Images/Lee Smith

Picture 65H: Andres Iniesta scores the first and only goal for Spain giving them enough goals to win the 2010 FIFA World Cup. He received a pass from Cesc Fabregas which displaced the goalkeeper laterally. He knew that he had to concentrate on striking the ball towards the middle of the goal making sure not to miss the goal in order to give him the best chance to score. Notice his deep concentration on making sure to keep his eyes on the ball. With close to a billion people watching all over the world, he did not let the pressure get to him despite visual distractions from the goalkeeper and the defender. Action Images/Jason Cairnduff

Picture 65I: This picture was taken right after his contact with the ball. Notice how Iniesta's head is still down, showing that he was fully concentrating on the ball at the time of contact and not being distracted by the keeper, defender, or the urge to see the final product before his "last touch". Action Images/Jason Cairnduff

by the keeper, defender, or the urge to see the final product before his last touch.

In picture 65J, you will see the ball going into the net to win Spain the World Cup. Notice that the ball did not go into the goal anywhere near the far post. The ball crossed the line almost 3 yards away from the post. A brilliant strike that showed the skill that the Spaniards had that enabled them to win their first ever World Cup.

In picture 65K, Manchester United's Peter Schmeichel comes off his line to close down the shooting angles against Manchester City's Niall Quinn. He has tried to distract the striker by jumping at him and making himself look very big. As you can tell, any shot at goal that does not accidentally hit Schmichael will be a goal but the illusionist that Schmeichel is in this picture wins over the situation. Unbelievably, Quinn fails to score because he misses the net.

Picture 65J: The 2010 World Cup winning goal crossed the goal line almost 3 yards away from the post. Iniesta made sure to hit the net rather than place his shot perfectly in a corner because the goalkeeper was displaced laterally before the shot. In situations where the goalkeeper is displaced from side to side, it is important for the striker to concentrate on the ball and make sure to hit the net because it's a great chance to be a hero. Too many players young and old miss these clear scoring opportunities. Action Images/Frank Faugere

When the strikers think there are no shooting options, then the goalkeepers have gained the edge in stopping the shot that they shouldn't really have because they do not control the strikers' last touch.

So how can the strikers make the goalkeeper do a poor job in covering the goal? Well, if strikers really want to guarantee that the keepers will mess up their ability to cover the goal properly, what they need to do is arrive at the field in the middle of the night before a game. They'll need some tools and helpers in order to move one of the goals so that they are not even with each other. This will guarantee lots of goals!

Picture 65K: Manchester United goalkeeper Peter Schmeichel cuts down the shooting angles and makes Manchester City's Niall Quinn believe that the only way to beat him is by placing the ball right inside the post. Consequently he misses the net altogether. Action Images/ Darren Walsh

IF YOU HEAR OR SEE COWS IN THE BACKGROUND, MAKE SURE YOUR STRIKERS AND KEEPERS CHECK THE FIELD!

I recall playing goal in a cup game away from home when I was young. The field and clubhouse were in a rural area in the middle of nowhere with farms everywhere. Our opponent's fans must have come from all over to watch their team play. The stadium's seating was only on one side of the field. Farmland surrounded the rest of the field. Cows were in a distant field, and they would moo every once in a while. The fence behind my goal was quite low and the grass in the ranch behind me was quite high. In the warm-up our players kept hitting the ball over the goal and into the long grass behind me. I was afraid to jump the fence to retrieve the ball because of the possibility that there might have been some cows or bulls hiding behind the tall grass. I did not want to get chased by any cows or bulls!

While I was warming up with players taking shots from outside the box, I kept getting scored on. After quite a few goals I was starting to question my psychological state of mind as I kept getting my angles all wrong. This was not normal for me, because I relied on my ability to cover my angles to make up for my lack of height.

After allowing a number of goals in the warm up, I took a quick look at the other goal at the other end of the field to check my sanity. I always look at the goal at the other end of the field to gauge where the centre of my goal is: to my surprise the other goal was off by about 4 yards. When I stood at the centre of my goal and looked directly across the field, I realized that I would be lining up with one of the posts at the other end of the field. Obviously, I had to adjust my angles for the game and kept looking back at my own goal to check my angles. Our team won that game and thankfully, we never had to play there again.

The point is that, most young players will not always be playing in perfect fields as they work their way up the ranks. Goalkeepers always use the other goal to judge their positioning. They cannot always keep looking back to find their own goal. Is there any kind of advantage that your strikers can gain by checking their surroundings prior to any game?

One other outcome of making it seem as though there are no shooting angles available is that strikers are likely to touch the ball one more time before attempting a shot at goal. With each touch, the keeper has more time to set up or close down the angles even more. Also, that extra touch can be a bad one, which once again would favour the goalkeeper. As we know, with each touch of the ball, the striker's chances to score diminish.

I'm sure the debate will linger on about the 2010 World Cup Final game between Spain and Holland in regards to the turning point in that game. With close to a billion viewers watching, I would say that Arjen Robben's breakaway chance to score in the second half could have been the deciding factor in that game. He received a through ball at full speed and took one touch to control the ball but then had to make a decision. Should he attempt to shoot to score on his next touch, or should he take an extra touch to get closer to the goal to shoot? Of course, we all know that Iker Casillas made a toe save on the shot which Robben took on his third touch (see picture 65L). Was it a lucky save or a touch too much?

You should know my thoughts about his decision. Robbens' second touch came when he was 22 yards out from the goal and at the edge of the D. Iker Casillas was at the penalty spot mark and in motion as he was coming out to narrow down the angle at that moment. Robben could have taken a shot on goal instead of taking an extra touch when the ball was 10 yards away from the goalkeeper. Robben decided to take an extra touch. By the time he caught up with the ball and got his body in place to take his last touch, the distance between Casillas and Robben was narrowed down to 3 yards. As you know, with each touch, the shooters chances to score go down.

Robben made a mistake by taking an extra touch. His chances to score dropped by about 50-57 % according to the facts from the previous 2 World Cups as stated in Chapter 46. But, on the other hand, he figured that Casillas would be guessing and moving before he took his last touch, which was correct and therefore he made sure not to miss the

Picture 65L: Arjen Robben took three touches and got too close to the goalkeeper in this opportunity. Spain's Iker Casillas guesses to make the save after cutting down the angle brilliantly but guesses wrong. Fortunately for him, the ball barely touches his toe to save a goal. Although Robben was correct in making sure to hit the net, he was unlucky that Casillas' toe nicked the ball denying him a goal and Holland a chance to win the World Cup. It's a game of inches. Action Images/Carl Recine

Picture 65M: Arjen Robben looks dejected after missing a chance to score in the 2010 FIFA World Cup Final. He knows he should have done better. Action Images/John Sibley

net. Robben made the right decision to make sure to hit the net. Casillas closed down the angle nicely but guessed instead of staying big and that in itself was an error on his part. But because Robben took an extra touch it allowed Casillas to get closer to Robben and narrow the angle. But as fate would have it, Robben's error to take an extra touch was greater than Casillas' error to guess where to go, which also happened to be in the wrong direction. Casillas got fortunate as his toe barely got in the way of Robben's shot and deflected the ball just past the post.

Maybe Robben's decision to take that extra touch was based on the illusion that Casillas looked bigger than he really was. In any event, Arjen Robben knew he should have done better as shown by his reaction in picture 65M. Spain got lucky in this situation. Holland ended up losing but the goalkeeper did his job of closing the distance between him and the shooter. You could say that Spain may have won the FIFA 2010 World Cup "by a toe"!

5) Think Inside the Posts to Score

Goalkeepers want strikers to think that the only way to beat them is with a perfect shot. If the keepers can get this impression in the strikers' brain, then they will force a lot of errors. Some goalkeepers can do this with their reputation alone. The goalkeeper with the best goals against average in the league may intimidate a striker. The coach may play up the opposing goalkeeper before a game reducing a striker's confidence by making him think that the only way to beat a particular keeper is by perfectly placing shots in the top corners or right inside the posts. The rules to scoring and facts to scoring are no different with the world's best goalkeepers or the average goalkeeper. Do not let statistics and reputation affect your strikers. Goals will still go in the goal in the same fashion if your strikers follow the rules to scoring goals. They always have and always will.

You may want to motivate your team by telling them that you'll need 110% from each player because the opponents are very good or the keeper is the league's best keeper, but make sure to talk to your strikers individually. Give them the confidence that all keepers are human and move in the same way. Tell them that when a chance to score develops, they just have to do the simple things without trying to score the perfect goal.

6) Feel Danger and Make the Striker Fear an Injury

Another way goalkeepers can be illusionists is that they can "scare" the strikers from attempting certain risky things if the strikers think they will get hurt. Goalkeepers who come out challenging for the ball by diving at feet or going up in the air with aggression, could make strikers think twice before going up to challenge for a ball. Unfortunately, as strikers move up the levels, these types of players will probably get weeded out because a striker must be brave. What you need to tell your strikers is that in many situations, the keepers are equally leery of getting hurt and that they may not always come out for the challenge. In picture 65N, the US goalkeeper and Canadian forward collide. Could the collision affect the striker's chances at scoring later in this game?

Just because the keeper may have come out for a cross or a through ball at an earlier point in the game, does not mean he will do so later with the same authority. It's possible that the keeper may have been totally "in the zone" to come out aggressively and with confidence to challenge for a ball. That same keeper, later in the game may misread a play, or be out of his "zone" and therefore may not come out as aggressively. The top strikers are always ready to pounce and challenge for tough balls. In picture 50G and 64C, Fernando Torres challenged for a ball despite a

Picture 65N: When a keeper comes out aggressively to challenge for the ball, opposing attackers may hold back in future situations because they are afraid of getting hurt. Hesitation on the part of the strikers can cause them to miss great scoring opportunities later in the game. They need to stay mentally alert and tough and be ready to pounce on balls and challenge for them all game long. Photo by Les Jones/Covershots

defender challenging him from behind and a goalkeeper rushing towards him. It turned out to be the only goal in the 2008 Euro final. He had enough time to get out of the way after his magical touch to avoid injury. In fact, it wasn't even close. Many players would have avoided the possible confrontation. Go back and check out picture 56B and see how Italy's Vieri does not let the keeper's big gloves and other distractions prevent him from getting to a ball and scoring.

7) Keepers will try and Trick Strikers to Shoot to Their Good Side

Most goalkeepers have a preferred side to dive or go down on (picture 65O). When a prediction is not clear as to which side the ball may go to, keepers are most likely to go towards their good side and even try and force the striker to shoot there. Thus, knowing a keeper's strong side should help a striker in situations where a ball could be placed either way. Sometimes a striker will choose one side or the other because it's easier to perform that shot based on the situation but when faced with the opportunity to make a choice, a clever striker will have studied the keeper and know his weak side.

Often when a keeper makes a save (especially on through balls or shots from angles), it's likely because the striker made a poor decision on when and where to shoot. The striker did not read the goalkeeper's motions well enough to make the correct decision. In the next chapter, I want to help the striker read the goalkeeper's body motions so that he will score more goals by shooting in areas where the keeper's body will not be able to stop the ball.

Picture 65O: Most goalkeepers prefer to dive to their good side. Knowing which side that may be, may help strikers decide where to shoot. Hope Solo goes down to her left on this shot. Photo by Les Jones/Covershots

CHAPTER 66

Human Motion and Goalkeeping

Goalkeepers Cannot Fly

As strange as it may seem, it's true, "goalkeepers cannot fly". I know that as a coach, you've thought that some keepers can fly. They are the keepers that have your players' number. Just when you're ready to cheer a goal, you see the goalkeeper "fly" across the goal to get to a ball. Trust me, they really cannot fly. I certainly wished that I could have when I played. The goalkeeper is only human and cannot do certain things. The keeper has to adhere to the same rules of human motion as anyone else to dive across the goal to get to a ball. To take off in any direction the keeper has to push off the ground in the opposite direction. To go further up or across the goalkeeper has to push down into the ground harder in the opposite direction. The goalkeeper's feet and legs have to act as a springboard and the reality is that to gain maximum thrust, he has to bend at the knees as much as possible to be able to push off, and regardless of how hard he thrusts, he will only be able to move his body so far to the side, so high, and so quickly. The laws of physics and gravity apply to the goalkeeper just like any other player.

After we have taught the strikers to make all the right decisions from a mental perspective as covered up to this point in this book, we need to move on to the advanced stage of perfecting our strikers. To do this, we need to teach strikers to read the human body movement of the goalkeeper (see chapters 39 and 40 for a detailed explanation of the physics of force and motion). In this chapter I break down some of these factors and explain them in a way that our strikers can learn, remember, and ultimately use them in the stressful situation of a game. If my strikers can visualize what a goalkeeper's movements must be every step of the way, then they can become even more powerful strikers.

When studying the goalkeeper's motions as it pertains to stopping a goal I focused on what the goalkeeper was doing at the moment of the striker's last touch. This moment in time was critical in my analysis. How can this information help coaches communicate to their players so that they can make decisions that will help them beat the goalkeeper more often? As a former goalkeeper, I knew exactly what needed to be done to score on me but explaining and simplifying this information for my strikers was not as easy. Like everyone else, some players tune in quickly while others need a different type of explanation.

I want to simplify and classify different goalkeeper movements that players can easily look for on their own before the keeper actually performs them. I want my strikers to react quickly to the goalkeeper's situation in any given set of circumstances. I want them to quickly know what the goalkeeper can and cannot do. For example, if my striker is approaching the goal focusing on a ball being crossed to him at head level, I want him to know what the goalkeeper in this situation is likely doing. I do not want the striker to take his eyes off the ball but rather use his peripheral vision to spot the goalkeeper and determine what the goalkeeper is doing based on some basic human motion rules I have set out for him. Then, based on these cues, he will pick the best action that will result in a goal. All of this has to happen quickly. I do not want my striker staring at the goalkeeper or taking his eyes off the ball and changing his mind while deciding what to do.

This is what we need to teach our strikers

Explaining how we want our Strikers to Read the Goalkeeper

1. When the striker is ready for his last touch, what different body positions can the goalkeeper possibly be in, in order to stop the attempt at goal?

2. Can he clearly identify these body positions and then determine how he can score on the goalkeeper for each situation? There may be one or two good options for the striker to use for each body position that the goalkeeper may be in.

3. Once we have given the striker some options to score for each body position that the goalkeeper will be in, we'll need to teach the striker to identify that position before it happens. Correctly predicting what the goalkeeper will be doing when the striker makes his last touch will be vital.

4. Finally, once the striker can correctly predict which body position the goalkeeper will be in when he gets the last touch on the ball, then we want the striker to pick one of the good options in his repertoire in order to score in that situation.

Making wrong predictions for the body positions of the goalkeeper at the moment of the striker's last touch will result in fewer goals. Making correct predictions for the goalkeeper's body position but choosing the wrong option on the last touch will also result in fewer goals. The coach will never really know what's going on in his striker's mind but we know from the previous chapter that the goalkeeper will do as much as humanly possible to confuse and distract the striker. Decisions have to be made quickly and accurately if the striker wants to score lots of goals.

If we can narrow the choices our strikers have to make when they get a scoring chance based on correctly predicting the goalkeepers body position to just one or two good options every time, then our strikers will score a load of goals. Hopefully, the action they choose will be correct more than 50% of the time and the only reason they do not score will be because the goalkeeper made a great save or a defender did something at the last second to prevent the goal. I would prefer to end a game knowing that my strikers always made the right choices when a chance to score presented itself. If this is the case, I'm sure my strikers will be amongst the top scorers in the league, provided of course that they get scoring chances and that they have the technical skills to shoot, head, or pass a ball.

To come up with methods to coach my strikers to make quick, accurate decisions, I had to relate them to the most important moment in their goal scoring efforts and analyze the possible goalkeeper's body positions when the striker is ready to take his last touch. I based this analysis on the position of the goalkeeper's feet. What's happening with the feet? While there seems to be only two possibilities, I have added a third in order to train the strikers to read the goalkeeper's ability to make a save more accurately. I want my strikers to be accurate in foreseeing the goalkeeper's exact position at the moment of their last touch and I want my strikers to feel the exhilaration of beating the goalkeeper by reading his motion. Everything that the goalkeeper does prior to a shot is out of control of the strikers and not important. What's important is what they are doing at the moment of the last touch or potential last touch. Here are the three things that the striker must assess right away about the goalkeeper in any given scoring situation.

At the moment of the striker's last touch the goalkeeper is:

1. In motion
2. Stationary
3. In a stationary – motion position

That's relatively simple isn't it? They are either moving or not moving. The third position I've called stationary-motion needs some explaining. I made these classifications based on watching the goalkeeper's feet at the moment of the last touch. The movement of the feet is very important because wherever the feet go, the rest of the body has to follow. We don't want the striker to be fooled by the hands when making decisions of where to aim or shoot because the hands will move with the body. If the feet are going from right to left, the hands will be heading in that direction as well. But the hands will be an obstacle that needs to be addressed. Before I go into details on each of the 3 situations in the next few chapters, I want to address the goalkeeper's reaction zone.

The Hand is Quicker Than the Eye

Each goalkeeper has a reaction zone covered by his hands and arms. This area is the one area of the body, where depending on the situation, the goalkeeper will be able to make a last second hand movement to stop a shot. The goalkeeper's reaction zone (pictured in diagram 66A) is like a bird's wing span. Apart from the goalkeeper's body including torso, legs, and head, this area can be covered by a goalkeeper very quickly based on reaction. This area is in the middle of the body and radiates from where the arms are set prior to the last touch by about 1 foot above and below the starting point of the arms. It's not a huge area, but it's there. The area will be bigger as the location of the shot is farther away because more time can elapse for the goalkeeper to move his hands. As the shooter moves closer to the goalkeeper, the wing span will be smaller since the keeper will have less time to move his hands. The interesting thing about what keepers will do instinctively is that their hands will move very quickly to protect their head. How often have you seen a ball hit the goalkeeper in the head regardless of how close the shooter is to the goalkeeper?

Diagram 66A- The goalkeeper's reaction zone or his wing span on a reaction save with his hands and arms is about a foot above and below where the hands are set before the shot. Also, the area by the head is covered very quickly.

Very few goalkeeper head injuries are a result of the ball. Head injuries occur in collisions with opponents or with the goalposts and not the ball. Strikers should avoid shooting the ball right by the goalkeeper's ears or above the head, as it will probably be stopped. You'll notice that I left a small area between the ears and shoulders unmarked. This is because I have seen cases where the arms overplayed this area and the goalkeeper did not stop the ball there. In those cases, the keeper's perception may have detected that the ball was going to strike the head and therefore moved quickly to protect the head. The ball may have missed the head and the goalkeeper's hand was faster than the ball as a result.

In picture 66B, Gianluigi Buffon of Juventus gets set to try and stop a shot from Kaka of AC Milan from in close. His hands are out in front of him. In this position he has already instinctively prepared to make sure a shot does not hit him in the head or face. He'll be able to cover a little bit of area around his arms but his wing span will be very small since the shooter is very close. You can see that his hands are on the way up and ready to intercept a shot to the face. We'll come back to this picture later as there is another interesting thing that he's doing to prepare to stop the shot.

In diagram 66A, I extended the wing span above the head. Goalkeepers will also be quick to react above their head because the eyes and the visual perception system will have detected the potential danger to the head. Even if the ball goes just above the head, the hands will have already been on their way to protect the head so going above the head is not going to take that much more time. How many times do you see the goalkeepers make a great reflex save above the head where they deflect the ball over the bar? Goalkeepers are very accurate in judging these shots. See pictures 66C and 66D as Buffon makes a great reflex save over his head in the 2006 World Cup Final against France.

When a ball is scored right above the goalkeeper's head, it's usually a result of a very hard shot taken from in close, usually around the 6-yard box, but still, goalkeepers avoid getting hit in the face.

Picture 66B: Gianluigi Buffon of Juventus gets set to try and stop a shot from Kaka from in close. His hands are out in front of him and intersect the potential path of the ball between the ball and his head. In this position he has already instinctively prepared to make sure a shot does not hit him in the head or face. He'll be able to cover a little bit of area around his arms but his wing span will be very small since the shooter is very close. Action Images/Tony Gentile

The important thing for strikers to know is that although the arms and hands may be able to stop a shot in the goalkeeper's reaction zone by making a reaction save, this area is not as big as one would imagine especially to either side of the keeper. The striker should not try too hard to avoid hitting this area if it will result in a shot that does not hit the goal at all. When the goalkeeper is in motion prior to the last touch by the striker, this reaction area will actually cover less area than when the keeper is stationary. Also, if the goalkeeper in motion is falling and changing planes, the reaction zone will tilt and once again cover less surface area. A good example of this can be seen in picture 63D in chapter 63. To further understand this point, imagine that the goalkeeper is lying on his back and starts to move his arms as in diagram 66A. The goalkeeper will actually cover a very small area of the goal.

1) Beating a Goalkeeper in Motion

Beating a moving goalkeeper should be easier than beating a stationary goalkeeper because the reason the keeper is moving is that he has probably been displaced. The goalkeeper could be moving forward towards the shooter in order to cut down the shooting angles or sideways to cover a pass or cross that's played across the face of the goal. A lot of goals are scored

Picture 66C: Buffon of Italy makes a great deflection save above his head. In many cases, the goalkeeper moves his head down to avoid getting hit in the head while at the same time extending the arm to deflect the ball over the bar. The arm instinctively came up to protect the head but once he realizes this has been accomplished, the keeper is in a great position to make a save on a ball that would have gone right under the bar. Most times, this save is easier than it looks because it's almost instinctive. As goalkeepers, we love these types of saves because they look great on TV and give us confidence. Did they get my good side? Picture Supplied by Action Images/Shaun Best

Picture 66D: Gianluigi Buffon of Italy stops a header from France's Zinedine Zidane by tipping the ball over the bar. Buffon's save preserved Italy's chance to win the 2006 FIFA World Cup at the Olympic Stadium in Berlin, Germany on July 9th, 2006. Action Images /Wolfgang Rattay

when the goalkeeper's feet are moving as the striker takes his last touch. As you already know, goalkeepers are often guessing to make a save. Also most goals are scored when the striker is less than 7 yards away from the goalkeeper.

As I stated before, the hands will go where the body takes them and quite often, when the body is in motion before the last touch, the hands become less effective in their reflex reaction. This is evident when the ball ends up going through the space that the hands once occupied. Go back and check pictures from chapters 60 and 63 and you'll see a number of situations where the goalkeeper's hands were in the right spot to make a save before the body moved. Unfortunately, once the body moved away from the area that the hands once occupied, they had to follow the body and hence were unable to make the save. This occurs in pictures 55C, 63D, 63E, 63F, 60H, and 60I.

The best position for a goalkeeper to be in to prepare to stop a shot is the stationary "set and ready" position. Craig Forrest demonstrates this in pictures 64A and 64B. Keepers should have both feet on the ground and be on the balls of their feet, crouched over with the weight slightly forward so that they are ready to move in either direction quickly. Strikers would prefer that the goalkeeper would not be ready for the shot or header. Can the striker get off a shot quickly before the goalkeeper is set up and while he is still moving to get into that preferred position? Doing so should be advantageous to the striker. I always tell my strikers, "shoot early", before the goalkeeper can get set. "Early shots often surprise goalkeepers". Also by "preparing to score" early, the striker can get away an early shot because a late shot may never happen. These are different ways of saying the same thing. Pick what works best for your strikers. The early shot is supposed to catch the goalkeepers in motion preparing for a shot they didn't expect.

Catch the Goalkeepers in Motion Before They Get Set!

- ✓ **Shoot Early:**
- ✓ **Early Shots Surprise Goalkeepers:**
- ✓ **Early Shots Pay, Late Shots May Never Happen!**

Let's break down situations where the goalkeeper is in motion at the time of a striker's last touch in more detail. We'll look at each situation.

Goalkeeper's Body Position when he is in Motion at the Time of the Striker's Last Touch

a) The goalkeeper is moving laterally from side to side, left to right, or right to left covering a ball played across the face of the goal

b) The goalkeeper is moving backwards

c) The goalkeeper is moving forward towards the shooter

a) The Goalkeeper is Moving Laterally

When the goalkeeper is moving laterally, the striker definitively must shoot as soon as possible because the goalkeeper is very vulnerable in that situation. When the goalkeeper moves from left to right or right to left, the keeper will do so in two methods. If the displacement is not very much, he may shuffle across the goal. That means that the legs will not cross. If he has to cover a large area, he will be crossing his feet and running across the goal while trying to stay square to the goal. The more goalkeepers get displaced, the more vulnerable they will be to a shot, or header in the direction they came from. As the goalkeeper moves his feet across, it's better to aim down low because the hands will be hard pressed to get to a low ball in the opposite direction to where he is travelling.

Many goals are scored because the goalkeeper will have shuffled to his new position but did not have enough time to stop and get in the 'set and ready' position properly. Sometimes, while the goalkeeper is going from side to side, he is also coming out towards the attacker. Let's identify each step as the goalkeeper moves laterally. In picture 66E, we see the goalkeeper go from his left to right. The first thing that the striker wants to assess is the speed of the goalkeeper as he is moving across the goal. Is he going very fast, fast, or slow, or is he stopped and in the set position? Can our strikers ascertain this while also keeping their eyes on the moving ball by using their peripheral vision?

A Mental Training Exercise for Strikers

To train your strikers to start reading and consciously thinking about what the goalkeeper is doing, set up a practice session similar to what you see in the photograph 66E. Have a server provide high balls and low balls across the face of the goal so that your strikers are receiving the ball between 5 and 8 yards out from the goal. Then have your goalkeeper move at different speeds across the goal. The striker's job is to tell you how fast he thought the goalkeeper was moving (or maybe not moving) at the time he made contact with the ball. You want your strikers to have a correct answer as to the keeper's speed before their last touch all while concentrating on the ball. Practice having your strikers shout out the answer early so that they can understand that they should know this information in order to make a better decision in regards to where to place the ball. If the striker is not detecting the correct speed of the goalkeeper, then you'll need to practice this more often in order for the striker to get it right most of the time.

The faster the goalkeeper is going from side to side, the more useless he will be to get a ball played to where he came from. At the same time, he will be able to catapult himself further in the direction he's already going. Can your strikers assess that quickly enough to make the best decision on where to place the ball? Are they even thinking about the keeper's speed? The natural striker is probably processing all this information instinctively. For strikers who are having problems converting enough chances from crosses, get them thinking about the goalkeeper's speed as they move to cover the goal. If the striker detects that the goalkeeper will have time to stop and get in the "set and ready" position, then he will have different options based on the keeper being in a stationary position as opposed to being in motion.

Picture 66E: To train your strikers to read the goalkeepers movements, practice serving them balls across the face of the goal making sure they keep their eyes on the ball and do not miss the ball. At the same time, ask them to tell you whether the goalkeeper was moving very fast, fast, slow, or was stationary at the moment of their last touch. It's a mental training exercise.

When the goalkeeper is in motion and is scrambling to cover the goal after a cross from one end of the goal to the other end of the goal, his body position is predictable. The faster the keeper is coming across the goal, the less chance he will have to stop and make a save in the opposite direction. In picture 66F, Owen scores by heading the ball against the path of the goalkeeper's. The striker needs to predict each step that the keeper takes and assess where the feet will land. Placing the ball low to the foot closest to the post where the ball came from is where to aim if the attacker is coming towards the ball. Many strikers will play the ball ahead of the keeper in the direction where they are going and often the keeper makes a save that looks heroic. The reality is that, in most cases, the striker should have put the ball in the opposite side of the goal. In picture 66F, focus on the right foot of the goalkeeper. A ball played right beside it would be impossible to stop since the keeper has committed too much to his left.

In picture 66F, based on the body motion of the goalkeeper and the speed at which he's moving across the goal, you can tell that he will be able to launch himself to his left much further than normal because he has had a running start. Any striker that aims to score in the same direction that the keeper is going needs to take this into account. Another option for the striker is to place the ball so that it lands right beside the keepers left foot as it touches the ground. For an instant, that foot is planted and frozen in time and vulnerable there, but the timing has to be perfect. This will be difficult to execute in comparison to heading the ball beside the goalkeeper's right foot.

In the 1970 World Cup, England goalkeeper Gordon Banks made an incredible save on Pele of Brazil when he went from post to post to cover a cross. Banks sprinted across the goal to cover the opposite post and Pele headed the ball down, as all good strikers do. But he placed the ball in the path that Banks was taking. Consequently, as shown in picture 66G, Banks dove to deflect the ball over the net. He was lucky that Pele didn't put the ball back in the direction he came from. The save looked brilliant since he started at the near post and got to the ball at the other end of the goal. What made the save incredible was that since Pele headed it down, Banks had to save a ball that was bouncing back up off the ground. Timing that reaction with his hand while diving at the same time was just as incredible as the distance he covered to get to the ball. Pele couldn't believe he didn't score and Banks' save has often been called "the save of the century".

Picture 66F: Owen scores by putting the ball in the opposite direction that the keeper is moving. The keeper is moving laterally from right to left. The faster he's going to his left, the more vulnerable he will be to his right. Based on the position of the striker, the best option is to place the ball to the keeper's right. Many players will put the ball in the path of the keeper. Action Images/Alex Morton

Pele should have put the ball in the other corner but he might have forgotten that he was playing against one of the world's best goalkeepers at the time. On any other goalkeeper, he probably

Picture 66G: Gordon Banks of England dove to deflect a ball headed towards his right by Pele of Brazil. When the cross was played, Banks was at the post to his left. He covered the other part of the goal quickly. Pele, not shown, has headed the ball down at the far post having jumped incredibly high with a defender in front of him to head the ball down to the ground. In the picture, the ball has already bounced off the ground and Banks has just touched it to deflect it over the bar. Since Pele arched his back and whipped his full body into the ball, it had a lot of momentum so that when Banks deflected it, the ball still had plenty of velocity to clear the bar. Photo supplied by Action Images/Frank Barro

would have scored. Pele actually had to perform quite a jump, at full speed to get to the ball. Incredibly, he still managed to get the ball on goal and down to the ground, but that time, he was denied. Good strikers will score more often when they make the right decisions most of the time. Notice that I didn't say all the time. There is no such thing in soccer. Not everything follows your typical textbook script. I hope I have changed some of the typical textbook concepts you have read in the past. Still, not everything I point out will work perfectly all the time. Every situation is different.

In picture 66H, Fabien Barthez of France is coming across the goal from his right to left and is in full motion laterally as Switzerland's Daniel Gygax is coming to head a cross. He puts the ball down to Barthez's feet but does not read the keeper's motion well enough. Notice how easy it would have been for him to score if he would have aimed the ball right beside the keeper's right foot. Instead, the ball is headed in the same direction that Barthez is moving. Barthez does his part to distract the striker from thinking properly by moving laterally and keeping his big hands up (also to protect his face). Gygax's peripheral vision would have noticed the big gloves moving from his left to right. The right side of the goal would have appeared open in his field of vision. The gloves may have covered the left part of the goal and the striker may have assumed that the keeper was covering that portion of the goal.

If Gygax had scored in this situation, his team would have beaten France 1-0 at this 2006 World Cup game. Just one different decision in this one second of play revolving around Gygax's last touch would have changed the results of a full 90 minutes of play. Here is where I believe Gygax's problem was from a decision-making standpoint. He did get two things right: he headed the ball down and he directed the ball towards the net and did not miss the net. But he did not properly read the speed of the goalkeeper moving laterally. He went with the easy decision based solely on vision without thinking about human body motion. This is one reason why Gygax is disappointed after the save. Gygax did well by being good enough to read the play and get into such a great scoring position, but he wasted that effort by being unable to finish the job (Pictures 66I, 66J, 66K).

Picture 66H: Switzerland's Daniel Gygax heads a ball against France's Fabien Barthez who's in full motion at his last touch and places the ball where the goalkeeper is going. At the moment of his last touch, he is barely 6 yards away from the goal. Picture supplied by Action Images/Oleg Popov

If the goalkeeper had been moving slower, then Gygax's decision may have been the correct one. Also, if a striker is at a fair distance past the outside post and inside the 6-yard line from the end line, then he may be at too poor an angle to aim for the post that the goalkeeper came from. Unless he lifts the ball over the goalkeeper's head in the opposite direction, he may end up playing it right at the keeper. If this is the case, the closest post may be the best option. If the striker is too far to the side of the goal, then another option to consider is to play the ball into the magic spot for a teammate. But this was not the case with Gygax's opportunity.

What's Going on in my Striker's Brain when the Keeper is in Motion Laterally?

When the goalkeeper is in motion laterally at the moment of the striker's last touch, I want my striker to be thinking to place the ball to the corner where the keeper is coming from. Strikers have to assess each situation separately but they should always put their body in a position to prepare to aim to the side of the goal that the ball is coming from. This will put them in a better position technically to perform the skill of directing the ball to either side of the goal. Should strikers choose to go to the other post because of the situation, then they will be less likely to miss the goal.

Goals are scored to the striker's near post. I don't want you to think that all goals are scored by placing the ball to the opposite side of where the goalkeeper is coming from. Scoring at the near post seems to occur more often if the last touch is inside the 6-yard line and when the goalkeeper is too slow or unable to react and come across his goal in time. Also if the goalkeeper is too far away from that post for whatever reason, the nearest post to the striker may provide an easier opportunity for a goal. In such instances, the striker is often so close to the goal that the goalkeeper has no chance of making a save. In diagram 66L, the striker (player 1) is outside the post. Playing the ball back towards the post the goalkeeper is coming from may result in the ball hitting the goalkeeper as he moves across the goal and thus forcing a save.

In the 2006 World Cup a lot of goals were scored at the far side as well as the near side but surprisingly, quite a number of goals went in very close to the goalkeeper's feet and body.

Picture 66I: These are a great series of photographs that clearly demonstrate my points. Although following my 4 golden rules to scoring is a great base for strikers to go by, moving to a more advanced stage of grasping the psychological factors that affect performance when it comes to scoring will separate good goal scorers from great goal scorers.

Unless it comes from instincts, most players will have to improve their psychological decision-making part of their game to score more goals. Learning how to read the keeper's movements is just one of these advanced skills.

In this picture, Gygax is all by himself without defenders challenging him, but makes a poor decision as he heads the ball to the post that Barthez is quickly moving towards, thus helping him make a save. Picture supplied by Action Images/Oleg Popov

Picture 66J: Fabien Barthez of France makes a great save on Gygax of Switzerland by coming across the face of the goal from the other post. Since he was moving very fast and in motion at the time that Gygax had his last touch, he was able to get to the other post. A header to the other post would have scored. Action Images/ Oleg Popov

Picture 66K: Gygax of Switzerland reacts to the missed opportunity at the World Cup 2006 game against France. A better decision could have won Switzerland the game. One bad decision can be so crucial in a soccer match where in a typical game, chances are few. Action Images/Pascal Lauener

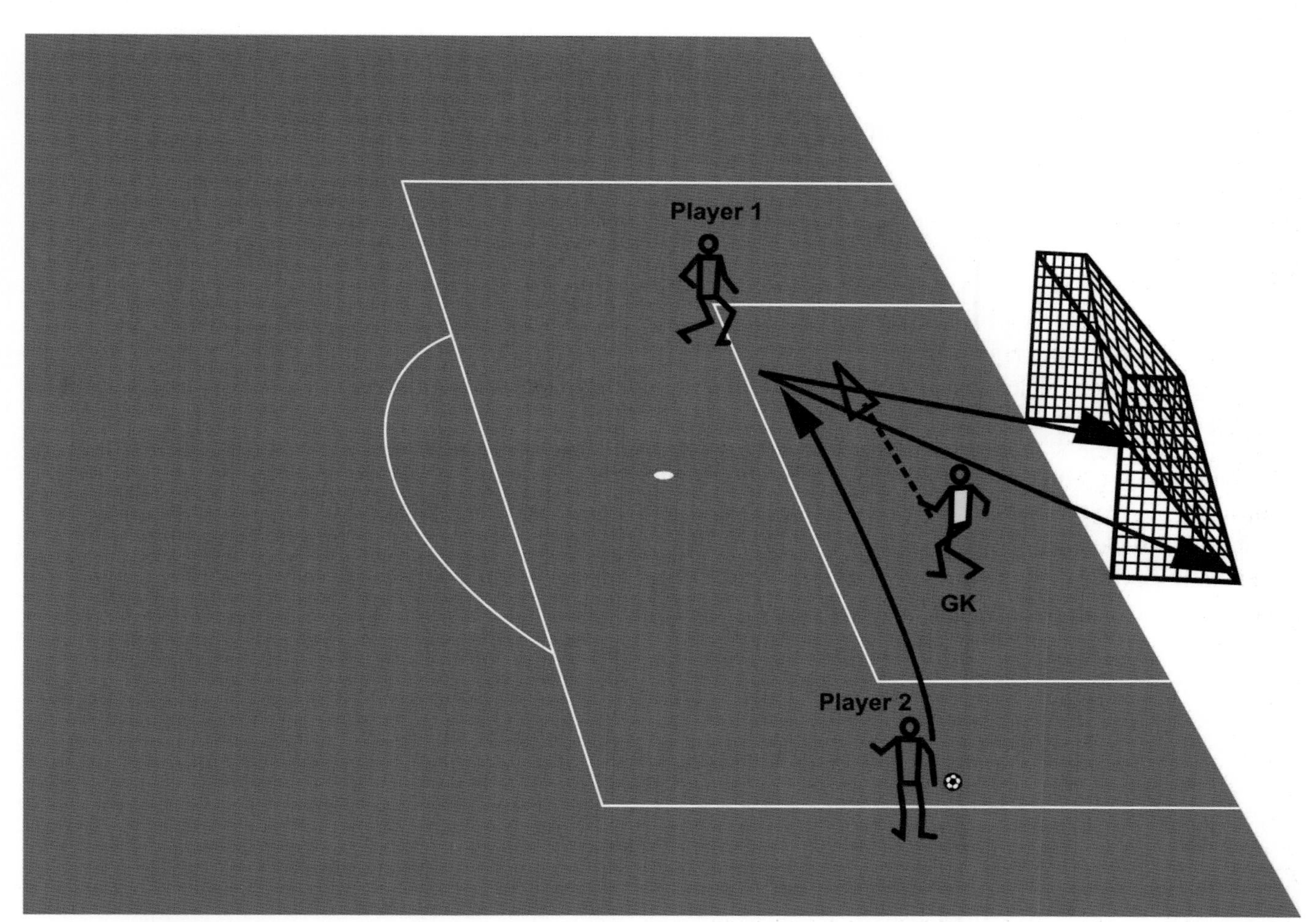

Diagram 66L: If the striker (player 1) receiving a ball from a cross is too far outside the post and the goalkeeper is still in motion across the face of the goal, then the striker may have no choice but to play the ball to the nearest post. Unlike in the example with Switzerland's Gygax, if the striker is at too much of an angle, then going in the opposite direction may not be the best option. If the goalkeeper is very quick and gets to a position where the keeper has stopped and been able to get in a "set and ready" position at the near post, then playing the ball to the far post may once again be the better option because good goalkeepers rarely give away a good scoring opportunity at the near post. Assessing the keeper's speed and future feet position will help strikers make better decisions on where to place the ball. Illustration by Jo-Anne Godawa

A Powerful Statistic That Coaches Need to Know

Another interesting note was that on goals that were scored when the goalkeeper was moving laterally at the moment of the striker's last touch, the ball did not tend to go into the goal very close to the posts. Balls that entered the goal while the goalkeeper was still in motion at the striker's last touch tended to be at least 1 yard towards the centre of the goal from the posts. Few goals were scored in the corners at all. The goalkeeper is very vulnerable when moving laterally and balls played to the corners were either saved or missed the net. Barely 10%, or 2-3 of 21 goals (it was hard to tell the exactly distance the ball was from the post on one of the goals) scored in the 2006 World Cup when the goalkeeper was moving laterally at the moment of the striker's last touch went in the goal closer than 1 yard from either post. This includes goals scored by the head and by the foot. I found this to be very interesting. Did world class strikers realize that, when a goalkeeper is in motion, hitting the goal was more important than picking corners on their last touch? Was this instinctive?

b) The Goalkeeper is Moving Backwards

Do not miss the net! That's all you have to tell your strikers. Good goalkeepers are seldom caught in this position. Sometimes it occurs when a goalkeeper has come out too far and realizes that he should not have done so. He starts moving backwards to get back into position but is usually in such a poor position that he is better off praying that the striker misses the net. Out of all the goals in the 2006 World Cup none were clearly in this category. Only one or two goals looked as though the goalkeeper was starting to take a step backwards before the goal went in. Generally, whenever goalkeepers are moving backwards at the moment of the striker's last touch, they are in trouble and will not be able to do much to stop a ball unless it hits them. The striker should never miss the net when the goalkeeper is in this situation because it's almost certain a goal will result if they hit the big 8 by 24-foot target.

c) The Goalkeeper is Moving Forward Towards the Shooter

One of the most common situations for strikers to be facing on their last touch is that the goalkeeper is moving forwards as they are moving towards the goal. The goalkeeper is usually coming out to cut down their angles and still in motion. Each situation is different based on any number of circumstances but by and large the majority of scoring chances occur when a player is coming towards the goal from an angle. Rarely, will a striker be running straight down the middle of the pitch against the goalkeeper. Young players miss these types of chances too often and in my opinion, not enough goals are converted. Players are prone to hit the ball at the goalkeeper, or miss the goal, or try and score that highlight reel goal into the top corner. This aspect of scoring is so important for strikers to grasp that I'll give it its own chapter called "shooting from angles".

In chapter 68 on "shooting from angles", I'll provide key coaching cues to guarantee success and wipe away many of the errors that players make. Some of the methods of beating a goalkeeper when shooting from angles are similar whether the goalkeeper is moving forward or in a stationary position. I'll cover the details of beating a goalkeeper in the stationary positions first in the next chapter and come back to scoring on a keeper who's moving towards the shooter from an angle in chapter 68.

CHAPTER 67

Scoring on the Goalkeeper who is in the 'Set and Ready' Stationary Position

The goalkeeper's best position to get ready to stop a shot is the 'set and ready' stationary position. When goalkeepers are in a perfect position to stop a shot it means that they have come out to cut down angles. They are in a well balanced position with their legs shoulder-width apart, crouched down a bit with their knees slightly bent and their hands up and out in front of them. Their weight is on the balls of their feet and they are ready to pounce. They have their eyes on the ball as the attacker gets set to shoot. See pictures 64A and 67A as Craig Forrest demonstrates this position. Sometimes, goalkeepers may have their hands down low. This is also considered a 'set and ready' position provided the keeper is not in motion.

In this chapter, I want the coaches to understand that I'm trying to find as many little things as possible to help the striker make correct decisions when faced with a goalkeeper who appears to be in the 'set and ready' position. Although I'm going to present you with a number of secrets that can help your strikers score when faced with a goalkeeper in a good 'set and ready' position, I want you to understand that it may take just one point that does the trick. I want to shift the balance of power from the goalkeeper, who will likely stop the shot (based on the number of goals scored per game), to the striker who can change that statistic. One mental cue that helps him make better decisions may be all that's needed to turn an average goal scorer into a great goal scorer. Please monitor your strikers closely to see if they have turned the corner with just one piece of advice. If you have noticed a difference and see a defining moment in your striker's performance, (as discussed in chapter 18), do not bombard them or confuse them with too much information.

Although one would assume that, when a goalkeeper is in the "set and ready" position, he will greatly reduce the striker's chances to score, I want my strikers to understand that in no way should this deter them from scoring lots of goals. Many times, what appears to be a great goalkeeping position to spectators, coaches, and to the shooter is not the case when you're in the goalkeeper's position. In fact, while the keepers are looking confident and poised to make a save when in the 'set and ready' position, in reality they may be panic-stricken.

I'll bet you that many of your strikers do not understand this point. Those instinctive goal scorers will be completely surprised by what I just wrote because they will not have a clue as to why this isn't common knowledge. The best strikers in the world would have never imagined that I would have to say this to players. When interviewing some of the best strikers I have played with, this point became apparent yet surprising to me at first. They expect to score and they know the goalkeeper is in panic-mode because they, 'the almighty', are going to score. As I stated in chapter 19, George Klas, a deadly goal scorer and an old teammate of mine said, "I knew some players who would get stressed out about how to score. I could never understand why a striker would not expect to score every time."

But most strikers I have coached tend to panic and worry about what will happen if they miss. They get down on themselves when they miss and, consequently, try harder the next time and are even more nervous as the pressure upon them to score continues to build. That's the total opposite to those natural strikers who can read the goalkeeper's motions and feel cool, calm, and confident that they are going to score all the time. It's the mental state of the striker that I want to work on. All the ideas presented in the rest of this chapter that pertains to reading the goalkeepers motions while in a stationary mode are meant to help your strikers experience an amazing "captivating and absorbing" (CAM) moment in their careers. As they learn some secret things about the goalkeeper's human motion possibilities and try things, they in turn can have a "defining moment" in their careers that catapults them to a renewed level of confidence. Understanding that it's the goalkeeper who is scared stiff and not them is step one. This is important because as a keeper, I played best when I turned the tables around in my mind. It's not as easy to do as it sounds. The striker will experience the same feelings.

Picture 67A: Craig Forrest is in the 'set and ready' position with legs shoulder-width apart, eyes on the ball, hands out, knees bent, and he is on the balls of his feet. The ball was played right into his hands and he was fortunate that he didn't have to move in either direction to make the save. Action Images/John Sibley

Picture 67B: In this picture, the goalkeeper simply falls backwards and to his left to cover a low ball to his left. He has to get his left foot out of the way as he falls. Even though he can usually fall rather quickly to his side, he can still only go down as fast as the speed of gravity. He cannot make himself fall down any faster. This is physics. If the goalkeeper starts from a more upright position, he will take longer to fall. If he is already very low, them he will get down quicker.

How many times have you seen goalkeepers fall down to make a save, but the ball goes under them? A well-struck ball from within 7 yards should beat the goalkeeper unless the striker happens to hit the keeper's legs where they are planted. In this picture, the striker placed the ball too high. There is space between the left knee and ground for a ball to go through to score. Photo by Les Jones/Covershots

2) Beating a Keeper in the Stationary-mode Position

The goalkeeper is in the stationary position when his feet are not in motion at the time of a striker's last touch. There are two different situations: the stationary-mode position and the stationary-motion position. This may sound confusing at first but follow closely as I describe the difference between the two stationary positions. Keep in mind that I'm trying to classify things so that the striker can eventually make better and quicker decisions. The striker has to quickly decide if the goalkeeper is in stationary-mode or stationary-motion position.

The stationary-mode position is when the goalkeeper is in a good 'set and ready' position. In this position the goalkeeper is ready to move in whichever direction that the ball will go to. The goalkeeper's possible movements are what I want to concentrate on next.

Without moving the feet, the goalkeeper will be able to do a few things quickly. As I have pointed out in chapter 66, the goalkeeper's hands will be able to move fairly quickly in the reaction zone, as shown in the save from Craig Forrest in picture 67A. Also, since the keeper has the knees bent, he will be able to reach up very quickly to cover a ball above the head by extending the knees and moving up. Also, the goalkeeper can fall or collapse by releasing the tension in the leg muscles and fall to either side. In either case, the leg closest to the side he is falling towards has to collapse and get out of the way so that he can fall on that side. In picture 67B, the goalkeeper falls to his left to get down to a low ball. The fall is often slightly backwards and thus the area that he can cover is not very much. Even though the goalkeeper can usually fall rather quickly to his side and backwards, he can still only go down as fast as the speed of gravity. He cannot make himself fall down any faster. These are the laws of physics. If the goalkeeper starts from a more upright position, he will take longer to go down. If he is already very low, then he will get down quicker.

How many times have you seen a goalkeeper fall down to make a save, but the ball squeezes under him? A well-struck ball from within 7 yards should beat the keeper unless the striker happens to aim to a side where the keeper is <u>already</u> thinking of making his way down. In picture 67B, the striker has placed the ball too high. There is space between the left knee and the ground for a ball to go through to score. Go back and check out Michael Owens's goal in picture 55I. The goalkeeper just tries to fall quickly to his right and cannot fall down fast enough even though the shot was taken from 12 yards out from the keeper.

Keepers are not in a 100% Perfect Position all the Time

When a goalkeeper gets in the 'set and ready' position, there is no guarantee that the goalkeeper's 'set and ready' position is always good. Strikers can't assume that the keepers are going to be in the perfect position 100% of the time. The less experienced they are, the more mistakes they will make in their judgment of the best possible position. That's another key reason I keep coming back to the golden rules of goal scoring. To hit the goal is paramount because although the goalkeepers may be in a 'set and ready' position, they can be in a poor 'set and ready' position. They can be leaning too much to one side of the goal or the other, or they can be leaning too far forward or too far backwards.

In Ronaldo's goal against Belgium in the 2002 World Cup as shown in picture 67C, the goalkeeper's legs were too far apart and consequently the ball went through his legs into the net. One thing to look for is to see if a goalkeeper's legs are the correct distance apart. If the goalkeeper's legs are too far apart as they get set to make a stop, then the striker has a huge advantage because the keeper will not have much quickness or ability to move from this position.

Picture 67C: Ronaldo is 8 yards away from the Belgian goalkeeper in this picture as the keeper is in a 'set and ready' stationary position to stop the ball after a cross along the ground. Ronaldo strikes the ball firmly and the keeper tries to collapse by falling down to stop the ball but the speed of gravity is too slow to help him fall to make a save. Consequently, the ball goes right through his legs and into the goal to seal a victory for Brazil in the 2002 World Cup. Action Images/Ruben Sprich

When you see the replay of Ronaldo's goal against Belgium over and over, you see that Ronaldo was focused exclusively on the ball and made sure to make good contact with it. Ronaldo also knew that the goalkeeper was no more than 7-10 yards away and that it was a great scoring opportunity. He made sure not to miss. I don't think that in his mind he said, "I'm going to aim to put it through the goalkeeper's legs". He was thinking about hitting the net, getting good contact on the ball so that he could give the ball good pace, and he knew that if he did those two things correctly, his chances to score would escalate dramatically.

What the Goalkeepers Must do When They Have to Move Their Feet to Make a Save

I want to cover what the goalkeepers need to do from a good 'set and ready' stationary position to make a save when they have to move their feet. First, to set up for the attempt at goal they have to stop moving forwards, backwards, or sideways and be in control of their body. Although the goalkeepers may be in the perfect 'set and ready' position, in reality, they still cannot be certain as to where the ball is going to go. It could go to their right, left, high, low, or straight at them. The goalkeeper can start to make a move in the direction that the ball is going only once the ball leaves the striker's foot or head. At this moment, there is a span of time where the goalkeeper picks up the visual cues as to where the ball is going. This information is then transferred to the brain where it is processed. Then the brain has to quickly tell the correct body parts to move to accomplish the goal of stopping the ball. This time span is called the reaction time of the goalkeeper. This reaction time can be different for each goalkeeper. In fact it can be different for the same goalkeeper based on his training. When you hear goalkeepers say that they need to get their timing back, it usually means that once there has been a layoff due to injury or an off-season break, they need to get this 'reaction time' back to mid-season form. Although one may have a hard time understanding why reaction time may deteriorate without practice, it does occur and can be a huge factor.

I really noticed that my reaction time was way off in pre-season training. To me, strikers seemed to get their shooting velocity back to normal even on the first day of training. For goalkeepers, it felt like I was so slow at the start of the season or once back from an injury that I wondered if I was going to be good enough to stop anything. It's unbelievable how fast a goalkeeper's reaction time can deteriorate. (But maybe it was not really my reaction time – see stationary-motion)

This decision (reaction) time has to be followed by a motion by the body to get to the ball. If the goalkeeper does not have to move his feet to get to the ball, then a save can be made quickly, as discussed. But if the goalkeeper has to move his feet, then there is a split second where the keeper has to do certain things in order to move. I want my strikers to know what the goalkeeper has to do in order to stop them from scoring. Here is a step by step analysis of the goalkeeper's movements.

Moving from a good 'set and ready' position, the goalkeeper's motions to stop a goal are as follows:

1) Shift in weight:

The first thing that will happen is that the goalkeeper needs to shift his weight to the foot that will start to push him in the direction that he needs to go. In picture 67D and 67E, you will see that both goalkeepers are barely touching the ground with their toes as they are in the midst of shifting their weight to the foot they need to push off with. Often this means going up in order to come down on the foot that will push off. They practically have to take a little hop to move into a position where they can start propelling themselves in a specific direction. Also, this slight upward motion helps them get a faster and deeper bend at the knees. The more the goalkeepers can bend their knees, the more they can spring off by straightening the knees.

When they straighten their knees they will be pushing into the ground in the opposite direction that they want to go in order to get to the ball. The harder the push, the farther they will be able to go in the opposite direction. If they feel that the ball is going further from them, then they will need a bigger push, which also means that they will need more bend at the knees before the push starts.

All this motion to shift weight and bend at the knees will take some time.

The goalkeeper usually has to get lower than the 'set and ready' position in order to get more push on a dive or jump. This takes time and sometimes there is not enough time to actually accomplish all this and still get to the ball. In picture 67D, we see goalkeeper Edwin Van der Sar of Manchester United moving off the ready position to get in another position that will prepare to send him in the direction of the ball. In picture 67E, Jerzy Dudek of Poland reacts by shifting his weight by slightly lifting his feet off the ground after being in the 'set and ready' stationary-mode position.

Picture 67D: The first reaction from the 'set and ready' stationary-mode position is for the goalkeeper to shift his weight towards the foot that needs to push off to send the body in the intended direction. As this is happening, the body tends to lift both feet off the ground to reposition itself. If both feet don't actually leave the ground, then the foot not starting the pushing will tend to lift as the body shifts and transfers its weight towards the other foot. In this picture Van der Sar has just started his little hop or lift to transfer his weight. Watford's Hameur Bouazza shoots on Manchester United's goalkeeper Edwin Van der Sar during their FA Cup semi-final soccer match at Villa Park in Birmingham. Action Images/ Eddie Keogh

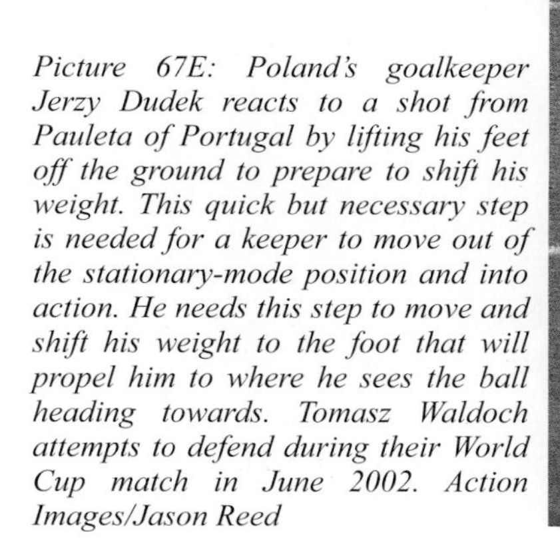

Picture 67E: Poland's goalkeeper Jerzy Dudek reacts to a shot from Pauleta of Portugal by lifting his feet off the ground to prepare to shift his weight. This quick but necessary step is needed for a keeper to move out of the stationary-mode position and into action. He needs this step to move and shift his weight to the foot that will propel him to where he sees the ball heading towards. Tomasz Waldoch attempts to defend during their World Cup match in June 2002. Action Images/Jason Reed

2) Coming down and starting the push from the furthest foot:

Once the goalkeepers have enough weight on the foot that they want to push off with, they will need to start to push themselves in the direction they want to go. This starts with the foot furthest from the direction they want to go. This foot will give them the initial thrust in the intended direction. Often, as this foot comes down to dig into the ground, the knee will bend and goalkeepers will start to lean the rest of their body in the other direction so that they can start gaining momentum in the direction they want to go. This will help them get a better angle on the push into the ground.

In picture 67F, taken just after picture 67D notice that Manchester United's Van der Sar's knees are bent as he is still planting his right foot. In Picture 67G and 67H, Czech Republic's goalkeeper Petr Cech has leaned towards the direction he wants to go and has started to push off with the foot furthest from the ball to take him to his left.

Picture 67F: Hameur Bouazza, on the ground, has taken his shot at Manchester United's goalkeeper Edwin Van der Sar. Van der Sar is still shifting his weight after picture 67E's initial reaction to the shot. At this point he is starting to lean to his left while planting his right foot to push off with that foot which will send him to his left to try to stop the shot. Action Images/Carl Recine

Picture 67G: Ghana's Asamoah Gyan takes a power shot against Petr Cech of the Czech Republic during their Group E World Cup 2006 soccer match in Cologne, Germany. Cech's right foot is starting to push off. He does this by straightening his right knee which will send him to his left. Also, notice Gyan's power shot which includes his back foot coming off the ground. Action Images/ Ina Fassbender

Picture 67H: Ghana's Asamoah Gyan's power shot on Czech Republic's goalkeeper Petr Cech as shown from a different angle. Cech's right foot is pushing off to try and get his body to the ball. He gains thrust by straightening his right knee. Action Images/Radu Sigheti

3) Straightening of the furthest knee:

Once the furthest leg has been planted and the body has started to lean in the intended direction, the next muscle movement that must occur is that the furthest leg must extend and the knee must straighten out. This quick leg extension will give the body its first full push towards its intended direction. The quality of this push will dictate how far and how quickly the goalkeeper will be able to get to the ball at the opposite side. It's the quadriceps muscles of the leg that will do most of the work to straighten the leg by extending the knee. If the goalkeeper's foot planted on the ground is not planted firmly or slips due to poor ground conditions or poor footwear, then the amount of thrust the body can produce will be reduced.

In pictures 67G and 67H you see Petr Cech in this part of the motion. In picture 67I, Kasey Keller of the USA is in the same motion as he pushes with his left leg and begins the knee extension and straightening of the furthest leg.

Picture 67I: Italy's Alberto Gilardino (on ground) heads the ball towards Kasey Keller of the U.S.A. during their Group E World Cup 2006 soccer match in Kaiserslautern, Germany. Keller is in the process of pushing off with his left leg by straightening his knee. Action Images / Dylan Martinez

4) Extension of the ankle of furthest foot:

The next step in the motion of the goalkeeper to get to the ball is the extension of the ankle furthest from the ball. Once the furthest knee and leg have been straightened, the last function of this leg and foot is to extend the ankle so that the most force can be put into the ground to send the body in the opposite direction. This motion must start right after the knee has been extended and leg straightened in order to transfer the most energy from the knee and upper leg to the lower leg and then to the ankle, foot, and toe. All this takes time. A bad grasp of the turf can negate all the good things that the body has done to try and get maximum thrust.

In picture 67J and 67K, you see Kasey Keller extend his left ankle to try and send his body to the right to make a save.

Picture 67J: Kasey Keller of the U.S.A. extends his left ankle after his leg has been straightened to continue the push towards the ball, which is heading to his right. Italy's Alberto Gilardino (on ground) headed the ball towards Kasey Keller's right while making contact with the ball just outside the 6-yard box. He dives to get to the ball and lands inside the 6-yard box. Keller's teammate Claudio Reyna (10) watches during their World Cup 2006 soccer match in Germany. Action Images/ Oleg Popov

Picture 67K: Kasey Keller of the U.S.A. has extended his left ankle to gain maximum push from that leg while shifting his weight to his right leg. The right leg is starting to dig into the ground to do its job of pushing the body towards the ball by extending the knee. Action Images/ Dylan Martinez

5) Planting and transferring weight to nearest foot:

Once the furthest leg and foot have done their job, the nearest foot must dig into the ground and get ready to do the last part of the take-off of the body to get to the ball. In pictures 67J, 67K, and 67L you see Keller's right leg get dug into the ground and the weight transferred to it.

Picture 67L: Kasey Keller of the U.S.A. is in the process of straightening his right knee by using the powerful thigh (quadriceps) muscles. Right after this is completed, his right ankle will get extended to offer the last bit of thrust towards the ball. Action Images/Tony Gentile

6) Straightening of the nearest knee.

Now the nearest leg must extend at the knee. It's the quadriceps muscle group which is responsible for extending the knee and getting maximum power. The quads are the body's most powerful muscle group.

7) Extending ankle of nearest foot.

As he extends his knees by applying force into the ground, the last portion of the movement is to extend the ankle to finish the motion. In picture 67L, you see this last action getting ready to take force as Keller's right knee has almost finished extending.

Kasey Keller is in full flight in picture 67M as we see the extension of the nearest leg (right) towards the direction that the ball is travelling.

My Main Point

Here is my main point about all the examples of the goalkeepers' efforts to stop the opposition from scoring when they are standing in a stationary-mode position as shown in most of the pictures up to this point in this chapter. All these scoring attempts resulted in goals. Gilardino scored on Keller by heading the ball from just outside the 6-yard line. Ghana's Asamoah Gyan's power shot beat Czech Republic's goalkeeper Petr Cech to score at 18 yards out from the goal and 12 yards away from Cech. Watford's Hameur Bouazza shoots and scores on Manchester

Picture 67M: Kasey Keller of the U.S.A. has extended his right knee and ankle to gain maximum push during this goal-scoring attempt. Unfortunately, although he reacted shortly after Italy's Alberto Gilardino (on ground) headed the ball, he was unable to get there quickly enough to stop the goal. Action Images/Oleg Popov

United's goalkeeper Edwin Van der Sar. Pauleta of Portugal scores on Jerzy Dudek of Poland and Brazil's Ronaldo scores by beating the Belgian keeper between the legs. I do not believe that on a well-struck ball, the human body will be fast enough to react to a situation and perform all the steps I have described. From purely a stationary-mode position, apart from the hand reaction zone, the body cannot move fast enough to make a save where the feet have to move the body.

Great Reaction Saves from a Goalkeeper's Perspective

I know that some readers will be questioning my point about goalkeeper's not being quick enough to react with their feet to make very many saves when starting from a 'set and ready' stationary-mode position and therefore resort to guessing. You may be one of them. You may say that you're sure that you have seen cases where goalkeepers have waited for the shot to be taken before making a move and witnessed them stopping the ball. And you're right. In many of those cases, the strikers may not have directed the ball as forcefully as they should have, which would allow for movement after the shot resulting in a save. In such instances it may have been partly as a result of a distraction provided by the keeper. Remember that the best goalkeepers are master illusionists.

However, consider this: If goalkeepers have time to make saves straight from a power shot a few meters from the goal without any sort of predicting where the ball may go, then how would one explain that the goalkeeper must form a wall to stop a shot on a free kick from 25 yards out from goal? Is it possible, that from that distance, the goalkeeper would need a wall at all? Especially when there is no movement of the ball or players. It's a dead ball! Everyone knows there will be a shot coming including the goalkeeper! Why do they need a wall at all?

Sometimes, although it may <u>not appear</u> that the goalkeepers have moved prior to a shot, they in fact may have made the decision in their minds to move in that direction but the resulting reaction was not noticeable in the game or video footage. It's possible at times that the goalkeeper is very quick to react but having played keeper, I'm convinced, that in most cases where a reaction save has taken place, an element of that motion or anticipated motion has already been made in the goalkeepers mind. It may have occurred in the form of preparing the body beforehand to be strong in a certain area so that a quick visual cue from a shot will send the correct body movement into action as anticipated. In that context, "reaction time" could also be called "anticipation time".

As a coach, my challenge was to get my strikers who were still having problems scoring to find better ways to communicate to them on how to read the goalkeeper's body movements in advance of their last touch. That's when I came up with the stationary-motion position concept. I found that I got through to some players better when other advice failed. They got better very quickly at predicting the goalkeeper's stance, or position at the moment of their last touch. This ability helped them decide where they thought the keeper was in their attempt to stop them from scoring from a human motion perspective. Hence, they could make better decisions on how to score in each situation.

3) The Stationary-Motion Keeper Position

I came up with this term to help my strikers identify the strengths and weaknesses in a goalkeeper's position at the moment of their last touch. Not all strikers will need this cue, but I started researching this after I gave a lecture in California at the Coaches conference in Santa Clara for the California Youth Soccer Association (CYSA). The question posed from one of the coaches at my session was, "What do I do when a player keeps shooting at a goalkeeper's chest after he adheres to the 4 golden rules to scoring?"

I did more research on this subject and came up with more detailed information which has really helped some players. The stationary-motion position is when the goalkeepers' feet are stationary but the rest of their body is in motion or in anticipated motion mode. I then classified stationary-motion into two types of stationary-motion positions. They are positive (+ve) stationary-motion and negative (-ve) stationary-motion. A further description follows.

THE TWO STATIONARY-MOTION POSITIONS for the Goalkeeper

1. **Negative Stationary-Motion Position.**

   This is when the goalkeepers are in a position when they are stopping their motion as they get into a position where they can stop the ball but before they can make any movements to actually stop the ball. Also, goalkeepers are in a negative stationary-motion position when they are in a position where they cannot make any further movements that can help them stop the ball. A negative stationary-motion position for the goalkeeper is always a good situation for the striker.

2. **Positive Stationary-Motion Position**

   This position explains most of the situations where goalkeepers make great reaction type saves. When goalkeepers are in a positive stationary-motion position it means that they have made up their minds as to where they have to go in order to stop the ball. It's positive because it's a position where the goalkeepers are working to make a save. The goalkeeper's body is already prepared to go in an intended direction. It's positive because the motion, if they have guessed what the striker is going to do correctly, will probably result in a save. It's positive because the keepers may have forced the striker to do a certain thing, which will lead the striker to shoot where they are already heading. It's positive because it has a better chance of resulting in a save than any other thing they do if the ball is played outside of the goalkeepers' reaction zone.

1. Negative Stationary-Motion Position

If my strikers can identify situations when the goalkeeper is or will be in a negative stationary-motion position before their last touch, then they should find goal-scoring easier. One such position is when the goalkeeper has just stopped his motion to get 'set and ready'. In picture 67N, I'm demonstrating human motion as it applies to the goalkeeper at an NSCAA coaching conference. In the picture, I'm about to crouch down to a lower 'set and ready' position by bending my knees. Usually, to get to this position, the goalkeeper has come out to block the angles or get square to a shooter. But at the instant that I'm stopping and setting, my muscles, especially my hamstring muscles, are in the process of putting the brakes on so that I don't fall forward. At this instant, I'm in a negative stationary-motion position because as I'm braking to gain my balance, I can't do anything else. My muscles are busy stopping me from falling forward. This is a critical time phase because the goalkeeper is frozen for this instant and will not be able to move to save a ball. If a striker has realized this and taken a shot while I'm in this position, I'm beat unless the ball hits me.

As a goalkeeper, the harder I have to stop my motion forwards, backwards, or sideways to get in a balanced position, the better chance the striker has to score. An early shot that surprises me may beat me. Let me repeat that:

An early shot that surprises me, will probably beat me. If the striker has caught me in a negative stationary-motion position and shot early so that I can't make a save, my very next series of actions will probably be to move and pretend I can stop the goal knowing full well that I will not. Why would I do this? So I don't look bad!

Another situation where I would identify the goalkeeper to be in a negative stationary-motion position is in pictures 67O and 67P. In both these pictures we see varying degrees of negative stationary-motion positions that the goalkeeper can be in. They are negative because until the goalkeeper can regain balance, he cannot do anything. In picture 67O, Fabien Barthez has just stopped himself to get set up for a shot but is not in the best body position yet. His weight is on his heels and he is using his powerful muscles of the quads and hamstrings to stop him from falling backwards. Until he stops using these muscles for the purpose of gaining balance he will be in this negative stationary-motion position. These muscles cannot do two things at once. It's like a car; you cannot put the brakes and accelerate at the same time and be effective in taking the car where you want it to go. Once these muscles have done the job of getting the body in a good, balanced position, then they will be ready to make the body move in order to make a save. I cannot tell from the picture if Barthez does eventually get in a preferred position but knowing him as a world class keeper, I'm sure he did.

Picture 67N: Lecturing at an NSCAA coaching conference in the USA, I demonstrate some finer points of Human Motion and Goalkeeping.

As the goalkeeper gets himself in the 'set and ready' position to stop a shot, with knees partly bent and hands out, a number of things take place within the body that will make some things possible and other things impossible.

While the goalkeeper's 'set and ready' position places him in a position to react quickly, in most cases, further motion is necessary before the goalkeeper can throw his body towards the ball.

I want my strikers to know what goalkeepers can and cannot do with their bodies at certain times. This information can be helpful in their decision-making process when shooting to score.

How the goalkeeper comes out to challenge the shooter and get in a 'set and ready' position will affect his ability to move in certain directions and how quickly it can be done. Photo by Craig Bohnert, NSCAA, 2004.

Let's assume that a striker had the ball in a favorable shooting position while Barthez was in the position shown in picture 67O. If he did not take the shot at this exact moment, a great goal-scoring situation for the striker would have evaporated. Can my strikers identify these seconds with their peripheral vision during a game? These moments are coming all the time because every time goalkeepers have to move to change their angle, they will have to re-set themselves into new positions. Each time they do this, these negative stationary-motion positions will be created. And the more goalkeepers are displaced, the longer they will be in a negative position where they cannot do anything to make a save unless it's in their reaction zone.

In picture 67P, Buffon is in an even poorer negative stationary-motion position than Barthez in picture 67O. Although his feet are stationary, his body is in motion falling backwards. At this instant, he cannot possibly do anything with his feet to make a save. His only chance is if the ball goes in the reaction zone covered by his hands or the ball hits him. What he has done well though, is to come out and narrow the shooting angle. By being as close as possible to the shooter, he gives himself a chance to make a save with his hands or by having the ball hit him. He's also done well by trying to distract the shooter by being so close to him. If the shooter has predicted this and makes good contact with the ball and places it by one of his feet, then he should score. Unfortunately for Radek Sirl of Zenit Saint Petersburg, he does not score. Juventus wins the game 1-0.

Another negative stationary-motion position exists when a goalkeeper moves sideways to get into a new position. At the moment that the goalkeeper is stopping to set up, his body cannot do anything with his feet to move to stop a shot. In picture 65F in Chapter 65, Jens Lehmann of Germany stops to get set for a shot but unfortunately cannot get his hands or body on the ball to stop Del Piero of Italy. Lehmann actually did well to do his best and get in this position but the ball did not hit him. So many players will try too hard to pick corners or not shoot when the decision should be to catch the goalkeeper in these negative moments and make sure to place the ball on goal.

2. Positive Stationary-Motion Position

Goalkeepers are in a positive stationary-motion position when they have made up their minds as to where they have to go in order to stop the ball. In other words, they are in motion in their minds to stop the ball and this is positive for the goalkeeper. It's not a guarantee that what they are planning to do will be the right choice but it's more positive than being in a negative stationary-motion position. I would also say that a goalkeeper who has experience and tries to dictate to the striker where to shoot will also have a better success rate than one not preparing his body. When in a positive stationary-motion position, the goalkeeper's body is already prepared to go in an intended direction. I recall from my days as a goalkeeper that I had to have made up my mind as to where I was going to go before the shot was taken. I prepared to do so without showing or giving away what I was going to do or where I may go. I could prepare my body to go left but I could not prepare to go both left and right at the same time and be fast enough to make a save in either direction. Keep in mind that I'm always referring to shots struck well and less than 18 yards away from me.

Picture 67O: Fabien Barthez's feet are not in motion but his muscles are working hard to regain his balance as he is back on his heels and in no position to move his feet to make a save. He has probably just shifted to get into a good 'set and ready' position in anticipation of a possible shot but until he has fully recovered his body from moving into that perfect position, he will be vulnerable and thus I call this position a negative stationary-motion position. Action Images/Michael Regan

I believe that many goalkeepers predetermine which direction their body will go thereby trying to eliminate their reaction time to zero. A goalkeeper's decision to go in a certain direction comes from the many experiences that he has faced over time. Since the body is already in motion in the brain, all the signals that each muscle must receive from the brain to perform a certain task have already taken place. The eyes, brain, and the nerve cells are already contemplating to spring to action in a certain direction. When a striker surprises the goalkeeper and places the ball in the opposite direction to where they were intending to go, they often simply remain frozen there. The only changes that can take place are a result of task-switching which can still play a part in some saves.

Task-switching saves are still possible when the ball is played close to the body and may require an arm save in the 'reaction zone' or sometimes a leg swing with the non-support leg. Sometimes goalkeepers can move their leg slightly to block a shot if that leg is not bearing any weight. I'll call this the 'leg reaction zone' as shown in diagram 67Q. The leg can make a reaction save on deflections as well as shots. In picture 67R, Seaman has no chance of making a leg or foot save if the ball is played by his right foot, but his left foot can swing to block a shot if he cannot get his body down fast enough on a low shot. Strikers should avoid placing a ball close to the goalkeeper's non-weight bearing foot.

In positive stationary-motion instances the spectator or striker may not actually see where the goalkeeper is going to move, but the goalkeeper has consciously or subconsciously already made this decision and therefore all his muscles are preparing to head in the intended direction.

In order to be at the top of their game, the goalkeepers must be "in the zone" to be able to read the strikers' body movements as they try to score. It takes deep concentration and focus for the goalkeepers to read the game and the

Picture 67P: Gianluigi Buffon of Juventus is in a negative stationary-motion position in a game against Zenit Saint Petersburg as Radek Sirl tries to score but does not. I classify this as a negative stationary-motion position as it's a good situation for a striker to score because the keeper is moving, not to make a save, but rather to stop the body from falling over. Action Images/Eric Bretagnon

finer details of the strikers as they try to score on them. Their timing also has to be accurate. If they signal their intentions too early as we see in picture 63D in Chapter 63, where the goalkeeper moves well ahead of Owen's last touch even though their feet do not move, then a good striker will spot that and react to score easily. Goalkeepers have to disguise where they are thinking of going. If the goalkeeper is half a second too late or too early then he will have problems making saves.

Goals Scorers are Worth Gold

Take a good look at picture 67S (also picture 66B). Having watched the scoring opportunity numerous times, Buffon of Juventus is actually in a positive stationary-motion position. Kaka, of A.C. Milan, is at the 6-yard line having received a ball from a cross. Buffon shuffled over to prepare to take a shot from Kaka who received the ball off a deflection. He got into a stationary 'set and ready' position. His goal is to remain as big as possible without giving away what he's doing too early. Kaka does well to get a shot away in this instance but Buffon does better to stay stationary until the last possible second before falling towards his right. The ball hits Buffon in the legs to his right and Kaka does not score.

Diagram 67Q: When goalkeepers are anticipating and moving or preparing to move in one direction, they can still make a foot and leg reaction save with the leg not bearing any weight. This reaction zone (shaded) for the leg is not as large as the arm reaction zones and is limited to one foot and leg. This limitation to only one foot being able to react quickly, is another reason players will score more goals if they keep the ball low.

Kaka did everything correctly in this situation. In this picture, he did a side volley to get his foot to the ball. Buffon did not have much time to do anything else. Although his legs were a bit far apart, he did not compromise his position as he tried to stay big and protect his head and as much of the goal as possible. Many keepers would have

Picture 67R: Alan Shearer shoots on David Seaman from in close. You can tell from this picture that Seaman was in a positive stationary-motion position before the shot was taken as he is already headed in the correct direction. He's already collapsing to his left to stop the shot. This would not be possible if he had not already made the decision in his mind. If Seaman was not preparing for this shot going to his left and had to rely on a leg reflex save, then the striker should place his shot away from the leg that is non-weight bearing as the keeper can still move it to try to block the shot. Can your striker read which way the goalkeeper will go before the last touch? Photo by Les Jones, Covershots

Picture 67S: Buffon has made the decision to go to his right based on his ability to read the situation accurately. Although his feet were not in motion prior to Kaka directing the ball towards the goal, his mind had already made that decision and hence he was able to move quickly enough to get in the way of the shot to make the save. Action Images/Tony Gentile

come out and been in motion instead of stationary prior to the shot and hence, not have saved the ball. Although Buffon was stationary and in the 'set and ready' position, he was anticipating moving to his right and fell that way and got in the way to make the save. When you look closely at the picture (and the replay in slow motion), you can tell that Buffon had anticipated that Kaka was going to send the ball to the right and he was heading that way. His mind was already made up and the muscles in his body already knew that. He was thus in a positive stationary-motion position according to my definition. His experience in reading human body motion and Kaka's physical possibilities probably helped him guess correctly. It's often that "sixth sense" that makes a great goalkeeper.

This is why Buffon is regarded as one of the best goalkeepers in the world. He's tall, big, and plays very soundly without being too acrobatic. Kaka probably congratulated Buffon and did not let this missed opportunity bother him. When a world class striker misses this type of opportunity it's probably more the result of great goalkeeping, or of physically not being able to do any better. In fact, Kaka was prepared to score early and miraculously turned a bouncing ball off a cross into a great shot at goal. Other strikers may have not gotten the shot away at all. It's this kind of composure that almost set a record transfer fee amount for a player moving from one club to another but A.C. Milan did not want to lose their prized possession even though Manchester City offered a ridiculously high amount of money for Kaka. Goal scorers are worth gold. In fact, they are worth so much that less than a year later, Real Madrid came knocking on the door for Kaka. Players who can score goals allow teams to go further in Champions League play and in their search for the league title which ultimately brings more fans to more games. It's the fans who help pay the bills!

The Frozen Keeper

How often have you seen the goalkeeper frozen and not move at all? Sometimes the goalkeeper remains frozen while the ball goes right by his side. From a spectator's point of view the ball seems to go into the goal very close to the keeper and seems savable. The goalkeeper looks bad since he just stands there and waves at a ball. If the goalkeeper does not subconsciously or consciously prepare his body movement for a particular action, then many of the saves would not be possible. But for that reason, when a ball goes in the direction where the keeper did not expect it to go, he appears frozen and hopeless. I believe that the keeper would not be able to get to many balls without being in a positive stationary-motion position unless a shot is weak and poor.

In picture 67T, the keeper, Marko Simeunovic of Slovenia watches the ball go right past him in the net, as he remains frozen. I have had this happen to me as well. In these cases, I'm sure the goalkeeper was in a positive stationary-motion position ready to go in one direction but making sure to stay big not to give away which way he was planning to go. Staying big and holding the feet position also allows the keepers to make a save on a ball shot right at them or within their reaction zone. But when the ball does not go where they expected it to go and misses their reaction zone, the keepers freeze knowing that they have no chance. That's because all their major muscles have prepared themselves to do one thing and there is not enough time to change that plan of action and still be able to get to the ball.

In picture 67T, had the ball gone to Marko Simeunovic's right, he may have made a great save. I'll guarantee you that he planned to go to his right in his mind and that this information got down to his quad and hamstring muscles. He started the weight shifting process before this picture was taken but elected to leave his body and feet in a stationary position in case the ball did not go to his right. That position would allow a reaction save involving the hands. Unfortunately, the ball was played outside his reaction zone in an unexpected way. The striker went to head the ball and was aiming at the post to the keeper's right but completely missed the ball. The ball hit the striker's thigh and went towards Simeunovic's left. You do not see Simeunovic guessing and start his motion towards where he thought the ball might go in case the ensuing shot may have been closer to his hands. But his mind was already made up because when the ball didn't go where he expected it to go and outside his 'reaction zone', he was left looking frozen and hopeless.

Sometimes strikers can try and get goalkeepers to get in a stationary-motion position by making them go in the wrong direction by faking to kick a ball in one direction and then placing it in the other direction. Whenever strikers can freeze the goalkeepers, they have a huge advantage. This often means the strikers have outsmarted the goalkeepers in where they place the ball.

Shooting Through Legs

Another way to freeze the goalkeepers is to shoot when they cannot see the ball. If goalkeepers lose a split second between when the ball is kicked towards the goal and when they actually spot the ball coming at them, this may cause them to freeze because they think that it's too late to get to a ball. How many times do you see a goalkeeper move late after a shot? This usually occurs when a striker shoots the ball even though it may seem that defenders are in the way. Directing the ball towards the goal especially if the striker is close to goal is usually a good decision because if there are a lot of legs in the way, the goalkeeper may not actually spot the ball until after it has left the striker's foot.

Often, in a freezing situation, it seems as though the goalkeeper has given up on making the save. I've been in this situation many times and often my wrong muscle group is tense and ready to go, but I realize that I'm too late to get it going because I've spotted the ball too late. If you take a close look at picture 67D, you will see Watford's Bouazza flying off the ground in a half scissors/bicycle kick position to get his foot on the ball and direct it at Van der Sar of Manchester United. The ball actually comes through two players and the position of the striker is unexpected. Therefore Van der Sar probably would not have expected the cross to turn into a shot on goal. In this sequence, I actually believe that Van der Sar spotted the ball just a bit too late and therefore went through the motions to try and make the save look good for the camera! It was a brilliant goal and one that requires the strikers to always be "prepared to score" on their first touch when close to goal, which is also their "Last Touch".

Picture 67T: Slovenia's goalkeeper Marko Simeunovic watches the ball as South Africa's Siyabonga Nomvethe scores in the opening minutes of the 2002 World Cup. The goalkeeper was mentally and physically prepared to go to his right and was fooled when the ball went to his left making him look as though he is frozen. Goalkeepers hate these types of goals because it makes them look bad. Action Images/Jason Reed

CHAPTER 68

Scoring From Angles

One of the most common types of goals in soccer comes from when the striker is at an angle to the goal and is presented with a goal scoring shooting opportunity. Many of these opportunities come from a pass being made behind the last defender and the striker running forward to the ball to shoot. Sometimes it comes from a pass or rebound that has come back from a deeper position and sometimes the chance comes from a cross. It may even come from dribbling past a defender but regardless of how the opportunity was created, chances to score from an angle with the foot are very common. When your strikers are not scoring when they get chances from an angle, then there are a variety of problem areas that can be analyzed. I want to tackle this topic from two perspectives. One is a perception perspective and the other is more related to beating the goalkeeper and performing the skill. Both are important and need attention. In chances from angles, the goalkeeper may be in motion, in the stationary-mode position, or in one of the two stationary-motion positions, but how to score is basically similar.

It's when players have chances to score from angles that often their mind starts to watch those highlight reel goals again. Players consistently try to score impossible goals that they see over and over on TV. Although everyone will score one of these types of goals eventually, they may miss 40 good chances to score while attempting this type of goal. But it's not just the TV cameras and fame that sit in their mind; it's their own visual system that gets in the way. What the eyes see and what the brain processes are totally normal. In order to overcome the urges of trying to score on the top corners, we need our conscious mind to override what the eyes have seen and the visual cortex has interpreted. Recall the chapter on perception and reality. Let's look at the reality of what the eyes see when shooting from angles and find ways to train the striker to score.

Step by Step Guide on how to Train your Strikers to Score from Angles all the Time

In picture 68A, I show the goalkeeper coming out to cut down the shooting options. The camera taking this picture is 7 yards away from the goalkeeper and at eye level. When the player with the opportunity to shoot takes a quick peek at the goal before shooting, he will notice that the goalkeeper does not cover the top corners. The hands cover the bottom portion of the goal making the top corners look attractive but aiming for them will not result in goals for the striker.

Picture 68A: The goalkeeper is 7 yards away from the ball and coming out with his hands up. It appears that the goalkeeper does not cover the top corners of the goal and that the hands block the view to the bottom portion of the goal. The camera is at eye level. The goalkeeper is Matthew Caldaroni. Photo by John DeBenedictis

I'm going to walk you through a step-by-step guide on how to train your strikers to score from angles almost every time. Follow the order I provide and do not miss any steps regardless of how simple they appear. I have strictly designed this program based on psychology with the end result being that my strikers will be able to recall how to score from angles every time. It's the psychological imprint in their minds that I want to make.

If the goalkeeper comes out with his hands in a lower position as shown in picture 68B, we see even more space at the top corners. This is what a player will see. It looks as though the top corners are easier to shoot for than the bottom corners. The hands do not cover them at all. It is no wonder that shooting for the top corners is appealing. "Not only does it look open,

Picture 68B: The goalkeeper is exactly 7 yards away from the striker and coming out with his hands down instead of up. In this picture the top portion of the goal is even more attractive as a shooting option than in picture 68A. When the eyes see this, they get excited and tell the foot to aim for the top corners.

but it will make me look like a superstar", is what the brain is telling the player's foot. I show players in my course these pictures.

The next thing to do is to bring the camera down to the level of the ball and take a picture from there as if the ball had eyes. See picture 68C and diagram 68D. This brings a whole new perspective to things doesn't it?

"The Ball has its Own Eyes"

In picture 68C the reality of the scoring situation becomes clearer. I show these photos to my strikers in my "Golden Goal Scoring" course to make my point. It's clear that the top corners of the goal are no longer open when the camera is on the ball and by the foot. The ball will see its way into the goal a lot easier if it's placed along the ground directed at the corners. This is a very powerful image and one that always draws the greatest reaction from players and coaches. In this scenario, if a goalkeeper makes a save with his hands, it signifies that the shooter was shooting for the top corners. That's how I analyze what's on the shooter's mind. Use this as your gauge to see when your strikers are making errors in deciding where to shoot.

In diagram 68D, I show the path of the ball to goal when the goalkeeper makes a save with the hands. The ball trajectory shows where the ball would go if the goalkeeper was not there. Not only do players aim for the wrong spot but they also try and go through the 'reaction zone' of the keeper, which happens to be in the path of the ball to the top corners of the goal. As their eyes see the top corners open, the brain agrees with the eyes, which is why the player shoots for the top corners which appear as being open. This is where the brain has to override the eyes in the default setting of how to score from angles. Players have to change the default setting in their brains, which is what I'm trying to do in these step-by-step instructions. Great strikers tend to make this decision automatically.

Picture 68C: In this picture, the camera is on the ball. The ball is exactly 7 yards away from the goalkeeper and at an angle to the goal. From this angle, the perspective on how to score changes completely. From the ball's perspective, the top corners are covered and the bottom corners are not.

Diagram 68D: The path of the ball from the shooter's foot to the top corner is intersected by the goalkeeper at the height of the goalkeeper's hands which indicates that whenever the goalkeeper makes a save with his hands, the striker was shooting for the top corner. This decision will not likely result in a goal.

When you set out a bunch of soccer balls on a field and watch players shoot in warm-up, you will see them all try and score goals that, for the most part don't happen in real games. When at an angle and without a goalkeeper, they will invariably attempt to score on the farthest post and in the top corner. This is fun, but ask your strikers to train differently. Tell them the fun starts when they score lots of goals in real games!

Here is what I say to strikers,

> ***"If the ball is on the ground and the goalkeeper has made a save at waist level, it means that the player was aiming for the top corner. Based on my statistics of how goals are scored, that player made a BAD DECISION. Remember that the ball has eyes and sees a chance to score when you place it low. Here is an interesting statistic based on facts!***
>
> ***In the 2002 World Cup, when a goal was scored by the foot on a through ball from an angle, out of 18 goals scored, only one entered the net high (top third of the goal), one went in the mid range and the rest went in low. In fact, on the one that went in the middle third of the goal, had the goalkeeper not moved, he would have made the save and therefore leaving zero goals that went through the mid-height of the goal. If you want to score, keep the ball low. Look at these pictures again and again to program your mind!"***

Scoring From Angles After Through Balls

- Out of 18 goals scored in the 2002 Men's World Cup when the ball was on the ground at an angle, only one entered the goal in the upper third of the goal.
- One out those goals went in the mid-portion of the goal but the keeper would have stopped that goal had he not moved out of the way by trying to guess.
- All the other goals entered the net in the bottom third of the goal.

The next step is to have your players come in at the goal from an angle and train them to shoot low. You can do a drill as shown in diagram 68E where players shoot on goal from angles. Player 1 passes the ball to player 2 who shoots in one or two touches (preferably on one touch). After a while move player 1 around to either side of player 2 to provide balls at different angles to emulate different situations in a game where the ball can be played past the last defender. You can even have the shooter dribble in from an angle starting outside the box to add variety. You do not need to have a goalkeeper in the goal at first. Just have someone stand there and make sure your players are running towards the goal from an angle and shooting from 3-9 yards away from the goalkeeper. Then repeatedly tell them over and over that they have to shoot low keeping the ball in the bottom third of the net.

When working with teenage players and adults too, what will happen? The success rate of goals will be between 20% and 60%. Players will not score on 100% of their chances with no pressure at all and with a coach standing 7 yards away as a goalkeeper. Why? Players will miss the goal too often under these circumstances because they will try and put the ball in off the goalpost or hit the ball incorrectly. Here is what I tell players at my courses:

> ***"Why are you missing the net half of the time? There is no pressure on you from a defender and the goalkeeper is just standing there. It's good that you are keeping the ball low but what's with trying to hit it in off the posts? Do you think that trying to score that perfect goal will get you on TV or are you interested in becoming a great striker? In this situation, with no pressure and a passive goalkeeper, you must score 100% of the time!"***

When you review diagrams 20C, 20D, 20E, 20F, and 20G from chapter 20 you will recall where goals are scored. Not all goals are going in off the posts. What I do next is place some pylons around 1 and 1/2 yards away from each post – see picture 68F. Then I ask my strikers to shoot a moving ball from an angle and aim for the pylons. They get a point for hitting the pylon. What happens when you place pylons there? All of a sudden players who tried to blast the ball will now shoot as though they are passing the ball. Most goals from angles, especially as the striker gets closer to the goal, are scored with a firm inside of the foot pass. What you will find is that players will all of a sudden start scoring by hitting the pylon or by just missing the pylon but still getting the ball inside the post. The success rate of the strikers will go up from barely 50% to 90 to 100%. Confidence grows instantly.

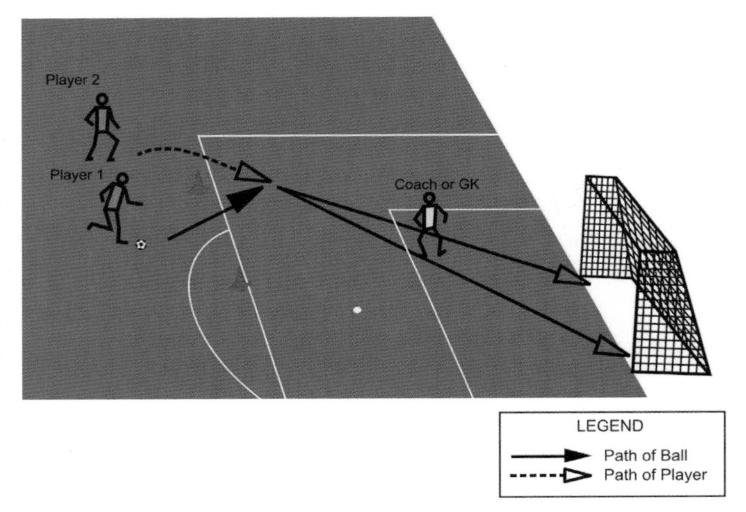

Diagram 68E: In this drill have your strikers come at the goal from an angle and force them to shoot low all the time on a passive goalkeeper. Move the passer, (player #1) around. Take note of their success rate in scoring. Try to get them to score on one touch making sure not to play weak hospital balls into the goal. Do not offer any feedback at this point. Illustration by Jo-Anne Godawa

The players who want to be on television by making the highlight reels will find that they are scoring more highlight reel goals by scoring just inside the post when they aim for the pylons than when they were actually aiming to put it in off the post. There is a big thrill in this for players. It actually gets so easy and the mood of my training session increases as players score all the time. Suddenly, half of the goals that they will score are what they perceive as beautiful goals going in just inside the posts. The body language of the players after scoring is visibly more confident and happy.

"Going over the Cliff"

Now the next step is to have the goalkeeper in motion and moving out from the centre of the goal towards the shooter on each shot. The goalkeeper is still fairly passive and remains tall but comes out and tries to make a save when the ball is close to his free foot. You will see that the conversion rate will go down again. The goalkeeper or coach will stick a foot out when they can to save a ball. At this point, the next step is to teach your strikers to read the goalkeeper's motion. What we plan at this stage is for the goalkeeper or coach to walk out from the centre of the goal, one exaggerated step at a time. If the goalkeeper is in motion and coming out towards the shooter, the striker should try to place the ball by the support foot as it touches the ground. The striker has to find the point in the goalkeeper's motion where he has "gone over the cliff." This means that there is a point in each step that anyone takes where the location of the planting foot cannot be changed because the rest of the body has committed to that position as if to go "over the cliff". This term resonates with players and it helps them 'get it'. Try it yourself.

Picture 68F: I place pylons about one and a half yards inside the posts, and then ask my strikers to aim for the pylons instead of just inside the posts. They will instantly score more goals when the goalkeeper is still passive. Even if players aim for the pylons and miss the pylon, there is a great chance the ball will still hit the net and go inside the post. During games, you want your strikers to imagine that there are imaginary pylons positioned in the goal as shown.

Take a step in your walk. There are various moments as you prepare to plant your foot for the next step where you can still alter where that foot will land. There are split seconds before you plant the foot with each step where you can change where to plant it. Almost right up until you plant your foot you are still able to move it a bit further to the left or the right. But there will be one critical moment when all your muscles of the feet and legs will no longer be able to change where the next footstep will land. If the striker can predict when and where the foot will land, then he can place the ball right beside that spot. The faster the goalkeeper will be in motion, the earlier he will "go over the cliff" in each step. If your striker can focus on the placement of the goalkeeper's support foot all while keeping his eyes on the ball and then aim for that place, then he will have a better chance of scoring.

Picture 68G: In this case, the goalkeeper is in motion coming out to cut down the angle from the centre of his goal. If the striker reads the goalkeeper's motions correctly with his peripheral vision, then the ball should be going right past the goalkeeper's right foot at this instant and towards the pylon at the far post. A ball shot to the other pylon may allow the goalkeeper to make a reaction save with his left foot because he has not gone 'over the cliff' with his left foot yet. Soon he will go 'over the cliff' in his next step and a perfectly timed shot just beside where his left foot will land should score. The goalkeeper is Shayne Branigan. Photo by John DeBenedictis

In the next step of the learning stage, I ask my goalkeeper to come out step by step and I ask my strikers to place the ball by the support foot and hit the pylon. In picture 68G, the striker has to aim where the goalkeeper's foot has to land. At this moment, the ball should be going right by the goalkeeper's right foot and hit the pylon at the far post if the striker hits the ball properly.

As my strikers get better at this, I ask the goalkeeper to pick up speed. In many instances, in a game situation the goalkeeper will be in motion. Decisions have to be made quickly. In picture 68G, the goalkeeper's left foot is getting ready to plant but has not gone "over the cliff" yet. He can still alter his left foot motion and change the location where it will land. But in a split second from this picture, he will have to plant his foot. Can my striker read this position and place the ball right beside where he will plant his foot so that he can hit the pylon and score? If the striker had shot earlier, he could have placed the ball by the goalkeeper's right foot at this instant to score on the far post.

Don't think that players will get this right the first time. The goalkeeper will stop a fair number of balls as the strikers misjudge where the support foot will land. They will also choose the wrong post to shoot at but allow them to experiment with this as they try to foresee where the goalkeeper will plant his foot. It will take focus and concentration from the strikers and unless they are a natural at this, they will succeed only by taking practice seriously. This simple exercise may tell you which players have a future and are coachable and which ones are not.

Here is how I explain it to players,

> ***"Find the point where you can predict accurately where his support foot is going to land. You have to find this point because if you can't read this quickly, you will not have enough time to react fast enough to kick the ball to that spot. You won't have time to shift your eyes from the ball to the goalkeeper and back fast enough. In fact, it's your peripheral vision that should read this motion. Your mind knows what it's looking for. Don't panic in this situation and don't forget to pass the ball with a well-paced ball. Knowing what you are going to do, (keep the ball low), where to aim, (pylons), what to look for in the goalkeeper's motions, (support foot), while under pressure will make your decisions easier to make. You will score more goals."***

Hear the Grass or Chip the Ball?

It will take practice as they learn to bring their minds into the scoring process. Some will start to lift the ball more than they should. Remind them to keep the ball low. I like to say to players that they should 'hear the grass' as the ball skirts along the ground into the goal. If the goalkeeper is coming out very very fast and will be very close to the striker when they get their next chance to touch the ball on their next step, then a small chip may be necessary in order to clear a rushing goalkeeper. This occasionally becomes a good option when the last touch will come when the ball is less than 2 yards away from the goalkeeper and the keeper has come out very low. But more often, if the goalkeeper is further than 2-3 yards away and trying to get into a stationary position, the goalkeeper should 'hear the grass' as the ball hugs the grass as it goes by his foot.

If the goalkeepers manage to get in a stationary position on a shot from an angle, the chances are that they will be in a stationary-motion position. If they are in a negative position, then the striker can place the ball in the goal by either foot. If they are in a positive stationary-motion position, then the striker should try and read which way the goalkeeper is leaning towards and place the ball in the other direction. This is not always easy. Remember that the ball is moving, the goalkeeper is cutting down the angles, and defenders are in a hurry to try and block the shot. Is there a preferred positive stationary-motion position that most goalkeepers lean towards? I would say that, when the striker is coming in from an angle, most of the times, the goalkeeper would lean to protect his near post. This makes the

Picture 68H: Switzerland's Johann Vonlanthen scores on France's Fabien Barthez at Euro 2004, low at the far post where the pylon would be in the practice session. Action Images/David Gray

chances of scoring increase at the far post and not the near post. In picture 68H, Switzerland's Johann Vonlanthen scores on France's Fabien Barthez at the far post. Notice that the ball would hit a pylon about 1 1/2 yards in from the post just as practiced.

In picture 68I, I want you to notice how easy it would be to score right by the goalkeeper's support foot. In this

Picture 68I: This keeper is not in a very good position at all. He will not be able to stop this shot by his right foot because that foot is planted firmly on the ground. His other foot is the foot that the striker should stay away from. In this case, the shooter has chosen the correct side to shoot on but the ball is not very close to the support foot. Wouldn't it be a shame if the striker did not score? A ball 2 inches from the support foot would score. Les Jones/Covershots

Picture 68J: Denmark's goalkeeper Thomas Sorensen attempts to stop the ball as Senegal's Salif Diao (not seen) scores during their 2002 World Cup match. The ball goes right by the goalkeeper's foot. Also note that the goalkeeper is leaning to protect his near post. Action Images/Jason Reed

shot, the striker has put the ball a fair distance from the goalkeepers support foot. It would be a shame if he did not score because the goalkeeper is in a very poor position to make the save. I could not find out if the striker scored in this picture. In picture 68J, you will notice that the ball just beats the goalkeeper by the foot. The ball will go in the net at the far post but not right at the post.

In picture 68K, Manchester United's Wayne Rooney is about to touch the ball as he gets close to the goalkeeper. Can you tell from this picture where he should place the ball so that a goal will result because it will be impossible for the goalkeeper to stop? Use photos like this one to train your strikers how to read the goalkeeper's motions. The goalkeeper's support foot that has just been planted on the ground is frozen for a moment. This little trick is applicable to all players on the field against defenders. I tell my strikers to look for these moments in training sessions when passing to teammates. I want them to look at placing a ball right by the support foot of the defending player all the time so that they get used to doing this. The more they practice this, the better they will get at predicting human motion and get their timing right.

Picture 68K: Wayne Rooney of Manchester United is ready to shoot on the goalkeeper, Mark Schwarzer of Middlesbrough, who is in motion. The goalkeeper is moving and can be easily beaten if Rooney places the ball right past the keepers left foot. Action Images/Jason Cairnduff

A striker can use this skill not only to score, but also to thread a pass to another striker or teammate to create a scoring chance. Of all players on the field, the strikers will find the least amount of room to maneuver in and have the least amount of time to make decisions. Practicing the placement of the pass is of vital importance to the strikers whether they are passing a ball to a teammate or into the goal. As I stated earlier, for the strikers, every passing drill should be a goal scoring drill in their minds and they should look for moments to pass the ball by an opponent's support foot.

In picture 68L, we see the results of Rooney's decision. Even some of the world's best players will make judgment errors in some situations, as did Rooney in picture 68L. Players who are successful just make less of them.

To enhance the training of this aspect of scoring I use my tiny perception techniques. I have my players help me instruct younger players in the camps that I run. I ask my players to join the kids and try some of the things we

Picture 68L: Rooney decides not to shoot on Schwarzek and therefore misses a great scoring opportunity. Yes, even the best make some bad decisions. Action Images/Jason Cairnduff

worked on at practice. When working with younger kids, they will find success more often as they concentrate on the skill of passing the ball by the defender's, or goalkeeper's foot. The younger kids also like playing with the camp instructors. When asking your players to perfect some of these skills, have them work with less talented players. They will find it easier to read little kids' natural body movements because they will be slower but their body movements will be the same as when they grow up.

To Shoot or not to Shoot!

Quite often when a through ball is played and a striker has a chance to score, the last defender will sprint to try and block the shot and the goalkeeper will probably be coming out. This is one of the biggest decision-making seconds for the striker and one of the most important moments in the game. Strikers will be saying to themselves, "can I get my shot away or will it be blocked"? It's also a moment when teammates and spectators pass judgment on the striker. If the shot is blocked, some people will say that the striker was too selfish and should have passed the ball to a teammate. Or they may say that he should have cut back to get a better shooting chance as in Rooney's (unsuccessful) attempt in picture 68L. But if cutting back was unsuccessful, fans may say that he should have shot or passed the ball to a teammate. If the goalkeeper makes a save, the same 'what if' questions will arise. If the striker shoots and scores, he will be a hero. It's almost a no-win situation because more often than not, a goal will not result. What we need to stress is that in most of these cases, it's better off to get a shot away than try anything else. And, here's why.

This is what I tell players at my "Golden Goal Scoring" course.

> ***"When you're coming in at an angle, you are probably facing the goal. The defender chasing you has probably had to turn to chase you and in most cases is coming at you from a more central position on the field. This means that, the longer you wait to shoot the poorer an angle you will be at. Also, the longer you wait to shoot, the more the defender can recover from turning to chase you and make up ground, and the more time the goalkeeper has to cut his angles. If you decide to cut back to get into a more central position, your move to cut back may fail and thus your shooting opportunity will disappear forever. Also, the defender may get lucky and defend you and get the ball away from you and, once again you will not be able to shoot. Lastly, even if you pulled a great move, there may be other defenders in the way to prevent you from shooting. If you shoot, you may get a shot on goal, which can result in a goal. If the ball is blocked, there is going to be a rebound. That may result in another chance for you or a teammate.***
>
> ***We have all seen goals where the striker cuts the ball back and then beats another one or two defenders to score and looks like a hero, but there are a lot more failures in trying this than successes. Go with the shot most of the time. Sometimes, you are in complete control of the situation and cutting back is the best option, but go into the goal scoring chance with the idea of shooting.***
>
> ***Let me tell you one more thing. As a goalkeeper, when a striker came through towards me on my right side of the field and the striker was under pressure, I expected him to cut***

back more often than when a player came through on my left side of the goal. If the ball came to my left, I was more apt to go out quickly to try and dive at the player's feet before they shot than when the ball was to my right. Why, do you think?"

At this point I would see if my strikers would guess the answer. It has something to do with math. Did I not say that goaltenders are mathematicians? Most players (80%) are right footed and thus many strikers do not like to shoot with their left foot. So if they are faced with a situation where they are in a position to shoot from an angle on the left side of the field and are pressured from the inside by a defender, then they are more likely <u>not</u> to shoot with their left foot. Many players will prefer to try and cut the ball back to their right foot. On the other side, a right-footed player would be more likely to shoot.

As a goalkeeper, I would try and figure out who could shoot with their left by studying the strikers in warm ups or try and remember them from a previous game. A right-footed player who would try and shoot with his left foot would often not have enough pace on the ball to beat me. On the other hand, if there was not enough pressure coming from one of my defenders from a central position and the striker could easily use his right foot as shown in pictures 68P and 68Q, then this presented a problem because the shooter would be at less of an angle to the goal than if he was shooting with his left foot. The goalkeeper would have to cover a bigger portion of the goal when the angle was not as sharp for the shooter.

Near Post or Far Post- What's the Goalkeeper Thinking?

When goalkeepers come out to challenge a shooter who is coming at them from an angle, they usually have to do so from another position. That is, they are not always coming out from the centre of their goal. Often they have to act quickly and they cannot take the time to look at their goal and make sure they have the angles covered properly. Their objective is to come out as far as possible to narrow the angle. Their ultimate goal is to prevent the shot altogether by coming out to get a ball before the shooter does. This is not always possible. The goalkeeper will always be fearful of giving up a goal at the near post. Take a look at picture 68F and 68G. Which pylon do you think would be easier to hit if you were the striker and there was no goalkeeper in the way? The answer is obvious. The one at the near post is closer and therefore would be easier to hit. Knowing this, the goalkeeper will know that, if he gives too much space at the near post, the striker will have an easy time picking this spot to score. Since it's closer to the striker, a shot at the near post will give the goalkeeper less time to make a save. Even a reaction save in his reaction zone may not be possible for the goalkeeper to make the save at the near post.

Goalkeepers are also told by coaches to never give up a goal at the near post. And last but not least, goals scored on the goalkeeper's near post make the goalkeeper look bad. The fans aren't happy and their teammates will give them that look that just deflates their confidence for the rest of the game. For these reasons, most goalkeepers will try and overprotect the near post.

If in motion or in the positive stationary-motion position, the goalkeeper will be planning to cover the nearest post most of the time. This will mean that in most cases, the striker should shoot for the far post along the ground to score. The striker must focus on this and must know that the goalkeeper is vulnerable down low on the far side of the goal. He must pay attention to the goalkeeper's foot that covers the far post and make sure the ball passes by it when that foot is in the support position. Most goalkeepers will knowingly give this post to the striker as opposed to the near post and challenge the shooter to hit the ball right inside the post. They are thinking, "go ahead, and try to score on me at the far post". They are also hoping that since the striker thinks the far post is further away, that they will feel that they have to strike the ball harder in order to beat the goalkeeper. Usually, the harder players try to kick a ball, the less accurate they will be.

Indecision can also cause the striker to miss. The striker may see the near post as being open especially if the ball is played across the goal but if the goalkeeper appears quickly to cover that post, then the striker may have some doubt as to where to aim. This all plays to the goalkeeper's benefit. The goalkeeper wants the striker to panic and feel as though he has to hit a perfect shot in order to score. Forcing a shot to the far post also gives the goalkeeper the hope that a defender may sprint back fast enough to stop the ball from crossing the line. On a muddy pitch, the extra distance that the ball has to travel may lead to it getting stuck in the mud in front of the goal. I mention this because it has happened to one of the teams I have coached. We started cheering for a goal when suddenly the ball stopped. The striker who shot the ball stopped following the ball and started celebrating, much to his disappointment. There are a lot of reasons why the goalkeeper will prefer to give the striker the far post to shoot at instead of the near post. This is what I tell my strikers:

> ***"The far post is easy for you to score on if you stay calm, think of passing the ball into the goal, aim for an imaginary pylon a yard and a half inside the far post and try to pass the ball by the goalkeepers support foot. Actually you are aiming for an imaginary pylon near the support foot which is much closer to you than the far post. It's amazing how easy it is to score when you stay focused on this task."***

In most cases, the goalkeeper will be less than 7 yards away from the shooter so you want your striker thinking that accuracy needed to score is less than 7 yards away. If your striker can place a ball right by a support foot, then the resulting shot should end up in the back of the net, unless of course the goalkeeper has totally botched up his angles. In order to hit the pylon at the posts, you may want to put some pylons by the keeper's foot as shown in picture 68M to get your players to understand how easy it should be to hit a target less than 7 yards away. They just have to focus on the keeper's movements and be sure to stay away from his free foot.

Picture 68M: To stress the point of aiming the ball by the support foot, place a pylon or cone by the support foot. This target is very close to the shooter and should be easy to hit. A pass striking this pylon with some pace will automatically hit the net unless the goalkeeper has completely misplayed his angles. The goalkeeper is Shayne Branigan/Photo by John DeBenedictis

Picture 68N: Align the pylons so that players get used to aiming for the near pylon. It will be easier to hit and make scoring seem easier than when players think that aiming for the far pylon may be too difficult. Once the player gets the idea of this exercise, he can feel more confident that he will not miss the net. How many times do coaches see the ball roll just wide of the goal in these situations? This exercise will help reduce those types of misses. And yes, occasionally the goalkeeper will get to the ball and make a save but as players get better at timing their shot, getting the right weight on the ball, and making their decisions early, they will miss less often and score more goals.

In picture 68N, you can see how I've aligned the pylons from the perspective of the ball. With the camera on the ball, if the striker hits the pylon by the goalkeeper's foot with good pace, then he will also hit the pylon on the goal line and therefore not miss the net.

Picture 68O: Sometimes the near post shot is the better option. The pylons are aligned for the near post in this photo. If the shooter shoots for the far post, in this picture the goalkeeper has not gone "over the cliff" yet and may be able to kick out his right leg to save a shot to the far post in his leg reaction zone. But in an instant, he will go "over the cliff" and a shot to the far post should score. I prefer that the striker shoots for the far post more often, making sure to aim for the pylon rather to put it in off the post.

In picture 68O, the pylon is by the keeper's foot at the near post, which can be the better option once in a while. But since keepers tend to protect the near post more and start moving in that direction before the shot, I believe the far post is the better option most of the time.

Thing Of Beauty - Brilliant!

In pictures 68P, 68Q, 68R, 68S, and 68T, you see cases where the goalkeeper gets beat to the far post because the striker has read the goalkeeper's motion properly. In each case, the ball is played to the far post along the ground and by the goalkeepers support foot. You can tell in picture 68Q that the goalkeeper has tried to guess which way to dive to stop Tevez. It almost seems as though the keeper is trying to get out of the way to allow a goal to be scored. Carlos Tevez shows real mental strength and poise to make the correct decision to score. He makes goal scoring seem so simple in this photograph.

All these far post goals are a thing of beauty for me because these types of goals really make goal-scoring look easy. If the strikers are concentrating on the task at hand, they can make these precision passes look simple. Kaka used his left foot to score and was at a poor angle but he was able to thread the needle to score. These goals are based on reading consciously or subconsciously where the goalkeeper's body will be at an instant in time and putting the ball where there is no way that the goalkeeper can stop it. It's perception, psychological composure, skill, and artistry at their best.

When you look at picture 68T and 68U, which show the conclusion of the goal by A.C. Milan's Kaka in pictures 68R and 68S, you can really appreciate the calm touch and surgeon-like precision skill of Kaka or any player who scores these types of goals. When looking at the last picture, (68U) it's like listening to the last note of a brilliant symphony overture as it puts the concluding note on the art of goal scoring. Similar to Andres Iniesta's goal in the 2010 World Cup Final as shown in picture 65J from chapter 65, the ball bulges the net but it enters the goal more than 1 yard away from the far post.

Brilliant!

Picture 68P: Argentina's Jorge Valdano scores the second goal in the 1986 World Cup Final against West Germany at Azteca Stadium in Mexico City. He places the ball right by the goalkeeper's left foot. Action Images/Tony Marshall

Picture 68Q: At the 2006 FIFA World Cup in Germany, Carlos Tevez of Argentina scores a goal against Serbia and Montenegro by placing the ball by the goalkeeper's left foot towards the far post. Action Images/Lee Smith

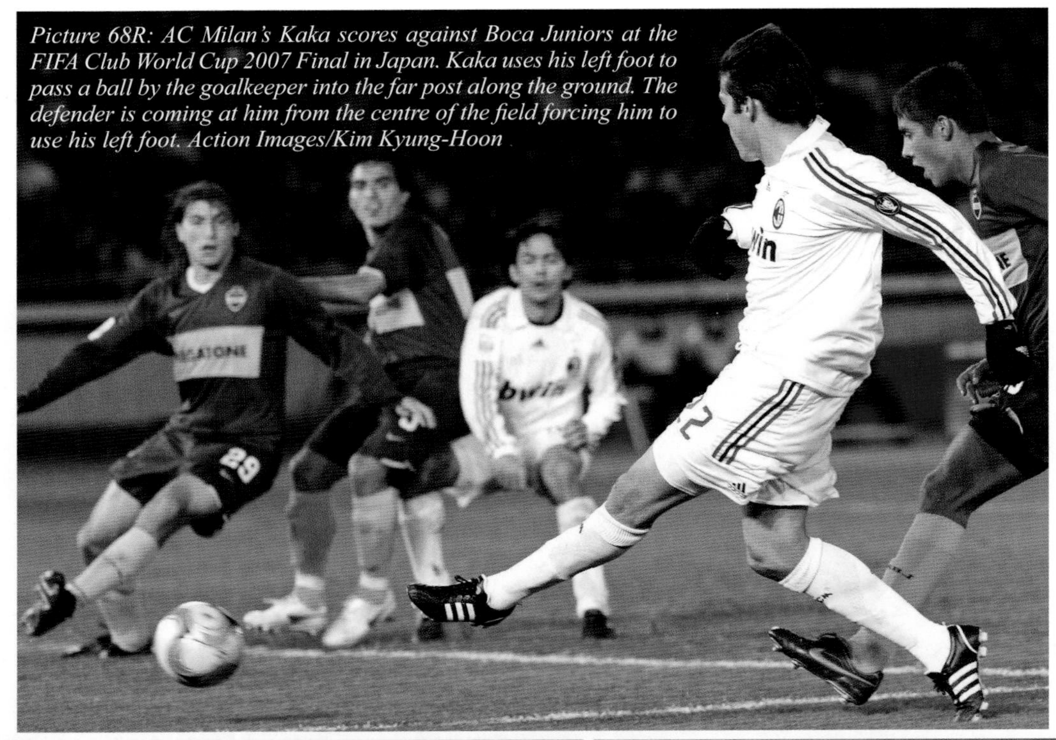

Picture 68R: AC Milan's Kaka scores against Boca Juniors at the FIFA Club World Cup 2007 Final in Japan. Kaka uses his left foot to pass a ball by the goalkeeper into the far post along the ground. The defender is coming at him from the centre of the field forcing him to use his left foot. Action Images/Kim Kyung-Hoon

Picture 68S: This picture taken right after picture 68R shows the ball going past the goalkeeper. Kaka placed the ball by the keeper's left foot as he came out to cut down the angle. Since the goalkeeper was in motion, Kaka found the spot where the goalkeeper could not block the ball by placing the ball in the opposite direction he was heading. Action Images/Issei Kato

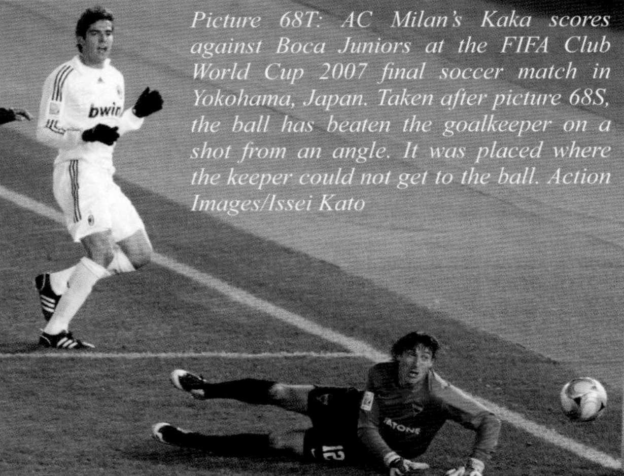

Picture 68T: AC Milan's Kaka scores against Boca Juniors at the FIFA Club World Cup 2007 final soccer match in Yokohama, Japan. Taken after picture 68S, the ball has beaten the goalkeeper on a shot from an angle. It was placed where the keeper could not get to the ball. Action Images/Issei Kato

Picture 68U: AC Milan's Filippo Inzaghi reacts to teammate Kaka's (not pictured) goal against Boca Juniors. Notice that the ball did not go in near the post. It's a perfectly placed shot that simply beats the goalkeeper right by his foot. Where the ball crosses the line is not as important as where the ball goes past the goalkeeper. The closer the ball goes right beside the goalkeeper, the more likely the resulting shot will hit the net. Brilliant! Action Images/Kim Kyung-Hoon

CHAPTER 69

The Psychology of the Goalkeeper and the Striker

As I move towards the end of the book, I wouldn't do justice to the topic if I didn't go into the psychological state of the goalkeeper as it relates to the striker. Some of this information was included in the chapter 65 about illusions. In this chapter I want to go into some more in-depth battles that the goalkeeper is having with himself and with the striker. If strikers know what type of things the goalkeeper is dealing with from a psychological standpoint, then it will help them with their own issues that may be affecting their performance.

The psychological state of the goalkeeper can play an important part in the number of goals that he stops or concedes. The goalkeeper's role is to prevent the other team from scoring goals. Any goal that the goalkeeper has allowed means he has not been successful in doing the job. This negative feeling can be quite depressing. To make matters worse, goalkeepers have little or no effect on the outcome of the game once they have allowed a goal against them unless their team makes that goal back. Even if they stop all remaining shots in the game but their teammates cannot score, their inability to stop that one goal from going into the goal would cost them the game. That can be pretty demoralizing, especially since soccer is such a low scoring game.

Goalkeepers hate giving up goals. As much as they don't like giving up goals, giving up the bad goals really affect them. As much as keepers want to forget about it, it really is hard not to think about a bad goal they may have given up. I know it did affect me. Mistakes affect most goalkeepers. Their gaffes are obvious to everyone and many goalkeepers are conscious of this as they stand there in front of all the spectators, players, and coaches while wishing to go somewhere and hide. In picture 69A, we see a dejected goalkeeper. This is not a pretty sight for the keeper but a delight in the eyes of the attacker.

Picture 69A: When a goalkeeper lets in a goal, it can be very depressing. Not fun: that's for sure. Photo by Les Jones/Covershots

In addition, the goalkeeper cannot truly make a save that everyone can see until someone takes a shot. Think about that statement for a second. The goalkeeper's game is totally based on other people's decisions and, in most cases, the goalkeeper has little or no decision making power. The keeper is expected to be there to stop all shots. It's not as if goalkeepers can call for a shot so they can make themselves look important. There can be moments in a game where they are totally irrelevant and unimportant. Sometimes it can last a fairly long time. But ten minutes later, when they actually get a shot taken at them, they are expected to perform miracles. God help the goalkeepers if that shot is a well taken shot that scores. All eyes will be on the goalkeepers for doing nothing all game yet being unable to save that one shot even if superman could not have saved it!

In an earlier chapter I discussed how depressing it is to be a parent of a young goalkeeper. It's the only position on the field where a mistake will usually lead to a goal by the opponent. The position is very negative in nature. It's no wonder everyone says that you have to be different to play goal. I think to some extent you have to be able to accept all the negativity around the position and turn it into a challenge of wits. This is one reason I suppose that I became a keeper. I find it quite amazing how many goalkeepers become coaches as a percentage of playing positions. As I mentioned at the start of this section, goalkeepers have to be students of the game.

In many cases, there is a psychological game going on between the goalkeeper and the strikers that most fans of the game don't even know about. I found that the best strikers I had the pleasure of playing with or against were special in a way that is hard to describe.

Two of the best strikers I played with both were successful for Canadians in the late 70s and in the 80s. Mike Burke was our leading goal scorer on our National Championship team at York University and also played on Canada's National team. He was also the National Soccer League's leading goal scorer on a few occasions. The other one was Aldo D'Alfonso who also played at York and went on to play for the Toronto Blizzard in the North American Soccer League. At practice, every shot from those players was a challenge. They wanted to score every time. It was pleasurable for them to score and they never let up.

The best goal scorers get in the goalkeeper's mind. They know how to beat the goalkeeper and enjoy beating the keeper in different ways. I noticed that these types of players carried over their pleasure of scoring and their attitude towards scoring in games to practices. For them it was important to take scoring seriously at practice just as much as in games. It wasn't just about shooting and scoring, it was about outsmarting you. For them, scoring on me at practice was important. After a goal, both Burke and D'Alfonso would turn around and give you that smirk that said, "I know what you were thinking. I didn't just score on you, I outsmarted you!" At the same time, they appreciated a save that I would make on them and would congratulate me in their own way. They also gave you that look that let you know that "they'll get you next time."

There is a special mutual respect between the strikers and the goalkeepers. Burke won the golden boot award numerous years in the National Soccer League. Had it not been for all the imports that gobbled up the striker positions in the NASL, he would have been one of the league's top goal scorers but at the time it was bad business to have a Canadian in such a high profile position on the NASL roster. I felt that he knew my tricks and thoughts. It's as if he saw things before they would happen and he knew what I would do. I loved stopping him as much as he liked scoring on me. If found that every shot at practice was a challenge for both of us. Every attempt at goal, even if it was insignificant, was exciting for these types of players. You could see it in his eyes, the smirk, and the attitude. He could shoot with power, accuracy, and quickness. It was different with him.

"I didn't just score on you, I outsmarted you!"

They appreciated a save that I would make on them and would congratulate me in their own way, with their look. But at the same time they would also let me know that, "they'll get you next time."

All goalkeepers have their unique stories about some of the strikers they played with or against and can tell you about a striker that seemed to have their number. Canadian goalkeeper Paul Dolan, who played in Canada's first game at a World Cup final in 1986 in Mexico against the almighty French, led by Michel Platini shares some stories. Canada lost that game by a close 1-0 score and almost upset the French. Dolan was the youngest goalkeeper to ever play in the World Cup and still holds that record for a goalkeeper at 20 years, 6 weeks old. He said that teammate Eddie Berdusco always seemed to have his number and that he was able to get his shot off deceptively quickly. Berdusco scored one of Canada's most famous goals in a 1994 warm-up game against Brazil in front of one of Canada's largest crowds ever in Edmonton. Canada tied Brazil's full squad 1-1 in Brazil's last warm-up game before the 1994 World Cup that they went on to win.

The pressure on a young goalkeeper at a major event such as the World Cup is immense. Strikers need to know that goalkeepers are under extreme pressure to perform. Here are some thoughts from Paul Dolan on the subject.

HANDLING PRESSURE

Paul Dolan recalls a moment in the World Cup game when Canada was still tied 0-0 well into the second half against the powerful French. "I had just made a save to force a corner kick and as we set up to defend I was saying to my players, 'c'mon guys, let's get picked up and don't let them get one now, this is too much fun'. For me that summed up my experience of that game, where, despite the enormity of the challenge, I was able to soak up my experience of what was the highlight of my soccer playing career."

About the pressure before that game as underdogs Dolan said, "Coach Tony Waiters was a huge mentor and helped me a lot. He just told me to do what I had been doing up until the finals and enjoy the experience. Being an underdog actually takes some of the pressure away. I took my practices and game warm-ups very seriously, and this probably got me into a good position going into games so that I was able to make saves early and get into that flow. Once you are in the zone, you have the confidence that comes from making those first couple of saves. At that point, you feel like you have banked enough goodwill that you don't have that fear of allowing a bad goal which I think weighs a lot on a keeper's mind during a game. If things don't start so well you might have a tendency to allow that worry to bother you rather than focus on just doing the best you can. In other words negative thinking can get you out of the zone very quickly.

One of my secrets was to never let my teammates, coaches, or opponents think that I made a mistake (hard to do if it was very obvious) or that I was bothered by making a mistake. I feel like you are beaten when you put your head down after a mistake so I tried not to let anyone see that even if I felt it."

I tell strikers, look at the reaction of the goalkeepers after they allow a goal or make a mistake that almost results in a goal. Their body reaction can tell you something about how their state of mind is. A goalkeeper in a poor state of mind will be easier to beat than one who is confident and attentive. When I was down because of a bad goal, I felt unsure of some of my actions and my own confidence was low. I felt unsure about coming off my line, or about my angles, and this hesitation would make it easier for someone to score on me. When I let in a bad goal that cost the game, the bus ride home was never pleasant. On the other hand, I felt confident especially as Dolan said, after making a good early save. I felt that no one could score on me unless it was a perfect shot. Picture 69B shows a dejected goalkeeper after allowing a goal. A striker should peek at a goalkeeper's reaction right after he has given up a goal. A weaker shot may beat a goalkeeper whose confidence is low. A goalkeeper without confidence may have problems handling crosses, or coming off the line to intercept a through ball. Any advantage that the striker can gain on the opponent will help your team.

As Paul Dolan stated in his quote about not looking bothered by giving up a goal, I believe that another part of that psychological battle the keepers and the strikers have is that the good goalkeepers will try and make everything look easy instead of difficult. I think that when a goalkeeper makes a save look easy, it sends a clear message to the striker that can be unnerving.

Picture 69B: This goalie is not very happy and may be vulnerable more than normal for the rest of the game. Photo by Les Jones/Covershots

Make Saves Look Easy

When a goalkeeper makes a save look easy or an attempt at goal looks as though it was not a problem for him, part of that may be an act to disrupt the concentration of the striker. It may frustrate the striker into thinking that the only way to beat the goalkeeper is by picking the corners. The keepers try to get into the striker's brain and if the goalkeepers succeed into making the striker believe that they are hard to beat then they will get the upper hand on the striker. For goalkeepers, most of the problems that are created when a striker shoots quickly and on target will be solved if the striker has to take extra time to think about picking a corner in order to score. The reason is that three things will happen.

- Firstly, this extra thought process could negate a shooting opportunity.
- Secondly, trying to pick a corner will cause more misses.
- And thirdly, if the keeper knows that the striker is feeling insecure about shooting and feels that he must pick corners, then the keepers can cheat a bit by moving early based on the shooter's body language prior to shooting.

If the goalkeeper can make a save when the striker actually places the ball to a corner of the net, then such a save can completely destroy the striker's confidence. The coach may as well pull some strikers off. The goalkeeper will have won that psychological battle with that player.

To make a save look easy the goalkeeper will need expert positioning and in many cases will need to guess. An experienced goalkeeper will take educated guesses. When making a save where the keeper has guessed correctly, he will need to make the save look easy. At this point even if he is sweating or is saying to himself, 'Whew, that was lucky that I guessed correctly', he cannot show it.

Making saves that do not require diving or major body exertion or extension can really play on a striker's mind. As a coach, when watching a goalkeeper pull those types of saves on my team, I really worry. I worry for a number of reasons. One is that I know my striker is going to second guess himself. Secondly, I know that when a goalkeeper makes saves look easy, his confidence level is way up. When the goalkeeper looks confident, it also makes the rest of the defenders more confident in how they play. The body language of the goalkeeper's teammates is also better because they don't fear making a mistake as much. If the defenders don't have much confidence in the goalkeeper, it can affect the whole game and how they defend and attack.

How can a goalkeeper make the striker believe that only a perfect shot will beat him? As a keeper, I believed that my best weapon was to make saves look easy. If I had to dive to make a save, I would be disappointed with myself because I knew that I did a poor job cutting down my angles. If I see a goalkeeper diving around as though they should be in the Olympics in a gymnastics competition, I feel that they have a poor grasp of geometry and should be easy to score on. Nothing can be more demoralizing for a striker than taking a brilliant shot at goal and having the goalkeeper just stand there and make a save look easy. Even as a coach, I get agitated and start to feel that the goalkeeper is unbeatable when he makes a seemingly difficult save look easy. The whole team can feel the let down when the goalkeeper looks as though he hardly had to make an effort to make a save. This is especially true if the play that created the chance was good and the shooting or heading effort itself was of good quality.

The Rules of Scoring Don't Change

Regardless of how hard or easy the goalkeeper makes a save look, you need to reassure your strikers that the rules to scoring goals do not change. In the next opportunity that comes your strikers' way, they must still hit the goal. They need to analyze what they could have done better on the opportunity that was stopped and get excited about their next opportunity.

The Goalkeeper's Inner Game

Another trick that goalkeepers use to make it seem as though they have everything under control and are confident, is to make chances where the striker has missed the net look as though they were well covered. Goalkeepers have to show that the shot would have been saved with no problem even if the striker had hit the net. Sometimes making things look easy is not just about making a save on a shot but also making a near miss look as though it would have been saved. Many goalkeepers follow a ball that is going wide of the goal or over the bar. I believe that part of this ritual is to show the striker that had the ball hit the net, that the keepers would have easily handled it. For goalkeepers, this ritual also provides them self assurance that they had the shot covered. It helps them with their own inner game.

In picture 69C, Gianluigi Buffon follows a ball that goes way over the bar with his hands. He knows full well that this ball will clearly miss the net but, nonetheless, goalkeepers will follow a ball over the bar or past a post as Buffon does in the picture. Besides showing everyone that he had it covered, he is also telling himself, "Yup I knew it was going over the net but just to convince myself that I got it right, I'll follow the ball over the goal just in case." Goalkeepers are always talking to themselves in their minds during the game. It gives them confidence. Another thing that gives goalkeepers confidence is when strikers miss the net. It gives them confidence because, when a shot misses the goal, the goalkeepers know they blocked their angles correctly. That results in a good feeling for the goalkeeper.

Picture 69C: Italian goalkeeper Gianluigi Buffon of Italy knows this ball is going to clear the bar at Euro 2008 but makes sure everyone knows he would have made the save had the ball hit the net. By following the ball as it goes over the bar, he creates an illusion that in order to beat him; the striker will need to be better than just being able to hit the net. The striker may get the feeling that he may have to pick the top corner in order to score. Or he may feel that he has to get closer to Buffon in order to score because he will easily cover any shots taken from a distance.

This non-save is more an ongoing psychological battle with the opponents than a necessary action. He also is clearly showing his defenders that he has everything under control. This allows them to play with more confidence knowing that their keeper is there for them. This ritual also assures the goalkeeper that he had things well covered and improves his inner game. Picture supplied by Action Images/Christian Charisius

Just as effective in distracting a striker is the goalkeeper's ability to come off his line to prevent a scoring chance by getting to a ball before the striker. In picture 69D, you see situations where a confident goalkeeper can put a striker off his game by coming off his line well. A goalkeeper who is good at reading the game especially as it comes to being able to intercept through balls also gives confidence to his defenders to play with less fear at the back, making a strikers' job even more difficult.

In picture 69E, goalkeeper Swiatek courageously comes off her line to get a ball at the penalty spot mark before the on-rushing attacker gets to the ball. A goalkeeper who comes off her line quickly and accurately under intense pressure exudes confidence. As a result, she deflates the strikers' confidence as they try to find holes through the defenders. The goalkeeper also helps boost the confidence of the defenders, who know that their keeper is there for them when tough situations present themselves. In younger players, sometimes goalkeepers are slightly afraid to dive at feet. Courageous strikers should take note of those types of goalkeepers and take advantage of great scoring situations that will help them score more goals and get noticed.

Another area where a striker can determine the mental state of the goalkeeper is in the goalkeeper's ability to handle crosses. Never an easy save, coming off a line to intercept a cross in heavy traffic conditions is very important for a goalkeeper. Some goalkeepers who are on their game seem to make this practice appear effortless while at other times, the same goalkeeper can be completely off his game and mistime or misread crosses. Have your strikers observe the keeper early in the game to see how he handles crosses. An insecure goalkeeper may give you and your strikers clues to how the defenders will react to crosses. Goalkeepers with height will obviously have an advantage over shorter goalkeepers in this department. In picture 69F, the goalkeeper comes off her line to intercept a cross effectively. Stephan Frei looks confident with the cross in the picture on page 246. Can your strikers take advantage of more scoring opportunities available if the goalkeeper does not look confident on crosses?

Picture 69D: The goalkeeper is quick to come off his line to thwart an attack. When strikers know that a goalkeeper is good at coming off his line, it means that they will have to be very alert to chase any through balls because they will have less margin for error in timing their runs. Photo by Les Jones/Covershots

Handling crosses and through balls are probably the toughest saves that goalkeepers have to make because it's more than just about catching or blocking a ball. It's about reading the play, being courageous, fighting through traffic, and making sure not to misjudge the ball. Make sure your strikers see which goalkeepers are strong and weak in these areas of their game so that they can capitalize on weaknesses. Many goalkeepers fail to make the pro level, even though they are great shot stoppers because of weaknesses in these areas of their game. The alert striker must be ready to score on keepers who are weak in these two areas.

Picture 69E: Canadian goalkeeper Swiatek comes off her line to chase down a penetrating pass with confidence. A keeper who comes off her line quickly and accurately exudes confidence. As a result, she deflates the strikers as they try to find holes through the defenders and helps boost the confidence of the defenders, who know that their keeper is there for them. Photo by Les Jones/Covershots.

Picture 69F: The goalkeeper picks out this cross with confidence. She lets everyone know that crosses will not be a problem for her. A goalkeeper that is confident on crosses will make her defenders more confident as well. If defenders have to worry about the goalkeeper's ability to handle every cross, then they will be more tentative. Can your strikers take advantage of more scoring opportunities available if the goalkeeper does not look confident on crosses? Photo by Les Jones/ Covershots

Even When Scored Upon, the Goalkeeper has to Look Good

If you haven't played goal, you'll be surprised how important the issue of looking good on a goal scored on goalkeepers is. Goalkeeping can be a very lonely position when things don't go their way. Fans, coaches, and teammates don't understand how hard it is to make a save in some circumstances. If the goalkeeper looks bad in allowing a goal it can bring everyone on the team down and affect the whole team's game as well. Players can feel as though that they are trying hard to win the game but when the goalkeeper lets in a goal that, to them, seems stoppable, they feel short-changed by the goalkeeper. Most often a goal that looks bad is actually unstoppable but players get dejected and down on themselves because they feel that the goalkeeper is not trying hard enough. And players hate the goalkeeper who makes excuses after a game or blames everyone but himself. Even if the striker has skillfully scored a goal that most goalkeepers could not stop regardless of how savable it looked, goalkeepers who don't take responsibility for the goal are despised by their defenders. Can your strikers score a goal and make the goalkeeper look bad? A bad looking goal can have a psychological effect on the goalkeeper and the opponents for the rest of the game.

As a coach, you may have to closely watch your opponents and their reactions to giving up a goal especially after a goal that looks bad. It may be an opportunity to attack more and put the game away. Similarly, your key attacking players should be aware of the state of mind of the goalkeeper and defenders after a bad goal. They may be hesitant to do certain things, which may allow a striker to take advantage of this situation. There are other things to watch out for that can help a striker get scoring chances. Does a certain defender have a yellow card, which may make him less effective in playing his normal game? The striker should always be looking for the mental edge.

The key is the goaltender. What kinds of goals look bad on the goalkeeper? Anything low that appears to be close to them looks bad whether or not the goalkeeper could have made the save. Many goals that are scored, as we covered in chapter 68, are scored from angles. The ball will go into the goal low along the ground and right by the goalkeeper's foot. This type of goal makes the keeper look bad. Some goalkeepers are more affected by bad goals than others. Top corner goals look OK and everyone feels the goalkeeper had no chance, but low balls that don't seem to have power and go in the net are the worst especially if the ball barely makes it over the line. Even goalkeepers want the net to bulge so fans can see how hard the shot was.

Goalkeepers also hate being dribbled around. So what the goalkeepers will often do is make an attempt at the ball so that it looks like they tried their best knowing full well that they have no chance of getting the ball. This is evident in pictures 61E and 61F from chapter 61 when Filippo Inzaghi dribbled around goalkeeper Petr Cech. Once Inzaghi touched the ball past Cech, it was apparent that Cech had no chance on the play but he bravely still did his best to show everyone that he tried his best. As a result, the coach and teammates are not going to question whether the keepers could have or should have done better. They won't stop talking to them or treat them as though they have bad breath or some incurable disease. Goalkeepers should always try to make an effort for the ball even if it's to make the strikers feel that they barely scored and to show their teammates that they made a valiant effort to make a save.

In picture 69G, the goalkeeper was unable to stop this shot. In this case, the shot was perfectly placed and most goalkeepers would have a feeling from when the moment the ball left the striker's foot that this shot would go in. In this picture, the goalkeeper gave the effort to try and go for the ball. While this is not the way a goalkeeper is supposed to dive for a ball, he made a late decision to show the fans that he tried hard to make the save. He may have also wanted the striker to know that it will take more shots like that to beat him.

MY WORST DECISION JUST TO LOOK GOOD!

It was my first season in the National Soccer League and I had just won the starting position against an imported goalkeeper from Russia a few games prior when I made one crucial mistake that would affect me up until today. I played for Toronto Ukrania of the National Soccer League and we played in St. Catharines against St. Catharines Roma. Their stadium was sold out with over 3,000 people in the stands and the game was being televised on local TV. This was a big thing in North America in the late seventies and early eighties.

Around the 20th minute, their striker took a long hard drive to the top corner of my goal similar to the goal shown in picture 69G. I knew I was beat. I wasn't going to even try for the ball but was it the crowd, TV cameras, my perception of things? I don't know exactly what came over me, but I made an attempt to dive to get the ball just as the goalkeeper did in this photo. But because the decision was made late, as I started flying, my body turned the wrong way. I was in the exact same position as the goalkeeper in the picture. I was also upset about giving up a goal, as all goalkeepers are.

Just as in the goalkeeper in the photo, my left knee was severely bent as shown in the picture. Not paying attention to my landing I landed directly on my left knee in the bent position with all my weight. I felt a crunch or two and tried to shake it off as I went to pick up the ball from the goal. Trying to not show pain or dejection I stayed on the field until the opponents played a through ball. As I tried to go out to intercept it, my knee locked and I went nowhere. The striker who beat me to the ball should have scored because I would not have been able to go in any direction to stop a ball. Thankfully for me, he missed the net completely.

I was done for the game and the rest of the season until the very last game. I had damaged my cruciate ligaments. That knee has never been the same and even today, I need to wear a knee brace whenever I play hockey.

The moral of this story: goalkeepers hate looking bad when giving up goals. In picture 67D and 67F, I'm sure Edwin Van der Sar knew that he could not stop this ball. He dove so late in relation to when the ball went in the net that I could tell that it was probably more for show than to really expect to make a save. Check out pictures 67L and 67M of Kasey Keller trying to make a save. He is flying towards the ball but the ball passed him by long before he took off. Goalkeepers do this to make themselves not feel bad by not looking bad.

Picture 69G: This goalkeeper is making an awkward attempt to stop this shot. It's not a normal diving position for a goalkeeper. In fact, I believe the goalkeeper decided to take off a bit late as an afterthought. In other words, the keeper probably knew right away that he was not going to get to this ball but then decided to go for it so that he would not look bad for not trying to make the save on this un-savable shot. This attempt will let the striker know that it will only take shots such as these to beat him and let his defenders know that he's trying his best for the team to stop the shots, including brilliantly taken shots. Talking of brilliant shots, isn't this just an incredible photograph taken by Les Jones of Covershots?

You may wonder why I mention these stories in a book about goal scoring. The strikers must know the psychology that's going on with goalkeepers as they try to put them off. The best strikers will turn these psychological games around to put their opponents off instead of the other way around. Hitting a moving ball and scoring is not easy even without opponents and on an empty net! That ball is not easy to put in the goal all the time. I want my strikers to win all psychological wars against the goalkeepers and knowing this element of the game will only make them better. And I want the young players who keep aiming for highlight reel goals to think that, by scoring those boring, along the ground goals, they are doing more than goal scoring. They are winning a psychological war with the goalkeeper. The temptation to shoot the ball off the ground is so strong that some very skilled and potentially great strikers continue to miss scoring opportunities when there is no reason they should. This aspect of explaining to your strikers how to score can make them make the right decisions more often. But the best I can say is this: You're the coach, if you have a player who gets chances to score, it's your duty to make sure he converts those chances. Plain and simple.

Dealing with Injuries to the Striker

Strikers are faced with more situations where they can sustain an injury than most players. This is because they are often with the goal and the defenders behind them. Also, they can be the difference between a team winning and losing. So if defenders have the option to stop a goal by challenging for a ball that they have no chance of winning legally but can stop a goal by bringing down a striker, then you'll probably agree that many defenders will try and stop the goal. Alan Shearer said, "You take a lot of knocks playing up front".

Although I'm sure most players do not want to seriously injure their opponents nor get called for a foul, sometimes the options are non-negotiable if they want to keep their spot on the team. Most players will hope that their tackle will not injure their opponent but often injuries result from tough tackles to prevent goals. How do strikers handle injuries?

Injuries, especially painful injuries, can cause a mental block in the future performance of players. I know all injuries are painful but in this case I mean injuries that are long lasting and tend to be of the more serious variety where players will miss some games. The painful but not long lasting bruise type injuries are part of the game and have little long-term effects. Athletes are usually quick to get up once an initial pain wears off. The resulting bruise rarely affects performances. But injuries that may have been caused by collisions and resulting in ligament damage, fractures, or concussions can have long-term effects even after the athlete has recovered. Memories of the condition that caused the injury are implanted in the brain forever. If players identify a situation where they are heading towards what resulted in a previous serious injury, they may hold back and try to avoid that confrontation. Your strikers may be less aggressive chasing a ball or making a move if the last time the same situation occurred, they were sidelined for 6 weeks or more. As Rafi Srebro states in his book *Winning with Your Head*, "Every injury is also a head injury". He states that an injury always harms our minds even if it occurs in the leg.

Injuries cause players to have less self-confidence, which also includes some fear and anxiety. I was always cognizant of how to land after diving for a ball and did not injure myself again in that way but I did injure the same knee and ankle playing hockey years later. With no opponents around me, my skate must have caught a rut in the ice and hence buckled ripping apart my ankle ligaments and re-injuring my knee ligaments. After a full year off, I returned to action but I always worry about the quality of the ice and know that I will try fewer things if the ice is bad than if it is good. I also make sure not to sharpen my skates too often so that I can avoid a similar injury. Fortunately, I only play recreational hockey but I can imagine how athletes would not be able to compete at the highest levels if they are hesitant due to a previous injury. In his book, Srebro goes through some mental training a player can do in order to come back from injury. I would recommend the book if any of your players were having problems getting back to their pre-injury form.

No Pat on The Back

Getting back to the psychology of scoring and the striker and goalkeeper, there were so many times that a player should have scored on me but they didn't. Somehow, I felt that I got in their minds to stop the shot by making them do the wrong things. Some of my best saves never happened. No one congratulated me and no one gave me a pat on the back because I didn't have to make the save. It was a save for me because if one had taken the goalkeeper away from that situation, the striker would probably have scored.

One of the biggest factors goalkeepers have going for them is that they don't have to worry about controlling a ball with defenders all around them. They can try to distract strikers. Strikers have a lot of things going on around them that affect their ability to perform the skills to score.

Truly great strikers have something different about them. They have an aura of confidence. I don't want to coach strikers to be cocky or arrogant but rather have an inner confidence to be able to score. It's also important to note that, unfortunately, some good strikers are difficult to handle. As a coach, you may need to walk on pins and needles a bit. Your ability to handle these strikers can make or break your season and even your personal coaching career especially if you're coaching at the higher levels that are results driven.

Scoring Slumps

Many of the ideas presented in this book are meant to help you build your strikers' inner confidence. The way these players need to practice is different. How they handle slumps and come out of those slumps is also different. Michael Owen said in Simon Kuper's article, "When confidence is high they (the goals) flow, when it's not, they dry up." A superstar like Alan Shearer had a big slump at one point in his career but came out of it. Great strikers persevere and get back to scoring like they always did. I found that most of the successful ones always practiced hard.

I had the pleasure of spending some time and talking with Jeff Cunningham towards the end of his time in Toronto (Picture 69H). He's one of the top goal scorers in the history of the MLS. He played with Columbus Crew and Real Salt Lake before coming to Toronto FC. When he arrived in Toronto, he had scored over 90 goals in the MLS but in the year and a half that he played for Toronto, he only scored 6 goals and was in a big slump and barely getting playing time. As a true professional striker he wanted to hear what I had to say about scoring goals. Shortly after our meetings, he was traded to F.C. Dallas. I kept in touch with him through e-mail and sent him the draft of this book's chapter 46 right after he left Toronto. He scored in his first game with Dallas to come out of his slump. In fact, in the following season, at 33 years of age, he had regained his form completely and won the MLS scoring title. Perhaps my advice helped him and maybe not. Like all good strikers who have an instinct to score, once he got his confidence back, he started scoring again.

Picture 69H: John with Jeff Cunningham formerly of Toronto FC. Jeff has scored over 130 goals in the MLS and is the all-time leading goal scorer as of 2012.

To Score Or Not To Score

Just like the striker who is confident, the confident goalkeeper is always harder to score on. When I was in "the zone", it felt great and I was into the game in many ways. I would be talking, instructing my defenders and the defenders were listening. When I let in a bad goal, I would not feel like talking because I would be assuming that my defenders would be saying to themselves, "Why is the goalkeeper telling me what to do and where to be if he can't stop a beach ball?" Sure, teammates tell you that it's ok, but inside you, you know that they are probably blaming you for the goal and the loss if you lose the game. Or you think everyone is talking about you.

As a coach, I even have a hard time talking to my goalkeeper after a game if he's had a bad game. What do you say? If you say, "Good game", he knows you're lying. If you say, "Nice try", he knows you're trying to make him feel good but it's not working. You can't say, "Bad game", as it's like punching him in the face. Goalkeepers just want to go home and come fresh the next day and hope that everyone forgets about the performance. So while you need to deal with the mental state of your goalkeepers, you want your strikers to have no mercy. They need to take advantage of the goalkeepers' volatile state of mind. The true strikers cannot have feelings for the goalkeepers and must always want to score. The answer is always to score.

How well does your Striker Study the Goalkeeper?

It's hard for the goalkeeper not to think about bad games or goals. I still remember some of my worst moments as much as my best. For the goalkeeper, after a bad goal in a game, once the team gets a goal back, it starts to feel better. Sometimes it never comes. The goalkeeper is the only player on the field that can't make a mistake. As a keeper I tried to get in the zone to help me play better, block out the crowd and fans and concentrate on the game and my role in it. To help me do this I became a student of the strikers. Strikers must become students of the goalkeepers to outsmart them.

Here is what I say to strikers:

> ***"As goalkeepers, we get to know certain players. Don't think goalkeepers aren't studying you. They will know if you like to shoot early or if you like to hold on to the ball or don't shoot enough. Do you use your right or left foot? Do certain players ever use their left? Goalkeepers will also relay this information to their defenders. The keepers have to try and know the strikers' tendencies so they can predict what they are more likely to do in different circumstances. Most goalkeepers will really know their teammates so if a particular teammate ends up playing against you down the road, you can bet that the goalkeeper will know a thing or two about him.***
>
> ***If you're a good striker, you'll know quite a bit about your goalkeeper as well and what his strengths and weaknesses are. If you don't know things about your goalkeeper on the team that you are playing with right now, then you are not doing very well. If you want to be a great goal scorer, you better start learning about this aspect of the game. Start by getting in the frame of mind of knowing your own goalkeeper in detail. What's his weak side or strong side to dive on? Does your keeper catch the ball cleanly? Which hand does he distribute the ball with? Which foot does he kick with? Which hand does he write with? How confident is he on coming off the line, on crosses, or through balls. How does your goalkeeper play the angles? What side of the goal is he most likely to give you? How does your goalkeeper play penalty shots? Does he wait for you to shoot or does he prefer to dive first? Does the goalkeeper like to dive a certain way based on the striker's approach?"***

Listen and Look Carefully

Ask your strikers to listen to the opposing goalkeeper talk to his defenders. How well does he command his box and how well does he communicate with his defenders?

Does the goalkeeper give his defenders clear, concise instructions or is the goalkeeper vague in giving directions? For example, does the goalkeeper say, "Johnny, cover number 4, behind you," or does he say, "Someone, cover this guy." How specific is the opposing goalkeeper with his instructions to the defenders when a ball is played from one player to another? Does the keeper like to come out on corner kicks or does he prefer to stay in the goal? How is the goalkeeper on crosses to the near post, and to the far post? Look at the opposition's goalkeeper's height. If the goalkeeper is tall, then he is probably better on crosses than a shorter goalkeeper will be. If the keeper is short then he is probably quick off his line. How safe are the keeper's hands? Is there anything that can put the keeper off? What is the goalkeeper's stress level?

My assistant and goalkeeper coach a few years back played semi-pro goalkeeper in England and he loved to practice. At our practice sessions with the kids, he was usually diving around making saves as though he was a young man. When he had a sore back the next day I would say to him, "You're not young anymore. Get some ice on it". But as good as he was in practice he said, "I loved to practice but hated games. My stress levels escalated to the point where I would get into a sweat. I rarely played any meaningful games because I couldn't handle the stress."

This is what I tell strikers in my course:

> ***"Are you really a striker? Because if you don't have answers to the questions I have posed, then I don't think you're ready to go to the next level unless you change. Think about this for a second: Even if you're the leading goal scorer in your league. You can bet that there is someone in another league, in another state or province, in another country, or in another continent that is at the same level as you are but has answers to all***

these questions. If you meet for a tryout with the same team and all else being equal, who do you think has a better chance of scoring more goals, and be selected for the team?

Study your opponents and in particular the defenders and the goalkeeper. If you are attending a tryout as a freshman or rookie camp for the first time, get to know some habits of the goalkeeper's you'll be trying to score against right away. Between breaks and after training, try and get to know them so you can gauge their personalities and their inner confidence level. The small edge you can gain by having as much information as possible on them is what will be needed to get to the top. Remember that you don't make pro without being good and smart. It's a competitive world out there. Even the worst player in the English Premier League is probably around the 600th best player in the world!"

PART FIVE

MORE PSYCHOLOGICAL INFORMATION TO COVER THE REST OF THE GAME

Penalty Shots, Set Plays, Beating Defenders, and More Psychological Stuff That Goes on the Field of Play That Affects Strikers.

PART FIVE

Les Jones/Covershots

THE REST OF THE GAME

CHAPTER 70

Penalty Shots and Set Plays

In his book, *Coaching Set-Plays*, Tony Waiters stated that between 25 and 60% of goals are scored from set plays. The exact statistics vary from year to year and from league to league but they always seem to fall between those figures. That's a lot of goals and strikers must be able to score from set plays if they want to be effective. Most strikers want to be involved in set plays. Usually the coach has to fend off all the players who want to take "the shot" and pick the players who do the job more consistently. It doesn't matter how hard one begs to be the 'go to guy', for the coach, actions speak louder than words. The striker that scores at practice may get the first choice but if he fails to score in the pressure of a game, you can bet that the coach will try someone else. Likewise, if a player scores in a game, the coach is likely to stick with that player giving him numerous chances to duplicate the effort.

I always tell young players that David Beckham didn't get good at free kicks just by taking a few at practice. He would go out on his own and practice free kicks over and over for hours on end.

Set plays are an important part of the game. Here are statistics from the 1998 World Cup.

Goals From Set Plays From the 1998 World Cup

- 11% of goals came from penalty shots
- 16% of goals came from free kicks (direct and indirect)
- 10% of goals came from corner kicks
- 4% of goals came from throw-ins

That's 41% of goals coming from set plays

(Source: Professor L. Harvey of *Centre for Research into Quality*)

Depending on the age group that you coach, you will need to be careful with these statistics. If you are coaching an U14 team, the percentage of goals scored from set plays will be lower. More goals will come from free play. At U18, there may be more goals scored from set plays than U14 but they probably will not reach the percentages of a World Cup with the best players, most organized defenses and best goalkeepers.

Goals from corner kicks and throw-ins have other components to them, many of which we have covered. Many goals from set plays come as a result of a rebound that started from a set play. Judge how much time you should spend on set plays in your practice sessions by analyzing your team's games. Set plays are the only time in a game where the ball is stopped and there is time to put pre-planned tactics into action. Make sure to take advantage of this opportunity as a coach and practice set plays but do not forget that all the pre-planning and practice in the world will go to waste if the last player to touch the ball that you will depend on to score fails. Make sure the player you designate to get the last touch on the ball in any set play situation is a player that is focused on finishing the job properly.

Penalty Shots

Of all the set plays, the penalty kick offers your team the best chance of scoring. Make sure you practice this. The 1994 and 2006 World Cup's were decided by penalty kicks and the 2010 World Cup almost got to penalty kicks. No one remembers the losers as much as the winners. For example when a World Cup champion is crowned, there is no asterisk beside their victory in the eyes of the fans. No one claims that Italy was the 2006 World Cup Champions via the penalty kicks or Brazil was the 1994 champion by way of the penalty kick shoot-out. They simply will be remembered as "The World Cup Champions".

Diagram 70A: Aiming for the two circles will make it impossible for a goalkeeper to stop the ball unless the keeper has moved to these areas, prior to a shot without diving. If the player shooting misses the two circles by just a little bit, there is enough room for error that the ball should still go into the goal especially if struck with good pace. The shot does not have to be a powerful drive but the shot must have good weight on it so that it's not going too slowly.

I recall being at a goalkeeping coaching session with Dick Howard, former goalkeeper for the Toronto Metros and Rochester Lancers of the old NASL and currently a TV soccer analyst as well as the chairman for FIFA's technical study group. He was lecturing about what some goalkeepers did to try and stop shots. The penalty shot is one of the most psychological points in a game. It's a one-on-one situation and the striker should score so the pressure is on the striker. The goalkeeper's best hope is that the striker makes a mistake and it becomes the goalkeeper's job to somehow, force the striker to make an error. Howard was up against the great Pele of Santos F.C. in a game in Toronto and was getting ready to try and stop Pele from scoring on the ensuing penalty shot. Before Pele took the shot, Howard went to Pele, shook his hand, and wished him luck. It was a gesture that took Pele by surprise since no one had done this to him before. Pele proceeded to bury the ball in the bottom corner of the goal to score. Pele then reminded Howard that he had recently scored his 1,000th professional goal signifying that psychological experiments such as this may work on other players but not him.

Pele and Howard have met on many occasions since then and Pele still recalls Howard's psychological ploy and called him the "Crazy Canuck". In my opinion, the reality of the situation is that the striker should score on 100% of the penalty shots taken. A well-placed shot should score every time if the shooter aims for two areas of the goal that are impossible for the goalkeeper to stop. The human body cannot fly and is not fast enough to react to shots taken in these areas of the goal assuming that the goalkeeper is standing in the middle of the goal when the ball is kicked. If the goalkeeper is standing off to one side, then the perfect spot to place the ball would be reduced to one side. The bottom line is that, a skilled player who can kick and pass a ball properly should score every time. The two areas of the goal are shown in diagram 70A and are designated by a circle. These areas are towards the upper corners of the goal but not exactly in the top corners. After the ball goes into the net, they will seem like highlight reel goals to the spectators but in reality they are not very close to the corners at all. The ball is to cross the goal line in the area of the two circles shown in the diagram. By aiming for these areas, there is enough room for error in accuracy that should still allow a striker to score every time.

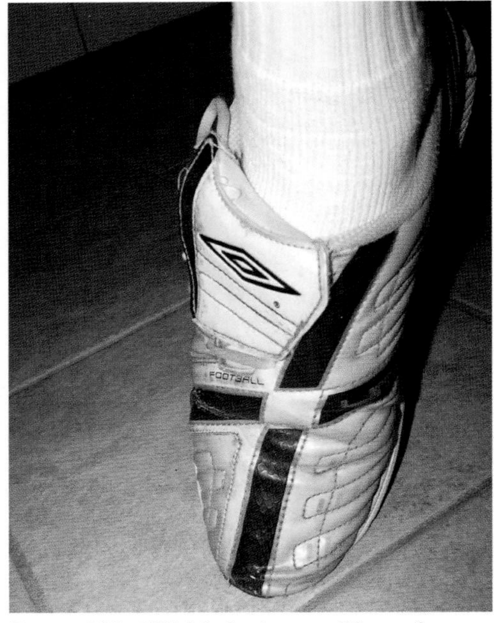

Picture 70B: "X" Marks the spot. The perfect spot to strike a ball on a penalty shot is on the inside front of the foot. The bone on the medial side of the foot provides the best part of the foot for accuracy, control, and enough power to place the ball where a player wants it to go. In this shoe design, "X" marks the spot nicely. The support foot should be beside the ball and aiming at the target. The support foot can be even with the ball or up to a half ball behind the front of the ball. If the support foot is further back behind the ball than that, there is a good chance that the shooter will start to lean back too much and send the ball high over the bar.

The shooter also has to be careful not to try to blast the ball with too much power and then compromise accuracy. How often do we see professional players send the ball with power over the bar or off the bar? A penalty shot should result in a goal.

The ball can be passed there with a well-paced ball, not a weak lob. It should not be taken with a power shot because accuracy will be compromised. The ball should be struck on the inside (medial side) of the foot in between where a power drive would be taken from and an inside of the foot pass would be taken from. In picture 70B, "X" marks the perfect spot on the foot to strike a ball with on a penalty shot. The important part of the skill is to make sure the shooter's support foot is even with the front of the ball or up to half a ball behind it and not completely behind the ball. Planting the support foot behind the ball would cause the ball to rise too quickly and possibly send the ball over the bar. Also, make sure the shooter keeps his eyes on the ball at the moment of contact.

The strikers should use visualization techniques to clearly see themselves scoring in either of these two spots all the time. At practice, the coach can place a hula-hoop hanging from the bar to get strikers to score by placing the ball in the hoop. Then prior to a kick, the players should block out the goalkeeper, spectators, and any background noise and visualize themselves scoring on one of the two hula-hoops. The visualization should always include keeping the eyes on the ball, the placement of the support foot, and the last step. In picture 70C, the USA player scores in the final of the 1999 Women's World Cup by aiming the ball in one of the areas depicted in diagram 70A. Even if the ball does not go directly in the hoop, anything close and well struck should score.

Picture 70C: In the 1999 Women's World Cup, the USA beat China in penalty shots by scoring on all 5 of their shots. The Chinese coach said that they were beaten because the US was better prepared psychologically. Dr. Colleen Hacker was their sport psychologist. She prepared each player on an individual basis for the competition. Tony DiCicco was their head coach. Photo by Les Jones/Covershots

The Lasko Effect

You'll notice that I said that the ball should go into the goal. The only way for the goalkeeper to get to any of those two areas is to be standing there when the ball arrives. That means that the goalkeeper would have to move towards one of those two areas prior to the kick being taken. The goalkeeper cannot be diving for those areas. If goalkeepers try to dive to any of those two circles from the centre of the goal, which is where most goalkeepers start from, then they will not be able to get to the ball because gravity will bring them down towards the ground. I watched all of Alan Shearer's goals in his career with Newcastle in a DVD called *Shearer, The Legend* and most of his goals from penalty shots were from these areas. He preferred to go to the goalkeeper's right. But there are situations where a goalkeeper may be able to predict what the striker is doing. And don't think for a moment that a good goalkeeper is not studying your strikers.

THE GOALKEEPER FACTOR

I played with a player called George Lasko for a season and we would practice penalty shots occasionally. He and I along with a few other players would stay after the training session to practice penalty shots. Usually penalty shot practice is not fun for goalkeepers but I enjoyed it and took on the challenge as though it was a game. Many young goalkeepers don't give the impression that they are trying and will not go for a lot of balls. A striker that sees a goalkeeper prepare to stop a shot as though they really want to stop the striker will get the striker to do likewise and for both parties there can be a lot to learn.

Every time George took a penalty shot, he would take a peek at one corner of the goal before he started his run to the ball. Then he would put his head down as he approached the ball to take his shot. On the first time he scored on me, I took note of what he did. He scored by placing the ball low to the opposite corner from where he peeked. The next time it was his turn to shoot, he did the same thing. I suspected that he would do the same thing but I didn't want to guess where he was going to shoot so I waited for the shot and he scored in the opposite corner to where he peeked again. This time I paid particular attention to see if he would look up as he ran to kick the ball. He did not. He kept his head down. Later in that practice when it was his turn again to take the penalty shot, he took his peek again so I knew exactly what he was going to do. So guess what I decided to do? I decided to dive in the direction he peeked at instead of the direction I knew the ball was going. Then after that I acted like I was mad at myself and that he completely fooled me.

For the rest of the season, every time he took a penalty shot at me, he would do the same thing and I would purposely let him score by diving to the side he peeked at and then acted as if I was upset because he fooled me. A year or two later, playing in the NSL pro league, we were on opposite sides. We greeted each other before the game and wished each other luck.

Later in that game, our team gave up a penalty shot. Guess who stepped up to take the shot? It would be my old teammate, George Lasko. I was wondering if he was going to do the same thing. I paid particular attention to his eyes prior to the kick. Just as predicted, he took a peak at the corner he was not going to shoot at and then proceeded to keep his head down during his approach to the ball to shoot. Knowing where he was going to go, I shifted over to the corner of the goal opposite to where he peeked and practically stood there waiting for the ball to come at me. I picked up the ball as though it was a simple pass; made the save look easy and we proceeded to win the game 1-0. If you think that goalkeepers are not studying you as a striker, then you're wrong!

Good strikers study goalkeepers as well. As I mentioned in the last chapter, your striker must learn how to concentrate and learn a thing or two about goalkeepers. I never once let George feel as though I knew what he was giving away while we were on the same team. This was my secret and you never know when it can make you a better player or make your team win as I was lucky enough to experience in that scenario.

Alan Shearer, who always took the team's penalty kicks while at Newcastle United, said that a good goal scorer should want the challenge and pressure of taking a penalty kick. He said, "I've never understood any goal scorer who doesn't want to take a penalty. I mean, if you put them in a one-on-one situation in general play, a goal scorer would want that. There are some players who are petrified to take a penalty."

He also said that the pressure is on the shooter, "When you miss a chance in open play, people don't remember. When you miss a chance on a penalty, people remember." When asked about a particular miss he said, "I took responsibility for that game. It was my responsibility that everyone went home miserable that evening. It took a while to get over that."

Shearer would think of the possibility of taking a penalty shot before each game and would recall something about the goalkeeper he would likely be facing in the game. He would stay and take penalty shots for 10 or 15 minutes after a Friday practice before a Saturday game. He said that he would know at dinner time the Friday night before a weekend game exactly where he would place the ball if confronted with a penalty shot. It was not always in the same corner but most of the time it was in his favourite spot. When watching Shearer's penalty shot goals, even the goalkeepers who knew which way he was going to shoot and dove that way, could not save the shot because Shearer hit the ball with enough pace and accuracy to score. His favourite side was high to his left or the goalkeeper's right. He would try and recall a number of things about the goalkeeper he might be facing in an upcoming game. Shearer said:

> "Who is the keeper and have I taken one against him before? Does he know my favourite side? Did I train with him before? At times I would change my mind at the last minute but more often than not, I missed. Penalty shots don't get any easier just because you have taken lots. It's a battle of the mind."

"I would know at dinner time the Friday night before a weekend game exactly where I was going to shoot."

Alan Shearer from the DVD, *Shearer, The Legend*

In the 1999 Women's World Cup Final, Brandi Chastain scored that memorable penalty shot goal that got her so excited that see took her shirt off after the ball went in the net to give the USA the World Cup. The picture of her with her shirt off and with her sports bra on made front page headlines in newspapers around the world. The pressure of taking the last shot in front of almost 100,000 spectators, (the most to ever witness a female sporting event) must have been immense. But fortunately for her, she had taken a shot on the Chinese goalkeeper, before. She said "She (Gao Hong), had psyched me out earlier. I looked up and caught her eye. Her gaze rattled me and my shot dinged off the crossbar."

In her book *It's Not About the Bra,* Chastain said, "There was no way I'd look into her eyes again. A penalty kick is as much a mental challenge as it is a physical one. No one really expects a keeper to save a PK, so she has nothing to lose. All the mental pressure weighs on the shooter."

Picture 70D: A penalty shot is an important part of the game and one in which strikers on your team should practice over and over. A goal scored on a penalty shot can win your team the game. In this case, it was penalty shots that won the US National Women's team the 1999 World Cup. Not a bad prize! Unfortunately, in 2011, a similar penalty shoot-out cost the US team the gold medal as they lost to Japan. Photo by Les Jones/Covershots

Picture 70D shows the jubilation of the US team as they were presented with the World Cup. A penalty shot is an important part of the game and one in which the strikers on your team should practice over and over. A goal scored on a penalty shot can win your team the game. In this case, it was penalty shots that won the US National Women's team the World Cup. They scored on all five shots. Not a bad prize for being good technically and mentally at taking penalty shots!

Here is what I say to strikers:

> ***"As a striker you have to make sure not to give anything away. Do not be predictable. In today's game with the use of video replays, players can go back and review goals to see what the goalkeeper tends to do and what the striker tends to do so a bit of variety is always good. The goalkeeper will try to distract you or find out something about you. You must do the same. That's what good strikers do."***

I don't play poker but I have heard the expression having a 'poker face'. From what I understand, poker players do not want to give away what they have in their hand. The striker is in the same boat as a poker player. The goalkeeper will be looking at things such as the striker's angle of approach to the ball, the eyes, the striker's composure, and he will want to see if the shooter is nervous. The goalkeeper may delay getting set to stop the penalty shot to try and throw the striker off. Goalkeepers often do this to make the strikers start thinking more and possibly changing their minds as to where to shoot.

Picture 70E: The goalkeeper has committed early before the shooter touches the ball. If the keeper has moved much too early, the striker can alter his decision and score easily in the opposite direction to where the goalkeeper has moved. Photo by Les Jones/Covershots

Uncertainty in the striker's mind can be a plus for the goalkeeper. In today's game the goalkeeper can move laterally along the line and although few goalkeepers are using this rule to maximum use, you should make sure to prepare your shooter for a goalkeeper that is moving back and forth along the line while your striker is getting set to shoot. Make sure that your strikers stay focused. In some cases, the goalkeeper commits to an action so early and goes "over the cliff" that the striker can alter his original plan and score easily. The striker must have played this scenario out in his mind often to make sure that he does not panic and make a mistake. In picture 70E, the goalkeeper has gone "over the cliff" and committed to one side prior to the kick. If the striker can spot this with his peripheral vision then he can change his original plan and score easily.

Despite what the goalkeepers are trying to do from a psychological standpoint to distract the shooters, the strikers must focus on the task of scoring in this ideal situation. The penalty shot is an ideal situation that can't be made any easier for the strikers. They must relax; take a deep breath, concentrate, and feel confident that they will score. By knowing in advance where they are going to shoot, and visualize their shot prior to taking it, then they should not miss. They should never change their mind unless, as stated, the goalkeeper makes his move much too early where the change of plans is going to result in an easy goal.

Picture 70F: In this goal, the ball is placed close to one of the two circles from diagram 70A. Even though the goalkeeper has guessed correctly and the ball would not have hit the circle perfectly, because the ball was struck with pace and the goalkeeper cannot fly, the shooter still scores. Gravity has made it impossible for the goalkeeper to get to this ball. Photo by Les Jones/Covershots.

The ability to consistently hit one of the two areas depicted in diagram 70A will come with practice. Players who do not know where to aim according to diagram 70A and picture 70F, and assume that they should place the ball into the top corner of the goal and therefore aim there, will miss more often than they should. When young players watch highlights of these types of goals on television they get fooled as to where the ball enters the net because of the bulging mesh. In diagram 70G, I show where the ball enters the net as opposed to where the ball bulges the mesh. The bulging mesh makes it appear as though the ball goes in the top corner of the goal. Picture 70H shows the bulging net in a perfectly placed shot by De Rossi of Italy in the 2006 World Cup final.

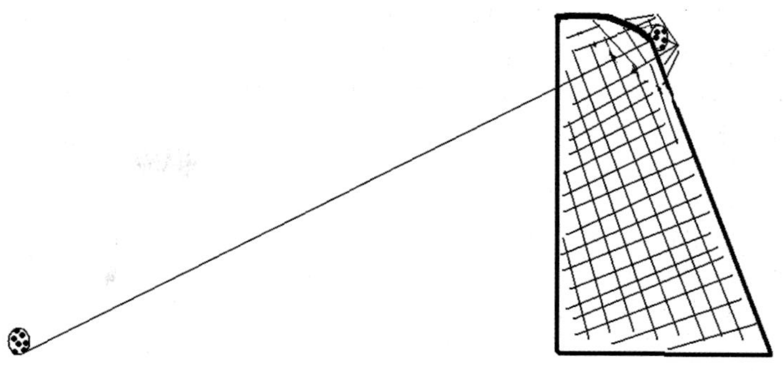

Diagram 70G: This diagram shows the reality of where the ball crosses the goal line when a ball bulges the goal and appears as though the shooter shoots for the top corner. In fact, the ball goes in one of the circles as depicted in diagram 70A.

Picture 70H: Daniele De Rossi places this ball in the hoop as depicted in diagram 70A. Even though the goalkeeper, Fabien Barthez, guesses correctly, this shot is unstoppable because gravity brings the keeper down. Although the ball appears to go in high close to the top bar and in the corner of the goal, it actually crosses the face of the goal almost 2 feet below the bar and about 2 feet away from the post. De Rossi's aim is perfect and his pace on the ball is equally perfect. Action Images/Michael Dalder

Daniele De Rossi places this ball in the hoop as depicted in diagram 70A if it were there. Even though the goalkeeper, Fabien Barthez guesses correctly, this shot is unstoppable because gravity brings the keeper down. Although the ball appears to go in high close to the top bar and in the corner of the goal, it actually crosses the face of the goal almost 2 feet below the bar and about 2 feet away from the post. De Rossi's aim is perfect and his pace on the ball is equally perfect.

Coaches should make a point of making sure young strikers get into the habit of studying goalkeepers because the goalkeepers will look for any edge but rarely would you expect strikers to tell goalkeepers what they are going to do. Paul Dolan had an interesting story about one player who did something different when he took a penalty shot on him.

WHY NOT TO TELL THE GOALKEEPER WHAT YOU ARE GOING TO DO?

Goalkeepers will keep secret information about a striker until such a time, if ever, that it will play to their advantage. The striker should do likewise but Paul Dolan found out that there is nothing like an honest opponent. He told me this story.

"Playing for the Vancouver Whitecaps against Colorado in the late 90s, Colorado was awarded a penalty kick, which Wolde Harris was stepping up to take. I asked him out loud with both sets of players lined up for the penalty kick which way he was going to shoot. I said to him, 'you've got to give me a chance because your shot is so hard' and bravado got the better of him. He pointed to where he was going to shoot and I dived to my right to stop him. I gave him a big smile right away but tipped my hat to him for keeping his word."

ONE MORE PENALTY SHOT STORY

I'm sure there are a lot of stories in regards to penalty shots but I'm always looking for the unique one. Sometimes, you will find that the best stories can be found in the recreational leagues where passion drives the game. Marcus Schultze, a goalkeeper in a recreational league in Brampton, Ontario was confronted with a penalty shot to deal with. As he prepared to get set to try to stop the shot, he could not identify the shooter as no player had stepped up to the centre of the field around the penalty spot. Then he spotted a player standing way at his own 18 yard box at the centre of the field and saw him start to run towards him. He explained what happened this way.

"I identified that he was the shooter as he started running from deep in his own end of the field around the 18 yard box. He ran right up the middle of the field towards me with a straight face and steady stride. He took no stutter steps and he didn't look at the ball. He ran as if he was out for a jog in the park. When he got to the ball he just nailed it inside my post, low to the left side. I didn't really move much and I was angry at what he did so I didn't even bother guessing. It was a case where the shooter out-psyched the goalie. I usually jump around to try to throw off the shooter. This time I didn't do anything. And to make matters worse, this player was the other team's goalkeeper."

Set Plays

Corner Kicks

A large number of goals from set plays come from corner kicks. In the 2002 World Cup goals from corner kicks actually surpassed goals from free kicks as well as goals from penalty kicks so do not underestimate the importance of practicing to convert a ball into the goal when there is a lot of traffic around. From a psychological standpoint, scoring goals from corner kicks is like scoring goals from crosses with a bit more traffic in front of the goal. Crosses are dealt with in chapters 56, 57, 58, 59, and 60. Many goals scored from corners are from rebounds, which are covered in chapter 73. Players will need to focus on the ball because there will be lots of distractions. Sometimes 20 of the 22 players on the field are in the box when a corner kick presents itself, especially towards the last seconds of a game with a trailing team trying to score. The player who gets the last touch on the ball will need to be focused on his last touch. He will need to compete for the ball and ultimately direct the ball at the goal. None of this is much different than converting crosses.

Free Kicks

Quite a few goals come as a result of free kicks and in this book I want to cover the psychology of scoring off a free kick. The main focus is on the shooter or the player with the last touch.

I was at a game recently where there were five free kicks all from around the edge of the box. No goals, no saves. One blocked shot, four shots that missed the post or bar by less than a yard. In some cases, depending on where the fans were seated and at which angle they were, the fans thought the ball had gone in. But none did. Zero for five. Each free kick took about 3-4 minutes to execute. Close to 20 minutes of my time was spent watching players fight for space in the wall, argue with the referee, and stand around and ultimately produce no goals. Yes, there were close calls but there were no goals and no saves.

There are so many free kicks where the shooter tries so hard to put the ball around a wall and tuck it into the post. Players practically aim to curl the ball in off the inside of the post or right under the crossbar. It's evident that players are more apt to miss the goal when aiming to place the ball inches or centimeters inside of the posts or under the crossbar. I would have preferred to see four out of five shots hit the net. I would have had a better chance of seeing a goal or at least a great save. From a spectator's point of view, I would have enjoyed the game more.

Fans love to see goals and great saves as well, especially if it's from the home team's goalkeeper. Hitting the ball towards the corners is OK but the shooters must adjust their aim so it's not right at the posts. They should focus on a spot about 1-2 yards inside the post and decide which part of the goal they want to shoot at. If the ball must be placed high rather than low for some reason, then the shooter must aim a foot below the bar.

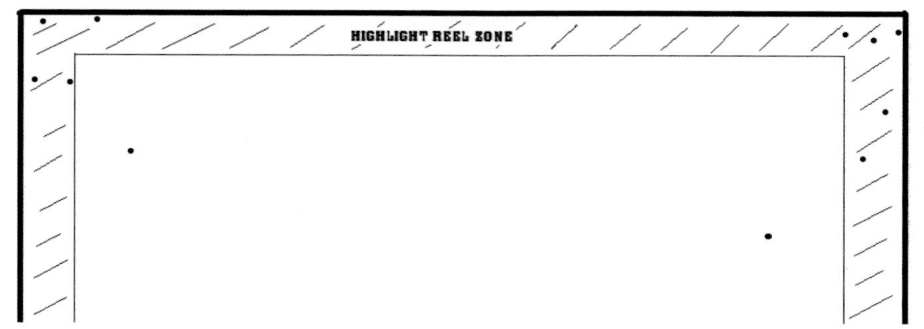

Diagram 70I: The shaded area represents the area where goals scored in this area end up on TV and shown in the highlights most often. The dots represent where the ball entered the net on the goals that were scored from a free kick in the 2002 World Cup. Goals scored from free kicks are more likely going to be shown in the highlights than most other goals due to where they cross the goal line.

In the 2002 World Cup only 11 goals were scored from a shot from a direct or indirect free kick out of 161 goals scored in all. More goals (13) were scored off a penalty shot. In the 2006 World Cup only 5 goals out of the 147 goals scored, were scored directly from a free kick. I would have thought that goals scored from free kicks were much higher than that. Why did I <u>think</u> this number was low? It's probably because free kick goals that are scored end up in the highlight reels for best goals. In fact, of the free kick goals scored in the 2002 World Cup, all but two were scored in the highlight reel zone. In diagram 70I, I show where these goals were scored. The area, which I consider "the highlight reel zone", is the area close to the posts or crossbar as shown by the shaded area of the goal in diagram 70I. Why were such few goals scored directly from free kicks? Were the walls impenetrable? Was the goalkeeper too good? I would say that more scoring opportunities were missed from direct free kicks from the shooter missing the net than from any other reason. I tell my strikers to make sure to aim inside the posts and hit the net. Then they should be ready for a rebound or deflection.

I believe that there are a couple of issues to deal with when scoring from free kicks. The accuracy of the shot is most important as the obstacles are quite great because of the wall, the defenders, and the goalkeeper. At what other point in the game can the defenders organize themselves to bring everyone back if they wish, then have the goalkeeper set a barrier to cover part of the goal as well? With this ability to organize the team to defend free kicks, the attacking team will need to fool the goalkeeper in order to beat him.

As I mentioned in chapter 65, if your players can get the goalkeeper to freeze, then all you need to do is make sure your shooter concentrates enough on his task and hits the net. The shooter doesn't have to aim for the perfect corner, which does not mean it won't actually end up there. In diagram 70I, the goal to the right of the diagram that does not fall in the highlight reel zone was scored without the goalkeeper even moving to try and stop the shot. He was totally fooled. The shooter will have to clear a wall but that can be done with practice. If the goalkeeper is not fooled, then the striker's chance of scoring will diminish because the goalkeeper's goal will be smaller since the wall covers part of it.

Work on deceiving the goalkeeper in your creative plans. Try to block the keeper's view of the ball and do your best to avoid complex free kicks but try to mask whom the shooter will be. A slight hesitation on behalf of the goalkeeper can result in a goal. Plan to hide the intent of who is shooting and where he is aiming.

Challenge your strikers to work on free kicks on their own. The problem with practicing free kicks is that no one wants to stand in the wall and get hit by a ball. Thankfully, there are portable walls on the market which will make the coaches life easier when coaching this aspect of the game.

Strikers have to visualize hitting the goal and fooling the goalkeeper in their minds instead of visualizing a highlight reel free kick. In this way, there is a better chance of hitting the goal every time. Keep in mind that even if the shot may be stopped by the keeper, there may be a rebound. Likewise, if the ball hits the wall, there may be a rebound. If the ball sails over the goal or wide of the goal, there is no further chance to score. How many times have you seen a goal scored from free kicks come off a deflection? This usually only occurs when the ball would have hit the goal in the first place. Low and mid height shots cause more deflections than high shots.

At the youth level, where defenders may be apt to turn or duck, hitting the goal will score more goals. I tell players who may be looking for a chance to get a soccer scholarship or a tryout somewhere that if they get chances to take free kicks, they need to take advantage of their scoring opportunity. Here is what I say to them:

> ***"If you get chances to take free kicks near the goal, it's your chance to add goals to your statistics. In order to score you better hit the net or you won't score. It's as simple as that. Aim 1 yard inside the post and at least a foot under the bar in the event you are shooting high. Hitting the ball through a wall at mid height with a shot is better than missing the goal altogether. Players may turn or move away and it may glance off one of them into the goal, and guess what? You'll get the goal and you can pad your statistics. Sure the defenders may be better at the college level but if this helps get you there, take the opportunity.***
>
> ***Don't try a perfectly placed Beckham or Carlos Alberto type shot or you'll never score. While you wait for that one highlight reel goal, your buddies will have scored 5 or 6 more goals than you will by simply hitting the net. And chances are that one or two of those 5 or 6 goals will accidentally be a highlight reel goal anyway. Direct free kicks are one of the few times where you can hit a dead ball directly into the net. The defenders are***

forced to stay 10 yards away and you can pre-plan the sequence of events. What more do you want? Do your job to focus, visualize and hit the target. Visualize the kick but you must take the time to practice this over and over at home with different soccer balls. Not all soccer balls fly exactly the same and you never know what you'll be playing with in a game, especially at the youth level.

The real key to scoring on a free kick from just outside the box is fooling the goalkeeper. If you can, in the slightest way, fool the goalkeeper or force him to react slower than he should, then your chances of scoring will go up substantially. As a goalkeeper, once I would set my wall, I felt confident that I could handle the shot if it came to where I was standing. I always worried about a ball that would go over my wall into the opposite corner but most of the time, the striker would miss the net making my life easier.

If you get a chance to move the ball a few inches to the left or right after the wall has been placed, then you can bet that the goalkeeper is feeling uneasy again if he does not have a chance to re-set the wall. An uncertain goalkeeper is more likely to react slower to a shot than a confident keeper because he may be favouring an area of the goal which he should not be worried about. In the times when I was beaten I would always kick myself because I knew I messed up for even the slightest second by going for a fake or not reading where the ball was going to go. And finally, don't forget the <u>Golden Rule</u> on all free kicks and penalty kicks, always place the ball yourself." (See picture 70J)

Picture 70J: Francesco Totti of Roma places the ball himself on an upcoming free kick attempt against Celtic. It's the "Golden Rule" of all free kicks and penalty shots. The player shooting must always place the ball just in case someone else places it in a rut in the field. Photo by Les Jones/Covershots.

How to Play with the Goalkeeper's Psyche on Free Kicks

I want to focus on the goalkeeper's state of mind when defending free kicks. Here are a few things that bothered me as a goalkeeper. Whenever I set up a wall I would feel pretty confident that I could make a save unless I was unhappy with one of the players in the wall. What worried me as a goalkeeper were deflections in the event that the wall buckled. I trusted some players more than others to not turn their backs or duck out of the way.

Not all goalkeepers have control over who is in the wall and when the goalkeeper is uncertain of his wall it can cause them to react slower than expected to get to a ball. Rarely will the striker or coach know which players should not be in the opponent's wall. This could be something to scout for when watching a future opponent. In picture 70K, we see Bayern Munich's goalkeeper, Hans Joerg Butt setting up his wall.

The two main things that are noticeable and affect the goalkeeper's state of mind have to do with the movement of the wall and the ball. Strikers need to keep their eye on the goalkeeper to see what they have done with their wall. Tell your strikers to look to see if the wall has been forced to move by the referee after the keeper originally set it up. A slight movement of the wall, usually backwards, can raise a doubt in a keeper's mind especially if he does not have time to reset it. Also, if possible, have your shooter re-adjust the ball slightly by a few inches laterally or backwards after the wall has been placed before shooting. Any time that the wall or ball is moved after the goalkeeper has set up his wall, he will feel uneasy unless he can double-check the placement of the wall. Most goalkeepers will frantically go back to the near post to double check and re-adjust their wall before the shot is taken. If the shooter is ready to shoot and the referee will allow it, the keeper may not be able to double-check the wall. This feeling of uncertainty can disturb a goalkeeper.

Picture 70K: Hans Joerg Butt, the goalkeeper for Bayern Munich is setting up his wall by lining up his players to cover the near post. Once the goalkeeper has set up his wall he feels confident that he can cover the rest of the goal unless the ball or the wall is moved. Action Images/ Michael Dalder

The problem for the goalkeeper is that he will want to go back to the near post to double check the wall but often his teammates will ignore him or not hear him when he wants to re-adjust the wall. This is because the players will assume that the wall has already been dealt with and needs no further attention. Other issues take precedence as players are shouting other instructions to each other such as what to watch out for or whom to cover.

In picture 70L, we see the referee move the wall back and the keeper tries to re-position the wall. None of his teammates have noticed his shout for attention as they worry about other players in front of the wall. If no one pays attention to the keeper and the wall is not re-adjusted then the goalkeeper will not feel confident. This is a time for your striker to take note of this and act quickly to shoot on goal before the goalkeeper gets the attention of his defenders to re-adjust the wall. Train your players to look to create those situations and work quickly to get away a shot.

Whatever you have planned for your team on a free kick, have your players act quickly if they notice panic with the goalkeeper. The goalkeeper may not show it but I'll guarantee you, it will be taking place in his mind. Movement of the ball or the wall after the wall has been set up can turn into a huge opportunity for your team to score because of the state of mind of the keeper. This is no time to miss the net because this doubt in the goalkeeper's mind will most likely freeze him into not moving at all for a ball. As you can tell, the striker has to be super alert to pick up on little things such as this.

Nothing feels better to goalkeepers than if they don't have to make a save on a free kick. Why? Because they feel as though they have erected the perfect wall and thus psyched out their attacker. Watch closely the reaction and body language of confident goalkeepers after a player misses the goal, even just by inches. The goalies will follow the ball giving the impression that he had it covered and they did a great job with the wall. Consciously or subconsciously, goalkeepers want to send a message to the striker that the free kick attempt was no problem. If the keeper has to make a difficult save, he will be thinking that, "we better not give up another free kick. It was too close for comfort." And when the keeper reads the ball well and makes a save look easy, he still feels that the ball got through and it could have been worse. Missing the net gives the goalkeepers more confidence than they should have. Tell your strikers to hit the net.

Picture 70L: In this game between Olympique Lyonnais and A.J. Auxerre, the wall has been forced to move by the referee. If the ball or the wall gets moved ever so slightly, the goalkeepers will feel uneasy about their wall unless they can double check it and re-position it. When trying to re-adjust a wall after the goalkeeper originally sets it up, they will find that it will be harder to get the attention of their teammates to do so because the players will think that the placement of the wall has already been dealt with. Other issues take precedence as players are shouting other instructions to each other such as what to watch out for or whom to cover as you see from this picture.

I have seen cases where the goalkeeper cannot get the attention of teammates to re-adjust their wall or where the referee does not allow any more time for the defensive team to delay the shot. Whenever the wall or ball has been moved and the goalkeeper has not had the chance to re-adjust the wall, the mental state of the goalkeeper is not where it should be. An air of doubt will fill the keeper's mind. Due to this self doubt, the keeper will feel that he may have to cover the whole goal instead of a certain portion of the goal. The keeper may be frozen when the shot is actually taken and this is no time to bail the goalkeeper out by missing the net. Action Images/Julien Crosnier.

In terms of what type of shot a player should take, that will depend on the distance. A power shot versus a chip or lofted curve shot or pass will depend on each situation. I suggest players practice all types of shots from all different distances and angles. The free kick should involve something that will cause the goalkeeper to guess wrong, get distracted, or feel unsure of himself. In other words, play with his psyche. The coach can involve other players in order to do this.

Free Kick Specialists Should Go to Hollywood

As funny as the above statement may sound, it's reality. The best actors and supporting actors will score more goals. If your players can move the ball or make it difficult for the keeper to know who is taking the shot so that he hesitates before trying to make a save, then your players will score more goals provided they hit the net. What a shame it would be for a player to completely fool the goalkeeper but miss the net. How many times have you seen a goalkeeper not move at all only to see the ball miss the net? A ball played one yard inside the post is more likely to result in a goal if the goalkeeper is fooled. A good acting job will make up for a perfectly placed shot. It may be easier to score by fooling the goalkeeper than by trying to beat the keeper who is not fooled with a perfectly placed shot.

In summary, get your players to sell the fake and disguise the shot. Work on these things at practice. Free kick practices can be boring for most of the players on the team but keep the statistics about scoring goals from set plays in mind. Make sure you spend the time with your players to practice them. Alert your players to the things that may affect the mental state of the goalkeeper. Bring out the academy award and get ready to present it to your best actor because they will help your team score most of your goals off free kicks. Most of the time, the academy award should go to the player who pretends to take the kick rather than the shooter. Can they fool the goalkeeper?

GOAL KICKS

Not too many coaches would think that the goal kick for his team can be planned to be an attacking set play. I devised an attacking goal kick set play with my team which actually worked fairly well.

A Set Play Story That has a Moral to the Story

So here is my secret goal kick set play that I devised for us to use when we needed a goal and it was our goal kick. (Picture 70M)

MY SECRET GOAL KICK SET PLAY?

Yes you read that correctly. I used to have a set play dedicated for goal kicks way back in the 80s. I saved this play for a key moment in a game and the conditions had to be right. It could only work once in a game and maybe only once a year against a certain opponent. I used this play with my U16s right up to when they were U21s. In the eighties, soccer balls were not like they are today. In today's game a player can kick the ball a long way down the field. That did not take place too often back then because of the technology of the ball. The Mitre Multiplex ball was the closest to today's soccer balls and would travel further than others but these balls were almost impossible to get in Canada at the time and they were very expensive. I made sure we had one for special games. This ball traveled further than most balls.

My defender, Norm Tsolakis, was one player on my team that could kick a ball quite far from a goal kick. We would use our goal kick set-play when the wind was at our back and when we needed a goal late in a game. I signaled to our team when we needed to try our special set play from our goal kick that we had practiced. This is how it worked.

As we got set for the goal kick, my striker Kenny Dodd, who won the league scoring title in the NSL at U18, would slowly walk up to the other teams penalty box. He would do so from as close to the sidelines as possible and tried to be inconspicuous. At the same time, my other striker, Paul Kumar, Bill Misener, or Greg Dac Bang, would walk back towards our own goal while my tallest player, Peter Norde would move up from his defensive midfield position towards the centre field line.

At this point the opposition would be trying to figure out whom to mark. Norm would start his run to take a big boot up the field. In a matter of seconds, the defenders from the defending team would notice our player standing all by himself near their box and they would not know what to do. One would shout, "Hey mark him", while the another player would be shouting,

"He's offside, ref, ref". While the ball was in the air, the other team would see the ball sail over the centre field mark and be shouting offside.

Mad hysteria would develop within the other team as everyone shouted for an offside call. Our striker, Dodd would pick up the bouncing ball all alone by the opponent's box with just the goalkeeper to beat. The goalkeeper would hardly try as he expected an offside call, and Dodd never failed to put the ball in the back of the net even if the goalkeeper did try to stop him. The opponents would always hound the referees for an offside call. The goal would stand on all occasions except once. Why did the goal count? Check the rules. You cannot be offside on your team's own goal kick.

On one occasion the lineman raised the flag and the referee blew the whistle before the ball entered the net. The linesman forgot that there cannot be an offside on a goal kick. The goal did not count as the whistle blew before our player shot the ball in the goal and hence we were not awarded a goal. We tied that game 0-0 instead of winning it 1-0.

The job of our big tall midfielder, Peter Norde, who moved up to centre field, was to jump if a challenge was needed to get the ball past everyone if the kick was not going far enough. He was to make sure not to touch the ball or we would be called offside. On one occasion when the goal kick did not quite have the distance required, his challenge made the last defender miss-head the ball and the ball went through to our striker waiting all by himself in the box to score.

The moral of the story: whatever great play you come up with as a coach for set plays, nothing will work successfully if whoever gets the last touch on the ball doesn't put in it the back of the net.

And the second moral to this story: read the Laws of the Game!

Picture 70M: Alex Yates from the Pickering Soccer Club's U21 team takes a goal kick. Photo by Philip Yates

CHAPTER 71

Dealing with Defenders

The Psychology

From a psychological point of view, defenders, just like goalkeepers, are most vulnerable after allowing a goal. This is especially true for the player who committed the biggest error. Sometimes defenders can even get down on themselves if they have not made a noticeable error. A player who made an error that may not be noticeable to the spectator will know that the coach will clearly identify his mistake. For example, a defender may be in the wrong position based on what the coach wants but fans may not know about the error. As a striker, this may be a good time to take a peek at the reaction of the opposing coach or manager and the nearest defenders. Can their reaction clarify the mental state of the defenders to see if they can be taken advantage of because their body and mind are in a depressed mode?

I was watching a National Hockey League (NHL) hockey game between the Toronto Maple Leafs and the Pittsburgh Penguins. The previous year, Pittsburgh got to the Stanley Cup Finals (the ultimate goal in hockey) but lost. In the following season the team was out of a play-off position two-thirds into the season. They had two of the best players in the league. Sidney Crosby and Evgeni Malkin were the top two scorers in the league at the time but the team was losing too many games for the talent that they had. I recall thinking to myself and then telling my son who was watching the game with me, "The Pittsburgh players are not really trying. I don't think they like this coach and it seems as though they are purposely trying to lose so that he gets replaced."

Toronto, a team well behind Pittsburgh in the standings, went on to win the game handily. The very next day, the Pittsburgh coach got fired and the team went on a winning streak after that and made the play-offs without any problems. In fact, they went on to win the Stanley Cup, one of the hardest trophies to win in a yearly sporting season. If you're a coach for whom the players don't want to play, then you can bet that they won't play well for you. Be careful how you treat your athletes but if you're coaching in a game and you have noticed that something was not right with the players on the opposing team, then the chance for your strikers to score more goals couldn't be better. Newcastle United of the EPL had similar issues in their 2008/2009 season.

But when defenders are on their game both physically and mentally, they are a tough and mean group. Coaches put their toughest players in these positions. Central defenders tend to be the toughest and biggest players on the field, although Fabio Cannavaro of Italy re-energized shorter and smaller players who play on the back line with his play at the World Cup in 2006. The typical defenders will do anything to prevent a scoring chance and goal. Their job is to prevent the striker from getting to the ball. They will use elbows, arms, and all parts of their bodies to try and stop or put off the striker. Many defenders will want to send a message early in the game to a striker with a tough, often illegal tackle just to let them know who they are dealing with and to put some fear in the striker's game. This psychological ploy can affect some strikers when confronted with a 50/50 ball later in the game.

Sometimes defenders will revert to some ugly tactics including verbal abuse in order to throw a striker off his game. This is often wrongly called 'gamesmanship.' If the defender can take a striker off his game by taking him out of "the zone", then he will if it can give his team a better chance to win. How to do this depends on the personality and ethics of the defender. This is a common ploy in all sports especially when the stakes are high. If you consider the money that players make or can make in pro sports and the number of players who want to take another player's job, you can start to gain the proper perspective in this aspect of gamesmanship. For the defender, one bad game where the player he has to mark scores, can affect his position on the team and potential future earnings. A striker will have to deal with many distractions including abuse from defenders.

A Head Butt that was Felt Around the World

A perfect example of this type of gamesmanship is the famous incident between Zinedine Zidane of France and Marco Materazzi of Italy in the 2006 World Cup Final. As shown in the now famous picture 71A, Zidane head-butts

Materazzi and was given a red card after Materazzi said something to Zidane. Italy went on to win the game. With their best player sent off and the team playing the rest of the game with 10 men, France went on to lose the final. The fact that Zidane could not hold his emotions in check after Materazzi said something definitively unprintable for this book confirms the type of antics strikers and goal scorers will always have to put up with. You'd better make sure your strikers understand this important aspect of their game. It will take place.

Picture 71A: Italy's Marco Materazzi receives a head butt from France's Zinedine Zidane after he tries to take Zidane off his game by making derogatory comments towards him and his family. Zinedine receives the red card for his actions. This occurred during the most important sporting event in the world, which is held once every 4 years. The World Cup 2006 final soccer match was held in Berlin on July 9, 2006. Picture Supplied by Action Images/Peter Schols

Many people have commented on the head-butting incident between Marco Materazzi and Zinedine Zidane at the 2006 World Cup Final, but how many have thought of it in this way?

This is how I see it from a striker's coach point of view. If strikers cannot control their emotions then they may not have a career at all. Zidane, Beckham, Rooney, Maradona, have all had a hot temper at times but if players are not capable of handling the stresses of the game on a week to week basis, then they will probably never get the opportunity to play at the highest levels.

In the case of Zidane and Materazzi, consider this. Since the first World Cup in 1930, there have been a total of 19 World Cups to 2010. If each team carries 23 players (teams in the 30's carried fewer players due to travel costs), then that means a total of only 437 players have received a gold medal for winning the World Cup. Think of that for a second. Only 437 male players (maximum) have ever won a World Cup. A few players have won it more than once so the actual number of players who have a gold medal is less. In the winning team's country, the champions are immortalized forever and can retire with personal autograph appearances for the rest of their lives.

This is one of the hardest medals to win. The Men's FIFA World Cup is the single most watched sporting event in the world. Almost ¾ of a billion people watched the 2006 final. The total cumulative TV audience over the month-long competition for the 2006 World Cup was 26.29 billion. In 2010, over a quarter of a billion people went on the FIFA World Cup web site to check up on their favourite teams or players. When so many people watch and follow such an important and popular event, it can be very beneficial financially for players in many ways.

Also, knowing that there are 7 billion people living in the world today and between 1930 and 2011 another 4 billion people have passed away, that means that only 437 individuals out of a total of 11 BILLION people that have been alive at some point between 1930 and 2010 have a World Cup gold medal. That statistic is mind boggling. What are the odds? Getting a World Cup gold medal is virtually impossible.

Now, if you're playing against a type of striker that you know can be influenced by some trash talking in such a big game that can make you and your team win the World Cup and be one of those rare individuals to have a World Cup gold medal, would you consider some trash talking to win one? If your team is looking unlikely to win but if trash talking would eliminate the key player on the opposition and change the game in your favour, would you consider trash talking? And finally, if you were not in agreement of this type of unfair play, would you oppose a teammate doing so if you could be one of those rare players to have a World Cup championship medal? It's an ethical question and an interesting point to ponder for sure!

Although I would never resort to these types of tactics as a coach or player, they do occur, which is why they persist. It happens right down at the kids' level of play even though it may not have any bearing on the future career of a child. Children in elementary schools get bullied all the time. What happened at the World Cup final is just another form of bullying but in a different context. I hate to put it this way but, for some people, trying to win using unfair play is worth it for them.

Often clashes occur when a game includes physical contact. Issues may have developed over a game or games that remain unsettled. Even in a non-contact and tame sport such as baseball, issues occur. For example, when one pitcher hits a batter, tempers can flair and a brawl can erupt. It's sport and that's just the way it is. The striker will be on the receiving end of most of the abuse, although many strikers have been known to harass defenders as well. Make your strikers aware of this part of the game and prepare them so that they don't cost your team a game or their personal careers a major blow.

I recall attending an excellent coaching session put on by Robert Iarusci, who played for the world famous New York Cosmos and Canada's National team. He explained his experiences covering players such as Johan Cruyff, George Best, Roberto Bettega, and Eusebio just to note a few players. He would try and change his method of defending against a striker constantly during a game to keep the striker guessing. Early in the game, he would go in hard a few times in a row but later he may pretend to go in hard and put the striker with the ball in a state of defending the ball instead of attacking him. By varying his method of covering or challenging for a ball he would often win balls from some the world's best strikers.

After he graduated, Iarusci would occasionally come back and join our varsity team in training sessions at York University while still playing for the Toronto Metros and New York Cosmos. I was always impressed with how well he defended in front of me in scrimmages, making my job simple. He played to outsmart the attacker without playing dirty. We were recently discussing why goals at the 2010 World Cup were down and he had this to say:

> "More goals would be scored if the referees would not allow defenders to grab, clutch, hold, and wrestle their opponents!! Defenders now know they can prevent their opponents by simply grabbing them before the ball comes to the area. When I played, I never touched my opponent. I positioned myself to anticipate him to the spot I felt he wanted to enter or to the spot where I felt he might have the best chance to score. Some obstruction with the body but I never raised my hands to my opponent! When the sport stops the mugging we'll see more goals."

Just as defenders try to be unpredictable so should strikers. The two big issues that strikers have to constantly try and figure out about defenders are the following:

1. Where are the defenders?
2. How do I move them out of the way so that a teammate or I can score?

In picture 71B, Paul Peschisolido has to play the ball but needs to know where the defenders are so that he can do the right thing with the ball. Strikers, just like all players on the field always have to be looking around to see where their opponents and teammates are. Most of the time, defenders are not straight ahead but to the side or at different positions around them. In picture 71C, Ryan Giggs of Manchester United is facing a defender who is not facing him at all.

The Skill

Coaches often spend a great deal of time with strikers working on beating players one-on-one with the defender facing the striker and the striker facing the defender. In pictures 67E and 67R from chapter 67 and pictures 65H and 65I from chapter 65, we see examples of where the defender is off to the side of the striker. Keep in mind that since most goals are scored on one touch, often the ball was played to the goal scorer from a teammate. The defender may have been defending the ball carrier that then passed the ball off to the eventual goal scorer. In most of those shots on goal, the striker has received the ball from another player and hence the defender has already been displaced. Look closely at those pictures in Chapters 65 and 67 to see what I mean. The defender is reaching to get in the way but is not in front of the striker. Quite often the player who makes the final pass is more likely to be faced with a typical one-on-one situation with a defender in front of him. Because of this, he will look for a pass to set up a fellow striker who is in a better shooting position. This does not mean that practicing one-on-one from a frontal position is not good because the goal scorer is also often the player who sets up most of the goals for his colleagues. This leads to the next issue for strikers. How do they move defenders out of the way to create a shooting opportunity for themselves or a shooting opportunity for a teammate?

Picture 71B: Paul Pecshisolido of Canada has defenders around him in different positions. Defenders are not always directly in front of strikers who are getting close to goal. Picture by Les Jones/Covershots

Picture 71C: Ryan Giggs of Manchester United is facing a defender but the defender is not facing him, as one would expect. Coaches often put strikers in drills where defenders are one-on-one facing them. Vary your one-on-one sessions so that they are more realistic as to the types of situations found in games. Les Jones/Covershots.

Moving Defenders out of the Way

There are a number of things that the strikers can do to move defenders out of the way so that they can shoot. Most of what they do has to be preplanned because it's part of 'preparing to score'. Before a ball comes to them, they should already have narrowed what they will do to just a few options. If they wait until the ball is upon them to decide what to do, it will be too late, most of the time. Ian Dawson, a former teammate of mine who played striker at York University phrased it perfectly at a recent team reunion, "The extra split second that it takes a player to decide what to do can be the difference between success and failure."

Strikers need to create time and space for themselves. Before receiving a ball, strikers should always look to take a defender that is marking them in a different direction from where they want the ball. Checking, or taking a step in the opposite direction to where they want the ball helps create space by moving the defender out of the way for them to receive a ball where the defender was or was going. The communication with fellow teammates will be vital in making sure all players are on the same page. This is best done at practice by repeating things over and over.

When a ball is played to the striker's feet with defenders behind him, he should always go and meet the ball to create space for himself where possible. The striker should create space for himself so that he can meet the ball in optimum conditions where he has room to turn and face the goal. If the striker is looking to run to a ball played into space, he can do a dummy run. A dummy run is a run in the opposite direction to where the striker wants the ball. The striker first has to take the defender in the wrong direction and then cut back to the opposite direction to where he originally wanted the ball. Taking the defender to a poor defending position is important. In diagram 71D we see where a player makes a dummy run before accepting a pass from a teammate to create a scoring chance. Once again, this has to be worked out in practice so all players involved know what the strategy or plan is. In essence, the striker is dictating to the defender where he should go. Strikers must always look to evade defenders but the passer has to know the plan or he will play the ball to the wrong spot.

There are times when it's beneficial to have a defender tight on the striker's back. If a ball is played to his feet, the striker can fake to turn in one direction before the ball gets to him and then quickly turn in another direction. The fact that the defender is right up his back can help the striker lean on the defender to turn and actually help him shield the ball. In picture 71E, Danny Dichio has his back to the defender and can use the defender to help him turn to face the goal. This can help him turn while shielding the ball.

Diagram 71D: In this example, player 9 runs in a different direction to where he wants the ball in order to take the defender (2) away in the wrong direction. This is called a dummy run. Player 10 (the passer) has to know the plan in order for it to work effectively. His pass will be important. The pace of the ball will need to be perfect so that the striker can shoot on his first touch. It also has to be away from a recovering defender and away from other defenders in the area. Finally, if the pass is too strong, it will lead to the possibility of the goalkeeper coming out to intercept the pass. Illustration by Jo-Anne Godawa

Here is the big secret for young kids. To get a shot away at goal, players do not need to move the defenders completely out of the way. All they need to do is move enough of them away so that a shot will not be blocked. Too often, young players think that they have to be clear of defenders and be completely away from them in order to shoot to score. Here is how I explain this aspect to them.

"To score, all you need to do is get the ball past the defender's body part that is closest to the ball. You may need to clear the foot or the head or arm. The defender's feet are not two feet long. The defender's legs can only stretch so far. And remember that the ball is usually at your feet and not at eye level unless of course you are heading a ball. The decision most players make to direct the ball towards goal is usually always correct when the ball is in the air because you know that you'll only get one touch on the ball. For some reason, when the ball is at feet, players usually take more touches than necessary and hence make wrong decisions. If you cannot see a clear path to the goal from your eyes, it does not mean that the ball cannot get to the goal from your feet!

Sometimes you will not beat a defender to a ball. Congratulate the defender for doing a good defensive job but let him pay when he allows you to get a touch on the ball before he can. Make your first touch your last touch. It would be a wasted effort if you were to get to a ball first and didn't get a shot off. When the ball comes to your feet, prepare to score by making your first touch also your last touch just like when the ball is in the air. Make the right decisions and try to get ball to the net on one touch."

Picture 71E: Preston's Danny Dichio takes a ball to his feet with his back to the defender, Ipswich's Sylvain Legwinski. He can try to turn using the defender to lean on and get a shot away. Also, the striker can lay the ball off to a teammate having engaged a central defender to him. This may allow space for a teammate to shoot and score. Good strikers will need to have good shielding skills. When two strikers work together to create space for one another, both will increase their scoring.

Sometimes coaches like to have players with good shielding skills to act as target players. They tend to be bigger players and are responsible for feeding faster and often smaller strikers the ball. But they will also need to score if a chance presents itself for them to keep their position on the team. Action Images/Carl Recine

Another key aspect to moving a defender out of the way is for the ball carrier to force the defender to commit to the player with the ball. The best way to challenge the defender is to go right at him. This will force the defender to make decisions and to commit to the player with the ball rather than enable the defender to dictate to the striker which way he should take the ball. Defenders don't like it when strikers come right at them because if they commit to trying to get the ball on the striker's terms, then they will find it harder to stop the striker from beating them. Also, they may be in a poor position to stop a pass to another opponent who may be in a good scoring position. In picture 71C, Giggs goes at the defender and gets him in an awkward position to defend. Most of the time, it's the teammate who plays the biggest role in getting the defenders out of the way for the player with the biggest chance to score by running at defenders to make them commit to try to get the ball and then passing it to the striker to score.

The Master Teacher

One of the best methods of moving defenders out of the way is by using a variety of dribbling and ball possession moves that were first introduced to North America by Dutch coach Wiel Coerver in 1984 at a presentation in Philadelphia at the National Soccer Coaches Association of America's Coaching Convention. He studied professional players closely and found out what certain players did in order to beat defenders or maintain possession of the ball. His methods now commonly called the "Coerver" methods have been used worldwide in youth training programs. I would recommend that every striker seeks his books and DVDs and works on these techniques. Although they sometimes seem as though they are just tricks and fancy ways to beat defenders, they in fact are very well thought-out methods to displace defenders based on visual perception, ball protection, and the ability to distinguish which move or skill to use in certain situations.

THE NATIONAL SOCCER COACHES ASSOCIATION OF AMERICA

The NSCAA coach's convention is the world's largest annual soccer coaching convention. Coaches from all over the world attend the coaching sessions to learn and stay abreast on the latest developments in the game. Also, a huge convention hall is dedicated to exhibitors that showcase their latest and most exciting soccer products and services. The convention has grown from an annual event that attracted 1,000 coaches a year to one where over 7,000 coaches attend regularly.

Coaches who would like to improve their coaching knowledge should make an effort to attend one of these annual events. Guest speakers included coaches from all over the world. Topics are covered in field sessions and lecture sessions. They cover a wide range of topics from the most basic geared for the youngest players in the game to the most advanced featuring World Cup coaches. Visit www.nscaa.com for information on this annual convention.

When Wiel Coerver devised his techniques, he paid particular attention to detail and created moves and ball possession strategies for many different circumstances that players would find themselves in. Unless the skills become instinctive through visual and motor muscular perception training, players will often use them to be fancy but will not be as successful as they should be with them. For example, some young players may do a fancy move that was designed for a player to execute with their right foot when a defender was to their right. If the young player tries the move when the defender is to the left, then it will not be effective. As a coach, make sure you understand the benefits to all your players of learning these moves and ball possession skills properly. When reviewing them, note that in all cases, the ball stays very close to and under the body and is rarely exposed without protection. Your first sign to determine if a player's move is performed correctly is to see where the ball is in relation to the body. If the ball does not stay very close to and under the body most of the time, then the move is probably being done incorrectly.

THE WIEL COERVER TECHNIQUES ARE A MUST FOR STRIKERS

Based on these techniques, in 1984, I produced a series of videos meant for my players and my camp instructors to make sure they understood the basic concepts of the moves and ball possession skills. The drills and exercises were devised to help develop the visual and motion perception situations that players would encounter in a game. I always wanted to make sure that players got the proper feelings of what would be tracked by their visual perception system in the exercises. They were designed so that the players knew what they should expect visually in each move. Thus, if they did not get the right visual feelings when using the moves in games or at practice, then they would feel that something was not right about what they were doing.

To provide the correct visual stimulus, the defenders or coaches in the drills, as shown in the videos, had to exaggerate the defender's movements so that the visual system felt the correct sensation. Also, when doing each move slower, the attacking moves were also exaggerated to further provide the perfect visual sensations and perception. I found that players learning these methods who were at a very late stage in their development by normal standards quickly learned the skills. One of these students is pictured in picture 71B. Paul Peschisolido took the moves to heart, practiced them over and over, and mastered them. He was already 15 when he was first introduced to them. He can be seen in the videos.

My good friend John Van der Kolk was the videographer and brilliantly shot close-ups and used super slow motion editing to catch the beauty of these skills of the game. He mixed them very nicely with music and they are often captivating to watch. They have been re-edited and are available at www.goldengoalscoring.com and on www.youtube.com. Excuse the older uniforms and hairstyles but the super slow motion scenes are still great to watch.

Today, I see players with an array of moves and often they are trying moves that are part of the Coerver repertoire but they have no idea when and when not to use them in a game. I stress to coaches that, they are a great tool but if players dribble when they should not or try the wrong move with the wrong foot, then they can hurt the team by giving up the ball. Also, a lot of young players try fancy moves to get a clearer shot on goal when they may already have a clear path to goal. Coaches need to remind strikers that a quick and simple move is often the best way to displace a defender. Often the defender only has to be displaced a few inches in order to clear a path to goal. They do not have to go all the way around their opponent in order to get a shot away. If you have players who want to show off all the time, simply remind them the rules to scoring when it comes to the number of touches that the world's top players need to score. The more players touch the ball, the less likely they are to score. Use this statistic over and over to cure any bad habits. Remind strikers who continuously want to take too many touches of the ball when they have it close to goal that they will be weeded out and not make it to the next level. Even Lionel Messi follows the rules when it comes to scoring. He takes fewer touches when he scores then one would assume.

There are a few Coerver skills that are absolutely essential to strikers when it comes to scoring goals and moving or eluding defenders to create scoring chances. The three most popular moves to displace defenders are "the chop", the "fake kick" and the "scissors or double scissors" (also called the "step over"). Since 1984 when the moves were first introduced, the names of each move have been changed to keep up with the times. We would name the moves after players who used them most. There was "the Rivelino" move or the "Sir Stanley Matthews" move, "the Maradona" move and "the Cryuff" moves but now wherever you go the names seem to change. Using names helps young players remember them until they become automatic in a game. Practicing them using my "tiny perception training techniques" as explained in chapter 42 will improve their ability to pick out which moves work best in each situation.

"The Chop"

The chop is when a player cuts back in a direction opposite to where he is going and the defender is also going. The key to chopping the ball is to keep the ball under the body while doing the skill and quickly shift weight from one foot to the other foot. The term chop comes from the fact that the player is swinging the leg down and over the ball as if chopping wood with an axe. In slightly different situations the chop comes from a quick jab of the ball to bring it back under the body with the inside front part of the foot. The important part of this skill is to make sure the hips are turned and the ball is cut back under the body and not left open for a defender to steal.

Young players will get away with cutting back without keeping the ball under the body with a motion that does not resemble a chop. But as defenders get bigger, older, and better, they will not have success without chopping the ball properly. A good chop is performed with a quick jab or chop of the ball with the inside of the foot as shown in picture 71F. The foot strikes the front part of the ball so that it comes back towards the body to safety. When the ball is cut back under the body, it is hard to take away. Often the toe is down and the ball is struck with the front inside part of the foot as shown in picture 71G. Pay particular attention to the hips. Make sure your strikers are getting over the ball by twisting their hips. The knee is often pointing down and inwards. After the chop, the player must accelerate or explode in the opposite direction to get the defender out of the way and then quickly get a shot away. Often the chop is the third last touch before the second last touch, before the last touch, which is a shot at goal or a pass to another striker who is in a better shooting position. See pictures 71F, 71G, 71H, 71I, and 71J for more examples of the inside of the foot chop and a description of this skill.

Picture 71F: Arjen Robben of Real Madrid chops the ball inside against an SV Hamburg player by turning his hips to get his foot in front of the ball. As he brings his foot down to hit the ball his chop or tap will make contact on the front part of the ball so that the ball will come back under his body. Action Images/Michael Regan

Picture 71G: Mauro Camoranesi of Juventus reaches to chop the ball with his right foot to bring the ball under his body to elude the defender. His toe is angled down as he twists his hips to get his foot in front of the ball. This will help bring the ball under the body so that the defender will not be able to intercept it. Action Images/Scott Heavey

Picture 71H: Lionel Messi (10) of Argentina has his hips twisted with his knee pointed down and inward in order to get his foot in front of the ball. This allows him to chop or cut the ball back and under his body. He will then shift his weight and accelerate in the opposite direction to clear the defender out of the way for a shot or pass. Action Images/ Enrique Marcarian

Picture 71I: Barcelona's Lionel Messi chops the ball to change direction against Manchester United's John O'Shea (22), Rio Ferdinand (L) and Michael Carrick during their Champions League final soccer match at the Olympic Stadium in Rome on May 27, 2009. Notice how his hips are turned. Picture Supplied by Action Images/Darren Staples

Picture 71J: Landon Donovan of the USA chops the ball with his right foot. Notice how the hips are turned and that he's starting to bring his knee in front of the ball and twisting it inward before he makes contact with the ball. Action Images/Guy Jeffroy

The Fake Kick

Any moves that are associated with faking to kick a ball used to be called the "Cryuff" moves. For the strikers, the ability to pretend to shoot a ball and then quickly get a real shot away is paramount to learn because there will be times when the defender is right in front of them. A fake kick can displace or freeze the defender for an instant. The action of faking to kick a ball will put the defending player in a protection position as opposed to an aggressive attacking position especially if the defender is not too close to the striker. If the defender is so close to the striker that a kick would hit him in the foot, then he would not want to turn his back because a shot blocked with the foot would not hurt. But if the striker is a yard or two away and a shot could potentially hit the defender in the mid section, then there is a good chance that he will turn his back and go into a protection position to avoid getting hit by the ball where it may hurt.

When performing a fake kick, the striker must sell the fake. Strikers have to be great actors in order to fool defenders. Not all defenders will go for a fake but it does tend to work more than most other moves when the striker wants to create a little space to shoot. Certainly, there is a better chance that a fake kick will work to freeze the defender if the effort is worthy of an "Academy Award" performance than if it's not delivered very well. Younger players will have more success by using the fake kick than older players especially at higher levels of play because if defenders want to make it to the pro level, they'd better not be turning their back very often or they will likely get cut from the team. Young strikers need to score lots of goals to get more opportunities for career advancement but they must also know that some of the things that work with younger defenders may not work as easily with more experienced players.

Even if the fake kick does not make the defender turn his back to avoid getting hit, he may stretch himself to try and block the shot. This can put him in an awkward position to defend the actual shot, which would be taken from a spot beyond his reach. A fake kick can also fool the goalkeeper who may react to the fake and not be in the best position to stop the actual shot. In picture 71K, Dwight Yorke fakes a kick to try and fool the defender.

Picture 71K: Dwight Yorke fakes a kick to try and displace the defender. The next touch is usually to the same side of the kicking foot and away from the defender. If the defender takes a big step to try and block the shot, then he will be in an awkward position to block an actual attempt at goal unless the striker does not sell the fake very well. Photo: Les Jones/ Covershots

Putting Moves Together

A striker can often put two moves together to move a defender out of the way. One of the most common combination-moves for a striker is the fake kick and chop. As shown in picture 71L, Del Piero fakes a kick but them chops the ball back behind his support leg to take the ball in the other direction. Since the defender has thrown his body in one direction to block the shot, sometimes the best option is to take the ball back in the opposite direction. Using the inside of the foot chop accomplishes this best. With the defender going with speed in the opposite direction, it would be difficult for him to get back in a good defending position to attempt to block another shot from the other foot.

Picture 71L: Italy's Alessandro Del Piero fakes a kick and then chops the ball back behind his standing leg in the opposite direction in this training session for the Italian National team. The defender is taking a big step in one direction making it difficult for him to defend the space behind him. If Del Peiro delivers a good chop, he should be able to get a shot on goal away with his left foot. Note how his hips are starting to turn as he brings his foot down to chop the ball. Photo supplied by Action Iamges/Tony Gentile

Being a good two-footed player will give a striker more options to score. Often right footed plays prefer chopping the ball with their right foot and do a good job of displacing the defenders but only to set up a shot with their left foot. Many players will then avoid using their left to shoot the ball and try to chop again to bring the ball back to their right foot to shoot. This will usually result in a missed goal scoring opportunity as the attempt more often than not, fails. It's often better to get a weaker, but accurate shot away with a player's weaker foot than not a shot at all because the goalkeeper may have also been fooled on the fake. Of course, the best scenario is for your strikers to be able to kick with both feet.

The Scissors Move (Step Over)

The scissors move tends to be another very effective way to displace defenders out of good defending positions to clear a path to goal. The

Picture 71M: AC Milan's Ronaldinho does the scissors move (also pictured on page 1). Notice that the ball is under the body. He has brought his left foot over and around the ball and is about to plant it towards the left of the ball. Note the position of the body and arms. The defender may see Ronaldinho going to his left which could make him go in that direction as well but once he plants his foot, he will take the ball to his right with the outside of his right foot. With the ball under Ronaldinho's body, the defender will have a hard time trying to stretch in the opposite direction to stop him. Because of his ability to shift weight convincingly, Ronaldinho has also put himself in a position to use his powerful quadriceps muscles in his left leg to spring him in the opposite direction to complete the move and move the defender out of the way.

When you watch Ronaldinho perform this move from a normal TV viewpoint, you do not notice how much he shifts his body from left to right as you can see from this picture. This is the correct way to perform the scissors. The player has to throw his body off to one side and sell the direction he wants the defender to go towards laterally. Action Images/Jason Cairnduff

scissors is done with the ball under the body as the player moves one leg in a circular motion over and in front of the ball from inside his body to the outside. He plants the circling foot to the outside of the ball and leans over to try and make the defender go in that direction and then quickly bursts in the opposite direction using the outside of the opposite foot to play the ball. Some players do the move twice by bringing the other foot across the body after the first motion. This is called the double scissors. If done correctly and with good foot speed and execution, the defender can get frozen with both feet stuck on the ground, opening up a spot for the striker to play a ball and then shoot. Ronaldinho of Brazil in picture 71M uses this move effectively. Sometimes he goes over the ball with his legs three or four times. You would have to call his move the triple or quadruple scissors move.

Each player will have his best or favourite moves and sometimes it's better to be great at one or two moves rather than be average in many of them. Don't discourage players from practicing the moves because it should be in their arsenal of ways to move defenders. For the strikers, the more options they have, the better. The important thing is that they don't become too predictable and that they don't overdo it and forget about team play.

A FEW OF MY FAVOURITE MOVES

One of my students was 15 year old Paul Peschisolido of the Scarboro Azzurri U16 soccer team coached by Tony La Ferrara. Tony brought me in to work with his team teaching them the Coerver techniques in the summer of 1984. Tony had developed some of the top players in the country and wanted to expose them to these new techniques. Paul was one of the first players in Canada to learn the Coerver techniques after I started teaching players the moves after having seen Wiel Coerver in January 1984 in Philadelphia. Paul was a player that really took to the techniques and practiced them intensely. I worked with the team every few weeks and I noticed that Paul was improving rapidly and was very keen on learning more moves and perfecting them. But I also noticed that he had developed a couple of favourites. His favourites were the inside of the foot chop and the scissors move.

Paul went on to play at the highest levels in Canada by making the U16 National team. Eventually he got a tryout in England thanks to Tony Taylor at Birmingham City. Once he mastered some of the moves, he gained confidence on the ball and was able to combine good timing of the moves with taking opportunities to score key goals. He scored a goal in his first reserve game and that immediately caught the eye of the manager and sent him on his way to a professional career. To make a long story short, he had a good professional career in England and also played for Canada's Men's National Team. He played for Birmingham City, West Bromwich Albion, Fulham, Sheffield United, and Derby County.

Each year, during the summer break from the English League, Paul would come back to Canada to his local community in Pickering Ontario, and do demonstrations to help inspire and teach kids at the Pickering Soccer Club. I would have him do some of his moves and then finish off doing bicycle kicks for the audience. He loved working with kids and he also loved doing bicycle kicks for the kids. In one session, after a couple of bicycle kicks I figured that it would be enough. I didn't want him to jeopardize his career with an off-season injury. But Paul kept asking to do more because he saw that the kids were enjoying watching him perform them. He must have done 20 or 25 bicycle kicks for the kids, not missing the ball once. A true gentleman who loved the game and loved inspiring kids.

One Saturday afternoon I was watching a play-off game between Sheffield United and Nottingham Forest that was televised live in Canada. I hadn't realized that Paul was playing in the game until he came on as a substitute towards the end of the game. It was an exciting match and the game was tied 2-2 when he came in. In the extra time session and with about 9 minutes remaining in the game Paul received the ball outside the box directly from his team's goal kick. He pulled the ball down, beat two opponents with a chop, then did a semi scissors move and another chop to displace three defenders and the goalkeeper, and then passed the ball into the net on a stunning goal. I jumped so high off the couch that afternoon shouting, "At a boy Paul".

Paul's favourite two moves a decade earlier when first introduced to the Coerver techniques combined to do the trick in a memorable goal that was a highlight reel goal because of the moves before the shot. It broke all the rules about number of touches but it concluded with a simple low pass into the bottom third of the goal.

Picture 71N: In this demonstration of the Coerver techniques I trained young kids called the "World of Soccer Stars" to perform across Ontario. Paul Peschisolido would be the special guest at the end of sessions performed in his hometown of Pickering. The player in the foreground on the left side (Christopher Stewart) went on to play for the Canadian U17 National team and captained the U19 National team. Other players pictured are Keith Binns and Billy Ellison Jr. I'm supervising and my two assistants, Tony Oliver and Dino Mastrogiannis are to the left of the photograph.

The important thing about these moves is that the striker must use each unsuccessful attempt at beating a defender as a learning experience. Strikers have to ask themselves, "Did I use the right move for the situation? Why did it not work? How can I make it work next time?" A real understanding of these moves occurs when the striker realizes that they are based on predicting human movement and not fancy footwork or tricks.

Here is what I say to my players:

> ***"Analyze yourself all the time. Test yourself. When the move does not work ask yourself why and ask yourself, was I thinking of the opponents' body motion? Do the moves over and over and over until it becomes automatic. You will need to consciously think while you're trying them in scrimmages. Try it with younger opponents, easy opponents, and concentrate on doing the moves based on the correct skills rather than the fact that you're bigger and faster than your smaller opponents are. Eventually, when successful, you'll get an exciting feeling and won't want to wait to do it over and over again on an opponent in a game. These feelings will help these moves become instinctive for you."***

All players will have their favourite moves and tricks to rid themselves of defenders. A player's body type will make some moves work better than others. Strikers need to be proficient at these skills especially when they need to displace an opponent. Outrunning a defender is not always the best method of scoring for players that tend to be a bit slower. The important point I want to make is that strikers do not have to beat a player one-on-one by completely going around them. All they have to do is find a way to move them just enough so that they can get a shot away.

CHAPTER 72

Forcing Key Mistakes by Defenders on the Ball

In today's game most goals are scored as a result of some sort of error made by a player. An error somewhere on the field by someone usually enables the scoring opportunity to exist. It may be a missed assignment by a player on the defensive team that triggers a reaction that puts the defending team in disarray. The error can be a result of a poor strategy by the defensive team or a great strategy by the attacking team to force the defensive team to make errors and exploit them. Mistakes can be a result of poor communication between teammates on the defensive side. The bottom line is that an error was made somewhere. It can also be a result of a single player getting beaten when he should not have been. Often, rain, snow, sun and wind and the field conditions cause errors. And we cannot forget that there are goals scored when the defenders have defended perfectly but the goalkeeper makes an error.

In this chapter I focus on the individual defending player who has possession of the ball and his mental state. Can our strikers force errors that can result in a goal for our team? I want to focus on the things that strikers need to know that can help their individual game. We know that, when defenders or goalkeepers make errors, the player who erred may be vulnerable to more errors due to low self-confidence. Keep an eye on these players. All of a sudden, the ball can become a 'hot potato' to them. Players in a depressed state may not want the ball and may prefer to hide. This is when the true strikers prey on these opponents. Strikers must be aware of defenders who may not be in their best mental state because they may make another mistake whereas, under normal conditions, they may not. Whether it is by applying more pressure or taking the affected players on, the strikers must be alert to these potential advantages.

Looking at individual mistakes by defenders, I want my strikers to ask these questions.

1. How can they cause more mistakes so that they can score more goals, and
2. How can my strikers predict when the defenders may make an error?

Are there some identifiable situations where we can read human behaviors where a player may be more prone to making errors? I have sorted defensive errors into 4 categories. While there is no guarantee that the defender will make an error, the chances for error are increased in these types of situations.

4 Reasons Why Mistakes are Made by Defenders on the Ball

1. Relaxed body
2. Overstressed body
3. Perceived stress
4. The elements

1. Relaxed Body

In this situation, which I call the 'relaxed mode' state, the player with the ball is in a state of mind that tells him that there is no danger ahead. You can also call this state the 'no danger state of mind'. The mistake is made because the mind is not ready for danger. The body is almost over-relaxed and the player is overconfident that he has the skills and time to do something constructive with the ball. The player in this situation allows his guard down a bit. Then, when a sudden state of danger presents itself, there is a quick state of panic or shock. The muscles act as though they get a jolt of energy that makes them hyperalert and this also takes away some of their ability to perform some of the more refined skills. The body basically has a panic attack caused by the realization that the 'no danger' assumption was wrong. In this situation, the body needs more time than normal to recompose itself and therefore the chance for error is great.

In picture 72A, we see Rio Ferdinand of Manchester United relaxed and looking to make a pass or kick the ball up the field. He is not aware that a pressuring opponent may be closer to him than he thinks.

2. Overstressed Body

This situation is simple to observe because the player with the ball is in too much danger. Pressure from opponents is at a maximum and therefore the chance for error is at the greatest. I hesitate to call this a case where a defender makes a mistake because there may be more than one opponent close to him. Close pressure will make performing a skill such as clearing a ball difficult. In picture 72B, the defender may make an error because she is under extreme pressure, which may include some physical contact. Coaches may want to call these good pressurizing skills by their attackers as opposed to a defensive error.

Picture 72A: Rio Ferdinand of Manchester United has the ball and is in relaxed state as he moves the ball forward looking for a teammate to pass it to. He feels as though he has plenty of time. When defensive players have the ball in this "relaxed state" the body is relaxed because the mind feels no apparent danger nearby. If a striker sneaks up on this player's blind side, he may be able to cause the body into a state of panic, which may lead to an error on his next touch. Identifying this 'relaxed state' is part of the psychological game that strikers need to be in tune with if they are to force mistakes by defenders on the ball. Mistakes can lead them or their teammates to score more goals. Picture Supplied by Action Images

Picture 72B: In this picture, Mia Hamm of the USA is pressurizing the Chinese defender with the ball. Close pressure like this will force players to make errors. She has even made slight contact with her arms, which will stress the player with the ball even more. Strikers should work hard to try to get this type of pressure on defenders with the ball because an error close to the opponent's net can result in goals. Photo by Les Jones/Covershots.

3. Perceived Stress

How often have you seen a player rush his pass or kick or next touch when there was no need to do so? Why do defenders make errors and think there is more pressure on them when there actually is not? It's good to note that close pressure without actually being close enough to touch the ball or player can cause the defender to rush his kick or pass and thus force an error.

In this situation, the player with the ball <u>thinks</u> he is in an overstressed situation such as in reason #2 but really is not. The player has perceived the situation incorrectly and therefore has made wrong assumptions as to how much time he has to perform a skill. I'll elaborate on how to create this perceived stress later in this chapter.

4. The Elements

The elements can cause mistakes. Rain, bumps on the field, wind, sun, mud, snow, ice and any other condition that is out of anyone's control and detrimental to performing a skill can be a cause for a player to make a mistake. Pressurizing defenders when the conditions are poor may cause defenders to make more errors.

But goal scoring does not necessarily go up when the conditions are bad. Poor footing can also cause errors for strikers while performing their last touch. Missed scoring chances due to poor conditions will just have to be accepted by the strikers as one of those things to forget about and move on.

Knowing the 4 reasons how players make mistakes can help any player on the field look for situations where they can force the opponents to make a mistake. Strikers won't be totally focussed on all the little things that can help their game for the full 90 minutes but we want to make sure they are focused in special moments, certainly when a scoring opportunity presents itself but also when they can be instrumental in forcing the defenders to make an error. Can they be focused enough to force a defender to make a mistake and turn that error into a goal?

How then do we train our strikers to cause mistakes to be made in each of these four situations?

Forcing Mistakes when the Defender is in Relaxed Mode

In this case, we need to make sure our strikers read the mental state of the player with the ball. Can they identify when the defender's body is in the 'relaxed mode' state? If the defender is, then he is vulnerable. Ask your players to see if the defender with the ball is looking relaxed and exhaling or breathing softly whilst in this mode. In a game, this state will exist when the player with the ball feels as though he has more time and space than he thinks. The striker may be a few yards away from the player with the ball. The striker may or may not be in the defender's peripheral field of vision. Preferably the striker should be a bit to the side of the defender with the ball and should try to get out of the defender's field of vision. If he is in the defender's field of vision, he should be looking relaxed as though he will not put on a challenge: he can be walking or jogging and looking away from the defender pretending not to exert any energy to go and challenge him.

We want the defender with the ball to stay in the "relaxed and confident" mode. The defender may look downfield and around for his next move. This cockiness is noticeable and the striker should drift to the side of the defender as much as possible and try to disappear from the player's radar. Then suddenly, with a sudden burst of speed, at the instant before the defender touches the ball forward again to set up even another touch, the striker can pounce.

If shocked and surprised by the sudden pressure, the first reaction of the defender may be a reflex panic-like jerk. His very next touch will probably be poor. Quickly after that, the defender may be able to make a play but if the striker is close enough to the defender at this point then he may be unable to make an intelligent play. The defender may be forced into a big mistake that the striker or a teammate can capitalize on. If the defender being preyed upon is tensed up, his finer motor skills may let him down. His next touch or pass may be poor and he may make a mistake that will allow the pressurizing striker or a teammate to get the ball in a good scoring position.

Direct Pressure to Defenders with the Ball Can Cause an Error due to Overstress

In this second type of error, extreme pressure will cause mistakes. Getting close enough to the defender where the striker can actually tackle for the ball is called pressure. The coach may have more detailed information on how they may want to pressurize opponents on different parts of the field but, generally, if a ball is in the possession of a defender and the striker is close by, he should apply pressure. In any ball that is 50/50 or even 25/75 in favour of the defender, the striker should challenge. A mistake by a defender in his third of the field can be converted to a scoring chance very quickly and usually in less than 9 seconds. The attacking team does not have to go very far to get to the net.

Coaches are demanding that strikers today get fit enough to do more pressurizing than ever before. When the ball is in your team's end it's a long way to the other end of the field. Also when attacking from your end of the field, the opposition is working hard to get back behind the ball to defend. There may be a lot of people to go through to score. When a defender has the ball in his own end of the field, teammates start to leave their defending positions to get into better attacking positions thereby leaving fewer defenders back to defend. Coaches want to take advantage of the field position of the ball to force errors, which may leave the defending team with fewer players to defend after an error.

In picture 72C, we see a player on Canada's U20 Women's team with a personal motivational reminder to work hard during games. Strikers need to train to sprint to close down opponents to try and force errors and then be able to possibly sprint again to try to score. If they are successful in causing an error and win the ball with a chance for them to score, they then must have the mental fortitude and be mentally composed to execute the fine skill of scoring. Often the aggressive effort needed to win a ball goes against the finer skills needed to score especially when the ball is on the ground. The urge to power the ball into the goal instead of calmly passing the ball into the goal is high. The mind must take over the striker's body and do the right thing to score instead of going with the instinctive urge to be overly aggressive in shooting.

*Picture 72C: In this picture taken during the national anthem, a player on Canada's U20 Women's World Cup team in Chile has a motivational note for herself. In particular, strikers need to do whatever it takes to get fit enough to meet the demands of today's game and what is expected of them from their coaches. I tell players, **"If you don't get fit and work hard, someone else will."** Having mental notes such as this to remind players what they need to do to succeed is fine. Photo by Les Jones/Covershots.*

English FA coach Dick Bate (picture 72D) made some interesting observations about fitness and playing at high intensity levels for pro players. He presented these findings at his lecture at the 2009 NSCAA convention in St. Louis. He stated that the number of sprints per game that players made in the English Premier League has doubled since 2002. Players were all running a minimum of 13km per game. Strikers and wide players covered the most distances. Picture 72C just puts it more bluntly.

Picture 72D: Dick Bate from the English FA first came to North America for a coaching session with The National Soccer Coaches Association of Canada. I have quoted Dick's work in this book. Dick Bate is a master clinician and this photo is from the NSCAA convention in Philadelphia in 2010, where he was a guest speaker. Photo by Alfonso Garcia

Forcing Mistakes by Pretending to be Close to the Defender with the Ball

Forcing mistakes by pretending to be close to the defender with the ball is probably the most intriguing method of causing mistakes. Is it possible to make a defender perceive pressure to cause him stress when in fact it's not there? Imagine your strikers applying pressure on a defender when they are not as close as they would like to be because they physically cannot be somewhere where they cannot be. Can we train strikers to make the defender with the ball feel as though he is under extreme pressure? How can this be done? As stated earlier, studying the mental state of the defender is one way to start.

Strikers should get into the habit of studying the defenders who are trying to prevent them from scoring just as defenders and goalkeepers are studying them. Train your strikers to find out what the defender's weak foot is. This information can help them cause an illusion. Have your nearest striker approach the defender with the ball from the side of his stronger foot. This should force the defender to play the ball to his weaker foot and away from where your striker is, even if your striker is too far away to cause any real threat. A less experienced defender will believe that there is more pressure on him than there really is when using his weaker foot. If the striker can enter the defender's field of vision so that he is spotted by his peripheral vision, then the defender with the ball may panic and think that the striker is closer than he really is. Although the defender with the ball may still have plenty of time to make a good play, if he thinks that he is under pressure as in situation 2, then he is more prone to making an error. Strikers who are too far to challenge can cause some defenders to become stressed by getting in their field of vision so that the defender with the ball has to think about them.

The difference between this situation and situation 1 is that in the first "relaxed body" type error, the striker is close enough to actually put pressure on the defender by sneaking up on the ball carrier. In this situation, the striker is too far away to realistically challenge the defender for the ball. Strikers who are too far to challenge for the ball can cause some defenders to become stressed by getting in their field of vision so that the defender with the ball will think about them. Therefore, getting on their blind side when they are too far away to pressure may not be the best choice. I hope you understand the difference to be able to explain to your strikers when they should be blind side of the ball carrier and when it's better not to be.

Generally, strikers should make the ball carrier feel more stressed than he should be so that he is more prone to making errors. A quick turn over of the ball to a midfield teammate can quickly turn to a scoring chance for the striker who put the visual stress on the defender with the ball. Getting in the visual field of a defender with the ball on his stronger foot's side especially in or near his own box can pay dividends. The exact opposite situation occurs when strikers have the ball and may be ready to shoot. Defenders want the strikers to believe that they are closer than they really are and therefore force them to hurry their shot. Soccer is a game of opposites isn't it?

In Rafi Srebro's book, *Winning with Your Head,* he writes about stress in competition. Here are a couple of priceless quotes from his book on stress. "In sport, most threatening situations are a result of thoughts and often they exist only in our imagination or mind. When our brain recognizes a real or imagined stressful situation, the body prepares for immediate reaction."

Srebro says that stress can come from a number of things. For example, an important game is stressful in itself for defenders. A mistake can cause a goal against their team. "The feeling of tension brings with it the stress reaction of the body that prevents players from playing well and leads to more mistakes than normal."

Can your strikers identify stressed defenders and escalate their stress level by being in positions that make them less confident of their game? Your strikers should be alert throughout the game to the mental state of the defenders covering them. This state can change drastically during a game.

The Own Goal

With that I bring you to another important psychological point that you and your team captain or team leaders can play a very important role in. "The own goal". Generally, strikers would prefer to get credit for goals and don't like the term 'own goals' but you as a coach love them, unless of course it happens to your team. If your team scores one, how well does the other team react? Do they blame each other and are they down after the kick-off? If they are, make sure your strikers are ready to take advantage of more possible errors. How does your team respond after giving up an own goal? Our championship team solved the dilemma of giving up an own goal in a key game with great leadership.

"THE OWN GOAL"

We were playing a key game against our archrivals, The University of Toronto. Midway in the second half we went down 2-1 when my centre back/sweeper, Paul D'Agostino, (who went on to play in the NASL with Memphis and Calgary) played the ball back to me as I was coming out for the ball away from the goal. Unfortunately we got our signals mixed up and we completely missed each other. He passed it back to where I had moved from and the ball went right into the back of our own net. We both knew we messed up but first on the scene of the accident was captain Nick Plessas who told us not to worry about it. Not that we weren't disappointed but he kept our spirits up and the team came back at the end of the game to score twice on goals by Mike Burke and Danny Iannuzziello to win the game off nicely played balls by Peter Kovacs and Mac Musabay.

How does your team react to adversity? If your players are uptight at each other, their tense body will make it harder for them to regain their finest motor skills needed for delicate passing and finishing. The value of your captain can really shine through in adverse situations.

Are your team leaders the types of players that can help your team regain composure or are they more apt to cause friction? If your strikers are too tensed up and pumped with anger, they may not be able to make their last touch a work of art.

CHAPTER 73

Garbage Goals, Rebounds, and Unexplainable Goals

I'm sure you heard of the term garbage goals. They are the types of goals that are somewhat of an accident that needed a set of circumstances to take place before they occurred. The ball had to end up at a place where a striker was where he was able to capitalize on the situation and put the ball in the net. If your team is a recipient of one of these goals, then you are happy, but if you are on the team that has conceded one of them, you're shocked at how unlucky your team is. Is it not quite surprising how certain players seem to get more than their fair share of these types of goals? Do these players have a sixth sense that allows them to predict where the ball will go in order to get into a scoring position?

These types of goals usually occur from rebounds off the goalkeeper or defenders. Often they come from deflections and partially blocked shots. The best advice I can give my players is to train for playing any ball in the box until the play is settled by way of a whistle (with the ball going out of bounds, a foul, or a goal), or when the ball ends up safely in the goalkeeper's hands.

Often, when players are in a shooting drill at a training session, everyone stops when the ball is partially stopped by the keeper. I'm always looking for that player who is alert and ready to pounce on any loose balls in the area. There is a natural tendency for players to relax after a shot instead of being alert for rebounds, deflections, and loose balls. This often starts with how you conduct practices. Encourage your strikers to always play rebounds. I find that when it's hot and humid or close to the end of a practice, players tend to get lazy and not play things until the end. Keep an eye on your strikers in particular and make sure that they are working hard till the end. See how they perform at the end of your practices. If your strikers are not the hardest working players on your team by the end of the training sessions, then this is not good because most goals are scored towards the end of the game. The last quarter of the game produces the most goals. True strikers are working hard until the very end.

Why is it that most goals are scored towards the end of games? There are a few reasons for this. One is that players are more physically and mentally tired. Also, since soccer is a bit of a chess match, teams can play a certain style only to set up a new formation or strategy to use later in a game when the opponent is less likely to make adjustments. Also, most teams bring on substitutes towards the end and thus there will be some fresh legs against some tired legs that can change the outcome of a game. And finally, if one team is down by a goal, then the team that is losing will take a bit more risks at the back as they bring players forward. This will create more chances at both ends of the field. If players are moving forward and crowding the box in an attack, there are going to be more chances of garbage goals scored towards the end of the game than in any other part of the game.

Other situations that create more garbage goals are whenever there is a chance to move more players up into the box easily. Set plays are good opportunities to bring players forward in attack because the play is stopped. This gives everyone time to move forward with fewer risks at the back. You will see quite a number of goals scored from rebounds off of corner kicks and more goals scored from deflections on free kicks than at any other times.

Rebounds

Here is some advice you can give your strikers to help them to prepare to score more goals from rebounds. If the shooter is at an angle and aims the ball to the goalkeeper's near post there is less chance for a rebound that can result in a goal. Any rebound from a near post shot may be at a poorer angle than the original shot or may go out of bounds. But, whenever a shot from an angle is taken towards the centre of the goal or the far post or back post then there is a better chance for a goal from the ensuing rebound. Since the goalkeeper will be coming from the center of the goal and heading towards the shooter to block a shot, any shot taken towards the post opposite the one he is moving to, will provide an opportunity for a rebound unless the goalkeeper:

a) saves the shot and maintains possession of the ball;
b) is able to deflect the ball just slightly and enough to clear the far post for a corner kick.

If the goalkeeper allows a rebound, it is more than likely going to end up towards his opposite side than where it came from. I have tracked hundreds of rebound goals and there is a pattern that I have identified that may help the strikers in some situations. Sometimes, things happen so fast that most strikers will not have time to prepare themselves to go to a specific spot. They are either lucky enough to be there or they are not. But if there is a better position where a player can go to when he anticipates a shot coming from a teammate then the information in diagrams 73A, 73B and 73C should help him make a better decision as to where to go.

In diagram 73A, we see that 9 out of 10 goals off of rebound shots are scored on a line opposite to where the ball came from using the centre of the goalkeeper and perpendicular to the goal line as reference points. Therefore, if a shot is taken to the right of this centre line, regardless of where the goalkeeper is stationed in his goal, then in 9 out of 10 shots, the ensuing rebound will end up on the other side of the centre line. Please note that the centre line is at right angles to the goal line and not necessarily square with the goalkeeper. In diagram 73A, I'm showing that if the ball is shot from the right of the centre line then most goals scored from the rebound will be scored from the left of the centre line. If the ball were shot from the left, then the same holds true and 90% of goals scored from rebounds will be to the right of this centre line. The length of the line of the shot, which indicates the distance travelled by the ball towards the keeper, is almost always longer than the length of the rebound. Where the goalkeeper stands in relation to the goal does not affect which side of the line the ball will go to on the rebound. Note that I am <u>not</u> saying that the ball does not rebound on the same side of the line in these proportions. What I am saying is that <u>goals scored</u> when the ball rebounds on the opposite side of the line are scored in this proportion.

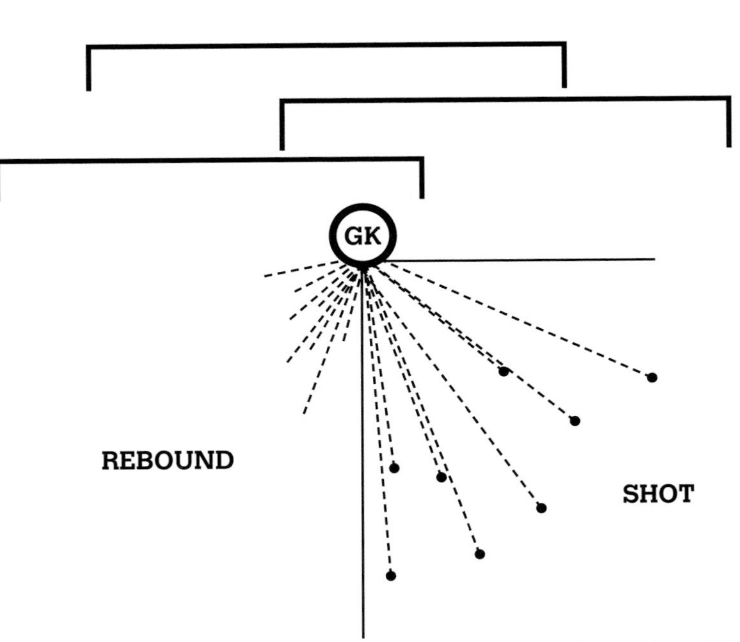

Picture 73A: In this diagram, the dots indicate where the shot is taken. GK is the goalkeeper or is some instances, a defender. Note that there are three goals behind the keeper. This is to show that in some cases the goalkeeper or defender is at the centre of his goal and at other times he is at the near post or at the far post. It does not matter if the goalkeeper is angled to the shooter; the key point is that the centre line from the goalkeeper is at 90 degrees to the goal line. In 9 out of 10 rebounds that result in goals, if the ball is shot from one side of this centre line, the ensuing rebound which results in most goals will be on the other side of this centre line. Only 1 in 10 goals scored off of a rebound will come from the same side of this centre line that the ball is originally shot from. I didn't expect such a large discrepancy from all the goals I have studied.

There is no guarantee that the ball will come out back towards the goal line, the 6-yard box or come out as far as the penalty spot. The most likely area where goals are scored from after a rebound from a shot from an angle is shown in diagram 73B and 73C. In diagram 73B I have indicated one dot (black) for the shooting player's last touch. The line from that dot is the path of the ball which takes you to another dot. This dot indicates where the ball rebounds from, which is usually the position of the goalkeeper or defender. From there, a line is drawn to another dot (red). This is where the eventual goal scorer scored from on his last touch. In some cases, the goal scorer was the same player that took the original shot but in most cases it was a different player that scored from a rebound. In diagram 73C, I give a more graphic picture of where balls will go to after there is a rebound. Hopefully I can train my strikers to look for these areas to give them a better chance of scoring from a rebound.

The trick for strikers is not to be too far behind the ball and have the ball roll across the face of the goal without anyone there to score on the rebound. Also you don't want your strikers to be too close to the goal as it would be impossible for them to go backwards to try and get to the ball. As a general rule, the following striker (non-shooting striker) should be behind the shooting striker when the shot originates from inside the box so that he is always in a position to go forward to get to a rebound. It's difficult to go backwards to get to a rebound and then turn to score. There will not be enough time. The following striker should usually be running forward and at a 45-degree angle to the goalkeeper.

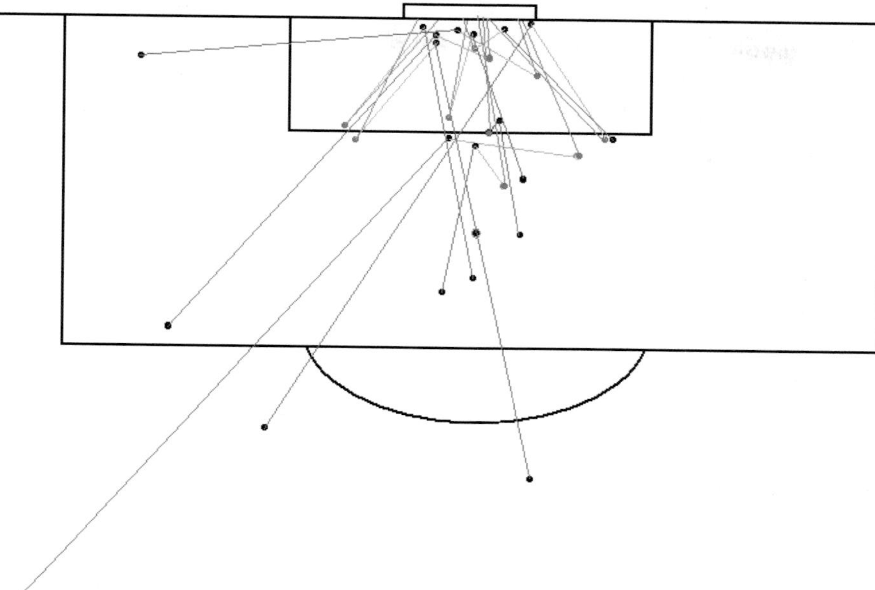

Picture 73B: In these actual goals, I show a black dot where the original shot is taken from. Then the red line indicates the path of the ball from the original shot to another black dot which indicates where it rebounded from. The next line, in blue, indicates the path the ball takes after the rebound. The next dot is red, and indicates the last touch of the goal scorer. The next line is in green and indicates the ball's path to the goal to score. Note that most goals from rebounds are scored between 2 and 9 yards out. These 10 actual examples reflect any group of 10 rebound goals I have analyzed.

These are just general rules and in no way gospel. The situation will be different each time based on the speed of the play and the type of shot that the strikers take (i.e. pass into goal or power shot).

Surprisingly, in World Cup play, not as many goals are scored from rebounds as one would assume. In the 2002 World Cup, only 7 goals came from a rebound and one of those rebounds came from a penalty shot. There were a number of goals that came off deflections either by the attacking player or a defending player, which indicates that a shot on goal is never a bad option. Rebound goals seem to make up between 3% and 8% of goals scored.

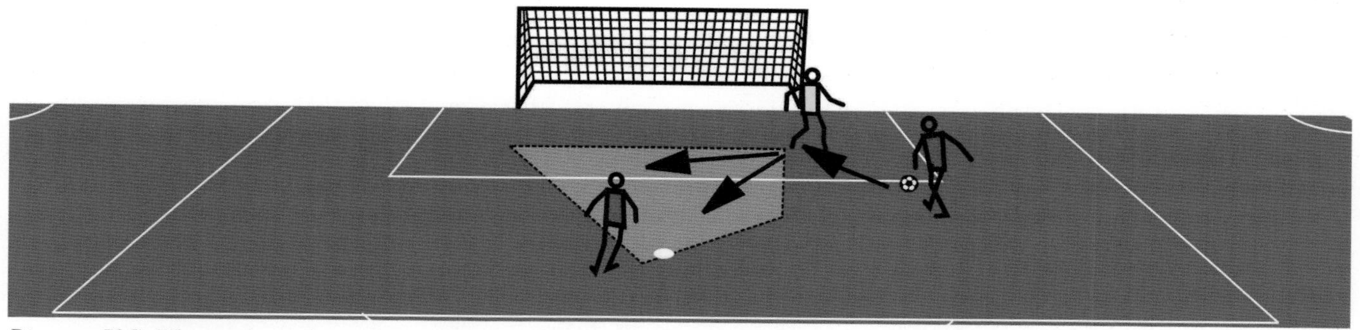

Diagram 73C: When a player shoots from an angle and there is a rebound, there is an area that most rebounds will end up going to as shown by the shaded area. The following striker should usually be behind the shooter and in a position where he has to run forward to get to a rebound. If the second striker is too close to goal and has to come backwards to get to a rebound, then he will probably not score. If he is too far behind the play he may miss a ball rebounding across the face of the goal. Being at a 45 degree angle from the goalkeeper and slightly behind the shooter will probably give him the best odds of scoring more goals on an ensuing rebound. Illustration by Jo-Anne Godawa

The Goalkeeper and Rebounds

Whenever a rebound results from a goalkeeper's save, the goalkeeper's chances of making a second save will be very low since he will have probably been displaced. Strikers should not miss the goal in this situation. If your strikers get a ball from a rebound make sure that they hit the net. There will be very little reason for them to aim since almost any shot on goal should score unless they hit the goalkeeper. Any action other than shooting on the first touch after a rebound is unacceptable. Also, any player who is anticipating a possible rebound should already know what part of the foot he will attempt to score with: the inside of the foot as in making inside of the foot passes because this area of the foot provides the largest surface area. Balls coming off rebounds are likely to be bouncing or spinning so you want to make sure your striker uses the largest part of the foot to score with.

Picture 73D: Ronaldo scores the first goal for Brazil in the 2002 World Cup Final past German goalkeeper Oliver Kahn on a rebound after Kahn could not hold on to the ball after a shot on goal. This goal was Ronaldo's 12th goal in a World Cup finals competition. In the 2006 World Cup he scored 3 more goals eclipsing West Germany's Gerd Mueller's mark of 14 (10 in 1970 and 4 in 1974). The goal was a result of Ronaldo working hard to anticipate a possible rebound. In 9 out of 10 shots, a rebound is not going to be available but a good goal scorer is always ready to score. Picture supplied by Action Images/Dan Chung

In picture 73D, Ronaldo practically wins the 2002 World Cup for Brazil by pouncing on a rebound after Kahn of Germany fails to hold onto the ball. Many players would have stopped after seeing a teammate take a shot right into the goalkeeper's arms. Ronaldo, the highest scoring player in World Cup history, did not stop running towards the goal just in case of a rebound. He anticipated correctly and consequently scored an easy goal to give Brazil a 1-0 lead in the World Cup Final. This goal changed the complexion of the game as Brazil went on to win 2-0 to capture the 2002 World Cup.

We know that many goals are scored from rebounds. Can we create a rebound? Pele used to purposely kick the ball at a defender's shins and wait for the ball to bounce off them and then retrieve it to go around them or take a shot at goal. In close quarters, sometimes it's the best play because there may not be a shooting option because of a defender in the way. There may be no room to try to do anything else. There may be no passing options either. When the striker kicks the ball at a defender, the defender is frozen for a second and is not able to do anything. No one knows where the rebound will go therefore all other defenders are in no position to predict what's going to happen next. This is not something I would suggest when there are better options but one to consider in some situations.

When a defender or goalkeeper blocks a shot and there is a rebound, who has the advantage, the player shooting or the player who blocked the ball? I would say that the player shooting has the advantage in that situation. Since the shot came before the block, the shooter has a split second advantage over the player blocking the shot to recover and play the rebound. However, one reason why more goals are not scored after a blocked shot and an ensuing rebound is that there are usually two or three defensive players for every attacking player around the ball. This will swing the chance of a defender clearing the ball versus a resulting goal to the defensive side. But that's the only reason the odds are in favour of the defensive team. Therefore, if your striker has to decide whether he should try to get a shot away or not and deal with it possibly being blocked then he should consider this. If there is only one defensive player close to him then your striker's odds of getting to a rebound are pretty good.

Another issue that defending players may be faced with is that they may turn their head away if the ball is near their head or chest area and this slows them down to get to a rebound. For example, how many times have you seen a defensive player block a shot with his side or his back as he turns away from the shot? Quite a few I'm sure. When a defender blocks a shot in this manner, he is not in a good position to get to the rebound before the shooter because he may have his back to the striker and the ball. The striker who is still facing the goal should have a great chance to score from the rebound especially if no other defenders are nearby. I want my strikers to always be expecting a rebound. Sometimes attacking players relax their bodies and lose focus or react negatively after their shot has been blocked and forget to expect a rebound. By the time they react, it's often too late to score. Make sure your players don't get down on themselves after a blocked shot and miss the opportunity to score on the rebound. Remind them that it doesn't matter how the ball goes in the net, all goals are beautiful.

Unexplainable Goals

You should have noted by now that I have tried to explain how most goals are scored focusing solely on the players with the chance to score. I've talked about the physical things they can do, the mental things they should do, and the skill related things that they should know and do. I've also tried to cover goals from different parts of the field and different circumstances. But one of the things that make this game so great is that not everything follows a set pattern of rules every time. There are goals that can be described as practically unexplainable. They are hard to practice and they are usually rare. Such unexplainable goals can come from gross goalkeeping errors. How does a striker practice that?

Another hard to explain type goal are goals coming from the famous bicycle kick or scissors kick. The striker still has to be ready for the chance but it happens so rarely that practicing them for any length of time may make no sense because the time can be better spent on trying things that are more likely to happen in a game.

Picture 73E: Brazil's Edmilson scores against Costa Rica in the 2002 World Cup on this bicycle kick. He was "prepared to score". Action Images/Tony O'Brien

Picture 73F: Juventus' Amauri attempts an overhead (bicycle) kick as AC Milan's Paolo Maldini (3) watches during their Italian Serie A soccer match at Olympic stadium in Turin in December, 2008. It's one of the most exciting type goals to watch and undoubtedly it will make all the highlight reels. Bicycle kicks don't need to be practiced. If the mind is always "prepared to score" it will happen without thinking. Action Images/Stefano Rellandini

The Bicycle Kick

The famous bicycle kick is a type of goal I would say is practically unexplainable except to say that strikers who score such goals need to be hyper alert when a chance presents itself. They must always be "prepared to score". It's not often that a ball will be exactly where it needs to be for bicycle kick type goals to occur. They are a thing of beauty and always make the highlight reels. Some strikers may be lucky enough to only score one bicycle kick goal per lifetime but it certainly is one that no one will ever forget, especially the goal scorer. In picture 73E, we see Edmilson of Brazil score a bicycle kick goal. In picture 67D (chapter 67); we see another bicycle kick goal by Watford's Hameur Bouazza on Manchester's Edwin Van der Sar. All I can say to strikers is that they should always be prepared to score on one touch. Goals will come at the most unexpected times. The true striker is always readying his body to score.

In all these goals, especially the 'once in lifetime goals', the player still has to know where the net is. Another bicycle kick attempt at goal is shown in picture 73F as Juventus' Amauri attempts an overhead (bicycle) kick as AC Milan's Paolo Maldini (3) watches during their Italian Serie A soccer match. Great unbelievable and unexplainable type goals can only come when the mind is "prepared to score".

You cannot score a bicycle kick goal without being "prepared to score". All I can say to strikers is that they should always be prepared to score on "one touch".

Be Prepared to Score

When strikers are prepared to score knowing that their only touch is also their last touch amazing things can happen, such as the bicycle kick or flying scissors kick or overhead kick and volleys of all varieties. Liam Davies (picture 73G), a student at my "Golden Goal Scoring Academy" course surprised himself when he directed the ball at the goal on his first (and last) touch at training and ended up doing a bicycle kick. We were not practicing bicycle kicks. We were just working on being "prepared to score" and it happened automatically. I see coaches working on the bicycle kick at training and especially at soccer camps where kids are asked to practice something that may never happen in their lifetime. Practicing the bicycle kick can be dangerous as players can hurt their shoulders or arms if they repeat it often at practice and land awkwardly.

Picture 73G: Liam Davies, a Golden Goal Scoring Academy student, plays with The Richmond Hill Soccer Club. After taking the golden goal scoring course Liam wrote, "Thank you so much for helping me with my scoring touch and the first game back I scored a hat trick". A year later, Liam came second in league scoring.

Sometimes, bicycle kick type goals occur when a player heads to where he expects the ball to go, but the passer misses the target and passes the ball behind the striker or the striker has made his run too soon. In such cases, the ball is crossed behind the striker who now has to stop, turn, and try to get to the ball by throwing his body in the air to get a foot to the ball. The true goal scorer is always prepared to score and only when the mindset is in this mode, can incredible bicycle kick or scissor kick type goals occur. In my view, these types of goals are solely based on the state of mind of the player. Practicing how to get in this mindset is more important than repeating bicycle kicks at training. In picture 73J, Wayne Rooney scores an incredible bicycle kick goal against Manchester City in an EPL game when the cross was played behind him. He had his mind set to prepare to score right from the start. There is no hesitation on what to do in his mind.

Picture 73H: Laurentian University's Lisa Watson prepares to score against RMC. Watson, a former student of the Golden Goal Scoring Academy course retained key psychological information from the course 5 years later. The material presented in this book must be presented in a unique intense fashion to have long lasting effects. Players who learn the psychological factors that help them score goals will continue to score them as they grow older. It by no means replaces training and ongoing coaching but all things being equal; it may be the difference between being average and being great at scoring goals. Photo by Action Event Photos with permission from Laurentian University.

Rooney was asked in an interview after the game if he felt that the goal was pure instinct. Rooney said, "Yea, I think so. You don't have time to think about what you're going to do." It was his first bicycle kick in his professional career indicating that even players who score a lot of goals, rarely get those types of goals.

Another one of my students at my goal scoring courses, Lisa Watson, (picture 73H) has been a great goal scorer ever since taking my course when she was 14. Her father Russ, also her coach at the time, accompanied her to the course and has continued to remind her about being prepared to score. Playing for Laurentian University in Sudbury, Ontario, Lisa was one of the top rookie goal scorers in the league and got invited to try out for the Canadian Intercollegiate team before an injury ended her season prematurely. In 2012, 9 years after taking the Golden Goal Scoring course, Watson became the all-time goal scoring leader for Laurentian University's Lady Vees.

She had this to say about being prepared to score:

> "The first thing I remember from the course was the in-class session about always being 'prepared to score'. This is something from the session I still keep in mind to this day. I remember on our way to the course after that lesson my dad would always point out the 'Be Prepared to Stop' (picture 73I) sign and would remind me that I should ALWAYS be 'prepared to score'. I remember working with John on the field on parts of shooting that some coaches don't stress upon in practice."

Picture 73I: This sign which is on the way to a soccer complex acted as a reminder for Lisa Watson to be "Prepared to Score". Photo by Lisa and Russ Watson

Picture 73J: Wayne Rooney scores and incredible goal for Manchester United against their cross-town rivals, Manchester City, in February 2011. Rooney made a run to the goal scoring area for the cross but the cross came behind him. He stopped, turned and threw his foot to the ball and directed the ball at the goal. The ball was still close enough for him to get to and a true goal scorer will do anything to try to get to a ball and direct it at the goal. Rooney said, "You don't have time to think about what you're going to do." Great strikers always have to be prepared to direct the ball at the net in any way they can. It's rule #1 to scoring goals. Photo provided by Action Images/Jason Cairnduff

CHAPTER 74

Why Goals Are Not Scored

I believe that if my strikers know how goals are not scored, then they will be apt to listen to a coach discuss ways to score. It's another way to connect with players who are having problems scoring. In the case of your strikers, assuming they are getting chances to score, their ability to finish can decide the fate of your whole team and season. A few more goal conversions here and there will make a huge difference. By bringing up my top 10 list of how goals are not scored, I hope to continue the psychological education of my key strikers by reminding them why they or their opponents don't score. Hopefully, this will get them to study their position and opponents better. I like lists and laws and rules when coaching players because it stresses key points. A top 10 list or top 5 list is easier to remember in the heat of the moment when analyzing one's performance. Here is my "top ten list" of reasons why goals are NOT scored. Make sure your strikers know them and relate to them. I'll explain some of them while others have already been explained or are self-explanatory.

10 Key Mistakes Strikers Make That Result in Goals NOT Being Scored

1. Player does not shoot.
2. Player misses the net.
3. Player takes eyes off the ball at the last second.
4. Player thinks that there is not a goal scoring opportunity when in fact there is.
5. Player takes too long to shoot.
6. Player relaxes body too much (i.e. the player is over confident and loses cognitive thought needed to finish the job of scoring).
7. Player aims to bulge the net (highlight reel).
8. Player tries ridiculous moves in close quarters.
9. Player goes offside.
10. Player gets panic attack.

Most of the above list is self-explanatory or has been explained in detail so far but a few may need a bit more explanation. The first two reasons indicate that the striker was not prepared to score. Reason 3 can be the number one reason for some players who do shoot but miss the net or get poor contact with the ball. It actually is related to reason 6. When a player becomes over confident and thinks that he will easily score in a situation that seems easy to finish, his body becomes too relaxed and overconfident. This leads to the player taking his eyes off the ball a bit too early to watch the ball go towards the net. Often, the scoring opportunity seems so simple that the thinking process and focus needed to finish the job of scoring also disappears. This is a typical error and when a miss occurs in such a situation, fans and coaches can't believe the missed opportunity and neither can the player who misses. The goalkeeper is counting his lucky stars and the striker usually prefers to go and hide somewhere. The eyes are so important and, as a coach, look to the eyes to see what's going on with the striker.

Reason 4, the striker thinking there is not a goal scoring opportunity, is a common problem and has been addressed extensively. Address reason 5 by reminding players that the more touches they take, the less chance of scoring they will have. In the case of a player coming through the middle but off to the side a bit, and the keeper coming out to challenge, every touch of the ball will put the shooter in a poorer angle to the goal. Also with every touch, the goalkeeper can take up to 3 to 5 steps to get closer to the shooter and reduce his shooting angles. Recall from chapter 64 that very few goals are scored on a goalkeeper when the keeper is 2 yards or less from the striker when shooting. Therefore, it's the keeper's mission to get as close to the shooter as possible. Each touch of the ball allows goalkeepers to get to that magical 2-yard distance from strikers who are about to shoot. It's amazing how fast a keeper can make up that distance with each touch of the ball that a striker takes. That distance closes fast especially when both parties are moving towards each other.

I have discussed reason 7, the highlight reel scenario, over and over. Reason 8 happens often with younger players. Players that try to dribble closer and closer to the goal will be unsuccessful as players get older and better at defending. Back-heels, other fancy moves and trying to do too much in the scoring area is usually going to result in failure. Tell your players to save the fancy stuff to celebrating the goal. Ask them to concentrate on doing the simple things right when presented with a scoring chance.

Coaching the Psychology of NOT Going Offside

Reason number 9 is new. I have written briefly about this in chapter 61 on through balls. Sometimes it takes a whole game to get a good goal scoring chance. I have seen time and time again cases where players are too eager or not aware of their surroundings and hence they break through past the last defender to receive a pass too early and go offside. It often negates a brilliant passing play or combination play that would have resulted in a great scoring chance. My editor Bernard Lecerf, who also coaches at Upper Canada College in Toronto and whose teams have won three National titles in a row at the private U13 boys tournaments, said that this is a much more important topic than I originally gave it credit for. Thinking about that for a second made me realize that he was correct. Young players in particular go offside a lot. Some players seem to always go offside. In the next few pages I want to present some ideas on how to get the message across to those players who tend to go offside too often. Avoiding going offside can make a great difference for some teams and players.

It's good that strikers are looking to find the space behind defenders to get into scoring positions but if they keep going offside, then they will become their own worst enemy in trying to score for the team. Before you go any further, make sure your players clearly understand the offside rule. You cannot correct an error if players are not clear on the offside law. It can be a confusing law for some, especially when some referees don't get it right all the time. I was recently watching an MLS game where the referee's assistant called an offside and negated a nice series of passes to create a potential chance. The replay clearly showed that the play was NOT offside but it was called. A young player may be confused by the rule when he follows your instructions and gets called offside.

But have you tried being the referee with the flag and had to call the play? It's not easy. While running or jogging to stay with the last defender, you also have to keep an eye on the attackers. But the hardest part is that you also have to see the ball and when it's played forward because it's at that instant that you have to decide which player or players are in an offside position. Then you have to wait to see if those players who are in an offside position actually get the ball. To top it off, there can be more than one player that you have to pay attention to at the same time to see if they are offside. This all happens in a matter of seconds and sometimes, your eyes have to switch back and forth between the ball and the last defenders, who, by the way, can change in a matter of seconds. What I'm saying is that it's not easy and there are bound to be errors. Your players need to understand this and don't let it affect their game.

How your attacking players avoid going offside can start with finding out the referee's position in the equation. Find out your situation in the league that you are playing in. Not all leagues, especially at the youth level, will have referee assistants to call offsides. If there are no referee assistants, then you may have to play the game a bit differently. Tell your strikers and attacking midfielders to hold that run a few extra seconds. Have your players be just a bit more patient even if they may be onside. This is because, on a close play, when a referee does not have assistants to call offside, he is most likely going to call a close play in favour of the defensive team. Many referees are taught that it's better to make a bad offside call than to give away a bad goal. Suggest to your strikers that maybe they can count 1000, 1001, 1002 in their head before the run to help make them hold their runs a bit more.

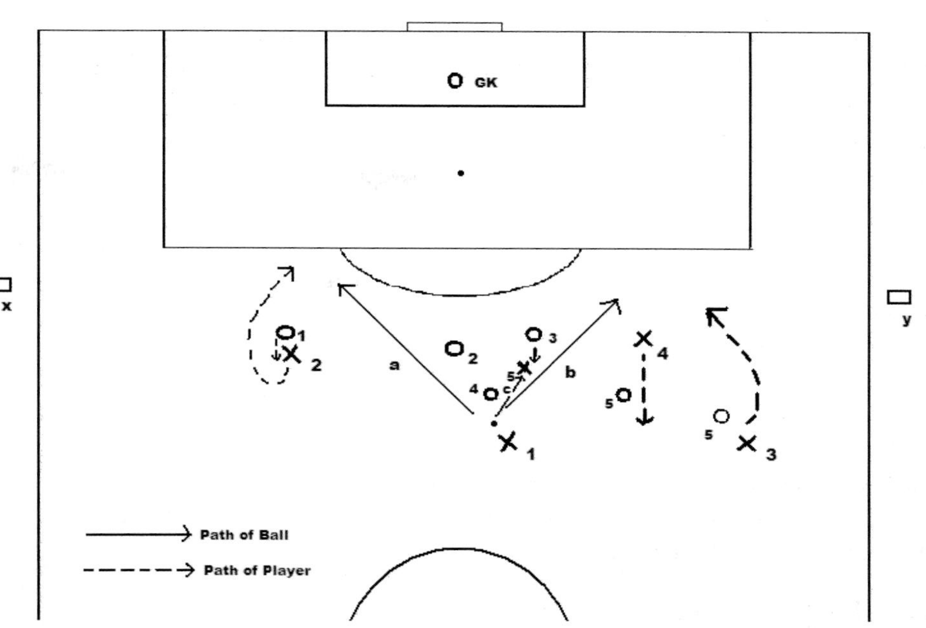

Diagram 74A: This diagram shows some different scenarios of players that can go off-side. X1 has the ball. X2, X3, X4, and X5 can all receive a pass. How can everyone who may get the last pass stay on side? What are some of the thoughts they can be thinking of to help them stay alert and onside?

Not going offside is often a case where the coach has to develop team strategies to beat teams that play the offside trap. Coaching your players to make sure they don't go offside within your strategies is what I want to cover. Timing is important. The striker's head needs to be on a swivel, as he keeps looking around to see if he is still onside. Quite often, your strikers come back to avoid an offside trap and your midfielders make advancing runs to collect passes that pierce the defense. They are more apt to stay onside since they can see more of the field in their runs. In diagram 74A, I have drawn different scenarios of different players who may receive a pass from the player with the ball (X1). In the example above, X3 can be the midfield player or fullback running forward to receive a ball past the last defenders from X1 (pass b). Still, players often make simple timing and mental errors that negate great scoring opportunities by going offside. I want to focus on the mental state of your players and offer some suggestions to help players who keep going offside.

Obviously, players running through defenders whether they are advancing midfielders, overlapping fullbacks, or strikers, need to time their runs to avoid getting behind the last defender before the ball is played forward. You may need to practice how to combat the offside trap with your team at training. Usually teams that like to play the offside trap will indicate that early in a game. As a coach, you may need to bring some key players over to alert your players of the opposition's strategies so that your attacking players change their mindset of how they will play the game. Going offside frequently often affects some players mentally and takes them out of the "zone". Some players get frustrated at themselves, the referees and their assistants, or their teammates for taking too long to play balls. Be quick to settle your players down so that they stay in the game mentally.

When making runs, a striker often has to straddle an imaginary line before breaking through as Filippo Inzaghi did in his breakaway goal at the 2006 World Cup. See diagram 61D from chapter 61 to recall how he makes a run sideways until the perfect moment to break through. Strikers have to be alert to where they are in relation to the other players on the field. Have them peek in both directions especially if their back is to the opposition's goal. Sometimes they need to come back towards their own goal before curling away from defenders to get in the space behind them as X2 does in diagram 74A.

In diagram 74A, X2 could be in a good position to receive a penetrating pass from teammate X1. Let's assume that all the defensive players, O1, O2, and O3 are all planning to move forward to catch the X players offside. X2 has to be careful not to mess up his one-on-one opportunity. Even if the marking player O1 is not pushing forward to play an offside trap, X2 must time his run perfectly. Think of what he needs to do. He needs to make sure he doesn't go offside by looking at all the defenders but which player is the most important? His marking player, O1 is the most important player to him. All he needs to do is make sure he is not offside with him and he will be safe. So what I'm suggesting is to make sure he remains onside with the closest player. This will be easier to do and now his next task is to time a run past O1 with his teammate's ability to send him a perfect ball. He can focus his attention on only two players, X1 and O1. He cannot break too soon. He can't be running through when his teammate, X1, is in no position to pass the ball.

For example, in a situation such as that in picture 74B, X2 cannot start to sprint forward at this instant assuming X1 is Giggs of Manchester United. He would have to wait for Giggs to step with his right foot to regain balance and push the ball forward and then be ready to take off as Giggs is set to get his left foot on the ball to pass it. But what if this player was a right footed player and rarely uses his left effectively? This is certainly a situation one would encounter with younger players. If that's the case, then the striker would have to hold his run even longer until Giggs would plant his left foot and then again bring his right foot up to make a pass. Is my striker really in "the zone" to pick the best moment to advance forward?

Picture 74B: Ryan Giggs of Manchester United has broken free of a defender and may have an opportunity to play a penetrating pass forward to a striker but he will need to regain his balance first on his next step before any passing attempt is possible. Can the striker time his run based on Ryan Giggs' movements? Photo by Les Jones/Covershots

Sometimes, there is no play because O1 is marking him closely and at other times there is. Many players may not have the speed to outrun a defender because often defenders are some of the fastest players on the team. When you combine a good central defender who can read the game well and has speed, your strikers will have to be very good at picking out precise moments to find space behind defenders while avoiding going offside. A defender who reads the game well will stay half turned while facing the ball and get a head start on beating a striker to a through ball. In such a case, the striker should try to get the defender as square as possible to the play so that he would have to make a complete 180 degree turn to try and track down and catch a striker running forward. The striker can do this by coming to meet the ball and taking the defender with him and then curling away to the defender's (O1 and O2) blind side as shown by the run of X2 in the diagram. The pass has to be played at the right time and perfectly (pass a). Running on the blind side of a defender keeps him and the ball carrier in the same view making it easier to see both of them over his right shoulder thus avoiding going offside.

To beat fast defenders who can read the game well, you may have to practice varying the type of balls that your midfield players play to your strikers. Young players have a tendency to run away from midfield players all the time expecting a through ball. At the younger ages a few fast players can provide your team with lots of goals. This habit will cause parents to be shouting "send it, send it" all game long. As defending players get better as they age, the constant through pass will not work as often because coaches will organize their defensive players better which may include playing the offside trap.

Train your strikers to receive the ball to their feet with their back to the goal. To vary your attack, have your midfielders give strikers the ball at their feet as they check and come towards the ball carrier. This will create numerous options and set up through balls later in a game by forcing a defender to come forward to follow a defender.

Now if X1 holds on to the ball too long and misses a great chance to send a player in on goal alone, then you'll need to talk to this player to make sure he finds teammates who are making the correct runs at the right time.

I had a super fast player who would often play in a central striker position as shown by X5 in diagram 74A but would always take off too early and always go offside. Despite telling him to hold his run and take a peek at the defenders to see where they were, he still kept going offside. He had problems coming back to meet the ball and always wanted to take off. It took constant training and repetition to get him to find the space to come back and meet the ball. He did well with that part of his game but when it was time to run for a through ball, he would take off too early or get beat by the offside trap by not knowing where the defenders were. He didn't even need a head start because he was so fast but he kept going offside because he didn't check to see where the defenders were. I suggested he take a peek to both sides of the field behind him very quickly before deciding. I told him to pretend to find his mom or dad standing on each side of the field to look at them quickly so that he would look both ways. I figured that would force him to look both ways and spot defenders and thus stay onside. In diagram 74A, I have marked these as x and y on the side of the field. Did this work? No. So after the next game, thinking that at 18 years old, looking for his parents wouldn't do the trick, I told him to picture two pretty girls, one at each side of the field and take a peek at them. Did this work? Much better. I had to get the message across some way so that he would turn his head to see where the defenders were so that he would avoid going offside.

As a coach, sometimes you practice making numerous passes to work the ball around only to create that final pass that sends a player through to get a chance to score. It will all be nullified if your players go offside. It happens so often that it is the number 9 reason as to why goals are not scored and once you figure out what's going wrong, do your best to communicate with the player who is most responsible for the team going offside. Be creative. You know that because that's just part of coaching. I'd like to hear your stories so e-mail me your most creative coaching moments at www.goldengoalscoring@rogers.com regardless of the problem.

10th and Final Reason why Goals are NOT Scored

The 10th and final reason why goals are not scored is "the panic attack". Some strikers get "panic attacks" when there is a chance to score. There are usually defenders nearby but not always near enough to stop them from scoring. Some players' bodies tense up and this causes skill to deteriorate. Players who don't get many scoring opportunities often panic when they get a chance because they feel that a defender is closer to them then they really are. Defenders moving forward usually encounter these situations. Make sure everyone gets a chance to practice shooting because you never know who will get the chance to score in a game. The chapters on handling stress earlier in the book will help players deal with stress-related problems that I classify as a "panic attack".

Excuses, Excuses!

There are many times when there are good reasons why your strikers will not score. You can't be negative with your strikers so it's good to allow them to have acceptable excuses for not scoring. Here are some acceptable excuses for missing goals or not scoring. This is what I tell my strikers in regards to acceptable excuses and how I explain it to them.

Top 5 Acceptable Excuses for not Scoring

1) "The Goalkeeper Made a Great Save."

"You need to congratulate the goalkeeper when he truly made a good save. But at the same time, you have to look forward to your next chance and make it a challenge. If you keep hitting the goalkeeper or he keeps stopping you, then you may need to do more to try and read the keeper's body motions. Make a conscious effort after each missed attempt to identify what the keeper did to stop you based on my classifications on human body motion. What position was the keeper in when he stopped you? Was the keeper in motion, stationary, or in a positive or negative stationary motion position? Once you think this through, what could you have done better? Don't miss this opportunity to analyze your performance and consciously think about what you will do next time. This is a great learning situation. Don't miss it by not thinking about it and just feeling that the goalkeeper was amazing or you messed up."

2) "Weather, Field Conditions"

"Sometimes there is nothing you can do if the elements are against you. A missed chance could be the result of a wet field, rain, snow, sleet, mud, the sun, or an unlucky bounce on the field. Life goes on so don't worry about it. In the case of a wet field, you may want to adjust your run patterns knowing that the ball may skid as it comes towards you. In a muddy pitch you may need to lift the ball off the ground a bit to avoid the mud from stopping the ball from rolling into the goal. Apart from these small adjustments, consider that it's just part of the game and enjoy the rest of the game."

3) "Referees, Fouls, and Physical Contact"

"Hopefully, if there was a foul, the referee will settle things properly. Don't lose your composure and concentration if the referee does not make the call because losing your composure can cost you a goal later in the game. Think about this for a second: I'll bet you that you will miss more scoring chances because of your mistakes than because of a referee's mistakes. Things happen fast and the referee can't always see everything clearly. Referees are also human and make mistakes. Do not let referees' decisions take you out of the game mentally or physically because of a red card. In both cases, whether you're out of the game mentally or physically as a result of a red card, you will not be able to score a goal that can change your career. One goal at the right time can be huge for you. Five of my players got scouted to the Toronto Blizzard reserve squad because of their performance in one game when the Toronto Blizzard head coach and assistant coaches Bob Houghton and Colin Toal were at the game." (Picture of my 1984 team in Appendix E) ***"Don't blow it.***

Physical contact is often part of the game. Don't let this affect your game. You must be brave and courageous to be a great goal scorer. If you score you can be the one person who can cause the other team to lose or be responsible for a player losing a spot on his team. Expect to get played physically. Put yourself in the other player's position under the circumstances I just gave you. Would you not be physical? Defenders often play physical right from the start to let you know that they are there and thus they will try to put you off your game early. It's part of the game, get used to it."

Illegal tactics by defenders such as committing physical fouls or fouls such as pulling the shirt are a common problem strikers need to get used to. In picture 74C, Kaka of Brazil gets his shirt pulled by US player Benny Feilhaber. Notice how hard it would be for a referee standing behind Kaka or to the side of them to notice the tug.

Picture 74C: Benny Feilhaber of the U.S. tries to stop Kaka of Brazil during their Confederations Cup final soccer match in Johannesburg, South Africa. Illegal tactics by defenders is an excuse that you can accept from your strikers. Hopefully, the officials will penalize the culprits. Picture Supplied by Action Images/Rogan Ward

Also in today's game, it seems that both strikers and defenders are using their arms to impede the progress of their opponents more than I've ever seen. Scenes like those in picture 74D, where players are holding each other, are very familiar. Some strikers get so upset if fouls are not called against them that it affects their game as they waste more energy arguing with the referee than getting on with the game (picture 74E). Tell your strikers to expect physical play against them and make sure it does not affect their mental state. Different personalities will be affected differently and sometimes the opposing team may have scouted the opposition and know which players are more likely to lose focus and as such try to put them off their game.

Picture 74D: Adrian Cann of Toronto FC has a good grasp of the striker he is marking from the Portland Timbers. Les Jones/Covershots

Picture 74E: In this photo the player is more concerned with the referee's decision than getting on with the game. Strikers can't let referee's decisions affect their game and take them out of "the zone." Photo by Philip Yates

Dealing with Injuries

Strikers are more apt to get injuries than are any other players on the team. This is because of the influence that they can impart on a game. They can lose a game for the opponent. They can beat a defender and that defender can get replaced if they get beaten too often. The goalkeeper's career is at stake if he lets in too many goals. In such a low scoring game as soccer, there are a lot of things at stake with every goal especially at the higher levels. It's hard for defenders to give up goals and thus they will get very physical to prevent them. As much as it is unfair sportsmanship to purposely bring a player down to stop a goal scoring chance, it will happen. That's because the defenders feel that they may get away without being called at all. If the referee does make a call against them, their team may have less chance of giving up a goal from a free kick than by allowing the striker to shoot.

Consequently, strikers will get injured. If the injury was painful and put them out of action for a while, it can play on the strikers' mental state in the future as stated in chapter 69. Rafi Srebro, in his book *Winning with your Head*, states that "Every body injury comes with injury to the mind." In his book he offers great advice on how to overcome injuries. Psychologically, players may recall the sound of a tackle resulting in a major bruise, ligament tear, or fracture whenever they are placed in a similar environment with similar conditions. Often they may need some psychological aid in overcoming their fears because they will try to avoid that situation in the future.

In fact, this is often a very big issue with players. The worse the injury was, the harder it will be for that particular player to do the exact same thing that put him in the situation where he got injured. For example, if the player who got injured was cutting to his inside with the left foot when he received the serious knee injury, then he will tend to avoid making that cut after his recovery. This will occur even if a similar cut provided most of his goal scoring chances before the injury. There is a fear factor in the brain that remembers traumatic moments. New information is coming out regularly on traumatic injuries or experiences. In the latest research, scientists may have identified a portion of the brain that stores this information and they are working on inhibiting the negative feelings that occur when this area of the brain is recalled.

Here are more excuses I accept from my strikers and what I tell them.

4) "Great Defensive Plays and Blocks"

"Just like you may congratulate a goalkeeper for making a great save, you can congratulate a defender for making a great clean defensive play to stop you from scoring. Maybe they blocked a shot or didn't get fooled by you, but in all cases get excited about the next opportunity to score and keep doing what you know will work. Don't try fancy things on your next chance just because of a great defensive play."

Now if on the other hand, your strikers get beaten by defenders who may seem to make great plays but they are a result of a bad decision by your strikers, then this is not an acceptable excuse. This is why it is important for them to learn to analyze their performance right away. After the game you may want to check with your strikers to see if their self analysis of specific plays matched your observations.

5) "Deflections and Misses due to Timing"

"You will miss chances by the slightest of seconds or inches. You may have gotten somewhere a split second too late to score but gave it your best to get there. Or there may have been a deflection that caused you to miss a goal. These things happen and don't worry about them. Try and learn from them to see what you could have done better, and then get excited for the next chance to score."

No More Excuses!

There you have it, the only excuses I'll accept from players for not scoring. And just so they don't use these excuses as a crutch, I have a list of 6+ not acceptable excuses for them. Here is what I tell players about non-acceptable excuses.

1) "I misplayed the ball."

"You cannot misplay the ball if you want to be a great goal scorer. Keep your eyes on the ball and focus on it on your last touch."

2) "I had no chance to shoot."

"You were not prepared to score!"

3) "I missed the goal by inches."

"Nice, but the last time I looked, the net did not move! You didn't aim for the right spots."

4) "I didn't expect the rebound."

"Why not? You want to be a great striker. Always expect a rebound. Tell yourself that there will be one and try and predict where it would be if there were one. In that case, whenever there is one, you will score."

5) "The ball was spinning or too hard."

"You were not prepared to score!"

6) "A whole bunch of other excuses."

"If you are saying things like, 'I just missed' or 'got there too late' or' too early' or 'I was covered' or 'just a step away', then you're not reading the game correctly. To solve some of these problems go over my rules to scoring on crosses, through balls, positioning, and reading human motion. Focus on your positioning and your mental aspect of the game. Small adjustments can turn close calls into goals. When you practice, take it seriously and analyze yourself rather than just ignore the situation. Make every chance at practice a learning opportunity.

Always give yourself a reason why you missed. Ask yourself, what could you have done that would have resulted in a goal instead of a miss? Blame yourself for missing but ask why? Don't get down on yourself. Look to finding the answer and then look forward to the next challenge where you can try to concentrate more on scoring.

Always look forward to the next challenge. The thrill of 'I can't wait to try it again' should be stronger than the urge to think 'Oh no, I don't want to look bad and miss again'. It's all about staying positive and looking forward to challenging yourself until you get it right. Once you get it right, it will leave you with an amazing feeling!"

The psychology of this section is to make your strikers realize that in the top 10 reasons why goals are not scored, not once does it state that it's because the goalkeeper or defender made a great play. I don't want strikers to keep blaming their inability to score on the goalkeeper or defenders. The goalkeeper cannot humanly save everything. He can and should give his opponents a pat on the back when they do a good job. Tell your strikers to congratulate their opponents for outsmarting them and challenge them to get excited for their next opportunity. Do your strikers have the skills to analyze their performance? These are very important personal skills. Do not forget to use some of the secrets to scoring as presented in this book. Like a magician, tell them to keep them as secrets.

CHAPTER 75

The Last Words

I hope I have cleared up some uncertainties about scoring goals. I have provided you with clear statistics and given in-depth psychologically based information for you to use to teach your players how to become effective at scoring goals. I hope that I have inspired you to read more books on sport psychology and find new ways to help your players make better decisions on the field to develop better strikers. Raw talent can never be replaced but when two players of equal talent are pitted against each other, the smarter player will always win in most sports. Sometimes the less talented player will overcome the player with more raw talent simply because of his mental makeup. I think this is more applicable for players in some positions than others. In my opinion, the strikers and goalkeepers are two positions where the psychology becomes very important in performance. I have seen many instances where less talented strikers who score goals get starting positions over more talented strikers who do not score.

For every rule I have pointed out there are probably going to be cases where the rule does not work. Players will always challenge you to find an exception to the rules. That smart kid will always point it out to you and try to make you look bad. That's just part of coaching. With some players, certain things will work while with others they may not, especially as it applies to psychology. I have given lectures on the material in this book to coaches and I have found that some coaches have not used it to their best advantage. Maybe they didn't "get it" completely or didn't deliver the message properly. If needed, go over the material again to understand the concepts. Just like a comedian relies on good timing and delivery of his comedy, the coach must work on the timing and delivery of the psychological material he provides the strikers. It can make a huge difference in how your strikers take in the information provided.

Before going out and using this material, realize that not all the points are good for every player. Also realize that too much information can confuse players. Strategically present key points to your strikers at the right time and try to deliver them to your key players one on one. In fact, within your own team, one striker may need some information from one chapter in this book while another would be much better with information from another part of the book. Trying to impress your players with all the information in this book is not what I have set out to do by writing it. I want you to use this book as a reference guide to help you help your players improve as strikers and deal with certain problems that your strikers may be having with a part of their game. Your players will be more successful and so will you as a coach. Practice your delivery. If you have attended any of my lectures you will notice that I try to deliver the message in the most powerful way that will make the player remember what to do in the most important time of the game. That is in "The Last 9 Seconds" prior to the most important moment of all, which is at the moment of "The Last Touch".

Generally, goal scoring is going down. Oh no! In the 2002 World Cup there were 161 goals scored and in the 2006 World Cup there were 147 goals scored. That's almost a 10% decrease. A further decrease in the number of goals occurred in the FIFA 2010 World Cup (See article on the next page, which was published in *Soccer Journal* and *Soccer 360 Magazine*).

Technology

Technological advances in the game seem to address two main areas of concern; safety and increasing goal scoring. Better shin pads are meant to protect players more. Better nutritional information including education on hydration and eating habits, injury prevention, and rehabilitation are all geared for safety. Players are more aware of nutritional requirements today than they were 20 years ago and new and better training methods are making players run for longer distances and longer periods of time at higher speeds than ever before. Dick Bate of the English FA in his lecture at the NSCAA coaches conference in St. Louis said that the future of the game is heading towards fitter and faster players. Coaches are demanding more running from them with more sprints per game. In his analysis, he found that it is normal for all players to run 13 km per game, 50% more than in 1965. He stated that in the English Premier League, the number of sprints a player makes per game has doubled since 2002. He also stated that defenders cover similar distances at high speed but less overall distances than attackers and wide players. Coaches are demanding that players run back and defend in numbers and new training methods have allowed them to do so.

All these things seem to be adding to the reduction in goals. And then there are the shoes. They are lighter with the idea that they help players run faster and move quicker, which will presumably help increase goal scoring. But there can be a flaw in this as I stated in this article which has been published in different publications.

GOALS AT WORLD CUP ARE DOWN AGAIN: IT MUST BE THE SHOES!

Another World Cup has come to an end and the number of goals scored in the competition is down again. Since 1998, when they allowed 32 teams in the finals, the number of goals scored has dropped steadily. In 1998 there were 171 goals scored in 64 games. In 2002, it went down to 161 goals and in 2006 it dropped even further to 147. And just when we figured that the new Adidas Jabulani ball was going to give the goalkeepers nightmares and result in more goals being scored, the opposite happened. In the 2010 World Cup, the total of goals scored dropped down to only 145. What has gone wrong?

Those who have been to any of my "Psychology of Goal Scoring" or "Secrets to Goal Scoring" lectures or courses would be looking for me to explain the drop in goal scoring, but they also know that I would probably come up with a most unique and thought provoking explanation. So, not to disappoint, let me give you something to ponder on the subject of why goals were down at the 2010 Men's FIFA World Cup.

First of all, let me state some of the obvious reasons as to why goals are down. To start with, athletes today are fitter than ever. Players are able to run at top speeds longer and faster than before. Advances in physiology, nutrition, and training methodology have allowed players to get fitter meaning that coaches can demand players to get back to defend in numbers more often and faster than ever before. No doubt this will have an effect on the number of goals teams give up over time. For example, trying to get past 7 players to get an attempt at goal is a lot easier than trying to get past 10 players to get a chance to score. The math is simple.

Another reason may be that third-world soccer countries are no longer easy to beat. For example, who would have thought that New Zealand would be the only team not to lose a game at the 2010 World Cup? When teams are fit, organized, and can defend well, they can upset any of the top nations or reduce the number of goals that they give up so that they do not have to go home feeling embarrassed. These two factors are probably the main reason why goals are down.

But on the other hand, one would assume that the new ball would have increased the number of goals scored at the World Cup. Goalkeepers have complained about the ball and in the 2010 World Cup I saw an unusual amount of goalkeeping errors that resulted in goals. Had those errors not occurred there would have been even less goals scored. Having said all that, I want to look at one other factor that may be affecting goals scored and that is the new shoes that the players are wearing today. Yes, the shoes! I think, they add to the equation a little bit.

I think that they are too flashy, colourful, and noticeable. The bright oranges and yellows that we see in a lot of the shoes that the players are wearing are easy to spot on the pitch. The eye can locate these colours quickly when there is motion involved. That can be motion of the player wearing the shoes or motion by a defending player. In fact, yellow as has been shown to be one of the most noticeable colors in the color spectrum when motion is involved. Bright orange is not far behind. This is simple to test. Next time you are in a vehicle, notice how quickly the eye can spot a yellow car, van, or truck. Also notice that the construction pylons are usually orange. This is not done by accident. When a car is moving, the driver can spot the bright orange pylons very quickly. These colors are picked so that drivers in motion avoid running over construction workers.

I believe that defenders are quick to find players that they need to cover when their opponents wear bright orange or yellow shoes. It's harder for an attacking player to disappear from the field of vision of a marking player because he can quickly pick out where he is in his peripheral vision because of his shoes!

Coaches talk to their strikers about getting on the "blind side" of defenders so that they can elude them. Getting on the "blind side" of a defender means getting to a position where they can't be seen. Coaches ask players to make "blind side runs" all the time meaning that they want their players to run behind defenders so that they can't be spotted until it's too late. Well that's all fine and dandy, but when players show up with bright colored shoes that can be spotted a mile away, what's the point of this whole coaching point? Wearing bright coloured shoes will make it even easier for the defender to find his man.

At the highest levels, a fraction of a second can be the difference between scoring and not scoring, winning and losing. Why would a striker in particular, want to give away any possible advantage?

So there you have it, my theory on why goal scoring was down at the 2010 World Cup but I expect goal scoring to be up at the next World Cup because this article will make its way to coaches around the world and they will ban their strikers from wearing bright colored shoes. Oh, and the fact that these new shoes are so lightweight, well, that's a whole other topic.

With every World Cup, Adidas comes out with new and better soccer balls with the intent of increasing the true flight of a ball and its ability to cut through air so that more goals can be scored. Eliminating stitches and seams helps reduce friction but in all cases, the main goal is to improve goal scoring. As you can see from the above article, that has not necessarily been the case.

Some of the biggest new developments have come from soccer shoes. The idea of making them lighter is based on the fact that if a lighter shoe increases foot speed, then a player will be able to increase the power of his shot. Also, a lighter shoe should allow players to run faster. But a lighter weight shoe also compromises on safety especially if a player gets stepped upon or is in a collision due to a hard tackle. We will see if there will be increases in foot injuries over time. Manufacturers are convinced that the stability of the shoe is just as strong with the new lightweight synthetics as it is with leathers. Lighter shoes can also cause a slight problem in the beginning as players swing their foot to kick a ball. Their timing may be off as they will be swinging a lighter object. While this may cause some initial problems, our brain has the capacity to make motor muscular corrections to fix this problem rather quickly with training. Just as tennis players quickly adjusted to lighter tennis rackets, golfers adjusted to lighter golf clubs, and hockey players adjusted to lighter hockey sticks, soccer players will make quick adjustments to lighter soccer shoes.

Most of the shoe advancements including lighter shoes have focused on players getting more power in their shots. But as you know by now, this is one of the problems of least concern when scoring. The biggest issue when strikers kick the ball is to hit the ball accurately and direct the ball at the net. It's more about accuracy than anything else. None of the shoe manufacturer's have made a big dent in this area. The major manufacturers such as Adidas, Nike, Puma, and Umbro have just touched on the subject.

The curve of the typical shoe follows the shape of the foot which is opposite to the curve of the ball. This makes the sweet spot for contact between the ball and the shoe very small allowing errors to occur. A new shoe company called Concave has redesigned the soccer shoe to make the shoe's sweet spot follow the curve of the ball. Their concept is so revolutionary that while patenting their shoe, they also had to check with FIFA to see if their shoe would be legal. FIFA has given it the go-ahead and players in the EPL have now started using the shoe. The Concave shoe is so different that I included it in this book because it actually addresses one of the top reasons (missing the target) why goals are not scored. It's shown in picture 75A. The shoe also provides a larger surface area when using the inside of the foot for passing a ball into the goal. Will it revolutionize future soccer shoes? Will it actually produce results? Will players like it? Only time will tell.

While these technological advances may help, most players will still need to practice their game from a technical, tactical, strategic, and psychological standpoint as pointed out in this book. For many of the technical or skill related

Picture 75A: Concave, the manufacturer of this new shoe, has made the front part of the shoe that makes contact with the ball, larger and opposite to the curvature of the foot but similar to the curvature of the ball. Concave, had to receive permission from FIFA to ensure the shoe was legal according to FIFA's "Laws of the Game" before going into marketing and production of the shoe. FIFA stated that it was a legal shoe according to their laws. The idea is that the larger front plate will increase accuracy when shooting. The theory is that the ball will adjust to the concave shape of the front of the shoe. As the ball makes contact with the shoe, it will adjust itself and leave the foot with more accuracy. Photo thanks to Jim Grimes, president of Concave Sports.

factors that affect goal scoring, players cannot substitute for the amount of practice and time needed in order to get better. But the mental aspect of goal scoring can be learned quickly and powerfully and can be long lasting. Most of my thoughts and ideas in this book should give you ways to help your strikers make more correct decisions when presented with goal scoring opportunities.

The Last Pass

Among the many different issues that may affect strikers, there is also the important issue of the ball that's played to the striker from his teammate. Good midfield players or associate strikers who can feed strikers perfect passes can make a huge difference in the number of goals scored by your team. Even if your striker's makes correct decisions all the time, they won't be able to score if the service they receive is not good. Think about this for a second; most goals are scored on "one touch" and that number is going up. At Euro 2008, a whopping 82% of goals were scored on only "one touch".

It's probably going up because there are more players to go through in order to get a scoring chance. Nutritional advances along with training and fitness advances allow for fitter players who can come back to defend in numbers faster. This means that there is less time and space around the box to get scoring chances. Also, fitter and faster players are harder to beat. And finally, as Robert Iarusci, former defender for the New York Cosmos and current sports analyst on a Toronto sports radio station pointed out, defenders who use illegal tactics to defend are getting away with it more and more. Either due to illegal methods of stopping players or better individual and team defending tactics, players rarely get beat one on one anymore with dazzling dribbles. That's sad but what has developed because of this is the new art of passing. Passing is not new but the importance placed on the last pass to create the goal is now regarded as a thing of beauty. It's no longer ignored.

If 80% of goals are scored on "one touch", then the previous touch by the teammate who delivered the ball to the striker who scored the goal becomes critical. That final pass has become so important. David Beckham has made the art of passing the ball like a work of art. Although it was always important, somehow, he has made young players bask in the glory of making that perfect pass, hasn't he? The beauty of soccer can be found in all sorts of aspects of the game and skills needed to play it but passing has traditionally not been as exciting to watch and appreciated as it is today.

The First 9 Seconds

For strikers, the ability to receive a ball, hold it, shield it, and then make a pass is vital because they are often the start of an attack. When they act as target players it is important for them to be in the zone. I call this the "first 9 seconds" of each goal. Strikers tend to have a key passing role in most goals including their own. They may start many of their own goals and the goals of their teammates whenever they are target men for the start of an attack. They may have to make a pass to keep an attack going after they receive the ball early in the attack. And they are quite likely to make the "last pass" for the "one touch" goal that a teammate will score. And sometimes, that "last pass" is the best option for the strikers. Here is what I say to players in this regard.

> ***"Don't shoot when there is no shot at all to score. This can deprive your team of a chance to score. Yes, you have to be selfish as a goal scorer but the 'last pass' is still very important. Hopefully your teammates will score when you pass them a ball that creates a scoring chance for your team. In fact, you may still end up being the goal scorer on***

that chance because you may score off a rebound from the goalkeeper. Be ready at all times for that. So often the passer ends up being the goal scorer. Many of the world's top goal scorers score this way. It's almost an art to score off rebounds by anticipating an unexpected chance. Remember that when you scored from a rebound the statistics will still say it's your goal regardless of how difficult or easy it looked.

Also when you pass the ball to a teammate when you should, he will reciprocate when he should by passing the ball to you instead of shooting. This will in turn increase your chances to score. When a teammate provides you with a scoring chance, remember to focus on your job and 'the last touch' to score. If you don't get the ball when you should, don't get disappointed. If that player keeps making bad decisions, he won't be on your team too long. So doing your job to set up teammates to score will help your game because you will also get great balls from teammates to score from. Getting in the game mentally to receive the ball when it arrives to start an attack is what I call the 'first 9 seconds' of each goal. It takes good concentration to make that great 'last pass' because it can lead to a goal. It all starts with teamwork."

The High Angle Camera

The statistics, facts, and psychological ideas I have presented are meant to give the players in the position to score an instant high angle camera in their head so they can see themselves on the field. I want my strikers to see themselves on the pitch from the high angle camera position when they are in a scoring position with the ball with a decision to be made. And by use of the psychological cues provided in this book, hopefully your strikers will make the right decisions to score more often.

Words and Secrets from "The King, Pele"

My goal scoring sessions and courses have changed a bit over time. I continue to experiment and learn what works best with both players and coaches. I must say that, as I have been on this mission to write this book and lecture on this topic, I have had great feedback from players and coaches and have also received many great ideas from coaches as well. The results from the players I have worked with have been truly amazing and almost unbelievable. It's been a wonderful journey and I have met some great people in the process. (You can check out some of their photos and quotes in the appendix.)

And one of those people is "The King" himself, Pele, who is also the best person to ask about the secrets to scoring goals. So I did just that. I had the opportunity to meet Pele personally for the very first time in New York City while he was there for his 70th birthday and to re-launch the world famous New York Cosmos and introduce his new brand of footwear and apparel called Pele Sports. In my chance to meet him I was picked to ask him a question for the audience and of course, I wanted to know his secret to scoring goals (picture 75B). While he gave a great answer, I don't think he gave it all away just as I expected. See a video of his answer to my question on my website at www.thelast9seconds.com or at www.goldengoalscoring.com.

Pele's answer was geared to the technical side of things and he stressed the importance of practicing things over and over. But his answer was a secret if you pick out exactly what he was saying in his own way. He said that his father was very good at heading the ball and scored lots of goals with his head so Pele, wanting to be like his father, practiced heading the ball to score. For someone who is 5'8" tall, he scored a large number of goals with his head. He questioned why a taller player such as Christiano Ronaldo does not score more goals with his head. He worked hard to practice this element of his game. He also realized that the left foot should be equally dangerous as his right for opposing defenders and goalkeepers, so he practiced this over and over as well.

That was the secret he shared with everyone there. I knew he wouldn't talk about where to shoot or what he was thinking in his head as he had a chance to score. It probably came to him instinctively or maybe it needed to stay a secret a bit longer. But he did say that being able to kick with both feet meant that he would always be prepared to kick the ball at the goal regardless of which foot the ball went to. This makes so much sense because, if most goals are going to be scored on only one touch, then it becomes imperative for a striker to be prepared to score with either foot because at least half (50%) of the chances to score with the feet would have to come to each foot. The chance to score cannot only go to one foot. That would be impossible so if a player cannot use both feet, then he will only be able to score on 50% of the chances that are available for him to score goals from that can be converted by the foot. In addition, a striker needs to be very good at heading the ball or he will not be able to score between 20 and 30% of <u>all</u> goals scored in soccer.

Picture 75B: I asked Pele his Secret to Scoring Goals in New York (Photo by Ian Gibson)

Pele made his point and he continues to promote the game at every opportunity. I thank you for taking the time to read this book and I want to remind you that the game of soccer and all that it has to offer is about fun, enjoyment, passion, health, and friendships that are built through the game for life. "The beautiful game" as Pele once said, says it all.

"Intuition"

Just recently York University won the National Championship; 31 years after my team won it. York soccer director at the time and former Canadian National Team player Paul James invited the alumni from our team to a special event to honour our accomplishment along with the new team's championship victory under coach Carmine Isacco. At the event I met old teammates. We have had a special bond that remains to this day. We see each other every few years for some reason or another. At the event I told my former teammates about my upcoming book on goal scoring. When I discussed the concept of the book with a former striker, Aldo D'Alfonso, who went on to play in the NASL for the Toronto Blizzard for a short time, he said, "In one appearance as a sub, I missed a great scoring chance that I should have scored on. If I had scored on that opportunity, I may have been given more chances to play regularly. You don't get many chances to prove yourself at the pro level."

The striker position is unforgiving. You don't get many chances in the big leagues to prove yourself. For a North American player, to get a chance to play in the NASL in those days as a striker was an accomplishment when all the striker positions were taken up by foreign players like Pele, Cryuff, Best, Eusebio, and Müller. D'Alfonso went on to offer this about strikers, "To me, goal scoring is about 'intuition'. You have to have intuition".

I'm glad he mentioned those words to me because I'm saying the same thing in Part 2 of this book. He summed up what I wrote about when I stated that some of the superstars and natural strikers seem to have that something special. It's intuition. The point that I want to make is if you see such a player, please leave him alone. If a player instinctively can do it, don't coach it. There will be other areas of his game to coach but don't mess with "intuition". Do not use very much of the psychological material you have read in this book because you'll probably just confuse him and take away his free play, improvisation abilities and "intuition". He doesn't need the extra help. Be brave enough to identify this athlete, don't over-coach him and let him have fun.

The Last Word

I want to end with something that should stay in the back of your mind all the time as you coach your strikers.

I recall playing a game of ice hockey (old timers) and in a key moment of a play-off game I took the puck up the wing and blasted a slap shot in the top corner of the net beating the goalie cleanly. It was a highlight reel goal if there ever was one, at least for me because, as a defender, I rarely score. We won the game on that goal and everyone was talking about it in the dressing room. It felt great! The players jumped on me on the ice after the goal. My teammates kept talking about my booming shot, which was a shock to all of them. They kept talking about the goal at the bar after the game even though I wanted them to stop.

When I went home that night I wasn't just feeling good, I was feeling great! It's one of those goals I'll never forget even if I had scored it at a less opportune time. The fact that it was "one of those goals" and beating the goalie felt great. I'm not one to go around bragging about my goals so I didn't bring it up at work the next day. But the very next day I met a client, Dale Russell, who had played a soccer game the day before. We talked about different things until I came up to the question of how his soccer team was doing. Well, that was just the cue he was looking for. Dale was in a great mood and probably couldn't wait to tell me. He told me that he scored the "best goal in Canada" that most people have ever seen. You could tell from his expression that he was delighted to tell me about it and even wanted to make sure I believed him by having his friend who was with him verify that he actually did score this goal. Of course his friend agreed with him that this was one of the best goals he had ever witnessed.

He explained it as a goal that came directly off a corner kick where he had to do a bicycle kick from outside the box in order to score. He was so excited about this goal and was thrilled that it was caught on camera. He wanted to bring it in to me to show me. Everyone likes talking about great accomplishments or having others talk about it. It's human nature.

After he left I realized, having scored my own highlight reel goal in hockey the night before, that in our own way, we were both rejuvenated about playing the sport. In fact, I couldn't wait for the next game. After that highlight reel goal I wanted to go play hockey again as soon as possible. This exhilarating feeling came over me. I'm sure it was the same emotion that Dale was feeling. This made me realize that highlight reel goals are actually a powerful incentive to go out and play more, play hard, and practice so that players can score more of them. It helps them build up the passion for the game. For the goalkeeper, it may be about making a great save. But even defenders and midfielders, even if just at practice or in that rare occasion in a game, the feeling of exhilaration and excitement that comes with scoring a highlight reel goal is infectious.

It's really what fans, players, the sport itself, wait for and need. It keeps us coming back for more. It's probably the backbone of sport as we see it in our media inspired world. But it also provides a great feeling of accomplishment and energy to do more, play more, and enjoy the game more. Keep this psychological fact in the back of your mind as you **teach** your players to play and **inspire** your players to **love to play** the game of soccer.

Enjoy the coaching experience and thanks for reading,

John DeBenedictis

FIELD EXERCISES
TESTIMONIALS
MEMORIES
FRIENDS
AND CLOSING REMARKS
APPENDIX

APPENDIX A

Field Exercises for Strikers

Practicing to become a better goal scorer is not as simple as it seems. Players that play other positions can go practice ball control and dribbling moves all the time on their own. A game can often break out in a nearby park and usually players put a couple of bags at each end to make small goals and the game goes on without real goalkeepers. Players can practice passing, dribbling, defending and moving into space or looking to support each other, all of which is part of a strikers tools to succeed, but the opportunity to score on a real goal with a real goalkeeper usually only takes place at practice with the rest of the team.

Also, since the coach has to deal with all the players on the team and the different aspects of the game, the striker does not get enough <u>specific</u> training. The main problem with a potential striker who wants to go out on his own to practice scoring is that if 82 out of every 100 goals are scored on just one touch, as per the statistics from Euro 2008, that means that in all those cases, the ball came from someone else and from somewhere. That means that another person is essential for training how to become a good goal scorer. To be realistic, it's hard to practice goal scoring on your own. You can't practice redirects, crosses, heading or just about any skill without help. But somehow, the striker has to make the best of this situation and what I have devised in all my field sessions are a series of drills or exercises that strikers can use to practice their scoring skills when they are alone or with a friend. In some cases, I have devised exercises with 2 friends. These exercises are meant to challenge and motivate the striker to go out on their own to perfect their craft.

I also show strikers how to take ordinary drills that they do with their team and convert them to their own scoring exercises. It's more about getting your striker to continuously focus on consistency in doing things that can be like scoring a goal. Passing, for example should be a skill that any striker considers as a goal scoring exercise. Get your striker to focus more than other players on executing the skills and be sharper mentally than any other player on your team at practice.

Challenge your strikers to take advantage of players who may be loose in practice to continuously get in the habit of doing the simple things right when it comes to scoring and passing so that they read every players state of consciousness in practice. For example, have them ascertain if one player is weaker because he may not be practicing as hard as he should. Expect your striker to take advantage of this all the time in practice. The key point is to get your strikers to identify body language of defenders so that it can help them pry on the weak in games.

I say this to players in my Golden Goal Scoring Academy course:

> ***"Practice to score on an empty goal often because if you can't score a goal without a goalkeeper in the goal, under no pressure, then how do you expect to score in a game when there is a goalkeeper in the game?***
>
> ***On the journey to become a better goal scorer, I will not show you how to become better at the skill of shooting but I will teach you the skill of scoring."***

Here is a simple drill that I teach my strikers to do on their own with a friend. They don't even need a goal. It can be fun especially when friends challenge each other. They can do it in a patch of grass. This drill was first introduced to me by Tony Waiters at a clinic that he did for coaches of young recreational players. The coaches, including me, at his session when he first introduced it were enjoying the drill. For the longest time, we didn't want to stop. It is such a simple drill but if two friends challenge each other as my partner and I were, it was fun. The drill is in his book, *Coaching 6, 7, & 8 Year Olds*.

Two players stand at opposite ends of a pylon and pass the ball to each other as shown in picture A1. If there is a circle around the pylon made out of disc cones or a circle on a field, then it's better. Starting with passing, the object of the game is for players to pass the ball and knock down the pylon in the middle. Also, to prevent "hospital balls",

Picture A1: In this exercise, two players, on opposite sides of a circle try and pass the pass through the circle and hit and knock down the pylon in the middle. They need to put enough power on their passes so that the ball exits the circle in order for it to count. The first to 3 wins.

Picture A2: Hit it! A good pass in this case as Alex Von Gemmingen hits the pylon to score a point. Thanks to Tony LaFerrara, Shelly Augustin, Mike Amato, and Mike Cancellara from the Pickering Soccer Club for allowing me to use the field for this photo shoot. Jan Lang is the receiving player and I'm the photographer.

Picture A3: The players move back and make this a shooting exercise. The emphasis here is to keep the ball low in order to hit the pylon. This simple drill can keep two or even three players practicing their scoring for hours without the need for a goal.

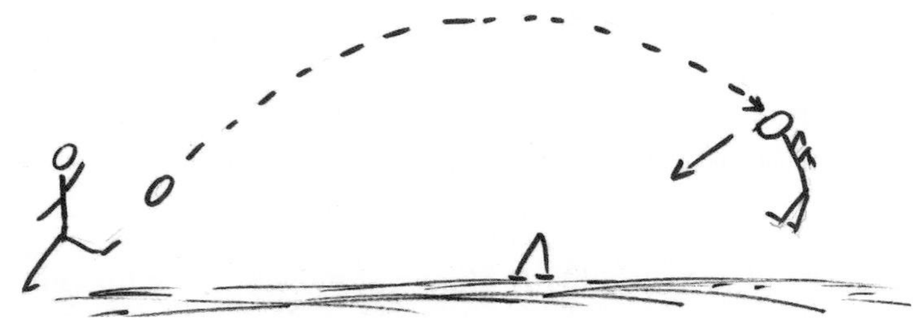

Diagram A4: This exercise is similar to the exercises before this one, except that this time one player passes the ball to his partner in the air who moves inside the circle to head the ball down to hit the pylon.

you want the ball to roll outside the circle after the pylon has been knocked over or it won't count. The first player to get to 3 (or whatever number you choose) wins the game. A simple drill like this teaches accuracy and keeping the ball low, which as you know, results in more goals. Also, passing the ball with enough force to knock over the pylon so that it's not a weak pass or shot prevents "hospital balls".

A simple drill like this can be set up anywhere. In a park, field, gym, or even a parking lot and it can be fun. Only two players are needed. The striker has to consider this a scoring drill. Players can put conditions on the game such as players can only use one or two touches as they collect a missed opportunity from their partner, or the ball has to be moving or many other conditions that can emulate real conditions.

The next step is to ask players to move back and then make this a shooting drill. Once again, the only way to score is to knock down the pylon which automatically makes the players force themselves to keep the ball low. This can become a simple challenge for players or friends. It's a way to practice shooting without the need of nets, goalkeepers, or even lots of balls because each player is retrieving the partner's ball. Pictures A2 and A3 show the friends shooting and knocking down the pylon.

Next, you can turn this drill into a heading drill as shown in diagram A4. One player chips the ball to his partner who enters the circle to head the ball down to hit the pylon to score a point. This exercise works on passing to set up a teammate for a goal, and on heading. The important thing is that the player has to head the ball down, which is perfect for teaching players how to score from a header. Add a third person in all these drills and you have a situation where players move around more and make the exercise include more crossing type situations without the need for a goal.

This is just one of many drills I do in my course. I give them more mental feedback in what they need to be thinking rather than technical feedback as I expect players to know this already. Players will leave the course with tons of things they can do on their own or with a friend to practice goal scoring.

More drills will be available in my upcoming DVDs.

APPENDIX B

Friends who have Helped me with this Book

Bernard Lecerf is my editor and worked with me to clarify some of my thinking and proofread my work. He played soccer at the junior level for Valenciennes and Rennes (French Ligue 1 teams) and for the University of Toronto Varsity team. He is Head of the Middle Division at Upper Canada College in Toronto. He is Head of Prep Soccer and coaches the U13A soccer team, which has won numerous Tier One U13 CISAA championships and the U13 Independent School National Tournament seven times over the last fifteen years.

His passions include coaching and playing the beautiful game, squash, jazz, and writing French as a second language educational materials. Bernard and I worked on this book for over four years!

Les Jones is the photographer who took many of the pictures in this book. Les Jones of Covershots has been to various World Cups and is Canada's top soccer sports photographer.

John Van Der Kolk (Left), videographer, encouraged me to film my methods of teaching the Wiel Coerver ball possession and dribbling techniques specifically to help North American players. View them at www.goldengoalscoring.com. Les Jones, my main photographer, is on right.

Paul Di Murro, Layout Designer for Direct Image.

Jo-Anne Godawa has designed most of the illustrations in this book and has been patient with the many revisions I have asked her to do. Jo-Anne is also the graphic artist behind my "That's Soccer Talk" T-shirt collection for Jato Sport.

Mike Salvatore
Mike is the web site designer for my www.goldengoalscoring.com, www.thelast9seconds.com, www.thesecretstoscoringgoals.com web sites and blog.

Anton Tielemans designed the book cover.

Tielemans' web site is www.tielemansdesign.com

People who have Inspired me with Their Coaching Sessions, Advice, Quotes, and Feedback

Tony Waiters is a former goalkeeper with the England National team. He was the coach of England's youth team before coming to North America to coach in the NASL with the Vancouver Whitecaps. He then coached Canada's National Men's team to their only World Cup appearance. He is now president of World of Soccer and Byte Size Coaching and has authored many books and is a respected clinician around the world.
www.bytesizecoaching.com
www.worldofsoccer.com

Dick Howard is shown with the World Cup and with the FIFA Technical Committee seated beside Sepp Blatter. Howard played goal for the Toronto Metros and Rochester Lancers in the NASL. He provided me with a CAM experience as I watched him play against Pele and Santos of Brazil in Toronto. It was a memorable experience. The stadium was packed with fans that came to see Pele and his World Champions team, Santos of Brazil. Fans were on the roofs of nearby buildings by the stadium just to get a glimpse of Pele. After Howard's performance in that game, I wanted to become a goalkeeper and it was a Captivating and Absorbing Moment for me, which got me back playing again after quitting soccer, but this time, as a goalkeeper.

Currently, Howard is a TV soccer analyst and travels throughout the World for FIFA helping elevate the technical side of the game. He has also authored a book on Goalkeeping.

Karl Dewazien:

Coaching Director for the California Youth Soccer Association and author of the FUNdamental Soccer book series. Karl's coaching sessions are always unique and inspiring.
www.karldewazien.com and
www.fundamentalsoccer.com

I'm with Jim McPherson (far left) who had the confidence in me to give me my first team to coach at a very young age. He has dedicated over 40 years of volunteer time with the Clairlea Westview Soccer Club and was recently honored by having a field named after him in Toronto. His wife Marlene and Ken Pettigrew, (also pictured with me) have been with the club as directors for over 35 years.

Bill Beswick is pictured here with me at an NSCAA conference. He has lectured and written about sport psychology in soccer extensively and worked with English Premier League clubs. I have quoted him in this book.

I'm with Simon Kuper of the *Financial Times* who wrote about strikers in his column called "*ON THE GAME*". The article was titled, "How to score goals, and lots of them", which I've quoted various times in this book. Kuper has written many books including *Football Against the Enemy* and *Soccernomics*.

I'm with Paul Dolan who shared some goalkeeping information and stories with me for this book. Dolan remains the youngest goalkeeper ever to play in the World Cup setting that mark playing for Canada against France at the 1986 World Cup in Mexico.

I'm with Alan Shearer, who has won the English Premier League (EPL) scoring title more than once and is the all-time highest goal scorer for Newcastle United. Some of Shearer's quotes are in the book including his take on penalty shots. Shearer also played for England.

Pele and I share a laugh in New York City. After asking him earlier in the day what his secrets to scoring goals were, which I have written about in Chapter 75, we discuss his visit with children in Toronto, how he helped soccer in North America, and how soccer is played today. This is one person for whom my book would have done absolutely nothing for because he figured it all out on his own. Photo courtesy of Pele Sports

APPENDIX D

Do we call the Goal Scorer a Striker?

I always get players who tell me that they want to play as a striker. I also get parents who tell me that their son or daughter is a striker and should play there. They get upset if their child's coach may have not played them in the striker position. Coaches usually have a pretty good feeling where they see certain players play within their team. Regardless of the reason, the coach will have an inner feeling of where he thinks players should play within his squad. His concern is that the total unit plays better together and looks at things as a whole. Sometimes we compromise one player's position to fill in other gaps, but we're pretty much all the same in our convictions.

Part of being an armchair critic is to discuss with friends, fans, and relatives how the team should play and where players should play without knowing the inner workings and feelings of a coach and his team's inner dynamics. That's all part of the game and will be forever. Coaches often toss and turn at night when things aren't going well as to where to move players and what systems and styles to play. It's all part of the challenge and fun of coaching.

I recall one situation with my son's team a few years back when I was coaching and numerous players begged me for the opportunity to play as a striker. I had 15 players dressed for a game and had 3 players who normally played in the striker position who were not eager to try other positions. I had another 3 players who continuously begged me to play up front. So I used the 8 players who did not care where they played on the field in the 8 positions available on the field who were not strikers and played them for the full 90 minutes. And I rotated the 6 players who wanted to play as strikers. Since I played with 2 strikers, it meant that each player only got to play a third of a game. Did the players who don't normally play striker score? No. Did we get many chances to score? No. Did the players who only played a third of a game complain they didn't play much? Yes. Like in most teams, players prefer to play rather than sit on the bench and watch.

The message was that if they want to play a position where there aren't too many spots available for them, then they will have more competition for the job and possibly spend more time on the bench. We got fewer chances to score because the players who wanted to play striker were also the ones that won a lot of balls for our team and started attacks. In fact, they would have had more chances to score playing in their normal position than playing as a striker. This is because I like to see my midfielders and defenders move forward in attack on overlaps, set plays, and other opportunities during a match when the situation calls for it. Did these players beg to play striker the next game? No. Like most players, playing in a game is better than sitting on the bench. Sometimes, as coaches, we just can't talk our way of reasoning with some players (and their parents); you just got to prove it to them in other ways.

Dealing with the Parents who Think Their Child Should be Your Striker

One parent of a college age player complained to me that his son was moved from a striker position to a wing midfield position by his coach. This happened partly because the team switched systems to a system with only one striker. He complained that now his son could not score. This is nonsense. It doesn't matter what you call the positions on the field, more than one player will get a chance to score and when that chance comes, the player needs to know how to turn that chance into a goal as often as possible. It doesn't matter what you call that player (based on his position) at that moment in time. In many teams, midfielders score just as many goals as some true strikers do. Defenders also score goals. It's not just strikers.

In fact, over time, the total number of goals scored in a typical game has not changed that much over the past 80 years. Generally, soccer is a low scoring game. The number of goals scored has not dropped significantly in relation to the change in the number of strikers playing in a game. In the old days when soccer was in its infancy, except for the goalkeeper, everyone played as a striker and chased the ball. It was the 0-10 system. Then some smart coach decided that he should designate a player that stays back all the time in case someone with speed breaks away from the scrum and goes in alone to score. The system 1-9 was born. As teams adopted that strategy, another coach decided that having an extra player who could partly help the lone defender would be a good idea, creating the midfield position.

Then a bright coach asked his players to pass the ball once in a while instead of dribbling it as far as they could. That changed a few things and things evolved from there into the 2-3-5 system of play that had 2 defenders, 3 midfielders and 5 forwards. That system was modified to the WM system that ruled the pitches for years. Then the poorer Italian teams who kept getting beat by the richer clubs decided that bringing more players back including someone to play behind the defenders was a way of avoiding big losses and giving their teams a chance to tie or win. This new position was labeled the "sweeper" or "libero" and the new defensive system became known as the "catenaccio".

Generally, more and more players are taken from the striker position and are being brought back and called different names. Today, it's not uncommon to see teams play with only one true striker but the reduction of strikers has not reduced the number of goals in proportion to the number of true strikers in a game. For example, comparing when teams played with 5 strikers to today where teams play with only one striker does not correlate to an 80% reduction in the number of goals scored in a typical game from the 1930's to 2011. This means that players other than strikers will score goals. Players need to know that they are all strikers when they get the chance to move forward to score and they have an actual scoring opportunity. I say this to players:

> ***"The name of your position does not mean anything when a chance to score develops. It's you and the ball that counts. Not the fact that you're playing as a wide midfielder. Who cares? Just play the game. Don't play with anger at the coach because you're not the striker. In that case, you'll never score."***

When Italy won the World Cup in 2006, it was defender Marco Materazzi who tied for the lead in goal scoring for the Italian team with 2 goals. It was defenders Fabio Grosso and Gianluca Zambrotta that would score two of Italy's biggest goals in the lead up to the World Cup Final. In 2010, it was defender Carles Puyol who beat Germany to take Spain to the World Cup final. And Andres Iniesta, who scored the only goal in the 2010 World Cup final, was a midfielder. A player who can score goals regardless of his position on the field will always be highly sought after.

APPENDIX E

Some Special Teams I have Coached

The main team I coached and stayed with for a number of years was with the Clairlea Westview Soccer Club. The players were born in 1964 and 1965. This team changed names once they moved beyond the U18 age bracket to Clairlea/Azzurri which was run by both the Clairlea Westview Soccer Club and the Scarboro Azzurri Soccer Club as a joint partnership.

I started coaching at 15 with a U9 house league/recreational team and then started a rep team at U12 the year after. Besides staying with this team right up until U21, I also was selected to coach two select teams: the Scarborough Indianapolis Peace Games team and the National Soccer League U19 and U21 Selects. Also, I started the high school soccer program with the high school I graduated from the year after I left. I coached both the junior and senior teams and started a girl's program for someone else to coach. I also coached the Scarboro Azzurri Men's team. At one point I was volunteering to coach 5 different teams at the same time. I also started and organized coaching clinics and tournaments. Later, I started my own soccer camps. I would say that in hindsight, I probably spent too much time with soccer.

Please note that I was not able to remember the names of all the players that I coached and are in these pictures. They are identified with an x. If you are one of these individuals, please send me a note. I'd like to include it in future editions of this book.

1984 Scarboro Clairlea/Azzurri U21 National Soccer League Team: Top row (left to right) John DeBenedictis (Head Coach), Tony Spataro (Manager), Paul Kumar, Georgio Bassi, George Crook, Peter Norde, George Higgs, Ian Ellis, Richmond Remani, Mike Gallo, Nicola Cortese (Trainer), Tony Lupinacci (Assistant Coach). Bottom row: Dino Mastrogiannis, Billy Pagonis, Glen Cooper, Kenny Dodd, Peter Roussis, Norm Tsolakis, Gus Tsoraklidis, Greg Dac Bang (Absent: John Henning)

1982 Clairlea Westview Soccer Team: Top row: John DeBenedicts (C), Richmond Remani, Peter Roussis, Bill Misener, John Henning, Greg Dac Bang, Norm Tsolakis, Billy Pagonis, Tony Spataro (M), Ken Tsoraklidis (M). Bottom row: Mike Kosmas Mouratidis, George Yanovski, Dino Mastrogiannis, Ken Dodd, Gus Tsoraklidis, Georgio Bassi

1985 Scarboro Azzurri U21 National Soccer League Team: Top row (L to R) Tony Lupinacci (Assistant Coach), Keith Costello, Ken Dodd, Georgio Bassi, Norm Tsolakis, Bill Pagonis, Richmond Remani, John DeBenedictis (Head Coach). Bottom row: Peter Norde, Mark Gibbs, Stu Morrison, Cam Walker, Tony Ahou, Greg Dac Bang

1982 U19 National Soccer League Selects: Top row (L-R): Tony Spataro (Manager) Chris Short, David Hinton, Gus Tsoraklidis, Paul Thomas, Gino DiFlorio, Giulio Spatafora, John Siebner, Dave Kenny, John Farrin, Richard Sutter, Sergio Barbosa, Bernie Rilling, John DeBenedictis (Head Coach). Bottom row: Sam Foti, Mario Calabretta, Manny Apolinaro, Kevin Greig, Joe Fimiani, Carlo Bosco

1977 W.A. Porter Collegiate Senior High School Team: Top row: John DeBenedictis, John Houston, Mark DeBenedictis, Tony Spataro, Leon Richards, Domenic Piro, Peter Raponi, Andy Kyriazis, Peter Andreoglou, J. Remani, Steve Bethanis Bottom row: Ik-soo Yoon, Ken Schnorbush, Robert DeBenedictis, Billy Kim, James Zikos, John King Remani

March 1981: My team joined the Tampa Bay Rowdies of the NASL in a training session and scrimmage in Tampa Florida with Tampa coach Gordon Jago as part of an 8 day training camp. For that memorable trip we had to thank Tim Carter of Eckerd College in St. Petersburg, Florida for hosting us. Also, Jay Miller of Tampa University also provided help with a friendly game during our stay.

1981 National Soccer League U21 Selects: Top row: Tony Spataro (manager), Nino Adamo, Carlo Bosco, Julio Spatafora, John Farren, x, x, John DeBenedictis (Head Coach). Bottom row: Peter Nespecca, Sam Foti, Joe Fimiani, Frank Donato, Joe x, Bill Kenny, x.

First Team I ever coached in 1974 with my brother Mark with the Clairlea Westview Soccer Club's house leagues.

2010 U18 Pickering Power: Top row: John DeBenedictis (Head Coach), Eric Chin-Sang, Julian Brown, Sal Moncada, Shane Wall, Justin Humby, George Meszaros Jr., Jan Lang, Bogoja Nastoski, Marco DeBenedictis, Matt McCormick, Albert Chin-Sang (Assistant Coach), Dagmar Ueberfeld-Lang (Manager). Bottom row: Sam Gatto, Alex Von Gemmingen, Shayne Branigan, Nicholas Rodrigues, Evan Gonsalves, Lucas Caridi: Absent: Jamal Drysdale, Kyle Van Vliet, Ruth Smith (Assistant Manager), Dave Faria (Assistant Coach)

Winning the 1984 Robbie Tournament U21 Division was a special victory for us as many players got scouted for tryouts in the NASL, MISL, and US Colleges after that game.

APPENDIX F

Some Special Teams I Have Played With

York University, 1977 Canadian National Champions

Top row: Dave Buckley, John DeBenedictis, Pino Baldassara, Peter Kovacs, Paul D'Agostino, Mike Burke. Middle row: Norm Crandles (Manager), Diane St. Onge (Trainer), Claudio Travierso, Bob Cameron, Vic Mandatori, Ian Dawson, Danny Iannuzziello, Luigi Martelli, Eric Willis (Coach). Bottom row: Peter Landy, Mac Musabay, Nick Plessas, Simon Bennett, Aldo D'Alfonso (absent- Clive Banton)

1974 U18 Wexford Juniors of the NSL Minor Division. This was my first year with the team and only third year playing as a goalkeeper. Since we had three goalkeepers, I played as a striker for this game. I'm seated second from the left. I scored a couple of key goals that year and still remember the mob I was confronted with after each goal. It's certainly a better feeling than having just been scored on.

Top row: Barry Heaton (Coach), x, Sam Papaconstantinou , Donny Small, Wayne Shepherd, George Klas, Danny Storrer, x, x, John Shepherd (Manager). Bottom row: Luis Carreira, John DeBenedictis, Ian Kennedy, Gavin Craig, Gerry Robinson, Peter Roubos, Steve Harper, Peter Nikolovski, Absent: Greg Stamkos.

My Oldtimers Hockey Team (Pick Ups): Top row: Dennis Jacko, Gary Nasu, John Mason, Billy Rourke, Michael Brady, Sean Barr, Craig Vanderlaan, Alan Moffatt. Bottom row: John DeBenedictis, Rick May, John Ayres, Malcolm Whitton, Jeff Bowers, Mike Cardy

Committees I Have Worked With

I was part of the committee that was responsible for putting on the NHL Celebrity game at the Robbie International Soccer Tournament in support of Cystic Fibrosis.

1988 Scarboro Azzurri Directors with Tony Waiters: Top row: Kevin Scott, Vincey Angelone, Debbie Klien Cramarossa, Dino Cirone, Pompeo Morra, Tony Waiters (Guest), Angelo Pesce, Rick Trentadue, Toni LaFerrara. Bottom row: Tony Marmo, Vince Vitale, John DeBenedictis, Tony Lupinacci, Peter Angelone, Tony LaFerrara. Absent: Dr. Lou Lombardi, Joe Cirone, Don Lombardi, Mike Loschiavo

A Most Memorable Coaching Moment

A "Special" Coaching Experience You Can't Imagine Until You Try For Yourself

One of my most memorable coaching experiences was something completely opposite from one that you would expect. Dr. Lou Lombardi and his wife Serena, ran the Scarboro Azzurri Special Olympics Soccer Program for years. They asked me to be a special guest coach at one of their practices. I did my usual planning with notes and diagrams of what I wanted to do. I approached the field, assembled the players and was amazed to find out that I was not just dealing with kids. I had a group that ranged in age from 15 to 55. There were close to 25 boys, girls, men and women all there ready and eager to play.

What a shock that was! Then of course I tried the first drill I had prepared and nothing went as planned. It did not work at all and I quickly noticed that I had to completely scrap my plans. I realized you cannot coach a Special Olympics team like any team, not even a very young team, but instead you need to coach them all one-on-one all through practice, including your scrimmage.

I pulled parents, and had plenty of help from members of the Monteleone Old-Timers Soccer team who so graciously give their time each week to help bring the ratios down to as close as possible to a two to one ratio. But what impressed me most was that these players were all happy to be there. They tried their hardest to do what was said and they loved doing what they were doing. Even though some were physically unable to move properly they tried and were happy to be there. The players all listened and were eager to learn. It was such a gratifying feeling that I now know why they are called "special". These people can really bring you down to earth.

WOW! It Made My Day

The Special Olympics people make me realize that life need not be as complicated as we make it provided we all give and share that loving feeling for each other. Wow, it was a magical experience and one of my truly most memorable moments in coaching. We often define our best soccer memories by winning games and tournaments, exotic traveling and international experiences. By giving back some time right at home we can add to our soccer memories.

Even if you can only dedicate one session to them, they will appreciate you and you will appreciate the experience even more. You don't even need to have much soccer experience to help out. You will leave the practice session feeling good. That's a guarantee. And if you haven't had the opportunity to try it then there are many Special Olympians waiting to make your day.

Contact your local Special Olympics program in your area and I am sure that they will be grateful for your help. Don't miss this opportunity because it is truly is a window for personal growth.

I Made it a Mission to Find a Way to Give More

After this experience I wanted to go back and volunteer my services again but I had very little time. I was coaching more than one team at the time, running the World of Soccer camps in Ontario, and sat on the board of directors for the Scarboro Azzurri Soccer Club. I was also the club's technical director, which made it impossible for me to make more of their sessions. But years later, I did get the opportunity to organize a celebrity game with former Toronto Blizzard players, local media personnel, and distinguished ex-players from the NSL and coaches and raised $2,000.00 for the Special Olympics program. Picture A5 includes all the players who donated their time to help me raise funds for the program.

Picture A5: I was proud to put on a celebrity game in Toronto with ex-NASL, NSL, and NHL players and media personnel playing against ex-Toronto Blizzard players in order to raise funds for the Special Olympics program in Toronto.

Back row: Trevor McCallum, Pat Pietrantonio, Gordon Wallace (half kneeling), Frank Tropea, Paul Hammond, Aldo D'Alfonso, Gordon Sweetzer, Colin Franks, Dave Ashfield, Brian Budd, Nick Plessas, Adrian DiGirolomo, Rick Morandini, Joe Pellegrino, Orazio De Chiantis, Lucky Raso, Alf DeBlasis, Tony LaFerrara. Front row: Randy Ragan, Charlie Falzon, Gordon Arrowsmith, Peter Zezel, Special Olympian Soccer player, Serena Lombardi, John DeBenedictis, Carmen Marcantonio, Scott Granville, Joe Mancuso, Joe Pascale. Photo by Tony Pavia

APPENDIX H

Developing my Golden Goal Scoring Course

In my Golden Goal Scoring Academy course, I feel that I can make a major impact on a player's ability to score goals by working on the psychology of goal scoring in a 16-30 hour course delivered over a short period of time: Preferably between 3 and 7 days. When you coach a team for a few seasons, you get to go over things over a period of years. Spreading things out over years as the player ages by repeating things over and over will improve strikers. As described in the introduction I felt that I needed to find ways to improve goal scoring faster than that especially as I kept finding that many of the reasons why players didn't score had nothing to do with skill. Players who had unbelievable skills still missed too many opportunities. That's when I started developing ways to make an impact with players quickly. Experimenting with different ideas and timelines, it took me a while to come up with the ideal course that would have the greatest impact in goal scoring on most athletes.

For example, I found that working with players once a week for 16 sessions did not have the huge impact that I expected to make any major changes in their psychological state of mind towards scoring goals. I found the same poor results with 10 two-hour sessions. That was too much like regular practice and classroom sessions without field session didn't work. That's not to say it didn't work at all, it just didn't have the major impact that I expected and wanted to get.

I found that the best situation is to blend in classroom and field sessions. I knew that most of my material was psychological and had to be done in a classroom setting, but I also knew that kids preferred working on the field with a ball, especially after I introduced new ideas in the classroom. But since I knew I needed to work with them one-on-one I had to experiment with how many players I could handle at one time. The best numbers are between 6-10 players but I have had success with up to 18 players although I will say that you will lose a few. This is also based on age. The next question I had to answer is how can I take what I did in the class and make it work on the field? I wasn't looking at teaching players how to kick a ball but combine the mental aspects of scoring with each individual's skill set. That's where I developed different types of field sessions as I stated in Appendix A. What are players thinking in their head as they try to score or position themselves on the field? That's the mentality I take in my field sessions.

At the end of my course, I want a players mental game changed not for just the next week but for the rest of their lives. I want the players who come to my course to recall the information presented so that they can take my course just once in their lives and be new players for life. After my course, they will still need to practice their technical skills and put in lots of hours practicing them, but hopefully they will have acquired some new powerful information to help their thought processes to make better decisions specific to scoring goals. Having a coach reinforce the mental aspects of scoring covered in the course is helpful as well.

A Better Player for you to Coach

Also, after taking my course, players should be able to analyze each goal scoring opportunity by themselves. And finally, after the course, coaches should notice that they will have more focused players at their practice sessions. Hopefully they will be more attentive to what their coach has to say and encourage their teammates to work hard so that they can put their new mental skills to practice at every training session. Most players who have taken my course should also come back to your team sessions with a feeling that they have been let in on a big secret and will avoid sharing it with anyone. That's a good thing and something that I want to accomplish in my course. I want coaches who spend time with their players to teach them skills and techniques to see their hard and long hours of coaching get results because their players will score more goals on the chances that they get. Some refresher reading or a one day session a year or two later can be done occasionally just to recall some of the many things I present in the course, but that's it.

I developed this course because I wanted to address the psychological aspects of goal scoring so that players can change how they think about and play their position. My course is meant to help the coach, who may not

I'm lecturing to players and coaches at the Pro Soccer Camp in Bethany, West Virginia, USA, on the topic of Goal Scoring.

have time to work with his strikers one-on-one and get into the many psychological aspects of the position. When you speak to your strikers after they have taken my course, they will listen more intensely to you, be more focused in finding out the finer points of coaching that you make, work harder, and take your practices a notch up, which will be infectious for the rest of the team. Will my course be the reason you will win? Will my course replace your hard work? Not at all. Your hours and hours of work with kids will be the reason they will succeed. I'm just coming along to give them some expert advice from a psychological standpoint to pay more attention to the great information you already provide them. Just like a fitness trainer specializes on fitness, I have made it my goal to specialize on scoring from a psychological perspective delivered from a former goalkeeper.

Much of what I teach kids in the course is similar to what you will have been saying over and over. I just give them some specific mental skills based on the psychology of a striker. That's it. I provide a bit of outside help to make your sessions better. Players should leave my course ready to be more absorbent of everything you teach them.

While I was developing my course I put on various coaching sessions usually lasting 5-6 hours to get feedback. Here are some of the comments I received from coaches who attended some of my first sessions that resulted in this book. I have also included comments from some of the players who have attended my player Goal Scoring courses.

Comments

"A new way to make the forwards think about scoring goals. It was very interesting and very informative. If players or coaches come with an open mind, they will definitely learn a lot, which in turn will help all soccer players. Thanks John, I look forward to the next one."
Fausto Macri (Erin Mills S.C., Mississauga)

"Very good use of visuals. I liked how John showed facts from the World Cup to prove his points. Recommend the seminar for coaches who have trouble with their teams scoring and enjoyed the presentation"
Joey Lombardi (Ontario Soccer Association staff coach)

"An out of the ordinary, but effective way to get the point across about scoring. "It was interesting, informative and also entertaining. Excellent visual presentation in a relaxed atmosphere. I've never seen six hours go by so fast."
Gary Nasu (Ajax Soccer Club, Ajax, Ontario)

"Visual presentation was great! Kids and adults are all visual learners. Very good. At first, I asked myself how is John going to teach goal scoring in a class? Great ideas."
Bob Talmage (Technical Director- Peel Halton Soccer Association)

"Very informative from a variety of perspectives and research data; statistics on goals scored was noteworthy. Highlights and examples were excellent to view."
David Rumack (Armour Heights S.C., Toronto)

"A great session John. I look forward to seeing it grow. As a coach, I introduced many of the key elements taught in your course to all of our team players. The results have been dramatic with overall scoring this season that is 3 times better than any other year. Your methods are a regular component of our training sessions."
Bob Twidle, Mississauga, Ontario

"I thought your seminar was excellent. It definitively changes how I coach my team. After two exhibition games against strong competition we scored 3 goals in each game compared to last year where we struggled to score goals."
Neil Pinheiro (Brams Utd. Girls U15 Allstar Team, Brampton, Ontario)

"During the last 30 years I have been to countless soccer clinics. Many were excellent, few were a waste of time. Your clinic is different, and unique. I enjoyed your coaching session and as you fine-tune your Secrets, Tricks, and Facts to improve Scoring Goals, will have a powerful presentation for developing Goal Scoring. A "powerful tool", which no doubt will benefit and excite many coaches and players."
Alfons Rubbens, (Publisher, Inside Soccer Magazine)

"I just wanted to thank you for giving me a different perspective into goal scoring. Thanks again."
Gino Lombardi.

"I went to your session and truly enjoyed it. Thank You! Thanks so much!"
Rick Mullins (Director Coeur d'Alene Sting Soccer Club, Idaho)

"John, we would be happy to be quoted supporting your course. It was excellent and has made a difference. If anything else, it gave the girls that little mental edge required to end the slump they were on. The results have been dramatic. In the 7 games before taking your course we averaged 1.3 goals per game (9 goals in 7 games, 2 against the top 2 teams in the league). In the 5 league games following your course the average has increased to 2.4 goals per game (12 goals in 5 games, 2 of those 5 games were against the same top 2 teams). Since the Goal Scoring course, including League, Provincial Cup and League Cup games, we have played a total of 11 matches (4 versus the top 2 teams). Our average has increased from 1.3 goals per game to 3.5 goals per game (38 goals in 11 games)."

"Even without Analisa the girls scored four goals against Mississauga last week and created enough chances for more if not for the heroics of their keeper and the ref calling back goals. I think it is important to note that the course did wonders BUT, the application of the coaching scoring principles you preached at each of our practices is why it continues to produce results. I guess the message for the coaches is that it will not only transform your players but also you as a coach!"
Regards, Gerry Gentile (Coach: U16 Girls Vaughan Soccer Club, Ontario)

U16 Girls Vaughan SC: Top row: Petrice Gentile, Shannon Robertson, Christina Fantozzi, Samantha Cawkell, Rachael Goulding, Tania Pedron, Kesia Broome, Paula Ruscigno, Jenelle Niles. Bottom row: Daniel Blair, Analisa Romano, Nicole Currie, Monique Budani, Melissa Migliazza, Daneen Stevenato, Jasmine Merith

Coach: Gerry Gentile

Manager: Mike Ruscigno

"I sat in on your class about scoring goals at the convention and was blown away! I wanted you to do your entire course during the convention! It was awesome."
Doug Meade, (Cherokee Soccer Assoc. Woodstock, Ga)

"Absolutely loved your presentation in Charlotte this weekend. The idea of bringing scoring down to the simplest level is brilliant and I know it will help my high school girls team. I am going to teach them the 4 Golden Rules and I am going to explain the top 10 reasons why goals are not scored. Again, thank you for all of the help you have already given me."
Best regards, Jack Baer (Coach, Howland (Ohio) High School Girls Soccer)

"Your coaching session in Baltimore was "wicked-awesome. Very informative. The best part was you had everybody right from the start! Everyone was frantically taking notes. Cool."
Saverio Michielli

"I've been coming to these conventions since 1951 and this is the first session that really really piqued my interest. Enjoyed presentation. Great points on scoring and it was well done with repetition to get the points across. Lots of psychological stuff that also relates to basketball. Picture with Landon Donovan was perfect. Well done."
Rick Pizarro (Springfield College, Baltimore)

"I loved your presentation in Santa Clara and felt that there were points that where extremely valid, and gave us coaches an opportunity to re-evaluate our shooting sessions. Ciao".
Marco DiTano (California State Coach)

"Liam played again this weekend and scored another three goals including a highlight reel diving header ! To say that he is thrilled with what you taught him in a short time would be dramatic understatement. Your goal scoring course is truly wonderful. Thanks again John and keep up the great work! Cheers."
Chris Davies (Newmarket, Ontario)

Lisa Watson playing with Laurentian University. She was a top goal scorer in her rookie season and invited to the Canadian University team. In 2012, 9 years after taking the Golden Goal Scoring course, Watson became the all-time goal scoring leader for Laurentian University's Lady Vees. Photo thanks to Laurentian University.

Laura Twidle took the course when she was 13 and has improved her conversion rate on the chances she receives ever since. In 2010-2011, she is a top midfielder and goal scorer for Central Michigan. Photo courtesy of Bob Twidle.

I'm with Kosmas (Mike) Mouratidis at a camp in Bethany College, West Virginia in 2010. Mike is a USSF A licensed coach, coaching instructor, head coach, pro soccer camp director, and professor. I had the pleasure of coaching Mike when he was a kid and was one of the classiest players I ever coached.

I'm with Rob Mosele, president of Edmonton Juventus Soccer Club and coach of the boys U14 team in 2010. Rob brought me to Edmonton to work with the club's U13 and U14 boys in 2009. That year, the U14 boys won the National Title scoring a record breaking 41 goals in 5 matches. Rob said, "Even the subs were scoring."

"I guess the message for the coaches is that it will not only transform your players but also you as a coach!"

Coach: Gerry Gentile

APPENDIX I

Growing Up Soccer in Toronto

Growing up in Toronto, a multicultural Canadian city, the game was always played at the highest level available. Many immigrants that came to Toronto after World War II were Europeans and they brought the game with them. But other sports such as hockey, football, and baseball were the popular sports that most kids played and watched. Much of the soccer that was played in Toronto stayed within the immigrant community and they often started their own professional and semi-professional teams. Clubs like Toronto Italia, Toronto Portuguese, Toronto Croatia, Serbian White Eagles, Toronto Homer (Greeks), Toronto Ukrania, Toronto Hungaria, and more played in the National Soccer League that included teams from Montreal, Buffalo, Windsor/Detroit, and the Southern Ontario region. Some teams averaged attendances over 10,000 when the top teams played. Many of the top players in the league came to play in Toronto after finishing their season in Europe to make some extra money. Players like Sir Stanley Matthews and Eusebio played in Toronto.

While the NSL existed, Toronto also had a team that played in North America's top league, whatever it was at the time. Toronto always had a team. My father would take me to whatever game was played at Varsity Stadium, Toronto's top soccer stadium. He wanted us to follow Toronto's team as opposed to the team of his home country which played in the NSL. Therefore, I rarely went to go see Toronto Italia play, but rather Toronto's team. I recall watching the Toronto Falcons who turned into the Toronto Metros, and then Toronto Metros-Croatia (who went on to win the Soccer Bowl in the NASL) and then the Toronto Blizzard. After the NASL folded, there was not much hope for pro soccer in North America. Many great Canadian and American kids who worked so hard to practice their game to one day play in the NASL, had their dreams shattered after the NASL went from 24 teams in 1980 to 9 teams in 1984. In the end only Toronto and Minnesota wanted to continue and the league folded after that year. My dreams as a coach was also shattered and jobs in the soccer business practically disappeared.

When the NASL folded there was not much soccer to watch and the NSL had also started to lose its allure as the former fans that populated those games aged and preferred to go watch their kids and grandkids play ice hockey, baseball, or youth soccer. The NSL packed up things in 1997 where a good crowd was now 500 and not 10,000-12,000.

The media did a poor job covering our game in Toronto and throughout North America and this did not help promote the game. It wasn't until 1994, when the World Cup came to the USA, that things started to look brighter. But until the MLS came to Toronto with their new team, Toronto FC, 21 years had passed and for many young players and coaches across North America, a whole generation had their dreams shattered, except for the lucky few that were good enough to play in Europe. I've thought of writing a book on "The Lost Generation" of soccer players across North America whose dreams were shattered. I've met many such players but I figured that no one would buy it because it would be a depressing read.

Picture A6: A massive celebration broke out after Italy won the 2006 World Cup in Toronto's "Little Italy". Over 250,000 people blocked miles of roadway in Toronto right after the final whistle. Although the Italians had the biggest celebrations, all the other nationalities held their own celebrations as their teams won games. Photo by John DeBenedictis

The Best Place to Watch the World Cup Outside the Host Country

But Toronto still got their soccer fix through television and, in particular, the World Cup. Many people have stated that the next best place to watch a World Cup game other than at the World Cup would be in Toronto. With so many ethnic communities, parties break out in all parts of the city, blocking roads and traffic every time a particular team wins. In 1982 and 2006, when Italy won the World Cup, Toronto hosted the biggest World Cup party outside of Italy and bigger than many Italian cities. Over 250,000 people danced throughout the streets in Little Italy as everyone joined in the celebrations. With a large Italian population together with soccer fans of every nationality joining in, it made headlines across the country. Also in 2006, over 20,000 soccer fans attended the live broadcast at the SkyDome to watch the final between Italy and France on the Jumbo Screen. I took the picture of the celebration afterwards (picture A6).

But for me, it was my mom and dad that inspired me to go watch, play and then coach soccer. My dad took me and my brothers to Toronto games where I saw some of the world's best players including Pele, Roberto Bettega, Giorgio Chinaglia, George Best, Johan Cruyff, Gerd Müller, Franz Beckenbauer, Eusebio, Carlos Alberto, Gordon Banks and many more all mixed with Canadian and US players who worked hard to deserve to play with some of the best.

A Special Thanks to my Family Members and Friends

I appreciate my parent's support in the game which has provided me with not just great memories but also some great friends. While researching and testing my ideas for this book over the past decade, I received lots of positive comments and feedback from all members of my family and my wife's family. Most of all from my wife Angela, and our sons Joseph and Marco who have seen me disappear for hours on end while writing this book. I include photos of all those mentioned as a thank you for their support.

My wife Angela

My sons, Joseph and Marco, and our dog, Rex

Thanks to Lisa Furry, Alex Araya, Bob Talmage and Norm Tsolakis who held the fort at JMT METROSPORT while I was away writing this book.

DeBenedictis gang: Seated: Mark (brother), mom and dad, Uncle Tony and Aunt Domenica, me Standing: cousin Robert and wife Donna, Caroline, Joseph, Peter, Danny (brother), Marco, Lina, Stephen, Daniel, Michael, Angela

My in-laws: Top row: Joseph Cirone, Mike Cirone and wife Oriana, Bianca Cirone, Marco DeBenedictis, Peter Foley and wife Julie, Joseph and Angela DeBenedictis. Bottom Row: Joe Cirone, Julia Mastromarco, Grace Cirone Conor Foley, and Liam Foley.

Frank and Susie Cirone with sons Cameron and Nicolas. (Absent Matthew)

A key part of developing this book came when we visited our friends in Long Island NY and played soccer on their front lawn. Sal, Sue and Nicholas Formica, me, Thomas Formica, my wife Angela, Irene Formica and my son Joseph. My son Marco is in front of me.

Toughest goalie to score on: our dog, Rex

Do NOT Drink and Drive: Innocent Lives are in Your Hands

In memory of Roger, Paul, and Angela St. Denis

My two boys, Joseph and Marco (centre) are with Roger St. Denis (top right) playing a short round of golf with two of his kids. (Paul: far left and Angela: bottom right). I first met Roger at a coaching clinic that I was instructing at. He was a volunteer coach who donated time to help young kids even though he had little soccer experience. Roger always stayed after my sessions to ask more questions about the game so that he could become a better coach for the kids he coached. He also donated time to feed the homeless and helped many other charities and less fortunate people. A few years later he was best man at my wedding and also my uncle by marriage. His two kids were my wife's first cousins. Their home was always open to guests for food and fun times.

In December 2006, their family went on their first vacation in a long time after taking care of their elderly aunt who lived into her 90s. On their drive to Florida, an impaired driver, who was 3 times over the legal blood alcohol limit for driving, entered the interstate highway near Pittsburgh Pennsylvania going the wrong way and against traffic. The drunk driver hit Roger's driver side of the car head-on at full speed killing him, Paul and little Angela and ruining the lives of innocent family members. Survived by his wife, aunt Angela and cousin Therese, I think of them and their generosity and love for everyone every single day.

Enjoy every day of your life.

Enjoy your family, friends, and relatives.

Do NOT Drink and Drive.

When you drive, please drive carefully.

Lives are in your hands.

APPENDIX K

Coaches: you will not always win… …and I'm not talking about the game of soccer.

Karl Dewazien, coaching director for the California Youth Soccer Association states in his books, videos, DVDs, web site and lectures that "The outcome of our children is infinitely more important than the outcome of any game they will ever play."

As coaches, most of us know that most of the players we coach will not end up playing for the National Team or Manchester United, Real Madrid, or Juventus, and that one of our roles is to help kids through life. You will be dealing with kids of many different cultures and many different backgrounds. You'll probably coach some kids whose parents are wealthy and some whose parents are poor. You will probably see some brilliant players and some not very good players throughout your coaching career and some who are more passionate than others. If you stay with teams over years, you will see and watch players grow mentally, physically, socially and get to know their personalities as they develop. You'll meet some kids from good homes and some from broken homes, some others whose parents are together and some whose are not. And through all this, you know that sport can be a great thing for them to be involved in to learn many different aspects of life.

But although you will try and instill all the best in the players that you coach, I want you to know that at the end of the day, especially once the players have left you, there may not be much more you can do to influence their lives. For those who stay in soccer, you can usually follow them to some extent. I have heard some great stories about players I have coached and what they have gone on to do or be in their lives outside of soccer. But I have also heard some very sad stories and wished that I could have done more for them after they left my team. But in the end, I always felt that I did my best for every kid I coached and hoped that I instilled some good values in them. Things do not always work out for everyone and you as a coach cannot worry about the players that have gone astray provided that you have done your best.

If you have respected players and gained respect from them, then you will have positively influenced most of the players that you coached but there will be some that just go their own way. One of the better players that I coached ended up homeless and addicted to drugs and alcohol and played on Canada's National Homeless Team. I did not realize what happened to him until one day I picked up a copy of *Reader's Digest Magazine* (November, 2009) and read a story on him. You cannot worry about players who follow the wrong path. If you have done your best, the chances are that it's other factors that will cause some to go down the wrong path. But in this case, it was nice to hear that the game of soccer helped him gain his self-respect and lead him down a path to recovery.

But by and large, most of the players I have coached have done well and it's a great feeling when your ex-players seek you out years later and thank you for the time you spent with them. Many still play old-timers soccer while some now coach their sons and daughters. Others have started their own soccer academies and camps.

And with time, life has its own complexities but one thing we cannot stop is just that: time. Unfortunately it ages us but hopefully makes us wiser. I was recently at a friendly game between Manchester United and Glasgow Celtic in Toronto and two seats away from me was a face that looked familiar but I wasn't sure who he was. Since he didn't say anything, neither did I.

After the game as I was looking for my camera, he picked it up for me and handed it to me. As we looked at each other a bit closer, we both knew who each other was. Cam Walker (picture 33A), a player I coached and who went on to play on Canada's National U19 Youth team sat only two seats from me the whole game but we hadn't put the pieces together until later.

We hugged and exchanged stories and it was nice to know that although we age, lose some hair, add a few wrinkles, and go through life, the one thing that stays with us forever is the passion that many of us have for the wonderful game of soccer.

Thank You for Reading

John DeBenedictis

REFERENCES

Akiyoshi, Kitaoka. *"Akiyoshi's Illusion Pages."* Department of Psychology from Ritsumeikan University in Kyoto Japan.立命館大学: n.pag. Web. 20 Feb. 2011.

Ashby, F Gregory. et al. "A Neuropsychological Theory of Positive Affect and Its Influence on Cognition." *Psychological Review* 106. (3) (1999): 529-550. Print.

DeBenedictis, John. *"Scoring Goals".* 57th Annual National Soccer Coaches Association of America Convention, Charlotte Convention Center, Charlotte, NC. 16 January 2004. Guest Lecture.

DeBenedictis, John. "Goals are Down it Must Be The New Shoes." *Soccer 360* 30(2010): 51.Print

DeBenedictis, John. "Goals at World Cup Are Down Again: It Must Be the Shoes." *Soccer Journal* November-December 55.7 (2010): 11. Print.

Callaghan, Barry. "The Man." *Toronto Life* January 36.1 (2002): 64-70. Print.

Carnegie, Dale. *How to Stop Worrying and Start Living.* New York: Pocket Books, 1984. Print.

Chastain, Brandi. *It's Not About the Bra.* New York Harper Collins Publishers Inc, 2004. Print.

Coerver, Wiel. *Soccer Fundamentals for Players and Coaches.* Englewood Cliff: Prentice-Hall, 1986. Print.

Connolly, Marc. "A Star's Perspective- German World Cup legend Jüergen Klinsmann offered some frank observations during an open Q and A at the 2003 NSCAA Convention." *Soccer Journal* May/June. 2003: 29-30. Print.

Crowther, Don. "Systematizing your Business." *Great PR Newsletter*. n.pag. Web. 2004.

Csikszentmihalyi, Mihaly. "Creativity, Fulfillment and Flow." *TED: Ideas worth Spreading* Feb. (2004): n.pag. Web. Feb. 2004.

Dewazien, Karl. *Fundamental Soccer Practice of Champions.* Fresno: Karl Dewazien, 2001. Print.

Dewazien, Karl. "*Fundamental, Coaching Youth Soccer with Koach Karl Dewazien."* n. pag. Web. Apr. 2001.

Dewazien, Karl. *Fundamental Soccer with Koach Karl*. Apr. 2011. Print.

DiCicco, Tony, et al.. *Catch Them Being Good*. New York: Penguin Group, 2002. Print.

Fisher, David. *Mia Hamm.* Kansas City: Andrews McMeel Publishing, 2000. Print.

Goleman, D. P. *Emotional Intelligence: Why It Can Matter More Than IQ for Character, Health and Lifelong Achievement.* New York: Bantam Books, 1995. Print.

Harvey, Lee. *Scoring Goals: An Analysis of the World Cup, 1998.* Centre for Research in to Quality. n.pag. Web. 1998.

Horvitz, Jon. C, et al. "Burst Activity of Ventral Segmental Dopamine Neurons as Elicited by Sensory Stimuli." *Brain Research* 759 (1997): 251-258. Print.

Jones, Michael. "We're Losing our Late Bloomers." *Soccer Journal* July-Aug. 2009. Print.

Kaufman, Lloyd. *Perception: The World Transformed*. New York: Oxford University Press, 1979. Print.

Koepp, M.J, et al. " Evidence for striatal dopamine release during a video game." *Nature* 393 (1998): 266-268. Web. 29 Mar. 1998.

Kucey, Sam. "The 12th. Player". *Newsoccer* (2003). Print.

Kuper, Simon. "How to Score Goals- and Lots of Them." *Financial Times* Weekend March 29/March 30, 2003. Print.

Marr, Arthur J. " In the Zone: A Biobehavioral Theory of the Flow Experience." *Athletic Insight. Online Journal of Sport Psychology* 3.1 (2001): n. pag. Web. 29 Mar. 2001.

"Muller-Lyer Illusion." New World Encyclopedia. Web. 20 February 2011.

Murphy, Shane. *The Sport Psych Handbook.* Champaign: Human Kinetics, 2005. Print.

"Ouchi Illusion: from Wolfram MathWorld." Wolfram MathWorld: The Web's Most Extensive Mathematics Resource: n .pag. Web. 20 Feb. 2003.

Owen, Michael, and Harrison, Dave. *Michael Owen's Soccer Skills: How to Become a Complete Footballer.* London: Harper Collins, 2000. Print.

Rubinstein, Joshua S., et al. "Executive Control of Cognitive Processes in Task Switching." *Journal of Experimental Psychology: Human Perception and Performance* 27.4 (2001): 763-797. Print.

Schienberg, Dr. Paul. "Mental Training: Creative Visualization and Athletic Performance Part I-III." *Psyched Online*: n.pag. Web. Mar. 2003.

Schinke, Robert J, et al. "Understanding and Refining the Resilience of Elite Athletes: An Intervention Strategy". *Athletic Insight: The Online Journal of Sport Psychology* 4.3 (2001): Web. 2001.

Schneider, Marius. "Goals, Goals, Goals." *FIFA Magazine* Sep 2004: 38-43. Print.

Schum, Tim. "Soccer's Age of Innocence Lost?" *NSCAA Soccer Journal* July/Aug. 1998. Print.

Shearer The Legend. Executive Producer. Roger Tames. Producer: Gary Whalen. 2006. Nova production for Granada Ventures Ltd and Newcastle United FC Ltd in association with SFX. 2006. DVD.

Srebro, Rafi. *Winning with your Head, A Complete Mental Training Guide for Soccer.* Spring City: Reedswain Publishing, 2002. Print.

Strand, Fleur. L. *Physiology: A Regulatory Systems Approach.* New York: Macmillan, 1978. Print.

The Princess Bride. Dir. Rob Reiner, Perf. Peter Falk, Cary Elwes, Robin Wright, Mandy Patinkin. Twenty Century Fox, 1987. DVD.

Tortora, Gerald. J. *Principles of Human Anatomy & Physiology.* Hoboken: John Wiley & Sons, 2012. Print.

Vogelsinger, Hubert. *The Challenge of Soccer: A Handbook of Skills, Techniques, and Strategy*. Boston: Allyn & Bacon Inc. 1973. Print.

Waiters, Tony, and Howe, Bobby. *Coaching 6, 7, and 8 year olds, Micro Soccer.* South Surrey: World of Soccer, 1988. Print.

Waiters, Tony, and Howe, Bobby. *Coaching 6, 7, and 8 year olds.* Vancouver: World of Soccer, 1988. Print.

Waiters, Tony. *"Byte Sized Coaching."* n.pag. Web. April. 2011.

Waiters, Tony. *Keeper II. Incorporating the 10 Principles of Goalkeeping*. South Surrey: World of Soccer. 2005. Print.

Waiters, Tony. "*World of Soccer." n. pag. Web. Apr. 2011.*

"Wayne Gretzky, The Great One." *A & E Biography.* A & E Television Networks. Television.

Weber, Peter. C. *Vertigo and Disequilibrium: A Practical Guide to Diagnosis and Management.* New York: Thieme Medical Publishers Inc., 2008. Print.

Wiese, Jim. *Sports Science, 40 Goal Scoring, High Flying, Medal-Winning Experiments for Kids.* New York: John Wiley & Sons Inc., 2002. Print.

References revised by Rosana Brasil

INDEX OF SUBTITLES, SUB STORIES, AND SPECIAL BULLETS OR DIAGRAMS:

PART ONE

Coaching the Psychological Aspects of Scoring Goals

PART TWO

Understanding Human Movement and Muscular and Visual Perception and how it Affects Player Development

PART THREE

SOCCER FACTS and Simplifying the Mystique of Scoring Goals Psychologically Using "The Power of Statistics" and "Visual Cues"

PART FOUR

Beating The Goalkeeper: "Insight into shifting the advantage to the striker"

PART 5

More Psychological Information to Cover the Rest of the Game: "Penalty Shots, Set Plays, Beating Defenders, and More Psychological Stuff That Goes on the Field of Play That Affects Strikers."

APPENDIX

REFERENCES

ABOUT THE AUTHOR

John DeBenedictis

John DeBenedictis has been coaching for over 35 years and has coached at many levels. Most of his coaching has been at the youth level from the youngest of children right up to U21 league select teams playing in international competitions. He has also coached men's teams. He ran his own soccer camps with Tony Waiters, former English International goalkeeper and Canadian National Team coach in Ontario. He played goalkeeper for York University helping them win the National Title in 1977. He played as a semi-professional in the National Soccer League (a professional league based in southern Ontario, Upper New York State, Quebec, and Michigan), with Toronto Ukrania. He also runs his "Secrets to Goal Scoring" course as part of his Golden Goal Scoring Academy.

DeBenedictis has traveled throughout North America presenting his unique lecture on "The Secrets to Scoring Goals". He was one of the keynote speakers at the NSCAA (National Soccer Coaches Association of America) Coaching Convention in 2004 in Charlotte, North Carolina, 2005 in Baltimore, Maryland, and 2013 in Indianapolis, Indiana, USA. In 2007, DeBenedictis spoke in Santa Clara, California for the California Youth Soccer Association's annual coaching conference and convention. In 2009, he brought his course to the Edmonton Juventus Soccer Club. In 2010, 2011, and 2012 he was a special guest coach at the Pro Soccer Camp in West Virginia and Ohio.

DeBenedictis has an Honours Bachelor of Science degree with a major in Physical and Health Education as well as earning an advanced certificate of coaching from York University and holds a senior coaching license. DeBenedictis has always been interested in youth player development and the promotion of the game in North America. He has written numerous coaching articles for soccer publications and sport psychology web-sites across North America. Some of his articles have been instrumental in introducing change in player development programs with soccer clubs across North America.

DeBenedictis was also the first coach to bring the Wiel Coerver Dribbling and Ball Possession techniques to Canada demonstrating the techniques to coaches and players. DeBenedictis also produced a video on Ball Possession and Dribbling techniques geared to North American kids which is being re-issued and re-edited and will be available on www.YouTube.com as each part is finished. Many of the players he has coached or instructed went on to play professional soccer in Canada, the USA, and Europe. DeBenedictis taught the soccer course for the Physical Education Department at the University of Toronto, and also ran soccer camps for the Ontario Soccer Association in the 80"s.

DeBenedictis has concentrated on building a course that will help players score more goals. From a goalkeeping perspective, he could never understand why players did not score more goals on him. He feels that the game would take on much more interest in North America if players would score more goals on the chances that they get and turn 0-0 games into 2-2 games thereby silencing the critics of soccer. He has developed a psychology based course to increase goal scoring. He has consulted MLS players who have improved their goal conversion rate after having spent some time with him.

In developing his course, he did extensive research into the cognitive processes used for performing tasks as it relates to perceptual motor-muscular learning. He has focused his research to include studying visual motion perception as it relates to different situations that soccer player's encounter. DeBenedictis then used his experience as a goalkeeper and coach to tie in his research to coaching soccer players. He blended everything in with sport psychology which led him to seek out different socce facts that have helped players understand what it takes to be a great goal scorer. All this information formed the basis for his unique goal scoring course and this book.

John training in his youth.

As part of his research into goal scoring for his course and this book, he interviewed and studied the careers of some of th world's best goal scorers.

DeBenedictis also continues to volunteer his services as Executive Director of The National Soccer Coaches Association of Canada, coach his son's team, and help promote the great game of soccer.